16-BIT AND 32-BIT MICROPROCESSORS
Architecture, Software, and Interfacing Techniques

AVTAR SINGH
San Jose State University

WALTER A. TRIEBEL
Intel Corporation

PRENTICE HALL, Englewood Cliffs, New Jersey 07632

Library of Congress Cataloging-in-Publication Data

Avtar Singh
    16-bit and 32-bit microprocessors : architecture, software, and
interfacing techniques / Avtar Singh, Walter A. Triebel.
        p.   cm.
    Includes bibliographical references and index.
    ISBN 0-13-812157-5
    1. Microprocessors. 2. Computer architecture.   I. Triebel,
Walter A.   II. Title.
QA76.5.A93   1991
004.16--dc20   90-7955
                                                        CIP

Editorial/production supervision:
  Gretchen K. Chenenko
Cover design:
  Wanda Lubelska
Manufacturing buyers:
  Mary McCartney and Ed O'Dougherty

© 1991 by Prentice-Hall, Inc.
A Division of Simon & Schuster
Englewood Cliffs, New Jersey 07632

AVTAR SINGH
To my teachers
Dr. Thau, Dr. Lamba,
and Headmaster Raghbir Singh

WALTER A. TRIEBEL
To my mother
Marie F. Triebel

Portions of this text were previously published as
THE 16 BIT MICROPROCESSORS: Architecture, Software, and Interface Techniques
by Triebel and Singh (Prentice Hall, 1985)

Printed in the United States of America

10 9 8 7 6 5 4 3 2 1

ISBN 0-13-812157-5

Prentice-Hall International (UK) Limited, *London*
Prentice-Hall of Australia Pty. Limited, *Sydney*
Prentice-Hall Canada Inc., *Toronto*
Prentice-Hall Hispanoamericana, S.A., *Mexico*
Prentice-Hall of India Private Limited, *New Delhi*
Prentice-Hall of Japan, Inc., *Tokyo*
Simon & Schuster Asia Pte. Ltd., *Singapore*
Editora Prentice-Hall do Brasil, Ltda., *Rio de Janeiro*

Contents

3   8086 MICROPROCESSOR PROGRAMMING 1   46

4   8086 MICROPROCESSOR PROGRAMMING 2   79

5   THE 8086 MICROPROCESSOR AND ITS MEMORY INTERFACE   110

Preface

In the late 1970's, a number of 16-bit microprocessor architectures were introduced by semiconductor manufacturers. The architectures of two of these microprocessors, the 8086 by Intel Corporation and the 68000 by Motorola, Inc., became broadly accepted in the marketplace. Today, these two devices have defined industry-standard architectures. For this reason, they are the 16-bit microprocessors presented in this book.

Both devices have evolved into a complete family of microprocessor and peripheral ICs. For example, there are three 16-bit members of the 8086 family, the original 8086, the 8088, and the 80286. The 8088 is an 8-bit bus version of the 8086 that permits design of lower-cost systems. On the other hand, the 80286 offers the system designer an enhanced software architecture, new hardware features, and higher performance, at a higher cost. The 68000 family also has two other 16-bit members, the 68008 and the 68010.

Large scale integrated (LSI) and very large scale integrated (VLSI) peripheral ICs are an important part of both families. Availability of these standard building blocks has simplified the design of microcomputer systems. Examples are parallel I/O expander, interval timer, interrupt controller, and direct memory access controller ICs. One example of a peripheral device available in the 68000 family is the 6821 peripheral interface adapter. This device is used to implement parallel I/O for a 68000-based microcomputer system. Another device, the 68230, provides both parallel I/O expansion and an interval timer. Examples of peripheral devices for the 8086 family are the 8255 programmable peripheral interface and 8259 programmable interrupt controller.

In the mid 1980s, 32-bit microprocessors were introduced that employ these industry-standard architectures. The 32-bit 80386 microprocessor offers a mode that is software compatible with the 8086 microprocessor, but with enhanced hardware features and much higher performance. Moreover, just like the 80286, the 80386 has a second mode of operation that provides an enhanced software architecture. The first fully 32-bit member of the 68000 family was the 68020. Just as with the evolution of the 8086 to the 80386, the 68020 offers software compatibility with the 68000, an extended software architecture, advanced hardware features, and a higher level of performance. Today the 80386 and 68020 are the most widely used 32-bit microprocessors. Both of these devices are also studied in this book.

People involved in the design of modern microcomputer-based electronic equipment must have a thorough knowledge of two primary areas: software architecture and hardware interfacing. The material presented in *16-Bit and 32-Bit Microprocessors: Architecture, Software, and Interfacing Techniques* represents a thorough study of both of these subjects. In Chapters 2 through 4, the software architecture of the 8086 microprocessor is examined, and the hardware interfaces of its microcomputer system are covered in detail in Chapters 5 through 7. This material is followed by studies of the software architecture and hardware architecture of the 80386 microprocessor in Chapters 8 and 9, respectively. The focus in these two chapters is on how the 80386 differs from the 8086.

Coverage includes traditional microprocessor-related topics such as internal architecture, microcomputer system interfaces, addressing modes, instruction set, assembly language programming techniques, bus cycles, bus interface circuits, program memory, and data storage memory (SRAM and DRAM), input/output circuitry, LSI and VLSI peripheral ICs, and interrupts and exception processing. This material also contains more advanced concepts, such as pipelining, instruction prefetch and decode, memory management, virtual memory, virtual to physical address translation, protection, tasks, task switching, multi-tasking, and paging.

A similar study of the 68000 and 68020 microprocessors and their microcomputer systems is provided in Chapters 10 through 16. First, a thorough understanding of the software architecture of the 68000 microprocessor is developed in Chapters 10 through 12. This includes material on the software model, memory address space, organization of data, register set, stack, addressing modes, instruction set, and analysis and writing of assembly language programs. Chapters 11 and 12 explore the hardware of the 68000-based microcomputer system. Here the hardware architectural features of the microcomputer are introduced and circuit design techniques for the memory, input/output, and interrupt interfaces are covered.

The 68020 microprocessor brings an order of magnitude higher performance and a number of advanced features to the 68000 architecture. The software and hardware architecture of the 68020 are presented in Chapters 15 and 16, respectively. Again, the focus is on functions and features of the 68020 that are different from those of the original 68000. For instance, in Chapter 9, we examine the new addressing modes, enhancements made to instructions supported by the original 68000, and instructions that are new with the instruction set of the 68020, such as the bit field and BCD pack and unpack instructions. Chapter 10 explores the hardware architecture of the 68020 and includes information on signal interfaces, clock requirements, data organization, bus cycles, and cache memory.

This book is for use in electrical engineering and electrical engineering technology curricula offered at universities and community colleges. However, the wealth of practical information and applications that are included make the book a valuable reference for practicing engineers and technicians. An instructor's solutions manual is available from Prentice Hall.

Every effort has been made to provide up-to-date information on the devices we introduce. However, it is recommended that the reader check with the manufacturer of a device for the most recent data.

Avtar Singh
Walter A. Triebel

1

Introduction to Microprocessors and Microcomputers

1.1 INTRODUCTION

In the last decade, most of the important advances in computer system technology have been closely related to the development of high-performance 16-bit and 32-bit microprocessor architectures and the microcomputer systems built with them.

Today, both the 16-bit and 32-bit microprocessor markets are quite mature. Several complete microprocessor families are available. They include support products such as large-scale integrated peripheral devices, emulators, and high-level languages. These microprocessors have become widely used in the design of new electronic equipment and computers. This book presents a detailed study of some of the most popular 16-bit microprocessors, the 8086 and 68000, and 32-bit microprocessors, the 80386 and 68020.

In this chapter we begin our study of microprocessors and microcomputers. The topics that follow are discussed:

1. Digital computers
2. Mainframe computers, minicomputers, and microcomputers
3. Hardware elements of the digital computer system
4. General architecture of a microcomputer system
5. Types of microprocessors and single-chip microcomputers

1.2 DIGITAL COMPUTERS

As a starting point, let us consider what a *computer* is, what it can do, and how it does it. A computer is a digital electronic data-processing system. Data are input to

1

the computer in one form, processed within the computer, and the information that results is either output or stored for later use. Figure 1.1 shows a modern computer system.

Figure 1.1 Modern large-scale computer. (Courtesy of International Business Machines Corp.)

Computers cannot think about how to process the data that were input. Instead, the user must tell the computer exactly what to do. The procedure by which a computer is told how to work is called *programming,* and the person who writes programs for a computer is known as a *programmer.* The result of the programmer's work is a set of instructions for the computer to follow. This is the computer's *program.* When the computer is operating, the instructions of the program guide it step by step through the task that is to be performed.

For example, a large department store can use a computer to take care of bookkeeping for its customer charge accounts. In this application, data about items purchased by the customers, such as price and department, are entered into the computer by an operator. These data are stored in the computer under the customer's account number. On the next billing date, the data are processed and a tabular record of each customer's account is output by the computer. These statements are mailed to the customers as a bill.

In a computer, the program controls the operation of a large amount of electronic circuitry. It is this circuitry that actually does the processing of data. Electronic computers first became available in the 1940s. These early computers were built with vacuum-tube electronic circuits. In the 1950s, a second generation of computers was built. During this period, transistor electronic circuitry, instead of tubes, was used to produce more compact and more reliable computer systems. When the *integrated circuit* (IC) came into the electronic market during the 1960s, a third generation of computers appeared. With ICs, industry could manufacture more complex, higher-speed, and very reliable computers.

Today, the computer industry is continuing to be revolutionized by the advances made in integrated-circuit technology. It is now possible to manufacture *very large scale integrated circuits* (VLSI) that can form a computer with just a small group of ICs. In fact, in some cases, a single IC can be used. These new technologies are rapidly advancing in the computer marketplace by permitting simpler and more cost-effective designs.

1.3 MAINFRAME COMPUTERS, MINICOMPUTERS, AND MICROCOMPUTERS

For many years the computer manufacturers' aim was to develop larger and more powerful computer systems. These are what we call *large-scale* or *mainframe computers*. Mainframes are always *general-purpose computers*. That is, they are designed with the ability to run a large number of different types of programs. For this reason, they can solve a wide variety of problems.

For instance, one user can apply the computer in an assortment of scientific applications where the primary function of the computer is to solve complex mathematical problems. A second user can apply the same basic computer system to perform business tasks such as accounting and inventory control. The only difference between the computer systems used in these two applications is their programs. In fact, today many companies use a single general-purpose computer to resolve both their scientific and business needs.

Figure 1.1 is an example of a mainframe computer manufactured by International Business Machine Corporation (IBM). Because of their high cost, mainframes find use only in central computing facilities of large businesses and institutions.

The many advances that have taken place in the field of electronics over the past two decades have led to rapid advances in computer system technology. For instance, the introduction of *small-scale integrated* (SSI) *circuits,* followed by *medium-scale integrated* (MSI) *circuits, large-scale integrated* (LSI) *circuits,* and *very large-scale integrated* (VLSI) *circuits,* has led the way in expanding the capacity and performance of large mainframe computers. But, at the same time, these advances have also permitted the introduction of smaller, lower-performance, and lower-cost computer systems.

As computer use grew, it was recognized that the powerful computing capability of a mainframe was not needed by many customers. Instead, they desired easier access to a machine with smaller capacity. It was to satisfy this requirement that the *minicomputer* was developed. Minicomputers, such as that shown in Fig. 1.2, are also digital computers and are capable of performing the same basic operations as the earlier, larger systems. However, they are designed to provide a smaller functional capability. The processor section of this type of computer is typically manufactured using SSI and MSI electronic circuitry.

Minicomputers have found wide use as general-purpose computers, but their lower cost also allows their use in dedicated applications. A computer used in a

Figure 1.2 Minicomputer system.
(Courtesy of Digital Equipment Corp.)

dedicated application represents what is known as a *special-purpose computer,* by which we mean a system that has been tailored to meet the needs of a specific application. Examples are process control computers for industrial facilities, data-processing systems for retail stores, and medical analysis systems for patient care.

The newest development in the computer industry is the *microcomputer.* Today, the microcomputer represents the most important step in the evolution of the computer world. It is a computer that has been designed to provide reduced size and capability compared to a minicomputer, with a much lower cost.

The heart of the microcomputer system is the *microprocessor.* A microprocessor is a general-purpose processor built into a single IC. It is an example of a VLSI device. Through the use of VLSI circuitry in the microcomputer have come the benefits of smaller size, lighter weight, lower cost, reduced power requirements, and higher reliability.

The low cost of microprocessors, which can be as low as $1, has opened the use of computer electronics to a much broader range of products. Figures 1.3, 1.4,

Figure 1.3 Retail store data-processing system. (Courtesy of Hugin-Sweda, Inc.)

Figure 1.4 Calculator. (Courtesy of Texas Instruments, Inc.)

Figure 1.5 Electronic toy. (Courtesy of Texas Instruments, Inc.)

and 1.5 show some typical systems in which a microcomputer is used as a special-purpose computer.

Microcomputers are also finding wide use as general-purpose computers. Figure 1.6 is an example of a personal computer system. In fact, microcomputer systems designed for the high-performance end of the microcomputer market are rivaling the performance of minicomputers and at a much lower cost to the user.

Figure 1.6 McIntosh™ personal computer. (Courtesy Apple Computer Co.)

1.4 HARDWARE ELEMENTS OF THE DIGITAL COMPUTER SYSTEM

The hardware of a digital computer system is divided into four functional sections. The block diagram of Fig. 1.7 shows the four basic units of a simplified computer: the *input unit, central processing unit, memory unit,* and *output unit.* Each section has a special function in terms of overall computer operation.

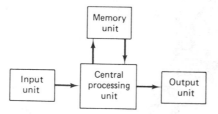

Figure 1.7 Block diagram of a digital computer. (Walter A. Triebel, *Integrated Digital Electronics,* © 1979. Adapted by permission of Prentice-Hall, Inc., Englewood Cliffs, N.J.)

The *central processing unit* (CPU) is the heart of the computer system. It is responsible for performing all arithmetic operations and logic decisions initiated by the program. In addition to arithmetic and logic functions, the CPU controls overall system operation.

On the other hand, the input and output units are the means by which the CPU communicates with the outside world. The *input unit* is used to input information and commands to the CPU for processing. For instance, a CRT terminal can be used by the programmer to input a new program.

After processing, the information that results must be output. This output of data from the system is performed under control of the *output unit.* Examples of ways of outputting information are as printed pages produced by a high-speed printer or displayed on the screen of a video display terminal.

The *memory unit* of the computer is used to store information such as numbers, names, and addresses. By "store," we mean that memory has the ability to hold this information for processing or for outputting at a later time. The programs that define how the computer is to process data also reside in memory.

In computer systems, memory is divided into two different sections, known as *primary storage* and *secondary storage*. They are also sometimes called *internal memory* and *external memory,* respectively. *External memory* is used for long-term storage of information that is not in use. For instance, it holds programs, files of data, and files of information. In most computers, this part of memory employs storage on magnetic media such as magnetic tapes, magnetic disks, and magnetic drums. This is because they have the ability to store large amounts of data.

Internal memory is a smaller segment of memory used for temporary storage of programs, data, and information. For instance, when a program is to be executed, its instructions are first brought from external memory into internal memory together with the files of data and information that it will affect. After this, the program is executed and its files updated while they are held in internal memory. When the processing defined by the program is complete, the updated files are returned to external memory. Here the program and files are retained for use at a later time.

The internal memory of a computer system uses electronic memory devices instead of storage on a magnetic media memory. In most modern computer systems, semiconductor read-only memory (ROM) and random access read/write memory (RAM) are in use. These devices make internal memory much faster-operating than external memory.

Neither semiconductor memory nor magnetic media memory alone can satisfy the requirements of most general-purpose computer systems. Because of this fact, both types are normally present in the system. For instance, in a personal computer system, working storage is typically provided with RAM, while long-term storage is provided with floppy disk memory. On the other hand, in special-purpose computer systems, such as a video game, semiconductor memory is used. That is, the program that determines how the game is played is stored in ROM, and data storage, such as for graphic patterns, is in RAM.

1.5 GENERAL ARCHITECTURE OF A MICROCOMPUTER SYSTEM

Now that we have introduced the *general architecture* of a digital computer, let us look at how a microcomputer fits this model. Looking at Fig. 1.8, we find that the architecture of the microcomputer is essentially the same as that of the digital computer in Fig. 1.7. It has the same functional elements: input unit, output unit, memory unit, and, in place of the CPU, a *microprocessor unit* (MPU). Moreover, each element serves the same basic function relative to overall system operation.

The difference between minicomputers, mainframe computers, and microcomputers does not lie in the fundamental blocks used to build the computer; instead, it relates to the capacity and performance of the electronics used to implement their blocks and the resulting overall system capacity and performance. As indicated earlier, microcomputers are typically designed with smaller capacity and lower performance than either minicomputers or mainframes.

Unlike the mainframe and minicomputer, a microcomputer can be implemented with a small group of components. Again, the heart of the computer system is the MPU (CPU) and it performs all arithmetic, logic, and control operations. However,

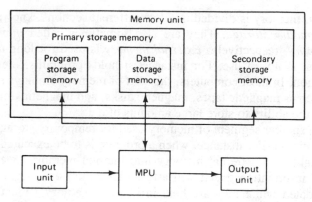

Figure 1.8 General microcomputer system architecture.

in a microcomputer the MPU is implemented with a single microprocessor chip instead of a large assortment of SSI and MSI logic functions such as in older minicomputers and mainframes. Notice that correct use of the term microprocessor restricts its use to the central processing unit in a microcomputer system.

Notice that we have partitioned the memory unit into an internal memory section for storage of active data and instructions and an external memory section for long-term storage. As in minicomputers, the long-term storage medium in a microcomputer is frequently a floppy disk. However, hard disk drives are used when storage requirements are higher than those provided by floppy disks.

Internal memory of the microcomputer is further subdivided into *program storage memory* and *data storage memory*. Typically, internal memory is implemented with both ROM and RAM ICs. Data, whether they are to be interpreted as numbers, characters, or instructions, can be stored in either ROM or RAM. But in most microcomputer systems, instructions of the program and data such as lookup tables are stored in ROM. This is because this type of information does not normally change. By using ROM, its storage is made *nonvolatile*. That is, if power is lost, the information is retained.

On the other hand, the numerical and character data that are to be processed by the microprocessor change frequently. These data must be stored in a type of memory from which they can be read by the microprocessor, modified through processing, and written back for storage. For this reason, they are stored in RAM instead of ROM.

Depending on the application, the input and output sections can be implemented with something as simple as a few switches for inputs and a few light-emitting diodes (LEDs) for outputs. In other applications, for example in a personal computer, the input/output (I/O) devices can be more sophisticated, such as video display terminals and printers, just like those employed in minicomputer systems.

Up to this point, we have been discussing what is known as a *multichip microcomputer system,* that is, a system implemented with a microprocessor and an assortment of support circuits, such as ROMs, RAMs, and I/O peripherals. This architecture makes for a very flexible system design. Its ROM, RAM, and I/O capacity can be easily expanded by just adding more devices. This is the circuit configuration used in most larger microcomputer systems. An example is the personal computer system shown in Fig. 1.9(a).

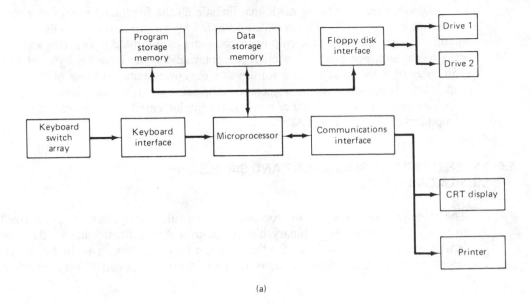

(a)

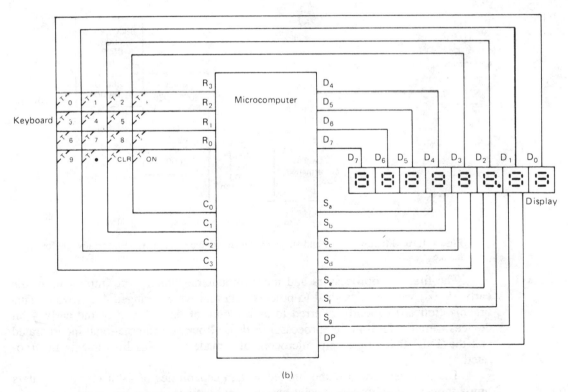

(b)

Figure 1.9 (a) Block diagram of a personal computer; (b) block diagram of a calculator.

Devices are now being made that include all the functional blocks of a microcomputer in a single IC. This is called a *single-chip microcomputer*. Unlike the multichip microcomputer, single-chip microcomputers are limited in capacity and not as easy to expand. For example, a microcomputer device can have 8K bytes of ROM, 256 bytes of RAM, and 32 lines for use as inputs or outputs. Because of this limited capability, single-chip microcomputers find wide use in special-purpose computer applications. A block diagram of a calculator implemented with a single-chip microcomputer is shown in Fig. 1.9(b).

1.6 TYPES OF MICROPROCESSORS AND SINGLE-CHIP MICROCOMPUTERS

The principal way in which microprocessors and microcomputers are categorized is in terms of the number of binary bits in the data they process, that is, their word length. Figure 1.10 shows that the three standard organizations used in the design of microprocessors and microcomputers are 4-bit, 8-bit, 16-bit and 32-bit data words.

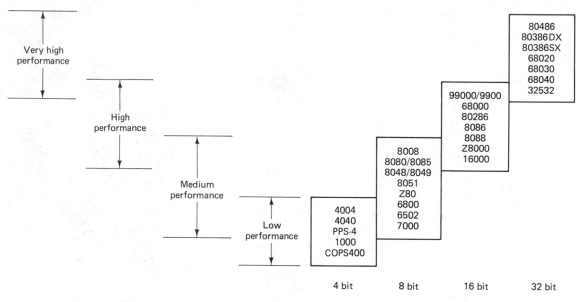

Figure 1.10 Microprocessor and single-chip microcomputer categories and relative performance.

The first microprocessors and microcomputers, which were introduced in the early 1970s, were all designed to process data that were arranged 4 bits wide. This organization is frequently referred to as a *nibble* of data. Some of the early 4-bit devices were the PPS-4 microprocessor made by Rockwell International Incorporated and the TMS1000 single-chip microcomputer made by Texas Instruments Incorporated.

The low performance and limited system capabilities of 4-bit microcomputers limits their use to simpler, special-purpose applications. Some common uses are in calculators and electronic toys. In this type of equipment, low cost, not high performance, is the overriding requirement in the selection of a processor. These kinds of applications are still implemented with 4-bit, single-chip microcomputers.

In the 1973–1974 period, second-generation microprocessors were introduced. These devices, such as Intel Corporation's 8008 and 8080, were 8-bit microprocessors. That is, they were designed to process 8-bit (1-byte-wide) data instead of 4-bit data.

The newer 8-bit microprocessors exhibited higher-performance operation, larger system capabilities, and greater ease of programming. They were able to provide the system requirements for many applications that could not be satisfied by 4-bit microcomputers. These extended capabilities led to widespread acceptance of multichip 8-bit microcomputers for special-purpose system designs. Examples of some of these dedicated applications are electronic instruments, cash registers, and printers.

Somewhat later, 8-bit microprocessors began to migrate into general-purpose microcomputer systems. In fact, the Z-80A was the host MPU in a number of personal computers.

Late in the 1970s, 8-bit, single-chip microcomputers, such as Intel 8048, became available. The full microcomputer capability of this single chip further reduces the cost of implementing designs for smaller, dedicated digital systems. In fact, 8-bit microcomputers are still being designed for introduction into the marketplace. An example is Intel's 80C51 family of 8-bit microcomputers. Newer devices, such as the 80C51FA, when compared to the 8048, offer a one-order-of-magnitude-higher performance, more powerful instruction sets, and special on-chip functions such as interval/event timers and universal asynchronous receiver/transmitters (UARTs).

The plans for development of third-generation 16-bit microprocessors were announced by many of the leading semiconductor manufacturers in the mid-1970s. The 9900 was introduced in 1977, followed by a number of other key devices, such as the 9981, 8086, 8088, Z8000, 68000, 99000, and 16000. These devices all provide high performance and have the ability to satisfy a broad scope of special- and general-purpose microcomputer applications. All the devices have the ability to handle 8-bit as well as 16-bit data words. Some can even process data organized as 32-bit words. Moreover, their powerful instruction sets are more in line with those provided by minicomputers instead of those of 8-bit microprocessors.

In terms of special-purpose applications, 16-bit microprocessors are replacing 8-bit processors in applications that require very high performance: for example, certain types of electronic instruments. A single-chip, 16-bit microcomputer, the 8096 is also available for use in this type of application.

Sixteen-bit microprocessors are also being used in applications that can benefit from some of their extended system capabilities. For instance, they are beginning to be used in word-processing systems. This type of system requires a large amount of character data to be temporarily active; therefore, it can benefit from the ability of a 16-bit microprocessor to access a much larger amount of data storage memory.

Most of the early personal computer designs were done with 16-bit microprocessors. For instance, IBM in its personal computer, the PC, uses the 8088 microprocessor to implement the microcomputer. The 8088 is an 8-bit bus version of the 8086 microprocessor that we cover in this book. Moreover, Apple Computer used the 68000 in its original McIntosh personal computer.

Today a new generation of personal computers is available that is designed with 32-bit microprocessors such as the 80386 and 68020. These 32-bit microprocessors are also widely used in high-performance computer interfaces and in telecommunications equipment.

ASSIGNMENT

Section 1.2

1. What tells a computer what to do, where to get data, how to process data, and where to put the results when done?
2. What is the name given for a sequence of instructions that is used to guide a computer through a task?
3. What type of electronic devices are revolutionizing the computer industry today?

Section 1.3

4. Name the three classes of computers.
5. What are the main similarities and differences between the minicomputer and the microcomputer?
6. What is meant by general-purpose computer?
7. What is meant by special-purpose computer?
8. What is the heart of the microcomputer system?

Section 1.4

9. What are the four building blocks of a digital computer system?
10. What is the heart of the digital computer called?
11. What is the function of the input unit?
12. What is the function of the output unit?
13. What is the purpose of memory in a computer system?
14. What is the difference between primary and secondary storage?
15. What does ROM stand for?
16. What does RAM stand for?

Section 1.5

17. What does MPU stand for?
18. Give two examples of devices used to implement external memory in a microcomputer system.
19. Into what two sections is the internal memory of a microcomputer partitioned?
20. Which part of the internal memory is normally implemented with RAM ICs?

21. Is ROM volatile or nonvolatile?
22. What is meant by volatile memory?
23. What is the difference between a multichip microcomputer and a single-chip microcomputer?

Section 1.6

24. What are the standard data word lengths for which microprocessors have been developed?
25. Give an example of a 4-bit microprocessor.
26. List two applications that are frequently implemented with a 4-bit microprocessor.
27. What 8-bit microprocessor was used in personal computers?
28. Name a modern 8-bit, single-chip microcomputer device.
29. Which microprocessor is used in IBM's original PC? Apple's original McIntosh?
30. Give the names of two 32-bit microprocessors.

2

Software Architecture of the 8086 Microprocessor

2.1 INTRODUCTION

In this chapter we begin our study of the 8086 microprocessor and assembly language programming. To program the 8086 using assembly language, we must understand how the 8086 microprocessor and its memory subsystem operate from a software point of view. For this reason, we will examine the *software architecture* of the 8086 microprocessor in this chapter. The following topics are covered:

1. Software model of the 8086 microprocessor
2. Memory address space and data organization
3. Segment registers and memory segmentation
4. Dedicated and general use of memory
5. Instruction pointer
6. Data registers
7. Pointer and index registers
8. Flag register
9. Generating a memory address
10. The stack
11. Input/output address space
12. Addressing modes of the 8086 microprocessor

14

2.2 SOFTWARE MODEL OF THE 8086 MICROPROCESSOR

The purpose of developing a *software model* is to aid the programmer in understanding the operation of the microcomputer system from a software point of view. To be able to program a microprocessor, we do not need to know all its hardware architecture features. For instance, we do not necessarily need to know the function of the signals at its various pins, their electrical connections, or their electrical switching characteristics. The function, interconnection, and operation of the internal circuits of the microprocessor also need not normally be considered.

What is important to the programmer is to know the various registers within the device and to understand their purpose, functions, operating capabilities, and limitations. Furthermore, it is essential to know how external memory is organized and how it is addressed to obtain instructions and data.

The software architecture of the 8086 microprocessor is illustrated with the software model shown in Fig. 2.1. Looking at this diagram, we see that it includes thirteen 16-bit internal registers: the *instruction pointer* (IP), four *data registers* (AX,

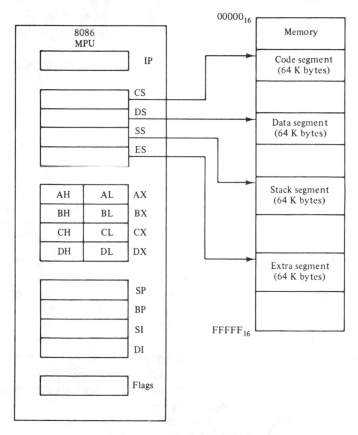

Figure 2.1 Software model of the 8086 microprocessor.

BX, CX, and DX), two *pointer registers* (BP and SP), two *index registers* (SI and DI), and four *segment registers* (CS, DS, SS, and ES). In addition to these registers, there is another register called the *status register* (SR), with nine of its bits implemented for status and control flags. The model also includes a *1,048,576 (1M) byte address space* for implementation of external memory. Our concern here is what can be done with this architecture and how to do it through software. For this purpose, we will now begin a detailed study of the elements of the model and their relationship to software.

2.3 MEMORY ADDRESS SPACE AND DATA ORGANIZATION

Now that we have introduced the idea of a software model, let us look at how information such as numbers, characters, and instructions are stored in memory.

As shown in Fig. 2.2, the 8086 microcomputer supports 1M bytes of external memory. This memory space is organized as bytes of data stored at consecutive addresses over the address range 00000_{16} tp $FFFFF_{16}$. From an addressing point of view, *even-* or *odd-addressed bytes of data* can be independently accessed. In this way, we see that the memory in an 8086-based microcomputer is actually organized as 8-bit bytes, not as 16-bit words. However, the 8086 can access any two consecutive bytes as a *word* of data. In this case, the *lower-addressed byte is the least significant byte* of the word and the *higher-addressed byte is its most significant byte*.

Figure 2.2 Address space of the 8086. (Reprinted by permission of Intel Corp. Copyright/Intel Corp., 1979.)

Figure 2.3(a) shows how a word of data is stored in memory. Notice that the storage location at the lower address, 00724_{16}, contains the value $00000010_2 = 02_{16}$. Moreover, the contents of the next-higher-addressed storage location 00725_{16} are $01010101_2 = 55_{16}$. These two bytes represent the word $0101010100000010_2 = 5502_{16}$.

To permit efficient use of memory, words of data can be stored at even- or odd-address boundaries. The least significant bit of the address determines the type of *word boundary*. If this bit is 0, the word is said to be held at an *even-address boundary*. That is, a word at an even-address boundary corresponds to two consecutive bytes, with the least significant byte located at an even address. For example, the word in Fig. 2.3(a) has its least significant byte at address 00724_{16}. Therefore, it is stored at an even-address boundary.

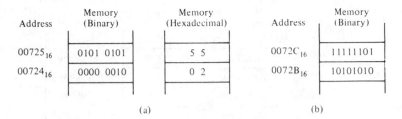

Figure 2.3 (a) Storing a word of data in memory; (b) an example.

EXAMPLE 2.1

What is the data word shown in Fig. 2.3(b)? Express the result in hexadecimal form. Is it stored at an even- or an odd-address boundary?

SOLUTION The most significant byte of the word is stored at address $0072C_{16}$ and equals

$$11111101_2 = FD_{16}$$

Its least significant byte is stored at address $0072B_{16}$ and is

$$10101010_2 = AA_{16}$$

Together these two bytes give the word

$$1111110110101010_2 = FDAA_{16}$$

Expressing the address of the least significant byte in binary form gives

$$0072B_{16} = 0000000001110010101011_2$$

Since the rightmost bit (LSB) is logic 1, the word is stored at an odd-address boundary in memory.

The *double word* is another data form that can be processed by the 8086 microcomputer. A double word corresponds to four consecutive bytes of data stored in memory. An example of double-word data is a *pointer* that is used to address data or code outside the current segment of memory. The word of this pointer that is stored at the higher address is called the *segment base address* and the word at the lower address is called the *offset value*.

An example showing the storage of a pointer in memory is given in Fig. 2.4(a). Here we find that the higher-addressed word, which represents the segment address, is stored starting at even-address boundary 00006_{16}. The most significant byte of this word is at address 00007_{16} and equals $00111011_2 = 3B_{16}$. Its least significant byte is at address 00006_{16} and equals $01001100_2 = 4C_{16}$. Combining these two values, we get the segment base address, which equals $0011101101001100_2 = 3B4C_{16}$.

The offset part of the pointer is the lower-addressed word. Its least significant byte is stored at address 00004_{16}. This location contains $01100101_2 = 65_{16}$. The most significant byte is at address 00005_{16}, which contains $00000000_2 = 00_{16}$. The resulting offset is $0000000001100101_2 = 0065_{16}$.

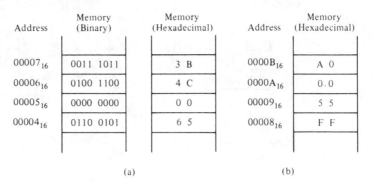

Address	Memory (Binary)	Memory (Hexadecimal)	Address	Memory (Hexadecimal)
00007_{16}	0011 1011	3 B	$0000B_{16}$	A 0
00006_{16}	0100 1100	4 C	$0000A_{16}$	0 . 0
00005_{16}	0000 0000	0 0	00009_{16}	5 5
00004_{16}	0110 0101	6 5	00008_{16}	F F

(a)   (b)

Figure 2.4   (a) Storing a 32-bit pointer in memory; (b) an example.

EXAMPLE 2.2

How should the pointer with segment-base address equal to $A000_{16}$ and offset address $55FF_{16}$ be stored at an even-address boundary starting at 00008_{16}?

SOLUTION   Storage of the two-word pointer requires four consecutive byte locations in memory starting at address 00008_{16}. The least significant byte of the offset is stored at address 00008_{16}. This value is shown as FF_{16} in Fig. 2.4(b). The most significant byte of the offset, which is 55_{16}, is stored at address 00009_{16}. These two bytes are followed by the least significant byte of the segment base address, 00_{16}, at address $0000A_{16}$, and its most significant byte, $A0_{16}$, at address $0000B_{16}$.

We just showed that data are stored in the memory of the 8086 microcomputer in one of three fundamental data formats, the byte (8 bits), word (16 bits), or double word (32 bits). These basic formats represent data elements that span one, two, or four consecutive bytes of memory, respectively.

2.4 SEGMENT REGISTERS AND MEMORY SEGMENTATION

Even though the 8086 has a 1M-byte memory address space, not all this memory can be active at one time. Actually, the 1M byte of memory can be partitioned into 64K (65,536) byte *segments*. Each segment represents an independently addressable unit of memory consisting of 64K consecutive byte-wide storage locations. Each segment is assigned a *base address* that identifies its starting point, that is, its lowest-addressed byte storage location.

Only four of these 64K-byte segments can be active at a time. They are the *code segment, stack segment, data segment,* and *extra segment.* The locations of the segments of memory that are active, as shown in Fig. 2.5 are identified by the value of address held in the 8086's four internal segment registers: CS (*code segment*), SS (*stack segment*), DS (*data segment*), and ES (*extra segment*). These four registers are shown in Fig. 2.5. Each contains a 16-bit base address that points to the lowest-addressed byte of the segment in memory. These four segments give a maximum of 256K bytes of active memory. Of this, 64K bytes are allocated for code (*program storage*), 64K bytes for a *stack,* and 128K bytes for *data storage.*

The values held in these registers are usually referred to as the *current segment*

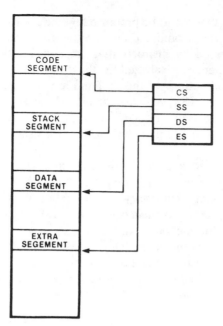

Figure 2.5 Active segments of memory. (Reprinted by permission of Intel Corp. Copyright/Intel Corp., 1979.)

register values. For example, the word in CS points to the first byte-wide storage location in the current code segment.

Figure 2.6 illustrates the *segmentation of memory*. In this diagram, we have identified 64K-byte segments with letters such as A, B, and C. The data segment (DS) register contains the value B. Therefore, the second 64K-byte segment of memory from the top, which is labeled B, acts as the current data storage segment. This is

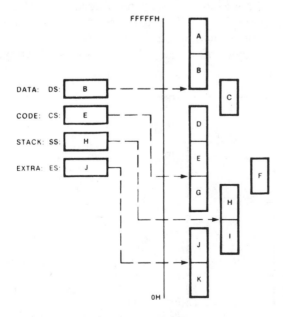

Figure 2.6 Contiguous, adjacent, disjointed, and overlapping segments. (Reprinted by permission of Intel Corp. Copyright/Intel Corp., 1979.).

the segment in which data that are to be processed by the microcomputer are stored. Therefore, this part of the microcomputer's memory must contain read/write storage locations that can be accessed by instructions as storage locations for source and destination operands. Segment E is selected for the code segment. It is this segment of memory from which instructions of the program are currently being fetched for execution. The stack segment (SS) register contains H, thereby selecting the 64K-byte segment labeled as H for use as a stack. Finally, the extra segment register ES is loaded with J such that segment J of memory can function as a second 64K-byte data storage segment.

The segment registers are said to be *user accessible*. This means that the programmer can change the value they hold through software. Therefore, for a program to gain access to another part of memory, it just has to change the value of the appropriate register or registers. For instance, a new 128K-byte data space can be brought in by simply changing the values in DS and ES.

There is one restriction on the value that can be assigned to a segment as a base address: it must reside on a 16-byte address boundary. Valid examples are 00000_{16}, 00010_{16}, and 00020_{16}. Other than this restriction, segments can be *contiguous, adjacent, disjointed*, or even *overlapping*.

2.5 DEDICATED AND GENERAL USE OF MEMORY

Any part of the 8086 microcomputer's 1M-byte address space can be implemented; however, some address locations have *dedicated functions*. These locations should not be used as general memory where data or instructions of the program are stored. Let us now look at these reserved and general-use parts of memory.

Figure 2.7 shows the *reserved* and *general-use (open) parts* of the 8086's *address space*. Notice that storage locations from address 00000_{16} to 00013_{16} are dedicated and those from address 00014_{16} to $0007F_{16}$ are reserved. These 128 bytes of memory are used for storage of pointers to interrupt service routines. As indicated earlier, each pointer requires 4 bytes of memory. Two bytes hold the 16-bit segment

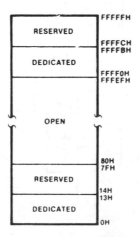

Figure 2.7 Dedicated and general use of memory. (Reprinted by permission of Intel Corp. Copyright/Intel Corp., 1979.).

address and the other two hold the 16-bit offset. Therefore, it can contain up to 32 pointers.

At the high end of the memory address space is another reserved pointer area. It is located from address $FFFFC_{16}$ through $FFFFF_{16}$. These four memory locations are reserved for use with future products and should not be used. Moreover, Intel Corporation, the manufacturer of the 8086, has identified the 12 storage locations from address $FFFF0_{16}$ through $FFFFB_{16}$ as dedicated for functions such as storage of the hardware reset jump instruction.

2.6 INSTRUCTION POINTER

The next register from the 8088's software model of Fig. 2.1 that we will consider is the *instruction pointer* (IP). It is also 16 bits in length and identifies the location of the next word of instruction code that is to be fetched in the current code segment. It is similar to a *program counter;* however, IP contains an offset instead of the actual address of the next instruction. This is because the 8086 contains 16-bit registers, but requires a 20-bit address for addressing memory. Internal to the 8086, the offset in IP is combined with the contents of CS to generate the address of the next word of instruction code.

During normal operation, the 8086 fetches words of instruction code one after the other from the code segment of memory and executes them. After an instruction is fetched from memory, it is decoded within the 8086 and, if necessary, operands are read from either the data segment of memory or internal registers. Next the operation specified in the instruction is performed on the operands and the result is written back to either an internal register or a storage location in memory. The 8086 is now ready to execute the next instruction.

Every time a word of code is fetched from memory, the 8086 updates the value in IP such that it points to the first byte of the next sequential word of instruction code. In this way, it is always ready to fetch more instructions of the program. Actually, the 8086 has an internal *code queue* and *prefetches* up to 6 bytes of instruction code and holds them internally by waiting for execution.

The active code segment can be changed by simply executing an instruction that loads a new value into the CS register. For this reason, we can use any 64K-byte segment of memory for storage of code.

2.7 DATA REGISTERS

As shown in Fig. 2.1, four *general-purpose data registers* are located within the 8086. During program execution, they are used for temporary storage of frequently used intermediate results. The advantage of storing these data in internal registers instead of memory is that they can be accessed much faster.

The data registers are shown in more detail in Fig. 2.8(a). Here we see that the four data registers are referred to as the *accumulator register* (A), the *base register* (B), the *count register* (C), and the *data register* (D). These names imply special functions that are performed by each register. Each of these registers can be accessed

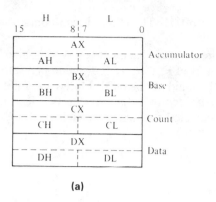

Register	Operations
AX	Word multiply, word divide, word I/O
AL	Byte multiply, byte divide, byte I/O, translate, decimal arithmetic
AH	Byte multiply, byte divide
BX	Translate
CX	String operations, loops
CL	Variable shift and rotate
DX	Word multiply, word divide, indirect I/O

(a)   (b)

Figure 2.8 (a) General-purpose data registers; (b) dedicated register functions. (Reprinted by permission of Intel Corp. Copyright/Intel Corp., 1979.)

either as a whole for 16-bit data operations or as two 8-bit registers for byte-wide data operations. References to a register as a word are identified by an X after the register letter. For instance, the 16-bit accumulator is referenced as AX. In a similar way, the other three registers are referred to as BX, CX, and DX.

On the other hand, when referencing one of these registers on a byte-wide basis, its high byte and low byte are identified by following the register name with the letter H or L, respectively. For the A register, the most significant byte is referred to as AH and the least significant byte as AL. The other byte-wide register pairs are BH and BL, CH and CL, and DH and DL.

Any of the general-purpose data registers can be used as the source or destination of an operand during an arithmetic operation such as ADD or a logic operation such as AND. However, for some operations, such as those performed by string instructions, specific registers are used. In the case of a string instruction, register C is used to store a count representing the number of bytes to be processed. This is the reason it is given the name *count register*. Another use of C is for the count of the number of bits by which the contents of an operand must be shifted or rotated during the execution of the multibit shift or rotate instructions.

Another example of dedicated use of data registers is that all I/O operations require the data that are to be input or output to be in the A register, while register D holds the address of the I/O port. Figure 2.8(b) summarizes the dedicated functions of the general-purpose data registers.

2.8 POINTER AND INDEX REGISTERS

Four other general-purpose registers are shown in Fig. 2.1: two *pointer registers* and two *index registers*. They are used to store offset addresses of memory locations relative to the segment registers. The values held in these registers can be read, loaded, or modified through software. This is done prior to executing the instruction that references the register for address offset. In this way, the instruction simply specifies which register contains the offset address.

Figure 2.9 shows that the two pointer registers are the *stack pointer* (SP) and *base pointer* (BP). The contents of SP and BP are used as offsets from the current value of SS during the execution of instructions that involve the stack segment of memory. In this way, they permit easy access to locations in the stack part of memory. The value in SP always represents the offset of the next stack location that can be accessed. That is, when combined with the value in SS, it results in a 20-bit address that points to the *top of the stack*.

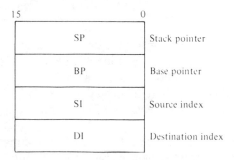

Figure 2.9   Pointer and index registers. (Reprinted by permission of Intel Corp. Copyright/Intel Corp., 1979.)

BP also represents an offset relative to the SS register. Its intended use is for access of data within the stack segment of memory. BP is employed as the offset in an addressing mode called the based addressing mode.

One common use of BP is within a subroutine that must reference parameters that were passed to the subroutine by way of the stack. In this case, instructions are written that use based addressing to examine the values of parameters held in the stack.

The index registers are used to hold offset addresses for instructions that access data stored in the data segment of memory. For this reason, they are always combined with the value in the DS register. In instructions that use indexed type of addressing, the *source index* (SI) register is used to store an offset address for a source operand, and the *destination index* (DI) register is used for storage of an offset that identifies the location of a destination operand. For example, a string instruction that requires an offset to the location of a source or destination operand would use these registers.

The index registers can also be used as source or destination registers in arithmetic and logical operations. Unlike the general-purpose registers, these registers must always be used for 16-bit operations and cannot be accessed as two separate bytes.

2.9 STATUS REGISTER

The *status register,* which is also called the *flag register,* is a 16-bit register within the 8086. However, as shown in Fig. 2.10 just nine of its bits are implemented. Six of these bits represent status flags. They are the *carry flag* (CF), the *parity flag* (PF), the *auxiliary carry flag* (AF), the *zero flag* (ZF), the *sign flag* (SF), and the *overflow flag* (OF). The logic state of these *status flags* indicates conditions that are produced

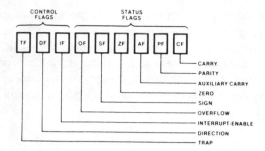

Figure 2.10 Status and control flags. (Reprinted by permission of Intel Corp. Copyright/Intel Corp., 1979.)

as the result of executing an arithmetic or logic instruction. That is, specific flag bits are reset (logic 0) or set (logic 1) at the completion of execution of the instruction.

Let us first summarize the operation of these flags:

1. *Carry flag* (CF): CF is set if there is a carry-out or a borrow-in for the most significant bit of the result during the execution of an arithmetic instruction. Otherwise, CF is reset.

2. *Parity flag* (PF): PF is set if the result produced by the instruction has even parity, that is, if it contains an even number of bits at the 1 logic level. If parity is odd, PF is reset.

3. *Auxiliary carry flag* (AF): AF is set if there is a carry-out from the low nibble into the high nibble or a borrow-in from the high nibble into the low nibble of the lower byte in a 16-bit word. Otherwise, AF is reset.

4. *Zero flag* (ZF): ZF is set if the result of an arithmetic or logic operation is zero. Otherwise, ZF is reset.

5. *Sign flag* (SF): The MSB of the result is copied into SF. Thus SF is set if the result is a negative number or reset if it is positive.

6. *Overflow flag* (OF): When OF is set, it indicates that the signed result is out of range. If the result is not out of range, OF remains reset.

For example, at the completion of execution of a byte-addition instruction, the carry flag (CF) could be set to indicate that the sum of the operands caused a carry-out condition. The auxiliary carry flag (AF) could also set due to the execution of the instruction. This depends on whether or not a carry-out occurred from the least significant nibble to the most significant nibble when the byte operands are added. The sign flag (SF) is also affected and it will reflect the logic level of the MSB of the result.

The 8086 provides instructions within its instruction set that are able to use these flags to alter the sequence in which the program is executed. For instance, ZF equal to logic 1 could be tested as the condition that would initiate a jump to another part of the program.

The other three implemented flag bits are *control flags*. They are the *direction flag* (DF), the *interrupt enable flag* (IF), and the *trap flag* (TF). These three flags are provided to control functions of the 8086 as follows:

1. *Trap flag* (TF): If TF is set, the 8086 goes into the *single-step mode*. When in the single-step mode, it executes one instruction at a time. This type of operation is very useful for debugging programs.

2. *Interrupt flag* (IF): For the 8086 to recognize *maskable interrupt requests* at

its INTR input, the IF flag must be set. When IF is reset, requests at INTR are ignored and the maskable interrupt interface is disabled.

3. *Direction flag* (DF): The logic level of DF determines the direction in which string operations will occur. When it is set, the string instruction automatically decrements the address. Therefore, the string data transfers proceed from high address to low address. On the other hand, resetting DF causes the string address to be incremented. In this way, transfers proceed from low address to high address.

The instruction set of the 8086 includes instructions for saving, loading, or manipulating specific bits of the status register. For instance, special instructions are provided to permit user software to set or reset CF, DF, and IF at any point in the program. For instance, just prior to the beginning of a string operation, DF could be set so that the string address automatically decrements.

2.10 GENERATING A MEMORY ADDRESS

A *logical address* in the 8086 system is described by a segment base and an offset. Both the segment base and offset are 16-bit quantities. This is because all registers and memory locations are 16 bits long. However, the *physical addresses* that are used to access memory are 20 bits in length. The generation of the physical address involves combining a 16-bit offset value that is located in a base register, an index register, or a pointer register and a 16-bit base value that is located in one of the segment registers.

The source of the offset address depends on which type of memory reference is taking place. It can be the base pointer (BP) register, base (BX) register, source index (SI) register, destination index (DI) register, or instruction pointer (IP). On the other hand, the base value always resides in one of the segment registers: CS, DS, SS, or ES.

For instance, when an instruction acquisition takes place, the source of the base address is always the code segment (CS) register and the source of the offset is always the instruction pointer (IP). On the other hand, if the value of a variable is being written to memory during the execution of an instruction, typically, the base address will be in the data segment (DS) register and the offset will be in the destination index (DI) register. Segment override prefixes can be used to change the segment from which the variable is accessed.

Another example is the stack address that is needed when pushing parameters onto the stack. This address is formed from the contents of the stack segment (SS) register and stack pointer (SP).

Remember that the segment base address represents the starting location of the 64K-byte segment in memory, that is, the lowest-addressed byte in the segment. The offset identifies the distance in bytes that the storage location of interest resides from this starting address. Therefore, the lowest-addressed byte in a segment has an offset of 0000_{16} and the highest-addressed byte has an offset of $FFFF_{16}$.

Figure 2.11 shows how a segment address and offset value are combined to give a physical address. What happens is that the value in the segment register is

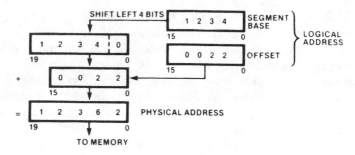

Figure 2.11 Generating a physical address. (Reprinted by permission of Intel Corp. Copyright/Intel Corp., 1979.)

shifted left by 4 bits, with its LSBs being filled with 0s. Then the offset value is added to the 16 LSBs of the shifted segment address. The result of this addition is the 20-bit physical address.

The example in Fig. 2.11 represents a segment base of 1234_{16} and an offset of 0022_{16}. First let us express the base in binary form. This gives

$$1234_{16} = 0001001000110100_2$$

Shifting left four times and filling with zeros results in

$$00010010001101000000_2 = 12340_{16}$$

The offset in binary form is

$$0022_{16} = 0000000000100010_2$$

Adding the shifted segment address and offset, we get

$$00010010001101000000_2 + 0000000000100010_2 = 00010010001101100010_2$$

$$= 12362_{16}$$

This address calculation is automatically done with the 8086 each time a memory access is initiated.

EXAMPLE 2.3

What would be the offset required to map to physical address location $002C3_{16}$ if the segment base is $002A_{16}$?

SOLUTION   The offset value can be obtained by shifting the segment base left 4 bits and then subtracting it from the physical address. Shifting left gives

$$002A0_{16}$$

Subtracting, we get the value of the offset:

$$002C3_{16} - 002A0_{16} = 0023_{16}$$

Actually, many different logical addresses can be mapped to the same physical address location in memory. This is done by simply changing the values of the base address in the segment register and its corresponding offset. The diagram in Fig. 2.12

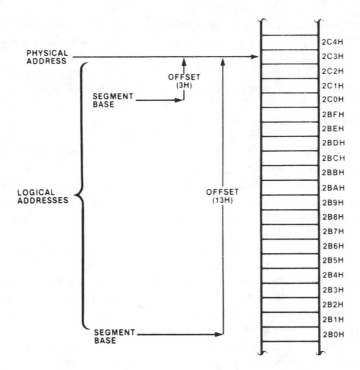

PHYSICAL
ADDRESS

OFFSET
(3H)

SEGMENT
BASE

LOGICAL
ADDRESSES

OFFSET
(13H)

SEGMENT
BASE

2C4H
2C3H
2C2H
2C1H
2C0H
2BFH
2BEH
2BDH
2BCH
2BBH
2BAH
2B9H
2B8H
2B7H
2B6H
2B5H
2B4H
2B3H
2B2H
2B1H
2B0H

Figure 2.12 Relationship between logical and physical addresses. (Reprinted by permission of Intel Corp. Copyright/Intel Corp., 1979.)

demonstrates this idea. Notice that base $002B_{16}$ with offset 0013_{16} maps to physical address $002C3_{16}$ in memory. However, if the segment base address is changed to $002C_{16}$ with a new offset of 0003_{16}, the physical address is still $002C3_{16}$

2.11 THE STACK

As indicated earlier, the *stack* is implemented in the memory of the 8086 microcomputer. It is 64K bytes long and is organized from a software point of view as 32K words. Moreover, we found that the lowest-addressed byte in the current stack is pointed to by the base address in the SS register.

During a *subroutine call* the contents of certain internal registers of the 8086 are pushed to the stack part of memory. Here they are maintained temporarily. At the completion of the subroutine, these values are popped off the stack and put back into the same internal registers where they originally resided.

For instance, when a *call* instruction is executed, the 8086 automatically pushes the current values in CS and IP onto the stack. As part of the subroutine, the contents of other registers can also be saved on the stack by executing *push* instructions. An example is the instruction PUSH SI. When executed, it causes the contents of the source index register to be pushed onto the stack.

At the end of the subroutine, *pop* instructions can be included to pop values from the stack back into their corresponding internal registers. For example, POP SI causes the value at the top of the stack to be popped back into the source index register.

Any number of stacks may exist in an 8086 microcomputer. A new stack can be brought in by simply changing the value in the SS register. For instance, executing the instruction MOV SS,DX loads a new value from DX into SS. Even though many stacks can exist, only one can be active at a time.

Another register, the stack pointer (SP), contains an offset from the value in SS. The address obtained from the contents of SS and SP is the physical address of the last storage location in the stack to which data were pushed. This is known as the *top of the stack*. The value in the stack pointer is initialized to $FFFF_{16}$ upon start-up of the microcomputer. Combining this value with the current value in SS gives the highest-addressed location in the stack, that is, the *bottom of the stack*.

The 8086 pushes data and addresses to the stack one word at a time. Each time the contents of a register are to be pushed onto the top of the stack, the value in the stack pointer is first automatically decremented by two and then the contents of the register are written into memory. In this way we see that the stack grows down in memory from the bottom of the stack, which corresponds to the physical address derived from SS and $FFFF_{16}$, toward the *end of the stack*, which corresponds to the physical address obtained from SS and offset 0002_{16}.

When a value is popped from the top of the stack, the reverse of this sequence occurs. The physical address defined by SS and SP points to the location of the last value pushed onto the stack. Its contents are first popped off the stack and put into the specific register within the 8086; then SP is automatically incremented by two. The top of the stack now corresponds to the previous value pushed onto the stack.

An example that shows how the contents of a register are pushed onto the stack is shown in Fig. 2.13(a). Here we find the state of the stack prior to execution of the PUSH instruction. Notice that the stack segment register contains 105_{16}. As indi-

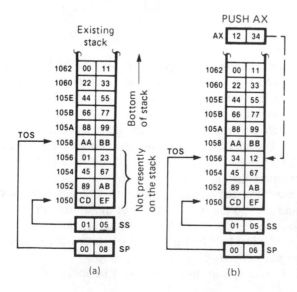

(a)

(b)

Figure 2.13 (a) Stack just prior to push operation (reprinted by permission of Intel Corp. Copyright/Intel Corp., 1979); (b) stack after execution of the PUSH AX instruction. (Reprinted by permission of Intel Corp. Copyright/Intel Corp., 1979.)

Software Architecture of the 8086 Microprocessor   Chap. 2

cated, the bottom of the stack resides at the physical address derived from SS with offset $FFFF_{16}$. This gives the bottom of stack address A_{BOS} as

$$A_{BOS} = 1050_{16} + FFFF_{16}$$

$$= 1104F_{16}$$

Furthermore, the stack pointer, which represents the offset from the beginning of the stack specified by the contents of SS to the top of the stack, equals 0008_{16}. Therefore, the current top of the stack is at physical address A_{TOS}, which equals

$$A_{TOS} = 1050_{16} + 0008_{16}$$

$$= 1058_{16}$$

Addresses that are equal to or higher than that of the top of stack, 1058_{16}, contain valid stack data. Those with lower addresses do not yet contain valid stack data. Notice that the last value pushed to the stack in Fig. 2.13(a) was $BBAA_{16}$.

Figure 2.13(b) demonstrates what happens when the PUSH AX instruction is executed. Here we see that AX contains the value 1234_{16}. Notice that execution of the PUSH instruction causes the stack pointer to be decremented by two but does not affect the contents of the stack segment register. Therefore, the next location to be accessed in the stack corresponds to address 1056_{16}. It is to this location that the value in AX is pushed. Notice that the most significant byte of AX, which equals 12_{16}, now resides in the least significant byte of the word in stack, and the least significant byte of AX, which is 34_{16}, is held in the most signficant byte.

Now let us look at an example in which stack data are popped back into the register from which they were pushed. Figure 2.14 illustrates this operation. In Fig. 2.14(a), the stack is shown to be in the state that resulted due to our prior PUSH AX example. That is, SP equals 0006_{16}, SS equals 105_{16}, the address of the top of the stack equals 1056_{16}, and the word at the top of the stack equals 1234_{16}.

Looking at Fig. 2.14(b), we see what happens when the instructions POP AX and POP BX are executed in that order. Here we see that execution of the first instruction causes the 8086 to read the value from the top of the stack and put it into the AX register as 1234_{16}. Next, SP is incremented to give 0008_{16} and another read cycle is initiated from the stack. This second read corresponds to the POP BX instruction, and it causes the value $BBAA_{16}$ to be loaded into the BX register. SP is incremented once more and now equals $000A_{16}$. Therefore, the new top of stack is at address $105A_{16}$.

From Fig. 2.14(b), we see that the values read out of 1056_{16} and 1058_{16} still remain at these addresses. But now they reside at locations that are considered to be above the top of the stack. Therefore, they no longer represent valid stack data.

2.12 INPUT/OUTPUT ADDRESS SPACE

The 8086 has separate memory and input/output (I/O) address spaces. The *I/O address space* is the place where I/O interfaces, such as printer and terminal ports, are

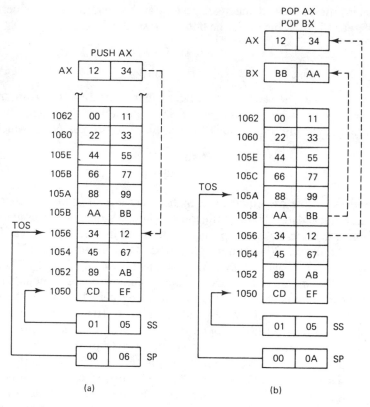

Figure 2.14 (a) Stack just prior to pop operation (reprinted by permission of Intel Corp. Copyright/Intel Corp., 1979); (b) stack after execution of the POP AX and POP BX instructions. (Reprinted by permission of Intel Corp. Copyright/Intel Corp., 1979.)

implemented. Figure 2.15 shows a map of the 8086's I/O address space. Notice that the address range is from 0000_{16} to $FFFF_{16}$. This represents just 64K byte addresses; therefore, unlike memory, I/O addresses are just 16 bits long.

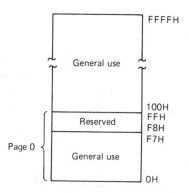

Figure 2.15 I/O address space. (Reprinted by permission of Intel Corp. Copyright/Intel Corp., 1979.)

The part of the map from address 0000_{16} through FF_{16} is referred to as *page 0*. Certain of the 8086's I/O instructions can only perform operations to I/O devices located in this part of the I/O address space. Other I/O instructions can input or output data from devices located anywhere in the I/O address space. Notice that the eight locations from address $00F8_{16}$ through $00FF_{16}$ are specified as reserved by Intel Corporation and should not be used.

2.13 ADDRESSING MODES OF THE 8086

When the 8086 executes an instruction, it performs the specified function on data. These data are called its *operands* and may be part of the instruction, reside in one of the internal registers of the 8086, stored at an address in memory, or held at an I/O port. To access these different types of operands, the 8086 is provided with various *addressing modes*. Here are the modes available on the 8086: *register addressing, immediate addressing, direct addressing, register indirect addressing, based addressing, indexed addressing and based indexed addressing*.

Of these seven modes, all but register addressing and immediate addressing make reference to an operand stored in memory. Therefore, they require the 8086 to initiate a read or write of memory. The addressing modes provide different ways of computing the address of an operand. Let us now consider in detail each of these addressing modes.

Register Addressing Mode

With the register addressing mode, the operand to be accessed is specified as residing in an internal register of the 8086. An example of an instruction that uses this addressing mode is

MOV AX, BX

This stands for move the contents of BX, the *source operand,* to AX, the *destination operand*. Both the source and destination operands have been specified as the contents of internal registers of the 8086.

Let us now look at the effect of executing the register addressing mode MOV instruction. In Fig. 2.16(a), we see the state of the 8086 just prior to fetching the instruction. Notice that IP and CS point to the MOV AX,BX instruction at address 01000_{16}. Prior to execution of this instruction, the contents of BX are $ABCD_{16}$ and the contents of AX represent a don't-care state. As shown in Fig. 2.16(b), the result of executing the instruction is that $ABCD_{16}$ is copied into AX.

Immediate Addressing Mode

If a source operand is part of the instruction instead of the contents of a register or memory location, it represents what is called an *immediate operand* and is accessed using the immediate addressing mode. Typically, immediate operands represent constant data.

Immediate operands can be either a byte or word of data. In the instruction

MOV AL, 15

the source operand 15_{16} is an example of a byte-wide immediate source operand. Note that the value of the immediate operand must always begin with one of the numbers 0 through 9. For example, if the immediate operand is to be $A5_{16}$, it must be written as 0A5H. The destination operand, which is the contents of AL, uses register addressing. Thus this instruction employs both the immediate and register addressing modes.

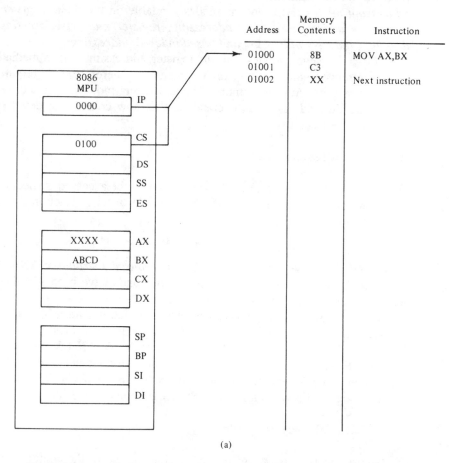

(a)

Figure 2.16 (a) Register addressing mode instruction before execution; (b) after execution.

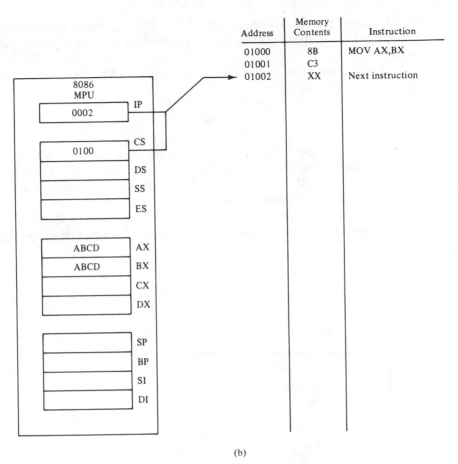

Address	Memory Contents	Instruction
01000	8B	MOV AX,BX
01001	C3	
01002	XX	Next instruction

(b)

Figure 2.16 (*continued*)

Figure 2.17(a) and (b) illustrates execution of this instruction. Here we find that the immediate operand 15_{16} is stored in the code segment of memory in the byte location immediately following the opcode of the instruction. This value is fetched, along with the opcode for MOV, into the instruction queue within the 8086. When it performs the move operation, the source operand is fetched from the instruction queue and not from the memory, and no external memory operations are performed. Notice that the result produced by executing this instruction is that the immediate operand, which equals 15_{16}, is loaded into the lower-byte part of the accumulator (AL).

Direct Addressing Mode

Direct addressing differs from immediate addressing in that the locations following the instruction opcode hold an *effective memory address* (EA) instead of data. This effective address is the 16-bit offset of the storage location of the operand from the location specified by the current value in the DS register. EA is combined with the contents of DS in the 8086 to produce the physical address of the operand in memory.

An example of an instruction that uses direct addressing for its source operand is

MOV CX, [BETA]

This stands for "move the contents of the memory location, which is labeled as BETA in the current data segment, into internal register CX." The assembler computes the offset of BETA from the beginning of the data segment and encodes it as part of the instruction's machine code.

In Fig. 2.18(a), we find that the value of the offset is stored in the two byte locations that follow the instruction. This value is also known as the *displacement*.

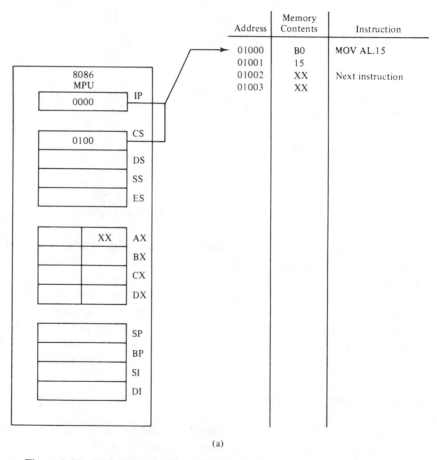

(a)

Figure 2.17 (a) Immediate addressing mode instruction before execution; (b) after execution.

Software Architecture of the 8086 Microprocessor   Chap. 2

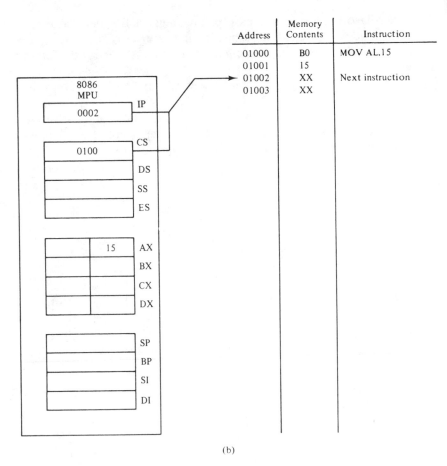

Address	Memory Contents	Instruction
01000	B0	MOV AL.15
01001	15	
01002	XX	Next instruction
01003	XX	

8086
MPU

IP 0002

CS 0100

DS

SS

ES

AX 15

BX

CX

DX

SP

BP

SI

DI

(b)

Figure 2.17   (*continued*)

Notice that the value assigned to constant BETA is 1234_{16}. As the instruction is executed, the 8086 combines 1234_{16} with 0200_{16} to get the physical address of the source operand. This gives

$$PA = 02000_{16} + 1234_{16}$$

$$= 03234_{16}$$

Then it reads the word of data starting at this address, which is $BEED_{16}$, and loads into the CX register. This result is illustrated in Fig. 2.18(b).

Register Indirect Addressing Mode

Register indirect addressing is similar to the direct addressing we just described in that an effective address is combined with the contents of DS to obtain a physical address. However, it differs in the way the offset is specified. This time EA resides in either a base register or an index register within the 8086. The base register can be either base register BX or base pointer register BP, and the index register can be source index register SI or destination index register DI.

An example of an instruction that uses register indirect addressing is

$$\text{MOV AX, [SI]}$$

This instruction moves the contents of the memory location offset by the value of EA in SI from the beginning of the current data segment to the AX register.

For instance, as shown in Fig. 2.19(a) and (b), if SI contains 1234_{16} and DS contains 0200_{16}, the result produced by executing the instruction is that the contents of memory location

$$PA = 02000_{16} + 1234_{16}$$

$$= 03234_{16}$$

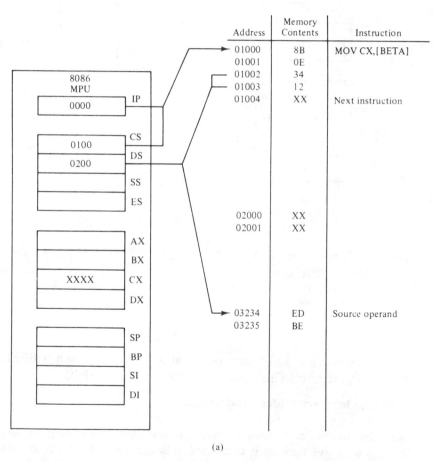

(a)

Figure 2.18 (a) Direct addressing mode instruction before execution; (b) after execution.

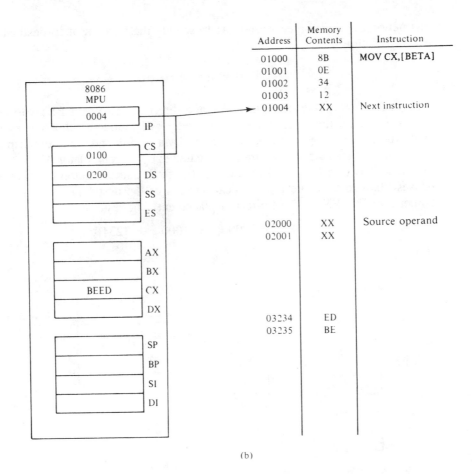

Address	Memory Contents	Instruction
01000	8B	MOV CX,[BETA]
01001	0E	
01002	34	
01003	12	
01004	XX	Next instruction
02000	XX	Source operand
02001	XX	
03234	ED	
03235	BE	

(b)

Figure 2.18 (*continued*)

are moved to the AX register. Notice in Fig. 2.19(b) that this value is $BEED_{16}$. In this example, the value 1234_{16} that was found in the SI register must have been loaded with another instruction prior to executing the MOV instruction.

Notice that the result produced by executing this instruction and the example for the direct addressing mode are the same. However, they differ in the way in which the physical address was generated. The direct addressing method lends itself to applications where the value of EA is a constant. On the other hand, register indirect addressing can be used when the value of EA is calculated and stored, for example, in SI by a previous instruction. That his, EA is a variable.

Based Addressing Mode

In the based addressing mode, the physical address of the operand is obtained by adding a direct or indirect displacement to the contents of either base register BX or base pointer register BP and the current value in DS or SS, respectively. A MOV instruction that uses based addressing to specify the location of its destination operand is as follows:

$$\text{MOV } [BX]+BETA, AL$$

This instruction uses base register BX and direct displacement BETA to derive the EA of the destination operand. The based addressing mode is implemented by specifying the base register in brackets followed by a + sign and the direct displacement. The source operand in this example is located in byte accumulator AL.

As shown in Fig. 2.20(a) and (b), the fetch and execution of this instruction causes 8086 to calculate the physical address of the destination operand from the contents of DS, BX, and the direct displacement. The result is

$$PA = 02000_{16} + 1000_{16} + 1234_{16}$$

$$= 04234_{16}$$

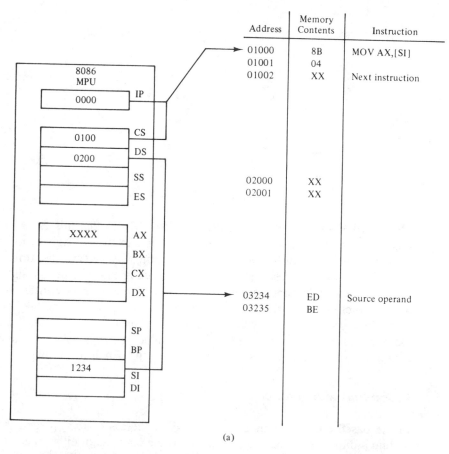

(a)

Figure 2.19 (a) Instruction using register indirect addressing before execution; (b) after execution.

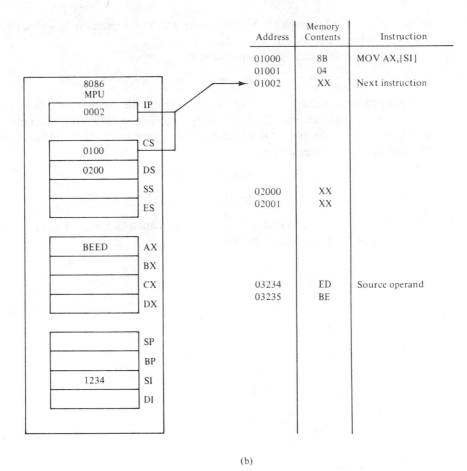

Address	Memory Contents	Instruction
01000	8B	MOV AX,[SI]
01001	04	
01002	XX	Next instruction
02000	XX	
02001	XX	
03234	ED	Source operand
03235	BE	

(b)

Figure 2.19 (*continued*)

Then it writes the contents of source operand AL into the storage location at 04234_{16}. The result is that ED_{16} is written into the destination memory location.

If BP is used instead of BX, the calculation of the physical address is performed using the contents of the stack segment (SS) register instead of DS. This permits access to data in the stack segment of memory.

Indexed Addressing Mode

Indexed addressing works identically to the based addressing we just described; however, it uses the contents of one of the index registers, instead of BX or BP, in the generation of the physical address. Here is an example:

```
MOV AL, [SI]+ARRAY
```

The source operand has been specified using direct indexed addressing. Notice that the notation this time is such that ARRAY, which is a *direct displacement,* is added to the selected index register, SI. Just as for the base register in based addressing, the index register is enclosed in brackets.

The effective address is calculated as

$$EA = (SI) + ARRAY$$

and the physical address is obtained by combining the contents of DS with EA.

The example in Fig. 2.21(a) and (b) shows the result of executing the MOV instruction. First the physical address of the source operand is calculated from DS, SI, and the direct displacement.

$$PA = 02000_{16} + 2000_{16} + 1234_{16}$$

$$= 05234_{16}$$

Then the byte of data stored at this location, which is BE_{16}, is read into the lower byte (AL) of the accumulator register.

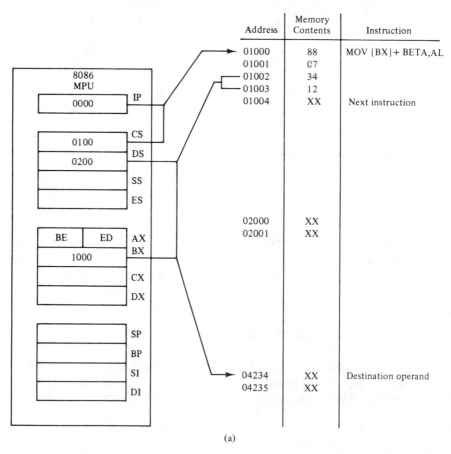

(a)

Figure 2.20 (a) Instruction using direct base pointer addressing before execution; (b) after execution.

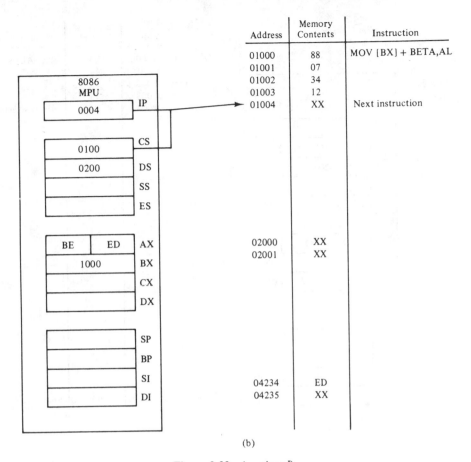

Address	Memory Contents	Instruction
01000	88	MOV [BX] + BETA,AL
01001	07	
01002	34	
01003	12	
01004	XX	Next instruction
02000	XX	
02001	XX	
04234	ED	
04235	XX	

(b)

Figure 2.20 (*continued*)

Based Indexed Addressing Mode

Combining the based addressing mode and the indexed addressing mode results in a new, more powerful mode known as based indexed addressing. Let us consider an example of a MOV instruction using this type of addressing.

$$\text{MOV AH, [BX] [SI]+BETA}$$

Notice that the source operand is accessed using based indexed addressing mode. Therefore, the effective address of the source operand is obtained as

$$EA = (BX) + (SI) + BETA$$

and the physical address of the operand from the current DS and the calculated EA.

In the example above if (DS) is equal to 200_{16}, $(DX) = 1000_{16}$, $(SI) = 2000_{16}$, and $BETA = 1234_{16}$; the address of the source operand is calculated as

$$PA = 02000_{16} + 1000_{16} + 2000_{16} + 1234_{16}$$

$$= 6234_{16}$$

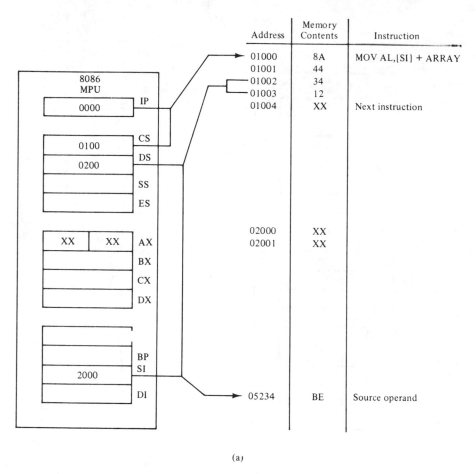

Address	Memory Contents	Instruction
01000	8A	MOV AL,[SI] + ARRAY
01001	44	
01002	34	
01003	12	
01004	XX	Next instruction
02000	XX	
02001	XX	
05234	BE	Source operand

(a)

Figure 2.21 (a) Instruction using direct indexed addressing before execution; (b) after execution.

Execution of the instruction causes the value stored at this location to be read into AH.

ASSIGNMENT

Section 2.2

1. What is the purpose of a software model for a microprocessor?
2. What must an assembly language programmer know about the registers within the 8086 microprocessor?
3. How many registers are located within the 8086?
4. How large is the 8086's memory address space?

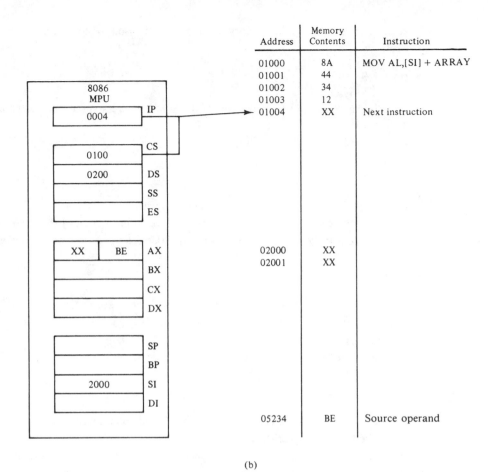

Address	Memory Contents	Instruction
01000	8A	MOV AL,[SI] + ARRAY
01001	44	
01002	34	
01003	12	
01004	XX	Next instruction
02000	XX	
02001	XX	
05234	BE	Source operand

(b)

Figure 2.21 (*continued*)

Section 2.3

5. What is the highest address in the 8086's memory address space? Lowest address?

6. Is memory in the 8086 microcomputer organized as bytes, words, or double words?

7. The contents of memory location $B0000_{16}$ are FF_{16}, and those at $B0001_{16}$ are 00_{16}. What is the even-addressed data word stored at address $B0000_{16}$?

8. Show how the double word 12345678_{16} will be stored in memory starting at address $A001_{16}$.

Section 2.4

9. How much memory can be active at a given time in the 8086 microcomputer?

10. Which of the 8086's internal registers are used for memory segmentation?

11. How much of the 8086's active memory is available as general-purpose data storage memory?

12. Which part of the 8086's memory address space is used to store instructions of a program?

Section 2.5

13. What is the dedicated use of the part of the 8086's address space from 00000_{16} through $0007F_{16}$?
14. What is stored at address $FFFF0_{16}$?

Section 2.6

15. What is the function of the instruction pointer register?
16. Give an overview of the fetch and the execution of an instruction by the 8086.
17. What happens to the value in IP each time the 8086 fetches a word of instruction code?

Section 2.7

18. Make a list of the general-purpose data registers of the 8086.
19. How is the word value of a data register labeled?
20. How are the upper and lower bytes of a data register denoted?
21. What dedicated operations are assigned to the CX register?

Section 2.8

22. What kind of information is stored in the pointer and index registers?
23. Name the two pointer registers.
24. For which segment register are the contents of the pointer registers used as an offset?
25. For which segment register are the contents of the index registers used as an offset?
26. What is the difference between SI and DI?

Section 2.9

27. Categorize each flag bit of the 8086 as either a control flag or a flag that monitors the status due to execution of an instruction.
28. Describe the function of each of the status flags.
29. How are the status flags used by software?
30. Which flag determines whether the address for a string operation is incremented or decremented?
31. Can the state of the flags be modified through software?

Section 2.10

32. What is the word length of the 8086's physical address?
33. What two address elements are combined to form a physical address?

34. If the current values in the code segment register and the instruction pointer are 0200_{16} and $01AC_{16}$, respectively, what is the physical address of the next instruction?

35. A data segment is to be located from address $A0000_{16}$ to $AFFFF_{16}$; what value must be loaded into DS?

36. If the data segment register contains the value found in Problem 35, what value must be loaded into DI if it is to point to a destination operand stored at address $A1234_{16}$ in memory?

Section 2.11

37. What is the function of the stack?

38. If the current values in the stack segment register and stack pointer are $0C00_{16}$ and $FF00_{16}$, respectively, what is the address of the top of the stack?

39. For the base and offset addresses in Problem 38, how many words of data are currently held in the stack?

40. Show how the value $EE11_{16}$ from register AX would be pushed onto the top of the stack as it exists in Problem 38.

Section 2.12

41. For the 8086 microprocessor, are the input/output and memory address spaces common or separate?

42. How large is the 8086's I/O address space?

43. What is the name given to the part of the I/O address space from 0000_{16} through $00FF_{16}$?

Section 2.13

44. Make a list of the addressing modes available on the 8086.

45. Identify the addressing modes used for the source and the destination operands in the instructions that follow.
   (a) MOV AL, BL
   (b) MOV AX, OFF
   (c) MOV [DI], AX
   (d) MOV DI, [SI]
   (e) MOV [BX]+XYZ, CX
   (f) MOV [DI]+XYZ, AH
   (f) MOV [BX][DX]+XYZ, AL

46. Compute the physical address for the specified operand in each of the following instructions from Problem 45. The register contents and variables are as follows: (CS) = $0A00_{16}$, (DS) = $0B00_{16}$, (SI) = 0100_{16}, (DI) = 0200_{16}, (BX) = 0300_{16}, and XYZ = 0400_{16}.
   (a) Destination operand of the instruction in (c)
   (b) Source operand of the instruction in (d)
   (c) Destination operand of the instruction in (e)
   (d) Destination operand of the instruction in (f)
   (e) Destination operand of the instruction in (g)

3

8086 Microprocessor Programming 1

3.1 INTRODUCTION

Chapter 2 was devoted to the general software architectural aspects of the 8086 microprocessor. In this chapter we begin a detailed study of the 8086's instruction set. A large part of the instruction set is introduced in this chapter. These instructions provide the ability to write simple straight-line programs. Chapter 4 covers the rest of the instruction set and more sophisticated programming concepts. The following topics are presented in this chapter:

1. Instruction set
2. Data transfer instructions
3. Arithmetic instructions
4. Logic instructions
5. Shift instructions
6. Rotate instructions

3.2 INSTRUCTION SET

The *instruction set* of a microprocessor defines the basic operations that a programmer can make the device perform. The 8086 microprocessor provides a powerful instruction set containing 117 basic instructions. The wide range of operands and addressing modes permitted for use with these instructions further expands the instruction set into many more instructions executable at the machine code level. For instance, the basic MOV instruction expands into 28 different machine-level instructions.

For the purpose of discussion, the instruction set will be divided into a number of groups of functionally related instructions. In this chapter we consider the data transfer instructions, arithmetic instructions, logic instructions, shift instructions, and rotate instructions. Advanced instructions such as those for program and processor control are described in Chapter 4.

3.3 DATA TRANSFER INSTRUCTIONS

The 8086 microprocessor has *data transfer instructions* that are provided to move data either between its internal registers or between an internal register and a storage location in memory. This group includes the *move byte or word* (MOV) instruction, *exchange byte or word* (XCHG) instruction, *translate byte* (XLAT) instruction, *load effective address* (LEA) instruction, *load data segment* (LDS) instruction, and *load extra segment* (LES) instruction. These instructions are discussed in this section.

MOV Instruction

The MOV instruction of Fig. 3.1(a) is used to transfer a byte or a word of data from a source operand to a destination operand. These operands can be internal registers of the 8086 and storage locations in memory. Figure 3.1(b) shows the valid source and destination operand variations. This large choice of operands results in many different MOV instructions. Looking at this list of operands, we see that data can be moved between registers, between a register and a segment register, between a register or segment register and memory, or between a memory location and the accumulator.

Notice that the MOV instruction cannot transfer data directly between a source and a destination that both reside in external memory. Instead, the data must first be moved from memory into an internal register, such as to the accumulator (AX), with one move instruction and then moved to the new location in memory with a second move instruction

All transfers between data registers and memory can involve either a byte or word of data. The fact that the instruction corresponds to byte or word data is designated by the way in which its operands are specified. For instance, AL or AH would be used to specify a byte operand, and AX a word operand. On the other hand, data moved between one of the registers and a segment register or between a segment register and a memory location must always be word-wide.

In Fig. 3.1(a) we also find additional important information. For instance, flag bits within the 8086 are not modified by execution of a MOV instruction.

An example of a segment register to general-purpose register MOV instruction shown in Fig. 3.1(c) is

MOV DX, CS

In this instruction, the code segment register is the source operand and the data register is the destination. It stands for "move the contents of CS into DX." That is,

$$(CS) \longrightarrow (DX)$$

Mnemonic	Meaning	Format	Operation	Flags Affected
MOV	Move	MOV D,S	(S) → (D)	None

(a)

Destination	Source
Memory	Accumulator
Accumulator	Memory
Register	Register
Register	Memory
Memory	Register
Register	Immediate
Memory	Immediate
Seg-reg	Reg16
Seg-reg	Mem16
Reg16	Seg-reg
Mem16	Seg-reg

(b)

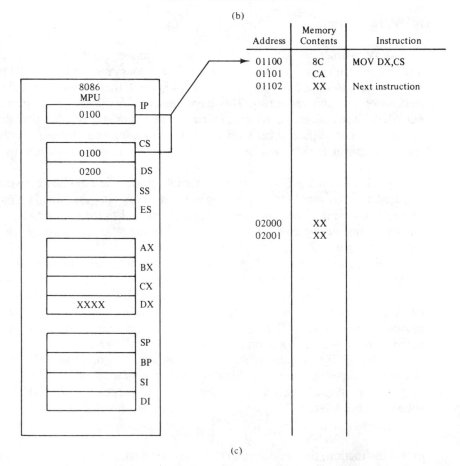

(c)

Figure 3.1   (a) Move data transfer instruction; (b) allowed operands; (b) MOV DX,CS instruction before execution; (d) after execution.

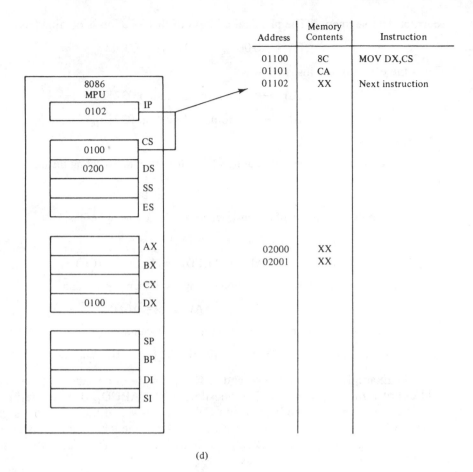

Address	Memory Contents	Instruction
01100	8C	MOV DX,CS
01101	CA	
01102	XX	Next instruction
02000	XX	
02001	XX	

(d)

Figure 3.1 (*continued*)

For example, if the contents of CS are 0100_{16}, execution of the instruction MOV DX,CS as shown in Fig. 3.1(d) makes

$$(DX) = (CS) = 0100_{16}$$

In all memory reference MOV instructions, the machine code for the instruction includes an offset address relative to the contents of the data segment register. An example of this type of instruction is

$$MOV \ [SUM], AX$$

In this instruction, the memory location identified by the variable SUM is specified using direct addressing. That is, the value of the offset is included in the two byte locations that follow its opcode in program memory.

Let us assume that the contents of DS equal 0200_{16} and that SUM corresponds to a displacement of 1212_{16}; then this instruction means "move the contents of accumulator AX to the memory location offset by 1212_{16} from the starting location of the current data segment." The physical address of this location is obtained as

$$PA = 02000_{16} + 1212_{16} = 03212_{16}$$

Thus the effect of the instruction is

$$(AL) \longrightarrow (\text{Memory Location } 03212_{16})$$

$$(AH) \longrightarrow (\text{Memory Location } 03213_{16})$$

EXAMPLE 3.1

If the DS register contains 1234_{16}, what is the effect of executing the instruction

```
MOV CX, [0ABCD]
```

SOLUTION Execution of this instruction has the following results:

$$((DS)0_{16} + ABCD_{16}) \longrightarrow (CL)$$

$$((DS)0_{16} + ABCD_{16} + 1_{16}) \longrightarrow (CH)$$

In other words, CL is loaded with the contents of memory location

$$12340_{16} + ABCD_{16} = 1CF0D_1$$

and CH is loaded with the contents of memory location

$$12340_{16} + ABCD_{16} + 1_{16} = 1CF0E_{16}$$

In Example 3.1, source operand $ABCD_{16}$ has been considered to be the direct address of a memory location. The question is why $ABCD_{16}$ does not represent immediate data that are to be loaded into CX. The answer to this question is given by how the 8086's assembler codes instructions. An immediate mode transfer is specified including the operand $ABCD_{16}$ without brackets. Therefore, the instruction would have to have been written as

```
MOV CX, 0ABCD
```

to represent an immediate data operand. The result produced by this instruction is

$$ABCD_{16} \longrightarrow (CX)$$

XCHG Instruction

In our study of the move instruction, we found that it could be used to copy the contents of a register or memory location into a register or contents of a memory location to a register. In all cases, the original contents of the source location are preserved and the original contents of the destination are destroyed. In some applications, it is required to interchange the contents of two registers. For instance, we might want to exchange the data in the AX and BX registers.

This could be done using multiple move instructions and storage of the data in a temporary register such as DX. However, to perform the exchange function more efficiently, a special instruction has been provided in the instruction set of the 8086. This is the exchange (XCHG) instruction. The format of the XCHG instruction and its allowed operands are shown in Fig. 3.2(a) and (b). Here we see that it can be used

Mnemonic	Meaning	Format	Operation	Flags Affected
XCHG	Exchange	XCHG D,S	(D) ↔ (S)	None

(a)

Destination	Source
Accumulator	Reg16
Memory	Register
Register	Register

(b)

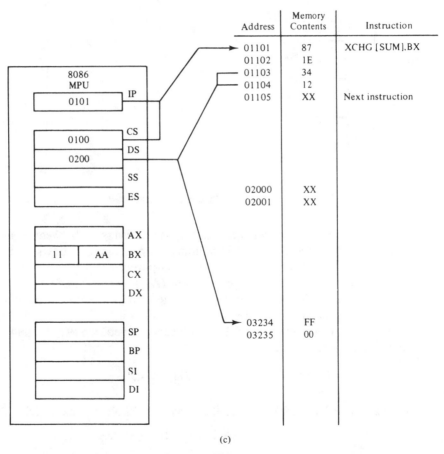

(c)

Figure 3.2 Exchange data transfer instruction; (b) allowed operands; (c) XCHG [SUM], BX instruction before execution; (d) after execution.

Sec. 3.3   Data Transfer Instructions

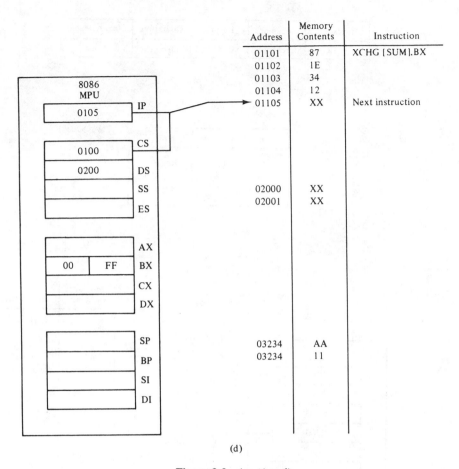

Address	Memory Contents	Instruction
01101	87	XCHG [SUM].BX
01102	1E	
01103	34	
01104	12	
01105	XX	Next instruction
02000	XX	
02001	XX	
03234	AA	
03234	11	

8086
MPU

IP 0105

CS 0100

DS 0200

SS

ES

AX

BX 00 FF

CX

DX

SP

BP

SI

DI

(d)

Figure 3.2 (*continued*)

to swap data between two general-purpose registers or between a general-purpose register and a storage location in memory. In particular, it allows for the exchange of words of data between one of the general-purpose registers, including the pointers and index registers, and the accumulator (AX); exchange of a byte or word of data between one of the general-purpose registers and a location in memory; or between two of the general-purpose registers.

Let us consider an example of an exchange between two internal registers. Here is a typical instruction:

XCHG AX, DX

Its execution by the 8086 swaps the contents of AX with that of DX. That is,

$$(AX \text{ original}) \longrightarrow (DX)$$

$$(DX \text{ original}) \longrightarrow (AX)$$

or

$$(AX) \longleftrightarrow (DX)$$

EXAMPLE 3.2

For the data shown in Fig. 3.2(c), what is the result of executing the instruction

$$XCHG \; [SUM], BX?$$

SOLUTION Execution of this instruction performs the function

$$((DS)0 + SUM) \longleftrightarrow (BX)$$

In Fig. 3.2(c) we see that $(DS) = 0200_{16}$ and the direct address $SUM = 1234_{16}$. Therefore, the physical address is

$$PA = 02000_{16} + 1234_{16} = 03234_{16}$$

Notice that this location contains FF_{16} and the address that follows contains 00_{16}. Moreover, note that BL contains AA_{16} and BH contains 11_{16}.

Execution of the instruction performs the following 16-bit swap.

$$(03234_{16}) \longleftrightarrow (BL)$$

$$(03235_{16}) \longleftrightarrow (BH)$$

As shown in Fig. 3.2(d), we get

$$(BX) = 00FF_{16}$$

$$(SUM) = 11AA_{16}$$

XLAT Instruction

The translate (XLAT) instruction has been provided in the instruction set of the 8086 to simplify implementation of the lookup table operation. This instruction is described in Fig. 3.3. When using XLAT, the contents of register BX represent the offset of the starting address of the *lookup table* from the beginning of the current data segment. Also the contents of AL represent the offset of the element to be accessed from the beginning of the lookup table. This 8-bit element address permits a table with up to 256 elements. The values in both of these registers must be initialized prior to execution of the XLAT instruction.

Execution of XLAT replaces the contents of AL by the contents of the accessed lookup table location. The physical address of this element in the table is derived as

$$PA = (DS)0 + (BX) + (AL)$$

Mnemonic	Meaning	Format	Operation	Flags Affected
XLAT	Translate	XLAT	$((AL) + (BX) + (DS)0) \rightarrow (AL)$	None

Figure 3.3 Translate data transfer instruction.

An example of the use of this instruction would be for software *code conversions:* for instance, an ASCII-to-EBCDIC conversion. This requires an EBCDIC table in memory. The individual EBCDIC codes are located in the table at element displacements (AL) equal to their equivalent ASCII character value. That is, the EBCDIC code $B1_{16}$ for letter A would be positioned at displacement 41_{16}, which equals ASCII A, from the start of the table. The start of this ASCII-to-EBCDIC table in the current data segment is identified by the contents of BX.

As an illustration of XLAT, let us assume that the contents of DS = 0300_{16}, BX = 0100_{16}, and AL = $0D_{16}$. $0D_{16}$ represents the ASCII character CR (carriage return). Execution of XLAT replaces the contents of AL by the contents of the memory location given by

$$PA = (DS)0 + (BX) + 0(AL)$$

$$= 03000_{16} + 0100_{16} + 0D_{16}$$

$$= 0310D_{16}$$

Thus the execution can be described by

$$(0310D_{16}) \longrightarrow (AL)$$

Assuming that this memory location contains EBCDIC CR 52_{16}, this value is placed in AL.

$$(AL) = 52_{16}$$

LEA, LDS, and LES Instructions

Another type of data transfer operation that is important is to load a segment or general-purpose register with an address directly from memory. Special instructions are provided in the instruction set of the 8086 to give a programmer this capability. These instructions are described in Fig. 3.4(a). They are load register with effective address (LEA), load register with data segment register (LDS), and load register and extra segment register (LES).

Looking at Fig. 3.4(a), we see that these instructions provide the ability to manipulate memory addresses by either loading a specific register with a 16-bit offset address or a 16-bit offset address together with a 16-bit segment address into either DS or ES.

The LEA instruction is used to load a specific register with a 16-bit offset address. An example of this instruction is

```
LEA SI, [INPUT]
```

When executed, it loads the SI register with an offset address value. The value of this offset is represented by the value of constant INPUT. INPUT is stored following the instruction opcode in program memory. This value is prefetched by the 8086; therefore, the instruction does not require any external bus cycles during its execution.

The other two instructions, LDS and LES, are similar to LEA except that they load the specified register as well as either the DS or ES segment register.

Mnemonic	Meaning	Format	Operation	Flags Affected
LEA	Load effective address	LEA Reg 16,EA	EA → (Reg 16)	None
LDS	Load register and DS	LDS Reg16,Mem32	(Mem32) → (Reg16) (Mem32+2) → (DS)	None
LES	Load register and ES	LES Reg16,Mem32	(Mem32) → (Reg16) (Mem32+2) → (ES)	None

(a)

(b)

Figure 3.4 (a) LEA, LDS, and LES data transfer instructions; (b) LDS SI,[200] instruction before execution; (c) after execution.

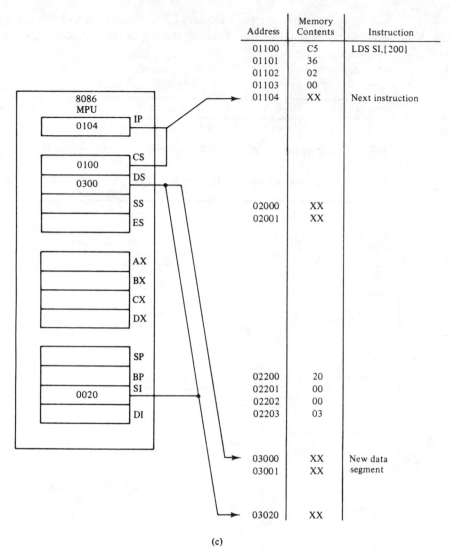

Address	Memory Contents	Instruction
01100	C5	LDS SI,[200]
01101	36	
01102	02	
01103	00	
01104	XX	Next instruction
02000	XX	
02001	XX	
02200	20	
02201	00	
02202	00	
02203	03	
03000	XX	New data
03001	XX	segment
03020	XX	

8086 MPU

IP 0104

CS 0100

DS 0300

SS

ES

AX

BX

CX

DX

SP

BP

SI 0020

DI

(c)

Figure 3.4 (*continued*)

┌ **EXAMPLE 3.3**

Assuming that the 8086 is set up as shown in Fig. 3.4(b), what is the result of executing the instruction

LDS SI, [200]

SOLUTION Execution of the instruction loads the SI register from the word location in memory whose offset address with respect to the current data segment is 200_{16}. Figure 3.4(b) shows that the contents of DS are 0200_{16}. This gives a physical address of

$$PA = 02000_{16} + 0200_{16} = 02200_{16}$$

It is the contents of this location and the one that follows that are loaded into SI. Therefore, in Fig. 3.4(c), we find that SI contains 0020_{16}. The next two bytes, that is, the contents of addresses 2202_{16} and 2203_{16}, are loaded into the DS register. As shown, this defines a new data segment starting at address 03000_{16}.

3.4 ARITHMETIC INSTRUCTIONS

The instruction set of the 8086 microprocessor contains an extensive complement of *arithmetic instructions*. They include instructions for the *addition, subtraction, multiplication,* and *division* operations. Moreover, these operations can be performed on numbers expressed in a variety of numeric data formats. They include *unsigned or signed binary bytes or words, unpacked or packed decimal bytes,* or *ASCII numbers.* By packed decimal, we mean that two BCD digits are packed into a byte register or memory location. Unpacked decimal numbers are stored one BCD digit per byte. These decimal numbers are always unsigned. Moreover, ASCII numbers are expressed in ASCII code and stored one number per byte.

The status that results from the execution of an arithmetic instruction is recorded in the flags of the 8086. The flags that are affected by the arithmetic instructions are carry flag (CF), auxiliary flag (AF), sign flag (SF), zero flag (ZF), parity flag (PF), and overflow flag (OF). Each of these flags was discussed in Chapter 2.

For the purpose of discussion, we will divide the arithmetic instructions into the subgroups shown in Fig. 3.5.

Addition	
ADD	Add byte or word
ADC	Add byte or word with carry
INC	Increment byte or word by 1
AAA	ASCII adjust for addition
DAA	Decimal adjust for addition
Subtraction	
SUB	Subtract byte or word
SBB	Subtract byte or word with borrow
DEC	Decrement byte or word by 1
NEG	Negate byte or word
AAS	ASCII adjust for subtraction
DAS	Decimal adjust for subtraction
Multiplication	
MUL	Multiply byte or word unsigned
IMUL	Integer multiply byte or word
AAM	ASCII adjust for multiply
Division	
DIV	Divide byte or word unsigned
IDIV	Integer divide byte or word
AAD	ASCII adjust for division
CBW	Convert byte to word
CWD	Convert word to doubleword

Figure 3.5 Arithmetic instructions. (Reprinted by permission of Intel Corp. Copyright/Intel Corp., 1979.)

Addition Instructions: ADD, ADC, INC, AAA, and DAA

The form of each of the instructions in the *addition group* is shown in Fig. 3.6(a) and their allowed operand variations, for all but the INC instruction, are shown in Fig. 3.6(b). Let us begin by looking more closely at the *add* (ADD) instruction. Notice in Fig. 3.6(b) that it can be used to add an immediate operand to the contents of the accumulator, the contents of another register, or the contents of a storage location in memory. It also allows us to add the contents of two registers or the contents of a register and a memory location.

Mnemonic	Meaning	Format	Operation	Flags Affected
ADD	Addition	ADD D, S	$(S) + (D) \rightarrow (D)$ Carry $\rightarrow (CF)$	OF, SF, ZF, AF, PF, CF
ADC	Add with carry	ADC D, S	$(S) + (D) + (CF) \rightarrow (D)$ Carry $\rightarrow (CF)$	OF, SF, ZF, AF, PF, CF
INC	Increment by 1	INC D	$(D) + 1 \rightarrow (D)$	OF, SF, ZF, AF, PF
AAA	ASCII adjust for addition	AAA		AF, CF OF, SF, ZF, PF undefined
DAA	Decimal adjust for addition	DAA		SF, ZF, AF, PF, CF, OF, undefined

(a)

Destination	Source
Register	Register
Register	Memory
Memory	Register
Register	Immediate
Memory	Immediate
Accumulator	Immediate

(b)

Destination
Reg16
Reg8
Memory

(c)

Figure 3.6 (a) Addition arithmetic instructions; (b) allowed operands for ADD and ADC; (c) allowed operands for INC.

In general, the result of executing the instruction is expressed as

$$(S) + (D) \longrightarrow (D)$$

That is, the contents of the source operand are added to those of the destination operand, and the sum that results is put into the location of the destination operand.

EXAMPLE 3.4

Assume that the AX and BX registers contain 1100_{16}, and $0ABC_{16}$, respectively. What are the results of executing the instruction ADD AX,BX?

SOLUTION Execution of the ADD instruction causes the contents of source operand BX to be added to the contents of destination register AX. This gives

$$(BX) + (AX) = 0ABC_{16} + 1100_{16} = 1BBC_{16}$$

This sum ends up in destination register AX.

$$(AX) = 1BBC_{16}$$

Execution of this instruction is illustrated in Fig. 3.7(a) and (b).

The instruction *add with carry* (ADC) works similarly to ADD. But in this case, the content of the carry flag is also added; that is,

$$(S) + (D) + (CF) \longrightarrow (D)$$

The valid operand combinations are the same as those for the ADD instruction.

Another instruction that can be considered as part of the addition subgroup of arithmetic instructions is the *increment* (INC) instruction. As shown in Fig. 3.6(c), its operands can be the contents of a 16-bit internal register, an 8-bit internal register, or a storage location in memory. Execution of the INC instruction adds 1 to the specified operand. An example of an instruction that increments the high byte of AX is

INC AH

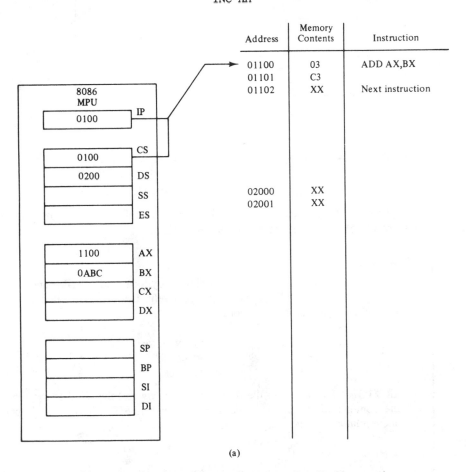

(a)

Figure 3.7 (a) ADD instruction before execution; (b) after execution.

Sec. 3.4   Arithmetic Instructions

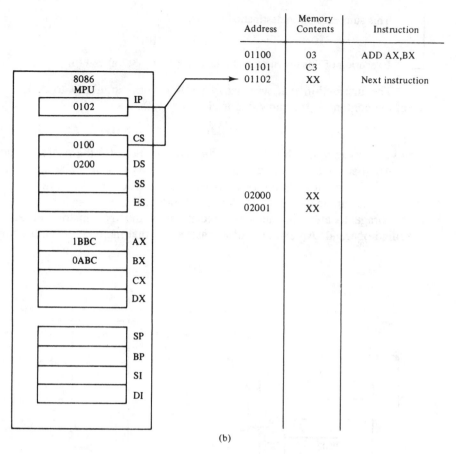

Address	Memory Contents	Instruction
01100	03	ADD AX,BX
01101	C3	
01102	XX	Next instruction
02000	XX	
02001	XX	

8086
MPU

0102	IP
0100	CS
0200	DS
	SS
	ES

1BBC	AX
0ABC	BX
	CX
	DX

	SP
	BP
	SI
	DI

(b)

Figure 3.7 (*continued*)

Looking at Fig. 3.6(a), we see that execution of any one of these three instructions affects all six of the flags mentioned earlier.

EXAMPLE 3.5

The original contents of AX, BL, word memory location DS:SUM, and carry flag (CF) are 1234_{16}, AB_{16}, $00CD_{16}$, and 0_{16}, respectively. Describe the results of executing the following sequence of instructions:

$$\text{ADD AX, [SUM]}$$
$$\text{ADC BL, 05}$$
$$\text{INC [SUM]}$$

SOLUTION By executing the first instruction, we add the word in the accumulator to the contents of the memory location identified as SUM. The result is placed in the accumulator. That is,

$$(AX) \longleftarrow (AX) + (SUM)$$

$$= 1234_{16} + 00CD_{16} = 1301_{16}$$

8086 Microprocessor Programming 1   Chap. 3

The carry flag remains reset.

The second instruction adds the lower byte of the base register (BL), immediate operand 5_{16}, and the carry flag, which is 0_{16}. This gives

$$(BL) \longleftarrow (BL) + IOP + (CF)$$

$$= AB_{16} + 5_{16} + 0_{16} = B0_{16}$$

Again CF stays reset.

The last instruction increments the contents of memory location SUM by 1. That is,

$$(SUM) \longleftarrow (SUM) + 1_{16}$$

$$= 00CD_{16} + 1_{16} = 00CE_{16}$$

These results are summarized in Fig. 3.8.

Instruction	(AX)	(BL)	(SUM)	(CF)
Initial state	1234	AB	00CD	0
ADD AX,[SUM]	1301	AB	00CD	0
ADC BL,05	1301	B0	00CD	0
INC [SUM]	1301	B0	00CE	0

Figure 3.8 Results due to execution of arithmetic instructions.

The addition instructions we just covered can also be used directly to add numbers expressed in ASCII code. This eliminates the need for doing a code conversion on ASCII form data prior to processing it with addition operations. Whenever the 8086 does an addition on ASCII format data, an adjustment must be performed on the result to convert it to a decimal number. It is specifically for this purpose that the *ASCII adjust for addition* (AAA) instruction is provided in the instruction set of the 8086. The AAA instruction should be executed immediately after the instruction that adds ASCII data.

Assuming that AL contains the result produced by adding two ASCII-coded numbers, execution of the AAA instruction causes the contents of AL to be replaced by its equivalent decimal value. If the sum is greater than 9, AL contains the LSDs, and AH is incremented by 1. Otherwise, AL contains the sum and AH is unchanged. Both the AF and CF flags can be affected. Since AAA can only adjust data that are in AL, the destination register for ADD instructions that process ASCII numbers should be AL.

EXAMPLE 3.6

What is the result of executing the following instruction sequence?

```
ADD  AL, BL
AAA
```

Assume that AL contains 32_{16}, which is the ASCII code for number 2, BL contains 34_{16}, which is the ASCII code for number 4, and AH has been cleared.

SOLUTION   Executing the ADD instruction gives

$$(AL) \longleftarrow (AL) + (BL)$$

$$(AL) = 32_{16} + 34_{16} = 66_{16}$$

Next the result is adjusted to give its equivalent decimal number. This is done by execution of the AAA instruction. The equivalent of adding 2 and 4 is decimal 6 with no carry. Therefore, the result after the AAA instruction is

$$(AL) = 06_{16}$$

$$(AH) = 00_{16}$$

and both AF and CF remain cleared.

The instruction set of the 8086 includes another instruction, called *decimal adjust for addition* (DAA). This instruction is used to perform an adjust operation similar to that performed by AAA but for the addition of packed BCD numbers instead of ASCII numbers. Information about this instruction is also provided in Fig. 3.6. Similar to AAA, DAA performs an adjustment on the value of AL. A typical instruction sequence is

```
ADD AL, BL
DAA
```

Remember that the contents of AL and BL must be packed BCD numbers. That is, two BCD digits packed into a byte. The adjusted result in AL is again a packed BCD byte.

Subtraction Instructions: SUB, SBB, DEC, AAS, DAS, and NEG

The instruction set of the 8086 includes an extensive group of instructions provided for implementing subtraction. As shown in Fig. 3.9(a), the subtraction subgroup is similar to the addition subgroup. It includes instructions for subtracting a source and destination operand, decrementing an operand, and for adjusting subtractions of ASCII and BCD data. An additional instruction in this subgroup is negate.

The *subtract* (SUB) instruction is used to subtract the value of a source operand from a destination operand. The result of this operation in general is given as

$$(D) \longleftarrow (D) - (S)$$

As shown in Fig. 3.9(b), it can employ the identical operand combinations as the ADD instruction.

The *subtract with borrow* (SBB) instruction is similar to SUB; however, it also subtracts the content of the carry flag from the destination. That is,

$$(D) \longleftarrow (D) - (S) - (CF)$$

Mnemonic	Meaning	Format	Operation	Flags affected
SUB	Subtract	SUB D,S	$(D) - (S) \rightarrow (D)$ Borrow $\rightarrow$ (CF)	OF, SF, ZF, AF, PF, CF
SBB	Subtract with borrow	SBB D,S	$(D) - (S) - (CF) \rightarrow (D)$	OF, SF, ZF, AF, PF, CF
DEC	Decrement by 1	DEC D	$(D) - 1 \rightarrow (D)$	OF, SF, ZF, AF, PF
NEG	Negate	NEG D	$0 - (D) \rightarrow (D)$ $1 \rightarrow$ (CF)	OF, SF, ZF, AF, PF, CF
DAS	Decimal adjust for subtraction	DAS		SF, ZF, AF, PF, CF OF undefined
AAS	ASCII adjust for subtraction	AAS		AF, CF OF, SF, ZF, PF undefined

(a)

Destination	Source
Register	Register
Register	Memory
Memory	Register
Accumulator	Immediate
Register	Immediate
Memory	Immediate

(b)

Destination
Reg16
Reg8
Memory

(c)

Destination
Register
Memory

(d)

Figure 3.9 (a) Subtraction arithmetic instructions; (b) allowed operands for SUB and SBB; (c) allowed operands for DEC; (d) allowed operands for NEG.

EXAMPLE 3.7

Assume that the contents of registers BX and CX are 1234_{16} and 0123_{16}, respectively, and the carry flag is 0. What will be the result of executing the instruction

$$\text{SBB BX, CX?}$$

SOLUTION Since the instruction implements the operation

$$(BX) - (CX) - (CF) \longrightarrow (BX)$$

we get

$$(BX) = 1234_{16} - 0123_{16} - 0_{16}$$
$$= 1111_{16}$$

Just as the INC instruction could be used to add 1 to an operand, the *decrement* (DEC) instruction can be used to subtract 1 from its operand. The allowed operands are shown in Fig. 3.9(c).

In Fig. 3.9(d) we see that the *negate* (NEG) instruction can operate on operands in a register or a storage location in memory. Execution of this instruction causes the value of its operand to be replaced by its negative. The way this is actually done is through subtraction. That is, the contents of the specified operand are subtracted from zero using 2's-complement arithmetic and the result is returned to the operand location.

Sec. 3.4   Arithmetic Instructions

63

EXAMPLE 3.8

Assuming that register BX contains $3A_{16}$, what is the result of executing the instruction

NEG BX ?

SOLUTION Executing the NEG instruction causes the 2's-complement subtraction that follows:

$$00_{16} - (BX) = 0000_{16} + 2\text{'s complement of } 3A_{16}$$
$$= 0000_{16} + FFC6_{16}$$
$$= FFC6_{16}$$

This value is returned to BX.

$$(BX) = FFC6_{16}$$

In our study of the addition instruction subgroup, we found that the 8086 is capable of directly adding ASCII and BCD numbers. The SUB and SBB instructions can also subtract numbers represented in these formats. Just as for addition, the results that are obtained must be adjusted to produce their corresponding decimal numbers. In the case of ASCII subtraction, we use the *ASCII adjust for subtraction* (AAS) instruction, and for packed BCD subtraction we use the *decimal adjust for subtract* (DAS) instruction.

An example of an instruction sequence for direct ASCII subtraction is

SUB AL,BL
AAS

ASCII numbers must be loaded into AL and BL before the execution of the subtract instruction. Notice that the destination of the subtraction should be AL. After execution of AAS, AL contains the difference of the two numbers, and AH is unchanged if no borrow takes place or is decremented by 1 if a borrow occurs.

Multiplication and Division Instructions: MUL, DIV, IMUL, IDIV, AAM, AAD, CBW, and CWD

The 8086 has instructions to support multiplication and division of binary and BCD numbers. Two basic types of multiplication and division instructions, those for the processing of unsigned numbers and signed numbers, are available. To do these operations on unsigned numbers, the instructions are MUL and DIV. On the other hand, to multiply or divide signed numbers, the instructions are IMUL and IDIV.

Figure 3.10(a) describes these instructions. Notice in Fig. 3.10(b) that only a byte-wide or word-wide operand is specified in a multiplication instruction. It is the source operand. As shown in Fig. 3.10(a), the other operand, which is the destination, is assumed already to be in AL for 8-bit multiplications or in AX for 16-bit multiplications.

Mnemonic	Meaning	Format	Operation	Flags Affected
MUL	Multiply (unsigned)	MUL S	$(AL) \cdot (S8) \rightarrow (AX)$ $(AX) \cdot (S16) \rightarrow (DX),(AX)$	OF, CF SF, ZF, AF, PF undefined
DIV	Division (unsigned)	DIV S	(1) $Q((AX)/(S8)) \rightarrow (AL)$ $R((AX)/(S8)) \rightarrow (AH)$ (2) $Q((DX,AX)/(S16)) \rightarrow (AX)$ $R((DX,AX)/(S16)) \rightarrow (DX)$ If Q is FF_{16} in case (1) or $FFFF_{16}$ in case (2), then type 0 interrupt occurs	OF, SF, ZF, AF, PF, CF undefined
IMUL	Integer multiply (signed)	IMUL S	$(AL) \cdot (S8) \rightarrow (AX)$ $(AX) \cdot (S16) \rightarrow (DX),(AX)$	OF, CF SF, ZF, AF, PF undefined
IDIV	Integer divide (signed)	IDIV S	(1) $Q((AX)/(S8)) \rightarrow (AL)$ $R((AX)/(S8)) \rightarrow (AH)$ (2) $Q((DX,AX)/(S16)) \rightarrow (AX)$ $R((DX,AX)/(S16)) \rightarrow (DX)$ If Q is positive and exceeds $7FFF_{16}$ or if Q is negative and becomes less than 8001_{16}, then type 0 interrupt occurs	OF, SF, ZF, AF, PF, CF undefined
AAM	Adjust AL for multiplication	AAM	$Q((AL)/10) \rightarrow AH$ $R((AL)/10) \rightarrow AL$	SF, ZF, PF OF, AF, CF undefined
AAD	Adjust AX for division	AAD	$(AH) \cdot 10 + AL \rightarrow AL$ $00 \rightarrow AH$	SF, ZF, PF OF, AF, CF undefined
CBW	Convert byte to word	CBW	(MSB of AL) $\rightarrow$ (All bits of AH)	None
CWD	Convert word to double word	CWD	(MSB of AX) $\rightarrow$ (All bits of DX)	None

(a)

Source
Reg8
Reg16
Mem8
Mem16

(b)

Figure 3.10 (a) Multiplication and division arithmetic instructions; (b) allowed operands.

The result of executing a MUL or IMUL instruction or byte data can be represented as

$$(AX) \longleftarrow (AL) \times (\text{8-bit operand})$$

That is, the resulting 16-bit product is produced in the AX register. On the other hand, for multiplications of data words, the 32-bit result is given by

$$(DX,AX) \longleftarrow (AX) \times (\text{16-bit operand})$$

where AX contains the 16 LSBs and DX the 16 MSBs.

For the division operation, again just the source operand is specified. The other operand is either the contents of AX for 16-bit dividends or the contents of both DX and AX for 32-bit dividends. The result of a DIV or IDIV instruction for an 8-bit divisor is represented by

$$(AH),(AL) \longleftarrow (AX)/(\text{8-bit operand})$$

where (AH) is the remainder and (AL) the quotient. For 16-bit divisions, we get

$$(DX),(AX) \longleftarrow (DX,AX)/(\text{16-bit operand})$$

Here AX contains the quotient and DX contains the remainder.

EXAMPLE 3.9

If the contents of AL equal -1_{10} and the contents of CL are -2_{10}, what will be the result produced in AX by executing the instructions

MUL CL

and

IMUL CL

SOLUTION The first instruction multiplies the contents of AL and CL as unsigned numbers.

$$-1_{10} = 11111111_2 = FF_{16}$$

$$-2_{10} = 11111110_2 = FE_{16}$$

Thus, executing the MUL instruction, we get

$$(AX) = (11111111_2) \times (11111110_2) = 1111110100000010_2$$

$$= FD02_{16}$$

The second instruction multiplies the same two numbers as signed numbers and gives

$$(AX) = 1_{16} \times 2_{16}$$

$$= 2_{16}$$

As shown in Fig. 3.10(a), adjust instructions for BCD multiplication and division are also provided. They are *adjust AX for multiply* (AAM) and *adjust AX for divide* (AAD). The multiplication performed just before execution of the AAM instruction is assumed to have been performed on two unpacked BCD numbers with the product produced in AL. The AAD instruction assumes that AH and AL contain unpacked BCD numbers.

The division instructions can also be used to divide an 8-bit dividend in AL by an 8-bit divisor. However, to do this, the sign of the dividend must first be extended to fill the AX register. That is, AH is filled with zeros if the number in AL is positive or with ones if it is negative. This conversion is automatically done by executing the *convert byte to word* (CBW) instruction.

In a similar way, the 32-bit by 16-bit division instructions can be used to divide a 16-bit dividend in AX by a 16-bit divisor. In this case, the sign bit of AX must be extended by 16 bits into the DX register. This can be done by another instruction, which is known as *convert word to double word* (CWD). These two sign-extension instructions are also shown in Fig. 3.10(a).

Notice that the CBW and CWD instructions are provided to handle operations where the result or intermediate results of an operation cannot be held in the correct word length for use in other arithmetic operations. Using these instructions, we can extend a byte or word of data to its equivalent word or double word.

EXAMPLE 3.10

What is the result of executing the following sequence of instructions?

```
MOV AL, 0A1
CBW
CWD
```

SOLUTION The first instruction loads AL with $A1_{16}$. This gives

$$(AL) = A1_{16} = 10100001_2$$

Executing the second instruction extends the most significant bit of AL, which is 1, into all bits of AH. The result is

$$(AH) = 11111111_2 = FF_{16}$$

$$(AX) = 1111111110100001_2 = FFA1_{16}$$

This completes conversion of the byte in AL to a word in AX.

The last instruction loads each bit of DX with the most significant bit of AX. This bit is also 1. Therefore, we get

$$(DX) = 1111111111111111_2 = FFFF_{16}$$

Now the word in AX has been extended to the double word

$$(AX) = FFA1_{16}$$

$$(DX) = FFFF_{16}$$

3.5 LOGIC INSTRUCTIONS

The 8086 has instructions for performing the logic operations *AND, OR, exclusive-OR,* and *NOT.* As shown in Fig. 3.11(a), the AND, OR, and XOR instructions perform their respective logic operations bit by bit on the specified source and destination operands, the result being represented by the final contents of the destination operand. Figure 3.11(b) shows the allowed operand combinations for the AND, OR, and XOR instructions.

For example, the instruction

```
AND AX, BX
```

Mnemonic	Meaning	Format	Operation	Flags Affected
AND	Logical AND	AND D,S	$(S) \cdot (D) \rightarrow (D)$	OF, SF, ZF, PF, CF AF undefined
OR	Logical Inclusive-OR	OR D,S	$(S) + (D) \rightarrow (D)$	OF, SF, ZF, PF, CF AF undefined
XOR	Logical Exclusive-OR	XOR D,S	$(S) \oplus (D) \rightarrow (D)$	OF, SF, ZF, PF, CF AF undefined
NOT	Logical NOT	NOT D	$(\overline{D}) \rightarrow (D)$	None

(a)

Destination	Source
Register	Register
Register	Memory
Memory	Register
Register	Immediate
Memory	Immediate
Accumulator	Immediate

(b)

Destination
Register
Memory

(c)

Figure 3.11 (a) Logic instructions; (b) allowed operands for AND, OR, and XOR; (c) allowed operands for NOT.

causes the contents of BX to be ANDed with the contents of AX. The result is reflected by the new contents of AX. If AX contains 1234_{16} and BX contains $000F_{16}$, the result produced by the instruction is

$$1234_{16} \cdot 000F_{16} = 0001001000110100_2 \cdot 0000000000001111_2$$

$$= 0000000000000100_2$$

$$= 0004_{16}$$

This result is stored in the destination operand.

$$(AX) = 0004_{16}$$

In this way we see that the AND instruction was used to mask off the 12 most significant bits of the destination operand.

The NOT logic instruction differs from those for AND, OR, and exclusive-OR in that it operates on a single operand. Looking at Fig. 3.11(c), which shows the allowed operands of the NOT instruction, we see that this operand can be either the contents of an internal register or a location in memory.

EXAMPLE 3.11

Describe the result of executing the following sequence of instructions.

```
MOV AL, 01010101B
AND AL, 00011111B
OR  AL, 11000000B
XOR AL, 00001111B
NOT AL
```

SOLUTION   The first instruction moves the immediate operand 01010101_2 into the AL register. This loads the data that are to be manipulated with the logic instructions. The next instruction performs a bit-by-bit AND operation of the contents of AL with immediate operand 00011111_2. This gives

$$01010101_2 \cdot 00011111_2 = 00010101_2$$

This result is produced in destination register AL. Note that this operation has masked off the three most significant bits of AL.

The next instruction performs a bit-by-bit logical OR of the present contents of AL with immediate operand $C0_{16}$. This gives

$$00010101_2 + 11000000_2 = 11010101_2$$

$$(AL) = 11010101_2$$

This operation is equivalent to setting the two most significant bits of AL.

The fourth instruction is an exclusive-OR operation of the contents of AL with immediate operand 00001111_2. We get

$$11010101_2 \oplus 00001111_2 - 11011010_2$$

$$(AL) = 11011010_2$$

Note that this operation complements the logic state of those bits in AL that are ones in the immediate operand.

The last instruction, NOT AL, inverts each bit of AL. Therefore, the final contents of AL become

$$(AL) = 11011010_2 = 00100101_2$$

These results are summarized in Fig. 3.12.

Instruction	(AL)
MOV AL,01010101B	01010101
AND AL,00011111B	00010101
OR AL,11000000B	11010101
XOR AL,00001111B	11011010
NOT AL	00100101

Figure 3.12   Results of example program using logic instructions.

3.6 SHIFT INSTRUCTIONS

The four *shift instructions* of the 8086 can perform two basic types of shift operations. They are the *logical shift* and the *arithmetic shift*. Moreover, each of these operations can be performed to the right or to the left. The shift instructions are *shift logical left* (SHL), *shift arithmetic left* (SAL), *shift logical right* (SHR), and *shift arithmetic right* (SAR).

The logical shift instructions, SHL and SHR, are described in Fig. 3.13(a). Notice in Fig. 3.13(b) that the destination operand, the data whose bits are to be shifted, can be either the contents of an internal register or a storage location in memory. Moreover, the source-operand can be specified in two ways. If it is as-

Mnemonic	Meaning	Format	Operation	Flags Affected
SAL/SHL	Shift arithmetic left/shift logical left	SAL/SHL D,Count	Shift the (D) left by the number of bit positions equal to Count and fill the vacated bits positions on the right with zeros	CF, PF, SF, ZF, OF AF undefined OF undefined if count $\neq$ 1
SHR	Shift logical right	SHR D,Count	Shift the (D) right by the number of bit positions equal to Count and fill the vacated bit positions on the left with zeros	CF, PF, SF, ZF, OF AF undefined OF undefined if count $\neq$ 1
SAR	Shift arithmetic right	SAR D,Count	Shift the (D) right by the number of bit positions equal to Count and fill the vacated bit positions on the left with the original most significant bit	OF, SF, ZF, PF, CF AF undefined

(a)

Destination	Count
Register	1
Register	CL
Memory	1
Memory	CL

(b)

Figure 3.13   (a) Shift instructions; (b) allowed operands.

signed the value 1, a 1-bit shift will take place. For instance, as illustrated in Fig. 3.14(a), executing

SHL AX, 1

causes the 16-bit content of the AX register to be shifted one bit position to the left. Here we see that the vacated LSB location is filled with 0 and the bit shifted out of the MSB is saved in CF.

On the other hand, if the source operand is specified as CL instead of 1, the count in this register represents the number of bit positions the operand is to be shifted. This permits the count to be defined under software control and allows a range of shifts from 1 to 256 bits.

An example of an instruction specified in this way is

SHR AX, CL

Assuming that CL contains the value 02_{16}, the logical shift right that occurs is shown in Fig. 3.14(b). Notice that the two MSBs have been filled with 0s and the last bit shifted out at the LSB, which is 0, is maintained in the carry flag.

In an arithmetic shift to the left, SAL operation, the vacated bits at the right of the operand are filled with zeros, whereas in an arithmetic shift to the right, SAR operation, the vacated bits at the left are filled with the value of the original MSB of the operand. Thus in an arithmetic shift to the right, the original sign of the number is extended. This operation is equivalent to division by 2 as long as the bit shifted out of the LSB is a zero.

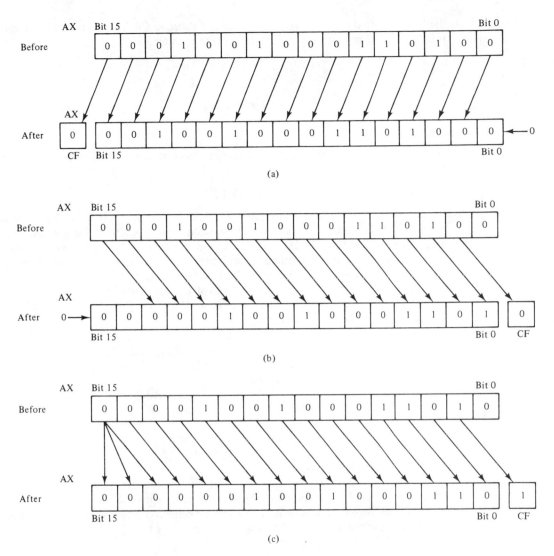

Figure 3.14 (a) Results of executing SHL AX,1; (b) results of executing SHR AX,CL; (c) results of executing SAR AX,CL.

┌ **EXAMPLE 3.12**

Assume that CL contains 02_{16} and AX contains $091A_{16}$. Determine the new contents of AX and the carry flag after the instruction

$$SAR \ AX, CL$$

is executed.

SOLUTION Figure 3.14(c) shows the effect of executing the instruction. Here we see that since CL contains 02_{16}, a shift right by two bit locations takes place and the original sign bit, which is logic 0, is extended to the two vacated bit positions. Moreover, the last bit shifted out from the LSB location is placed in CF. This makes CF 1. Therefore, the results produced by execution of the instruction are

$$(AX) = 0246_{16}$$

and

$$(CF) = 1_2$$

EXAMPLE 3.13

Write a program to implement the following expression using shift instructions to perform the arithmetic.

$$3(AX) + 7(BX) \rightarrow (DX)$$

SOLUTION   Shifting left by 1 bit position causes a multiplication by 2. To perform multiplication by an odd number, we can use a shift instruction to multiply to the nearest multiple of 2 and then add or subtract the appropriate value to get the desired result.

The algorithm for performing the arithmetic operations in the expression starts by shifting (AX) left by 1 bit. This gives 2 times (AX). Then adding the original (AX) gives multiplication by 3. Next, the contents of BX are shifted left by 3 bits to give eight times its value and subtracting the original (BX) once gives multiplication by 7. Expressing this with instructions, we get

```
MOV SI,AX   ;Copy (AX) into SI
SAL SI,1    ;2(AX)
ADD SI,AX   ;3(AX)
MOV DX,BX   ;Copy (BX) into DX
MOV CL,03   ;Load shift count
SAL DX,CL   ;8(BX)
SUB DX,BX   ;7(BX)
ADD DX,SI   ;Result
```

It is important to note that we have assumed that, to obtain any of the intermediate results and the final result, overflow does not occur. For instance, if 8(BX) cannot be accommodated in the 16 bits of BX, an overflow condition would occur and the result produced by executing the program may be incorrect.

3.7 ROTATE INSTRUCTIONS

Another group of instructions, known as the *rotate instructions,* are similar to the shift instructions we just introduced. This group, as shown in Fig. 3.15(a), includes the *rotate left* (ROL), *rotate right* (ROR), *rotate left through carry* (RCL), and *rotate right through carry* (RCR) instructions.

As shown in Fig. 3.15(b), the rotate instructions are similar to the shift instructions in several ways. They have the ability to shift the contents of either an internal register or storage location in memory. Also, the shift that takes place can be from 1 to 256 bit positions to the left or to the right. Moreover, in the case of a multibit shift, the number of bit positions to be shifted is again specified by the contents of CL. Their difference from the shift instructions lies in the fact that the bits moved out at either the MSB or LSB end are not lost; instead, they are reloaded at the other end.

Mnemonic	Meaning	Format	Operation	Flags Affected
ROL	Rotate left	ROL D,Count	Rotate the (D) left by the number of bit positions equal to Count. Each bit shifted out from the leftmost bit goes back into the rightmost bit position.	CF OF undefined if count ≠ 1
ROR	Rotate right	ROR D,Count	Rotate the (D) right by the number of bit positions equal to Count. Each bit shifted out from the rightmost bit goes into the leftmost bit position.	CF OF undefined if count ≠ 1
RCL	Rotate left through carry	RCL D,Count	Same as ROL except carry is attached to (D) for rotation.	CF OF undefined if count ≠ 1
RCR	Rotate right through carry	RCR D,Count	Same as ROR except carry is attached to (D) for rotation.	CF OF undefined if count ≠ 1

(a)

Destination	Count
Register	1
Register	CL
Memory	1
Memory	CL

(b)

Figure 3.15 (a) Rotate instructions; (b) allowed operands.

As an example, let us look at the operation of the ROL instruction. Execution of ROL causes the contents of the selected operand to be rotated left the specified number of bit positions. Each bit shifted out at the MSB end is reloaded at the LSB end. Moreover, the contents of CF reflect the state of the last bit that was shifted out. For instance, the instruction

ROL AX, 1

causes a 1-bit rotate to the left. Figure 3.16(a) shows the result produced by executing this instruction. Notice that the original value of bit 15 is 0. This value has been rotated into both CF and bit 0 of AX. All other bits have been rotated one bit position to the left.

The ROR instruction operates the same way as ROL except that it causes data to be rotated to the right instead of to the left. For example, execution of

ROR AX, CL

causes the contents of AX to be rotated right by the number of bit positions specified in CL. The result for CL equal to 4 is illustrated in Fig. 3.16(b).

The other two rotate instructions, RCL and RCR, differ from ROL and ROR in that the bits are rotated through the carry flag. Figure 3.17 illustrates the rotation that takes place due to execution of the RCL instruction. Notice that the bit returned to bit 0 is the prior contents of CF and not bit 15. The bit shifted out of bit 15 goes into the carry flag. Thus the bits rotate through carry.

EXAMPLE 3.14

What is the result in BX and CF after execution of the following instruction

RCR BX, CL?

Assume that prior to execution of the instruction $(CL) = 04_{16}$, $(BX) = 1234_{16}$, and $(CF) = 0_2$.

SOLUTION The original contents of BX are

$$(BX) = 0001001000110100_2 = 1234_{16}$$

Execution of the RCR instruction causes a 4-bit rotate right through carry to take place on the data in BX. Therefore, the original content of bit 3, which is 0, resides in carry; $CF = 0_2$ and 1000_2 has been reloaded from bit 15. The resulting contents of BX are

$$(BX) = 1000000100100011_2 = 8123_{16}$$

and

$$(CF) = 0_2$$

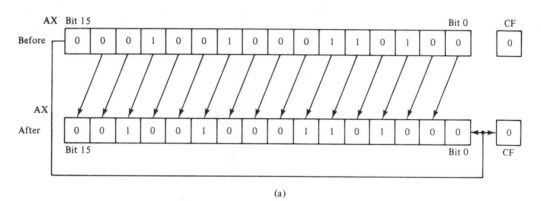

(a)

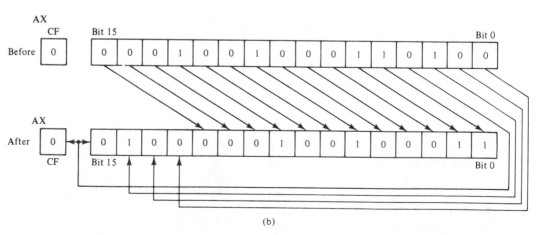

(b)

Figure 3.16 (a) Results of executing ROL AX,1; (b) results of executing ROR AX,CL.

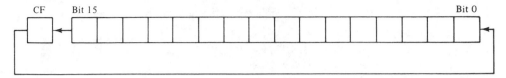

Figure 3.17 Rotation caused by executing an RCL instruction.

ASSIGNMENT

Section 3.3

1. Explain what operation is performed by each of the instructions that follows.
   (a) MOV AX,0110   (e) MOV [BX+DI],AX
   (b) MOV DI,AX   (f) MOV [DI]+0004,AX
   (c) MOV BL,AL   (g) MOV [BX][DI]+0004,AX
   (d) MOV [0100],AX

2. Assume that registers AX, BX, and DI are all initialized to 0000_{16} and that all data storage memory has been cleared. Determine the location and value of the destination operand as instructions (a) through (g) from Problem 1 are executed as a sequence.

3. Write an instruction sequence that will initialize the ES register with the immediate value 1010_{16}.

4. Write an instruction that will save the contents of the ES register in memory at address DS:1000.

5. Why will the instruction MOV CL,AX result in an error when it is assembled?

6. Describe the operation performed by each of the instructions that follows:
   (a) XCHG AX,BX   (c) XCHG DATA,AX
   (b) XCHG BX,DI   (d) XCHG [BX+DI],AX

7. If register BX contains the value 0100_{16}, register DI contains 0010_{16}, and register DS contains 1075_{16}, what physical memory location is swapped when the instruction in Problem 6(d) is executed?

8. Assume that (AL) = 0010_{16}, (BX) = 0100_{16}, and (DS) = 1000_{16}; what happens if the XLAT instruction is executed?

9. Write a single instruction that will load AX from address 0200_{16} and DS from address 0202_{16}.

10. Two code-conversion tables starting with offsets TABL1 and TABL2 in the current data segment are to be accessed. Write a routine that initializes the needed registers and then replaces the contents of memory locations MEM1 and MEM2 (offsets in the data segment) by the equivalent converted codes from the code-conversion tables.

Section 3.4

11. What operation is performed by each of the following instructions?
   (a) ADD   AX,00FF   (g) NEG   BYTE PTR [DI]+0010
   (b) ADC   SI,AX   (h) MUL   DX
   (c) INC   BYTE PTR [0100]   (i) IMUL BYTE PTR [BX+SI]
   (d) SUB   DL,BL   (j) DIV   BYTE PTR [SI]+0030
   (e) SBB   DL,[0200]   (k) IDIV BYTE PTR [BX][SI]+0030
   (f) DEC   BYTE PTR [DI+BX]

12. Assume that the state of 8086's registers and memory is as follows

(AX) = 0010_{16}	(DS:130) = 08_{16}
(BX) = 0020_{16}	(DS:131) = 00_{16}
(CX) = 0030_{16}	(DS:150) = 02_{16}
(DX) = 0040_{16}	(DS:151) = 00_{16}
(SI) = 0100_{16}	(DS:200) = 30_{16}
(DI) = 0200_{16}	(DS:201) = 00_{16}
(CF) = 1_{16}	(DS:210) = 40_{16}
(DS:100) = 10_{16}	(DS:211) = 00_{16}
(DS:101) = 00_{16}	(DS:220) = 30_{16}
(DS:120) = FF_{16}	(DS:221) = 00_{16}
(DS:121) = FF_{16}	

just prior to execution of each of the instructions in Problem 11. What is the result produced in the destination operand by executing instructions (a) through (k)?

13. Write an instruction that will add the immediate value $111F_{16}$ and the carry flag to the contents of the data register.

14. Write an instruction that will subtract the word contents of the storage location pointed to by the base register and the carry flag from the accumulator.

15. Two word-wide unsigned integers are now stored at the memory addresses $0A00_{16}$ and $0A02_{16}$, respectively. Write an instruction sequence that computes and stores their sum, difference, product, and quotient. Store these results at consecutive memory locations starting at address $0A10_{16}$ in memory. To obtain the difference, subtract the integer at $0A02_{16}$ from the integer at $0A00_{16}$. For the division, divide the integer at $0A00_{16}$ by the integer at $0A02_{16}$. Use register indirect relative addressing mode to store the various results.

16. Assuming that (AX) = 0123_{16} and (BL) = 10_{16}, what will be the new contents of AX after executing the instruction DIV BL?

17. What instruction is used to adjust the result of an addition that processes packed BCD numbers?

18. Which instruction is provided in the instruction set of the 8086 to adjust the result of a subtraction that involved ASCII coded numbers?

19. If AL contains $A0_{16}$, what happens when the instruction CBW is executed?

20. If the value in AX is $7FFF_{16}$, what happens when the instruction CWD is executed?

21. Two byte-sized BCD integers are stored at the symbolic addresses NUM1 and NUM2, respectively. Write an instruction sequence to generate their difference and store it at NUM3. The difference is to be formed by subtracting the value at NUM1 from that at NUM2.

Section 3.5

22. Describe the operation performed by each of the following instructions.
(a) AND BYTE PTR [0300], 0F
(b) AND DX, [SI]
(c) OR   [BX+DI], AX
(d) OR   BYTE PTR [BX] [DI]+10, F0
(e) XOR AX, [SI+BX]
(f) NOT BYTE PTR [0300]
(g) NOT WORD PTR [BX+DI]

23. Assume that the state of 8086's registers and memory is as follows

$(AX) = 5555_{16}$	$(DS:111) = FF_{16}$
$(BX) = 0010_{16}$	$(DS:200) = 30_{16}$
$(CX) = 0010_{16}$	$(DS:201) = 00_{16}$
$(DX) = AAAA_{16}$	$(DS:210) = AA_{16}$
$(SI) = 0100_{16}$	$(DS:211) = AA_{16}$
$(DI) = 0200_{16}$	$(DS:220) = 55_{16}$
$(DS:100) = 0F_{16}$	$(DS:221) = 55_{16}$
$(DS:101) = F0_{16}$	$(DS:300) = AA_{16}$
$(DS:110) = 00_{16}$	$(DS:301) = 55_{16}$

just prior to execution of each of the instructions in Problem 22. What is the result produced in the destination operand by executing instructions (a) through (g)?

24. Write an instruction that when executed will mask off all but bit 7 of the the contents of the data register.

25. Write an instruction that will mask off all but bit 7 of the word of data stored at address DS:0100.

26. Specify the relation between the old and new contents of AX after executing the following instructions.

```
NOT AX
ADD AX, 1
```

27. Write an instruction sequence that generates a byte-sized integer in the memory location identified by label RESULT. The value of the byte integer is to be calculated as follows:

$$(RESULT) = (AL) \cdot (NUM1) + (\overline{NUM2}) \cdot (AL) + BL)$$

Assume that all parameters are byte sized.

Section 3.6

28. Explain what operation is performed by each of the instructions that follows.
  (a) SHL DX, CL
  (b) SHL BYTE PTR [0400], CL
  (c) SHR BYTE PTR [DI], 1
  (d) SHR BYTE PTR [DI+BX], CL
  (e) SAR WORD PTR [BX+DI], 1
  (f) SAR WORD PTR [BX] [DI]+0010, CL

29. Assume that the state of 8086's registers and memory is as follows

$(AX) = 0000_{16}$	$(DS:200) = 22_{16}$
$(BX) = 0010_{16}$	$(DS:201) = 44_{16}$
$(CX) = 0105_{16}$	$(DS:210) = 55_{16}$
$(DX) = 1111_{16}$	$(DS:211) = AA_{16}$
$(SI) = 0100_{16}$	$(DS:220) = AA_{16}$
$(DI) = 0200_{16}$	$(DS:221) = 55_{16}$
$(CF) = 0_{16}$	$(DS:400) = AA_{16}$
$(DS:100) = 0F_{16}$	$(DS:401) = 55_{16}$

just prior to execution of each of the instructions in Problem 28. What is the result produced in the destination operand by executing instructions (a) through (f)?

30. Write an instruction that shifts the contents of the count register left by 1 bit position.

31. Write an instruction sequence that when executed shifts the contents of the word-wide memory location pointed to by the address in the destination index register left by eight bit positions.

32. Identify the condition under which the contents of AX would remain unchanged after executing any of the instructions that follow.

$$\begin{aligned}&\text{MOV CL, 4}\\&\text{SHL AX, CL}\\&\text{SHR AX, CL}\end{aligned}$$

33. Implement the following operation using shift and arithmetic instructions.

$$7(AX) - 5(BX) - \tfrac{1}{4}(BX) \rightarrow (AX)$$

Assume that all parameters are word sized.

Section 3.7

34. Describe what happens as each of the instructions that follow is executed by the 8086.
    (a) ROL DX, CL
    (b) RCL BYTE PTR [0400], CL
    (c) ROR BYTE PTR [DI], 1
    (d) ROR BYTE PTR [DI+BX], CL
    (e) RCR WORD PTR [BX+DI], 1
    (f) RCR WORD PTR [BX][DI]+0010, CL

35. Assume that the state of 8086's registers and memory is as follows

$(AX) = 0000_{16}$	$(DS:200) = 22_{16}$
$(BX) = 0010_{16}$	$(DS:201) = 44_{16}$
$(CX) = 0105_{16}$	$(DS:210) = 55_{16}$
$(DX) = 1111_{16}$	$(DS:211) = AA_{16}$
$(SI) = 0100_{16}$	$(DS:220) = AA_{16}$
$(DI) = 0200_{16}$	$(DS:221) = 55_{16}$
$(CF) = 1_{16}$	$(DS:400) = AA_{16}$
$(DS:100) = 0F_{16}$	$(DS:401) = 55_{16}$

    just prior to execution of each of the instructions in Problem 34. What is the result produced in the destination operand by executing instructions (a) through (f)?

36. Write an instruction sequence that when executed rotates the contents of the word-wide memory location pointed to by the address in the base register left through carry by one bit position.

37. Write a program that saves the content of bit 5 in AL in BX as a word.

4

8086 Microprocessor Programming 2

4.1 INTRODUCTION

In Chapter 3 we discussed many of the instructions that can be executed by the 8086 microprocessor. Furthermore, we used these instructions to write simple programs. In this chapter we introduce the rest of the instruction set and at the same time cover more complicated programming techniques. The following topics are discussed in this chapter:

1. Flag control instructions
2. Compare instruction
3. Jump instructions
4. Subroutines and subroutine-handling instructions
5. Loops and loop-handling instructions
6. String and string-handling instructions

4.2 FLAG CONTROL INSTRUCTIONS

The 8086 microprocessor has a set of flags that either monitor the status of executing instructions or control options available in its operation. These flags were described in detail in Chapter 2. The instruction set includes a group of instructions that when executed directly affect the setting of the flags. These instructions, shown in Fig. 4.1a, are *load AH from flags* (LAHF), *store AH into flags* (SAHF), *clear carry* (CLC), *set carry* (STC), *complement carry* (CMC), *clear interrupt* (CLI), and *set interrupt* (STI). A few more instructions exist that can directly affect the flags; however, we will not cover them until later in the chapter when we introduce the subroutine and string instructions.

Mnemonic	Meaning	Operation	Flags Affected
LAHF	Load AH from flags	$(AH) \leftarrow (Flags)$	None
SAHF	Store AH into flags	$(Flags) \leftarrow (AH)$	SF, ZF, AF, PF, CF
CLC	Clear carry flag	$(CF) \leftarrow 0$	CF
STC	Set carry flag	$(CF) \leftarrow 1$	CF
CMC	Complement carry flag	$(CF) \leftarrow (\overline{CF})$	CF
CLI	Clear interrupt flag	$(IF) \leftarrow 0$	IF
STI	Set interrupt flag	$(IF) \leftarrow 1$	IF

(a)

```
LAHF

MOV      MEM1, AH

MOV      AH, MEM2

SAHF
```

(b)

Figure 4.1 Flag control instructions; (b) program for Example 4.1.

Looking at Fig. 4.1a, we see that the first two instructions, LAHF and SAHF, can be used either to read the flags or to change them, respectively. Notice that the data transfer that takes place is always between the AH register and the flag register. For instance, we may want to start an operation with certain flags set or reset. Assume that we want to preset all flags to logic 1. To do this, we can first load AH with FF_{16} and then execute the SAHF instruction.

EXAMPLE 4.1

Write an instruction sequence to save the current contents of the 8086's flags in memory location MEM1 and then reload the flags with the contents of memory location MEM2. Assume that MEM1 and MEM2 are in the same data segment defined by the current contents of DS.

SOLUTION To save the current flags, we must first load them into the AH register and then move them to the location MEM1. The instructions that do this are

```
LAHF
MOV    [MEM1] , AH
```

Similarly, to load the flags with the contents of MEM2, we must first copy the contents of MEM2 into AH and then store the contents of AH into the flags. The instructions for this are

```
MOV   AH, [MEM2]
SAHF
```

The entire instruction sequence is shown in Fig. 4.1(b).

The next three instructions, CLC, STC, and CMC, are used to manipulate the carry flag. They permit CF to be cleared, set, or complemented to its inverse logic level, respectively. For example, if CF is 1 when a CMC instruction is executed, it becomes 0.

The last two instructions are used to manipulate the interrupt flag. Executing the clear interrupt (CLI) instruction sets IF to logic 0 and disables the interrupt interface. On the other hand, executing the STI instruction sets IF to 1, and the microprocessor starts accepting interrupts from that point on.

EXAMPLE 4.2

Of the three carry flag instructions CLC, STC, and CMC, only one is really an independent instruction. That is, the operation that it provides cannot be performed by a series of the other two instructions. Determine which one of the carry instructions is the independent instruction.

SOLUTION Let us begin with the CLC instruction. The clear carry operation can be performed by an STC instruction followed by a CMC instruction. Therefore, CLC is not an independent instruction. Moreover, the operation of the set carry (STC) instruction is equivalent to the operation performed by a CLC instruction followed by a CMC instruction. Thus STC is also not an independent instruction. On the other hand, the operation performed by the last instruction, complement carry (CMC), cannot be expressed in terms of the CLC and STC instructions. Therefore, it is the independent instruction.

4.3 COMPARE INSTRUCTION

There is an instruction included in the instruction set of the 8086 that can be used to compare two 8-bit or 16-bit numbers. It is the *compare* (CMP) instruction of Fig. 4.2(a). Figure 4.2(b) shows that the operands can reside in a storage location in

Mnemonic	Meaning	Format	Operation	Flags Affected
CMP	Compare	CMP D,S	(D) − (S) is used in setting or resetting the flags	CF, AF, OF, PF, SF, ZF

(a)

Destination	Source
Register	Register
Register	Memory
Memory	Register
Register	Immediate
Memory	Immediate
Accumulator	Immediate

(b)

Figure 4.2   (a) Compare instruction; (b) allowed operands.

memory, a register within the MPU, or as part of the instruction. For instance, a byte-wide number in a register such as BL can be compared to a second byte-wide number that is supplied as immediate data.

The result of the comparison is reflected by changes in six of the status flags of the 8086. Notice in Fig. 4.2(a) that it affects the overflow flag, sign flag, zero flag, auxiliary carry flag, parity flag, and carry flag. The logic state of these flags can be referenced by instructions in order to make a decision whether or not to alter the sequence in which the program executes.

The process of comparison performed by the CMP instruction is basically a subtraction operation. The source operand is subtracted from the destination operand. However, the result of this subtraction is not saved. Instead, based on the result the appropriate flags are set or reset. For example, let us assume that the destination operand equals $10011001_2 = -103_{10}$ and that the source operand equals $00011011_2 = +27_{10}$. Subtracting the source from the destination, we get

$$
\begin{array}{rcl}
10011001_2 & = & -103_{10} \\
-\ 00011011_2 & = & -(+27_{10}) \\
\hline
01111110_2 & = & +126_{10}
\end{array}
$$

In the process of obtaining this result, we set the status that follows:

1. No carry is generated from bit 3 to bit 4; therefore, the auxiliary carry flag AF is at logic 0.
2. There is a carry out from bit 7. Thus carry flag CF is set.
3. Even through a carry out of bit 7 is generated, there is no carry from bit 6 to bit 7. This is an overflow condition and the OF flag is set.
4. There are an even number of 1s; therefore, this makes parity flag PF equal to 1.
5. Bit 7 is zero and therefore sign flag SF is at logic 0.
6. The result that is produced is nonzero, which makes zero flag ZF logic 0.

Notice that the result produced by the subtraction of the two 8-bit numbers is not correct. This condition was indicated by setting the overflow flag.

EXAMPLE 4.3

Describe what happens to the status flags as the sequence of instructions that follow is executed.

```
MOV AX, 1234
MOV BX, 0ABCD
CMP AX, BX
```

Assume that flags ZF, SF, CF, AF, OF, and PF are all initially reset.

SOLUTION The first instruction loads AX with 1234_{16}. No status flags are affected by the execution of a MOV instruction. The second instruction puts $ABCD_{16}$ into the BX register. Again status in not affected. Thus, after execution of these two move instructions, the contents of AX and BX are

$$(AX) = 1234_{16} = 0001001000110100_2$$

and

$$(BX) = ABCD_{16} = 1010101111001101_2$$

The third instruction is a 16-bit comparison with AX representing the destination and BX the source. Therefore, the contents of BX are subtracted from that of AX.

$$(AX) - (BX) = 0001001000110100_2 - 1010101111001101_2$$

$$= 0110011001100111_2$$

The flags are either set or reset based on the result of this subtraction. Notice that the result is nonzero and positive. This makes ZF and SF equal to zero. Moreover, the carry, auxiliary carry, and no overflow conditions have occurred. Therefore, CF and AF are at logic 1 while OF is at logic 0.

Finally, the result has odd parity; therefore, PF is set to 0. These results are summarized in Fig. 4.3.

Instruction	ZF	SF	CF	AF	OF	PF
Initial state	0	0	0	0	0	0
MOV AX,1234	0	0	0	0	0	0
MOV BX,ABCD	0	0	0	0	0	0
CMP AX,BX	0	0	1	1	0	0

Figure 4.3 Effect on flags of executing instructions.

4.4 JUMP INSTRUCTIONS

The purpose of a *jump* instruction is to alter the execution path of instructions in the program. In the 8086 microprocessor, the code segment register and instruction pointer keep track of the next instruction to be fetched for execution. Thus a jump instruction involves altering the contents of these registers. In this way, execution continues at an address other than that of the next sequential instruction. That is, a jump occurs to another part of the program. Typically, program execution is not intended to return to the next sequential instruction after the jump instruction. Therefore, no return linkage is saved when the jump takes place.

Unconditional and Conditional Jump

The 8086 microprocessor allows two different types of jump instructions. They are the *unconditional jump* and the *conditional jump*. In an unconditional jump, no status requirements are imposed for the jump to occur. That is, as the instruction is executed, the jump always takes place to change the execution sequence.

This concept is illustrated in Fig. 4.4(a). Notice that, when the instruction JMP AA in part I is executed, program control is passed to a point in part III identified by the label AA. Execution resumes with the instruction corresponding to AA. In this way, the instructions in part II of the program have been bypassed. That is, they have been jumped over.

On the other hand, for a conditional jump instruction, status conditions that exist at the moment the jump instruction is executed decide whether or not the jump

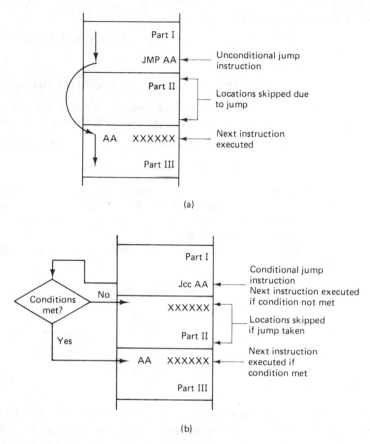

Figure 4.4 (a) Unconditional jump program sequence; (b) conditional jump program sequence.

will occur. If this condition or conditions are met, the jump takes place; otherwise, execution continues with the next sequential instruction of the program. The conditions that can be referenced by a conditional jump instruction are status flags such as carry (CF), parity (PF), and overflow (OF).

Looking at Fig. 4.4(b), we see that execution of the conditional jump instruction in part I causes a test to be initiated. If the conditions of the test are not met, the NO path is taken and execution continues with the next sequential instruction. This corresponds to the first instruction in part II. However, if the result of the conditional test is YES, a jump is initiated to the segment of the program identified as part III and the instructions in part II are bypassed.

Unconditional Jump Instruction

The unconditional jump instruction of the 8086 is shown in Fig. 4.5(a) together with its valid operand combinations in Fig. 4.5(b). There are two basic kinds of unconditional jumps. The first, called an *intrasegment jump,* is limited to addresses within the current code segment. This type of jump is achieved by just modifying the value

Mnemonic	Meaning	Format	Operation	Flags Affected
JMP	Unconditional jump	JMP Operand	Jump is initiated to the address specified by Operand	None

(a)

(b)

Figure 4.5   (a) Unconditional jump instruction; (b) allowed operands.

in IP. The other kind of jump, the *intersegment jump,* permits jumps from one code segment to another. Implementation of this type of jump may require modification of the contents of both CS and IP.

Jump instructions specified with a *Short-label, Near-label, Memptr16,* or *Regptr16 operand* represent intrasegment jumps. The Short-label and Near-label operands specify the jump relative to the address of the jump instruction itself. For example, in a Short-label jump instruction an 8-bit number is coded as an immediate operand to specify the *signed increment* of the next instruction to be executed from the location of the jump instruction. When the jump instruction is executed, IP is reloaded with a new value equal to the updated value in IP, which is (IP) + 2, plus the signed increment. The new value of IP and current value in CS give the address of the next instruction to be fetched and executed. With an 8-bit displacement, the Short-label operand can only be used to initiate a jump in the range from −126 to +129 bytes from the location of the jump instruction.

On the other hand, Near-label operands specify a new value of IP with a 16-bit immediate operand. This size of offset corresponds to the complete address range of the current code segment. The value of the offset is automatically added to IP upon execution of the instruction. In this way, program control is passed to the location identified by the new IP. An example is the instruction

JMP LABEL

This means to jump to the point in the program corresponding to the tag LABEL. The programmer does not have to worry about counting the number of bytes from the jump instruction to the location to which control is to be passed. Moreover, the fact that it is coded as a Short- or Near-label is determined by the assembler.

The jump to address can also be specified indirectly by the contents of a memory location or the contents of a register. These two types correspond to the Memptr16 and Regptr16 operands, respectively. Just as for the Near-label operand, they both permit a jump to any address in the current code segment.

For example,

$$\text{JMP BX}$$

uses the contents of register BX for the offset. That is, the value in BX is copied into IP. Then the physical address of the next instruction is obtained by using the current contents of CS and this new value in IP.

To specify an operand to be used as a pointer, the various addressing modes available with the 8086 can be used. For instance,

$$\text{JMP WORD PTR [BX]}$$

uses the contents of BX as the address of the memory location that contains the offset address (Memptr16 operand). This offset is loaded into IP, where it is used together with the current contents of CS to compute the "jump to" address.

The intersegment unconditional jump instructions correspond to the *Far-label* and *Memptr32 operands* that are shown in Fig. 4.5(b). Far-label uses a 32-bit immediate operand to specify the jump to address. The first 16 bits of this 32-bit pointer are loaded into IP and are an offset address relative to the contents of the code segment register. The next 16 bits are loaded into the CS register and define the new 64K-byte code segment.

An indirect way to specify the offset and code segment address for an intersegment jump is by using the Memptr32 operand. This time, four consecutive memory bytes starting at the specified address contain the offset address and the new code segment address, respectively. Just like the Memptr16 operand, a Memptr32 operand may be specified using any one of the various addressing modes of the 8086.

An example is the instruction

$$\text{JMP DWORD PTR [DI]}$$

It uses the contents of DS and DI to calculate the address of the memory location that contains the first word of the pointer that identifies the location to which the jump will take place. The two-word pointer starting at this address is read into IP and CS to pass control to the new point in the program.

Conditional Jump Instruction

The second type of jump instructions are those that perform conditional jump operations. Figure 4.6(a) shows a general form of this instruction, and Fig. 4.6(b) is a list of each of the conditional jump instructions in the 8086's instruction set. Notice that each of these instructions tests for the presence or absence of certain conditions.

For instance, the *jump on carry* (JC) instruction makes a test to determine if carry flag (CF) is set. Depending on the result of the test, the jump to the location specified by its operand either takes place or does not. If CF equals 0, the test fails and execution continues with the instruction at the address following the JC instruction. On the other hand, if CF is set to 1, the test condition is satisfied and the jump is performed.

Mnemonic	Meaning	Format	Operation	Flags Affected
Jcc	Conditional jump	Jcc Operand	If the specific condition cc is true, the jump to the address specified by the Operand is initiated; otherwise, the next instruction is executed	None

(a)

Mnemonic	Meaning	Condition
JA	above	CF = 0 and ZF = 0
JAE	above or equal	CF = 0
JB	below	CF = 1
JBE	below or equal	CF = 1 or ZF = 1
JC	carry	CF = 1
JCXZ	CX register is zero	(CF or ZF) = 0
JE	equal	ZF = 1
JG	greater	ZF = 0 and SF = OF
JGE	greater or equal	SF = OF
JL	less	(SF xor OF) = 1
JLE	less or equal	((SF xor OF) or ZF) = 1
JNA	not above	CF = 1 or ZF = 1
JNAE	not above nor equal	CF = 1
JNB	not below	CF = 0
JNBE	not below nor equal	CF = 0 and ZF = 0
JNC	not carry	CF = 0
JNE	not equal	ZF = 0
JNG	not greater	((SF xor OF) or ZF) = 1
JNGE	not greater nor equal	(SF xor OF) = 1
JNL	not less	SF = OF
JNLE	not less nor equal	ZF = 0 and SF = OF
JNO	not overflow	OF = 0
JNP	not parity	PF = 0
JNS	not sign	SF = 0
JNZ	not zero	ZF = 0
JO	overflow	OF = 1
JP	parity	PF = 1
JPE	parity even	PF = 1
JPO	parity odd	PF = 0
JS	sign	SF = 1
JZ	zero	ZF = 1

(b)

Figure 4.6 (a) Conditional jump instruction; (b) types of conditional jump instructions.

Notice that for some of the instructions in Fig.4.6(b) two different mnemonics can be used. This feature can be used to improve program readability. That is, for each occurrence of the instruction in the program, it can be identified with the mnemonic that best describes its function.

For instance, the instruction *jump on parity* (JP)/*jump on parity even* (JPE) can be used to test parity flag PF for logic 1. Since PF is set to 1 if the result from a computation has even parity, this instruction can initiate a jump based on the occurrence of even parity. The reverse instruction JNP/JNPE is also provided. It can be used to initiate a jump based on the occurrence of a result with odd parity instead of even parity.

In a similar manner, the instructions *jump if equal* (JE) and *jump if zero* (JZ) have the same function. Either notation can be used in a program to determine if the result of a computation was zero.

All other conditional jump instructions work in a similar way except that they test different conditions to decide whether or not the jump is to take place. The status conditions for each instruction are shown in Fig. 4.6(b). Examples of these conditions are that the contents of CX are zero, an overflow has occurred, or the result is negative.

To distinguish between comparisons of signed and unsigned numbers by jump instructions, two different names, which seem to be the same, have been devised. They are above and below for comparison of unsigned numbers and less and greater for comparison of signed numbers. For instance, the number $ABCD_{16}$ is above the number 1234_{16} if considered as an unsigned number. On the other hand, if they are considered as signed numbers, $ABCD_{16}$ is negative and 1234_{16} is positive. Therefore, $ABCD_{16}$ is less than 1234_{16}.

EXAMPLE 4.4

Write a program to move a block of N bytes of data starting at offset address BLK1ADDR to another block starting at offset address BLK2ADDR. Assume that both blocks are in the same data segment, whose starting point is defined by the data segment address DATASEGADDR.

SOLUTION The steps to be implemented to solve this problem are outlined in the flowchart in Fig. 4.7(a). It has four basic operations. The first operation is initialization. Initialization involves establishing the initial address of the data segment. This is done by loading the DS register with the value DATASEGADDR. Furthermore, source index register SI and destination index register DI are initialized with addresses BLK1ADDR and BLK2ADDR, respectively. In this way, they point to the beginning of the source block and the beginning of the destination block, respectively. To keep track of the count, register CX is initialized with N, the number of points to be moved. This leads us to the following assembly language statements.

```
MOV AX, DATASEGADDR
MOV DS, AX
MOV SI, BLK1ADDR
MOV DI, BLK2ADDR
MOV CX, N
```

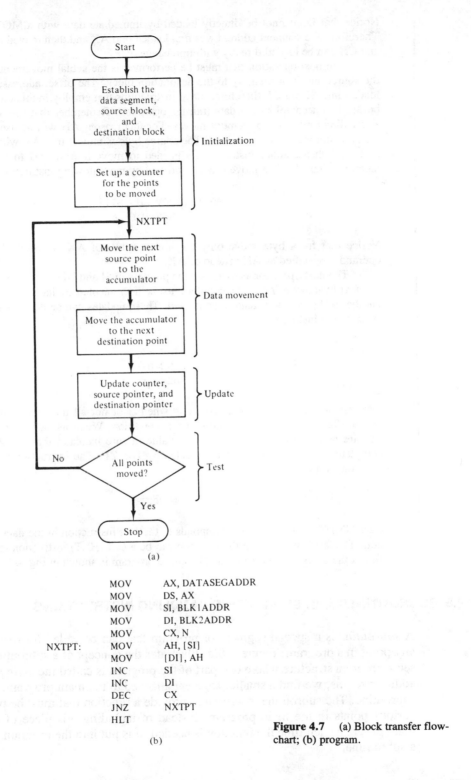

```
            MOV    AX, DATASEGADDR
            MOV    DS, AX
            MOV    SI, BLK1ADDR
            MOV    DI, BLK2ADDR
            MOV    CX, N
NXTPT:      MOV    AH, [SI]
            MOV    [DI], AH
            INC    SI
            INC    DI
            DEC    CX
            JNZ    NXTPT
            HLT
                   (b)
```

Figure 4.7 (a) Block transfer flow-chart; (b) program.

Notice that DS cannot be directly loaded by immediate data with a MOV instruction. Therefore, the segment address was first loaded into AX and then moved to DS. SI, DI, and CX can be loaded directly with immediate data.

The next operation that must be performed is the actual movement of data from the source block of memory to the destination block. The offset addresses are already loaded into SI and DI; therefore, move instructions that employ indirect addressing can be used to accomplish the data transfer operation. Remember that the 8086 does not allow direct memory-to-memory moves. For this reason, AH will be used as an intermediate storage location for data. The source byte is moved into AH with one instruction, and then another instruction is needed to move it from AH to the destination location. Thus the data move is accomplished by the following instructions:

```
NXTPT: MOV AH, [SI]
       MOV [DI], AH
```

Notice that for a byte move only the higher 8 bits of AX are used. Therefore, the operand is specified as AH instead of AX.

The next operation is to update the pointers in SI and DI so that they are ready for the next byte move. Also, the counter must be decremented so that it corresponds to the number of bytes that remain to be moved. These updates can be done by the following sequence of instructions:

```
INC SI
INC DI
DEC CX
```

The test operation involves determining whether or not all the data points have been moved. The contents of CX represent this condition. When its value is nonzero, there still are points to be moved, whereas a value of zero indicates that the block move is complete. This zero condition is reflected by 1 in ZF. The instruction needed to perform this test is

```
JNZ NXTPT
```

Here NXTPT is a label that corresponds to the first instruction in the data move operation. The last instruction in the program can be a *halt* (HLT) instruction to indicate the end of the block move operation. The entire program is shown in Fig. 4.7(b).

4.5 SUBROUTINES AND SUBROUTINE-HANDLING INSTRUCTIONS

A *subroutine* is a special segment of program that can be called for execution from any point in a program. Figure 4.8(a) illustrates the concept of a subroutine. Here we see a program structure where one part of the program is called the *main program*. In addition to this, we find a smaller segment attached to the main program, known as a subroutine. The subroutine is written to provide a function that must be performed at various points in the main program. Instead of including this piece of code in the main program each time the function is needed, it is put into the program just once as a subroutine.

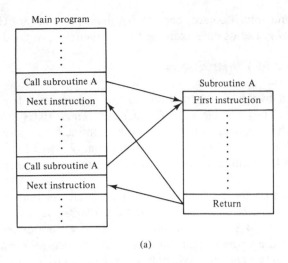

Main program

| Call subroutine A |
| Next instruction |

Subroutine A

| First instruction |

| Call subroutine A |
| Next instruction |

| Return |

(a)

Mnemonic	Meaning	Format	Operation	Flags Affected
CALL	Subroutine call	CALL operand	Execution continues from the address of the subroutine specified by the operand. Information required to return back to the main program such as IP and CS are saved on the stack.	None

(b)

Operand
Near-proc
Far-proc
Memptr16
Regptr16
Memptr32

(c)

Figure 4.8 (a) Subroutine concept; (b) subroutine call instruction; (c) allowed operands.

Wherever the function must be performed, a single instruction is inserted into the main body of the program to *call* the subroutine. Remember that the physical address CS:IP identifies the next instruction to be executed. Thus, to branch to a subroutine that starts elsewhere in memory, the value in the IP or CS and IP must be modified. After executing the subroutine, we want to return control to the instruction that follows the one that called the subroutine. In this way, program execution resumes in the main program at the point where it left off due to the subroutine call. A return instruction must be included at the end of the subroutine to initiate the *return sequence* to the main program environment.

The instructions provided to transfer control from the main program to a subroutine and return control back to the main program are called *subroutine-handling instructions*. Let us now examine the instructions provided for this purpose.

CALL and RET Instructions

There are two basic instructions in the instruction set of the 8086 for subroutine handling. They are the *call* (CALL) and *return* (RET) instructions. Together they provide the mechanism for calling a subroutine into operation and returning control back to the main program at its completion. We will first discuss these two instructions and later introduce other instructions that can be used in conjunction with subroutines.

Just like the JMP instruction, CALL allows implementation of two types of operations, the *intrasegment call* and the *intersegment call*. The CALL instruction is shown in Fig. 4.8(b) and its allowed operand variations are shown in Fig. 4.8(c).

It is the operand that initiates either an intersegment or an intrasegment call. The operands Near-proc, Memptr16, and Regptr16 all specify intrasegment calls to a subroutine. In all three cases, execution of the instruction causes the contents of IP to be saved on the stack. Then the stack pointer (SP) is decremented by 2. The saved values of IP is the address of the instruction that follows the CALL instruction. After saving this return address, a new 16-bit value, which corresponds to the storage location of the first instruction in the subroutine, is loaded into IP.

The three types of intrasegment operands represent different ways of specifying this new value of IP. In a Near-proc operand, the offset of the first instruction of the subroutine from the CALL instruction is supplied directly by the CALL instruction. An example is

CALL LABEL

Here LABEL identifies the 16-bit offset for a Near-proc operand that gets added to IP. This offset is coded as an immediate operand following the opcode for the call instruction. With a 16-bit offset, the subroutine can reside anywhere in the current code segment.

The Memptr16 and Regptr16 operands provide indirect subroutine addressing by specifying a memory location or an internal register, respectively, as the source of a new value for IP. The value specified is the actual offset that is to be loaded into IP. An example of a Regptr16 operand is

CALL BX

When this instruction is executed, the contents of BX are loaded into IP and execution continues with the subroutine starting at a physical address derived from CS and the new value of IP.

By using one of the various addressing modes of the 8086, a pointer to an operand that resides in memory can be specified. This represents a Memptr16 type of operand. In this case, the value of the physical address of the offset is obtained from the address specified by the pointer. For instance, the instruction has its subroutine offset address at the memory location whose physical address is derived from the contents of DS and BX. The value stored at this memory location is loaded into IP. Again the current contents of CS and the new value in IP point to the first instruction of the subroutine.

Notice that in both intrasegment call examples the subroutine was located within the same code segment as the call instruction. The other type of CALL instruction, the intersegment call, permits the subroutine to reside in another code segment. It corresponds to the Far-proc and Memptr32 operands. These operands specify both a new offset address for IP and a new segment address for CS. In both cases, execution of the call instruction causes the contents of the CS and IP registers to be saved on the stack and then new values are loaded into IP and CS. The saved values of CS and IP permit return to the main program from a different code segment.

Far-proc represents a 32-bit immediate operand that is stored in the 4 bytes that follow the opcode of the call instruction in program memory. These two words are loaded directly from code segment memory into IP and CS with execution of the CALL instruction.

On the other hand, when the operand is Memptr32, the pointer for the subroutine is stored as 4 consecutive bytes in data memory. The location of the first byte of the pointer can be specified indirectly by one of the 8086's addressing modes. An example is

CALL DWORD PTR [DI]

Here the physical address of the first byte of the 4-byte pointer in memory is derived from the contents of DS and DI.

Every subroutine must end by executing an instruction that returns control to the main program. This is the return (RET) instruction. It is described in Fig. 4.9(a) and (b). Notice that its execution causes the value of IP or both the values of IP and

Mnemonic	Meaning	Format	Operation	Flags Affected
RET	Return	RET or RET Operand	Return to the main program by restoring IP (and CS for fat-proc). If Operand is present, it is added to the contents of SP.	None

(a)

Operand
None
Disp16

(b)

Figure 4.9 (a) Return instruction; (b) allowed operands.

CS that were saved on the stack to be returned back to their corresponding registers. In general, an intrasegment return results from an intrasegment call and an intersegment return results from an intersegment call. In this way, program control is returned to the instruction that follows the call instruction in program memory.

There is an additional option with the return instruction. It is that a 2-byte code following the return instruction can be included. This code gets added to the stack pointer after restoring the return address either into IP (intrasegment return) or IP and CS (intersegment return). The purpose of this stack pointer displacement is to provide a simple means by which the *parameters* that were saved on the stack before the call to the subroutine was initiated, can be discarded. For instance, the instruction

RET 2

when executed adds 2 to SP. This discards one word parameter as part of the return sequence.

PUSH and POP Instructions

After the context switch to a subroutine, we find that it is usually necessary to save the contents of certain registers or some other main program parameters. These values are saved by pushing them onto the stack. Typically, these data correspond to registers and memory locations that are used by the subroutine. In this way, their original contents are kept intact in the stack segment of memory during the execution of the subroutine. Before a return to the main program takes place, the saved registers and main program parameters are restored. This is done by popping the saved values from the stack back into their original locations. Thus a typical structure of a subroutine is that shown in Fig. 4.10.

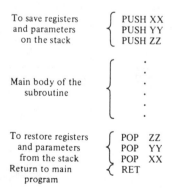

Figure 4.10   Structure of a subroutine.

The instruction that is used to save parameters on the stack is the *push* (PUSH) instruction and that used to retrieve them back is the *pop* (POP) instruction. Notice in Fig. 4.11(a) that the standard PUSH and POP instructions can be written with a general-purpose register, a segment register (excluding CS), or a storage location in memory as their operand.

Execution of a PUSH instruction causes the data corresponding to the operand to be pushed onto the top of the stack. For instance, if the instruction is

Mnemonic	Meaning	Format	Operation	Flags Affected
PUSH	Push word onto stack	PUSH S	$((SP)) \leftarrow (S)$	None
POP	Pop word off stack	POP D	$(D) \leftarrow ((SP))$	None

(a)

Operand (S or D)
Register Seg-reg (CS illegal) Memory

(b)

Figure 4.11 (a) Push and pop instructions; (b) allowed operands.

PUSH AX

the result is as follows:

$$((SP) - 1) \leftarrow (AH)$$

$$((SP) - 2) \leftarrow (AL)$$

$$(SP) \leftarrow (SP) - 2$$

This shows that the 2 bytes of AX are saved in the stack part of memory and the stack pointer is decremented by 2 such that it points to the new top of the stack.

On the other hand, if the instruction is

POP AX

its execution results in

$$(AL) \leftarrow ((SP))$$
$$(AH) \leftarrow ((SP) + 1)$$
$$(SP) \leftarrow (SP) + 2$$

In this manner, the saved contents of AX are restored back into the register.

At times, we also want to save the contents of the flag register and if saved we will later have to restore them. These operations can be accomplished with the *push flags* (PUSHF) and *pop flags* (POPF) instructions, respectively. These instructions are shown in Fig. 4.12. Notice that PUSHF saves the contents of the flag register on the top of the stack. On the other hand, POPF returns the flags from the top of the stack to the flag register.

Mnemonic	Meaning	Operation	Flags Affected
PUSHF	Push flags onto stack	$((SP)) \leftarrow (Flags)$	None
POPF	Pop flags from stack	$(Flags) \leftarrow ((SP))$	OF, DF, IF, TF, SF, ZF, AF, PF, CF

Figure 4.12 Push flags and pop flags instructions.

EXAMPLE 4.5

Write a program to generate the first 20 elements of a Fibonacci series. In this series, the first and second elements are 0 and 1, respectively. Each element that follows is obtained by adding the previous two elements. Use a subroutine to generate the next element from the previous two elements. Store the elements of the series starting at address FIBSER.

SOLUTION   Our plan for the solution of this problem is shown in Fig. 4.13(a). This flowchart shows the use of a subroutine to generate an element of the series, store it in memory, and prepare for generation of the next element.

The first step in the solution is initialization. It involves setting up a data segment, generating the first two numbers of the series, and storing them at memory locations with offset addresses FIBSER and FIBSER + 1. Then a pointer must be established to address the locations for other terms of the series. This address will be held in the DI register. Finally, a counter with initial value equal 18 can be set up in CX to keep track of how many numbers remain to be generated. The instructions needed for initialization are:

```
MOV   AX, DATASEGSTART
MOV   DS, AX
MOV   NUM1, 0
MOV   NUM2, 1
MOV   FIBSER, 0
MOV   FIBSER+1, 1
LEA   DI, FIBSER+2
MOV   CX, 12
```

Notice that the data segment address that is defined by variable DATASEGSTART is first moved into AX and then DS is loaded from AX with another MOV operation. Next the memory locations assigned to NUM_1 and NUM_2 are loaded with immediate data 0 and 1 respectively. These same values are then copied into the storage locations for the first two series elements, FIBSER and FIBSER + 1. Now DI is loaded with the address of FIBSER + 2, which is a pointer to the storage location of the third element of the series. Finally, CX is loaded with 12_{16}, which is the hexadecimal equivalent of 18_{10}.

To generate the next term in the series we call a subroutine. This subroutine generates and stores the elements. Before returning to the main program, it also updates memory locations NUM_1 and NUM_2 with the values of the immediate past two elements. After this, the counter in CX is decremented to record that a series element has been generated and stored. This process must be repeated until the counter becomes equal to zero. This leads to the following assembly language code:

```
NXTNM:   CALL   SBRTF
         DEC    CX
         JNZ    NXTNM
         HLT
```

The call is to the subroutine labeled SBRTF. After the subroutine runs to completion, program control returns to the DEC CX statement. This statement causes the count in CX to be decremented by 1. Next, a conditional jump instruction tests the zero flag to

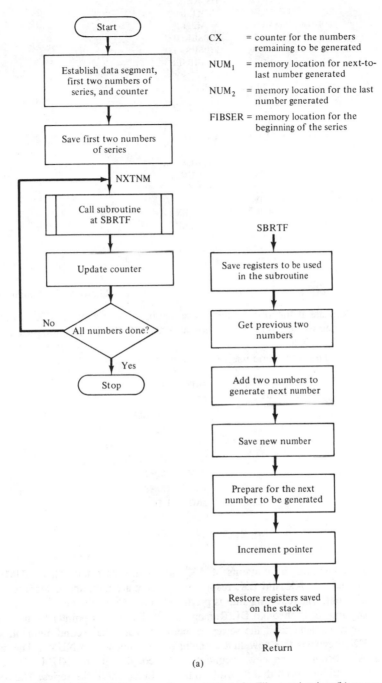

CX = counter for the numbers remaining to be generated

NUM₁ = memory location for next-to-last number generated

NUM_1 = memory location for next-to-last number generated

NUM_2 = memory location for the last number generated

FIBSER = memory location for the beginning of the series

(a)

Figure 4.13   (a) Flowchart for generation of a Fibonacci series; (b) program.

```
                    MOV       AX, DATASEGSTART
                    MOV       DS, AX
                    MOV       NUM1, 0
                    MOV       NUM2, 1
                    MOV       FIBSER, 0
                    MOV       FIBSER+1, 1
                    LEA       DI, FIBSER+2
                    MOV       CX, 12
        NXTNM:      CALL      SBRTF
                    DEC       CX
                    JNZ       NXTNM
                    HLT
        SBRTF:      PUSH      AX
                    PUSH      BX
                    MOV       AX, NUM1
                    MOV       BX, NUM2
                    ADD       AX, BX
                    MOV       [DI], AX
                    MOV       NUM1, BX
                    MOV       NUM2, AX
                    INC       DI
                    POP       BX
                    POP       AX
                    RET
```

(b)

Figure 4.13 (*continued*)

determine if the result after decrementing CX is zero. If CX is not zero, control is returned to the CALL instruction at NXTNM. If it is zero, the program is complete and execution halts.

The subroutine itself is given next.

```
        SBRTF:    PUSH    AX
                  PUSH    BX
                  MOV     AX, NUM1
                  MOV     BX, NUM2
                  ADD     AX, BX
                  MOV     [DI], AX
                  MOV     NUM1, BX
                  MOV     NUM2, AX
                  INC     DI
                  POP     BX
                  POP     AX
                  RET
```

First we save the contents of AX and BX on the stack. Then NUM_1 and NUM_2 are copied into AX and BX, respectively. They are then added together to form the next element. The resulting sum is produced in AX. Now the new element is stored in memory indirectly through DI. Remember that DI holds a pointer to the storage location of the next element of the series in memory. Then the second element, which is held in BX, becomes the new first element by copying it into NUM_1. The sum, which is in AX, becomes the new second term by copying it into NUM_2. Finally, DI is incremented by 1 such that it points to the next element of the series. The registers saved on the stack are restored and then we return back to the main program.

Notice that both the subroutine call and its return have Near-proc operands. The entire program is presented in Fig. 4.13(b).

4.6 LOOP AND LOOP-HANDLING INSTRUCTIONS

The 8086 microprocessor has three instructions specifically designed for implementing *loop operations*. These instructions can be used in place of certain conditional jump instructions and give the programmer a simpler way of writing loop sequences. The loop instructions are listed in Fig. 4.14.

Mnemonic	Meaning	Format	Operation
LOOP	Loop	LOOP Short-label	$(CX) \leftarrow (CX) - 1$ Jump is initiated to location defined by short-label if $(CX) \neq 0$; otherwise, execute next sequential instruction
LOOPE/LOOPZ	Loop while equal/loop while zero	LOOPE/LOOPZ Short-label	$(CX) \leftarrow (CX) - 1$ Jump to location defined by short-label if $(CX) \neq 0$ and $(ZF) = 1$; otherwise, execute next sequential instruction
LOOPNE/LOOPNZ	Loop while not equal/loop while not zero	LOOPNE/LOOPNZ Short-label	$(CX) \leftarrow (CX) - 1$ Jump to location defined by short-label if $(CX) \neq 0$ and $(ZF) = 0$; otherwise, execute next sequential instruction

Figure 4.14 Loop instructions.

The first instruction, *loop* (LOOP), works with respect to the contents of the CX register. CX must be preloaded with a count representing the number of times the loop is to be repeated. Whenever LOOP is executed, the contents of CX are first decremented by 1 and then checked to determine if they are equal to zero. If equal to zero, the loop is complete and the instruction following LOOP is executed; otherwise, control is returned to the instruction at the label specified in the loop instruction. In this way, we see that LOOP is a single instruction that functions the same as a decrement CX instruction followed by a JNZ instruction.

For example the LOOP instruction sequence shown in Fig. 4.15(a) will cause the part of the program from the label NEXT through the instruction LOOP to be repeated a number of times equal to the value of count stored in CX. For example, if CX contains $000A_{16}$, the sequence of instructions included in the loop is executed 10 times.

The other two instructions in Fig. 4.14 operate in a similar way except that they check for two conditions. For instance, the instruction *loop while equal* (LOOPE)/ *loop while zero* (LOOPZ) checks the contents of both CX and the ZF flag. Each time the loop instruction is executed, CX decrements by 1 without affecting the flags, its contents are checked for zero, and the state of ZF that results from execution of the previous instruction is tested for 1. If CX is not equal to 0 and ZF equals 1, a jump is initiated to the location specified with the Short-label operand and the loop continues. If either CX or ZF is 0, the loop is complete and the instruction following the loop instruction is executed.

Instruction *loop while not equal*(LOOPNE)/*loop while not zero* (LOOPNZ)

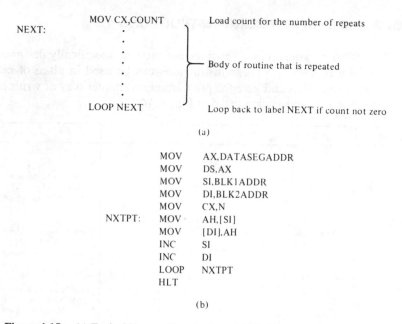

```
NEXT:        MOV CX,COUNT          Load count for the number of repeats
                .
                .
                .                     Body of routine that is repeated
                .
                .
         LOOP NEXT                    Loop back to label NEXT if count not zero
```

(a)

```
              MOV     AX,DATASEGADDR
              MOV     DS,AX
              MOV     SI,BLK1ADDR
              MOV     DI,BLK2ADDR
              MOV     CX,N
NXTPT:        MOV     AH,[SI]
              MOV     [DI],AH
              INC     SI
              INC     DI
              LOOP    NXTPT
              HLT
```

(b)

Figure 4.15 (a) Typical loop routine structure; (b) block move program employing the LOOP instruction.

works in a similar way to the LOOPE/LOOPZ instruction. The difference is that it checks ZF and CX looking for ZF equal to 0 together with CX not equal to 0. If these conditions are met, the jump back to the location specified with the Short-label operand is performed and the loop continues.

Figure 4.15(b) shows a practical implementation of a loop. Here we find the block move program that was developed in Example 4.4 rewritten using the LOOP instruction. Comparing this program to the one in Fig. 4.7(b), we see that the instruction LOOP NXTPT has replaced the DEC and JNZ instructions.

EXAMPLE 4.6

Given the following sequence of instructions:

```
              MOV     AX, 0
              MOV     DS, AX
              MOV     AL, 5
              MOV     DI, 0A000
              MOV     CX, 0F
AGAIN:        INC     DI
              CMP     [DI] , AL
              LOOPNE  AGAIN
NEXT:
```

explain what happens as they are executed..

SOLUTION The first four instructions are for initializing internal registers. Data segment register DS is cleared; accumulator register AL is loaded with the 5_{16}; destination index register DI is loaded with $A000_{16}$; and count register CX is loaded with F_{16} (15_{10}). After initialization, a data segment is set up at address 00000_{16} and DI points to the memory location at offset $A000_{16}$ in this data segment. Moreover, AL contains the data 5 and the CX register contains the loop count 15.

The part of the program that starts at the label AGAIN and ends with the LOOPNE instruction is a software loop. The first instruction in the loop increments DI by one. Therefore, the first time through the loop DI contains $A001_{16}$. The next instruction compares the contents of this memory location with the contents of AL, which is 5. If the data held at $A001_{16}$ is 5, the zero flag is set; otherwise, it is left at logic 0. The LOOPNE instruction then decrements CX (making it E_{16}) and then checks for CX $= 0$ or ZF $= 1$. If neither of these two conditions is satisfied, program control is returned to the instruction with the label AGAIN. This causes the comparison to be repeated for the examination of the contents of the next byte in memory. On the other hand, if either condition is satisfied, the loop is terminated and execution continues with the instruction identified by the label NEXT. In this way, we see that the loop is repeated until either a number 5 is found or all locations in the address range $A001_{16}$ through $A00F_{16}$ have been tested and found to not contain 5.

4.7 STRINGS AND STRING-HANDLING INSTRUCTIONS

The 8086 microprocessor is equipped with special instructions to handle *string operations*. By string we mean a series of data words or bytes that reside in consecutive memory locations. The string instructions of the 8086 permit a programmer to implement operations such as to move data from one block of memory to a block elsewhere in memory. A second type of operation that is easily performed is to scan a string of data elements stored in memory looking for a specific value. Other examples arc to compare the elements of two strings together in order to determine whether they arc the same or different and to initialize a set of consecutive memory locations. Complex operations such as these typically require several nonstring instructions to be implemented.

There are five basic string instructions in the instruction set of the 8086. These instructions, as listed in Fig. 4.16, are *move byte* or *word string* (MOVSB, MOVSW), *compare strings* (CMPS), *scan string* (SCAS), *load string* (LODS), and *store string* (STOS). They are called the *basic string instructions* because each defines an operation for one element of a string. Thus these operations must be repeated to handle a string of more than one element. Let us first look at the basic operations performed by these instructions.

Move String: MOVSB, MOVSW

The instructions MOVSB, and MOVSW perform the same basic operation. An element of the string specified by the source index (SI) register with respect to the current data segment (DS) register is moved to the location specified by the destination index (DI) register with respect to the current extra segment (ES) register. The move can be performed on a byte (MOVSB) or a word (MOVSW) of data. After the move is complete, the contents of both SI and DI are automatically incremented or decremented by 1 for a byte move and by 2 for a word move. Remember the fact that

Mnemonic	Meaning	Format	Operation	Flags affected
MOVSB	Move string byte	MOVSB	$((ES)0 + (DI)) \leftarrow ((DS)0 + (SI))$ $(SI) \leftarrow (SI) \pm 1$ $(DI) \leftarrow (DI) \pm 1$	None
MOVSW	Move string word	MOVSW	$((ES)0 + (DI) \leftarrow ((DS)0 + (SI))$ $((ES)0 + (DI) + 1) \leftarrow ((DS)0 + (SI) + 1)$ $(SI) \leftarrow (SI) \pm 2$ $(DI) \leftarrow (DI) \pm 2$	None
CMPSB/ CMPSW	Compare string	CMPSB/ CMPSW	Set flags as per $((DS)0 + (SI)) - ((ES)0 + (DI))$ $(SI) \leftarrow (SI) \pm 1$ or 2 $(DI) \leftarrow (DI) \pm 1$ or 2	CF, PF, AF, ZF, SF, OF
SCASB/ SCASW	Scan string	SCASB/ SCASW	Set flags as per $(AL$ or $AX) - ((ES)0 + (DI))$ $(DI) \leftarrow (DI) \pm 1$ or 2	CF, PF, AF, ZF, SF, OF
LODSB/ LODSW	Load string	LODSB/ LODSW	$(AL$ or $AX) \leftarrow ((DS)0 + (SI))$ $(SI) \leftarrow (SI) \pm 1$ or 2	None
STOSB/ STOSW	Store string	STOSB/ STOSW	$((ES)0 + (DI)) \leftarrow (AL$ or $AX) \pm 1$ or 2 $(DI) \leftarrow (DI) \pm 1$ or 2	None

Figure 4.16   Basic string instructions.

the address pointers in SI and DI increment or decrement depends on how the direction flag DF is set.

For example, to move a byte the instruction

MOVSB

can be used.

An example of a program that uses MOVSB is shown in Fig. 4.17. This program is a modified version of the block move program of Fig. 4.15(b). Notice that the two MOV instructions that performed the data transfer and INC instructions that update the pointer have been replaced with one move string byte instruction. We have also made DS equal to ES.

```
        MOV     AX,DATASEGADDR
        MOV     DS,AX
        MOV     ES,AX
        MOV     SI,BLK1ADDR
        MOV     DI,BLK2ADDR
        MOV     CX,N
        CDF
NXTPT:  MOVSB
        LOOP    NXTPT
        HLT
```

Figure 4.17   Block move program using the move string instruction.

Compare Strings and Scan Strings: CMPS/CMPW and SCASB/SCASW

The compare strings instruction can be used to compare two elements in the same or different strings. It subtracts the destination operand from the source operand and adjusts flags CF, PF, AF, ZF, SF, and OF accordingly. The result of subtraction is not saved; therefore, the operation does not affect the operands in any way.

An example of a compare strings instruction for bytes of data is

Again, the source element is pointed to by the address in SI with respect to the current value in DS and the destination element is specified by the contents of DI relative to the contents of ES. When executed, the operands are compared, the flags are adjusted, and both SI and DI are updated such that they point to the next elements in their respective strings.

The scan strings instruction is similar to compare strings; however, it compares the byte or word element of the destination string at the physical address derived from DI and ES to the contents of AL or AX, respectively. The flags are adjusted based on this result and DI incremented or decremented.

Figure 4.18 shows a program that reimplements the string scan operation described in Example 4.6 using the SCAS instruction. Again, we have set DS equal to ES.

```
            MOV      AX,0
            MOV      DS,AX
            MOV      ES,AX
            MOV      AL,5
            MOV      DI,0A000
            MOV      CX,0F
            CDF
AGAIN:      SCASB
            LOOPNE   AGAIN
NEXT:
```

Figure 4.18 Block scan operation using the SCASB instruction.

Load and Store Strings: LODSB/LODSW and STOSB/STOSW

The last two instructions in Fig. 4.16, load string and store string, are specifically provided to move string elements between the accumulator and memory. LODSB loads a byte from a string in memory into AL. The address in SI is used relative to DS to determine the address of the memory location of the string element. Similarly, the instruction

LODSW

indicates that the word string element at the physical address derived from DS and SI is to be loaded into AX. Then the index in SI is automatically incremented by 2.

On the other hand, STOSB stores a byte from AL into a string location in memory. This time the contents of ES and DI are used to form the address of the storage location in memory. For example, the program in Fig. 4.19 will clear the block of memory locations from $A000_{16}$ through $A00F_{16}$ to 00_{16}. STOSW would be used to store a word from AX into a string location in memory.

Repeat String: REP

In most applications, the basic string operations must be repeated in order to process arrays of data. This is done by inserting a repeat prefix before the instruction that is

```
                MOV        AX,0
                MOV        DS,AX
                MOV        ES,AX
                MOV        AL,05
                MOV        DI,0A000
                MOV        CX,0F
                CDF
AGAIN:          STOSB
                LOOPNE     AGAIN
        NEXT:
```

Figure 4.19 Clearing a block of memory with a STOSB operation.

to be repeated. The *repeat prefixes* of the 8086 are shown in Fig. 4.20.

The first prefix, REP, causes the basic string operation to be repeated until the contents of register CX become equal to zero. Each time the instruction is executed, it causes CX to be tested for zero. If CX is found to be nonzero, it is decremented by 1 and the basic string operation is repeated. On the other hand, if it is 0, the repeat string operation is done and the next instruction in the program is executed. The repeat count must be loaded into CX prior to executing the repeat string instruction. Figure 4.21 is the memory clear routine of Fig. 4.19 modified by using the REP prefix.

Prefix	Used with:	Meaning
REP	MOVS STOS	Repeat while not end of string $CX \neq 0$
REPE/REPZ	CMPS SCAS	Repeat while not end of string and strings are equal $CX \neq 0$ and $ZF = 1$
REPNE/REPNZ	CMPS SCAS	Repeat while not end of string and strings are not equal $CX \neq 0$ and $ZF = 0$

Figure 4.20 Prefixes for use with the basic string operations.

```
                MOV        AX,0
                MOV        DS,AX
                MOV        ES,AX
                MOV        AL,05
                MOV        DI,0A000
                MOV        CX,0F
                CDF
                REPSTOSB
        NEXT:
```

Figure 4.21 Clearing a block of memory by repeating STOSB.

The prefixes REPE and REPZ stand for the same function. They are meant for use with the CMPS and SCAS instructions. With REPE/REPZ, the basic compare or scan operation can be repeated as long as both the contents of CX are not equal to zero and the zero flag is 1. The first condition CX not equal to zero indicates that the end of the string has not yet been reached and the second condition $ZF = 1$ indicates that the elements that were compared are equal.

The last prefix, REPNE/REPNZ, works similarly to REPE/REPZ except that now the operation is repeated as long as CX is not equal to zero and ZF is zero. That is, the comparison or scanning is to be performed as long as the string elements are unequal and the end of the string is not yet found.

Autoindexing for String Instructions

Earlier we pointed out that during the execution of a string instruction the address indices in SI and DI are either automatically incremented or decremented. Moreover, we indicated that the decision to increment or decrement is made based on the setting of the direction flag DF. The 8086 provides two instructions, clear direction flag (CLD) and set direction flag (STD), to permit selection between *autoincrement* and *autodecrement modes* of operation. These instructions are shown in Fig. 4.22. When CLD is executed, DF is set to 0. This selects autoincrement mode and each time a string operation is performed SI and/or DI are incremented by 1 if byte data are processed and by 2 if word data are processed.

Mnemonic	Meaning	Format	Operation	Flags Affected
CLD	Clear DF	CLD	(DF) ← 0	DF
STD	Set DF	STD	(DF) ← 1	DF

Figure 4.22 Instructions for autoincrementing and autodecrementing in string instructions.

EXAMPLE 4.7

Describe what happens as the following sequence of instructions is executed.

```
CLD
MOV AX, DATA_SEGMENT
MOV DS, AX
MOV AX, EXTRA_SEGMENT
MOV ES, AX
MOV CX, 20
MOV SI, OFFSET MASTER
MOV DI, OFFSET COPY
REPMOVSB
```

SOLUTION The first instruction clears the direction flag and selects autoincrement mode of operation for string addressing. The next two instructions initialize DS with the value DATA_SEGMENT. It is followed by two instructions that load ES with the value EXTRA_SEGMENT. Then the number of repeats, 20_{16}, is loaded into CX. The next two instructions load SI and DI with beginning offset addresses MASTER and COPY for the source and destination strings. Now we are ready to perform the string operation. Execution of REPMOVSB moves a block or 32 consecutive bytes from the block of memory locations starting at offset address MASTER with respect to the current data segment (DS) to a block of locations starting at offset address COPY with respect to the current extra segment (ES).

ASSIGNMENT

Section 4.2

1. Explain what happens when the instruction sequence

```
LAHF
MOV [BX+DI], AH
```

is executed.

2. What operation is performed by the instruction sequence that follows

$$\text{MOV AH, [BX+SI]}$$
$$\text{SAHF}$$

3. Which instruction should be executed to assure that the carry flag is in the carry state? The no carry state?

4. Which instruction when executed disables the interrupt interface?

5. Write an instruction sequence to configure the 8086 as follows: interrupts not accepted; save the original contents of flags SF, ZF, AF, PF, and CF at the address $A000_{16}$; and then clear CF.

Section 4.3

6. Describe the difference in operation and the effect on status flags due to the execution of the subtract words and compare words instructions.

7. Describe the operation performed by each of the instructions that follow
   (a) CMP [0100],AL   (b) CMP AX,[SI]   (c) CMPWORD PTR [DI],1234

8. What is the state of the 8086's flags after executing the instructions in Problem 7(a) through (c)? Assume the following initial state exists before executing the instructions.

$$(AX) = 8001_{16}$$

$$(SI) = 0200_{16}$$

$$(DI) = 0300_{16}$$

$$(DS:100) = F0_{16}$$

$$(DS:200) = F0_{16}$$

$$(DS:201) = 01_{16}$$

$$(DS:300) = 34_{16}$$

$$(DS:301) = 12_{16}$$

9. What happens to the ZF and CF status flags as the following sequence of instructions is executed? Assume that they are both initially cleared.

$$\text{MOV BX,1111}$$
$$\text{MOV AX,BBBB}$$
$$\text{CMP BX,AX}$$

Section 4.4

10. What is the key difference between the unconditional jump instruction and conditional jump instruction?

11. Which registers have their contents changed during an intrasegment jump? Intersegment jump?

12. How large is a Short-label displacement? Near-label displacement? Memptr16 operand?

13. Is a Far-label used to initiate an intrasegment jump or intersegment jump?

14. Identify the type of jump, the type of operand, and the operation performed by each of the instructions that follows.

(a) JMP 10   **(b)** JMP 1000   **(c)** JMP WORD PTR[SI]

15. If the state of the 8086 is

$$(CS) = 1075_{16}$$

$$(IP) = 0300_{16}$$

$$(SI) = 0100_{16}$$

$$(DS:100) = 00_{16}$$

$$(DS:101) = 10_{16}$$

after executing each of the instructions in Problem 14, to what address is program control passed?

16. Which flags are tested by the various conditional jump instructions?

17. What flag condition is tested by the instruction JNS?

18. What flag conditions are tested by the instruction JA?

19. Identify the type of jump, the type of operand, and operation performed by each of the instructions that follows.

(a) JNC 10   **(b)** JNP PARITY_ERROR   **(c)** JO DWORD PTR [BX]

20. What value must be loaded into BX such that execution of the instruction JMP BX transfers control to the memory location offset from the beginning of the current code segment by 256_{10}?

21. The program that follows implements what is known as a *delay loop*.

```
          MOV   CX, 1000
DLY:      DEC   CX
          JNZ   DLY
NXT:      ---   ---
```

(a) How many times does the JNZ DLY instruction get executed?
(b) Change the program so that JNZ DLY is executed just 17 times.
(c) Change the program so that JNZ DLY is executed 2^{32} times.

22. Given a number N in the range $0 < N \le 5$, write a program that computes its factorial and saves the result in memory location FACT.

23. Write a program that compares the elements of two arrays, A(I) and B(I). Each array contains 100 16-bit signed numbers. The comparison is to be done by comparing the corresponding elements of the two arrays until either two elements are found to be unequal or all elements of the arrays have been compared and found to be equal. Assume that the arrays start at addresses $A000_{16}$ and $B000_{16}$, respectively. If the two arrays are found to be unequal, save the address of the first unequal element of A(I) in memory location FOUND; otherwise, write all 0s into this location.

24. Given an array A(I) of 100 16-bit signed numbers that are stored in memory starting at address $A000_{16}$, write a program to generate two arrays from the given array such that one P(J) consists of all the positive numbers and the other N(K) contains all the negative numbers. Store the array of positive numbers in memory starting at address $B000_{16}$ and the array of negative numbers starting at address $C000_{16}$.

25. Given a 16-bit binary number in DX, write a program that converts it to its equivalent BCD number in DX. If the result is bigger than 16 bits, place all 1s in DX.

26. Given an array A(I) with 100 16-bit signed integer numbers, write a program to generate a new array B(I) as follows:

$$B(I) = A(I), \quad \text{for } I = 1, 2, 99, \text{ and } 100$$

and

$$B(I) = \text{median value of } A(I - 2), A(I - 1), A(I),$$

$$A(I + 1), \text{ and } A(I + 2), \quad \text{for all other } I's$$

Section 4.5

27. Describe the difference between a jump and call instruction.

28. Why are intersegment and intrasegment call instructions provided in the 8086?

29. What is saved on the stack when a call instruction with a Memptr16 operand is executed? A Memptr32 operand?

30. Identify the type of call, the type of operand, and operation performed by each of the instructions that follows
   (a) CALL 1000   **(b)** CALL [0100]   **(c)** CALL DWORD PTR [BX + SI]

31. If the state of the 8086 is

$$(CS) = 1075_{16}$$

$$(IP) = 0300_{16}$$

$$(BX) = 0100_{16}$$

$$(SI) = 0100_{16}$$

$$(DS:100) = 00_{16}$$

$$(DS:101) = 10_{16}$$

$$(DS:200) = 00_{16}$$

$$(DS:201) = 01_{16}$$

$$(DS:202) = 00_{16}$$

$$(DS:203) = 10_{16}$$

after executing each of the instructions in Problem 30, to what address is program control passed?

32. What function is performed by the RET instruction?

33. Describe the operation performed by each of the instructions that follow:
   (a) PUSH DS   **(d)** POP [BX + DI]
   (b) PUSH SI   **(e)** POPF
   (c) POP DI

34. At what addresses will the bytes of the immediate operand in Problem 33(a) be stored after the instruction is executed?

35. Write a subroutine that converts a given 16-bit BCD number to its equivalent binary number. The BCD number is to be passed to a subroutine through register DX and the routine returns the equivalent binary number in DX.

36. When is it required to include PUSHF and POPF instructions in a subroutine?

37. Given an array A(I) of 100 16-bit signed integer numbers, write a subroutine to generate a new array B(I) such that

$$B(I) = A(I), \quad \text{for I} = 1 \text{ and } 100$$

and

$$B(I) = \tfrac{1}{4}[A(I - 1) - 5A(I) + 9A(I + 1)], \quad \text{for all other I's}$$

The values of A(I − 1), A(I), and A(I + 1) are to be passed to the subroutine in registers AX, BX, and CX and the subroutine returns the result B(I) in register AX.

38. Write a segment of main program and show its subroutine structure to perform the following operations. The program is to check continuously the three most significant bits in register DX and, depending on their setting, execute one of three subroutines: SUBA, SUBB, or SUBC. The subroutines are selected as follows:
(a) If bit 15 of DX is set, initiate SUBA.
(b) If bit 14 of DX is set and bit 15 is not set, initiate SUBB.
(c) If bit 13 of DX is set and bits 14 and 15 are not set, initiate SUBC.
If the subroutine is executed, the corresponding bits of DX are to be cleared and then control returned to the main program. After returning from the subroutine, the main program is repeated.

Section 4.6

39. Which flags are tested by the various conditional loop instructions?

40. What two conditions can terminate the operation performed by the instruction LOOPNE?

41. How large a jump can be employed in a loop instruction?

42. What is the maximum number of repeats that can be implemented with a loop instruction?

43. Using loop instructions, implement the program in Problem 22.

44. Using loop instructions, implement the program in Problem 23.

Section 4.7

45. What determines whether the SI and DI registers increment or decrement during a string operation?

46. Which segment register is used to form the destination address for a string instruction?

47. Write equivalent string instruction sequences for each of the following:

(a) MOV AX, [SI]	**(c)** MOV AL, [DI]
MOV [DI], AX	CMP AL, [SI]
INC SI	DEC SI
INC DI	DEC DI
(b) MOV AX, [SI]	
INC SI	
INC SI	

48. Use string instructions to implement the program in Problem 23.

49 Write a program to convert a table of 100 ASCII characters stored starting at offset address ASCII_CHAR into their equivalent table of EBCDIC characters and store them at offset address EBCDIC_CHAR. The translation is to be done using an ASCII to EBCDIC conversion table starting at offset address ASCII_TO_EBCDIC. Assume that all three tables are located in different segments of memory.

5

The 8086
Microprocessor and its
Memory Interface

5.1 INTRODUCTION

Up to this point, we have studied the 8086 microprocessor from a software point of view. We have covered its software architecture, instruction set, and how to write programs in assembly language. Now we will begin to examine the hardware architecture of the 8086-based microcomputer. This chapter is devoted to its signal interfaces, memory interface, and external memory subsystems. For this purpose, we have included the following topics in the chapter:

1. The 8086 microprocessor
2. Minimum-mode and maximum-mode systems
3. Minimum-system-mode interface
4. Maximum-system-mode interface
5. System clock
6. Bus cycle
7. Memory interface
8. Hardware organization of the memory address space
9. Memory bus status codes
10. Read and write bus cycles
11. Memory control signals

110

12. Demultiplexing the address/data bus

13. 4K-byte program storage memory, 2K-byte data storage memory circuit

5.2 THE 8086 MICROPROCESSOR

The 8086, first announced in 1978, was the first 16-bit microprocessor introduced by Intel Corporation. It has been followed by a steady stream of family components such as the 8088 microprocessor, the 8087 numeric coprocessor, and the 8089 I/O processor.

The 8086 is manufactured using *high-performance metal-oxide-semiconductor* (HMOS) *technology* and the circuitry on its chip is equivalent to approximately 29,000 transistors. It is enclosed in a 40-pin package as shown in Fig. 5.1. Many of its pins have multiple functions. For example, in the pin layout we see that address lines A_0 through A_{15} and data bus lines D_0 through D_{15} are multiplexed. For this reason, these leads are labeled AD_0 through AD_{15}.

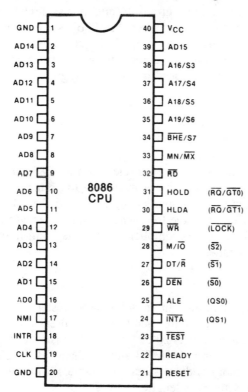

Figure 5.1 Pin layout of the 8086 microprocessor. (Reprinted by permission of Intel Corp. Copyright/Intel Corp., 1979.)

The 8086 is a true 16-bit microprocessor with 16-bit internal and external data paths. It has the ability to address up to 1M byte of memory via a 20-bit-wide address bus. Moreover, it can address up to 64K of byte-wide input/output ports or 32K of word-wide ports.

5.3 MINIMUM-MODE AND MAXIMUM-MODE SYSTEMS

The 8086 microprocessor can be configured to work in either of two modes. These modes are known as the *minimum system mode* and the *maximum system mode*. The minimum system mode is selected by applying logic 1 to the MN/$\overline{\text{MX}}$ input lead. Minimum 8086 systems are typically smaller and contain a single microprocessor. Changing MN/$\overline{\text{MX}}$ to logic 0 selects the maximum mode of operation. This configures the 8086 system for use in larger systems and with multiple processors. This mode-selection feature lets the 8086 better meet the needs of a wide variety of system requirements.

Depending on the mode of operation selected, the assignments for a number of the pins on the 8086's package are changed. As shown in Fig. 5.1, the pin functions specified in parentheses are those that pertain to a maximum-mode system.

The signals that are common to both modes of operation, those unique to minimum mode, and those unique to maximum mode are listed in Fig. 5.2(a), (b), and (c), respectively. Here we find the name, function, and type for each signal. For example, the signal $\overline{\text{RD}}$ is in the common group. It functions as a read control output and is used to signal memory or I/O devices when the 8086's system bus is set up for input of data. Moreover, notice that the signals hold request (HOLD) and hold acknowledge (HLDA) are produced only in the minimum-mode system. If the 8086 is set up for maximum mode, they are replaced by the request/grant bus access control lines $\overline{\text{RQ}}/\overline{\text{GT}}_0$ and $\overline{\text{RQ}}/\overline{\text{GT}}_1$.

5.4 MINIMUM-SYSTEM-MODE INTERFACE

When the minimum system mode of operation is selected, the 8086 itself provides all the control signals needed to implement the memory and I/O interfaces. Figure 5.3 shows a block diagram of a minimum-mode configuration of the 8086. The minimum-mode signals can be divided into the following basic groups: address/data bus, status, control, interrupt, and DMA. For simplicity in the diagram, multiplexed signal lines are shown to be independent.

Address/Data Bus

Let us first look at the address/data bus. In an 8086-based system these lines serve two functions. As an *address bus,* they are used to carry address information to the memory and I/O ports. The address bus is 20 bits long and consists of signal lines A_0 through A_{19}. Of these, A_{19} represents the MSB and A_0 the LSB. A 20-bit address gives the 8086 a 1M-byte memory address space. Moreover, it has an independent I/O address space which is 64K bytes in length.

The 16 *data bus* lines D_0 through D_{15} are actually multiplexed with address lines A_0 through A_{15}, respectively. By multiplexed we mean that the bus works as an address bus during one period of time and as a data bus during another period. D_{15} is the MSB and D_0 the LSB. When acting as a data bus, they carry read/write data for memory, input/output data for I/O devices, and interrupt-type codes from an interrupt controller.

Common Signals		
Name	Function	Type
AD15–AD0	Address/Data Bus	Bidirectional, 3-State
A19/S6– A16/S3	Address/Status	Output, 3-State
$\overline{BHE}$/S7	Bus High Enable/ Status	Output, 3-State
MN/$\overline{MX}$	Minimum/Maximum Mode Control	Input
$\overline{RD}$	Read Control	Output, 3-State
$\overline{TEST}$	Wait On Test Control	Input
READY	Wait State Control	Input
RESET	System Reset	Input
NMI	Non-Maskable Interrupt Request	Input
INTR	Interrupt Request	Input
CLK	System Clock	Input
V_{CC}	+5 V	Input
GND	Ground	

(a)

Minimum Mode Signals (MN/$\overline{MX}$ = V_{CC})		
Name	Function	Type
HOLD	Hold Request	Input
HLDA	Hold Acknowledge	Output
$\overline{WR}$	Write Control	Output, 3-State
M/$\overline{IO}$	Memory/IO Control	Output, 3-State
DT/$\overline{R}$	Data Transmit/ Receive	Output, 3-State
$\overline{DEN}$	Data Enable	Output, 3-State
ALE	Address Latch Enable	Output
$\overline{INTA}$	Interrupt Acknowledge	Output

(b)

Maximum Mode Signals (MN/$\overline{MX}$ = GND)		
Name	Function	Type
$\overline{RQ}/\overline{GT}$1, 0	Request/Grant Bus Access Control	Bidirectional
$\overline{LOCK}$	Bus Priority Lock Control	Output, 3-State
$\overline{S2}$–$\overline{S0}$	Bus Cycle Status	Output, 3-State
QS1, QS0	Instruction Queue Status	Output

(c)

Figure 5.2 (a) Signals common to both minimum and maximum modes (reprinted by permission of Intel Corp. Copyright/Intel Corp., 1979); (b) unique minimum-mode signals (reprinted by permission of Intel Corp. Copyright/Intel Corp., 1979); (c) unique maximum-mode signals (reprinted by permission of Intel Corp. Copyright/Intel Corp., 1979).

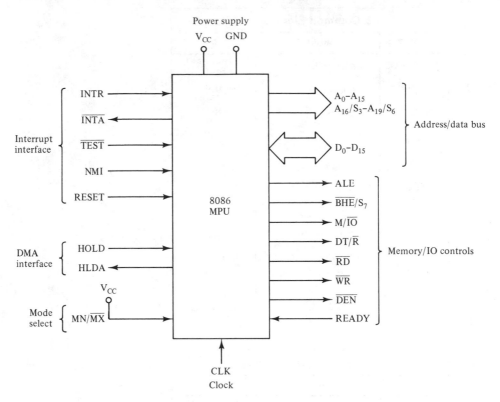

Figure 5.3 Block diagram of the minimum-mode 8086 MPU.

Status Signals

The four most significant address lines, A_{19} through A_{16} are also multiplexed, but in this case with status signals S_6 through S_3. These status bits are output on the bus at the same time the data are transferred over the other bus lines. Bits S_4 and S_3 together form a 2-bit binary code that identifies which of the 8086's internal segment registers was used to generate the physical address that was output on the address bus during the current bus cycle. These four codes and the register they represent are shown in Fig. 5.4. Notice that the code $S_4S_3 = 00$ identifies a register known as the *extra segment register* as the source of the segment address.

Status line S_5 reflects the status of another internal characteristic of the 8086. It

S_4	S_3	Segment register
0	0	Extra
0	1	Stack
1	0	Code/none
1	1	Data

Figure 5.4 Memory segment status codes.

is the logic level of the internal interrupt enable flag. The last status bit S_6 is always at the 0 logic level.

Control Signals

The *control signals* are provided to support the 8086's memory and I/O interfaces. They control functions such as when the bus is to carry a valid address, in which direction data are to be transferred over the bus, when valid write data are on the bus, and when to put read data on the system bus. For example, *address latch enable* (ALE) is a pulse to logic 1 that signals external circuitry when a valid address word is on the bus. This address must be latched in external circuitry on the 1-to-0 edge of the pulse at ALE.

Another control signal that is produced during the bus cycle is $\overline{\text{BHE}}$ (*bank high enable*). Logic 0 on this line is used as a memory enable signal for the most significant byte half of the data bus, D_8 through D_{15}. This line also serves a second function, which is as the S_7 status line.

Using the M/$\overline{\text{IO}}$ (*memory/IO*) and DT/$\overline{\text{R}}$ (*data transmit/receive*) lines, the 8086 signals which type of bus cycle is in progress and in which direction data are to be transferred over the bus. The logic level of M/$\overline{\text{IO}}$ tells external circuitry whether a memory or I/O transfer is taking place over the bus. Logic 1 at this output signals a memory operation, and logic 0 an I/O operation. The direction of data transfer over the bus is signaled by the logic level output at DT/$\overline{\text{R}}$. When this line is logic 1 during the data transfer part of a bus cycle, the bus is in the transmit mode. Therefore, data are either written into memory or output to an I/O device. On the other hand, logic 0 at DT/$\overline{\text{R}}$ signals that the bus is in the receive mode. This corresponds to reading data from memory or input of data from an input port.

The signals *read* ($\overline{\text{RD}}$) and *write* ($\overline{\text{WR}}$), respectively, indicate that a read bus cycle or a write bus cycle is in progress. The 8086 switches $\overline{\text{WR}}$ to logic 0 to signal external devices that valid write or output data are on the bus. On the other hand, $\overline{\text{RD}}$ indicates that the 8086 is performing a read of data off the bus. During read operations, one other control signal is also supplied. This is $\overline{\text{DEN}}$ (*data enable*), and it signals external devices when they should put data on the bus.

There is one other control signal that is involved with the memory and I/O interface. This is the READY signal. It can be used to insert wait states into the bus cycle such that it is extended by a number of clock periods. This signal is provided by way of an external clock generator device and can be supplied by the memory or I/O subsystem to signal the 8086 when they are ready to permit the data transfer to be completed.

Interrupt Signals

The key interrupt interface signals are *interrupt request* (INTR) and *interrupt acknowledge* ($\overline{\text{INTA}}$). INTR is an input to the 8086 that can be used by an external device to signal that it needs to be serviced. This input is sampled during the final clock period of each *instruction acquisition cycle*. Logic 1 at INTR represents an active interrupt request. When an interrupt request has been recognized by the 8086, it indicates this fact to external circuits with pulses to logic 0 at the $\overline{\text{INTA}}$ output.

The $\overline{\text{TEST}}$ input is also related to the external interrupt interface. Execution of a WAIT instruction causes the 8086 to check the logic level at the $\overline{\text{TEST}}$ input. If logic 1 is found, the MPU suspends operation and goes into what is known as the *idle state*. The 8086 no longer executes instructions; instead, it repeatedly checks the logic level of the $\overline{\text{TEST}}$ input waiting for its transition back to logic 0. As $\overline{\text{TEST}}$ switches to 0, execution resumes with the next instruction in the program. This feature can be used to synchronize the operation of the 8086 to an event in external hardware.

There are two more inputs in the interrupt interface: the *nonmaskable interrupt* (NMI) and *reset* (RESET). On the 0-to-1 transition of NMI, control is passed to a nonmaskable interrupt service routine. The RESET input is used to provide a hardware reset for the 8086. Switching RESET to logic 0 initializes the internal registers of the 8086 and initiates a reset service routine.

DMA Interface Signals

The *direct memory access* (DMA) interface of the 8086 minimum-mode system consists of the HOLD and HLDA signals. When an external device wants to take control of the system bus, it signals this fact to the 8086 by switching HOLD to the 1 logic level. At the completion of the current bus cycle, the 8086 enters the hold state. When in the hold state, signal lines AD_0 through AD_{15}, A_{16}/S_3 through A_{19}/S_6, $\overline{\text{BHE}}$, M/$\overline{\text{IO}}$, DT/$\overline{\text{R}}$, $\overline{\text{RD}}$, $\overline{\text{WR}}$, $\overline{\text{DEN}}$, and INTR are all in the high-Z state. The 8086 signals external devices that it is in this state by switching its HLDA output to the 1 logic level.

5.5 MAXIMUM-SYSTEM-MODE INTERFACE

When the 8086 is set for the maximum-mode configuration, it produces signals for implementing a *multiprocessor/coprocessor system environment*. By multiprocessor environment we mean that more than one microprocessor exists in the system and that each processor is executing its own program. Usually in this type of system environment, some system resources are common to all processors. They are called *global resources*. Other resources are assigned to specific processors. These dedicated resources are known as *local* or *private resources*.

Coprocessor also means that there is a second processor in the system. However, in this case, the two processors do not access the bus at the same time. One passes control of the system bus to the other and then may suspend its operation. In the maximum-mode 8086 system, facilities are provided for implementing allocation of global resources and passing bus control to other microcomputers or coprocessors.

8288 Bus Controller: Bus Commands and Control Signals

Looking at the maximum-mode block diagram in Fig. 5.5, we see that the 8086 does not directly provide all the signals that are required to control the memory, I/O, and

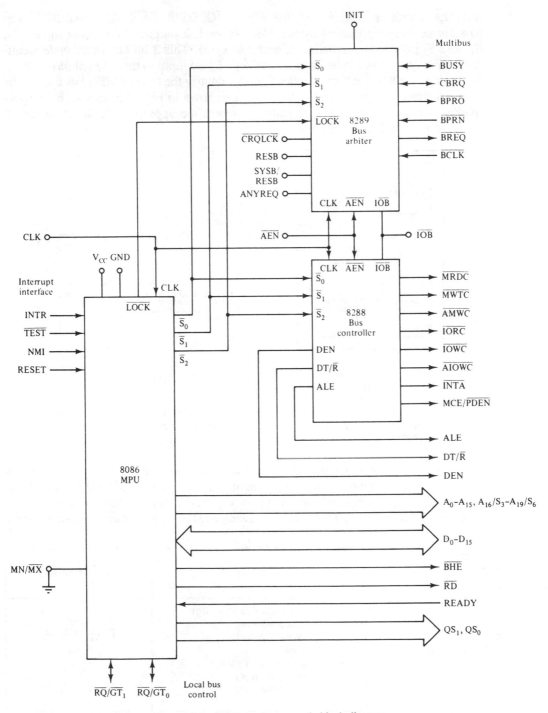

Figure 5.5   8086 maximum-mode block diagram.

interrupt interfaces. Specifically, the $\overline{\text{WR}}$, M/$\overline{\text{IO}}$, DT/$\overline{\text{R}}$, $\overline{\text{DEN}}$, ALE, and $\overline{\text{INTA}}$ signals are no longer produced by the 8086. Instead, it outputs three status signals $\overline{\text{S}}_0$, $\overline{\text{S}}_1$, and $\overline{\text{S}}_2$ prior to the initiation of each bus cycle. This 3-bit *bus status code* identifies which type of bus cycle is to follow. $\overline{\text{S}}_2\overline{\text{S}}_1\overline{\text{S}}_0$ are input to the external *bus controller* device, the 8288, which decodes them to identify the type of MPU bus cycle. The block diagram and pin layout of the 8288 are shown in Figs. 5.6(a) and (b), respectively. In response, the bus controller generates the appropriately timed command and control signals at its outputs.

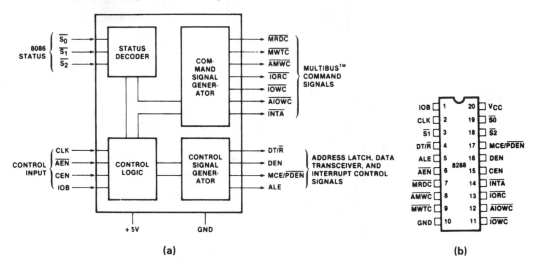

(a)   (b)

Figure 5.6 (a) Block diagram of the 8288 (reprinted by permission of Intel Corp. Copyright/Intel Corp., 1987); (b) pin layout (reprinted by permission of Intel Corp. Copyright/Intel Corp., 1987).

Figure 5.7 shows the relationship between the bus status codes and the types of bus cycles. Also shown are the output signals that are generated to tell external circuitry which type of bus cycle is taking place. These output signals are *memory read command* ($\overline{\text{MRDC}}$), *memory write command* ($\overline{\text{MWTC}}$), *advanced memory write*

Status Inputs			CPU Cycle	8288 Command
$\overline{\text{S2}}$	$\overline{\text{S1}}$	$\overline{\text{S0}}$		
0	0	0	Interrupt Acknowledge	$\overline{\text{INTA}}$
0	0	1	Read I/O Port	$\overline{\text{IORC}}$
0	1	0	Write I/O Port	$\overline{\text{IOWC}}$, $\overline{\text{AIOWC}}$
0	1	1	Halt	None
1	0	0	Instruction Fetch	$\overline{\text{MRDC}}$
1	0	1	Read Memory	$\overline{\text{MRDC}}$
1	1	0	Write Memory	$\overline{\text{MWTC}}$, $\overline{\text{AMWC}}$
1	1	1	Passive	None

Figure 5.7 Bus status codes. (Reprinted by permission of Intel Corp. Copyright/Intel Corp., 1979.)

command ($\overline{\text{AMWC}}$), *I/O read command* ($\overline{\text{IORC}}$), *I/O write command* ($\overline{\text{IOWC}}$), *advanced I/O write command* ($\overline{\text{AIOWC}}$), and *interrupt acknowledge command* ($\overline{\text{INTA}}$).

The 8288 produces one or two of these seven command signals for each bus cycle. For instance, when the 8086 outputs the code $\overline{S}_2\overline{S}_1\overline{S}_0$ equals 001, it indicates that an I/O read cycle is to be performed. In turn, the 8288 makes its $\overline{\text{IORC}}$ output switch to logic 0. On the other hand, if the code 111 is output by the 8086, it is signaling that no bus activity is to take place.

The control outputs produced by the 8288 are DEN, DT/$\overline{\text{R}}$, and ALE. These three signals provide the same functions as those described for the minimum system mode. This set of bus commands and control signals is compatible with the *Multibus,* an industry standard for interfacing microprocessor systems.

The 8289 Bus Arbiter: Bus Arbitration and Lock Signals

Looking at Fig. 5.5, we see that an 8289 *bus arbiter* has also been added in the maximum-mode system. This device permits multiple processors to reside on the system bus. It does this by implementing the *Multibus arbitration protocol* in an 8086-based system. Figures 5.8(a) and (b) show a block diagram and pin layout of the 8289, respectively.

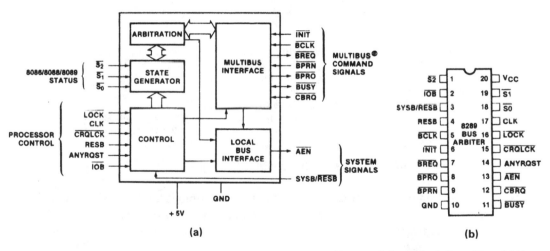

(a)   (b)

Figure 5.8 (a) Block diagram of the 8289 (reprinted by permission of Intel Corp. Copyright/ Intel Corp., 1987); (b) pin layout (reprinted by permission of Intel Corp. Copyright/Intel Corp., 1987).

Addition of the 8288 bus controller and 8289 bus arbiter frees a number of the 8086's pins for use to produce control signals that are needed to support multiple processors. *Bus priority lock* ($\overline{\text{LOCK}}$) is one of these signals. It is input to the bus arbiter together with status signals $\overline{S}$ through $\overline{S}_2$. The outputs of the 8289 are bus arbitration signals: *bus busy* ($\overline{\text{BUSY}}$), *common bus request* ($\overline{\text{CBRQ}}$), *bus priority out* ($\overline{\text{BPRO}}$), *bus priority in* ($\overline{\text{BPRN}}$), *bus request* ($\overline{\text{BREQ}}$), and *bus clock* ($\overline{\text{BCLK}}$). They correspond to the *bus exchange* signals of the Multibus and are used to lock other processors off the system bus during the execution of an instruction by the 8086. In this way the processor can be assured of uninterrupted access to *common system resources* such as *global memory*.

Queue Status Signals

Two new signals that are produced by the 8086 in the maximum-mode system are queue status outputs QS_0 and QS_1. Together they form a 2-bit *queue status code*, QS_1QS_0. This code tells the external circuitry what type of information was removed from the queue during the previous clock cycle. Figure 5.9 shows the four different queue statuses. Notice that $QS_1QS_0 = 01$ indicates that the first byte of an instruction was taken off the queue. As shown, the next byte of the instruction that is fetched is identified by the code 11. Whenever the queue is reset due to a transfer of control, the reinitialization code 10 is output.

QS1	QS0	Queue Status
0 (low)	0	No Operation. During the last clock cycle, nothing was taken from the queue.
0	1	First Byte. The byte taken from the queue was the first byte of the instruction.
1 (high)	0	Queue Empty. The queue has been reinitialized as a result of the execution of a transfer instruction.
1	1	Subsequent Byte. The byte taken from the queue was a subsequent byte of the instruction.

Figure 5.9 Queue status codes. (Reprinted by permission of Intel Corp. Copyright/Intel Corp., 1979.)

Local Bus Control Signals: Request/Grant Signals

In a maximum-mode configuration, the minimum-mode HOLD, HLDA interface is also changed. These two signals are replaced by *request/grant lines* $\overline{RQ}/\overline{GT}_0$ and $\overline{RQ}/\overline{GT}_1$, respectively. They provide a prioritized bus access mechanism for accessing the *local bus*.

5.6 SYSTEM CLOCK

The time base for synchronization of the internal and external operations of the 8086 microprocessor is provided by the CLK input signal. At present, the 8086 is available in three different speeds. The standard part operates at 5 MHz, the 8086-2 operates at 8 MHz, and the 8086-1 can be run at 10 MHz. CLK is externally generated by the 8284 clock generator and driver IC. Figure 5.10 is a block diagram of this device.

The normal way in which this clock chip is used is to connect a 15-MHz crystal

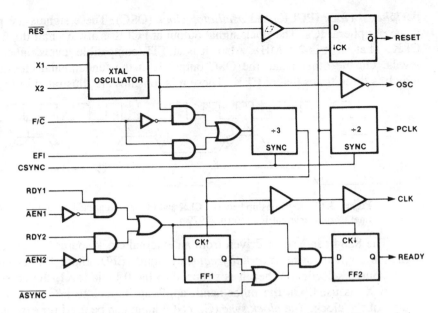

Figure 5.10 Block diagram of the 8284 clock generator. (Reprinted by permission of Intel Corp. Copyright/Intel Corp., 1979.).

between its X_1 and X_2 inputs. This circuit connection is shown in Fig. 5.11. Notice that a series capacitor C_L is also required. Its typical value when used with the 15-MHz crystal is 12 pF. The *fundamental crystal frequency* is divided by 3 within the 8284 to give a 5-MHz clock signal. This signal is buffered and output at CLK. CLK can be directly connected to CLK of the 8086.

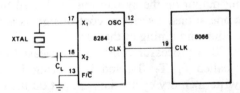

Figure 5.11 Connecting the 8284 to the 8086. (Reprinted by permission of Intel Corp. Copyright/Intel Corp., 1979.)

The waveform of CLK is shown in Fig. 5.12. Here we see that the signal is at *MOS-compatible voltage levels* and not TTL levels. Its minimum and maximum low logic levels are $V_{Lmin} = -0.5$ V and $V_{Lmax} = 0.6$ V, respectively. Moreover, the minimum and maximum values for high logic levels are $V_{Hmin} = 3.9$ V and $V_{Hmax} = V_{CC} + 1$ V, respectively. The *period* of the 5-MHz clock signal is 200 ns, and the maximum *rise* and *fall times* of its edges equal 10 ns.

In Fig. 5.10 we see that there are two more clock outputs on the 8284. They are

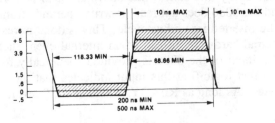

Figure 5.12 CLK voltage and timing characteristics. (Reprinted by permission of Intel Corp. Copyright/Intel Corp., 1979.)

peripheral clock (PCLK) and *oscillator clock* (OSC). These signals are provided to drive peripheral ICs. The clock signal output at PCLK is always half the frequency of CLK. That is, it is 2.5 MHz. Also, it is at TTL-compatible levels rather than MOS levels. On the other hand, the OSC output is at the fundamental clock frequency, which is three times that of CLK. These relationships are illustrated in Fig. 5.13.

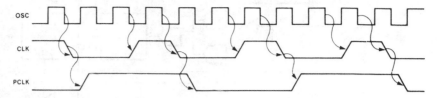

Figure 5.13 Relationship between CLK and PCLK. (Reprinted by permission of Intel Corp. Copyright/Intel Corp., 1979.)

The 8284 can also be driven from an external clock source. The external clock signal is applied to the *external frequency input* (EFI). Input F/$\overline{\text{C}}$ is provided for clock source selection. When it is strapped to the 0 logic level, the crystal between X_1 and X_2 is used. On the other hand, applying logic 1 to F/$\overline{\text{C}}$ selects EFI as the source of the clock. The *clock sync* (CSYNC) input can be used for external synchronization in systems that employ multiple clocks.

5.7 BUS CYCLE

The *bus cycle* of the 8086 is used to access memory, I/O devices, or the interrupt controller. As shown in Fig. 5.14(a), it corresponds to a sequence of events that starts with an address being output on the system bus, followed by a read or write data transfer. During these operations, a series of control signals is also produced by the 8086 to control the direction and timing of the bus.

The bus cycle of the 8086 processor consists of at least four clock periods. These four time states are called T_1, T_2, T_3, and T_4. During T_1, the 8086 puts an address on the bus. For a write memory cycle, data are put on the bus during period T_2 and maintained through T_3 and T_4. When a read cycle is to be performed, the bus is first put in the high-Z state during T_2 and then the data to be read must be put on the bus during T_3 and T_4. These four clock states give a *bus cycle duration* of 125 ns × 4 = 500 ns in an 8-MHz 8086 system.

If no bus cycles are required, the 8086 performs what are known as *idle states*. During these states no bus activity takes place. Each idle state is one clock period long and any number of them can be inserted between bus cycles. Figure 5.14(b) shows two bus cycles separated by idle states. Idle states are also performed if the instruction queue is full and the 8086 does not read or write operands from memory.

Wait states can also be inserted into a bus cycle. This is done in response to a request by an event in external hardware instead of an internal event such as a full queue. In fact, the READY input of the 8086 is provided specifically for this purpose. Figure 5.14(c) shows that logic 0 at this input indicates that the current bus cycle should not be completed. As long as READY is held at the 0 level, wait states

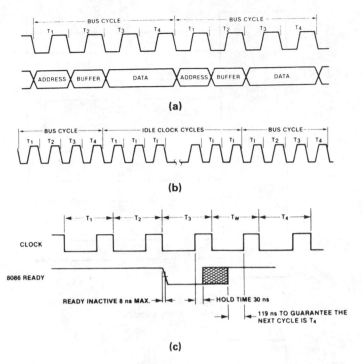

Figure 5.14 (a) Bus cycle clock periods (reprinted by permission of Intel Corp. Copyright/Intel Corp., 1979); (b) bus cycle with idle states (reprinted by permission of Intel Corp. Copyright/Intel Corp., 1979); (c) bus cycle with wait states (reprinted by permission of Intel Corp. Copyright/Intel Corp., 1979).

are inserted between periods T_3 and T_4 of the current bus cycle and in the case of a write cycle, data that were on the bus during T_3 are maintained. The bus cycle is not completed until the external hardware returns READY back to the 1 logic level. This extends the duration of the bus cycle, thereby permitting the use of slower memory devices in the system.

5.8 MEMORY INTERFACE

In either the minimum- or maximum-mode system configuration, the 8086 microprocessor can address up to 1M bytes of memory. However, the interface to the memory subsystem is different for each of these two modes of operation. The block diagram in Fig. 5.15 is that of the minimum-system memory interface. Here we find that it consists of the *multiplexed address/data bus lines* AD_0 through AD_{15} together with *additional address lines* A_{16} through A_{19} and *bank high enable* ($\overline{BHE}$). Notice that *memory control signals* ALE, $\overline{RD}$, $\overline{WR}$, M/$\overline{IO}$, DT/$\overline{R}$, and $\overline{DEN}$ are produced by the 8086.

The maximum-mode memory interface is shown in Fig. 5.16. This configuration includes an 8288 bus controller device. Notice that bus *status signals* $\overline{S}_0$ through $\overline{S}_2$ are input to this device. It decodes this 3-bit code to identify the type of bus cycle

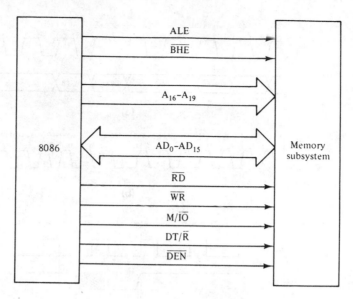

Figure 5.15 Minimum-mode 8086 system memory interface.

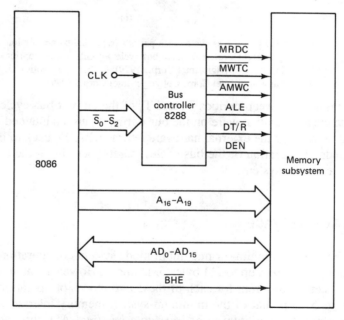

Figure 5.16 Maximum-mode 8086 system memory interface.

that is to be initiated. In turn, it generates *read/write signals* $\overline{\text{MRDC}}$, $\overline{\text{MWTC}}$, and $\overline{\text{AMWC}}$ as well as *control signals* ALE, DT/$\overline{\text{R}}$, and DEN. In this way we see that in the maximum-mode system the bus controller instead of the 8086 generates most of the timing and control signals for the memory interface.

The 8086 Microprocessor and its Memory Interface   Chap. 5

5.9 HARDWARE ORGANIZATION OF THE MEMORY ADDRESS SPACE

From a hardware point of view, the memory address space of the 8086 is implemented as two independent 512K-byte banks. They are called the *low (even) bank* and the *high (odd) bank*. Data bytes associated with an even address (00000_{16}, 00002_{16}, etc.) reside in the low bank and those with odd addresses (00001_{16}, 00003_{16}, etc.) reside in the high bank.

Looking at the block diagram in Fig. 5.17, we see that address bits A_1 through A_{19} select the storage location that is to be accessed. Therefore, they are applied to both banks in parallel. A_0 and bank high enable ($\overline{BHE}$) are used as bank select signals. Logic 0 at A_0 identifies an even-addressed byte of data and causes the low bank of memory to be enabled. On the other hand, $\overline{BHE}$ equal to 0 enables the high bank for access of an odd-addressed byte of data. Each of the memory banks provides half of the 8086's 16-bit data bus. Notice that the lower bank transfers bytes of data over data lines D_0 through D_7, while data transfers for the high bank use D_8 through D_{15}.

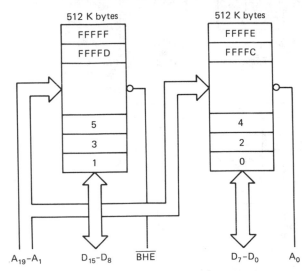

Figure 5.17 High and low memory banks. (Reprinted by permission of Intel Corp. Copyright/Intel Corp., 1979.)

Figure 5.18(a) shows that when a byte memory operation is performed to address X, which is an even address, a storage location in the low bank is accessed. Therefore, A_0 is set to logic 0 to enable the low bank of memory and $\overline{BHE}$ to logic 1 to disable the high bank. As shown in the circuit diagram, data are transferred to or from the lower bank over data bus lines D_0 through D_7. D_7 carries the MSB of the byte and D_0 the LSB.

On the other hand, to access a byte of data at an odd address such as X + 1 in Fig. 5.18(b), A_0 is set to logic 1 and $\overline{BHE}$ to logic 0. This enables the high bank of memory and disables the low bank. Data are transferred between the 8086 and the high bank over bus lines D_8 through D_{15}. Here D_{15} represents the MSB and D_8 the LSB.

Whenever an even-addressed word of data is accessed, both the high and low banks are accessed at the same time. Figure 5.18(c) illustrates how a word at even

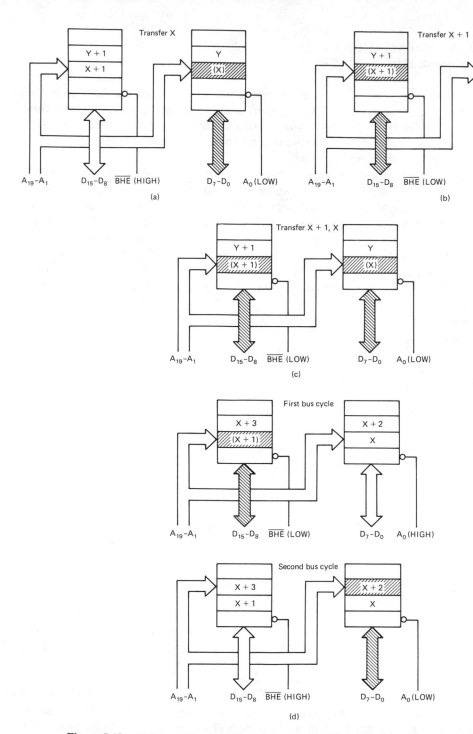

Figure 5.18 (a) Even-addressed byte transfer (reprinted by permission of Intel Corp. Copyright/Intel Corp., 1979); (b) odd-addressed byte transfer (reprinted by permission of Intel Corp. Copyright/Intel Corp., 1979); (c) even-addressed word transfer (reprinted by permission of Intel Corp. Copyright/Intel Corp., 1979); (d) odd-addressed word transfer (reprinted by permission of Intel Corp. Copyright/Intel Corp., 1979).

address X is accessed. Notice that both A_0 and $\overline{BHE}$ equal 0; therefore, both banks are enabled. In this case, a byte of data is transferred from or to both the low and high banks at the same time. This 16-bit word is transferred over the complete data bus D_0 through D_{15}. The bytes of an even-addressed word are said to be aligned and can be transferred with a memory operation that takes just one bus cycle.

A word at an odd-addressed boundary is different. It is said to be unaligned. That is, the least significant byte is at the lower address location in the high memory bank. This is demonstrated in Fig. 5.18(d). Here we see that the odd byte of the word is located at address $X + 1$ and the even byte at address $X + 2$.

Two bus cycles are required to access this word. During the first bus cycle, the odd byte of the word, which is located at address $X + 1$ in the high bank, is accessed. This is accompanied by select signals $A_0 = 1$ and $\overline{BHE} = 0$ and a data transfer over D_8 through D_{15}.

Next the 8086 automatically increments the address such that $A_0 = 0$. This represents the next address in memory that is even. Then a second memory bus cycle is initiated. During this second cycle, the even byte located at $X + 2$ in the low bank is accessed. The data transfer takes place over bus lines D_0 through D_7. This transfer is accompanied by $A_0 = 0$ and $\overline{BHE} = 1$.

5.10 MEMORY BUS STATUS CODES

Whenever a memory bus cycle is in progress, an address bus status code S_3S_4 is output on the multiplexed address lines A_{16} and A_{17}. This 2-bit code is output at the same time the data are carried over the other bus lines.

Bits S_3 and S_4 together form a 2-bit binary code that identifies which one of the four segment registers was used to generate the physical address that was output during the address period in the bus cycle. The four *address bus status codes* are listed in Fig. 5.19. Here we find that code $S_3S_4 = 00$ identifies the extra segment register, 10 identifies the stack segment register, 01 identifies the code segment register, and 11 identifies the data segment register.

S_3	S_4	Address Status
0	0	Alternate (relative to the ES segment)
1	0	Stack (relative to the SS segment)
0	1	Code/None (relative to the CS segment or a default of zero)
1	1	Data (relative to the DS segment)

Figure 5.19 Address bus status code. (Reprinted by permission of Intel Corp. Copyright/Intel Corp., 1979.)

These status codes are output in both the minimum and the maximum system modes. They can be decoded with external circuitry to enable separate 1M-byte address spaces for ES, SS, CS, and DS. In this way, the memory address reach of the 8086 can be expanded to 4M bytes.

5.11 MEMORY CONTROL SIGNALS

Earlier in the chapter we saw that similar control signals are produced in the maximum-and minimum-mode systems. Moreover, we found that in the minimum system mode, the 8086 produces all the control signals. But in the maximum system mode, they are produced by the 8288 bus controller. Here we will look more closely at each of these signals and their function with respect to the memory interface.

Minimum-System Memory Control Signals

In the 8086 microcomputer system of Fig. 5.15, which is configured for the minimum system mode of operation, we found that the control signals provided to support the interface to the memory subsystem are ALE, $\overline{BHE}$, M/$\overline{IO}$, DT/$\overline{R}$, $\overline{RD}$, $\overline{WR}$, and $\overline{DEN}$. These control signals are required to tell the memory subsystem when the bus is carrying a valid address, in which direction data are to be transferred over the bus, when valid write data are on the bus, and when to put read data on the bus.

For example, *address latch enable* (ALE) signals external circuitry that a valid address is on the bus. It is a pulse to the 1 logic level and is used to latch the address in external circuitry. Another important control signal involved in the memory interface is bank high enable ($\overline{BHE}$). Logic 0 is output on this line during the address part of the bus cycle whenever the high-bank part of the memory subsystem must be enabled.

The *memory/input-output* (M/$\overline{IO}$) and *data transmit/receive* (DT/$\overline{R}$) lines signal external circuitry whether a memory or I/O bus cycle is in progress and whether the 8086 will transmit or receive data over the bus. During all memory bus cycles, M/$\overline{IO}$ is held at the 1 logic level. Moreover, when the 8086 switches DT/$\overline{R}$ to logic 1 during the data transfer part of the bus cycle, the bus is in the transmit mode and data are written into memory. On the other hand, it sets DT/$\overline{R}$ to logic 0 to signal that the bus is in the receive mode. This corresponds to reading of memory.

The signals *read* ($\overline{RD}$) and *write* ($\overline{WR}$), respectively, identify that a read or write bus cycle is in progress. The 8086 switches $\overline{WR}$ to logic 0 to signal memory that a write cycle is taking place over the bus. On the other hand, $\overline{RD}$ is switched to logic 0 whenever a read cycle is in progress. During all memory operations, the 8086 produces one other control signal. It is *data enable* ($\overline{DEN}$). Logic 0 at this output is used to enable the data bus.

Maximum-System Memory Control Signals

When the 8086 is configured to work in the maximum mode, it does not directly provide all the control signals to support the memory interface. Instead, an external *bus controller,* the 8288, provides memory commands and control signals that are compatible with the *Multibus.* Figure 5.18 shows an 8086 connected in this way.

Specifically, the $\overline{WR}$, M/$\overline{IO}$, DT/$\overline{R}$, $\overline{DEN}$, ALE, and $\overline{INTA}$ signal lines on the 8086 are changed. They are replaced with *multiprocessor lock* signal ($\overline{LOCK}$), a *bus status code* ($\overline{S}_2$ through $\overline{S}_0$), and a *queue status code* (QS_1QS_0). The 8086 still does produce $\overline{BHE}$ and $\overline{RD}$ signals. Moreover, these two signals provide the same functions as they did in minimum system mode.

The 3-bit bus status code $\overline{S_2}\overline{S_1}\overline{S_0}$ is output prior to the initiation of each bus cycle. It identifies which type of bus cycle is to follow. This code is input to the 8288 bus controller. Here it is decoded to identify which type of bus cycle command signals must be generated.

Figure 5.20 shows the relationship between the bus status codes and the types of 8086 bus cycle produced. Also shown in this chart are the names of the corresponding command signals that are generated at the outputs of the 8288. The CPU cycles that correspond to memory operations have been highlighted in the table. For instance, the input code $\overline{S_2}\overline{S_1}\overline{S_0}$ equal to 100 indicates that an instruction fetch cycle is to take place. This memory read makes the $\overline{MRDC}$ command output switch to logic 0.

Status Inputs			CPU Cycle	8288 Command
$\overline{S_2}$	$\overline{S_1}$	$\overline{S_0}$		
0	0	0	Interrupt acknowledge	$\overline{INTA}$
0	0	1	Read I/O port	$\overline{IORC}$
0	1	0	Write I/O port	$\overline{IOWC}$, $\overline{AIOWC}$
0	1	1	Halt	None
1	0	0	Instruction fetch	$\overline{MRDC}$
1	0	1	Read memory	$\overline{MRDC}$
1	1	0	Write memory	$\overline{MWTC}$, $\overline{AMWC}$
1	1	1	Passive	None

Figure 5.20 Memory bus cycle status codes. (Reprinted by permission of Intel Corp. Copyright/Intel Corp., 1979.)

Another bus command that is provided for the memory subsystem is $\overline{S_2}\overline{S_1}\overline{S_0}$ equal to 110. This represents a memory write cycle and it causes both the *memory write command* ($\overline{MWTC}$) and *advanced memory write command* ($\overline{AMWC}$) outputs to switch to the 0 logic level.

The control outputs produced by the 8288 are DEN, DT/$\overline{R}$, and ALE. These signals provide the same functions as those produced by the corresponding pins on the 8086 in the minimum system mode.

The other two status signals, QS_0 and QS_1, form an instruction queue code. This code tells external circuitry what type of information was removed from the queue during the previous clock cycle. Figure 5.21 shows the four different queue statuses. Notice that $QS_1QS_0 = 01$ indicates that the first byte of an instruction was taken from the queue. The next byte of the instruction that is fetched is identified by queue status code. 11. Whenever the queue is reset, for instance due to a transfer of control, the reinitialization code 10 is output. Moreover, if no queue operation occured, status code 00 is output.

The last signal is bus priority lock ($\overline{LOCK}$). This signal is to be used as an input

QS$_1$	QS$_0$	Queue Status
0 (low)	0	No Operation. During the last clock cycle, nothing was taken from the queue.
0	1	First Byte. The byte taken from the queue was the first byte of the instruction.
1 (high)	0	Queue Empty. The queue has been reinitialized as a result of the execution of a transfer instruction.
1	1	Subsequent Byte. The byte taken from the queue was a subsequent byte of the instruction.

Figure 5.21 Queue status code. (Reprinted by permission of Intel Corp. Copyright/Intel Corp., 1979.)

to the 8289 bus arbiter together with bus status code $\overline{S}_0$ through $\overline{S}_2$, and CLK. They are used to lock other processors off the system bus during execution of an instruction. In this way the processor can be assured of uninterrupted access to common system resources such as *global memory*.

The *bus arbitration* signals produced by the 8289 are *bus clock* ($\overline{BCLK}$), *bus request* ($\overline{BREQ}$), *bus priority in* ($\overline{BPRN}$), *bus priority out* ($\overline{BPRO}$), and *I/O busy* ($\overline{BUSY}$). These are the bus exchange signals of the Multibus. This bus arbiter permits multiple processors to reside on the system bus by implementing the Multibus arbitration protocol in the 8086 microcomputer system.

5.12 READ AND WRITE BUS CYCLES

In the preceding section we introduced the status and control signals associated with the memory interface. Here we continue by studying the sequence in which they occur during the read and write bus cycles of memory.

Read Cycle

The memory interface signals of a minimum-mode 8086 system are shown in Fig. 5.22. Here their occurrence is illustrated relative to the four *time states* T_1, T_2, T_3, and T_4 of the 8086's bus cycle. Let us trace through the events that occur as data or instructions are read from memory.

The *read bus cycle* begins with state. T_1. During this period, the 8086 outputs the 20-bit address of the memory location to be accessed on its multiplexed address/data bus AD$_0$ through AD$_{15}$ and A$_{16}$ through A$_{19}$. $\overline{BHE}$ is also output during this time. Notice that a pulse is also produced at ALE. The trailing edge of this pulse should be used to latch the address and $\overline{BHE}$ is external circuitry.

Also we see that at the start of T_1, signals M/$\overline{IO}$ and DT/$\overline{R}$ are set to the 1 and 0 logic levels, respectively. This indicates to circuitry in the memory subsystem that a memory cycle is in progress and that the 8086 is going to receive data from the bus. Notice that both of these signals are maintained at these logic levels through out all four periods of the bus cycle.

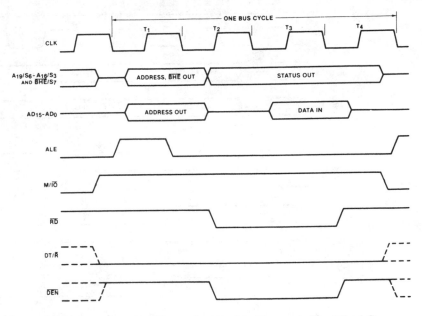

Figure 5.22 Memory read bus cycle. (Reprinted by permission of Intel Corp. Copyright/Intel Corp., 1979.)

Beginning with state T_2, status bits S_3 through S_6 are output on the upper four bus lines A_{16} through A_{19}. Remember that bits S_3 and S_4 identify to external circuitry which segment register was used to generate the address just output. This status information is maintained through periods T_3 and T_4. The rest of the address/data bus lines, AD_0 through AD_{15}, are put in the high-Z state during T_2.

Late in period T_2, $\overline{RD}$ is switched to logic 0. This indicates to the memory subsystem that a read cycle is in progress. Then $\overline{DEN}$ is switched to logic 0 to tell external circuitry to put the data that are to be read from memory onto the bus.

As shown in the waveforms, input data are read by the 8086 during T_3, after which, as shown in T_4, the 8086 returns $\overline{RD}$ and $\overline{DEN}$ to the 1 logic level. The read cycle is now complete.

Write Cycle

The *write bus cycle* timing, shown in Fig. 5.23, is similar to that given for a read cycle in Fig. 5.22. Looking at the write cycle waveforms, we find that during T_1 the address and $\overline{BHE}$ are output and latched with the ALE pulse. This is identical to the read cycle. Moreover, $M/\overline{IO}$ is set to logic 1 to indicate that a memory cycle is in progress. However, this time DT/$\overline{R}$ is also switched to logic 1. This signals external circuits that the 8086 is going to transfer data over the bus.

As T_2 starts, the 8086 switches $\overline{WR}$ to logic 0. This tells the memory subsystem that a write operation is to follow over the bus. The 8086 puts the data on the bus late in T_2 and maintains the data valid through T_4. The write of data into memory should be initiated as $\overline{WR}$ returns from 0 to 1 early in T_4. This completes the write cycle.

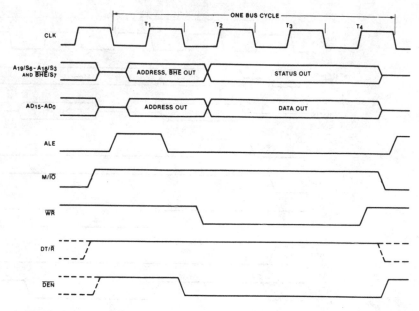

Figure 5.23 Memory write bus cycle. (Reprinted by permission of Intel Corp. Copyright/Intel Corp., 1979.)

Wait States in the Memory Bus Cycle

Wait states can be inserted to lengthen the memory bus cycles of the 8086. This is done with the *ready input* signal. Upon request from an event in hardware, for instance slow memory, the READY input is switched to logic 0. This signals the 8086 that the current bus cycle should not be completed. Instead, it is extended by inserting wait states with duration t_W equal to 125 ns (for 8-MHz clock operation) between periods T_3 and T_4. The data that were on the bus during T_3 are maintained throughout the wait-state period. In this way, the bus cycle is not completed until READY is returned back to logic 1.

In the 8086 microcomputer system, the READY input of the 8086 is supplied by the READY output of the 8284 clock generator circuit.

EXAMPLE 5.1

What is the duration of the bus cycle in the 8086-based microcomputer if the clock is 8 MHz and two wait states are inserted through wait state logic?

SOLUTION The duration of the bus cycle in an 8-MHz system is given in general by the expression

$$t_{cyc} = 500 \text{ ns} + N (125 \text{ ns})$$

In this expression N stands for the number of wait states. For a bus cycle with two wait states, we get

$$t_{cyc} = 500 \text{ ns} + 2(125 \text{ ns}) = 500 \text{ ns} + 250 \text{ ns}$$
$$= 750 \text{ ns}$$

The 8086 Microprocessor and its Memory Interface   Chap. 5

5.13 DEMULTIPLEXING THE ADDRESS/DATA BUS

In an 8086 microcomputer system, memory, I/O devices, and the interrupt interface share use of the multiplexed address/data bus lines. In all three cases, a stable address is required and it must be available at the same time that data are to be transferred over the bus. For this reason, the address and data signals must be separated using external demultiplexing circuits to give a system bus. This *demultiplexed system bus* consists of the 20 address lines A_0 through A_{19}, 16 data bus lines D_0 through D_{15}, and memory control signals $\overline{BHE}$, $M/\overline{IO}$, $\overline{WR}$, and $\overline{RD}$.

Several different techniques can be used to demultiplex the system bus. One approach is shown in Fig. 5.24. Here the microprocessor's bus is demultiplexed into a system bus just once at the MPU and then distributed to all other system elements. This is known as *local demultiplexing* and has the advantage of requiring minimal circuitry.

During bus cycles, a 20-bit address is output by the 8086 on AD_0 through A_{19} during period T_1 of the bus cycle. This address is accompanied by a pulse on the ALE (address latch enable) line. In this circuit, ALE tells external circuitry that a stable address is available and it should be latched.

In the circuit of Fig. 5.24 we have used three 8282 noninverting latches to demultiplex the address. These devices are octal latches. The ALE output of the 8086 is applied to the strobe (STB) input of all three latches. When pulsed at STB, the address applied to the DI_0 through DI_7 inputs of the 8282s is latched into their internal flip-flops. This happens on the 1-to-0 edge of ALE. Even though the address is latched, it is not yet available at address outputs A_0 through A_{19}. This is because the outputs of the octal latches are not yet enabled. To do this, we must switch the output enable ($\overline{OE}$) input on the 8282s to the 0 logic level. In many applications, $\overline{OE}$ can be fixed at the 0 logic level. This permanently enables the outputs of the 8282s and the address is made available at A_0 through A_{19} as soon as it is latched. Notice that signal $\overline{BHE}$ is latched together with the address. In this way, the address is latched and maintained stable throughout the bus cycle.

This circuit configuration also increases the drive capability at the system bus. The outputs of the 8282 are rated to drive up to 32 mA. However, a propagation delay of 30 ns is introduced as signals pass through it.

The data bus D_0 through D_{15} can be directly formed from the AD_0 through AD_{15} lines or buffered with bidirectional bus transceivers to increase drive capability. It is usually necessary to do this buffering because a large number of memory and peripheral devices are attached to the bus.

Two 8286 8-bit bidirectional transceiver devices can be used for this purpose. They are connected as shown in Fig. 5.24. Data can be passed in either direction between its A and B terminals. The direction of data transfer is determined by the logic level applied at the transfer (T) input. When T is logic 1, data are passed from A to B. This corresponds to the direction required for data transfers during write bus cycles. Changing the logic level of T to 0 causes data to be passed from B to A such as needed for read cycles. Moreover, logic 0 is needed at the $\overline{EN}$ input of the 8286 to enable the input and output drive circuitry selected by T. The bus side of the 8286 is able to drive up to 32 mA with propagation delays through the device equal to 30 ns.

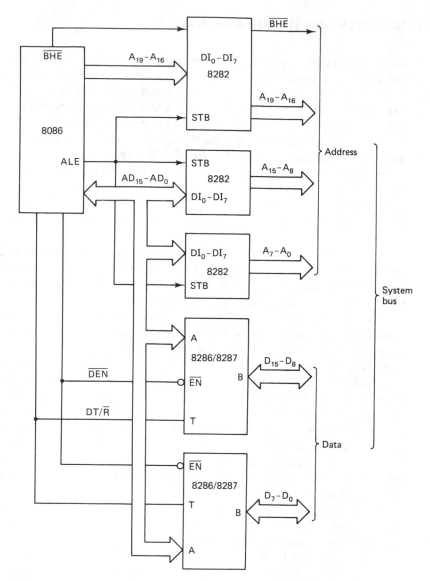

Figure 5.24 Local demultiplexing of the system bus. (Reprinted by permission of Intel Corp. Copyright/Intel Corp., 1979.)

From the circuit in Fig. 5.24, we see that the 8086 controls the direction and timing of data transfers through the 8286s with signals DT/$\overline{R}$ at the T input and $\overline{DEN}$ at its $\overline{EN}$ input. When DT/$\overline{R}$ is set to logic 1, the 8286s are set to pass data from MPU to memory. This sets the bus for a write operation. Switching DT/$\overline{R}$ to logic 0 changes the direction of data transfer through the 8286s such that the MPU can read data out of memory. $\overline{DEN}$ is switched to logic 0 whenever a data transfer is to take place over the bus and enables the output buffers of the 8286.

A second approach is shown in Fig. 5.25. This configuration is known as *remote demultiplexing*. In this case, the microprocessor's local bus signals are distributed to each part of the system and then demultiplexed by circuits provided in the memory or I/O sections.

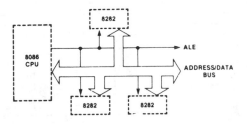

Figure 5.25 Remote demultiplexing of the system bus. (Reprinted by permission of Intel Corp. Copyright/Intel Corp., 1979.)

5.14 4K-BYTE PROGRAM STORAGE MEMORY, 2K-BYTE DATA STORAGE MEMORY CIRCUIT

In Section 5.13 we showed how the 8086's multiplexed bus is demultiplexed to give a system bus consisting of an independent 20-bit address bus and 16-bit data bus. Here we will look at how EPROM and RAM devices are connected to the system bus to implement program and data storage memory subsystems, respectively.

Program Storage Memory

The program storage memory part of a microcomputer is used to store fixed information such as instructions of the program or tables of data. Typically, it is read only, and for this reason is implemented with ROM. PROM, or EPROM devices. EPROM devices, such as the 2716, 2764, and 27256, are organized with a byte-wide output; therefore, a minimum of two devices is required to supply the 16-bit data bus of the 8086.

Figure 5.26 shows how two 2716s are connected to the demultiplexed system bus of a minimum-mode 8086-based microcomputer. These devices supply 4K bytes of program storage memory. To select one of the 4K of storage locations within the 2716s, 11 bits of address are applied to address inputs A_0 through A_{10} of the EPROMS. Assuming that bits A_1 through A_{11} of the 8086's address bus supply these inputs, the address range corresponding to program memory is from

$$A_{11}A_{10}A_9 \ . \ . \ A_1A_0 = 00000000000_2 = 00000_{16}$$

to

$$A_{11}A_{10}A_9 \ . \ . \ A_1BHE = 11111111111_2 = 00FFF_{16}$$

Data outputs D_0 through D_7 of the two EPROMs are applied to data bus lines D_0 through D_{15} respectively, of the 8086's system data bus. Data held at the addressed storage location are enabled onto the data bus by the control signal $\overline{RD}$ (read), which is applied to the $\overline{OE}$ (output enable) input of the EPROM.

In most applications, the capacity of program storage memory is expanded by attaching several EPROM devices to the system bus. In this case, additional high-order bits of the 8086's address are decoded to produce chip select signals. For instance, two address bits, A_{13} and A_{12}, can be decoded to provide four chip select

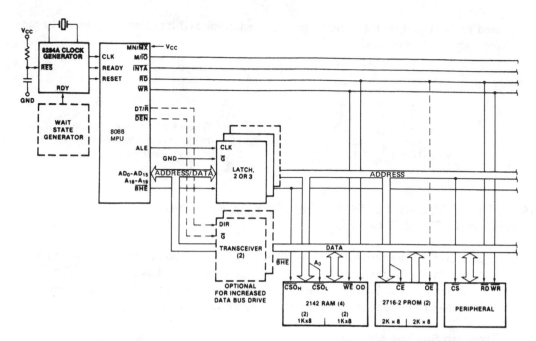

Figure 5.26 Minimum-mode system memory interface. (Reprinted by permission of Intel Corp. Copyright/Intel Corp., 1979.)

signals. Each of these chip selects is applied to the $\overline{CE}$ (chip enable) input of both EPROMs in a bank. When an address is on the bus, just one of the outputs of the decoder becomes active and enables the corresponding EPROMs for operation. By using eight 2716s, the program storage memory is increased to 16K bytes.

Now that we have explained how EPROMs are attached to the 8086s system bus, let us trace through the operation of the circuit for a bus cycle in which a word of code is fetched from program storage memory. During an instruction acquisition bus cycle, the instruction fetch sequence of the 8086 causes the instruction to be read from memory word by word. The values in CS and IP are combined within the 8086 to give the address of a storage location in the address range of the program storage memory. This address is output on A_0 through A_{19} and latched into the address latches synchronously with the signal ALE. Bits A_1 through A_{11} of the system address bus are applied to the address inputs of the 2716s. This part of the address selects the word of code to be output. When the 8086 switches $\overline{RD}$ to logic 0, the outputs of the 2716s are enabled and the word of data at the addressed storage location is output onto system data bus lines D_0 through D_{15}. Early in the read bus cycle, the 8086 switches DT/$\overline{R}$ to logic 0 to signal the bus transceivers that data are to be input to the microprocessor, and later in the bus cycle $\overline{DEN}$ is switched to logic 0 to enable the transceiver for operation. Now the word of data is passed from the system data bus onto the multiplexed address data bus from which it is read by the MPU.

The circuit in Fig. 5.27 shows a similar program storage memory implementation for a maximum-mode 8086 microcomputer system.

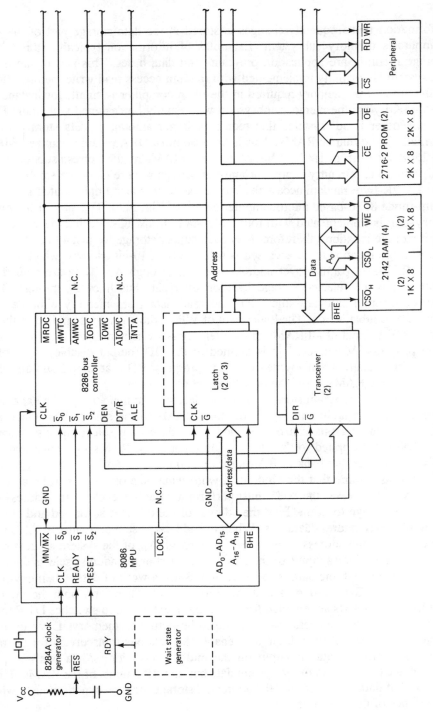

Figure 5.27 Maximum-mode system memory interface. (Reprinted by permission of Intel Corp. Copyright/Intel Corp., 1979.)

Data Storage Memory

Information that frequently changes is stored in the data storage part of the microcomputer's memory subsystem. Examples of information typically stored in data storage memory are application programs and data bases. This part of the memory subsystem is normally implemented with random access read/write memory (RAM). If the amount of memory required in the microcomputer is small, for instance, less than 64K bytes, the memory subsystem will usually be designed with static RAMs. On the other hand, systems that require a larger amount of data storage memory normally use dynamic RAMs. This is because most DRAMs are organized 64K by 1 bit 256K by 1 bit, or 1M by 1 bit. Moreover DRAMs require refresh support circuits. This additional circuitry is not warranted if storage requirements are small.

A 2K-byte random access read/write memory is also implemented in the minimum-mode 8086-based microcomputer circuit of Fig. 5.26. This part of the memory subsystem is implemented with four 2142 static RAM ICs. Each 2142 contains 1K, 4-bit storage locations; therefore, they each supply storage for just 4 bits of the word. The storage location to be accessed is selected by a 10-bit address, which is applied to all RAMs in parallel over address lines A_1 through A_{10}. Data are read from or written into the selected storage location over data bus lines D_0 through D_{15}. Of course, through software, the 8086 can read data from memory either as bytes, words, or double words. The logic level of $\overline{WR}$ (write), which is applied to the write enable ($\overline{WE}$) input of all RAMs in parallel, signals whether a read or write bus cycle is in progress. Moreover, $\overline{RD}$ is applied to the OD (output disable) input of both RAMs in parallel. When a write cycle is in progress, $\overline{RD}$ is at logic 1 and disables the outputs of the RAMs. Now the data lines act as inputs.

Just as for program storage memory, data storage memory can be expanded by simply attaching additional banks of static RAMs to the system bus. Once again, high-order address bits can be decoded to produce chip select signals. Each chip select output is applied to the chip enable input of all RAMs in a bank and, when active, it enables that bank of RAMs for operation.

Let us assume that the value of a word-wide data operand is to be updated in memory. In this case, the 8086 must perform a write bus cycle to the address of the operand's storage location. First the address of the operand is formed and output on the multiplexed address/data bus. When the address is stable, a pulse at ALE is used to latch it into the address latches. Bits A_1 through A_{10} of the system address bus are applied to the address inputs of the 2142s. This part of the address selects the storage location into which the data is to be written. Since a word of data is being written to memory, both $\overline{BHE}$ and A_0 are at the 0 logic level. Therefore, both the high bank and low bank RAMs are enabled for operation. Next the 8086 switches DT/$\overline{R}$ to logic 1 to signal the transceivers that data are to be output to memory. Later in the bus cycle, $\overline{DEN}$ is switched to logic 0 to enable the data bus transceivers for operation. Now the word of data is output on the multiplexed address/data bus and passed through the transceivers to the system data bus and data inputs of the RAMs. Finally, the word of data is written into the addressed storage location synchronously with the occurrence of the $\overline{WR}$ control signal.

Figure 5.27 shows a maximum-mode 8086-based microcomputer system that implements a similar data storage memory.

ASSIGNMENT

Section 5.2

1. Name the technology used to fabricate the 8086 microprocessor.
2. What is the transistor count of the 8086?
3. Which pin is used as the NMI input?
4. Which pin provides the $\overline{BHE}$ and S_7 output signals?
5. How much memory can the 8086 directly address?
6. How large is the I/O address space of the 8086?

Section 5.3

7. How is minimum or maximum mode of operation selected?
8. Describe the difference between the minimum-mode 8086 system and maximum-mode 8086 system.
9. What output function is performed by pin 29 when in the minimum mode? Maximum mode?
10. What type of signal is $M/\overline{IO}$?

Section 5.4

11. What are the word lengths of the 8086's address bus and data bus?
12. Does the 8086 have a multiplexed address/data bus or independent address and data buses?
13. What mnemonic is used to identify the least significant bit of the address bus? The most significant bit of the data bus?
14. What does status code $S_4 S_3 = 01$ mean in terms of the memory segment being accessed?
15. Which output is used to signal external circuitry that a byte of data is available on the upper half of the data bus?
16. What does the logic level on $M/\overline{IO}$ signal to external circuitry?
17. Which output is used to signal external circuitry that valid data are on the bus during a write cycle?
18. What signal does a minimum-mode 8086 respond with when it acknowledges an active interrupt request?
19. Which signals implement the DMA interface?
20. List the signals that go to the high-Z state in response to a DMA request.

Section 5.5

21. Identify the signal lines of the 8086 that are different for the minimum-mode and maximum-mode interfaces.

22. What status outputs of the 8086 are input to the 8288?
23. What maximum-mode control signals are generated by the 8288?
24. What function is served by the 8289 in a maximum-mode 8086 microcomputer system?
25. What status code is output by the 8086 to the 8288 if a memory read bus cycle is taking place?
26. What command output becomes active if the status inputs of the 8288 are 100_2?
27. If the 8086 executes a jump instruction, what queue status code would be output?
28. Which pins provide signals for local bus control in a maximum-mode 8086 system?

Section 5.6

29. What speed 8086s are available today?
30. What frequency crystal must be connected between the X_1 and X_2 inputs of the clock generator if an 8086-2 is to run at full speed?
31. What clock outputs are produced by the 8284? What would be their frequencies if a 30-MHz crystal was used?
32. What are the logic levels of the clock waveforms applied to the 8086?

Section 5.7

33. How many clock states are in an 8086 bus cycle that has no wait states? How are these states denoted?
34. What is the duration of the bus cycle for an 8086-1 that is running at full speed and with no wait states?
35. What is an idle state?
36. What is a wait state?
37. If an 8086 running at 10 MHz performs bus cycles with two wait states, what is the duration of the bus cycle?

Section 5.8

38. Which device products the ALE control signal in a minimum-mode 8086 microcomputer system? Maximum-mode system?
39. Is the minimum-mode signal M/$\overline{\text{IO}}$ produced in the maximum-mode memory interface?

Section 5.9

40. In which bank of memory are odd-addressed bytes of data stored? What bank select signal is used to enable this bank of memory?
41. Over which data bus lines are even-addressed bytes of data transferred and which bank select signal is active?
42. List the memory control signals together with their active logic levels that occur when a word of data is written to memory address $A0000_{16}$.
43. List the memory control signals together with their active logic levels that occur when a byte of data is written to memory address $B0003_{16}$. Over which data lines is the byte of data transferred?

Section 5.10

44. In a maximum-mode 8086 microcomputer, what code is output on S_3S_4 when an instruction fetch bus cycle is in progress?

45. What is the value of S_3S_4 if the operand of a pop instruction is being read from memory? The microcomputer employs the 8086 in the maximum mode.

Section 5.11

46. What memory bus status code is output when a word of instruction code is fetched from memory? Which memory control output(s) is (are) produced by the 8288?

47. What memory bus status code is output when a destination operand is written to memory? Which memory control output(s) is (are) produced by the 8288?

48. When the instruction PUSH AX is executed, what address bus status code and memory bus cycle code are output by the 8086 in a maximum-mode microcomputer system? Which command signals are output by the 8288?

Section 5.12

49. What does T_1 stand for? What happens in this part of the bus cycle?

50. Describe the bus activity that takes place as the 8086 writes a word of data into memory address $B0010_{16}$.

51. Which input is used to initiate a wait state?

Section 5.13

52. List the signals of the 8086's multiplexed local bus and the signals of the demultiplexed system bus.

53. In Fig. 5.24 which types of devices are used to latch the local address? Control the direction of data transfer over the data bus?

54. Explain the operation of the circuit in Fig. 5.24 as a word-wide read takes place from address $A0000_{16}$.

Section 5.14

55. Make a diagram showing how four 2764 EPROMs are connected to form a 16K-word program storage memory subsystem.

56. If we assume that the high-order address bits in the circuit formed in Problem 55 are all logic 0, what is the address range of the program memory subsystem?

57. How many 2142 static RAMs would be needed in the memory array of the circuit in Fig. 5.26 if the capacity of data storage memory is to be expanded to 64K bytes?

58. How many 2716 EPROMs would be needed in the program memory array in the circuit of Fig. 5.27 to expand its capacity to 96K bits?

6

Input/Output Interface of the 8086 Microprocessor

6.1 INTRODUCTION

In Chapter 5 we studied the memory interface of the 8086. Here we will study another important interface of the 8086 microcomputer system, the input/output interface. These are the topics in the order in which they are covered:

1. Input/output interface
2. I/O data transfers
3. I/O instructions
4. Input and output bus cycles
5. Eight-byte-wide output ports
6. 8255A programmable peripheral interface
7. 8255A implementation of parallel I/O ports

6.2 INPUT/OUTPUT INTERFACE

The *input/output interface* of the 8086 microcomputer permits it to communicate with the outside world. The way in which the 8086 deals with input/output circuitry is similar to the way in which it interfaces with memory circuitry. That is, input/output data transfers also take place over the multiplexed address/data bus. This parallel bus permits easy interface to LSI peripherals such as parallel I/O expanders and communication controllers. Through these I/O interfaces, the 8086 can input or output data in bit, byte, or word formats.

Minimum-Mode Interface

Let us begin by looking at the I/O interface for a minimum-mode 8086 system. Figure 6.1 shows the minimum-mode interface. Here we find the 8086, interface circuitry, and I/O ports for devices 0 through N. The circuits in this interface section must perform functions such as select the I/O port, latch output data, sample input data, synchronize data transfers, and translate between TTL voltage levels and those required to operate the I/O devices.

The data path between the 8086 and I/O interface circuits is the multiplexed address/data bus. Unlike the memory interface, this time just the 16 least significant lines of the bus, AD_0 through AD_{15}, are in use. This interface also involves the control signals that we discussed as part of the memory interface. They are: ALE, $\overline{BHE}$, $\overline{RD}$, $\overline{WR}$, $M/\overline{IO}$, $DT/\overline{R}$, and $\overline{DEN}$.

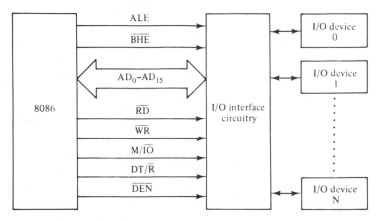

Figure 6.1 Minimum-mode 8086 system I/O interface.

Maximum-Mode Interface

When the 8086 system is strapped to operate in the maximum mode, the interface to the I/O circuitry changes. Figure 6.2 illustrates this configuration.

As in the maximum-mode memory interface, the 8288 bus controller produces the control signals for the I/O subsystem. The 8288 decodes bus command status codes output by the 8086 at $\overline{S}_2\overline{S}_1\overline{S}_0$. These codes tell which type of bus cycle is in progress. If the code corresponds to an I/O read bus cycle, the 8288 generates the I/O *read command output* $\overline{IORC}$ and for an I/O write cycle it generates I/O *write command outputs* $\overline{IOWC}$ and $\overline{AIOWC}$. The 8288 also produces control signals ALE, $DT/\overline{R}$, and DEN. Moreover, the address and data transfer path between 8086 and maximum-mode I/O interface remains address/data bus lines AD_0 through AD_{15}. In this configuration the control signal $\overline{BHE}$ is still produced by the 8086 microprocessor.

The table in Fig. 6.3 shows the bus command status codes together with the command signals that they produce. Those for I/O bus cycles have been highlighted. The 8086 indicates that data are to be input (Read I/O port) by code $\overline{S}_2\overline{S}_1\overline{S}_0 = 001$. This input causes the bus controller to produce control output I/O read command ($\overline{IORC}$). There is one other code that represents an output bus cycle. This is the

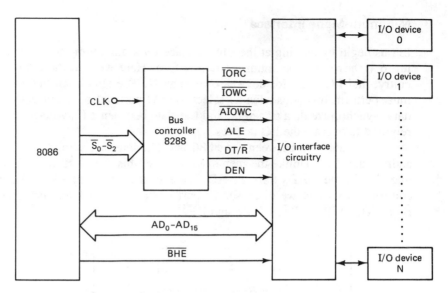

Figure 6.2 Maximum-mode 8086 system I/O interface.

Status inputs			CPU cycle	8288 command
$\overline{S}_2$	$\overline{S}_1$	$\overline{S}_0$		
0	0	0	Interrupt acknowledge	$\overline{INTA}$
0	0	1	Read I/O port	$\overline{IORC}$
0	1	0	Write I/O port	$\overline{IOWC}$, $\overline{AIOWC}$
0	1	1	Halt	None
1	0	0	Instruction fetch	$\overline{MRDC}$
1	0	1	Read memory	$\overline{MRDC}$
1	1	0	Write memory	$\overline{MWTC}$, $\overline{AMWC}$
1	1	1	Passive	None

Figure 6.3 I/O bus cycle status codes. (Reprinted by permission of Intel Corp. Copyright/Intel Corp., 1979.)

Write I/O port code $\overline{S}_2\overline{S}_1\overline{S}_0 = 010$. It produces two output command signals I/O write command ($\overline{IOWC}$) and advanced I/O write command ($\overline{AIOWC}$). These command signals are used to enable data from the I/O circuitry onto the system bus and control the direction in which data are transferred.

6.3 I/O DATA TRANSFERS

Earlier we indicated that input/output ports in the 8086 microcomputer can be either byte wide or word wide. The port that is accessed for input or output of data is selected by an *I/O address*. This address is specified as part of the instruction that performs the I/O operation.

I/O addresses are 16 bits in length and are output by the 8086 to the I/O interface over bus lines AD_0 through AD_{15}. As for memory addresses, AD_0 represents the LSB and AD_{15} the MSB. The most significant bits, A_{16} through A_{19}, of the memory address are held at the 0 logic level during the address period (T_1) of all I/O bus cycles.

The 8086 signals to external circuitry that the address on the bus is for an I/O port instead of a memory location by switching the $M/\overline{IO}$ control line to the 0 logic level. This signal is held at the 0 level during the complete input or output bus cycle. For this reason, it can be used to enable the address latch or address decoder in external I/O circuitry. Since 16 address lines are used to address I/O ports, the 8086's I/O address space consists of 64K word-wide I/O ports. Figure 6.4 shows a map of the *I/O address space* of the 8086 system.

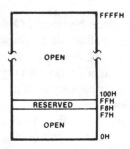

Figure 6.4 I/O address space. (Reprinted by permission of Intel Corp. Copyright/Intel Corp., 1979.)

Data transfers between the MPU and I/O devices are performed over the data bus. Word transfers take place over the complete data bus, D_0 through D_{15}, and can require either one or two bus cycle. To assure that just one bus cycle is required for the word data transfer, word-wide I/O ports should be aligned at even address boundaries.

On the other hand, data transfers to byte-wide I/O ports always require one bus cycle. Therefore, they can be located at either an even or odd address. Byte data transfers to a port at an even address are performed over bus line D_0 through D_7, and those to an odd-addressed port are performed over D_8 through D_{15}.

To input or output consecutive bytes of data to an LSI peripheral device, it should be connected such that all registers reside at either even or odd addresses. In this way, all data transfers take place over the same part of the bus. For this reason, A_0 cannot be used as a register select bit when addressing peripheral devices.

6.4 INPUT/OUTPUT INSTRUCTIONS

Input/output operations are performed by the 8086 using its *in* (IN) and *out* (OUT) instructions together with the I/O port addressing mode. There are two types of IN and OUT instructions: the *direct I/O instructions* and *variable I/O instructions*. These instructions are listed in the table of Fig. 6.5. Their mnemonics and names are provided together with a brief description of their operations.

Mnemonic	Meaning	Format	Operation
IN	Input direct	IN Acc,Port	$(Acc) \leftarrow (Port)$ Acc = AL or AX
	Input indirect (variable)	IN Acc,DX	$(Acc) \leftarrow ((DX))$
OUT	Output direct	OUT Port,Acc	$(Port) \leftarrow (Acc)$
	Output indirect (variable)	OUT DX,Acc	$((DX)) \leftarrow (Acc)$

Figure 6.5 Input/output instructions.

Either of these two types of instructions can be used to transfer a byte or word of data. In the case of byte transfers, data can be input/output over the upper or lower part of the bus. This is achieved by specifying an even or odd address, for the I/O port.

All data transfers take place between I/O devices and the 8086's AL or AX register. For this reason, this method of performing I/O is known as *accumulator I/O*. Byte transfers involve the AL register and word transfers the AX register. In fact, specifying AL as the source or destination register in an I/O instruction indicates that it corresponds to a byte transfer instead of a word transfer.

In a direct I/O instruction, the address of the I/O port is specified as part of the instruction. Eight bits are provided for this direct address. For this reason, its value is limited to the address range from 0_{10} equal 0000_{16} to 255_{10} equal $00FF_{16}$. This range corresponds to page 0 in the I/O address space of Fig. 6.4. An example is the instruction

IN   AL, FE

Execution of this instruction causes the contents of the byte-wide I/O port at address FE_{16} of the I/O address space to be input to the AL register.

EXAMPLE 6.1

Write a sequence of instructions that will output FF_{16} to a byte-wide output port at address AB_{16} of the I/O address space.

SOLUTION   First the AL register is loaded with FF_{16} as an immediate operand using the instruction

MOV   AL, FF

Now the data in AL can be output to the byte-wide output port with the instruction

OUT   AB, AL

The difference between the direct and variable I/O instructions lies in the way in which the address of the I/O port is specified. We just saw that for direct I/O instructions an 8-bit address is specified as part of the instruction. On the other hand, the variable I/O instructions use a 16-bit address that resides in the DX register within the 8086. The value in DX is not an offset. It is the actual address that is to be output on AD_0 through AD_{15} during the I/O bus cycle. Since this address is a full 16 bits in length, variable I/O instructions can access ports located anywhere in the 64K-byte I/O address space.

When using either type of I/O instruction, the data must be loaded into or removed from the AL or AX register before another input or output operation can be performed. Moreover, in the case of the variable I/O instructions, the DX register must be loaded with an address. This requires execution of additional instructions.

For instance, the instruction sequence

```
MOV   DX, A000
IN    AL, DX
```

inputs the contents of the byte-wide input port at $A000_{16}$ of the I/O address space.

EXAMPLE 6.2

Write a series of instructions that will output FF_{16} to an output port located at address $B000_{16}$ of the I/O address space.

SOLUTION   The DX register must first be loaded with the address of the output port. This is done with the instruction

```
MOV   DX, B000
```

Next the data that are to be output must be loaded into AL.

```
MOV   AL, FF
```

Finally, the data are output with the instruction

```
OUT   DX, AL
```

EXAMPLE 6.3

Data are to be read in from two byte-wide input ports at addresses AA_{16} and $A9_{16}$, respectively, and then output as a word to a word-wide output port at address $B000_{16}$. Write a sequence of instructions to perform this input/output operation.

SOLUTION   We can first read in the byte from the port at address AA_{16} into AL and move it to AH. This is done with the instructions

```
IN    AL, AA
MOV   AH, AL
```

Now the other byte can be read into AL by the instruction.

```
IN    AL, A9
```

To write out the word of data in AX, we can load DX with the address $B000_{16}$ and use a variable output instruction. This leads to the following

```
MOV   DX, B000
OUT   DX, AX
```

6.5 INPUT AND OUTPUT BUS CYCLES

In Section 6.2 we found that the I/O interface signals for the minimum-mode 8086 system are essentially the same as those involved in the memory interface. In fact, the function, logic levels, and timing of all signals other than M/$\overline{\text{IO}}$ are identical to those already described for the memory interface in Chapter 5.

Waveforms for the *I/O input (I/O read) bus cycle* and *I/O output (I/O write) bus cycle* are shown in Figs. 6.6 and 6.7, respectively. Looking at the input and output bus cycle waveforms, we see that the timing of M/$\overline{\text{IO}}$ does not change. The 8086 switches it to logic 0 to indicate that an I/O bus cycle is in progress. It is maintained at the 0 logic level for the duration of the I/O bus cycle. As in memory cycles, the address (ADDRESS OUT) is output together with ALE during clock period T_1. For the input bus cycle, $\overline{\text{DEN}}$ is switched to logic 0 to signal the I/O interface circuitry when to put the data onto the bus and the 8086 reads data off the bus during period T_3.

On the other hand, for the output bus cycle in Fig. 6.7, the 8086 puts write data (DATA OUT) on the bus late in T_2 and maintains them during the rest of the bus cycle. This time $\overline{\text{WR}}$ switches to logic 0 to signal the I/O section that valid data are on the bus.

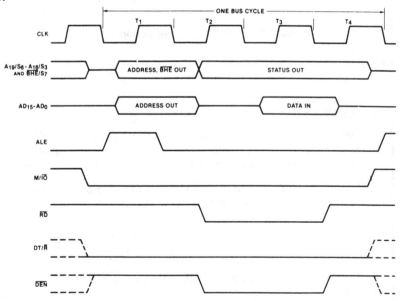

Figure 6.6 Input bus cycle. (Reprinted by permission of Intel Corp. Copyright/ Intel Corp., 1979.)

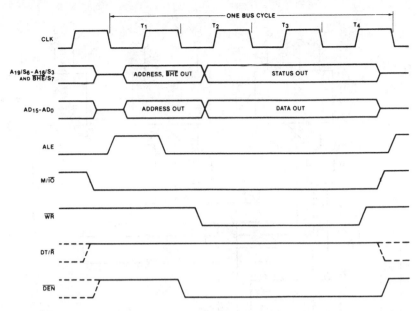

Figure 6.7 Output bus cycle. (Reprinted by permission of Intel Corp. Copyright/Intel Corp., 1979.)

The same bus cycle requirements exist for data transfers for I/O ports as were found for memory. That is, all byte transfers and word transfers to even-addressed ports require just one bus cycle. However, two bus cycles are required to perform data transfers for odd-addressed word-wide ports. Eight bits are transferred during each of these two bus cycles.

6.6 EIGHT-BYTE-WIDE OUTPUT PORTS

Up to this point in the chapter, we have introduced the I/O interface of the 8086-based microcomputer, the I/O address space, the I/O instructions, and I/O bus cycles. Now we will show a circuit that can be used to implement parallel output ports in an 8086 system. Figure 6.8 is such a circuit. It provides eight-byte-wide output ports that are implemented with 8282 octal latches. In this circuit, the ports are labeled PORT 0 through PORT 7. These eight ports give a total of 64 parallel output lines which are labeled O_0 through O_{63}.

Looking at the circuit, we see that the 8086's address/data bus is demultiplexed just as was done for the memory interface. Notice that two 8282 octal latches are used to form a 16-bit address latch. These devices latch the address A_0 through A_{15} synchronously with the ALE pulse. The latched address outputs are labeled A_{OL} through A_{15L}. Remember that address lines A_{16} through A_{19} are not involved in the I/O interface. For this reason they are not shown in the circuit diagram.

Actually, this circuit is designed such that the I/O ports reside at even byte addresses. This is the reason that only bus lines AD_0 through AD_7 are shown connecting to the output latches. It is over these lines that the 8086 writes data into the output ports.

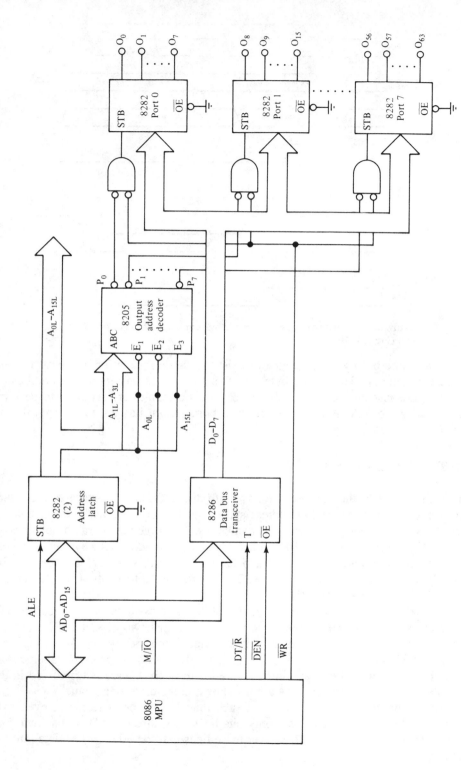

Figure 6.8 Sixty-four-output lines circuit.

Address lines A_{0L} and A_{15L} provide two of the three enable inputs of the 8205 output address decoder. These signals are applied to enable inputs $\overline{E}_1$ and E_3, respectively. The decoder requires one more enable signal at its $\overline{E}_2$ input. It is supplied by $M/\overline{IO}$. These enable inputs must be $\overline{E}_1\overline{E}_2E_3$ equal to 001 to enable the decoder for operation. The condition $\overline{E}_1$ equal 0 corresponds to an even address and $\overline{E}_2$ equal 0 represents the fact that an I/O bus cycle is in progress. The third condition, E_3 equal 1, is an additional requirement that A_{15L} be at logic 1 during all data transfers for this section of parallel output ports.

Notice that the 3-bit code $A_{3L}A_{2L}A_{1L}$ is applied to select inputs ABC of the 8205 1-of-8 decoder. When the decoder is enabled, the P output corresponding to this select code switches to logic 0. Notice that logic 0 at this output enables the $\overline{WR}$ signal to the strobe (STB) input of the corresponding output latch. In this way, just one of the eight ports is selected for operation.

When valid output data are on D_0 through D_7, the 8086 switches $\overline{WR}$ to logic 0. This change in logic level causes the selected 8282 device to latch in the data from the bus. The outputs of the latches are permanently enabled by the 0 logic level at their $\overline{OE}$ inputs. Therefore, the data appear at the appropriate port outputs.

The 8286 in the circuit allows data to move from 8086 to the output ports. This is accomplished by enabling the 8286's T and $\overline{OE}$ pins with the DT/$\overline{R}$ and $\overline{DEN}$ signals which are at logic 1 and 0, respectively.

EXAMPLE 6.4

To which output port in Fig. 6.8 are data written when the address put on the bus during an output bus cycle is 8002_{16}?

SOLUTION Expressing the address in binary form, we get

$$A_{15}\ldots A_0 = A_{15L}\ldots A_{0L} = 1000000000000010_{16}$$

The important address bits are

$$A_{15L} = 1$$

$$A_{0L} = 0$$

and

$$A_{3L}A_{2L}A_{1L} = 001$$

Moreover, whenever an output bus cycle is in progress, $M/\overline{IO}$ is logic 0. Therefore, the enable inputs of the 8205 decoder are

$$\overline{E}_1 = A_{0L} = 0$$

$$\overline{E}_2 = M/\overline{IO} = 0$$

$$E_3 = A_{15L} = 1$$

These inputs enable the decoder for operation. At the same time, its select inputs are supplied with the code 001. This input causes output P_1 to switch to logic 0.

$$P_1 = 0$$

The gate at the strobe input of Port 1 has as its inputs P_1 and $\overline{WR}$. When valid data are on the bus, $\overline{WR}$ switches to logic 0. Since P_1 is also 0, the STB input of the 8282 for

Port 1 switches to logic 1. This causes the data on D_0 through D_7 to be latched at output lines O_8 through O_{15} of Port 1.

EXAMPLE 6.5

Write a series of instructions that will output the byte contents of the memory location called DATA to output port 0 in the circuit of Fig. 6.8.

SOLUTION To write a byte to output port 0, the address that must be output on the 8086's address bus must be

$$A_{15}A_{14} \ldots \ldots A_0 = 1XXXXXXXXXXX0000_2$$

Assuming that the don't-care bits are all made logic 0, we get

$$A_{15}A_{14} \ldots \ldots A_0 = 1000000000000000_2$$
$$= 8000_{16}$$

Then the instruction sequence needed to output the contents of memory location DATA is

```
MOV    DX, 8000
MOV    AL, DATA
OUT    DX, AL
```

6.7 8255A PROGRAMMABLE PERIPHERAL INTERFACE (PPI)

The *8255A* is an LSI peripheral designed to permit easy implementatin of *parallel I/O* in the 8086 microcomputer. It provides a flexible parallel interface that includes features such as single-bit, 4-bit, and byte-wide input and output ports; level-sensitive inputs; latched outputs; strobed inputs or outputs; and strobed bidirectional input/outputs. These features are selected under software control.

A block diagram of the 8255A is shown in Fig. 6.9(a) and its pin layout in Fig. 6.9(b). The left side of the block represents the *microprocessor interface*. It includes an *8-bit bidirectional data bus* D_0 through D_7. Over these lines, commands, status information, and data are transferred between the 8086 and 8255A. These data are transferred whenever the 8086 performs an input or output bus cycle to an address of a register within the device. Timing of the data transfers to the 8255A is controlled by the *read/write* ($\overline{RD}$ and $\overline{WR}$) *control* signals.

The source or destination register within the 8255A is selected by a 2-bit *register select code*. The 8086 must apply this code to the *register select inputs*, A_0 and A_1 of the 8255A. The *PORT A, PORT B,* and *PORT C registers* correspond to codes $A_1A_0 = 00$, $A_1A_0 = 01$, and $A_1A_0 = 10$, respectively.

Two other signals are shown on the microprocessor interface side of the block diagram. They are the *rest* (RESET) and *chip select* ($\overline{CS}$) inputs. $\overline{CS}$ must be logic 0 during all read or write operations to the 8255A. It enables the microprocessor interface circuitry for an input or output operation.

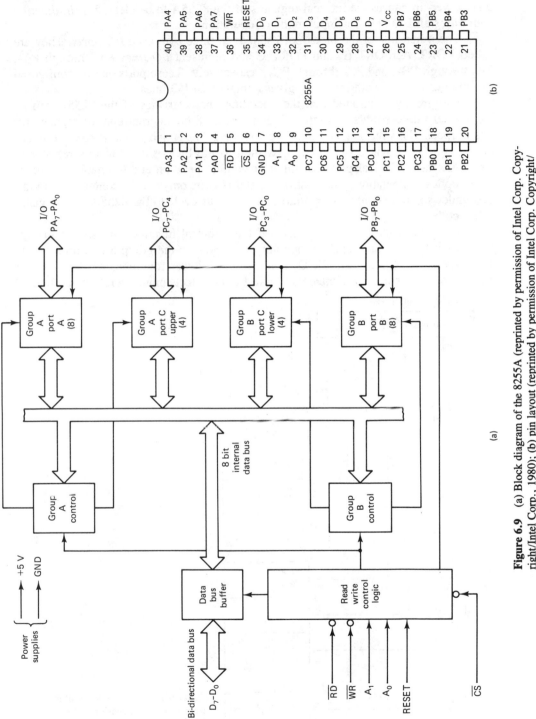

Figure 6.9 (a) Block diagram of the 8255A (reprinted by permission of Intel Corp. Copyright/Intel Corp., 1980); (b) pin layout (reprinted by permission of Intel Corp. Copyright/Intel Corp., 1980).

153

On the other hand, RESET is used to initialize the device. Switching it to logic 0 at power-up causes the internal registers of the 8255A to be cleared. *Initialization* configures all I/O ports for input mode of operation.

The other side of the block corresponds to three *byte-wide I/O ports*. They are called PORT A, PORT B, and PORT C and represent *I/O lines* PA_0 through PA_7, PB_0 through PB_7, and PC_0 through PC_7, respectively. These ports can be configured for input or output operation. This gives a total of 24 I/O lines.

We already mentioned that the operating characteristics of the 8255A can be configured under software control. It contains an 8-bit internal control register for this purpose. This register is represented by the *group A* and *group B control blocks* in Fig. 6.9(a). Logic 0 or 1 can be written to the bit positions in this register to configure the individual ports for input or output operation and to enable one of its three modes of operation. The control register is write only and its contents are modified under software control by initiating a write bus cycle to the 8255A with register select code $A_1A_0 = 11$.

The bits of the control register and their control functions are shown in Fig. 6.10. Here we see that bits D_0 through D_2 correspond to the group B control block in the diagram of Fig. 6.9(a). Bit D_0 configures the lower four lines of PORT C for input or output operation. Notice that logic 1 at D_0 selects input operation and logic 0

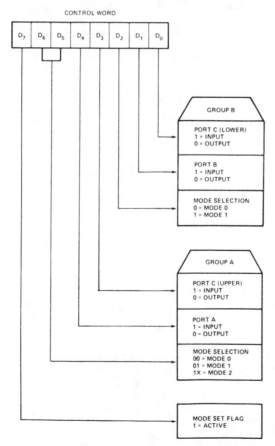

Figure 6.10 Control word bit functions. (Reprinted by permission of Intel Corp. Copyright/Intel Corp., 1980.)

selects output operation. The next bit, D_1, configures PORT B as an 8-bit-wide input or output port. Again, logic 1 selects input operation and logic 0 selects output operation.

The D_2 bit is the mode select bit for PORT B and the lower 4 bits of PORT C. It permits selection of one of two different modes of operation called *MODE 0* and *MODE 1*. Logic 0 in bit D_2 selects MODE 0, while logic 1 selects MODE 1. These modes will be discussed in detail shortly.

The next 4 bits in the control register, D_3 through D_6, correspond to the group A control block in Fig. 6.9(a). Bits D_3 and D_4 of the control register are used to configure the operation of the upper half of PORT C and all of PORT A, respectively. These bits work in the same way as D_0 and D_1 configure the lower half of PORT C and PORT B. However, there are now two mode select bits D_5 and D_6 instead of just 1. They are used to select between three modes of operation known as *MODE 0, MODE 1,* and *MODE 2.*

The last control register bit, D_7, is the *mode set flag*. It must be at logic 1 (active) whenever the mode of operation is to be changed.

MODE 0 selects what is called *simple I/O operation*. By simple I/O, we mean that the lines of the port can be configured as level-sensitive inputs or latched outputs. To set all ports for this mode of operation, load bit D_7 of the control register with logic 1, bits $D_6 D_5 = 00$, and $D_2 = 0$. Logic 1 at D_7 represents an active mode set flag. Now PORT A and PORT B can be configured as 8-bit input or output ports and PORT C can be configured for operation as two independent 4-bit input or output ports. This is done by setting or resetting bits D_4, D_3, D_1, and D_0.

For example, if $80_{16} = 10000000_2$ is written to the control register, the 1 in D_7 activates the mode set flag. MODE 0 operation is selected for all three ports because bits D_6, D_5, and D_2 are logic 0. At the same time, the 0's in D_4, D_3, D_1, and D_0 set up all port lines to work as outputs. This configuration is illustrated in Fig. 6.11(a).

By writing different binary combinations into bit locations D_4, D_3, D_1, and D_0, any one of 16 different MODE 0 I/O configurations can be obtained. The control word and I/O setup for the rest of these combinations are shown in Fig. 6.11(b) through (p).

EXAMPLE 6.6

What is the mode and I/O configuration for ports A, B, and C of an 8255A after its control register is loaded with 82_{16}?

SOLUTION Expressing the control register contents in binary form, we get

$$D_7 D_6 D_5 D_4 D_3 D_2 D_1 D_0 = 10000010_2$$

Since D_7 is 1, the modes of operation of the ports are selected by the control word. The three least significant bits of the word configure PORT B and the lower 4 bits of PORT C. They give

$D_0 = 0$ Lower 4 bits of PORT C are outputs

$D_1 = 1$ PORT B bits are inputs

$D_2 = 0$ MODE 0 operation for both PORT B and the lower 4 bits of PORT C

The next 4 bits configure the upper part of PORT C and PORT A.

$$D_3 = 0 \qquad \text{Upper 4 bits of PORT C are outputs}$$

$$D_4 = 0 \qquad \text{PORT A bits are outputs}$$

$$D_6D_5 = 00 \qquad \text{MODE 0 operation for both PORT}$$
$$\text{A and the upper part of PORT C}$$

This MODE 0 I/O configuration is shown in Fig. 6.11(c).

MODE 1 operation represents what is known as *strobed I/O*. The ports of the 8255A are put into this mode of operation by setting $D_7 = 1$ to activate the mode set flag and setting $D_6D_5 = 01$ and $D_2 = 1$.

In this way, the A and B ports are configured as two independent *byte-wide I/O ports* each of which has a *4-bit control/data port* associated with it. The control/data ports are formed from the lower and upper nibbles of PORT C, respectively.

When configured in this way, data applied to an input port must be strobed in with a signal produced in external hardware. Moreover, an output port is provided

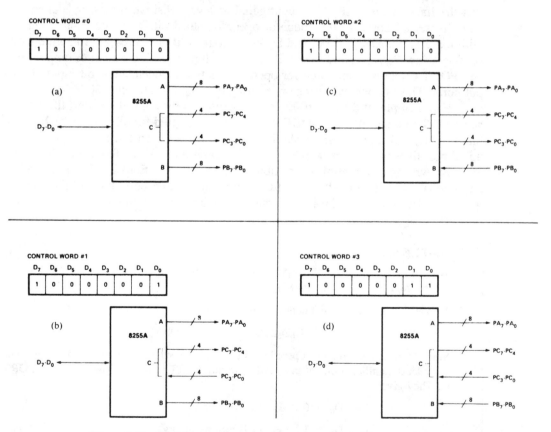

Figure 6.11 Mode 0 control words and corresponding input/output configurations. (Reprinted by permission of Intel Corp. Copyright/Intel Corp., 1980.)

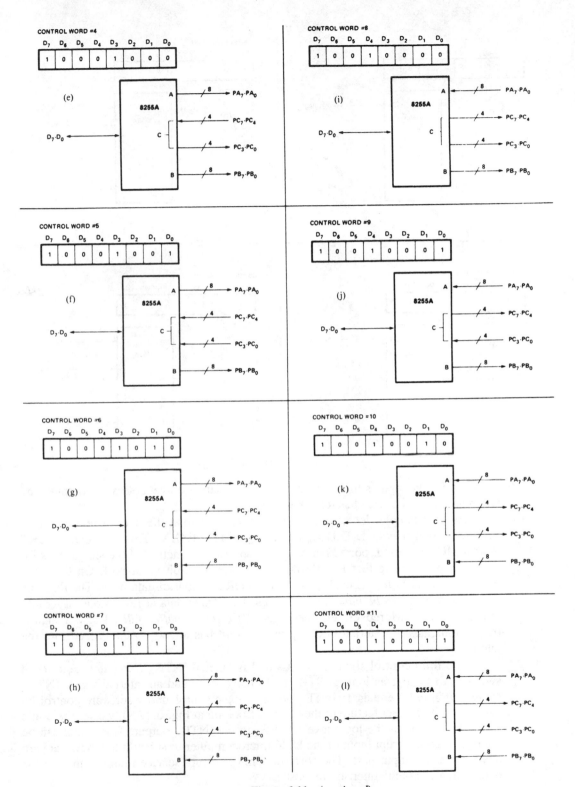

Figure 6.11 (*continued*)

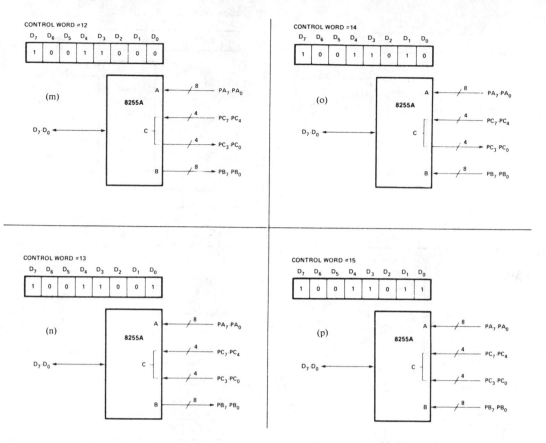

Figure 6.11 (*continued*)

with handshake signals that indicate when new data are available at its outputs and when an external device has read these values.

As an example, let us assume for the moment that the control register of an 8255A is loaded with $D_7D_6D_5D_4D_3D_2D_1D_0 = 10111XXX$. This configures PORT A as a MODE 1 input port. Figure 6.12(a) shows the function of the signal lines for this example. Notice that PA_7 through PA_0 form an 8-bit input port. On the other hand, the upper PORT C leads provide the PORT A control/data lines. The PC_4 line becomes $\overline{STB}_A$ (*strobe input*), which is used to strobe data at PA_7 through PA_0 into the input latch. Moreover, PC_5 becomes IBF_A (*input buffer full*). Logic 1 at this output indicates to external circuitry that a word has already been strobed into the latch.

The third control signal is at PC_3 and is labeled $INTR_A$ (*interrupt request*). It switches to logic 1 as long as $\overline{STB}_A = 1$, $IBF_A = 1$, and an internal signal $INTE_A$ (*interrupt enable*) equals 1. $INTE_A$ is set to logic 0 or 1 under software control by using the bit set/reset feature of the 8255A. Looking at Fig. 6.12(a), we see that logic 1 in $INTE_A$ enables the logic level of IBF_A to the $INTR_A$ output. This signal can be applied to an interrupt input of the 8086 microcomputer to signal it that new data are available at the input port. The corresponding interrupt service routine can read the data which clears the interrupt request.

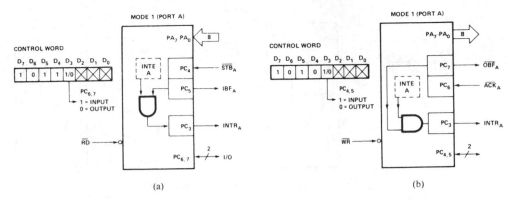

Figure 6.12 (a) Mode 1 port A input configuration (reprinted by permission of Intel Corp. Copyright/Intel Corp., 1980); (b) Mode 1 port A output configuration (reprinted by permission of Intel Corp. Copyright/Intel Corp., 1980).

As another example, let us assume that the contents of the control register are changed to $D_7D_6D_5D_4D_3D_2D_1D_0 = 10100XXX$. This I/O configuration is shown in Fig. 6.12(b). Notice that PORT A is now configured for output operation instead of input operation. PA_7 through PA_0 are now an 8-bit output port. The control line at PC_7 is $\overline{OBF}_A$ (*output buffer full*). When data have been written into the output port, $\overline{OBF}_A$ switches to the 0 logic level. In this way, it signals external circuitry that new data are available at the port outputs.

Signal line PC_6 becomes $\overline{ACK}_A$ (*acknowledge*), which is an input. An external device can signal the 8255A that it has accepted the data provided at the output port by switching this input to logic 0. The last signal at the control port is output $INTR_A$ (*interrupt request*), which is produced at the PC_3 lead. This output is switched to logic 1 when the $\overline{ACK}_A$ input is active. It is used to signal the 8086 with an interrupt that indicates that an external device has accepted the data from the outputs. $INTR_A$ switches to the 1 level when $\overline{OBF}_A = 1$, $\overline{ACK} = 0$, and $INTE_A = 1$. Again the interrupt enable ($INTE_A$) bit must be set to 1 under software control.

⌐ **EXAMPLE 6.7**

Figure 6.13(a) and (b) shows how PORT B can be configured for MODE 1 operation. Describe what happens in Fig. 6.13(a) when the $\overline{STB}_B$ input is pulsed to logic 0. Assume that $INTE_B$ is set to 1.

SOLUTION   As $\overline{STB}_B$ is pulsed, the byte of data at PB_7 through PB_0 is latched into the PORT B register. This causes the IBF_B output to switch to 1. Since $INTE_B$ is 1, $INTR_B$ also switches to logic 1.
⌐

The last mode of operation, MODE 2, represents what is known as *strobed bidirectional I/O*. The key difference is that now the port works as either input or output and control signals are provided for both functions. Only PORT A can be configured to work in this way.

To set up this mode, the control register is set to $D_7D_6D_5D_4D_3D_2D_1D_0 = 11XXXXXX$. The I/O configuration that results is shown in Fig. 6.14. Here we find that PA_7 through PA_0 operate as an *8-bit bidirectional port* instead of a unidirectional

Sec. 6.7   8255A Programmable Peripheral Interface (PPI)   **159**

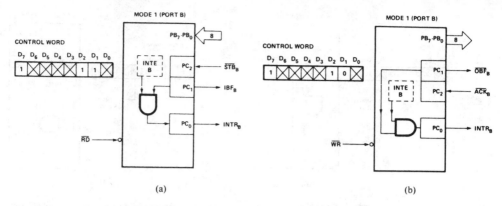

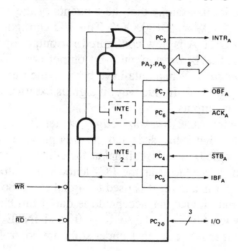

Figure 6.13 (a) Mode 1 port B input configuration (reprinted by permission of Intel Corp. Copyright/Intel Corp., 1980); (b) Mode 1 port B output configuration (reprinted by permission of Intel Corp. Copyright/Intel Corp., 1980).

Figure 6.14 Mode 2 input/output configuration. (Reprinted by permission of Intel Corp. Copyright/Intel Corp., 1980.)

port. Its control signals are $\overline{OBF}_A$ at PC_7, $\overline{ACK}_A$ at PC_6, $\overline{STB}_A$ at PC_4, IBF_A at PC_5, and $INTR_A$ at PC_3. Their functions are similar to those already discussed for MODE 1. One difference is that $INTR_A$ is produced by either gating $\overline{OBF}_A$ with $INTE_1$ or IBF_A with $INTE_2$.

In our discussion of MODE 1, we mentioned that the *bit set/reset* feature could be used to set the INTE bit to logic 0 or 1. This feature also allows the individual bits of PORT C to be set or reset. To do this, we write logic 0 to bit D_7 of the control register. This resets the bit set/reset flag. The logic level that is to be latched at a PORT C line is included as bit D_0 of the control word. This value is latched at the output line of PORT C, which corresponds to the 3-bit code at $D_3D_2D_1$.

The relationship between the set/reset control word and input/output lines is illustrated in Fig. 6.15. For instance, writing $D_7D_6D_5D_4D_3D_2D_1D_0 = 00001111_2$ into the control register of the 8255A selects bit 7 and sets it to 1. Therefore, output PC_7 at PORT C is switched to the 1 logic level.

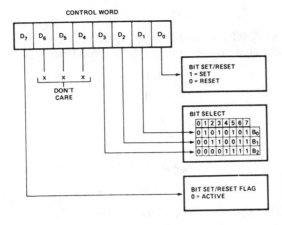

CONTROL WORD

BIT SET/RESET
1 = SET
0 = RESET

BIT SELECT

BIT SET/RESET FLAG
0 = ACTIVE

DON'T CARE

Figure 6.15 Bit set/reset format. (Reprinted by permission of Intel Corp. Copyright/Intel Corp., 1980.)

EXAMPLE 6.8

The interrupt control flag $INTE_A$ is controlled by bit set/reset of PC_6 (Fig. 6.12(b)). What command code must be written to the control register of the 8255A to set its value to logic 1?

SOLUTION To use the set/reset feature, D_7 must be logic 0. Moreover, $INTE_A$ is to be set to logic 1; therefore, D_0 must be logic 1. Finally, to select PC_6, the code at bits $D_3D_2D_1$ must be 110. The rest of the bits are don't-care states. This gives the control word

$$D_7D_6D_5D_4D_3D_2D_1D_0 = 0XXX1101_2$$

Replacing the don't-care states with the 0 logic level, we get

$$D_7D_6D_5D_4D_3D_2D_1D_0 = 00001101_2 = 0D_{16}$$

We have just described and given examples of each of the modes of operation that can be assigned to the ports of the 8255A. In practice, the A and B ports are frequently configured with different modes. For example, Fig. 6.16(a) shows the control word and port configuration of an 8255A set up for bidirectional MODE 2 operation of PORT A and input MODE 0 operation of PORT B.

EXAMPLE 6.9

What control word must be written into the control register of the 8255A such that PORT A is configured for bidirectional operation and PORT B is set up with MODE 1 outputs?

SOLUTION To configure the mode of operation of the ports of the 8255A, D_7 must be 1.

$$D_7 = 1$$

PORT A is set up for bidirectional operation by making D_6 logic 1. In this case, D_5 through D_3 are don't-care states.

$$D_6 = 1$$

$$D_5D_4D_3 = XXX$$

MODE 1 is selected for PORT B by logic 1 in bit D_2 and output operation by logic 0 in D_1. Since MODE 1 operation has been selected, D_0 is a don't-care state.

$$D_2 = 1$$

$$D_1 = 0$$

$$D_0 = X$$

This gives the control word

$$D_7D_6D_5D_4D_3D_2D_1D_0 = 11XXX10X_2$$

Assuming logic 0 for the don't-care states, we get

$$D_7D_6D_5D_4D_3D_2D_1D_0 = 11000100_2 = C4_{16}$$

This configuration is shown in Fig. 6.16(b)

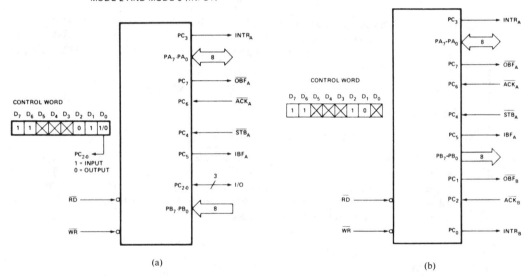

Figure 6.16   (a) Combined mode 2 and mode 0 (input) control word and I/O configuration (reprinted by permission of Intel Corp. Copyright/Intel Corp., 1980); (b) combined mode 2 and mode 1 (output) control word and I/O configurations (reprinted by permission of Intel Corp. Copyright/Intel Corp., 1980).

EXAMPLE 6.10

Write the sequence of instructions needed to load the control register of an 8255A with the control word formed in Example 6.9. Assume that the 8255A resides at address $0C_{16}$ of the I/O address space.

SOLUTION   First we must load AL with $C4_{16}$. This is the value of the control word that is to be output to the control register at address $0F_{16}$. The move instruction used to load AL is

MOV AL, C4

These data are output to the control register that resides at $0F_{16}$ ($0C_{16} + 3_{16}$) with the OUT instruction

OUT 0F, AL

6.8 8255A IMPLEMENTATION OF PARALLEL I/O PORTS

The circuit in Fig. 6.17 shows how PPI devices can be connected to the bus of the 8086 to implement parallel input/output ports. This circuit configuration is for a minimum-mode 8086 microcomputer. Here we find that two groups each of up to eight 8255A devices are connected to the data bus. Each group has its own 8205 address decoder. This decoder selects one of the devices at a time for input or output data transfers. The ports in the upper group are connected at odd-address boundaries and those in the lower group are at even-address boundaries. Each of these PPI devices provide up to 3-byte-wide ports. In the circuit, they are labeled PORT A, PORT B, and PORT C. These ports can be individually configured as inputs or outputs through software. Therefore, each group is capable of implementing up to 192 I/O lines.

Let us look more closely at the connection of the upper port. Starting with the inputs of the 8205 address decoder, we see that its enable inputs are $E_1 = \overline{BHE}$ and $E_2 = M/\overline{IO}$. $\overline{BHE}$ is logic 0 whenever the 8086 outputs an odd address on the bus. Moreover, $M/\overline{IO}$ is switched to logic 0 whenever an I/O bus cycle is in progress. For this reason, the upper decoder is enabled for I/O bus cycles to an odd address in its part of the I/O address range.

When the 8205 decoder is enabled, the code at its A_0 through A_2 inputs causes one of the eight 8255A PPIs to get enabled for operation. Bits A_5 through A_3 of the I/O address are applied to these inputs of the decoder. It responds by switching the output corresponding to this 3-bit code to the 0 logic level. Decoder outputs O_0 through O_7 are applied to the chip select ($\overline{CS}$) inputs of the odd-addressed PPIs. For instance, $A_5A_4D_3 = 000$ switches output O_0 to logic 0. This enables the first 8255A, which is numbered 1 in Fig. 6.17.

At the same time that the PPI chip is selected, the 2-bit code A_2A_1 at inputs A_1A_0 of the 8255A selects the port for which data are input or output. For example, A_2A_1 equal 00 indicates that PORT A is to be accessed.

Since the upper group is located at odd-address boundaries, input/output data transfers take place over data bus lines D_8 through D_{15}. The timing of these read/write transfers is controlled by signals $\overline{RD}$ and $\overline{WR}$.

EXAMPLE 6.11

What must be the address inputs of the even-addressed group of 8255As in Fig. 6.17 if PORT C of PPI 14 is to be accessed?

SOLUTION To enable PPI 14, the 8205 must be enabled for operation and its O_7 output switched to logic 0. This requires enable input $A_0 = 0$ and chip select code $A_5A_4A_3 = 111$.

$$A_0 = 0 \qquad \text{Enables 8205}$$

$$A_5A_4A_3 = 111 \qquad \text{Selects PPI 14}$$

PORT C of PPI 14 is selected with $A_1A_0 = 10$.

$$A_2A_1 = 10 \qquad \text{Accesses PORT C}$$

The rest of the address bits are don't-care states.

EXAMPLE 6.12

Assume in Fig. 6.17 that PPI 14 is configured such that port A is an output port and both port B and C are input ports and that all three ports are set up for MODE 0 operation. Write a program that will input the data at ports B and C, find the difference C-B, and output this difference to port A.

SOLUTION From the circuit diagram in Fig. 6.17, we find that the addresses of the three I/O ports on PPI 14 are

$$\text{PORT A} = 00111000_2 = 38_{16}$$

$$\text{PORT B} = 00111010_2 = 3A_{16}$$

$$\text{PORT C} = 00111100_2 = 3C_{16}$$

The data at ports B and C can be input with the instruction sequence

```
IN    AL, 3A        ; Read port B
MOV   BL, AL        ; Save data from port B
IN    AL, 3C        ; Read port C
```

Now the data from port B are subtracted from the data at port C with the instruction

```
SUB   AL, BL        ; Subtract B from C
```

Finally, the difference is output to port A with the instruction

```
OUT   38, AL        ; Write to port A
```

ASSIGNMENT

Section 6.2

1. What are the functions of the 8086's address and data bus lines relative to I/O operation?
2. Which signal indicates to the bus controller and external circuitry that the current bus cycle is for the I/O interface and not the memory interface?
3. In a maximum-mode system, which device produces the input (read), output (write), and bus control signals for the I/O interface?
4. Briefly describe the function of each block in the I/O interface circuit in Fig. 6.2.

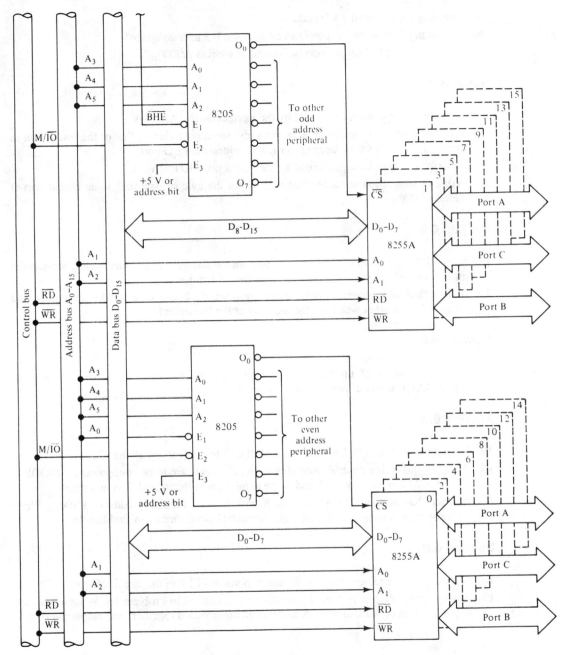

Figure 6.17 8255A parallel I/O ports at even and odd address boundaries. (Reprinted by permission of Intel Corp. Copyright/Intel Corp., 1979.)

Section 6.3

5. How large is the 8086's I/O address?
6. How many byte-wide I/O ports can exist in the I/O address space?
7. Can an I/O mapped output port be located at address $A0000_{16}$?

Section 6.4

8. Describe the operation performed by the instruction IN AX, 1A.
9. Write an instruction sequence to perform the same operation as that of the instruction in Problem 8, but this time use register DX to address the I/O port.
10. Describe the operation performed by the instruction OUT 2A,AL.
11. Write an instruction sequence that will output the byte of data $0F_{16}$ to an output port at address 1000_{16}.

Section 6.5

12. If an 8086 running at 10 MHz inserts two wait states into all I/O bus cycles, what is the duration of a bus cycle in which a byte of data is being output?
13. If the 8086 in Problem 12 was outputting a word of data to a word-wide port at I/O address $1A1_{16}$, what would be the duration of the bus cycle?

Section 6.6

14. Write a sequence of instructions to output the word contents of the memory location called DATA to output ports 0 and 1 in the circuit of Fig. 6.8.

Section 6.7

15. Describe the MODE 0, MODE 1, and MODE 2 I/O operations of the 8255A PPI.
16. What should be the control word if ports A, B, and C are to be configured for MODE 0 operation? Moreover, ports A and B are to be used as inputs and C as an output.
17. Assume that the control register of an 8255A resides at memory address 00100_{16}. Write an instruction sequence to load it with the control word formed in Problem 16.

Section 6.8

18. What are the addresses of the A, B, and C ports of PPI 2 in the circuit of Fig. 6.17?
19. Assume that PPI 2 in Fig. 6.17 is configured as defined in Problem 16. Write a program that will input the data at ports A and B, add these values together, and output the sum to port C.

7

Interrupt Interface of the 8086 Microprocessor

7.1 INTRODUCTION

In Chapter 6 we covered the input/output interface of the 8086 microcomputer system. Here we continue with a special input interface, the *interrupt interface*. The following topics are presented in this chapter:

1. Types of interrupts
2. Interrupt address pointer table
3. Interrupt instructions
4. Enabling/disabling the interrupts
5. External hardware interrupt interface
6. External hardware interrupt sequence
7. 8259A programmable interrupt controller
8. 8259A minimum-mode system interrupt interface
9. 8259A maximum-mode system interrupt interface
10. Internal interrupt functions

7.2 TYPES OF INTERRUPTS

Interrupts provide a mechanism for changing program environment. Transfer of program control is initiated by either the occurrence of an event internal to the 8086 microprocessor or an event in its external hardware. For instance, when an interrupt signal occurs indicating that an external device, such as a printer, requires service, the 8086 must suspend what it is doing in the main part of the program and pass control to a special routine that performs the function required by the device.

The section of program to which control is passed is called the *interrupt service routine*. When the 8086 terminates execution in the main program, it remembers the location where it left off and then picks up execution with the first instruction in the service routine. After this routine has run to completion, program control is returned to the point where the 8086 originally left the main body of the program.

The 8086 microcomputer is capable of implementing any combination of up to 256 interrupts. They are divided into five groups: *external hardware interrupts, software interrupts, internal interrupts,* the *nonmaskable interrupt,* and the *reset.* The function of the external hardware, software, and nonmaskable interrupts can be defined by the user. On the other hand, the internal interrupts and reset have dedicated system functions.

Hardware, software, and internal interrupts are serviced on a *priority* basis. Priority is achieved in two ways. First the interrupt processing sequence implemented in the 8086 tests for the occurrence of the various groups based on the hierarchy that follows: internal interrupt, nonmaskable interrupt, software interrupt, and external hardware interrupt. Thus we see that internal interrupts are the *highest-priority group* and the external hardware interrupts are the *lowest-priority group*. Second, the various interrupts are given different priority levels within a group by assigning to each a *type number*. *Type 0* identifies the highest-priority interrupt and *type 255* identifies the lowest-priority interrupt. Actually, a few of the type numbers are not available for use with software or hardware interrupts. This is because they are reserved for special interrupt functions of the 8086 such as internal interrupts. For instance, within the internal interrupt group an interrupt known as divide error is assigned to type number 0. Therefore, it has the highest-priority of the internal interrupts. Another internal interrupt is called *overflow* and is assigned the type number 4. Overflow is the lowest-priority internal interrupt.

The importance of priority lies in the fact that, if an interrupt service routine has been initiated to perform a function at a specific priority level, only devices with higher priority can interrupt the active service routine. Lower-priority devices will have to wait until the routine is completed before their request for service can be acknowledged. For this reason, the user normally assigns tasks that must not be interrupted frequently to higher-priority levels and those that can be interrupted to lower-priority levels. An example of a high-priority service routine that should not be interrupted is that for a power failure.

We just pointed out that once an interrupt service routine is initiated it can be interrupted only by a function that corresponds to a higher-priority level. For example, if a type 50 external hardware interrupt is in progress, it can be interrupted by any software interrupt, the nonmaskable interrupt, all internal interrupts, or any external interrupt with type number less than 50. That is, external hardware interrupts with priority levels equal to 50 or greater are *masked out*.

7.3 INTERRUPT ADDRESS POINTER TABLE

An *address pointer table* is used to link the interrupt type numbers to the locations of their service routines in the program storage memory. Figure 7.1 shows a map of the pointer table in the memory of the 8086 microcomputer system. Looking at this

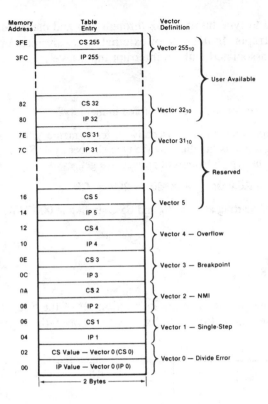

Memory Address	Table Entry	Vector Definition
3FE	CS 255	Vector 255$_{10}$
3FC	IP 255	
		User Available
82	CS 32	Vector 32$_{10}$
80	IP 32	
7E	CS 31	Vector 31$_{10}$
7C	IP 31	
		Reserved
16	CS 5	Vector 5
14	IP 5	
12	CS 4	Vector 4 — Overflow
10	IP 4	
0E	CS 3	Vector 3 — Breakpoint
0C	IP 3	
0A	CS 2	Vector 2 — NMI
08	IP 2	
06	CS 1	Vector 1 — Single-Step
04	IP 1	
02	CS Value — Vector 0 (CS 0)	Vector 0 — Divide Error
00	IP Value — Vector 0 (IP 0)	

← 2 Bytes →

Figure 7.1 Interrupt vector table. (Reprinted by permission of Intel Corp. Copyright/Intel Corp., 1979.)

table, we see that it contains 256 *address pointers (vectors)*. One pointer corresponds to each of the interrupt types 0 through 255. These address pointers identify the starting locations of their service routines in program memory.

Notice that the pointer table is located at the low-address end of the memory address space. It starts at address 00000_{16} and ends at $003FE_{16}$. This represents the first 1K bytes of memory.

Each of the 256 pointers requires two words (4 bytes) of memory. These words are stored at even-address boundaries. The higher-addressed word of the two-word vector is called the *base address*. It identifies the program memory segment in which the service routine resides. For this reason, it is loaded into the code segment (CS) register within the 8086. The lower-addressed word of the vector is the *offset* of the first instruction of the service routine from the beginning of the code segment defined by the base address loaded into CS. This offset is loaded into the instruction pointer (IP) register. For example, the vector for type number 255, IP_{255} and CS_{255}, is stored at addresses $003FC_{16}$ and $003FE_{16}$.

Looking more closely at the table in Fig. 7.1, we find that the first five pointers have *dedicated functions*. Pointers 0, 1, 3, and 4 are required for the 8086's internal interrupts: *divide error, single step, breakpoint,* and *overflow*. Pointer 2 is used to identify the starting location of the nonmaskable interrupt's service routine. The next 27 pointers, 5 through 31, represent a *reserved portion* of the pointer table and should not be used. The rest of the table, the 224 pointers in the address range 00080_{16} through $003FF_{16}$, are available to the user for storage of interrupt vectors.

These pointers correspond to type numbers 32 through 255 and can be employed by hardware or software interrupts. In the case of external hardware interrupts, the type number (priority level) is associated with an interrupt input level.

EXAMPLE 7.1

At what address should vector, $CS_{50}:IP_{50}$ be stored in memory?

SOLUTION Each vector requires four consecutive bytes of memory for storage. Therefore, its address can be found by multiplying the type number by 4. Since CS_{50} and IP_{50} represent the words of the type 50 interrupt pointer, we get

$$\text{Address} = 4 \times 50 = 200 = C8_{16}$$

Therefore, IP_{50} is stored starting at $000C8_{16}$ and CS_{50} starting at $000CA_{16}$.

7.4 INTERRUPT INSTRUCTIONS

A number of instructions are provided in the instruction set of the 8086 for use with interrupt processing. These instructions are listed with a brief description of their functions in Fig. 7.2.

Mnemonic	Meaning	Format	Operation	Flags Affected
CLI	Clear interrupt flag	CLI	$0 \rightarrow (IF)$	IF
STI	Set interrupt flag	STI	$1 \rightarrow (IF)$	IF
INT n	Type n software interrupt	INT n	$(\text{Flags}) \rightarrow ((SP) - 2)$ $0 \rightarrow TF,IF$ $(CS) \rightarrow ((SP) - 4)$ $(2 + 4 \cdot n) \rightarrow (CS)$ $(IP) \rightarrow ((SP) - 6)$ $(4 \cdot n) \rightarrow (IP)$	TF, IF
IRET	Interrupt return	IRET	$((SP)) \rightarrow (IP)$ $((SP) + 2) \rightarrow (CS)$ $((SP) + 4) \rightarrow (\text{Flags})$ $(SP) + 6 \rightarrow (SP)$	All
INTO	Interrupt on overflow	INTO	INT 4 steps	TF, IF
HLT	Halt	HLT	Wait for an external interrupt or reset to occur	None
WAIT	Wait	WAIT	Wait for $\overline{\text{TEST}}$ input to go active	None

Figure 7.2 Interrupt instructions.

For instance, the first two instructions, which are STI and CLI, permit manipulation of the 8086's interrupt flag through software. STI stands for *set interrupt enable flag*. Execution of this instruction enables the external interrupt input (INTR) for operation. That is, it sets interrupt flag (IF). On the other hand, execution of CLI (*clear interrupt enable flag*) disables the external interrupt input. It does this by resetting IF.

The next instruction listed in Fig. 7.2 is the *software interrupt* instruction INT n. It is used to initiate a software vector call of a subroutine. Executing the instruction causes transfer of program control to the subroutine pointed to by the vector for type number n specified in the instruction.

For example, execution of the instruction INT 50 initiates execution of a subroutine whose starting point is identified by vector 50 in the pointer table. That is, the 8086 reads IP_{50} and CS_{50} from addresses $000C8_{16}$ and $000CA_{16}$, respectively, in memory, loads these values into IP and CS, calculates a physical address, and starts to fetch instructions from this new location in program memory.

An *interrupt return* (IRET) instruction must be included at the end of each interrupt service routine. It is required to pass control back to the point in the program where execution was terminated due to the occurrence of the interrupt. When executed, IRET causes the three words IP, CS, and flags to be popped from the stack back into the internal registers of the 8086. This restores the original program environment.

INTO is the *interrupt on overflow* instruction. This instruction must be included after arithmetic instructions that can generate an overflow condition. It tests the overflow flag and if the flag is found to be set, a type 4 internal interrupt is initiated. This causes program control to be passed to an overflow service routine that is located at the starting address identified by the vector IP_4 at 00010_{16} and CS_4 at 00012_{16} of the pointer table.

The last two instructions associated with the interrupt interface are *halt* (HLT) and *wait* (WAIT). They produce similar responses by the 8086 and permit the operation of the 8086 to be synchronized to an event in external hardware. For instance, when HLT is executed, the 8086 suspends operation and enters the idle state. It no longer executes instructions; instead, it remains idle waiting for the occurrence of an external hardware interrupt or reset interrupt. With the occurrence of either of these two events, the 8086 resumes execution with the corresponding service routine.

If the WAIT instruction is used instead of the HLT instruction, the 8086 checks the logic level of the $\overline{TEST}$ input prior to going into the idle state. Only if $\overline{TEST}$ is at logic 1, will the MPU go into the idle state. While in the idle state, the 8086 continues to check the logic level at $\overline{TEST}$ looking for its transition to the 0 logic level. As $\overline{TEST}$ switches to 0, execution resumes with the next sequential instruction in the program.

7.5 ENABLING/DISABLING THE INTERRUPTS

An interrupt enable flag bit is provided within the 8086. Earlier we found that it is identified as IF. It affects only the external hardware interrupt interface, not the software or internal interrupts. The ability to initiate an external hardware interrupt at the INTR input is enabled by setting IF or masked out by resetting it. Through software, this can be done by executing the STI instruction or the CLI instruction, respectively.

During the initiation sequence of an interrupt service routine, the 8086 automatically clears IF. This disables the acceptance of any additional external hardware interrupt. If necessary, the interrupt flag bit can be set with an STI instruction at the beginning of the service routine to reenable the INTR input. Otherwise, it gets set at the end of the service routine to reenable the external hardware interrupt interface.

7.6 EXTERNAL HARDWARE INTERRUPT INTERFACE

Up to this point in the chapter, we have introduced the interrupts of the 8086, its pointer table, interrupt instructions, and masking of interrupts. Let us now look at the *external hardware interrupt interface* of the 8086.

Minimum-Mode Interrupt Interface

We will begin with an 8086 microcomputer configured for the minimum system mode. The interrupt interface for this system is illustrated in Fig. 7.3. Here we see that it includes the multiplexed address/data bus and dedicated interrupt signal lines INTR and $\overline{\text{INTA}}$. Moreover, external circuitry is required to interface the interrupt inputs, INT_{32} through INT_{255}, to the 8086's interrupt interface. This interface circuitry must identify which of the pending active interrupts has the highest priority and then pass its type number to the 8086.

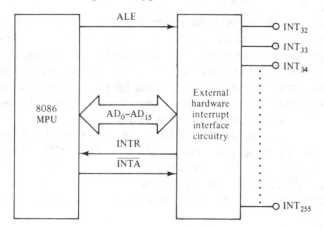

Figure 7.3 Minimum-mode 8086 system external hardware interrupt interface.

In this circuit we see that the key interrupt interface signals are *interrupt request* (INTR) and *interrupt acknowledge* ($\overline{\text{INTA}}$). The logic-level input at the INTR line signals the 8086 that an external device is requesting service. The 8086 samples this input during the last clock period of each instruction execution cycle. Logic 1 represents an active interrupt request. INTR is *level triggered;* therefore, its active 1 level must be maintained until tested by the 8086. If it is not maintained, the request for service may not be recognized. Moreover, the 1 at INTR must be removed before the service routine runs to completion; otherwise, the same interrupt may be acknowledged a second time.

When an interrupt request has been recognized by the 8086, it signals this fact to external circuitry. It does this with pulses to logic 0 at its $\overline{\text{INTA}}$ output. Actually, just two pulses are produced at $\overline{\text{INTA}}$ during the *interrupt acknowledge bus cycle*. The first pulse signals external circuitry that the interrupt request has been acknowledged and to prepare to send its type number to the 8086. The second pulse tells the external circuitry to put the type number on the data bus.

Notice that the lower 16 lines of the address/data bus, AD_0 through AD_{15}, are also part of the interrupt interface. During the second cycle in the interrupt acknowledge bus cycle, external circuitry must put an 8-bit type number on bus lines AD_0 through AD_7. The 8086 reads this number off the bus to identify which external device is requesting service. It uses the type number to generate the address of the interrupt's vector in the pointer table and to read the new values of CS and IP into the corresponding internal registers. CS and IP are transferred over the full 16-bit data bus. The old values of CS, IP, and the internal flags are automatically pushed to the stack part of memory. These word-wide transfers take place over the complete data bus.

Maximum-Mode Interrupt Interface

The maximum-mode interrupt interface of the 8086 microcomputer is shown in Fig. 7.4. The primary difference between this interrupt interface and that shown for the minimum mode in Fig. 7.3 is that the 8288 bus controller has been added. In the maximum-mode system, the bus controller produces the $\overline{\text{INTA}}$ and ALE signals. Whenever the 8086 outputs an interrupt acknowledge bus status code, the 8288

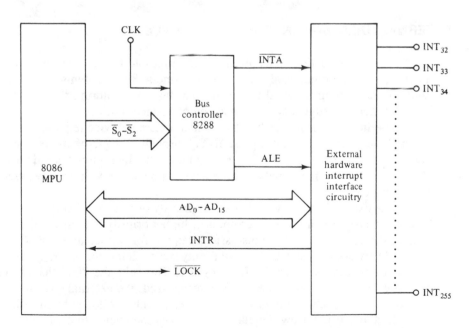

Figure 7.4 Maximum-mode 8086 system external hardware interrupt interface.

generates pulses at its $\overline{INTA}$ output to signal external circuitry that the 8086 has acknowledged an interrupt request. This interrupt acknowledge bus status code, $\overline{S}_2\overline{S}_1\overline{S}_0 = 000$, is highlighted in Fig. 7.5.

A second change in Fig. 7.4 is that the 8086 provides a new signal for the interrupt interface. This output, which is labeled $\overline{LOCK}$, is called the *bus priority lock* signal. $\overline{LOCK}$ is applied as an input to the *bus arbiter circuit*. In response to this signal, the arbitration logic assures that no other device can take over control of the system bus until the interrupt acknowledge bus cycle is completed.

Status inputs			CPU cycle	8288 command
$\overline{S}_2$	$\overline{S}_1$	$\overline{S}_0$		
0	0	0	Interrupt acknowledge	$\overline{INTA}$
0	0	1	Read I/O port	$\overline{IORC}$
0	1	0	Write I/O port	$\overline{IOWC}$, $\overline{AIOWC}$
0	1	1	Halt	None
1	0	0	Instruction fetch	$\overline{MRDC}$
1	0	1	Read memory	$\overline{MRDC}$
1	1	0	Write memory	$\overline{MWTC}$, $\overline{AMWC}$
1	1	1	Passive	None

Figure 7.5 Interrupt bus status code. (Reprinted by permission of Intel Corp. Copyright/Intel Corp., 1979.)

7.7 EXTERNAL HARDWARE INTERRUPT SEQUENCE

In the preceding section we showed the interrupt interfaces for the external hardware interrupts in minimum-mode and maximum-mode 8086 systems. Now we will continue by describing in detail the events that take place during the interrupt request, interrupt acknowledge bus cycle, and device service routine.

The interrupt sequence begins when an external device requests service by activating one of the interrupt inputs, INT_{32} through INT_{255}, of the external interrupt interface circuit in Fig. 7.3 or 7.4. For example, the INT_{50} input could be switched to the 1 logic level. This signals that the device associated with priority level 50 wants to be serviced.

The external circuitry evaluates the priority of this input. If there is no interrupt already in progress or if this interrupt is of higher priority than that which is presently active, the external circuitry must issue a request for service to the 8086.

Let us assume that INT_{50} is the only active interrupt input. In this case, the external circuitry switches INTR to logic 1. This tells the 8086 that an interrupt is pending for service. To assure that it is recognized, the external circuitry must maintain INTR active until an interrupt acknowledge pulse is issued by the 8086.

Figure 7.6 is a flow diagram that outlines the events that take place when the 8086 processes an interrupt. The 8086 tests for an active interrupt during the last clock state of the current instruction. Notice that it tests first for the occurrence of an

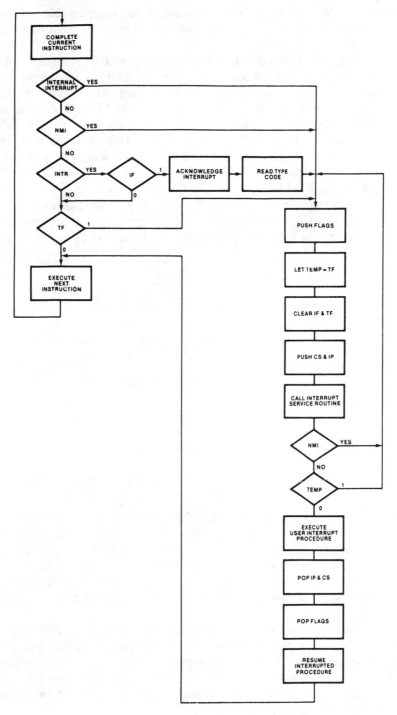

Figure 7.6 Interrupt processing sequence of the 8086 microprocessor. (Reprinted by permission of Intel Corp. Copyright/Intel Corp., 1979.)

internal interrupt, then the occurrence of the nonmaskable interrupt, and finally checks the logic level of INTR to determine if an external hardware interrupt has occurred.

If INTR is at logic 1, a request for service is recognized. Before the 8086 initiates the interrupt acknowledge sequence, it checks the setting of IF. If it is logic 0, external interrupts are masked out and the request is ignored. In this case, the next sequential instruction is executed. On the other hand, if IF is at logic 1, external hardware interrupts are enabled and the service routine is to be initiated.

Let us assume that IF is set to permit interrupts to occur when INTR is tested as 1. The 8086 responds by initiating the interrupt acknowledge bus cycles. This bus cycle is illustrated in Fig. 7.7. During T_1 of the first bus cycle, we see that a pulse is output on ALE but at the same time the address/data bus is put in the high-Z state. It stays in this state for the rest of the bus cycle. During periods T_2 and T_3, $\overline{\text{INTA}}$ is switched to logic 0. This signals external circuitry that the request for service has been granted. In response to this pulse, the logic 1 at INTR can be removed.

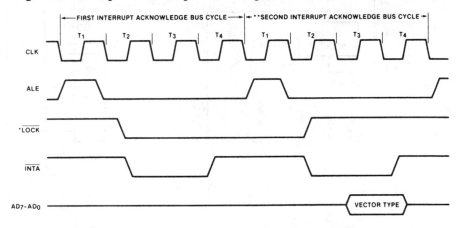

Figure 7.7 Interrupt acknowledge bus cycle. (Reprinted by permission of Intel Corp. Copyright/Intel Corp., 1979.)

The signal identified as $\overline{\text{LOCK}}$ is produced only in maximum-mode systems. Notice that $\overline{\text{LOCK}}$ is switched to logic 0 during T_2 of the first INTA bus cycle and is maintained at this level until T_2 of the second INTA bus cycle. During this time, the 8086 is prevented from accepting a HOLD request. Moreover, the $\overline{\text{LOCK}}$ ouput is used in external logic to lock other devices off the system bus, thereby assuring that the interrupt acknowledge sequence continues through to completion without interruption.

During the second interrupt acknowledge bus cycle, a similar signal sequence occurs. However, this interrupt acknowledge pulse tells the external circuitry to put the type number of the active interrupt on the data bus. External circuitry gates one of the interrupt codes $32 = 20_{16}$ through $255 = FF_{16}$ onto data bus lines AD_0 through AD_7. This code must be valid during periods T_3 and T_4 of the second interrupt acknowledge bus cycle.

The 8086 sets up its bus control signals for an input data transfer to read the type number off the data bus. DT/$\overline{R}$ and $\overline{DEN}$ are set to logic 0 to enable the external data bus circuitry and set it for input of data. Also, M/$\overline{IO}$ is set to 0, indicating that data are to be input from the interrupt interface. During this input operation, the byte interrupt code is read off the data bus. For the case of INT_{50}, this code would be $00110010_2 = 32_{16}$. This completes the interrupt acknowledge part of the interrupt sequence.

Looking at Fig. 7.6, we see that the 8086 first saves the contents of the flag register by pushing it to the stack. This requires one write cycle and 2 bytes of stack. Then it clears IF. This disables further external interrupts from requesting service. Actually, the TF flag is also cleared. This disables the single-step mode of operation if it happens to be active. Next, the 8086 automatically pushes the contents of CS and IP onto the stack. This requires two write cycles to take place over the system bus. The current value of the stack pointer is decremented by 2 as each of these values is put onto the top of the stack.

Now the 8086 knows the type number associated with the external device that is requesting service. It must next call the service routine by fetching the vector that defines its starting point from memory. The type number is internally multiplied by 4, and this result is used as the address of the first word of the interrupt vector in the pointer table. Two word read operations (two bus cycles) are performed to read the two-word vector from memory. The first word, which is the lower-addressed word, is loaded into IP. The second, higher-addressed word, is loaded into CS. For instance, the vector for INT_{50} would be read from addresses $000C8_{16}$ and $000CA_{16}$.

The service routine is now initiated. That is, execution resumes with the first instruction of the service routine. It is located at the address generated from the new value in the CS and IP. Figure 7.8 shows the structure of a typical interrupt service routine. The service routine must include PUSH instructions to save the contents of those internal registers that it will use. In this way, their original contents are saved in the stack during execution of the routine.

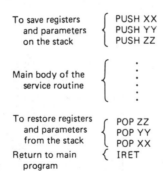

Figure 7.8 Structure of an interrupt service routine.

At the end of the service routine, the original program environment must be restored. This is done by first popping the contents of the appropriate registers from the stack by executing POP instructions. Then an IRET instruction must be executed as the last instruction of the service routine. This instruction causes the old contents of the flags, CS, and IP to be popped from the stack back into the internal registers of the 8086. The original program environment has now been completely restored and execution resumes at the point in the program where it was interrupted.

7.8 8259A PROGRAMMABLE INTERRUPT CONTROLLER

The 8259A is an LSI peripheral IC that is designed to simplify the implementation of the interrupt interface in an 8086 system. This device is known as a *programmable interrupt controller* or *PIC*. It is manufactured using the NMOS technology.

The operation of the PIC is programmable under software control and it can be configured for a wide variety of applications. Some of its programmable features are the ability to accept level-sensitive or edge-triggered inputs, the ability to be easily cascaded to expand from 8 to 64 interrupt inputs, and its ability to be configured to implement a wide variety of priority schemes.

Block Diagram of the 8259A

Let us begin our study of the PIC with its block diagram in Fig. 7.9(a). We just mentioned that the 8259A is treated as a peripheral in the 8086 microcomputer. Therefore, its operation must be initialized by the 8086 processor. The *host processor interface* is provided for this purpose. This interface consists of eight *data bus* lines D_0 through D_7 and control signals *read* ($\overline{RD}$, *write* ($\overline{WR}$), and *chip select* ($\overline{CS}$).

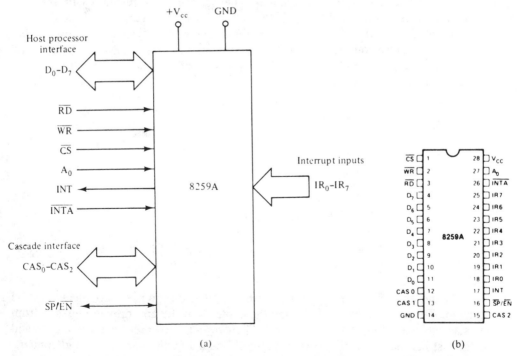

Figure 7.9   (a) Block diagram of the 8259A; (b) pin layout. (Reprinted by permission of Intel Corp. Copyright/Intel Corp., 1979.)

The data bus is the path over which data are transferred between the 8086 and 8259A. These data can be command words, status information, or interrupt type numbers. Control input $\overline{CS}$ must be at logic 0 to enable the host processor interface. Moreover, $\overline{WR}$ and $\overline{RD}$ signal the 8259A whether data are to be written into or read from its internal registers. They also control the timing of these data transfers.

Two other signals are identified as part of the host processor interface. They are INT and $\overline{INTA}$. Together, these two signals provide the handshake mechanism by which the 8259A can signal the 8086 of a request for service and receive an acknowledgment that the request has been accepted. INT is the interrupt request output of the 8259A. It is applied directly to the INTR input of the 8086. Logic 1 is produced at this output whenever the 8259A receives a valid interrupt request.

On the other hand, $\overline{INTA}$ is an input of the 8259A. It is connected to the $\overline{INTA}$ output of the 8086. The 8086 pulses this input of the 8259A to logic 0 twice during the interrupt acknowledge bus cycle, thereby signaling the 8259A that the interrupt request has been acknowledged and that it should output the type number of the highest-priority active interrupt on data bus lines D_0 through D_7 such that it can be read by the 8086. The last signal line involved in the host processor interface is the A_0 input. This input is normally supplied by an address line of the 8086 such as A_0. The logic level at this input is involved in the selection of the internal register that is accessed during read and write operations.

At the other side of the block in Fig. 7.9(a), we find the eight *interrupt inputs* of the PIC. They are labeled IR_0 through IR_7. It is through these inputs that external devices issue a request for service. One of the software options of the 8259A permits these inputs to be configured for *level-sensitive* or *edge-triggered operation*. When configured for level-sensitive operation, logic 1 is the active level of the IR inputs. In this case, the request for service must be removed before the service routine runs to completion. Otherwise, the interrupt will be requested a second time and the service routine initiated again. Moreover, if the input returns to logic 0 before it is acknowledged by the 8086, the request for service will be missed.

Some external devices produce a short-duration pulse instead of a fixed logic level for use as an interrupt request signal. If the 8086 is busy servicing a higher-priority interrupt when the pulse is produced, the request for service could be completely missed. To overcome this problem, the edge-triggered mode of operation is used.

Inputs of the 8259A that are set up for edge-triggered operation become active on the transition from the inactive 0 logic level to the active 1 logic level. This represents what is known as a *positive edge-triggered input*. The fact that this transition has occurred at an IR line is latched internal to the 8259A. If the IR input remains at the 1 logic level even after the service routine is completed, the interrupt is not reinitiated. Instead, it is locked out. To be recognized a second time, the input must first return to the 0 logic level and then be switched back to 1. The advantage of edge-triggered operation is that if the request at the IR input is removed before the 8086 acknowledges service of the interrupt, its request is maintained latched internal to the 8259A until it can be serviced.

The last group of signals on the PIC implement what is known as the *cascade interface*. As shown in Fig. 7.9(a), it includes bidirectional *cascading bus lines*

CAS_0 through CAS_2 and a multifunction control line labeled $\overline{SP}/\overline{EN}$. The primary use of these signals is in cascaded systems where a number of 8259A ICs are interconnected in a master/slave configuration to expand the number of IR inputs from 8 to as high as 64.

In a cascaded system, the CAS lines of all 8259As are connected together to provide a private bus between the master and slave devices. In response to the first $\overline{INTA}$ pulse during the interrupt acknowledge bus cycle, the master PIC outputs a 3-bit code on the CAS lines. This code identifies the highest-priority slave that is to be serviced. It is this device that is to be acknowledged for service. All slaves read this code off the *private cascading bus* and compare it to their internal ID code. A match condition at one slave tells that PIC that it has the highest-priority input. In response, it must put the type number of its highest-priority active input on the data bus during the second interrupt acknowledge bus cycle.

When the PIC is configured through software for the cascaded mode, the $\overline{SP}/\overline{EN}$ line is used as an input. This corresponds to its $\overline{SP}$ (*slave program*) function. The logic level applied at $\overline{SP}$ tells the device whether it is to operate as a master or slave. Logic 1 at this input designates master mode and logic 0 designates slave mode.

If the PIC is configured for single mode instead of cascade mode, $\overline{SP}/\overline{EN}$ takes on another function. In this case, it becomes an enable output which can be used to control the direction of data transfer through the bus transceiver that buffers the data bus.

A pin layout of the 8259A is given in Fig. 7.9(b).

Internal Architecture of the 8259A

Now that we have introduced the input/output signals of the 8259A, let us look at its internal architecture. Figure 7.10 is a block diagram of the PIC's internal circuitry. Here we find eight functional parts: the *data bus buffer, read/write logic, control logic, in-service register, interrupt request register, priority resolver, interrupt mask register,* and *cascade buffer/comparator.*

We will begin with the function of the data bus buffer and read/write logic sections. It is these parts of the 8259A that let the 8086 have access to the internal registers. Moreover, it provides the path over which interrupt type numbers are passed to the 8086. The data bus buffer is an 8-bit bidirectional three-state buffer that interfaces the internal circuitry of the 8259A to the data bus of the 8086. The direction, timing, and source or destination for data transfers through the buffer are under control of the outputs of the read/write logic block. These outputs are generated in response to control inputs $\overline{RD}$, $\overline{WR}$, A_0, and $\overline{CS}$.

The interrupt request register, in-service register, priority resolver, and interrupt mask register are the key internal blocks of the 8259A. The interrupt mask register (IMR) can be used to enable or mask out individually the interrupt request inputs. It contains 8 bits identified by M_0 through M_7. These bits correspond to interrupt inputs IR_0 through IR_7, respectively. Logic 0 in a mask register bit position enables the corresponding interrupt input and logic 1 masks it out. This register can be read from or written into under software control.

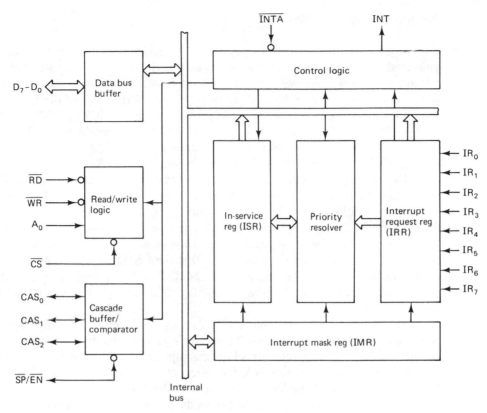

Figure 7.10 Internal architecture of the 8259A. (Reprinted by permission of Intel Corp. Copyright/Intel Corp., 1979.)

On the other hand, the interrupt request register (IRR) stores the correct status of the interrupt request inputs. It also contains one bit position for each of the IR inputs. The values in these bit positions reflect whether the interrupt inputs are active or inactive.

Which of the active interrupt inputs is identified as having the highest priority is determined by the priority resolver. This section can be configured to work using a number of different priority schemes through software. Following this scheme, it identifies the highest priority of the active interrupt inputs and signals the control logic that an interrupt is active. In response, the control logic causes the INT signal to be issued to the 8086.

The in-service register differs in that it stores the interrupt level that is presently being serviced. During the first $\overline{\text{INTA}}$ pulse in an interrupt acknowledge bus cycle, the level of the highest priority active interrupt is strobed into ISR. Loading of ISR occurs in response to output signals of the control logic section. This register cannot be written into by the microprocessor; however, its contents may be read as status.

The cascade buffer/comparator section provides the interface between master and slave 8259As. As we mentioned earlier, it is this interface that permits easy expansion of the interrupt interface using a master/slave configuration. Each slave has an *ID code* that is stored in this section.

Programming the 8259A

The way in which the 8259A operates is determined by how the device is programmed. Two types of command words are provided for this purpose. They are the *initialization command words* (ICW) and the *operational command words* (OCW). ICW commands are used to load the internal control registers of the 8259A. There are four such command words and they are identified as ICW_1, ICW_2, ICW_3, and ICW_4. On the other hand, the three OCW commands permit the 8086 to initiate variations in the basic operating modes defined by the ICW commands. These three commands are called OCW_1, OCW_2, and OCW_3.

Depending on whether the 8259A is I/O mapped or memory mapped, the 8086 issues commands to the 8259A by initiating output or write cycles. This can be done by executing either the OUT or MOV instruction, respectively. The address put on the system bus during the output bus cycle must be decoded with external circuitry to chip select the peripheral. When an address assigned to the 8259A is on the bus, the output of the decoder must produce logic 0 at the $\overline{CS}$ input. This signal enables the read/write logic within the PIC and data applied at D_0 through D_7 are written into the command register within the control logic section synchronously with a write strobe at $\overline{WR}$.

The interrupt request input (INTR) of the 8086 must be disabled whenever commands are being issued to the 8259A. This can be done by clearing the interrupt enable flag by executing the CLI (clear interrupt enable flag) instruction. After completion of the command sequence, the interrupt input can be reenabled. To do this, the 8086 must execute the STI (set interrupt enable flag) instruction.

The flow diagram in Fig. 7.11 shows the sequence of events that the 8086 must

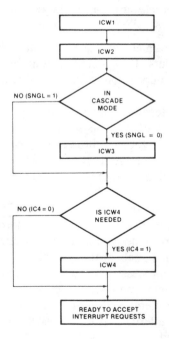

Figure 7.11 Initialization sequence of the 8259A. (Reprinted by permission of Intel Corp. Copyright/Intel Corp., 1979.)

perform to initialize the 8259A with ICW commands. The cycle begins with the 8086 outputting initialization command word ICW_1 to the address of the 8259A.

The moment that ICW_1 is written into the control logic section of the 8259A certain internal setup conditions automatically occur. First the internal sequence logic is set up such that the 8259A will accept the remaining ICWs as designated by ICW_1. It turns out that, if the least significant bit of ICW_1 is logic 1, command word ICW_4 is required in the initialization sequence. Moreover, if the next least significant bit of ICW_1 is logic 0, the command word ICW_3 is also required.

In addition to this, writing ICW_1 to the 8259A clears ISR and IMR. Also three operation command word bits, *special mask mode* (SMM) in OCW_3, *interrupt request register* (IRR) in OCW_3, and *end of interrupt* (EOI) in OCW_2, are cleared to logic 0. Furthermore, the *fully masked mode* of interrupt operation is entered with an initial priority assignment such that IR_0 is the highest-priority input and IR_7 the lowest-priority input. Finally, the edge-sensitive latches associated with the IR inputs are all cleared.

If the LSB of ICW_1 was initialized to logic 0, one additional event occurs. This is that all bits of the control register associated with ICW_4 are cleared.

In Fig. 7.11 we see that once the 8086 starts initialization of the 8259A by writing ICW_1 into the control register, it must continue the sequence by writing ICW_2 and then optionally ICW_3 and ICW_4 in that order. Notice that it is not possible to modify just one of the initialization command registers. Instead, all words that are required to define the device's operating mode must be output once again.

We found that all four words need not always be used to initialize the 8259A. However, for its use in the 8086 system, words ICW_1, ICW_2, and ICW_4 are always required. ICW_3 is optional and is needed only if the 8259A is to function in the cascade mode.

Initialization Command Words

Now that we have introduced the initialization sequence of the 8259A, let us look more closely at the functions controlled by each of the initialization command words. We will begin with ICW_1. Its format and bit functions are identified in Fig. 7.12(a). Notice that address bit A_0 is included as a ninth bit and it must be logic 0. This corresponds to an even address boundary.

Here we find that the logic level of the LSB D_0 of the initialization word indicates to the 8259A whether or not ICW_4 will be included in the programming sequence. As we mentioned earlier, logic 1 at D_0 (IC_4) specifies that it is needed. The next bit, D_1 (SNGL), selects between *single device* or *multidevice cascaded mode* of operation. When D_1 is set to logic 0, the internal circuitry of the 8259A is configured for cascade mode. Selecting this state also sets up the initialization sequence such that ICW_3 must be issued as part of the initialization cycle. Bit D_2 specifies address interval for the 8080/85 mode. However, it can be ignored when the 8259A is being connected to the 8086 and is a don't-care state. D_3, which is labeled LTIM, defines whether the eight IR inputs operate in the level-sensitive or edge-triggered mode. Logic 1 in D_3 selects level-triggered operation and logic 0 selects edge-triggered

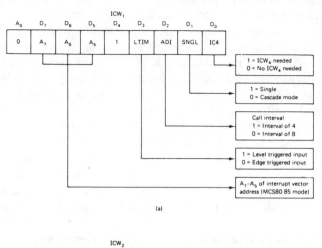

(a)

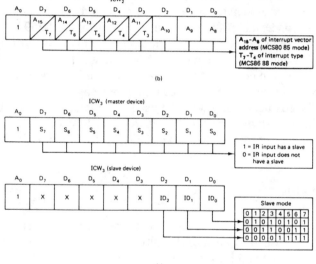

(b)

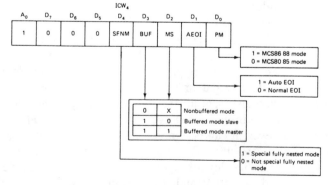

Figure 7.12 (a) ICW_1 format (reprinted by permission of Intel Corp. Copyright/Intel Corp., 1979); (b) ICW_2 format (reprinted by permission of Intel Corp. Copyright/Intel Corp., 1979); (c) ICW_3 format (reprinted by permission of Intel Corp. Copyright/Intel Corp., 1979); (d) ICW_4 format (reprinted by permission of Intel Corp. Copyright/Intel Corp., 1979).

operation. Finally, bit D_4 is fixed at the 1 logic level and the three MSBs D_5 through D_7 are not required in 8086-based microcomputer systems.

EXAMPLE 7.2

What value should be written into ICW_1 in order to configure the 8259A such that ICW_4 is needed in the initialization sequence, the system is going to use multiple 8259As, and its inputs are to be level sensitive? Assume that all unused bits are to be logic 0. Give the result in both binary and hexadecimal form.

SOLUTION   Since ICW_4 is to be initialized, D_0 must be logic 1.

$$D_0 = 1$$

For cascaded mode of operation, D_1 must be 0,

$$D_1 = 0$$

and for level-sensitive inputs D_3 must be 1.

$$D_3 = 1$$

Bits D_2 and D_5 through D_7 are don't care states and are all made logic 0.

$$D_2 = D_5 = D_6 = D_7 = 0$$

Moreover, D_4 must be fixed at the 1 logic level.

$$D_4 = 1$$

This gives the complete command word

$$D_7 D_6 D_5 D_4 D_3 D_2 D_1 D_0 = 00011001_2 = 19_{16}$$

The second initialization word, ICW_2, has a single function in the 8086 microcomputer. As shown in Fig. 7.12(b), its five most significant bits D_7 through D_3 define a fixed binary code T_7 through T_3 that is used as the most significant bits of its type number. Whenever the 8259A puts the 3-bit interrupt type number corresponding to its active input onto the bus, it is automatically combined with the value T_7 through T_3 to form an 8-bit type number. The three least significant bits of ICW_2 are not used. Notice that logic 1 must be output on A_0 when this command word is put on the bus.

EXAMPLE 7.3

What should be programmed into register ICW_2 if the type numbers output on the bus by the device are to range from $F0_{16}$ through $F7_{16}$?

SOLUTION   To set the 8259A up such that type numbers are in the range $F0_{16}$ through $F7_{16}$, its device code bits must be

$$D_7 D_6 D_5 D_4 D_3 = 11110_2$$

The lower 3 bits are don't-care states and all can be 0s. This gives the command word

$$D_7 D_6 D_5 D_4 D_3 D_2 D_1 D_0 = 11110000_2 = F0_{16}$$

The information of initialization word ICW_3 is required by only those 8259As that are configured for the cascaded mode of operation. Figure 7.12(c) shows its bits. Notice that ICW_3 is used for different functions depending on whether the device is a master or slave. In the case of a master, bits D_0 through D_7 of the word are labeled S_0 through S_7. These bits correspond to IR inputs IR_0 through IR_7, respectively. They identify whether or not the corresponding IR input is supplied by either the INT output of a slave or directly by an external device. Logic 1 loaded in an S position indicates that the corresponding IR input is supplied by a slave.

On the other hand, ICW_3 for a slave is used to load the device with a 3-bit identification code $ID_2 ID_1 ID_0$. This number must correspond to the IR input of the master to which the slave's INT output is wired. The ID code is required within the slave so that it can be compared to the cascading code output by the master on CAS_0 through CAS_2.

EXAMPLE 7.4

Assume that a master PIC is to be configured such that its IR_0 through IR_3 inputs are to accept inputs directly from external devices but IR_4 through IR_7 are to be supplied by the INT outputs of slaves. What code should be used for the initialization command word ICW_3?

SOLUTION For IR_0 through IR_3 to be configured to allow direct inputs from external devices, bits D_0 through D_3 of ICW_3 must be logic 0.

$$D_3 D_2 D_1 D_0 = 0000_2$$

The other IR inputs of the master are to be supplied by INT outputs of slaves. Therefore, their control bits must be all 1.

$$D_7 D_6 D_5 D_4 = 1111_2$$

This gives the complete command word

$$D_7 D_6 D_5 D_4 D_3 D_2 D_1 D_0 = 11110000_2 = F0_{16}$$

The fourth control word, ICW_4, which is shown in Fig. 7.12(d), is used to configure the device for use with the 8086 and selects various features that are available in its operation. The LSB D_0, which is called microprocessor mode (μPM), must be set to logic 1 whenever the device used is connected to the 8086. The next bit, D_1, is labeled AEOI for *automatic end of interrupt*. If this mode is enabled by writing logic 1 into the bit location, the EOI (*end of interrupt*) command does not have to be issued as part of the service routine.

Of the next 2 bits in ICW_4, BUF is used to specify whether or not the 8259A is to be used in a system where the data bus is buffered with a bidirectional bus transceiver. When buffered mode is selected, the $\overline{SP}/\overline{EN}$ line is configured as $\overline{EN}$. As indicated earlier, $\overline{EN}$ is a control output that can be used to control the direction of data transfer through the bus transceiver. It switches to logic 0 whenever data are transferred from the 8259A to the 8086.

If buffered mode is not selected, the $\overline{SP}/\overline{EN}$ line is configured to work as the master/slave mode select input. In this case, logic 1 at the $\overline{SP}$ input selects master mode operation and logic 0 selects slave mode.

Assume that the buffered mode was selected; then the $\overline{SP}$ input is no longer available to select between the master and slave modes of operation. Instead, the MS bit of ICW_4 defines whether the 8259A is a master or slave device.

Bit D_4 is used to enable or disable another operational option of the 8259A. This option is known as the *special fully nested mode*. This function is only used in conjunction with the cascaded mode. Moreover, it is enabled only for the master 8259A, not for the slaves. This is done by setting the SFNM bit to logic 1.

The 8259A is put into the fully nested mode of operation as command word ICW_4 is loaded. When an interrupt is initiated in a cascaded system that is configured in this way, the occurrence of another interrupt at the slave corresponding to the original interrupt is masked out even if it is of higher priority. This is because the bit in ISR of the master 8259A that corresponds to the slave is already set; therefore, the master 8259A ignores all interrupts of equal or lower priority.

This problem is overcome by enabling special fully nested mode of operation at the master. In this mode, the master will respond to those interrupts that are at lower or higher priority than the active level.

The last three bits of ICW_4, D_5 through D_7, must always be logic 0 and the word must be written to an odd-address boundary.

Operational Command Words

Once the appropriate ICW commands have been issued to the 8259A, it is ready to operate in the programmed mode. Three operational command words are also provided for controlling the operation of the 8259A. These commands permit further modifications to be made to the operation of the interrupt interface after it has been initialized. Unlike the initialization sequence, which requires that the ICWs be output in a special sequence after power-up, the OCWs can be issued under program control whenever needed and in any order.

The first operational command word, OCW_1, is used to access the contents of the interrupt mask register (IMR). A read operation can be performed to the register to determine its present status. Moreover, write operations can be performed to set or reset its bits. This permits selective masking of the interrupt inputs. Notice in Fig. 7.13(a) that bits D_0 through D_7 of command word OCW_1 are identified as mask bits M_0 through M_7, respectively. In hardware, these bits correspond to interrupt inputs IR_0 through IR_7, respectively. Setting a bit to logic 1 masks out the associated interrupt input. On the other hand, clearing it to logic 0 enables the interrupt input.

For instance, writing $F0_{16} = 11110000_2$ into the register causes inputs IR_0 through IR_3 to be enabled and IR_4 through IR_7 to be disabled. Input A_0 must be logic 1 whenever the OCW_1 command is issued.

EXAMPLE 7.5

What should be the OCW_1 code if interrupt inputs IR_0 through IR_3 are to be disabled and IR_4 through IR_7 enabled?

SOLUTION For IR_0 through IR_3 to be disabled, their corresponding bits in the mask register must be made logic 1.

The second operational command word OCW_2 selects the appropriate priority scheme and assigns an IR level for those schemes that require a specific interrupt level. The format of OCW_2 is given in Fig. 7.13(b). Here we see that the three LSBs define the interrupt level. For example, using $L_2L_1L_0 = 000_2$ in these locations specifies interrupt level 0, which corresponds to input IR_0.

The other three active bits of the word D_7, D_6, and D_5 are called *rotation* (R), *specific level* (SL), and *end of interrupt* (EOI), respectively. They are used to select a priority scheme according to the table in Fig. 7.13(b). For instance, if these bits are all logic 1, the priority scheme known as *rotate on specific EOI command* is enabled. Since this scheme requires a specific interrupt, its value must be included in $L_2L_1L_0$. A_0 must be logic 0 whenever this command is issued to the 8259A.

EXAMPLE 7.6

What OCW_2 must be issued to the 8259A if the priority scheme rotate on nonspecific EOI command is to be selected?

SOLUTION To enable the rotate on nonspecific EOI command priority scheme, bits D_7 through D_5 must be set to 101. Since a specific level does not have to be specified, the rest of the bits in the command word can be 0. This gives OCW_2 as

$$D_7D_6D_5D_4D_3D_2D_1D_0 = 10100000_2 = A0_{16}$$

The last control word OCW_3, which is shown in Fig. 7.13(c), permits reading of the contents of the ISR or IRR registers through software, issue of the poll command, and enable/disable of the special mask mode. Bit D_1, which is called *read register* (RR), is set to 1 to initiate reading of either the in-service register (ISR) or interrupt request register (IRR). At the same time, bit D_0, which is labeled RIS, selects between ISR and IRR. Logic 0 in RIS selects IRR and logic 1 selects ISR. In response to this command, the 8259A puts the contents of the selected register on the bus, where it can be read by the 8086.

If the next bit, D_2, in OCW_3 is logic 1, a *poll command* is issued to the 8259A. The result of issuing a poll command is that the next $\overline{RD}$ pulse to the 8259A is interpreted as an interrupt acknowledge. In turn, the 8259A causes the ISR register to be loaded with the value of the highest-priority active interrupt. After this, a *poll word* is automatically put on the data bus. The 8086 must read it off the bus.

Figure 7.14 illustrates the format of the poll word. Looking at this word, we see that the MSB is labeled 1 for interrupt. The logic level of this bit indicates to the 8086 whether or not an interrupt input was active. Logic 1 indicates that an interrupt is active. The three LSBs $W_2 W_1 W_0$ identify the priority level of the highest-priority

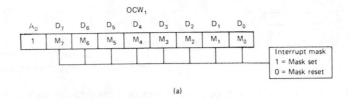

(a)

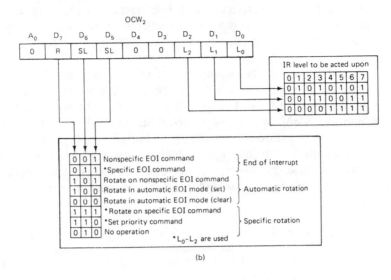

(b)

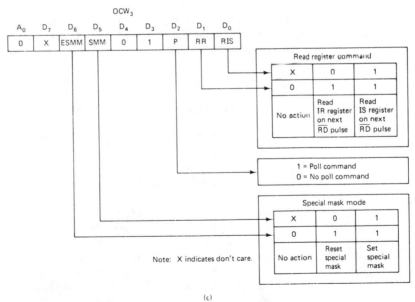

Note: X indicates don't care.

(c)

Figure 7.13 (a) OCW$_1$ format (reprinted by permission of Intel Corp. Copyright/ Intel Corp., 1979); (b) OCW$_2$ format (reprinted by permission of Intel Corp. Copyright/Intel Corp., 1979); (c) OCW$_3$ format (reprinted by permission of Intel Corp. Copyright/Intel Corp., 1979).

Sec. 7.8   8259A Programmable Interrupt Controller

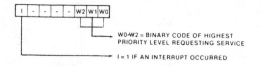

W0-W2 = BINARY CODE OF HIGHEST
PRIORITY LEVEL REQUESTING SERVICE

I = 1 IF AN INTERRUPT OCCURRED

Figure 7.14 Poll word format. (Reprinted by permission of Intel Corp. Copyright/Intel Corp., 1979.)

active interrupt input. This poll word can be decoded through software and when an interrupt is found to be active a branch is initiated to the starting point of its service routine. The poll command represents a software method of identifying whether or not an interrupt has occurred; therefore, the INTR input of the 8086 should be disabled.

D_5 and D_6 are the remaining bits of OCW_3 for which functions are defined. They are used to enable or disable the special mask mode. ESMM (*enable special mask mode*) must be logic 1 to permit changing of the status of the special mask mode with the SMM (*special mask mode*) bit. Logic 1 at SMM enables the special mask mode of operation. If the 8259A is initially configured for the fully nested mode of operation, only interrupts of higher priority are allowed to interrupt an active service routine. However, by enabling the special mask mode, interrupts of higher or lower priority are enabled, but those of equal priority remain masked out.

EXAMPLE 7.7

Write a program that will initialize an 8259A with the initialization command words ICW_1, ICW_2, and ICW_3 derived in Examples 7.2, 7.3, and 7.4, respectively. Moreover, ICW_4 is to be equal to $1F_{16}$. Assume that the 8259A resides at address $0A000_{16}$ in the memory address space.

SOLUTION Since the 8259A resides in the memory address space, we can use a series of move instructions to write the initialization command words into its registers. However, before doing this, we must first disable interrupts. This is done with the instruction

```
        CLI                     ;Disable  interrupts
```

Next we will set up a data segment starting at address 00000_{16}.

```
        MOV    AX, 0            ; Create a data segment at 0000₁₆
        MOV    DS, AX
```

Now we are ready to write the command words to the 8259A.

```
        MOV    AL, 19           ; Load ICW 1
        MOV    [A000] , AL      ; Write ICW 1 to 8259A
        MOV    AL, F0           ; Load ICW 2
        MOV    [A001] , AL      ; Write ICW 2 to 8259A
        MOV    AL, F0           ; Load ICW 3
        MOV    [A001] , AL      ; Write ICW 3 to 8259A
        MOV    AL, 1F           ; Load ICW 4
        MOV    [A001] , AL      ; Write ICW 4 to 8259A
```

Initialization is now complete and the interrupts can be enabled.

```
        STI                     ; Enable interrupts
```

7.9 MINIMUM-MODE SYSTEM AND MAXIMUM-MODE SYSTEM INTERRUPT INTERFACES USING THE 8259A

Now that we have introduced the 8259A programmable interrupt controller, let us look at how it is used to implement the interrupt interface in the 8086 microcomputer system. The circuit in Fig.7.15 shows three 8259A devices connected in a *master/ slave configuration* to construct an interrupt interface for a minimum-mode 8086 microcomputer system.

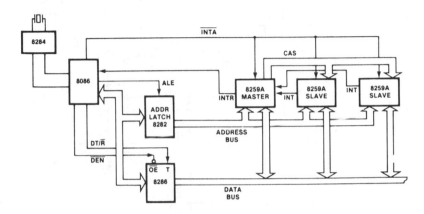

Figure 7.15 Minimum-mode interrupt interface using the 8259A. (Reprinted by permission of Intel Corp. Copyright/Intel Corp., 1979.)

Let us begin by tracing the path taken from the interrupt request inputs of the slaves to the interrupt request input of the 8086. A request for interrupt service is initiated at an IR input of a slave. This causes the INT output of the corresponding slave to switch to logic 1. Looking at the circuit, we see that the INT output of the slave PICs are applied to separate interrupt inputs on the master PIC. Then the INT output of the master is supplied directly to the interrupt request input of the 8086.

Notice that the demultiplexed address bus and data bus lines connect to all three 8259As in parallel. It is over these lines that the 8086 initializes the internal registers of the 8259As, reads the contents of these registers, and reads the type number of the active interrupt during the interrupt acknowledge bus cycle. Each 8259A should reside at a unique address. In this way, during read or write cycles to the interrupt interface, the address output on the bus can be decoded to produce an enable signal to chip-select the appropriate device.

The last group of signals in the interrupt interface are the CAS bus. Notice that these lines on all three PICs are connected in parallel. It is over these lines that the master signals the slaves whether or not the interrupt request has been acknowledged. The master/slave connection is shown in more detail in Fig. 7.16.

Whenever an interrupt input is active at the master or at slave and the priority is higher than that of an already active interrupt, the master controller switches INTR to logic 1. This signals the 8086 that an external device needs to be serviced. As long as

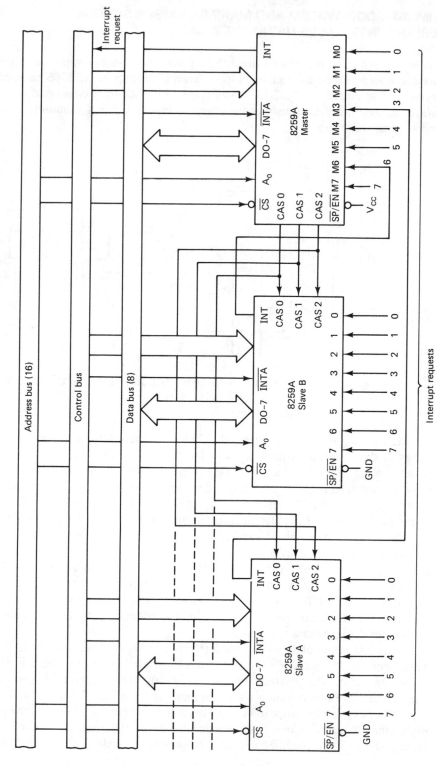

Figure 7.16 Master/slave connection. (Reprinted by permission of Intel Corp. Copyright/Intel Corp., 1979.)

the interrupt flag within the 8086 is set to 1, the interrupt interface is enabled and the interrupt request will be accepted. Therefore, the interrupt acknowledge bus cycle is initiated. As the first pulse is output at interrupt acknowledge ($\overline{\text{INTA}}$), the master PIC is signaled to output the 3-bit cascade code of the device whose interrupt request is being acknowledged on the CAS bus. The slaves read this code and compare it to their internal code. In this way, the slave corresponding to the code is signaled to output the type number of its highest-priority active interrupt onto the data bus during the second interrupt acknowledge bus cycle. The 8086 reads this number off the bus and then initiates a vectored transfer of control to the starting point of the corresponding service routine in program memory.

Figure 7.17 illustrates a similar interrupt interface implemented in a maximum-mode 8086 microcomputer system.

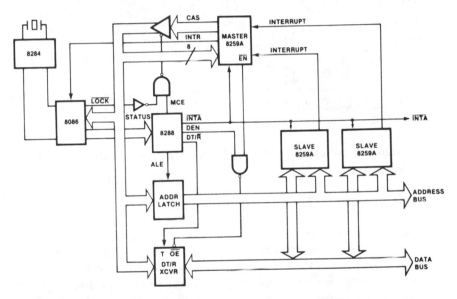

Figure 7.17 Maximum-mode interrupt interface using the 8259A. (Reprinted by permission of Intel Corp. Copyright/Intel Corp., 1979.)

7.10 INTERNAL INTERRUPT FUNCTIONS

Earlier we indicated that the first 32 of the 256 interrupts of the 8086 are reserved. Four of them are dedicated to the 8086's internal functions: divide error, overflow error, single step, and breakpoint. They are assigned unique type numbers, as shown in Fig. 7.18. Notice that they are the highest-priority type numbers. Moreover, in Fig. 7.6 we find that they are not masked out with the interrupt enable flag.

The occurrence of any one of these internal conditions is automatically detected by the 8086 and causes an interrupt of program execution and a vectored transfer of control to a corresponding service routine. During the control transfer sequence, no

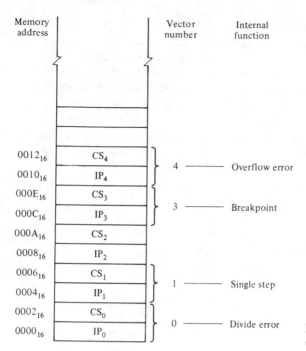

Figure 7.18 Internal interrupt vector locations.

external bus cycles are produced. Let us now look at each of these internal functions in more detail.

Divide Error

The *divide error* function represents an error condition that can occur in the execution of the division instructions. If the quotient that results from a DIV (divide) instruction or an IDIV (integer divide) instruction is larger than the specified destination, a divide error has occurred. This condition causes automatic initiation of a type 0 interrupt and passes control to a service routine whose starting point is defined by the values of IP_0 and CS_0 at addresses 0000_{16} and 0002_{16}, respectively, in the pointer table.

Overflow Error

The *overflow error* is an error condition similar to that of divide error. However, it can result from the execution of any arithmetic instruction. Whenever an overflow occurs, the overflow flag gets set. In this case, the transfer of program control to a service routine is not automatic at occurrence of the overflow condition. Instead, the INTO (interrupt on overflow) instruction must be executed to test the overflow flag and determine if the overflow service routine should be initiated. If the overflow flag is found to be set, a type 4 interrupt service routine is initiated. Its vector consists of IP_4 and CS_4, which are stored at 0010_{16} and 0012_{16}, respectively, in memory. The routine pointed to by this vector can be written to service the overflow condition. For instance, it could cause a message to be displayed to identify that an overflow has occurred.

Single Step

The *single-step* function relates to an operating option of the 8086. If the trap flag (TF) bit is set, the single-step mode of operation is enabled. This flag can be set or reset under software control.

When TF is set, the 8086 initiates a type 1 interrupt to the service routine defined by IP_1 and CS_1 at 0004_{16} and 0006_{16}, respectively, at the completion of execution of every instruction. This permits implementation of the single-step mode of operation such that the program can be executed one instruction at a time. For instance, the service routine could include a WAIT instruction. In this way, a transition to logic 0 at the $\overline{TEST}$ input of the 8086 could be used as the mechanism for stepping through a program one instruction at a time. This single-step operation can be used as a valuable software debugging tool.

Breakpoint Interrupt

The *breakpoint* function can also be used to implement a software diagnostic tool. A breakpoint interrupt is initiated by execution of the breakpoint instruction (*one-byte instruction*). This instruction can be inserted at strategic points in a program that is being debugged to cause execution to be stopped. This option can be used in a way similar to that of the single-step option. The service routine could again be put in the wait state, and resumption of execution down to the next breakpoint can be initiated by applying logic 0 to the $\overline{TEST}$ input.

ASSIGNMENT

Section 7.2

1. What are the five groups of interrupts supported on the 8086 MPU?
2. What name is given to the special software routine to which control is passed when an interrupt occurs?
3. List in order the interrupt groups; start with the lowest priority and end with the highest priority.
4. What is the range of type numbers assigned to the interrupts in the 8086 microcomputer system?
5. Is the interrupt assigned to type 21 at a higher or lower priority than the interrupt assigned to type 35?

Section 7.3

6. Where are the interrupt pointers held?
7. How many bytes of memory does an interrupt vector take up?

8. What two elements make up an interrupt vector?

9. Which interrupt function's service routine is specified by $CS_4:IP_4$?

10. The breakpoint routine in an 8086 microcomputer system starts at address $AA000_{16}$ in the code segment located at address $A0000_{16}$. Specify how the breakpoint vector will be stored in the interrupt vector table.

11. At what addresses is the interrupt vector for type 40 stored in memory?

Section 7.4

12. What does STI stand for?

13. Which type of instruction does INTO normally follow? Which flag does it test?

14. What happens when the instruction HLT is executed?

Section 7.5

15. Explain how the CLI and STI instructions can be used to mask out external hardware interrupts during the execution of an uninterruptible subroutine.

16. How can the interrupt interface be reenabled during the execution of an interrupt service routine?

Section 7.6

17. Explain the function of the INTR and $\overline{\text{INTA}}$ signals in the circuit diagram of Fig. 7.4.

18. Which device produces $\overline{\text{INTA}}$ in a minimum-mode system? In a maximum-mode system?

19. Over which data bus lines does external circuitry send the type number of the active interrupt to the 8086?

20. What bus status code is assigned to interrupt acknowledge?

Section 7.7

21. Give an overview of the events in the order they take place during the interrupt request, interrupt acknowledge, and interrupt vector-fetch cycles of an 8086 microcomputer system.

22. If an 8086-based microcomputer is running 10 MHz with two wait states, how long does it take to perform the interrupt-acknowledge bus cycle sequence?

23. How long does it take the 8086 in Problem 22 to push the values of the flags, CS and IP, to the stack? How much stack space do these values use?

24. How long does it take the 8086 in Problem 22 to fetch its vector from memory?

Section 7.8

25. Specify the value of ICW_1 needed to configure an 8259A as follows: ICW_4 not needed, single-device interface, and edge-triggered inputs.

26. Specify the value of ICW_2 if the type numbers produced by the 8259A are to be in the range 70_{16} through 77_{16}.

27. Specify the value of ICW_4 such that the 8259A is configured for use in an 8086 system, with normal EOI, buffered-mode master, and special fully nested mode disabled.

28. Write a program that will initialize an 8259A with the initialization command words derived in Problems 25, 26, and 27. Assume that the 8259A resides at address $0A000_{16}$ in the memory address space.

29. Write an instruction that when executed will read the contents of OCW_1 and place it in the AL register. Assume that the 8259A has been configured by the software of Problem 28.

30. What priority scheme is enabled if OCW_2 equals 67_{16}?

31. Write an instruction sequence that when executed will toggle the state of the read register bit in OCW_3. Assume that the 8259A is located at memory address $0A000_{16}$.

Section 7.9

32. How many interrupt inputs can be directly accepted by the circuit in Fig. 7.15?

33. How many interrupt inputs can be directly accepted by the circuit in Fig. 7.17?

34. Summarize the interrupt request/acknowledge handshake sequence for an interrupt initiated at an input to slave B in the circuit of Fig. 7.17.

Section 7.10

35. List the internal interrupts serviced by the 8086.

36. Which vector numbers are reserved for internal interrupts?

8

Software Architecture of the 80386 Microprocessor

8.1 INTRODUCTION

In this chapter, we study the software architecture of the 80386 microprocessor and its assembly language instruction set. The 80386 supports three modes of operation called the *real-address mode* (real mode), the *protected-address mode* (protected mode), and *virtual 86 mode*. Here we will first examine the real-address-mode software architecture and its extended instruction set. This material is followed by a detailed study of the 80386's protected-address mode of operation and system control instruction set. The chapter ends with a description of the virtual 86 mode. The following topics are covered in the chapter.

1. Real-address-mode software model
2. Real-address-mode instruction set
3. Protected-address-mode software architecture
4. Descriptor and page table entries
5. Protected-mode system control instruction set
6. Multitasking and protection
7. Virtual 86 mode

8.2 REAL-ADDRESS-MODE SOFTWARE MODEL

We will begin our study of the 80386 microprocessor by exploring its real-address-mode software model and operation. Whenever the 80386 is reset, it comes up in the real mode. The 80386 will remain in the real mode unless it is switched to protected mode under software control. In fact, in many applications it is simply used in real mode.

In real mode, the 80386 operates like a very high performance 8086. For example, the standard 16-MHz 80386 provides more than 10 times higher performance than the standard 5-MHz 8086.

When in the real mode, the 80386 can be used to execute the base instruction set of the 8086/8088 architecture. Object code for the base instructions of the 80386 is identical to that of the 8086/8088. This means that operating systems and programs written for the 8086 and 8088 can be run directly on the 80386 without modification. For this reason, we can say that the 80386 is *object code compatible* with the 8086 and 8088 microprocessors.

A number of new instructions have been added to the instruction set of the 80386 to enhance performance and functionality. For example, instructions have been added to push or pop the complete register set, perform string input/output, and check the boundaries of data array accesses. We also say that object code is *upward compatible* within the 8086 architecture. By this, we mean that 8086/8088 object code will run on the 80386. Of course, the reverse is not true if any of the new instructions are in use.

The real-mode software model of the 80386 is shown in Fig. 8.1. Here we have highlighted the 17 internal registers that are used in real-mode application programming. Nine of them, the data registers (EAX, EBX, ECX, and EDX), pointer registers (EBP and ESP), index registers (ESI and EDI), and the flag register (EFLAGS) are identical to the corresponding registers in the 8086's software model except that they are now 32 bits in length. The segment registers (CS, DS, SS, and ES) and instruction pointer (IP) are identical to those of the 8086. Notice that they are still 16 bits long. Moreover, they serve the same functions from a software point of view. For instance, CS:IP points to the next instruction that is to be fetched.

Several new registers are found in the real-mode 80386's software model. For instance, it has two more data segment registers, denoted FS and GS. These registers are not implemented in the 8086 microprocessor. Another new register called *control register zero* (CR_0) is included in the model. The only bit in (CR_0) that is active in the real mode is bit 0, which is the *protection enable* (PE) bit. This is the bit that is used to switch the 80386 from real to protected mode. At reset, PE is set to 0 and selects real-mode operation.

Looking at Fig. 8.1, we find that the 80386 microcomputer's real-mode address space is also identical to that of the 8086 microcomputer. It is partitioned into a 1MB memory address space and a separate 64KB input/output address space. The memory address space resides in the range from address 00000_{16} to $FFFFF_{16}$. I/O addresses overlap the first 64KB of this range, 0000_{16} to $FFFF_{16}$. Since the 80386 has six segment registers, not four like the 8086, six 64KB segments of the memory address space are active at a time. This gives a maximum of 384KB of active memory. 64KB of the active memory are allocated for code storage, 64KB for stack, and 256KB for data storage.

Figures 8.2(a) and (b) show that the real-mode 80386 memory and I/O address spaces are partitioned into general-use and reserved areas in the same way as for the 8086. For instance, in Fig. 8.2(a), we find that the first 1K bytes of the memory

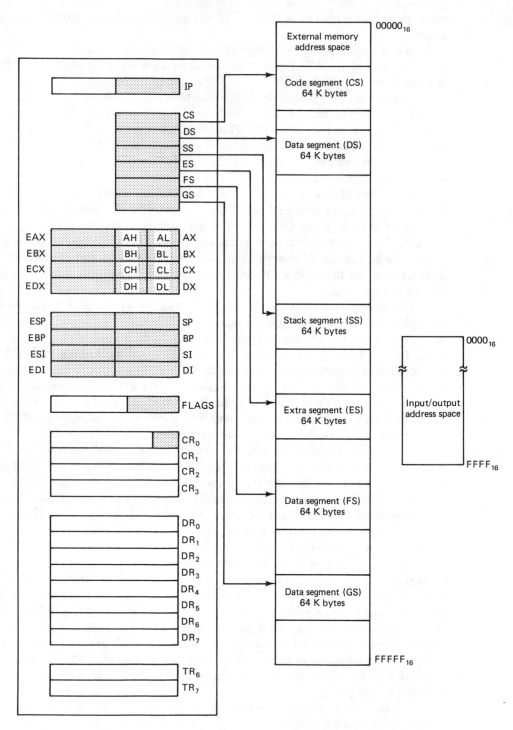

Figure 8.1 Real-mode software model of the 80386 microprocessor.

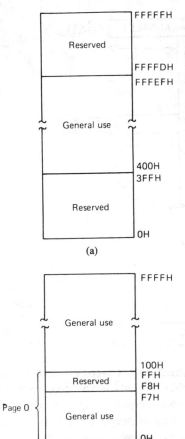

Figure 8.2 (a) Dedicated and general use of memory in the real mode (reprinted by permission of Intel Corp. Copyright/Intel Corp., 1979); (b) I/O address space (reprinted by permission of Intel Corp. Copyright/Intel Corp., 1979).

address space, addresses 0_{16} through $3FF_{16}$, are reserved. They are again used for storage of the interrupt vector table. Moreover, Fig. 8.2(b) shows that the first 256-byte I/O addresses are again identified as page 0. Ports at these addresses can be directly accessed by I/O instructions.

Finally, the real-mode 80386 generates physical addresses in the same manner as the 8086. This address generation is illustrated in Fig. 8.3. Notice that the 16-bit contents of a segment register, such as CS, are shifted left by four bit positions, the four least significant bits are filled with 0s, and then it is added to a 16-bit offset, such as the value in IP, to form the 20-bit physical memory address CS:IP.

8.3 REAL-ADDRESS-MODE INSTRUCTION SET

Figure 8.4 illustrates the evolution of the instruction set for the 8086 architecture. The instruction set of the 8086 and 8088 microprocessors that is called the *basic instruction set* is a subset of the 80386's real-address-mode instruction set. The in-

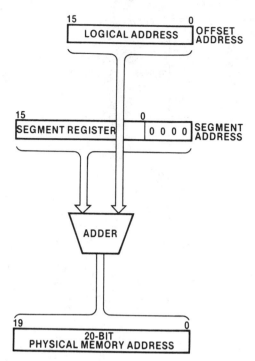

Figure 8.3 Real-address-mode physical address generation. (Reprinted by permission of Intel Corp. Copyright/Intel Corp., 1981.)

structions of the basic instruction set were covered in detail in Chapters 3 and 4. However, a number of enhancements have been made to these instructions in the 80386. First, the data registers, pointer registers, and index registers of the 80386 have been made into truly general purpose registers. That is, the contents of any of these registers can be used either as a data operand or as an offset or index in an address calculation. In addition, the basic instructions now support processing of double-word (32-bit) data in addition to bytes and words.

The basic instruction set was enhanced in the 80286 microprocessor with a group of instructions known as the *extended instruction set*. All these instructions are also available in the real-mode instruction set of the 80386. The last group of instructions, that is identified in Fig. 8.4 as the *80386 specific instruction set* is only implemented with the 80386 microprocessor. In this way, we see that the 80386's real-mode instruction set is a superset of the 8086's basic instruction set.

Extended Instruction Set

Figure 8.5(a) shows the three elements of the 80386's real-mode instruction set. Here we will continue by examining the instructions of the extended instruction set. The extended instruction set includes several new instructions and implements additional addressing modes for a few of the instructions already available in the basic instruction set. For example, in Fig. 8.5(b), we find that two of the instructions added as extensions to the basic instruction set are *push all* (PUSHA) and *pop all* (POPA). Moreover, the PUSH and IMUL instructions have been enhanced to permit the use of

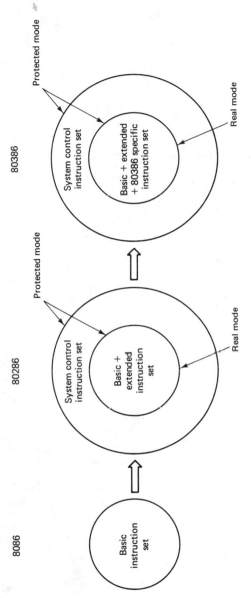

Figure 8.4 Evolution of the 8086 family instruction set.

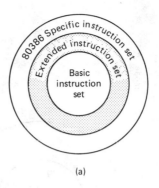

(a)

Mnemonic	Meaning	Format	Operation
PUSH	Push	PUSH dw/db	Push the specified data word (dw) or sign extended data byte (db) onto the stack.
PUSHA	Push all	PUSHA	Push the contents of registers AX, CX, DX, BX, original SP, BP, SI, and DI onto the stack.
POPA	Pop all	POPA	Pop the stack contents into the registers DI, SI, BP, SP, BX, DX, CX, and AX.
IMUL	Integer multiply	IMUL rw, ew, dw/db	Perform the signed multiplication as follows: rw = ew*dw/db where rw is the word size register, ew is the effective word size operand, and the third operand is the immediate data word (dw) or a byte (db).
Logic instructions		Instruction db	Perform the logic instruction using the specified byte (db) as the count.
INS	Input string	INSB, INSW	Input the byte or the word size element of the string from the port specified by DX to the location ES:[DI].
OUTS	Output string	OUTSB, OUTSW	Output the byte or the word size element of the string from ES:[SI] to port specified by DX.
ENTER	Enter procedure	ENTER dw, 0/1/db	Make stack frame for procedure parameters.
LEAVE	Leave procedure	LEAVE	Release the stack space used by the procedure.
BOUND	Check array index against bounds	BOUND rw, md	Interrupt 5 occurs if the register word (rw) is not greater than or equal to the memory word at md and not less than or equal to the second memory word at md + 1.

Figure 8.5   (a) Extended instruction group of the 80386's real-mode instruction set; (b) instructions of the extended instruction set.

immediate operand addressing. Let us now look at just the new instructions in more detail.

Push all and pop all instructions: PUSHA and POPA. When writing the compiler for a high-level language like C, it is common to push the contents of all the general purpose registers of the 80386 to the stack in the beginning of a subroutine. If we use the PUSH instruction to perform this operation, many instructions would be needed. To simplify this and the pop operation, special instructions are provided in the instruction set of the 80386. They are called *push all* (PUSHA) and *pop all* (POPA).

Looking at Fig. 8.5(b), we see that execution of PUSHA causes the values in AX, CX, DX, BX, SP, BP, SI, and DI to be pushed, in that order, onto the top of the stack. Figure 8.6 shows the state of the stack before and after execution of the instruction. As shown in Fig. 8.7, executing a POPA instruction at the end of the subroutine restores the old state of the registers of the 80386.

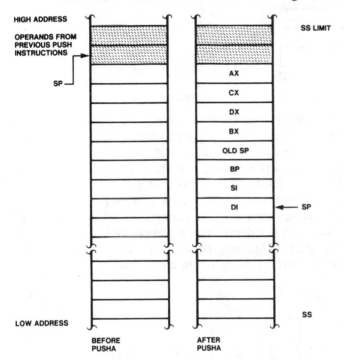

Figure 8.6 State of the stack before and after executing PUSHA. (Reprinted by permission of Intel Corp. Copyright/Intel Corp., 1987.)

Stack frame instructions: ENTER and LEAVE. Before the main program calls a subroutine, it is often necessary for the calling program to pass the values of some *parameters* to the subroutine. It is a common practice to push these parameters onto the stack before calling the routine. Then, during the execution of the subroutine, they are accessed by reading them from the stack and used in computations. Two instructions are provided in the extended instruction set of the 80386 to allocate and deallocate a data area called a *stack frame*. This data area, which is located in the stack part of memory, is used for local storage of parameters and other data.

Normally, high-level languages allocate a stack frame for each procedure in a

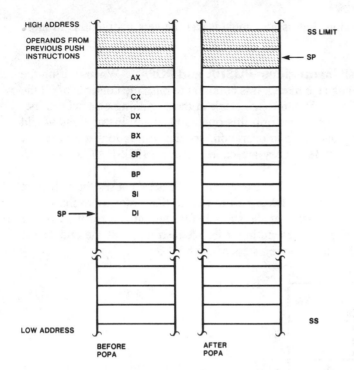

HIGH ADDRESS

OPERANDS FROM
PREVIOUS PUSH
INSTRUCTIONS

SS LIMIT

SP

AX
CX
DX
BX
SP
BP
SI
DI

SP

LOW ADDRESS

BEFORE
POPA

AFTER
POPA

SS

Figure 8.7 State of the stack before and after executing POPA. (Reprinted by permission of Intel Corp. Copyright/Intel Corp., 1987.)

program. The stack frame provides a dynamically allocated local storage space for the procedure and contains data such as variables, pointers to the stack frames of the previous procedures from which the current procedure was called, and a return address for linkage to the stack frame of the calling procedure. This mechanism also permits access to data in stack frames of the calling procedures.

The instructions used for allocation and deallocation of stack frames are given in Fig. 8.5(b) as *enter* (ENTER) and *leave* (LEAVE). Execution of an ENTER instruction allocates a stack frame, and it is deallocated by executing LEAVE. For this reason, as shown in Fig. 8.8, the ENTER instruction is used at the beginning of a subroutine and LEAVE at the end just before the return instruction.

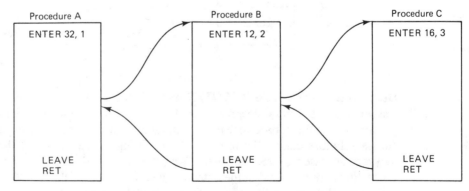

Procedure A

ENTER 32, 1

LEAVE
RET

Procedure B

ENTER 12, 2

LEAVE
RET

Procedure C

ENTER 16, 3

LEAVE
RET

Figure 8.8 Enter/leave example.

Software Architecture of the 80386 Microprocessor   Chap. 8

Looking at Fig. 8.5(b), we find that the ENTER instruction has two operands. The first operand, which is identified as *dw,* is a word-size immediate operand. This operand specifies the number of bytes to be allocated on the stack for local data storage of the procedure. The second operand, *db,* which is a byte-size immediate operand, specifies what is called the *lexical nesting level* of the routine. This lexical level defines how many pointers to previous stack frames can be stored in the current stack frame. The value of the lexical-level byte must be limited to a maximum of 32 in 80386 programs. This list of previous stack frame pointers is called a *display.*

An example of an ENTER instruction is

ENTER 12,2

Execution of this instruction allocates 12 bytes of local storage on the stack for use as a stack frame. It does this by decrementing SP by 12. This defines a new top of stack at address SS:SP-12. Also, the base pointer (BP) that identifies the beginning of the previous stack frame is copied into the stack frame created by the ENTER instruction. This value is called the *dynamic link* and is held in the first storage location of the stack frame. The number of stack frame pointers that can be saved in a stack frame is equal to the value of the byte that specifies the lexical level of the procedure. Therefore, in our example, just two levels of nesting are permitted.

The BP register is used as a pointer into the stack segment of memory. When a procedure is entered, the value in BP points to the stack frame location that contains the previous stack frame pointer (dynamic link). Therefore, base-indexed addressing can be used to access variables in the stack frame by referencing the BP register.

The LEAVE instruction reverses the process of an ENTER instruction. That is, its execution deallocates the stack frame. This is done by first automatically loading SP from the BP register. This returns the storage locations of the current stack frame to the stack. Now SP points to the location where the dynamic link (pointer to the previous stack frame) is stored. Next, popping the contents of the stack into BP returns the pointer to the stack frame of the previous procedure.

To illustrate the operation of the stack frame instructions, let us consider the example of Fig. 8.8. Here we find three procedures. Procedure A is used to call procedure B, which in turn calls procedure C. It is assumed that the lexical levels for these procedures are 1, 2, and 3, respectively. The ENTER, LEAVE, and RET instructions for each procedure are shown in the diagram. Notice that the ENTER instructions specify the lexical levels for the procedures.

The stack frames created by executing the ENTER instructions in the three procedures are shown in Fig. 8.9. As the ENTER instruction in procedure A is executed, the old BP from the procedure that called procedure A is pushed on the stack. BP is loaded from SP to point to the location of the old BP. Since the second operand is 1, only the current BP, that is, the BP for procedure A, is pushed onto the stack. To allocate 32 bytes for the stack frame, 32 is subtracted from the stack pointer.

After entering procedure B, a second ENTER instruction is encountered. This time the lexical level is 2. The instruction first pushes the old BP that is the BP for procedure A onto the stack, then pushes the BP previously stored on the stack frame

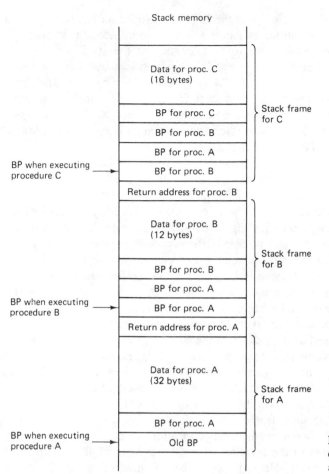

Stack memory

Data for proc. C
(16 bytes)

BP for proc. C

BP for proc. B

BP for proc. A

BP when executing
procedure C

BP for proc. B

Return address for proc. B

Stack frame
for C

Data for proc. B
(12 bytes)

Stack frame
for B

BP for proc. B

BP for proc. A

BP when executing
procedure B

BP for proc. A

Return address for proc. A

Data for proc. A
(32 bytes)

Stack frame
for A

BP for proc. A

BP when executing
procedure A

Old BP

Figure 8.9 Stack after execution of
enter instructions for procedures A, B,
and C.

for A to the stack, and last it pushes the current BP for procedure B to the stack. This mechanism provides access to the stack frame for procedure A from procedure B. Next, 12 bytes, as specified by the instruction, are allocated for local storage.

The ENTER instruction in procedure C is next executed. This instruction has the lexical level of 3 and therefore it pushes the BPs for the two previous procedures, that is, B and A, to the stack in addition to the BP for C and the BP for the calling procedure B.

Input string and output string instructions: INS and OUTS. In Fig. 8-5(b), we find that there are input and output string instructions in the extended instruction set of the 80386. Using these string instructions, a programmer can either input data from an input port to a storage location directly in memory or output data from a memory location to an output port.

The first instruction, called *input string,* has two forms: INSB and INSW. INSB stands for *input string byte* and INSW means *input string word.* Let us now look at the operation performed by the INSB instruction. INSB assumes that the address of the input port that is to be accessed is in the DX register. This value must be loaded prior to executing the string instruction. Moreover, the address of the memory storage location into which the byte of data is input is identified by the current values in ES and DI. That is, when executed, the input operation performed is

$$(ES:DI) \longleftarrow ((DX))$$

Just as for the other byte string instructions, the value in DI is incremented or decremented by 1 after the data transfer takes place.

$$(DI) \longleftarrow (DI) \pm 1$$

In this way, it points to the next storage location in memory to be accessed. Whether the value in DI is incremented or decremented depends on the setting of the DF flag. Notice in Fig. 8.5(b) that INSW performs the same data transfer operation except that, since the word contents of the I/O port are stored in memory, the value in DI is incremented or decremented by 2.

The INSB instruction performs the operation we just described on one data element, not an array of elements. However, this basic operation can be repeated to handle a block input operation. Block operations are done by inserting a repeat (REP) prefix in front of the string instruction. For example, the instruction

REP INSW

will cause the contents of the word-wide port pointed to by the I/O address in DX to be input and saved in the memory location at address ES:DI. Then the value in DX is incremented by 2 (assuming that DF equals 0), the count in CX is decremented by 1, and the value in CX is tested to determine if it is zero. As long as the value in CX is not zero, the input operation is repeated. When CX equals zero, all elements of the array have been input and the input string operation is complete. Remember that a count representing the number of times the string operation is to be repeated must be loaded into the CX register prior to executing the repeat input string instruction.

In Fig. 8.5(b), we also see that OUTSB and OUTSW are the two forms of the *output string* instruction. These instructions operate similarly as the input string instructions; however, they peform an output operation. For instance, executing OUTSW causes the operation that follows:

$$(ES:SI) \rightarrow ((DX))$$

$$(SI) \pm 2 \rightarrow (SI)$$

That is, the word of data held at the memory location pointed to by address ES:SI is output to the word-wide port located at the I/O address in DX. After the output data transfer is complete, the value in SI is either incremented or decremented by 2.

An example of an output string instruction that can be used to output an array of data is

REP OUTSB

When executed, this instruction causes the data elements of the array of byte-wide data pointed to by ES:SI to be output one after the other to the output port located at the I/O address in DX. Again, the count in CX defines the size of the array.

Check array index against bounds instruction: BOUND. The *check array index against bounds* (BOUND) instruction, as its name implies, can determine if the contents of a register, known as the *array index,* lie within a set of minimum/maximum values, called the *upper and lower bounds.* This type of operation is important when accessing elements of an array of data in memory.

The format of the BOUND instruction is given in Fig. 8.5(b). An example is the instruction

```
BOUND  SI,LIMITS
```

Notice that the instruction contains two operands. The first represents the register whose word contents are to be tested to verify whether or not they lie within the boundaries. In our example, this is source index register (SI). The second operand is the effective relative address of the first of two word storage locations in memory that contain the values of the lower and upper boundaries. In the example, the word of data starting at address LIMITS is the value of the lower bound and that stored at address LIMITS+2 is the value of the upper bound.

When this BOUND instruction is executed, the contents of SI are compared to both the value of the lower bound at LIMITS and upper bound at LIMITS+2. If it is found to be either less than the lower bound or more than the upper bound, an exception occurs and control is passed to a service routine through the vector for type number 5; otherwise, the next sequential instruction is performed.

80386 Specific Instruction Set

The enhancements to the 80386's real-mode instruction set, which are highlighted in Fig. 8.10(a), represent the 80386 specific instruction set. For example, it includes instructions to directly load a pointer into the FS, GS, and SS registers and bit test and bit scan instructions. Moreover, it contains additional forms of existing instructions that have been added to perform the identical operation in a more general way, on special registers or on a double word of data. First, we will look briefly at some of the instructions with expanded functions.

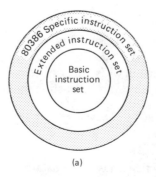

(a)

Figure 8.10 (a) 80386 specific instructions of the 80386's real-mode instruction set; (b) instructions of the 80386 specific instruction set.

Mnemonic	Meaning	Format	Operation
MOV	Move	MOV D, S	Moves the contents of a special register to/from a general purpose register. Special registers are CR0, CR2, CR3, DR0–DR3, DR6, DR7, TR6, and TR7.
Double word operand instructions	–	–	Operation extended to double word, operands. The instructions include: MOVSD, CMPSD, SCASD, LODSD, STOSD, INSD, OUTSD, JMP rel/32, JMP r/m32, CMPSD, CWD/CDQ, POPAD, POPFD, PUSHAD, PUSHFD, SHLD, AND SHRD.
MOVSX	Move with sign-extend	MOVSX D, S	Sign extend the S and place in D. Allows for 8 to 16 or 16 to 32 bit sign extension from a source (r/m8, or r/m16) to a destination (r16 or r32).
MOVZX	Move with zero-extend	MOVZX D, S	Zero extend the S and place in D. Allows for 8 to 16 or 16 to 32 bit zero extension from a source (r/m8, or r/m16) to a destination (r16 or r32).
LSS	Load register and SS	LSS r16, m16:16 LSS r32, m16:32	Load stack segment register and the specified register with the pointer from memory.
LFS	Load register and FS	LFS r16, m16:16 LFS r32, m16:32	Load data segment register FS and the specified register with the pointer from memory.
LGS	Load register and GS	LGS r16, m16:16 LGS r32, m16:32	Load data segment register GS and the specified register with the pointer from memory.
BT	Bit test	BT opr1, opr2	CF ← BIT (opr1, opr2)
BTR	Bit test and reset	BTR opr1, opr2	CF ← BIT (opr1, opr2), BIT(opr1, opr2) ← 0
BTS	Bit test and set	BTR opr1, opr2	CF ← BIT (opr1, opr2), BIT(opr1, opr2) ← 1
BTC	Bit test and complement	BTC opr1, opr2	CF ← BIT (opr1, opr2), BIT(opr1, opr2) ← NOT BIT(opr1, opr2)
BSF	Bit scan forward	BSF r16, r/m16 BSF r32, r/m32	Scan the second operand starting from bit 0. ZF = 0 if all bits are 0, else ZF = 1 and the register (r16 or r32) contains the bit index of the first set bit.
BSR	Bit scan reverse	BSR r16, r/m16 BSR r32, r/m32	Scan the second operand starting from the MSB. ZF = 0 if all bits are 0, else ZF = 1 and the register (r16 or r32) contains the bit index of the first set bit.
SETcc	Set byte on condition	SETcc r/m8	r/m8 ← 1 if cc is true, r/m8 ← 0 if cc is not true

(b)

Figure 8.10 (*continued*)

Figure 8.10(b) shows that the MOV instructions can be written with a control register (CR), debug register (DR), or test register (TR) as its source or destination operand. As an example, let us look at what function the instruction

```
MOV  EAX, CR0
```

performs. Execution of this instruction causes the value of the flags in CR_0 to be copied into the EAX register.

Looking at Fig. 8.10(b), we see that the string instructions have been expanded to support double-word operands. The instruction mnemonics for the double-word string operations are MOVSD, CMPSD, SCASD, LODSD, STOSD, INSD, and OUTSD. In all seven cases, the basic operation performed by the instruction is the same as described earlier; however, a double-word data transfer takes place. The same is true for the shift, convert, compare, jump, push, and pop instructions in Fig. 8.10(b). They simply perform their normal operation on double-word operands. One exception is that the 80386 limits the count for shift instructions to a count of 32, instead of 256 as on the 8086. Let us now look at the instructions that are only implemented on the 80386.

Sign-extend and zero-extend move instructions: MOVSX and MOVZX. In Fig. 8.10(b), we find that a number of special-purpose move instructions have been added to the instruction set of the 80386. The first two instructions, *move with sign-extend* (MOVSX) and *move with zero-extend* (MOVZX), are used to sign extend or zero extend, respectively, a source operand as it is moved to the destination operand location. The source operand is either a byte or a word of data in a register or a storage location in memory, while the destination oparand is either a 16 or 32-bit register.

For example, the instruction

```
MOVSX  EBX, AX
```

is used to copy the 16-bit value in AX into EBX. As the copy is performed, the value in the sign bit, which is bit 15 of AX, is extended into the 16 higher-order bits of EBX. If AX contains $FFFF_{16}$, the sign bit is logic 1. Therefore, after execution of the MOVSX instruction, the value that results in EBX is $FFFFFFFF_{16}$. The MOVZX instruction performs a similar function to the MOVSX instruction except that it extends the value moved to the destination operand location with zeros.

EXAMPLE 8.1

Explain the operation performed by the instruction

```
MOVZX  CX, BYTE  PTR  DATA_BYTE
```

if the value of data at memory address DATA_BYTE is FF_{16}.

SOLUTION When the MOVZX instruction is executed, the value FF_{16} is copied into the lower byte of CX and the upper 8 bits are filled with 0s. This gives

$$(CX) = 00FF_{16}$$

Load full pointer instructions: LSS, LFS, and LGS. The basic instruction set of the 8086 includes two *load full pointer instructions*, LDS and LES. Three additional instructions of this type are performed by the 80386. Looking at Fig. 8.10(b), we find that they are: LSS, LFS, and LGS. Notice that executing the *load register and SS* (LSS) instruction causes both the register specified in the instruction and the stack segment register to be loaded from the source operand. For example, the instruction

```
LSS  ESP, STACK_POINTER
```

causes the first 32 bits starting at memory address STACK_POINTER to be loaded into the 32-bit register ESP and the next 16 bits into the SS register.

The other two instructions, *load register and FS* (LFS) and *load register and GS* (LGS) perform a function similar to LSS. However, they load the specified register and the FS or GS register, respectively.

EXAMPLE 8.2

Write an instruction that will load the 48-bit pointer starting at memory address DATA_G_ADDRESS into the ESI and GS registers.

SOLUTION This operation is performed with the instruction

```
LGS  ESI, DATA_G_ADDRESS
```

Bit test and bit scan instructions: BT, BTR, BTS, BTC, BSF, and BSR. The *bit test and bit scan instructions* of the 80386 enable a programmer to test the logic level of a bit in either a register or storage location in memory. Let us begin by examining the bit test instructions. They are used to test the state of a single bit in a register or memory location. When the instruction is executed, the value of the tested bit is saved in the carry flag. Moreover, instructions are provided that can also reset, set, or complement the contents of the bit during the execution of the instruction.

In Fig. 8.10(b), we see that the *bit test* (BT) instruction has two operands. The first operand identifies the register or memory location that contains the bit that is to be tested. The second operand contains an index that selects the bit that is to be tested. Notice that the index may be either an immediate operand or the value in register. When this instruction is executed, the state of the tested bit is simply copied into the carry flag.

Once the state of the bit is saved in CF, further processing can be performed through software. For instance, a conditional jump instruction could be used to test the value in CF, and if CF equals 1, program control could be passed to a service routine. On the other hand, if CF equals 0, the value of the index could be incremented, a jump performed back to the BT instruction, and the next bit in the operand tested. Notice that this routine scans the bits of the first operand looking for the first bit that is logic 1.

Another example is the instruction

$$\texttt{BTR\ \ EAX,EDI}$$

Execution of this instruction causes the bit in 32-bit register EAX that is selected by the index in EDI to be tested. The value of the tested bit is first saved in the carry flag and then it is reset in the register EAX.

EXAMPLE 8.3

Describe the operation that is performed by the instruction

$$\texttt{BTC\ \ BX,7}$$

Assume that register BX contains the value $03F0_{16}$.

SOLUTION   Let us first express the value in BX in binary form. This gives

$$(BX) = 0000001111110000_2$$

Execution of the *bit test and complement* instruction causes the value of the eighth bit to be first tested and then complemented. Since this bit is logic 1, CF is set to 1. This gives

$$(CF) = 1$$

$$(BX) = 0000001101110000_2 = 0370_{16}$$

The *bit scan forward* (BSF) and *bit scan reverse* (BSR) instructions are used to scan through the bits of a register or storage location in memory to determine whether or not they are all 0. For example, by executing the instruction

$$\texttt{BSF\ \ ESI,EDX}$$

the bits of 32-bit register EDX are tested one after the other starting from bit 0. If all bits are found to be 0, the ZF is cleared. On the other hand, if the contents of EDX are not zero, ZF is set to 1 and the index value of the first bit tested as 1 is copied into ESI.

Byte set on condition: SETcc.   The *byte set on condition* (SETcc) instruction can be used to test for various states of the flags. In Fig. 8.10(b), we see that the general form of the instruction is denoted as

$$\texttt{SETcc\ \ S}$$

Here the cc part of the mnemonic stands for a general flag relationship and must be replaced with a specific relationship when writing the instruction. Figure 8.11 is a list of the mnemonics that can be used to replace cc and their corresponding flag relationships. For instance, replacing cc by A gives the mnemonic SETA. This stands for *set byte if above* and tests the flags to determine if

Instruction	Meaning	Conditions code relationship
SETA r/m8	Set byte if above	CF = 0 · ZF = 0
SETAE r/m8	Set byte if above or equal	CF = 0
SETB r/m8	Set byte if below	CF = 1
SETBE r/m8	Set byte if below or equal	CF = 1 + ZF = 1
SETC r/m8	Set if carry	CF = 1
SETE r/m8	Set byte if equal	ZF = 1
SETG r/m8	Set byte if greater	ZF = 0 + SF = OF
SETGE r/m8	Set byte if greater	SF = OF
SETL r/m8	Set byte if less	SF <> OF
SETLE r/m8	Set byte if less or equal	ZF = 1 · SF <> OF
SETNA r/m8	Set byte if not above	CF = 1
SETNAE r/m8	Set byte if not above	CF = 1
SETNB r/m8	Set byte if not below	CF = 0
SETNBE r/m8	Set byte if not below	CF = 0 · ZF = 0
SETNC r/m8	Set byte if not carry	CF = 0
SETNE r/m8	Set byte if not equal	ZF = 0
SETNG r/m8	Set byte if not greater	ZF = 1 + SF <> OF
SETNGE r/m8	Set if not greater or equal	SF <> OF
SETNL r/m8	Set byte if not less	SF = OF
SETNLE r/m8	Set byte if not less or equal	ZF = 1 · SF <> OF
SETNO r/m8	Set byte if not overflow	OF = 0
SETNP r/m8	Set byte if not parity	PF = 0
SETNS r/m8	Set byte if not sign	SF = 0
SETNZ r/m8	Set byte if not zero	ZF = 0
SETO r/m8	Set byte if overflow	OF = 1
SETP r/m8	Set byte if parity	PF = 1
SETPE r/m8	Set byte if parity even	PF = 1
SETPO r/m8	Set byte if parity odd	PF = 0
SETS r/m8	Set byte if sign	SF = 1
SETZ r/m8	Set byte if zero	ZF = 1

Figure 8.11 SET instruction conditions.

$$(CF) \ = \ 0 \ \text{and} \ (ZF) \ = \ 0$$

If these conditions are satisfied, a byte of 1s is written to the register or memory location specified as the source operand. On the other hand, if the conditions are not valid, a byte of 0s is written to the source operand.

An example is the instruction

```
SETE   AL
```

Looking at Fig. 8.11, we find that execution of this instruction causes the ZF to be tested. If ZF equals 1, 11111111_2 is written into AL; otherwise, it is loaded with 00000000_2.

EXAMPLE 8.4

Write an instruction that will load memory location EVEN_PARITY with the value FF_{16} if the result produced by the last instruction had even parity.

SOLUTION In Fig. 8.11, the instruction for (PF) = 1 is

```
SETPE  EVEN_PARITY
```

8.4 PROTECTED-ADDRESS-MODE SOFTWARE ARCHITECTURE

Having completed our study of the real-mode operation and instruction set of the 80386 microprocessor, we are now ready to turn our attention to its protected-address mode (protected mode) of operation. Earlier we indicated that whenever the 80386 microprocessor is reset it comes up in real mode. Moreover, we indicated that the PE bit of control register zero (CR_0) can be used to switch the 80386 into the protected mode under software control. When configured for protected mode, the 80386 provides an advanced software architecture that supports memory management, virtual addressing, paging, protection, and multitasking. In this section we will examine the 80386's protected-mode register model, virtual memory address space, and memory management.

Protected-Mode Register Model

The protected-mode register set of the 80386 microprocessor is shown in Fig. 8.12. Looking at this diagram, we see that its application register set is a superset of the real-mode register set shown in Fig. 8.1. Comparing these two diagrams, we find four new registers in the protected-mode model: the *global descriptor table register* (GDTR), *interrupt descriptor table register* (IDTR), *local descriptor table register* (LDTR), and *task register* (TR). Furthermore, the functions of a few registers have been extended. For example, the instruction pointer, which is now called EIP, is 32 bits in length; more bits of the flag register (EFLAGS) are active; and all four control registers, CR_0 through CR_3, are functional. Let us next discuss the purpose of each new and extended register, and how they are used in the segmented protected-mode operation of the microprocessor.

Global descriptor table register. As shown in Fig. 8.13, the contents of the global descriptor table register define a table in the 80386's physical memory address space called the *global descriptor table* (GDT). This global descriptor table is one important element of the 80386's memory management system.

GDTR is a 48-bit register that is located inside the 80386. The lower 2 bytes of this register identified as LIMIT in Fig. 8.13, specify the size in bytes of the GDT. The decimal value of LIMIT is one less than the actual size of the table. For instance, if LIMIT equals $00FF_{16}$, the table is 256 bytes in length. Since LIMIT has 16 bits, the GDT can be up to 65,536 bytes long. The upper 4 bytes of the GDTR, which are labeled BASE in Fig. 8.13, locate the beginning of the GDT in physical memory. This 32-bit base address allows the table to be positioned anywhere in the 80386's 4-GB linear address space.

EXAMPLE 8.5

If the limit and base in the global descriptor table register are $0FFF_{16}$ and 00100000_{16}, respectively, what is the beginning address of the descriptor table, size of the table in bytes, and ending address of the table?

SOUTION The starting address of the global descriptor table in physical memory is given by the base. Therefore,

$$GDT_{START} = 00100000_{16}$$

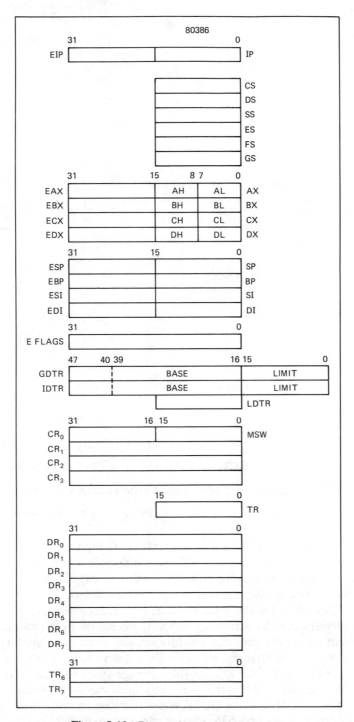

Figure 8.12 Protected-mode register model.

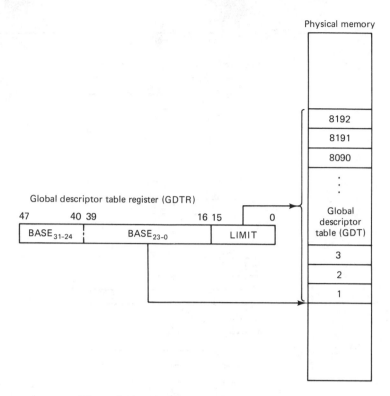

Figure 8.13 Global descriptor table mechanism.

The limit is the offset to the end of the table. This gives

$$GDT_{END} = 00100000_{16} + 0FFF_{16} = 00100FFF_{16}$$

Finally, the size of the table is equal to the decimal value of the limit plus 1.

$$GDT_{SIZE} = FFF_{16} + 1_2 = 4096 \text{ bytes}$$

The GDT provides a mechanism for defining the characteristics of the 80386's *global memory* address space. Global memory is a general system resource that is shared by many or all software tasks. That is, storage locations in global memory are accessible by any task that runs on the microprocessor.

This table contains what are called *system segment descriptors*. These descriptors identify the characteristics of the segments of global memory. For instance, a segment descriptor provides information about the size, starting point, and access rights of a global memory segment. Each descriptor is 8 bytes long; thus our earlier example of a 256-byte table provides storage space for just 32 descriptors. Remember that the size of the global descriptor table can be expanded by simply changing the value of LIMIT in the GDTR under software control. If the table is increased to its maximum size of 65,536 bytes, it can hold up to 8192 descriptors.

EXAMPLE 8.6

How many descriptors can be stored in the global descriptor table defined in example 8.5?

SOLUTION   Each descriptor takes up 8 bytes; therefore, a 4096-byte table can hold

$$4096/8 = 512 \text{ descriptors}$$

The value of the BASE and LIMIT must be loaded into the GDTR before the 80386 is switched from the real mode of operation to the protected mode. Special instructions are provided for this purpose in the system control instruction set of the 80386. These instructions will be introduced later in this chapter. Once the 80386 is in the protected mode, the location of the table is typically not changed.

Interrupt descriptor table register.   Just like the global descriptor table register, the interrupt descriptor table register (IDTR) defines a table in physical memory. However, this table contains what are called *interrupt descriptors,* not segment descriptors. For this reason, it is known as the *interrupt descriptor table* (IDT). This register and table of descriptors provide the mechanism by which the microprocessor passes program control to interrupt and exception service routines.

As shown in Fig. 8.14, just like the GDTR, the IDTR is 48 bits in length. Again, the lower 2 bytes of the register (LIMIT) define the table size. That is, the size of the table equals LIMIT+1 bytes. Since 2 bytes define the size, the IDT can also be up to 65,536 bytes long. But the 80386 supports only up to 256 interrupts and exceptions; therefore, the size of the IDT should not be set to support more than 256 interrupts. The upper 4 bytes of IDTR (BASE) identify the starting address of the IDT in physical memory.

The types of descriptors used in the IDT are what are called *interrupt gates.* These gates provide a mean for passing program control to the beginning of an interrupt service routine. Each gate is 8 bytes long and contains both attributes and a starting address for the service routine.

EXAMPLE 8.7

What is the maximum value that should be assigned to the limit in the IDTR?

SOLUTION   The maximum number of interrupt descriptors that can be used in an 80386 microcomputer system is 256. Therefore, the maximum table size in bytes is

$$IDT_{SIZE} = 8 \times 256 = 4096 \text{ bytes}$$

Thus

$$LIMIT = 0FFF_{16}$$

This table can also be located anywhere in the linear address space addressable with the 80386's 32-bit address. Just like the GDTR, the IDTR needs to be loaded before the 80386 is switched from the real mode to protected mode. Special instructions are provided for loading and saving the contents of the IDTR. Once the location of the table is set, it is typically not changed after entering protected mode.

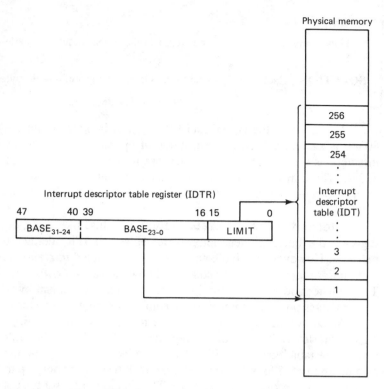

Figure 8.14 Interrupt descriptor table mechanism.

EXAMPLE 8.8

What is the address range of the last descriptor in the interrupt descriptor table defined by base address 00011000_{16} and limit $01FF_{16}$?

SOLUTION From the values of the base and limit, we find that the table is located in the address range

$$IDT_{START} = 00011000_{16}$$

$$IDT_{END} = 000111FF_{16}$$

The last descriptor in this table takes up the 8 bytes of memory from address $000111F8_{16}$ through $000111FF_{16}$.

Local descriptor table register. The *local descriptor table register* (LDTR) is also part of the 80386's memory management support mechanism. As shown in Fig. 8.15(a), each task can have access to its own private descriptor table in addition to the global descriptor table. This private table is called the *local descriptor table* (LDT) and defines a *local memory* address space for use by the task. The LDT holds segment descriptors that provide access to code and data in segments of memory that are reserved for the current task. Since each task can have its own segment of local memory, the protected-mode software system may contain many local descrip-

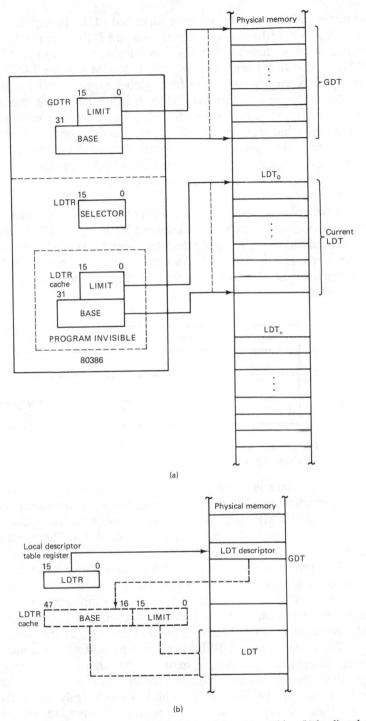

(a)

(b)

Figure 8.15 (a) Task with global and local descriptor tables; (b) loading the local descriptor table register to define a local descriptor table.

tor tables. For this reason, we have identified LDT$_1$ through LDT$_N$ in Fig. 8.15(a).

Figure 8.15(b) shows us that the 16-bit LDTR does not directly define the local descriptor table. Instead, it holds a selector that points to an *LDT descriptor* in the GDT. Notice that whenever a selector is loaded into the LDTR, the corresponding descriptor is transparently read from global memory and loaded into the *local descriptor table cache* within the 80386. It is this descriptor that defines the local descriptor table. As shown in Fig. 8.15(b), the 32-bit base value identifies the starting point of the table in physical memory, and the value of the 16-bit limit determines the size of the table. Loading of this descriptor into the cache creates the LDT for the current task. That is, everytime a selector is loaded into the LDTR, a local descriptor table descriptor is cached and a new LDT is activated.

Control registers. The protected-mode model includes the four system control registers, identified as CR$_0$ through CR$_3$ in Fig. 8.12. Figure 8.16 shows these registers in more detail. Notice that the lower 5 bits of CR$_0$ are system control flags. These bits make up what is known as the *machine status word* (MSW). The most significant bit of CR$_0$ and registers CR$_2$ and CR$_3$ are used by the 80386's paging mechanism.

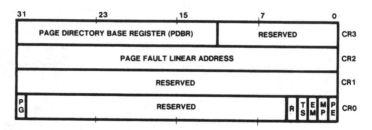

Figure 8.16 Control registers. (Reprinted by permission of Intel Corp. Copyright/ Intel Corp., 1986.)

Let us continue by examining the machine status word bits of CR$_0$. They contain information about the 80386's protected-mode configuration and status. The 4 bits labeled PE, MP, EM, and ET are control bits that define the protected-mode system configuration. The fifth bit, TS, is a status bit. These bits can be examined or modified through software.

The *protected-mode enable* (PE) bit determines if the 80386 is in the real or protected mode. At reset, PE is cleared. This enables real-mode of operation. To enter protected mode, we simply switch PE to 1 through software. Once in protected mode, the 80386 cannot be switched back to real mode under software control. The only way to return to real mode is by initiating a hardware reset.

The *math present* (MP) bit is set to 1 to indicate that a numeric coprocessor is present in the microcomputer system. On the other hand, if the system is to be configured so that a software emulator instead of a coprocessor is used to perform numeric operations, the *emulate* (EM) bit is set to 1. Only one of these two bits can be set at a time. Finally, the *extension-type* (ET) bit is used to indicate whether an 80287 or 80387 numeric coprocessor is in use. Logic 1 in ET indicates that an 80387 is installed.

The last bit in the MSW, *task switch* (TS), automatically gets set whenever the 80386 switches from one task to another. It can be cleared under software control.

The paging of the 80386 is turned on by switching the PG bit in CR_0 to logic 1. Paging is implemented with an address translation mechanism that consists of a page directory and page table that are both held in physical memory. Looking at Fig. 8.16, we see that CR_3 contains the *page directory base register* (PDBR). This register holds a 20-bit *page directory base address* that points to the beginning of the page directory. These 20 bits are actually the MSBs of the base address. The 12 lower bits are assumed to start at 000_{16} at the beginning of the directory and range to FFF_{16} at its end. Therefore, the page directory contains 4-KB memory locations and is organized as 1K, 32-bit addresses. These addresses each point to a separate page table, which is also in physical memory. Just like the page directory, each page table is also 4 KB long and contains 1K, 32-bit addresses. However, these addresses are called *page frame addresses*. Each page frame address points to a 4K frame of data storage locations in physical memory. The most recently used page table address and page frame address are held in the *page translation cache* inside the 80386.

If a page fault occurs during the page translation process, the 80386 saves the linear address at which the page fault occurred in register CR_2. This address is denoted as *page fault linear address* in Fig. 8.16.

Task register. The *task register* (TR) is a key element in the protected-mode task switching mechanism of the 80386 microprocessor. This register holds a 16-bit index value called a *selector*. The initial selector must be loaded into TR under software control. This starts the initial task. After this is done, the selector is automatically changed whenever the 80386 executes an instruction that performs a task switch.

As shown in Fig. 8.17, the selector in TR is used to locate a descriptor in the global descriptor table. Notice that when a selector is loaded into the TR the corresponding *task state segment* (TSS) *descriptor* automatically gets read from memory

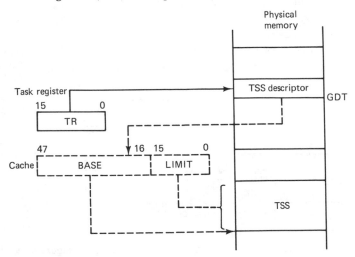

Figure 8.17 Task register and the task-switching mechanism.

and loaded into the on-chip *task descriptor cache*. This descriptor defines a block of memory called the *task state segment* (TSS). It does this by providing the starting address (BASE) and the size (LIMIT) of the segment. Every task has its own TSS. The TSS holds the information needed to initiate the task, such as initial values for the user-accessible registers.

EXAMPLE 8.9

What is the maximum size of a TSS? Where can it be located in the linear address space?

SOLUTION Since the value of LIMIT is 16 bits in length, the TSS can be as long as 64KB. Moreover, the base is 32 bits in length. Therefore, the TSS can be located anywhere in the 80386's 4-GB address space.

EXAMPLE 8.10

Assume that the base address of the global descriptor table is 00011000_{16} and the selector in the task register is 2108_{16}. What is the address range of the TSS descriptor?

SOLUTION The beginning address of the TSS descriptor is

$$\text{TSS\_DESCRIPTOR}_{start} = 00011000_{16} + 2108_{16}$$

$$= 00013108_{16}$$

Since the descriptor is 8 bytes long, it ends at

$$\text{TSS\_DESCRIPTOR}_{end} = 0001310F_{16}$$

Registers with changed functionality. Earlier we pointed out that the function of a few of the registers that are common to both the real-mode and protected-mode register models changes as the 80386 is switched into the protected mode of operation. For instance, the segment registers are now called the *segment selector registers,* and instead of holding a base address they are loaded with what is known as a *selector*.

The format of a selector is shown in Fig. 8.18. Here we see that the two least significant bits are labeled RPL, which stands for *requested previlege level*. These

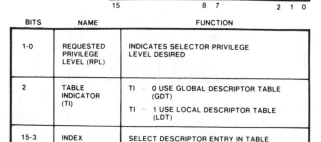

Figure 8.18 Selector format. (Reprinted by permission of Intel Corp. Copyright/Intel Corp., 1986.)

bits contain either $00 = 0$, $01 = 1$, $10 = 2$, or $11 = 3$ and assign a request protection level to the selector. The next bit, which is identified as *task indicator* (TI) in Fig. 8.18, selects the table to be used when accessing a segment descriptor. Remember that in protected mode two descriptor tables are active at a time, the global descriptor table and a local descriptor table. Looking at Fig. 8.18, we find that if TI is 0 the selector corresponds to a descriptor in the global descriptor table. Finally, the 13 most significant bits contain an *index* that is used as a pointer to a specific descriptor in the table selected by the TI bit.

EXAMPLE 8.11

Assume that the base address of the LDT is 00120000_{16} and the GDT base address is 00100000_{16}. If the value of the selector loaded into the CS register is 1007_{16}, what is the request privilege level? Is the segment descriptor in the GDT or LDT? What is the address of the segment descriptor?

SOLUTION   Expressing the selector in binary form, we get

$$(CS) = 0001000000000111_2$$

Since the two least significant bits are both 1,

$$RPL = 3$$

The next, bit, bit 2, is also 1. This means that the segment descriptor is in the LDT. Finally, the value in the 13 most significant bits must be scaled by 8 to give the offset of the descriptor from the base address of the table. Therefore,

$$OFFSET = 0001000000000_2 \times 8 = 512 \times 8 = 4096$$

$$= 1000_{16}$$

and the address of the segment descriptor is

$$DESCRIPTOR_{ADDRESS} = 00120000_{16} + 1000_{16}$$

$$= 00121000_{16}$$

Another register whose function changes when the 80386 is switched to protected mode is the flag register. As shown in Fig. 8.12, the flag register is now identified as EFLAGS and expands to 32 bits in length. The functions of the bits in EFLAGS are given in Fig. 8.19. Comparing this illustration to the 8086 flag register in Fig. 2.15, we see that five additional bits are implemented. These bits are only active when the 80386 is in protected mode. They are the 2-bit *input/output privilege level* (IOPL) code, the *nested task* (NT) flag, the *resume* (RF) flag, and the *virtual 8086 mode* (VM) flag.

Notice in Fig. 8.19 that each of these flags is identified as a system flag. That is, they represent protected-mode system operations. For example, the IOPL bits are used to assign a maximum privilege level to input/output. For instance, if 00 is loaded into IOPL, I/O can only be performed when the 80386 is in the highest privilege level, which is called *level 0*. On the other hand, if IOPL is 11, I/O is assigned to the least privilege level, level 3.

The NT flag identifies whether or not the current task is a nested task, that is, if

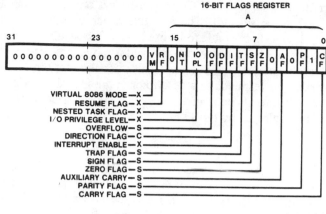

VIRTUAL 8086 MODE —X
RESUME FLAG — X
NESTED TASK FLAG— X
I/O PRIVILEGE LEVEL— X
OVERFLOW — S
DIRECTION FLAG — C
INTERRUPT ENABLE — X
TRAP FLAG — S
SIGN FLAG —S
ZERO FLAG — S
AUXILIARY CARRY — S
PARITY FLAG — S
CARRY FLAG — S

S = STATUS FLAG,   C = CONTROL FLAG,   X = SYSTEM FLAG

NOTE: 0 OR 1 INDICATES INTEL RESERVED. DO NOT DEFINE.

Figure 8.19   Protected-mode flag register. (Reprinted by permission of Intel Corp. Copyright/Intel Corp., 1986.)

it was called from another task. This bit is automatically set whenever a nested task is initiated and can only be reset through software.

Protected-Mode Memory Management and Address Translation

Up to this point in the section, we have introduced the register set of the protected-mode software model for the 80386 microprocessor. However, the software model of a microprocessor also includes its memory structure. Because of the memory management capability of the 80386, the organization of protected mode memory appears quite complex. Here we will examine how the *memory management unit* of the 80386 implements the address space and how it translates virtual (logical) addresses to physical addresses.

Virtual address and virtual address space.   The protected-mode memory management unit employs memory pointers that are 48 bits in length and consist of two parts, the *selector* and the *offset*. This 48-bit memory pointer is called a *virtual address* and is used by the program to specify the memory locations of instructions or data. As shown in Fig. 8.20, the selector is 16 bits in length and the offset is 32 bits long. Earlier we pointed out that one source of selectors is the segment selector registers within the 80386. For instance, if code is being accessed in memory, the active segment selector will be that held in CS. This part of the pointer selects a unique segment of the 80386's *virtual address space*.

The offset is held in one of the 80386's other user-accessible registers. For our example of a code access, the offset would be in the EIP register. This part of the pointer is the displacement of the memory location that is to be accessed within the selected segment of memory. In our example, it points to the first byte of the instruction that is to be fetched for execution. Since the offset is 32 bits in length, segment

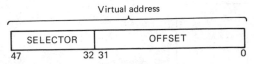

Figure 8.20 Protected-mode memory pointer.

size can be as large as 4 GB. We say as large as 4-GB bytes because segment size is actually variable and can be defined to be as small as 1 byte to as large as 4-GB bytes.

Figure 8.21 shows that the 16-bit selector breaks down into a *13-bit index, table select bit,* and 2 bits used for a *request privilege level.* The two RPL bits are not used in the selection of the memory segment. That is, just 14 of its 16 bits are employed in addressing memory. Therefore, the virtual address space can consists of 14^2 (16,384) unique segments of memory, each of which has a maximum size of 4 GB. These segments are the basic element into which the memory management unit of the 80386 organizes the virtual address space.

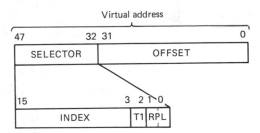

Figure 8.21 Segment selector format.

Another way of looking at the size of the virtual address space is that, by combining the 14-bit segment selector with the 32 bit offset, we get a 46-bit virtual address. Therefore, the 80386's virtual address space can contain 2^{46} = 64 terabytes (TB).

Segmented partitioning of the virtual address space. The memory managemet unit of the 80386 implements a segmented model of virtual memory. In this model, the 80386's 64-TB virtual address space is partitioned into a 32-TB *global memory address space* and a 32-TB *local memory address space*. This partitioning is illustrated in Fig. 8.22. The TI bit of the selector shown in Fig. 8.21 is used to select between the global or local descriptor tables that define the virtual address space. Within each of these address spaces, as many as 8192 segments of memory may exist. This assumes that every descriptor in both the global descriptor table and local descriptor table is in use. These descriptors define the attributes of the corresponding segment. However, in practical system applications not all the descriptors are normally in use. Let us now look briefly at how global and local segments of memory are used by software.

In the multiprocessing software environment of the 80386, an application is expressed as a collection of tasks. By *task* we mean a group of program routines that together perform a specific function. When the 80389 initiates a task, it can have both global and local segments of memory active. This idea is illustrated in Fig. 8.23. Notice that tasks 1, 2, and 3 each have a reserved segment of the local address space. This part of memory stores data or code that can only be accessed by the

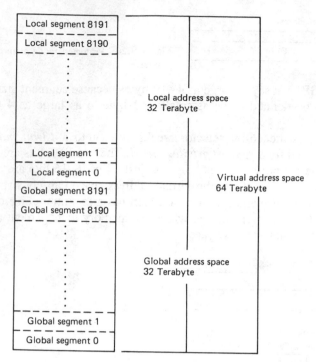

Local segment 8191

Local segment 8190

⋮

Local segment 1

Local segment 0

Global segment 8191

Global segment 8190

⋮

Global segment 1

Global segment 0

Local address space
32 Terabyte

Virtual address space
64 Terabyte

Global address space
32 Terabyte

Figure 8.22 Partitioning the virtual address space.

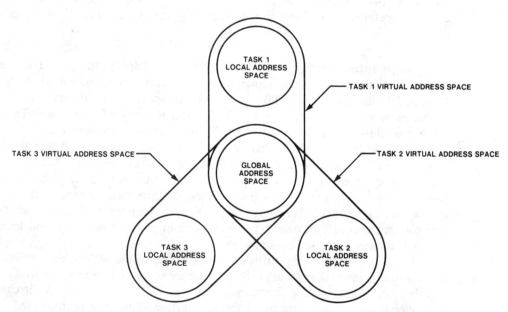

Figure 8.23 Global and local memory for a task. (Reprinted by permission of Intel Corp. Copyright/Intel Corp., 1987.)

corresponding task. That is, task 2 cannot access any of the information in the local address space of task 1. On the other hand, all the tasks are shown to share the same segment of the global address space. This segment typically contains operating system resources and data that are to be shared by all or many tasks.

Physical address space and virtual to physical address translation. We have just found that the virtual address space available to the programmer is 64 TB in length. However, the 32-bit protected-mode address bus of the 80386 supports just a 4-GB *physical address space.* For this reason, systems that employ a virtual address space that is larger than the implemented physical memory are equipped with a secondary storage device such as a hard disk. In this way, segments that are not currently in use are stored on disk.

The segmentation and paging memory management units of the 80386 provide the mechanism by which 48-bit virtual addresses are mapped into the 32-bit physical addresses needed by hardware. This address translation is illustrated in general with the diagram in Fig. 8.24. Notice that, first, a *segment translation* is performed on the virtual (logical) address. Then, if paging is disabled, the *linear address* produced is equal to the physical address. However, if paging is enabled, the linear address goes through a second translation process, known as *page translation,* to produce the physical address.

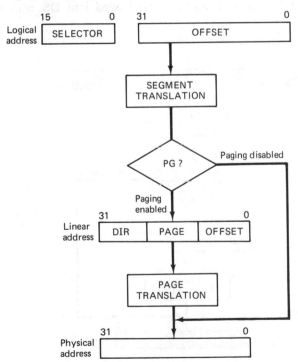

Figure 8.24 Virtual to physical address translation. (Reprinted by permission of Intel Corp. Copyright/Intel Corp., 1986.)

As part of the segment translation process, the MMU determines whether or not the corresponding segment of the virtual address space currently exists in physical memory. If the segment is not present, it signals this condition as an error. Once this condition is signaled, the operating system can initiate loading of the segment from the external storage device to physical memory. This operation is called a *swap*. That is, an old segment gets swapped out to disk to make room in physical memory, and then the new segment is swapped into this space. Even though a swap has taken place, it appears to the program that all segments are available in physical memory. Let us now look more closely at the address translation process.

We will begin by assuming that paging is turned off. In this case, the address translation sequence that takes place is that highlighted in Fig. 8.25(a). Figure 8.25(b) details the operations that take place during the segment traslation process. Earlier we found that the 80386's segment selector registers, CS, DS, ES, FS, GS, and SS, provide the segment selectors that are used to index into either the global descriptor table or the local descriptor table. Whenever a selector value is loaded into a segment register, the descriptor pointed to by the index in the table selected by the TI bit is automatically fetched from memory and loaded into the corresponding *segment descriptor cache register*.

Notice in Fig. 8.26 that the 80386 has one 64-bit internal segment descriptor cache register for each segment selector register. These cache registers are not accessible by the programmer. Instead, they are transparently loaded with a complete descriptor whenever an instruction is executed that loads a new selector into a segment register. For instance, if an operand is to be accessed from a new data segment, a local memory data segment selector would be first loaded into DS with the instruction

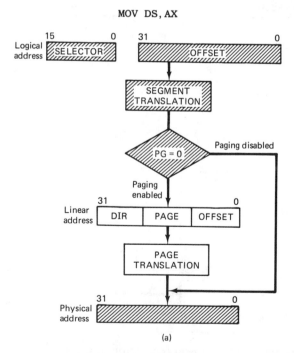

Figure 8.25 (a) Virtual to linear address translation (reprinted by permission of Intel Corp. Copyright/Intel Corp., 1986); (b) translating a virtual address into a physical (linear) address.

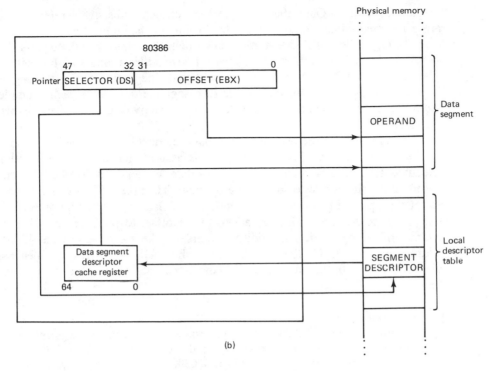

Figure 8.25 (continued)

As this instruction is executed, the selector in AX is loaded into DS and then the corresponding descriptor in the local descriptor table is read from memory and loaded into the data segment descriptor cache register.

In this way, we see that the segment descriptors held in the caches dynamically change as a task is performed. At any one time, the memory management unit permits just six segments of memory to be active. These segments correspond to the six segment selector registers, CS, DS, ES, FS, GS, and SS, and an reside in either local

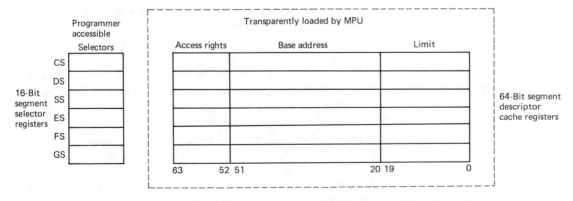

Figure 8.26 Segment selector registers and the segment descriptor cache registers.

or global memory. Once the descriptors are cached, subsequent references to them are performed without any overhead for loading of the descriptor.

In Fig. 8.26, we find that this data segment descriptor has three parts, 12 bits of *access rights* information, a 32-bit *segment base address,* and a 20-bit *segment limit.* The value of the 32-bit base address identifies the beginning of the data segment that is to be accessed. The loading of the data segment descriptor cache completes the table lookup that maps the 16-bit selector to its equivalent 32-bit data segment base address.

The location of the operand in this data segment is determined by the offset part of the virtual address. For example, let us assume that the next instruction to be executed needs to access an operand in this data segment and that the instruction uses based addressing mode to specify the operand. Then the EBX register holds the offset of the operand from the base address of the data segment. Figure 8.25(a) shows that the base address is directly added to the offset to produce the 32-bit physical address of the operand. This addition completes the translation of the 48-bit virtual address into the 32-bit linear address. As shown in Fig. 8.25(a), when paging is disabled, PG = 0, the linear address is the physical address of the storage location to be accessed in memory.

EXAMPLE 8.12

Assume that in Fig. 8.25(b) the virtual address is made up of a segment selector equal to 0100_{16} and offset equal 00002000_{16} and that paging is disabled. If the segment base address read in from the descriptor is 00030000_{16}, what is the physical address of the operand?

SOLUTION   The virtual address is

$$\text{VIRTUAL ADDRESS} = 0100{:}00002000_{16}$$

This virtual address translates to the physical address

$$\text{LINEAR ADDRESS} = \text{BASE ADDRESS} + \text{OFFSET}$$
$$= 00030000_{16} + 00002000_{16}$$
$$= 00032000_{16}$$

The paging memory management unit works beneath the segmentation memory management unit and, when enabled it organizes the 80386's address space in a different way. Earlier we pointed out that when paging is not in use the 4-GB physical address space is organized into segments that can be any size from 1 byte to 4GB. However, when paging is turned on, the paging unit arranges the physical address space into 1,048,496 pages that are each 4096 bytes long. Figure 8.27 shows the physical address space organized in this way. Let us continue by looking at what happens to the address translation process when paging is enabled.

In Fig. 8.28, we see that the linear address produced by the segment translation process is no longer used as the physical address. Instead, it undergoes a second translation called the *page translation.* Figure 8.29 shows the format of a linear address. Notice that it is composed of three elements, a 20-bit offset field, a 10-bit page field, and a 10-bit directory field.

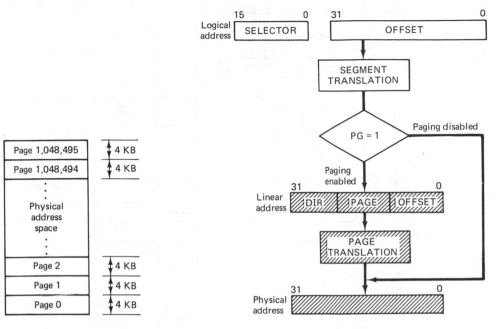

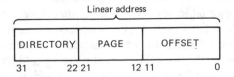

Logical address: SELECTOR (15 0) OFFSET (31 0)

SEGMENT TRANSLATION

PG = 1 — Paging disabled

Paging enabled

Linear address (31 0): DIR PAGE OFFSET

PAGE TRANSLATION

Physical address (31 0)

Page 1,048,495 — 4 KB
Page 1,048,494 — 4 KB
⋮
Physical address space
⋮
Page 2 — 4 KB
Page 1 — 4 KB
Page 0 — 4 KB

Figure 8.27 Paged organization of the physical address space.

Figure 8.28 Paged translation of a linear address to a physical address. (Reprinted by permission of Intel Corp. Copyright/Intel Corp., 1986.)

The diagram in Fig. 8.30 illustrates how a linear address is translated into its equivalent physical address. Earlier we found that the location of the *page directory table* in memory is identified by the value in the page directory base register (PDBR) in CR_3. Notice that the 10-bit directory field of the linear address is the offset from the value in PDBR that selects one of the 1K 32-bit *page directory entries* in the *page directory table*. This pointer is cached inside the 80386 in what is called the *translation lookaside buffer*. Its value is used as the base address of a *page table* in memory. Next the 10-bit page field of the linear address selects one of the 1K, 32-bit *page table entries* from the page table. This table entry is also cached in the translation lookaside buffer. In Fig. 8.30 we see that it is another base address and defines a 4K-byte *page frame* in memory. This frame of memory locations is used for storage of data. The 12-bit offset part of the linear address identifies the location of the operand in the active page frame.

The 80386's translation lookaside buffer is actually capable of maintaining 32 sets of table entries. For this reason, an attempt to reuse any of these 32 pages is implemented without a need for additional memory accesses. In this way, we see that

Linear address

DIRECTORY	PAGE	OFFSET
31 22	21 12	11 0

Figure 8.29 Linear address format.

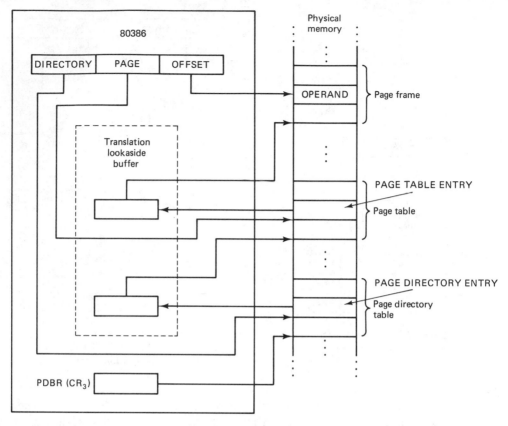

Figure 8.30 Translating a linear address to a physical address.

128KB of paged memory is always directly accessible. That is, operands in this part of memory can be accessed without first reading new entries from the page tables.

8.5 DESCRIPTOR AND PAGE TABLE ENTRIES

In the previous section of this chapter we frequently used the terms *descriptor* and *page table entry*. We talked about the descriptor as an element of the global descriptor, local descriptor, and interrupt descriptor tables. Actually, there are several kinds of descriptors supported by the 80386, and they all serve different functions relative to overall system operation. Some examples are the *segment descriptor, system segment descriptor, local descriptor table descriptor, call gate descriptor, task state segment descriptor,* and *task gate descriptor*. Moreover, we discussed page table entries in our description of the 80386's page translation of linear addresses. There are just two types of page table entries, the *page directory entry* and the *page table entry*. Let us now explore the structure of descriptors and page table entries.

Descriptors are the elements by which the on-chip memory manager manages the segmentation of the 80386's 64-TB virtual memory address space. One descriptor exists for each segment of memory in the virtual address space. Descriptors are assigned to the local descriptor table, global descriptor table, task state segment, call gate, task gate, and interrupts. The contents of a descriptor provide mapping from virtual addresses to linear addresses for code, data, stack, and the task state segments and assign attributes to the segment.

Each descriptor is 8 bytes long and contains three kinds of information. Earlier we identified the 20-bit *LIMIT* field and showed that its value defines the size of the segment or the table. Moreover, we found that the 32-bit *BASE* value provides the beginning address for the segment or the table in the 64-GB linear address space. The third element of a descriptor, which is called the *access rights byte,* is different for each type of descriptor. Let us now look at the format of just two types of descriptors, the segment descriptor and system segment descriptor.

The segment descriptor is the type of descriptor that is used to describe code, data, and stack segments. Figure 8.31(a) shows the general structure of a segment

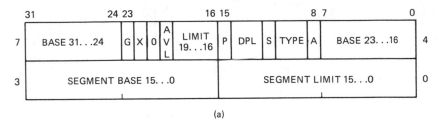

(a)

Bit Position	Name		Function	
7	Present (P)	P = 1	Segment is mapped into physical memory.	
		P = 0	No mapping to physical memory exists, base and limit are not used.	
6–5	Descriptor Privilege Level (DPL)		Segment privilege attribute used in privilege tests.	
4	Segment Descriptor (S)	S = 1	Code or Data (includes stacks) segment descriptor	
		S = 0	System Segment Descriptor or Gate Descriptor	
3	Executable (E)	E = 0	Data segment descriptor type is:	If
2	Expansion Direction (ED)	ED = 0	Expand up segment, offsets must be ≤ limit.	Data
		ED = 1	Expand down segment, offsets must be > limit.	Segment
1	Writeable (W)	W = 0	Data segment may not be written into.	(S = 1,
		W = 1	Data segment may be written into.	E = 0)
3	Executable (E)	E = 1	Code Segment Descriptor type is:	If
2	Conforming (C)	C = 1	Code segment may only be executed when CPL ≥ DPL and CPL remains unchanged.	Code Segment
1	Readable (R)	R = 0	Code segment may not be read	(S = 1,
		R = 1	Code segment may be read.	E = 1)
0	Accessed (A)	A = 0	Segment has not been accessed.	
		A = 1	Segment selector has been loaded into segment register or used by selector test instructions.	

Type Field Definition (bracket spanning rows 3 through 1)

(b)

Figure 8.31 (a) Segment descriptor format; (b) access byte bit definitions. (Reprinted by permission of Intel Corp. Copyright/Intel Corp., 1987.)

descriptor. Here we see that the two lowest addressed bytes, byte 0 and 1, hold the 16 least significant bits of the limit, the next 3 bytes contain the 24 least significant bits of the base address, byte 5 is the access rights byte, the lower 4 bits of byte 6 are the four most significant bits of the limit, the upper 4 bits include the *granularity* (G) and the *programmer available* (AVL) bits, and byte 7 is the eight most significant bits of the 32-bit base. Segment descriptors are only found in the local and global descriptor tables.

Figure 8.32 shows how a descriptor is loaded from the local descriptor table in

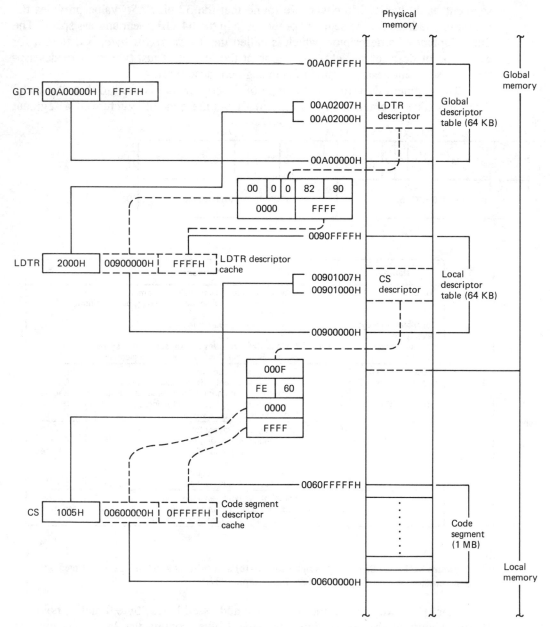

Figure 8.32 Creating a code segment.

global memory to define a code segment in local memory. Notice that the LDTR descriptor defines a local descriptor table between addresses 00900000_{16} and $0090FFFF_{16}$. The value 1005_{16}, which is held in the code segment selector register, causes the descriptor at offset 1000_{16} in the local descriptor table to be cached into the code segment descriptor cache. In this way, a 1-MB code segment is activated starting at address 00600000_{16} in local memory.

The bits of the access rights byte define the operating characteristics of a segment. For example, they contain information about a segment such as whether the descriptor has been accessed, if it is a code or data segment descriptor, its privilege level, if it is readable or writable, and if it is currently loaded into internal memory.

The function of each bit in the access rights byte is listed in Fig. 8.31(b). Notice that if bit 0 is logic 1 the descriptor has been accessed. A descriptor is marked this way to indicate that its value has been cached on the 80386. Bit 4 identifies whether the descriptor represents a code/data segment or is a control descriptor. Let us assume that this bit is 1 to identify a segment descriptor. Then, the type bits, bits 1 through 3, determine whether the descriptor describes a code segment or a data segment. The DPL bits, bits 5 and 6, assign a privilege level to the segment. Finally, the present bit indicates whether or not the segment is currently loaded into physical memory. This bit can be tested by the operating system software to determine if the segment should be loaded from a secondary storage device such as a hard disk. For example, if the access rights byte has logic 1 in bit 7, the data segment is already available in physical memory and does not have to be loaded from an external device. Figure 8.33(a) shows the general form of a code segment descriptor and Fig. 8.33(b) a general data/stack segment descriptor.

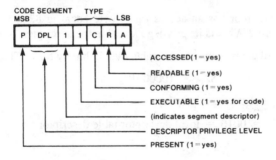

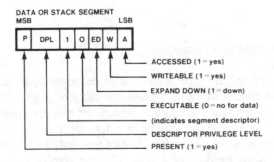

Figure 8.33 (a) Code segment descriptor access byte configuration (reprinted by permission of Intel Corp. Copyright/Intel Corp., 1987); (b) data or stack segment access byte configuration (reprinted by permission of Intel Corp. Copyright/Intel Corp., 1987).

EXAMPLE 8.13

The access rights byte of a segment descriptor contains FE_{16}. What type of segment descriptor does it describe and what are its characteristics?

SOLUTION   Expressing the byte in binary form, we get

$$FE_{16} = 11111110_2$$

Since bit 4 is 1, the access rights byte is for a code/data segment descriptor. This segment has the characteristics that follow:

$$P = 1 = \text{segment is mapped into physical memory}$$

$$DPL = 11 = \text{privilege level 3}$$

$$E = 1 = \text{executable code segment}$$

$$C = 1 = \text{conforming code segment}$$

$$R = 1 = \text{readable code segment}$$

$$A = 0 = \text{segment has not been accessed}$$

An example of a system segment descriptor is the descriptor used to define the local descriptor table. This descriptor is located in the GDT. Looking at Fig. 8.34, we find that the format of a system segment descriptor is similar to the segment descriptor we just discussed. However, the type field of the access rights byte takes on new functions.

EXAMPLE 8.14

If a system segment descriptor has an access rights byte equal to 82_{16}, what type of descriptor does it represent? What is its privilege level? Is the descriptor present?

SOLUTION   First, we will express the access rights byte in binary form. This gives

$$82_{16} = 10000010_2$$

Now we see that the type of the descriptor is

$$TYPE = 0010 = \text{local descriptor table descriptor}$$

The privilege level is

$$DPL = 00 = \text{privilege level 0}$$

and since

$$P = 1$$

the descriptor is present in physical memory.

Now that we have explained the format and use of descriptors, let us continue with page table entries. The format of either a page directory or page table entry is shown in Fig. 8.35. Here we see that the 20 most significant bits are either the base address of the page table if the entry is in the page directory table or the base address of the page frame if the entry is in the page table. Notice that only bits 12 through 31 of the base address are supplied by the entry. The 12 least significant bits are as-

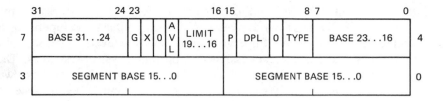

Name	Value	Description
TYPE	0	Reserved by Intel
	1	Available 80286 TSS
	2	LDT
	3	Busy 80286 TSS
	4	Call gate
	5	Task gate
	6	80286 interrupt gate
	7	80286 trap gate
	8	Reserved by Intel
	9	Available 80386 TSS
	A	Reserved
	B	Busy 80386 TSS
	C	80386 call gate
	D	Reserved by Intel
	E	80386 interrupt gate
	F	80386 trap gate
P	0	Descriptor contents are not valid
	1	Descriptor contents are valid
DPL	0-3	Descriptor privilege level 0, 1, 2 or 3
BASE	32-bit number	Base address of special system data segment in memory
LIMIT	20-bit number	Offset of last byte in segment from the base

Figure 8.34 System segment descriptor format and field definitions.

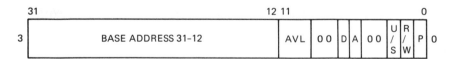

Figure 8.35 Directory or page table entry format.

sumed to be equal to 0. In this way, we see that page tables and page frames are always located on a 4-KB address boundary. In Fig. 8.30, we found that these entries are cached into the translation lookaside buffer when they are accessed.

The 12 lower bits of the entry supply protection characteristics or statistical information about the use of the page table or page frame. For example, the *user/ supervisor* (U/S) and *read/write* (R/W) bits implement a two-level page protection mechanism. Setting U/S to 1 selects user-level protection. User is the low privilege level and is the same as protection level 3 of the segmentation model. That is, user is the protection level assigned to pages of memory that are accessible by application software. On the other hand, making U/S equal to 0 assigns supervisor-level protection to the table or frame. Supervisor corresponds to levels 0, 1, and 2 of the segmentation model and is the level assigned to operating system resources. The *read/write* (R/W) bit is used to make a user-level table or frame read-only or read/write. Logic 1 in R/W selects read-only operation. Figure 8.36 summarizes the access characteristics for each setting of U/S and R/W.

U/S	R/W	User	Supervisor
0	0	None	Read/write
0	1	None	Read/write
1	0	Read-only	Read/write
1	1	Read/write	Read/write

Figure 8.36 User- and supervisor-level access rights.

Protection characteristics assigned by a page directory entry are applied to all page frames defined by the entries in the page table. On the other hand, the attributes assigned to a page table entry only apply to the page frame that it defines. Since two sets of protection characteristics exist for all page frames, the page protection mechanism of the 80386 is designed to always enforce the higher-privileged (more restricting) of the two protection rights.

EXAMPLE 8.15

If the page directory entry for the active page frame is $F1000007_{16}$ and its page table entry is 010000005_{16}, is the frame assigned to the user or supervisor? What access is permitted to the frame from user mode and from supervisor mode?

SOLUTION   First, the page directory entry is expressed in binary form. This gives

$$F10000003_{16} = 11110001000000000000000000000111_2$$

Therefore, the page protection bits are

$$U/SR/W = 11$$

This assigns user-mode and read/write accesses to the complete page frame.
   Next the page table entry for the frame is expressed in binary form as

$$01000005_{16} = 00000001000000000000000000000101_2$$

Here we find that

$$U/SR/W = 10$$

This defines the page frame as a user-mode, read-only page. Since the page frame attributes are the more restrictive, they apply. Looking at Fig. 8.36, we see that user software (application software) can only read data in this frame. On the other hand, supervior software (operating system software) can either read data from or write data into the frame.

The other implemented bits in the directory and page table entry of Fig. 8.35 provide statistical information about the table or frame usage. For instance, the *present* (P) bit identifies whether or not the entry can be used for page address translation. P equal to logic 1 indicates that the entry is valid and is available for use in address translation. On the other hand, if P equals 0, the entry is either undefined or not present in physical memory. If an attempt is made to access a page table or page frame that has its P bit marked 0, a page fault is results. This page fault needs to be serviced by the operating system.

The 80386 also records the fact that a page table or page frame has been accessed. Just before a read or write is performed to any address in a table or frame, the *accessed* (A) bit of the entry is set to 1. This marks it as having been accessed. For page frame accesses, it also records whether the access was for a read or write operation. The *dirty* (D) bit is only defined for a page table entry, and it gets set if a write is performed to any address in the corresponding page frame. In a virtual demand paged memory system, the operating system can check the state of these bits to determine if a page in physical memory needs to be updated on the virtual storage device (hard disk) when a new page is swapped into its physical memory address space. The last three bits are labeled AVL and are available for use by the programmer.

8.6 PROTECTED-MODE SYSTEM CONTROL INSTRUCTION SET

In Chapters 3 and 4, we studied the instruction set of the 8086 microprocessor. The part of the instruction set introduced in these chapters represents the basic instruction set of the 8086 architecture. In Section 8.3, we introduced a number of new instructions that are available in the real-mode instruction set of the 80386. In protected mode, the 80386 executes all the instruction that are available in the real mode. Moreover, it is enhanced with a number of additional instructions that either apply only to protected-mode operation or are used in the real mode to prepare the 80386 for entry into the protected mode. As shown in Fig. 8.37, these instructions are known as the *system control instruction set*.

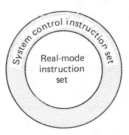

Figure 8.37 Protected-mode instruction set.

The instructions of the system control instruction set are listed in Fig. 8.38. Here we find the format of each instruction along with a description of its operation. Moreover, the mode or modes in which the instruction is available are identified. Let us now look at the operation of some of these instructions in detail.

Looking at Fig. 8.38, we see that the first six instructions can be executed in either the real or protected mode. They provide the ability to load (L) or store (S) the contents of the global descriptor table (GDT) register, interrupt descriptor table (IDT) register, and machine status word (MSW) part of CR_0. Notice that the instruction *load global descriptor table register* (LGDT) is used to load the GDTR from memory. Operand S specifies the location of the 6 bytes of memory that hold the limit and base that specifies the size and beginning address of the GDT. The first word of

Instruction	Description	Mode
LGDT S	Load the global descriptor table register. S specifies the memory location that contains the first byte of the 6 bytes to be loaded into the GDTR.	Both
SGDT D	Store the global descriptor table register. D specifies the memory location that gets the first byte of the 6 bytes to be stored from the GDTR.	Both
LIDT S	Load the interrupt descriptor table register. S specifies the memory location that contains the first byte of the 6 bytes to be loaded into the IDTR.	Both
SIDT D	Store the interrupt descriptor table register. D specifies the memory location that gets the first byte of the 6 bytes to be stored from the IDTR.	Both
LMSW S	Load the machine status word. S is an operand to specify the word to be loaded into the MSW.	Both
SMSW D	Store the machine status word. D is an operand to specify the word location or register where the MSW is to be stored.	Both
LLDT S	Load the local descriptor table register. S specifies the operand to specify a word to be loaded into the LDTR.	Protected
SLDT D	Store the local descriptor table register. D is an operand to specify the word location where the LDTR is to be saved.	Protected
LTR S	Load the task register. S is an operand to specify a word to be loaded into the TR.	Protected
STR D	Store the task register. D is an operand to specify the word location where the TR is to be stored.	Protected
LAR D, S	Load access rights byte. S specifies the selector for the descriptor whose access byte is loaded into the upper byte of the D operand. The low byte specified by D is cleared. The zero flag is set if the loading completes successfully; otherwise it is cleared.	Protected
LSL R16, S	Load segment limit. S specifies the selector for the descriptor whose limit word is loaded into the word register operand R16. The zero flag is set if the loading completes successfully; otherwise it is cleared.	Protected
ARPL D, R16	Adjust RPL field of the selector. D specifies the selector whose RPL field is increased to match the PRL field in the register. The zero flag is set if successful; otherwise it is cleared.	Protected
VERR S	Verify read access. S specifies the selector for the segment to be verified for read operation. If successful the zero flag is set; otherwise it is reset.	Protected
VERW S	Verify write access. S specifies the selector for the segment to be verified for write operation. If successful the zero flag is set; otherwise it is reset.	Protected
CLTS	Clear task switched flag.	Protected

Figure 8.38 Protected-mode system control instruction set.

memory contains the limit and the next 4 bytes contain the base. For instance, executing the instruction

```
LGDT  [INIT_GDTR]
```

loads the GDTR with the base and limit pointed to by address INIT_GDTR to create a global descriptor table in memory. This instruction is meant to be used during system initialization and before switching the 80386 to the protected mode.

Once loaded, the current contents of the GDTR can be saved in memory by executing the *store global descriptor table* (SGDT) instruction. An example is the instruction

```
SGDT    [SAVE_GDTR]
```

The instructions LIDT and SIDT perform similar operations for the IDTR. The IDTR is also set up during initialization.

The instructions *load machine status word* (LMSW) and *store machine status word* (SMSW) are provided to load and store the contents of the machine status word (MSW), respectively. These are the instructions that are used to switch the 80386 from real to protected mode. To do this, we must set the least significant bit in the MSW to 1. This can be done by first reading the contents of the machine status word, modifying the LSB (PE), and then writing the modified value back into the MSW part of CR_0. The instruction sequence that follows will switch an 80386 operating in real mode to the protected mode:

```
SMSW    AX        ; Read from the MSW
OR      AX, 1     ; Modify the PE bit
LMSW    AX        ; Write to the MSW
```

The next four instructions in Fig. 8.38 are also used to initialize or save the contents of protected-mode registers. However, they can be used only when the 80386 is in the protected mode. To load and to save the contents of the LDTR, we have the instructions LLDT and SLDT, respectively. Moreover, for loading and saving the contents of the TR, the equivalent instructions are LTR and STR.

The rest of the instructions in Fig. 8.38 are for accessing the contents of descriptors. For instance, to read a descriptor's access rights byte, the *load access rights byte* (LAR) instruction is executed. An example is the instruction

```
LAR    AX, LDIS_1
```

Execution of this instruction causes the access rights byte of local descriptor 1 to be loaded into AH. To read the segment limit of a descriptor, we use the *load segment limit* (LSL) instruction. For instance, to copy the segment limit for local descriptor 1 into register EBX, the instruction

```
LSL    EBX, LDIS_1
```

is executed. In both cases, ZF is set to 1 if the operation is performed correctly.

The instruction *adjust RPL field of selector* (ARPL) can be used to increase the RPL field of a selector in memory or a register, destination (D), to match the protection level of the selector in a register, source (S). If an RPL-level increase takes place, ZF is set to 1. Finally, the instructions VERR and VERW are provided to test the accessibility of a segment for a read or write operation, respectively. If the descriptor permits the type of access tested for by executing the instruction, ZF is set to 1.

8.7 MULTITASKING AND PROTECTION

We say that the 80386 microprocessor implements a *multitasking* software architecture. By this we mean that it contains on-chip hardware that both permits multiple tasks to exist in a software system and allows them to be scheduled for execution in a time-shared manner. That is, program control is switched from one task to another after a fixed interval of time elapses. For instance, the tasks can be executed in a round-robin fashion. This means that the most recently executed task is returned to the end of the list of tasks being executed.

Earlier we defined a task as a collection of program routines that performs a specific function. This function is also called a *process*. Software systems typically need to perform many processes. In the protected-mode 80386-based microcomputer, each process is identified as an independent task. The 80386 provides an efficient mechanism, called the *task switching mechanism,* for switching between tasks. For instance, an 80386 running at 16 MHz can perform a task switch operation in just $19\mu s$.

We also indicated earlier that when a task is called into operation it can have both global and local memory resources. The local memory address space is divided between tasks. This means that each task normally has its own private segments of local memory. Segments in global memory can be shared by all tasks. Therefore, a task can have access to any of the segments in global memory. As shown in Fig. 8.39, task A has both a private address space and a global address space available for its use.

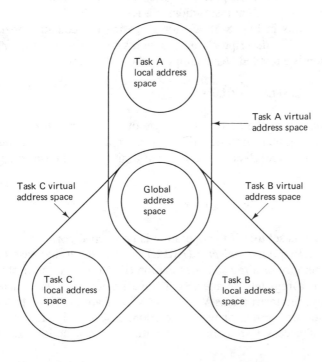

Figure 8.39 Virtual address space of a task. (Reprinted by permission of Intel Corp. Copyright/Intel Corp., 1987.)

Protection and the Protection Model

Safeguards can be built into the protected-mode software system to deny unauthorized or incorrect accesses of a task's memory resources. The concept of safeguarding memory is known as *protection*. The 80386 includes on-chip hardware that implements a *protection mechanism*. This mechanism is designed to put restrictions on the access of local and system resources by a task and to isolate tasks from each other in a multitasking environment.

Segmentation, paging, and descriptors are the key elements of the 80386's protection mechanism. We already identified that, when using a segmented memory model, a segment is the smallest element of the virtual memory address space that has unique protection attributes. These attributes are defined by the access rights information and limit fields in the segment's descriptor. As shown in Fig. 8.40(a), the on-chip protection hardware performs a number of checks during all memory accesses. Figure 8.40(b) is a list of the protection checks and restrictions imposed on software by the 80386. For example, when a data storage location in memory is written to, the type field in the access rights byte of the segment is tested to assure that its attributes are consistent with the register cache being loaded, and the offset is checked to verify that it is within the limit of the segment.

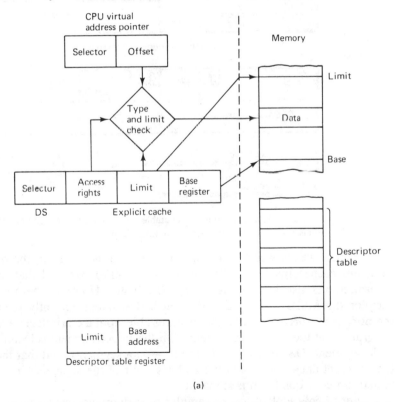

(a)

Figure 8.40 (a) Testing the access rights of a descriptor (reprinted by permission of Intel Corp. Copyright/Intel Corp., 1982); (b) protection checks and restrictions.

Type check
Limit check
Restriction of addressable domain
Restriction of procedure entry point
Restriction of instruction set

(b)   **Figure 8.40**   (*continued*)

Let us just review the attributes that can be assigned to a segment with the access rights information in its descriptor. Figure 8.41 shows the format of a data segment descriptor and a executable (code) segment descriptor. The P bit defines whether a segment of memory is present in physical memory. Assuming that a segment is present, bit 4 of the type field makes it either a code segment or data segment. Notice that this bit is 0 if the descriptor is for a data segment and it is 1 for code segments. Segment attributes such as readable, writable, conforming, expand up or down, and accessed are assigned by other bits in the type field. Finally, a privilege level is assigned with the DPL field.

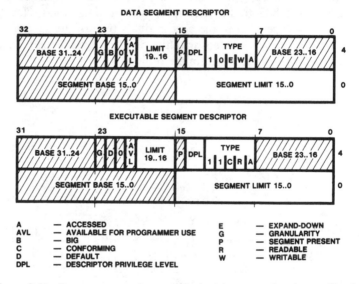

Figure 8.41   Data segment and executable (code) segment descriptors. (Reprinted by permission of Intel Corp. Copyright/Intel Corp., 1986.)

Earlier we showed that whenever a segment is accessed, the base address and limit are cached inside the 80386. In Fig. 8.40(a), we find that the access rights information is also loaded into the cache register. However, before loading the descriptor the MMU verifies that the selected segment currently present in physical memory is at a privilege level that is accessible from the privilege level of the current program, that the type is consistent with the target segment selector register (CS = code segment, DS, ES, FS, GS, or SS = data segment), and that the reference into the segment does not exceed the address limit of the segment. If a violation is detected, an error condition is signaled.

Let us now look at some examples of memory accesses that result in protection violations. For example, if the selector loaded into the CS register points to a descriptor that defines a data segment, the type check leads to a protection violation. Another example of an invalid memory access is an attempt to read an operand from a code segment that is not marked as readable. Finally, any attempt to access a byte of data at an offset greater than LIMIT, a word at an offset equal to or greater than LIMIT, or a double word at an offset equal to or greater than LIMIT-2 extends beyond the end of the data segment and results in a protection violation.

The 80386's protection model provides four possible privilege levels for each task. They are called *levels 0, 1, 2, and 3* and can be illustrated by concentric circles as in Fig. 8.42. Here level 0 is the most privileged and level 3 is the least privileged level.

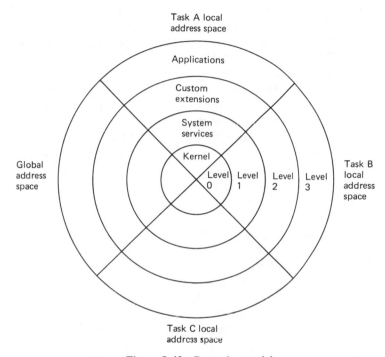

Figure 8.42 Protection model.

System and application software are typically partitioned in the manner shown in Fig. 8.42. The kernel represents application-independent software that provides microprocessor-oriented functions such as I/O control, task sequencing, and memory management. For this reason, it is kept at the most privileged level, level 0. Level 1 contains processes that provide system services such as file accessing. Level 2 is used to implement custom routines to support special-purpose system operations. Finally, the least privileged level, level 3, is the level at which user applications are run. This example also demonstrates how privilege levels are used to isolate system-level software (operating system software in levels 0 through 2) from the user's application software (level 3). Tasks at a level can use programs from the more privileged levels but cannot modify the contents of these routines in any way. In this way, applications are permitted to use system software routines from the three higher privilege levels without affecting their integrity.

Earlier we indicated that protection restrictions are put on the instruction set.

One example of this is that the system control instructions can only be executed in a code segment that is at protection level 0.

We also pointed out that each task is assigned its own local descriptor table. Therefore, as long as none of the descriptors in a task's local descriptor table references code or data available to another task, it is isolated from all other tasks. For instance, in Fig. 8.42 multiple applications running at level 3 are isolated from each other by assigning them different local resources. This shows that segments, privilege levels, and the local descriptor table provide protection for both code and data within a task. These types of protection result in improved software reliability because errors in one application will not affect the operating system or other applications.

Let us now look more closely at how the privilege level is assigned to a code or data segment. Remember that when a task is running it has access to both local and global code segments, local and global data segments, and stack segments. A privilege level is assigned to each of these segments through the access rights information in its descriptor. A segment may be assigned to any privilege level simply by entering the number for the level into the DPL bits.

To provide more flexibility, input/output has two levels of privilege. First, the I/O drivers, which are normally system resources, are assigned to a privilege level. For the software system of Fig. 8.42, we indicate that the I/O control routines were part of the kernel and are at level 0.

The IN, INS, OUT, OUTS, CLI, and STI instructions are what are called *trusted instructions*. This is because the protection model of the 80386 puts additional restrictions on their use in protected mode. They can only be executed at a privilege level that is equal to or more privileged than the *input/output privilege level* (IOPL) code. IOPL supplies the second level of I/O privilege. Remember that the IOPL bits exist in the protected-mode flag register. These bits must be loaded with the value of the privilege level that is to be assigned to input/output instructions through software. The value of IOPL may change from task to task. Assigning the I/O instructions to a level higher that 3 restricts applications from directly performing I/O. Instead, to perform an I/O operation, the application must request service by an I/O driver through the operating system.

Accessing Code and Data Through the Protection Model

During the running of a task, the 80386 may need to either pass control to program routines at another privilege level or access data in a segment that is at a different privilege level. Accesses to code or data in segments at a different privilege level are governed by strict rules. These rules are designed to protect the code or data at the more privileged level from contamination by the less privileged routine.

Before looking at how accesses are made for routines or data at the same or different privilege levels, let us first look at some terminology used to identify privilege levels. We have already been using the terms descriptor privilege level (DPL) and I/O privilege level (IOPL). However, when discussing the protection mechanisms by which processes access data or code, two new terms come into play. They are *current privilege level* (CPL) and *requested privilege level* (RPL). CPL is defined as the privilege level of the code or data segment that is currently being accessed by a task. For example, the CPL of an executing task is the DPL of the access rights byte in the descriptor cache for the CS register. This value normally equals the DPL of the code segment. RPL is the privilege level of the new selector loaded into a segment register. For instance, in the case of code, it is the privilege level of the code segment that contains the routine that is being called. That is, RPL is the DPL of the code segment to which control is to be passed.

As a task in an application runs, it may require access to program routines that reside in segments at any of the four privilege levels. Therefore, the current privilege level of the task changes dynamically with the programs it executes. This is because the CPL of the task is normally switched to the DPL of the code segment currently being accessed.

The protection rules of the 80386 determine what code or data can be accessed by a program. Before looking at how control is passed to code at different protection levels, let us first look at how data segments are accessed by code at the CPL. Figure 8.43 illustrates the protection level checks that are made for a data access. The general rule is that code can only access data that are at the same or a less privileged level. For instance, if the current privilege level of a task is 1, it can access operands that are in data segments with DPL equal to 1, 2, or 3. Whenever a new selector is loaded into the DS, ES, FS, or GS register, the DPL of the target data segment is checked to make sure that it is equal to or less privileged than the most privileged of either CPL or RPL. As long as DPL satisfies this condition, the descriptor is cached inside the 80386 and the data access takes place.

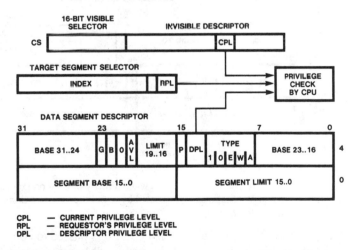

CPL — CURRENT PRIVILEGE LEVEL
RPL — REQUESTOR'S PRIVILEGE LEVEL
DPL — DESCRIPTOR PRIVILEGE LEVEL

Figure 8.43 Privilege-level checks for a data access. (Reprinted by permission of Intel Corp. Copyright/Intel Corp., 1986.)

One exception to this rule is when the SS register is loaded. In this case, the DPL must always equal the CPL. That is, the active stack (one is required for each privilege level) is always at the CPL.

EXAMPLE 8.16

Assuming that, in Fig. 8.43, DPL = 2, CPL = 0, and RPL = 2, will the data access take place?

SOLUTION   DPL of the target segment is 2 and this value is less privileged than CPL = 0, which is the more privileged of CPL and RPL. Therefore, the protection criterion is satisfied and the access will take place.

Different rules apply to how control is passed between code at the same privilege level and between code at different privilege levels. To transfer program control to another instruction in the same code segment, we can simply use a near jump or call instruction. In either case, just a limit check is made to assure that the destination of the jump or call does not exceed the limit of the current code segment.

To pass control to code in another segment that is at the same or a different privilege level, a far jump or call instruction is used. For this transfer of program control, both type and limit checks are performed and privilege level rules are applied. Figure 8.44 shows the privilege checks made by the 80386. There are two conditions under which the transfer in program control will take place. First, if CPL equals the DPL, the two segments are at the same protection level and the transfer occurs. Second, if the CPL represents a more privileged level then DPL, but the conforming code (C) bit in the type field of the new segment is set, the routine is executed at the CPL.

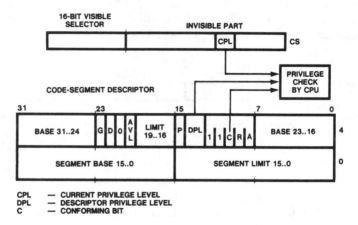

Figure 8.44   Privilege-level checks when directly passing program control to a program in another segment. (Reprinted by permission of Intel Corp. Copyright/ Intel Corp., 1986.)

The general rule that applies when control is passed to code in a segment that is at a different privilege level is that the new code segment must be at a more privileged level. A special kind of descriptor called a *gate descriptor* comes into play to implement the change in privilege level. An attempt to transfer control to a routine in a code segment at a higher privilege level is still initiated with either a far call or far jump instruction. This time the instruction does not directly specify the location of the destination code; instead, it references a gate descriptor. In this case the 80386 goes through a much more complex program control transfer mechanism.

The structure of a gate descriptor is shown in Fig. 8.45. Notice that there are four types of gate descriptors: the *call gate,* the *task gate,* the *interrupt gate,* and the *trap gate.* The call gate implements an indirect transfer of control within a task from code at the CPL to code at a higher privilege level. It does this by defining a valid entry point into the more privileged segment. The contents of a call gate are the virtual address of the entry point: the *destination selector* and the *destination offset.* In Fig. 8.45, we see that the destination selector identifies the code segment that contains the program to which control is to be redirected. The destination offset points to the instruction in this segment where execution is to resume. Call gates can reside in either the GDT or a LDT.

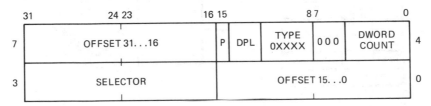

Name	Value	Description
TYPE	4 5 6 7	— Call gate — Task gate — Interrupt gate — Trap gate

P	0
	
	1
		— Descriptor contents are
		  not valid
		— Descriptor contents are
		  valid

DPL	0-3	Descriptor privilege level
WORD COUNT	0-31	Number of double words to copy from callers stack to called procedures stack. Only used with call gate
DESTINATION SELECTOR	16-Bit selector	Selector to the target code segment (call interrupt or trap gate) Selector to the target task state segment (task gate)
DESTINATION OFFSET	32-Bit offset	Entry point within the target code segment

Figure 8.45 Gate descriptor format. (Reprinted by permission of Intel Corp. Copyright/Intel Corp., 1987.)

The operation of the call gate mechanism is illustrated in Fig. 8.46. Here we see that the call instruction includes an offset and a selector. When the instruction is executed, this selector is loaded into CS and points to the call gate. In turn, the call gate causes its destination selector to be loaded into CS. This leads to the caching of the descriptor for the called code segment (executable segment descriptor). The executable segment descriptor provides the base address for the executable segment (code segment) of memory. Notice that the offset in the call gate descriptor locates

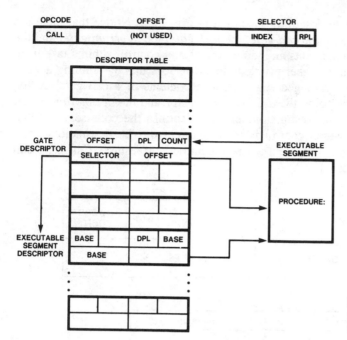

Figure 8.46 Call gate operation. (Reprinted by permission of Intel Corp. Copyright/Intel Corp., 1986.)

the entry point of the procedure in the executable segment.

Whenever the task's current privilege level is changed, a new stack is activated. As part of the program context switching sequence, the old ESP and SS are saved on the new stack along with parameters and the old EIP and CS. This information is needed to preserve linkage for return to the old program environment.

Now the procedure at the higher privilege level begins to execute. At the end of the routine, a RET instruction must be included to return program control back to the calling program. Execution of RET causes the old values of EIP, CS, the parameters, ESP, and SS to be popped from the stack. This restores the original program environment. Now program execution resumes with the instruction following the call instruction in the lower privileged code segment.

Figure 8.47 shows the privilege checks that are performed when program control transfer is initiated through a call gate. For the call to be successful, the DPL of the gate must be the same as the CPL and the RPL of the called code must be higher than the CPL.

Task Switching and the Task State Segment Table

Earlier we identified the task as the key program element of the 80386's multitasking software architecture and that another important feature of this architecture is the high-performance task switching mechanism. A task can be invoked either directly or indirectly. This is done by executing either the intersegment jump or intersegment call instruction. When a jump instruction is used to initiate a task switch, no return linkage to the prior task is supported. On the other hand, if a call is used to switch to the new task instead of a jump, back linkage information is automatically saved. This information permits a return to be performed to the instruction that follows the

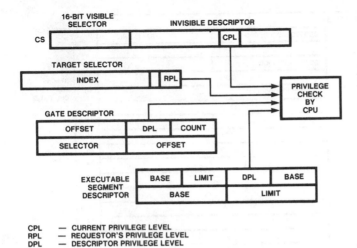

CPL — CURRENT PRIVILEGE LEVEL
RPL — REQUESTOR'S PRIVILEGE LEVEL
DPL — DESCRIPTOR PRIVILEGE LEVEL

Figure 8.47 Privilege-level checks for program control transfer with a call gate. (Reprinted by permission of Intel Corp. Copyright/Intel Corp., 1986.)

calling instruction in the old task at completion of the new task.

Each task that is to be performed by the 80386 is assigned a unique selector called a *task state selector*. This selector is an index to a corresponding *task state segment descriptor* in the global descriptor table. The format of a task state segment descriptor is given in Fig. 8.48.

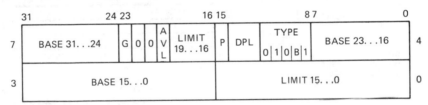

Figure 8.48 TSS descriptor format. (Reprinted by permission of Intel Corp. Copyright/Intel Corp., 1986.)

If a jump or call instruction has a task state selector as its operand, a direct entry is performed to the task. As shown in Fig. 8.49, when a call instruction is executed the selector is loaded into the 80386's task register (TR). Then the corresponding task state segment descriptor is read from the GDT and loaded into the task register cache. This only happens if the criteria specified by the access rights information of the descriptor are satisfied. That is, the descriptor is present (P = 1); the task is not busy (B = 0); and protection is not violated (CPL must be equal to DPL). Looking at Fig. 8.49, we see that, once loaded, the base address and limit specified in the descriptor define the starting point and size of the task's *task state segment* (TSS). This TSS contains all the information that is needed to either start or stop a task.

Before explaining the rest of the task switch sequence, let us first look more closely at what is contained in the task state segment. A typical TSS is shown in Fig. 8.49. Its minimum size is 103 bytes. For this reason, the minimum limit that can be specified in a TSS descriptor is 00065_{16}. Notice that the segment contains information such as the state of the microprocessor (general registers, segment selectors,

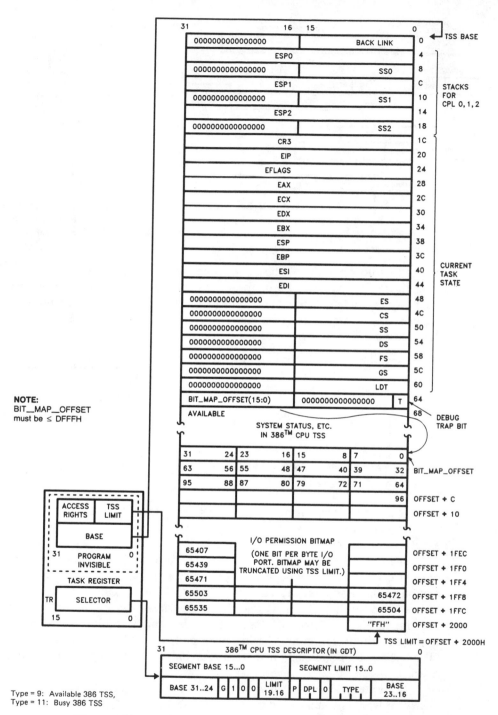

Figure 8.49 Task state segment table. (Reprinted by permission of Intel Corp. Copyright/Intel Corp., 1987.)

instruction pointer, and flag word) needed to initiate the task, a back link selector to the TSS of the task that was active when this task was called, the local descriptor table register selector, a stack selector and pointer for privilege levels 0, 1, and 2, and an I/O permission bit map.

Now we will continue with the procedure by which a task is invoked. Let us assume that a task was already active when a new task was called. Then the new task is what is called a *nested task* and causes the NT bit of the flag word to be set to 1. In this case, the current task is first suspended and then the state of the 80386's user-accessible registers is saved in the old TSS. Next, the B bit in the new task's descriptor is marked busy; the TS bit in the machine status word is set to indicate that a task is active; the state information from the new task's TSS is loaded into the MPU; and the selector for the old TSS is saved as the back-link selector in the new task state segment. The task switch operation is now complete and execution resumes with the instruction identifies by the new contents of the code segment selector (CS) and instruction pointer (EIP).

The old program context is preserved by saving the selector for the old TSS as the back-link selector in the new TSS. By executing return instruction at the end of the new task, the back-link selector for the old TSS is automatically reloaded into TR. This activates the old TSS and restores the prior program environment. Now program execution resumes at the point where it left off in the old task.

The indirect method of invoking a task is by jumping to or calling a *task gate*. This is the method used to transfer control to a task at an RPL that is higher than the CPL. Figure 8.50 shows the format of a task gate. This time the instruction includes a selector that points to the task gate, which is in either the LDT or GDT, instead of a task state selector. The TSS selector held in this gate is loaded into TR to select the TSS and initiate the task. Figure 8.51 illustrates a task initiated through a task gate.

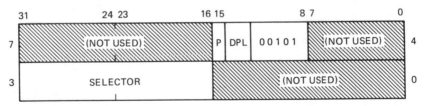

Figure 8.50 Task gate descriptor format. (Reprinted by permission of Intel Corp. Copyright/Intel Corp., 1986.)

Let us consider an example to illustrate the principle of task switching. In Fig. 8.52, we have a table that contains TSS descriptors SELECT0 through SELECT3. These descriptors contain access rights and a selector for tasks 0 through 3, respectively. To invoke the task corresponding to selector SELECT2 in the data segment where these selectors are stored, we can use the following procedure. First, the data segment register is loaded with the address SELECTOR_DATA_SEG_START to point to the segment that contains the selectors. This is done with the instructions

```
MOV   AX, SELECTOR_DATA_SEG_START
MOV   DS, AX
```

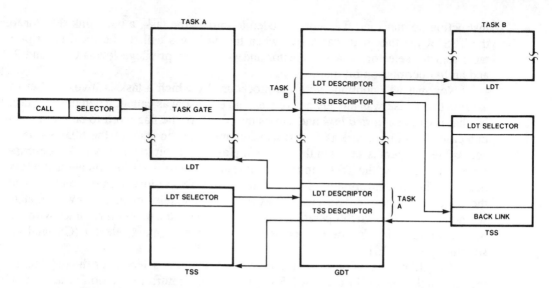

Figure 8.51 Task switch through a task gate. (Reprinted by permission of Intel Corp. Copyright/Intel Corp., 1987.)

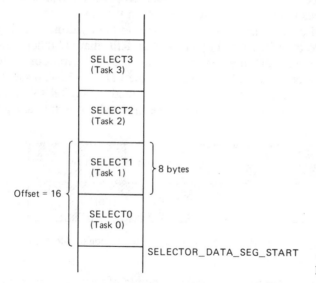

Figure 8.52 Task gate selectors.

Since each selector is 8 bytes long, SELECT2 is offset from the beginning of the segment by 16 bytes. Let us load the offset into register EBX.

```
MOV   EBX, 0F
```

At this point we can use SELECT2 to implement an intersegment jump with the instruction

```
JMP   DWORD PTR [EBX]
```

Execution of this instruction switches program control to the task specified by the selector in descriptor SELECT2. In this case, no program linkage is preserved. On the other hand, by calling the task with the instruction

CALL   DWORD PTR [EBX]

linkage is maintained.

8.8 VIRTUAL 86 MODE

8086 and 8088 application programs, such as those written for the PC DOS operating system, can be directly run on the 80386 in real mode. A protected-mode operating system, such as UNIX, can also run DOS applications without change. This is done through what is called *virtual 86 mode*. When in this mode, the 80386 supports an 8086 microprocessor programming model and can directly run programs written for the 8086. That is, it creates a virtual 8086 machine for executing programs.

In this kind of application, the 80386 is switched back and forth between protected mode and virtual 86 mode. The UNIX operating system and UNIX applications are run in protected mode, and when the DOS operating system and a DOS application are to be run, the 8086 is switched to the virtual 86 mode. This mode switching is controlled by a program known as a *virtual 86 monitor*.

Virtual 86 mode of operation is selected by the bit called *virtual mode* (VM) in the extended flag register. VM must be switched to 1 to enable virtual 86 mode of operation. Actually, the VM bit in EFLAGS is not directly switched to 1 by software. This is because virtual 86 mode is normally entered as a protected-mode task. Therefore, the copy of EFLAGS in the TSS for the task would include VM equal 1. These EFLAGS are loaded as part of the task switching process. In turn, virtual 86 mode of operation is initiated. The virtual 86 program is run at privilege level 3. The virtual 86 monitor is responsible for setting and resetting the VM bit in the task's copy of EFLAGS and permits both protected-mode tasks and virtual-86-mode tasks to coexist in a multitasking program environment.

Another way of initiating virtual 86 mode is through an interrupt return. In this case, the EFLAGS are reloaded from the stack. Again the copy of EFLAGS must have the VM bit set to 1 to enter the virtual 86 mode of operation.

ASSIGNMENT

Section 8.2

1. How does the performance of a 16-MHz 80386 compare to that of a 5-MHz 8086?
2. What is meant when we say that the 80386 is object code compatible with the 8086?
3. In the real mode, is the AX register 16 bits or 32 bits in length? The DS register?
4. What new registers are found in the 80386's real-mode software model?

Section 8.3

5. Describe the operation performed by the instruction PUSH 1234.
6. Which registers and in what order does the instruction POPA pop from the stack?
7. What is a stack frame?
8. How much stack does the instruction ENTER 1F,4 allocate for the stack frame? What is the lexical level?
9. If (DS) = (ES) = 1075_{16}, (DI) = 100_{16}, (DF) = 0, and (DX) = 1000_{16}, what happens when the instruction INSW is executed?
10. If (DS) = (ES) = 1075_{16}, (SI) = 100_{16}, (DF) = 1, (CX) = $000F_{16}$, and (DX) = 2000_{16}, what happens when the instruction REPOUTSB is executed?
11. Explain the function of the bound instruction in the sequence

```
SCAN:   DEC    DI
        BOUND  DI,LIMITS
        .
        .
        .
        JNZ    SCAN
```

Assume that address LIMITS contains the value 0000_{16} and LIMITS + 2 holds the value $00FF_{16}$.

12. Write an instruction that wil move the contents of control register 1 to the extended base register.
13. What instruction does the mnemonic SHLD stand for?
14. Describe the operation performed by the instruction

```
MOVSX   EAX, BL
```

15. Write an instruction that will zero-extend the word of data at address DATA_WORD and copy it into register EAX.
16. What operation is performed when the instruction LFS EDI,DATA_F_ADDRESS is executed?
17. If the values in AX and CL are $F0F0_{16}$ and 04_{16}, what is the result in AX and CF after execution of each of the instructions that follow:
   (a) BT AX,CL (b) BTR AX,CL (c) BTC AX,CL
18. What does the mnemonic SETNC stand for? What flag condition does it test for?

Section 8.4

19. List the protected-mode registers that are not part of the real-mode model.
20. What are the two parts of the GDTR called?
21. What is the function of the GDTR?
22. If the contents of the GDTR are $0021000001FF_{16}$, what are the starting and ending addresses of the table? How large is the table? How many descriptors can be stored in the table?
23. What is stored in the GDT?
24. What do IDTR and IDT stand for?

25. What is the maximum limit that should be used in the IDTR?

26. What is stored in the IDT?

27. What descriptor table defines the local memory address space?

28. What gets loaded into the LDTR? What happens when it gets loaded?

29. Which control register contains the MSW?

30. Which bit is used to switch the 80286 from real-address mode to protected-address mode?

31. What MSW bit settings identify that floating-point operations are to be performed by an 80387 coprocessor?

32. What does TS stand for?

33. What must be done to turn on paging?

34. Where is the page directory base register located?

35. How large is the page directory?

36. What is held in the page table?

37. What gets loaded into TR? What is its function?

38. What is the function of the task descriptor cache?

39. What determines the location and size of a task state segment?

40. What is the name of the CS register in the protected mode? The DS register?

41. What are the names and sizes of the three fields in a selector?

42. What does TI equals 1 mean?

43. If the GDT register contains $0013000000FF_{16}$ and the selector loaded into the LDTR is 0040_{16}, what is the starting address of the LDT descriptor that is to be loaded into the cache?

44. What does NT stand for? RF?

45. If the IOPL bits of the flag register contain 10, what is the privilege level of the I/O instructions?

46. How large is the 80386's virtual address?

47. What are the two parts of a virtual address called?

48. How large can a data segment be? How small?

49. How large is the 80386's virtual address space? What is the maximum number of segments that can exist in the virtual address space?

50. How large is the global memory address space? How many segments can it contain?

51. In Fig. 8.23, which segments of memory does task 3 have access to? Which segments does it not have access to?

52. What part of the 80386 is used to translate virtual addresses to physical addresses?

53. What happens when the instruction sequence that follows is executed?

```
MOV   AX,[SI]
MOV   CS,AX
```

54. If the descriptor accessed in Problem 53 has the value $00200000FFFF_{16}$ and IP contains 0100_{16}, what is the physical address of the next instruction to be fetched?

55. Into how many pages is the 80386's address space mapped when paging is enabled? What is the size of a page?

56. What are the three elements of the linear address that is produced by page translation? Give the size of each element.

57. What is the purpose of the translation lookaside buffer?
58. How large is a page frame? What selects the specific storage location in the page frame?

Section 8.5

59. How many bytes are in a descriptor? Name each of its fields and give their size.
60. Which registers are segment descriptors associated with? System segment descriptors?
61. The selector 0224_{16} is loaded into the data segment register. This value points to a segment descriptor starting at address 00100220_{16} in the local descriptor table. If the words of the descriptor are

$$(00100220) = 0110_{16}$$

$$(00100222) = 0000_{16}$$

$$(00100224) = 1A20_{16}$$

$$(00100226) = 0000_{16}$$

what are the LIMIT and BASE?
62. Is the segment of memory identified by the descriptor in Problem 61 already loaded into physical memory? A code segment or data segment?
63. If the current value of IP is 0226_{16}, what is the physical address of the next instruction to be fetched from the code segment of Problem 61?
64. What do the 20 most significant bits of a page directory or page table entry stand for?
65. The page mode protection of a page frame is to provide no access from the user protection level and read/write operation at the supervisor protection level. What are the settings of R/W and U/S?
66. What happens when an attempt is made to access a page frame that has $P = 0$ in its page table entry?
67. What does the D bit in a page directory entry stand for?

Section 8.6

68. If the instruction LGDT [INIT_GDTR] is to load the limit $FFFF_{16}$ and base 00300000_{16}, show how the descriptor must be stored in memory.
69. Write an instruction sequence that can be used to clear the task-switched bit of the MSW.
70. Write an instruction sequence that will load the local descriptor table register with the selector $02F0_{16}$ from register BX.

Section 8.7

71. Define the term multitasking.
72. What is a task?
73. What two safeguards are implemented by the 80386's protection mechanism?
74. What happens if either the segment limit check or segment attributes check fails?
75. What is the highest privilege level of the 80386 protection model called? Lowest level called?
76. At what protection level are applications run?

77. What is the protection mechanism used to isolate local and global resources?

78. What protection mechanism is used to isolate tasks?

79. What is the privilege level of the segment defined by the descriptor in Problem 61?

80. What does CPL stand for? RPL?

81. Overview the data access protection rule.

82. Which privilege-level data segments can be accessed by an application running at level 3?

83. Summarize the code access protection rules.

84. If an application is running at privilege level 3, what privilege-level operating system software is available to it?

85. What purpose does a call gate serve?

86. Explain what happens when the instruction CALL [NEW_ROUTINE] is executed within a task. Assume that NEW_ROUTINE is at a privilege level that is higher than the CPL.

87. What is the purpose of the task state descriptor?

88. What is the function of a task state segment?

89. Where is the state of the prior task saved? Where is the linkage to the prior task saved?

90. Into which register is the TSS selector loaded to initiate a task?

91. Give an overview of the task switch sequence illustrated in Fig. 8.51.

Section 8.8

92. Which bit position in EFLAGS is VM?

93. Is 80386 protection active or inactive in virtual 86 mode? If so, what is the privilege level of a virtual 86 program?

94. Can both protected mode and virtual 86 tasks coexist in an 80386 multitasking environment?

95. Can multiple virtual 86 tasks be active in an 80386 multitasking environment?

9

Hardware Architecture of the 80386 Microprocessor

9.1 INTRODUCTION

In Chapter 8, we studied the software architecture of the 80386 microprocessor. We covered its real- and protected-mode software architectures, extended instruction set, 80386 specific instruction set, and system control instruction set. Now we will turn our attention to the hardware architecture of the 80386-based microcomputer system. In this chapter, we examine the signal interface of the 80386, its memory interface, input/output interface, and interrupts and exception processing. For this purpose, we have included the following topics in the chapter:

1. 80386 microprocessor
2. Signal interfaces of the 80386
3. System clock
4. Bus states and bus cycles
5. Memory interface
6. Input/output interface
7. Interrupt and exception processing

9.2 80386 MICROPROCESSOR

The 80386, first announced in 1985, was the sixth member of Intel Corporation's 8086 family of microprocessors. We already have learned that from the software point of view the 80386 offers several modes of operation: real-address mode, protected-address mode, and virtual 80 mode. The real mode is for compatibility with the large existing 8088/8086 software base; protected mode offers designer-enhanced, system-level features such as memory management, multitasking, and protection; and virtual 86 mode provides 8086 real-mode compatibility while in the protected mode.

Hardware compatibility of the 80386 with either the 8086 or 80286 microprocessors is much less of a concern. In fact, a number of changes have been made to the hardware architecture of the 80386 to improve both its versatility and performance. For example, additional pipelining has been provided within the 80386, and the address and data buses have both been made 32 bits in length. These two changes in the hardware result in increased performance for 80386-based microcomputers. Another feature, *dynamic bus sizing* for the data bus, provides more versatility in system hardware design.

The 80386 is manufactured using Intel's complementary high-performance metal-oxide-semiconductor III (CHMOSIII) process. Its circuitry is equivalent to approximately 275,000 transistors, more than twice those used in the design of the 80286 MPU and almost 10 times that of the 8086. It is available in a 132-pin ceramic *pin grid array* (PGA) package. An 80386 in this package is shown in Fig. 9.1.

The signal at each lead of the package is shown in Fig. 9.2(a). Notice that all the 80386's signals are supplied at separate pins on the package. This is intended to simplify the microcomputer circuit design.

Figure 9.1 80386 IC. (Courtesy of Intel Corporation.)

Looking at Fig. 9.2(a), we see that the rows of pins on the package are identified by row numbers 1 through 14 and the columns of pins are labeled A through P. Therefore, the location of the pin for each signal is uniquely defined by a column and row coordinate. For example, in Fig. 9.2(a) address line A_{31} is at the junction of

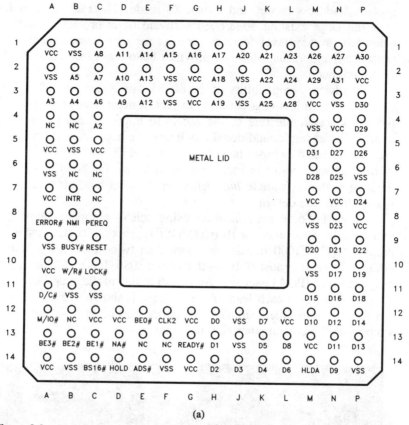

Figure 9.2 (a) Pin layout of the 80386 (reprinted by permission of Intel Corp. Copyright/Intel Corp., 1987); (b) signal pin numbering (reprinted by permission of Intel Corp. Copyright/Intel Corp., 1987).

column N and row 2. That is, it is at pin N2. The pin locations for all of the 80386's signals are listed in Fig. 9.2(b).

EXAMPLE 9.1

At what pin location is the signal D_0?

SOLUTION Looking at Fig. 9.2(a), we find the pin for D_0 is located in column H at row 12. Therefore, its pin is identified as H12 in Fig. 9.2(b).

9.3 SIGNAL INTERFACES OF THE 80386

A block diagram of the 80386 microprocessor is shown in Fig. 9.3. Here we have grouped its signal lines into four interfaces: the *memory/IO interface, interrupt interface, DMA interface,* and *coprocessor interface.* Figure 9.4 lists each of the signals at the 80386's interfaces. Included in this table are a mnemonic, function, type, and active level for each signal. For instance, we find that the memory/IO interface signal with the mnemonic M/$\overline{\text{IO}}$ stands for memory/IO indication. This signal is an output

Pin / Signal	Pin / Signal	Pin / Signal	Pin / Signal
N2 A31	M5 D31	A1 V_{CC}	A2 V_{SS}
P1 A30	P3 D30	A5 V_{CC}	A6 V_{SS}
M2 A29	P4 D29	A7 V_{CC}	A9 V_{SS}
L3 A28	M6 D28	A10 V_{CC}	B1 V_{SS}
N1 A27	N5 D27	A14 V_{CC}	B5 V_{SS}
M1 A26	P5 D26	C5 V_{CC}	B11 V_{SS}
K3 A25	N6 D25	C12 V_{CC}	B14 V_{SS}
L2 A24	P7 D24	D12 V_{CC}	C11 V_{SS}
L1 A23	N8 D23	G2 V_{CC}	F2 V_{SS}
K2 A22	P9 D22	G3 V_{CC}	F3 V_{SS}
K1 A21	N9 D21	G12 V_{CC}	F14 V_{SS}
J1 A20	M9 D20	G14 V_{CC}	J2 V_{SS}
H3 A19	P10 D19	L12 V_{CC}	J3 V_{SS}
H2 A18	P11 D18	M3 V_{CC}	J12 V_{SS}
H1 A17	N10 D17	M7 V_{CC}	J13 V_{SS}
G1 A16	N11 D16	M13 V_{CC}	M4 V_{SS}
F1 A15	M11 D15	N4 V_{CC}	M8 V_{SS}
E1 A14	P12 D14	N7 V_{CC}	M10 V_{SS}
E2 A13	P13 D13	P2 V_{CC}	N3 V_{SS}
E3 A12	N12 D12	P8 V_{CC}	P6 V_{SS}
D1 A11	N13 D11		P14 V_{SS}
D2 A10	M12 D10		
D3 A9	N14 D9	F12 CLK2	A4 N.C.
C1 A8	L13 D8		B4 N.C.
C2 A7	K12 D7	E14 ADS#	B6 N.C.
C3 A6	L14 D6		B12 N.C.
B2 A5	K13 D5	B10 W/R#	C6 N.C.
B3 A4	K14 D4	A11 D/C#	C7 N.C.
A3 A3	J14 D3	A12 M/IO#	E13 N.C.
C4 A2	H14 D2	C10 LOCK#	F13 N.C.
A13 BE3#	H13 D1		
B13 BE2#	H12 D0	D13 NA#	C8 PEREQ
C13 BE1#		C14 BS16#	B9 BUSY#
E12 BE0#		G13 READY#	A8 ERROR#
	D14 HOLD		
C9 RESET	M14 HLDA	B7 INTR	B8 NMI

(b)

Figure 9.2 (*continued*)

produced by the 80386 that is used to tell external circuitry whether the current address available on the address bus is for memory or an I/O device. Its active level is listed as 1/0, which means that logic 1 on this line identifies a memory bus cycle and logic 0 an I/O bus cycle. On the other hand, the signal INTR at the interrupt interface is the maskable interrupt request input of the 80386. This input is active when at logic 1. By using this input, external devices can signal the 80386 that they need to be serviced.

Memory/IO Interface

In a microcomputer system, the address bus and data bus signal lines form a parallel path over which the MPU talks with its memory and I/O subsystems. Like the 80286

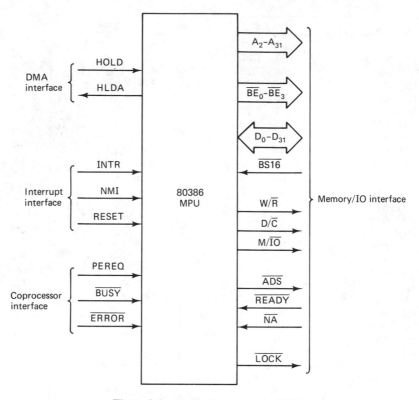

Figure 9.3 Block diagram of the 80386.

microprocessor, but unlike the older 8086 and 8088, the 80386 has a demultiplexed address/data bus. Notice in Fig. 9.2(b) that the address bus and data bus lines are located at different pins of the IC.

From a hardware point of view, there is only one difference between an 80386 configured for the real-address mode or protected virtual-address mode. This difference is the size of the address bus. When in real mode, just the lower 18 address lines, A_2 through A_{19}, are active, while in the protected mode all 30 lines, A_2 through A_{31}, are functional. Of these, A_{19} and A_{31} are the most significant address bits, respectively. Actually, real-mode addresses are 20 bits long and protected-mode addresses are 32 bits long. The other 2 bits, A_0 and A_1 are decoded inside the 80386, along with information about the size of the data to be transferred, to produce *byte enable* outputs, $\overline{BE}_0$, $\overline{BE}_1$, $\overline{BE}_2$, and $\overline{BE}_3$.

As shown in Fig. 9.4, the address lines are outputs. They are used to carry address information from the 80386 to memory and I/O ports. In real-address mode, the 20-bit address gives the 80386 the ability to address a 1-MB physical memory address space. On the other hand, in protected mode the extended 32-bit address results in a 4-GB physical memory address space. Moreover, when in protected mode, virtual addressing is provided through software. This results in a 64-TB virtual memory address space.

In both the real and protected modes, the 80386 microcomputer has an independent I/O address space. This I/O address space is 64K bytes in length. Therefore, just

Name	Function	Type	Level
CLK2	System clock	I	—
A_{31}–A_1	Address bus	O	1
BE_3–BE_0	Byte enables	O	0
D_{31}–D_0	Data bus	I/O	1
$\overline{BS}_{16}$	Bus size 16	I	0
W/$\overline{R}$	Write/read indication	O	1/0
D/$\overline{C}$	Data/control indication	O	1/0
M/$\overline{IO}$	Memory I/O indication	O	1/0
$\overline{ADS}$	Address status	O	0
$\overline{READY}$	Transfer acknowledge	I	0
$\overline{NA}$	Next address request	I	0
$\overline{LOCK}$	Bus lock indication	O	0
INTR	Interrupt request	I	1
NMI	Nonmaskable interrupt request	I	1
RESET	System reset	I	1
HOLD	Bus hold request	I	1
HLDA	Bus hold acknowledge	O	1
PEREQ	Coprocessor request	I	1
$\overline{BUSY}$	Coprocessor busy	I	0
$\overline{ERROR}$	Coprocessor error	I	0

Figure 9.4 Signals of the 80386.

address lines A_2 through A_{15} and the $\overline{BE}$ outputs are used when addressing I/O devices.

Since the 80386 is a 32-bit microprocessor, its data bus is formed from the 32 data lines D_0 through D_{31}. D_{31} is the most significant bit and D_0 the least significant bit. These lines are identified as bidirectional in Fig. 9.4. This is because they have the ability to either carry data in or out of the MPU. The kinds of data transferred over these lines are read/write data for memory, input/output data for I/O devices, and interrupt type codes from an interrupt controller.

Earlier we indicated that the 80386 supports dynamic bus sizing. Even though the 80386 has 32 data lines, the size of the bus can be dynamically switched to 16 bits. This is done by simply switching the *bus size 16* ($\overline{BS\ 16}$) input to logic 0. When in this mode, 32-bit data transfers are performed as two successive 16-bit data transfers over bus lines D_0 through D_{15}.

Remember that the 80386 supports byte, word, and double-word data transfers over its data bus. Therefore, it must signal external circuitry what type of data transfer is taking place and over which part of the data bus the data will be carried. The bus unit does this by activating the appropriate byte enable ($\overline{BE}$) output signals.

Figure 9.5 lists each byte enable output and the part of the data bus it is intended to enable. For instance, here we see that $\overline{BE_0}$ corresponds to data bus lines D_0 through D_7. If a byte of data is being read from memory, just one of the $\overline{BE}$ outputs is made active. For instance, if the most significant byte of an aligned double word is

Byte Enable	Data Bus Lines
$\overline{BE}_0$	$D_0 - D_7$
$\overline{BE}_1$	$D_8 - D_{15}$
$\overline{BE}_2$	$D_{16} - D_{23}$
$\overline{BE}_3$	$D_{24} - D_{31}$

Figure 9.5 Byte enable outputs and data bus lines.

read from memory, $\overline{BE}_3$ is switched to logic 0. On the other hand, if a word of data is being read, two outputs become active. An example would be to read the most significant word of an aligned double word from memory. In this case, $\overline{BE}_2$ and $\overline{BE}_3$ are both switched to logic 0. Finally, if an aligned double word read is taking place, all four $\overline{BE}$ outputs are made active.

EXAMPLE 9.2

What code is output on the $\overline{BE}$ lines whenever the address on the bus is for an instruction acquisition bus cycle?

SOLUTION Since code is always fetched as 32-bit words (aligned double words), all the byte enable outputs are made active. Therefore,

$$\overline{BE}_3\overline{BE}_2\overline{BE}_1\overline{BE}_0 = 0000_2$$

The byte enable lines work exactly the same way when write data transfers are performed over the bus. Figure 9.6(a) identifies what type of data transfer takes place for all the possible variations of the byte enable outputs. Here we find that $\overline{BE}_3\overline{BE}_2\overline{BE}_1\overline{BE}_0 = 1110_2$ means that a byte of data is written over data bus lines D_0 through D_7.

EXAMPLE 9.3

What type of data transfer takes place and over which data bus lines are data transferred if the $\overline{BE}$ code output is

$$\overline{BE}_3\overline{BE}_2\overline{BE}_1\overline{BE}_0 = 1100_2$$

SOLUTION Looking at the table in Fig. 9.6(a), we see that a word of data is transferred over data bus lines D_0 through D_{15}.

The 80386 performs what is called *data duplication* during certain types of write cycles. Data duplication is provided in the 80386 to optimize the performance of the data bus when it is set for 16-bit mode. Notice that whenever a write cycle is performed in which data are only transferred over the upper part of the 32-bit data bus the data are duplicated on the corresponding lines of the lower part of the bus. For example, looking at Fig. 9.6(b), we see that, when $\overline{BE}_3\overline{BE}_2\overline{BE}_1\overline{BE}_0 = 1011_2$, data (denoted as XXXXXXXX) are actually being written over data bus lines D_{16} through D_{23}. However, at the same time, the data denoted as DDDDDDDD in Fig. 9.6(b) are automatically duplicated on data bus lines D_0 through D_7. In spite of the fact that the byte is available on the lower eight data bus lines, $\overline{BE}_0$ stays inactive. The same thing happens when a word of data is transferred over D_{16} through D_{31}. In

$\overline{BE}_3$	$\overline{BE}_2$	$\overline{BE}_1$	$\overline{BE}_0$	$D_{31}-D_{24}$	$D_{23}-D_{16}$	$D_{15}-D_8$	D_7-D_0
1	1	1	0				XXXXXXXX
1	1	0	1			XXXXXXX	
1	0	1	1		XXXXXXXX		
0	1	1	1	XXXXXXXX			
1	1	0	0			XXXXXXXX	XXXXXXXX
1	0	0	1		XXXXXXXX	XXXXXXXX	
0	0	1	1	XXXXXXXX	XXXXXXXX		
1	0	0	0		XXXXXXXX	XXXXXXXX	XXXXXXXX
0	0	0	1	XXXXXXXX	XXXXXXXX	XXXXXXXX	
0	0	0	0	XXXXXXXX	XXXXXXXX	XXXXXXXX	XXXXXXXX

(a)

$\overline{BE}_3$	$\overline{BE}_2$	$\overline{BE}_1$	$\overline{BE}_0$	$D_{31}-D_{24}$	$D_{23}-D_{16}$	$D_{15}-D_8$	D_7-D_0
1	1	1	0				XXXXXXXX
1	1	0	1			XXXXXXX	
1	0	1	1		XXXXXXXX		DDDDDDDD
0	1	1	1	XXXXXXXX		DDDDDDDD	
1	1	0	0			XXXXXXXX	XXXXXXXX
1	0	0	1		XXXXXXXX	XXXXXXXX	
0	0	1	1	XXXXXXXX	XXXXXXXX	DDDDDDDD	DDDDDDDD
1	0	0	0		XXXXXXXX	XXXXXXXX	XXXXXXXX
0	0	0	1	XXXXXXXX	XXXXXXXX	XXXXXXXX	
0	0	0	0	XXXXXXXX	XXXXXXXX	XXXXXXXX	XXXXXXXX

(b)

Figure 9.6 (a) Types of data transfers for the various byte enable combinations; (b) data transfers that include duplication.

this example, $\overline{BE}_3\overline{BE}_2\overline{BE}_1\overline{BE}_0 = 0011_2$, and Fig. 9.6(b) shows that the word is duplicated on data lines D_0 through D_{15}.

EXAMPLE 9.4

If a word of data that is being written to memory is accompanied by the byte enable code 1001_2, over which data bus lines are the data carried? Is data duplication performed for this data transfer?

SOLUTION In the tables of Fig. 9.6, we find that for the byte enable code 1001_2, the word of data is transferred over data bus lines D_8 through D_{23}. For this transfer, data duplication does not occur.

Control signals are required to support information transfers over the 80386's address and data buses. They are needed to signal when a valid address is on the address bus, in which direction data are to be transferred over the data bus, when valid write data are on the data bus, and when an external device can put read data on the data bus. The 80386 does not directly produce signals for all these functions. Instead, it outputs bus cycle definition and control signals at the beginning of each bus cycle. These bus cycle identification signals must be decoded in external circuitry to produce the needed memory and I/O control signals.

Three signals are used to identify the type of 80386 bus cycle that is in progress. In Figs. 9.3 and 9.4, they are labeled *write/read indication* (W/$\overline{R}$), *data/control indication* (D/$\overline{C}$), and *memory/input–output indication* (M/$\overline{IO}$). The table in Fig. 9.7 lists all possible combinations of the bus cycle definition signals and the corresponding type of bus cycle. Here we find that the logic level of memory/input–output (M/$\overline{IO}$) tells whether a memory or I/O cycle is to take place over the bus. Logic 1 at this output signals a memory operation, and logic 0 signals an I/O operation. The next signal in Fig. 9.7, data/control indication (D/$\overline{C}$), identifies whether the current bus cycle is a data or control cycle. In the table, we see that it signals control cycle (logic 0) for instruction fetch, interrupt acknowledge, and halt/shut down operation and data cycle (logic 1) for memory and I/O data read and write operations. Looking more closely at the table in Fig. 9.7, we find that if the code on these two lines, M/$\overline{IO}$ D/$\overline{C}$, is 00 an interrupt is to be acknowledged; if it is 01, an input/output operation is in progress; if it is 10, instruction code is being fetched; and, finally, if it is 11, a data memory read or write is taking place.

M/$\overline{IO}$	D/$\overline{C}$	W/$\overline{R}$	Type of Bus Cycle
0	0	0	Interrupt acknowledge
0	0	1	Idle
0	1	0	I/O data read
0	1	1	I/O data write
1	0	0	Memory code read
1	0	1	Halt/shutdown
1	1	0	Memory data read
1	1	1	Memory data write

Figure 9.7 Bus cycle definition signals and types of bus cycles.

The last signal identified in Fig. 9.7, write/read indication (W/$\overline{R}$), identifies the specific type of memory or input/output operation that will occur during a bus cycle. For example, when W/$\overline{R}$ is logic 0 during a bus cycle, data are to be read from memory or an I/O port. On the other hand, logic 1 at W/$\overline{R}$ says that data are to be written into memory or an I/O device. For example, all bus cycles that read instruction code from memory are accompanied by logic 0 on the W/$\overline{R}$ line.

EXAMPLE 9.5

What type of bus cycle is taking place if the bus cycle definition code M/$\overline{IO}$D/$\overline{C}$W/$\overline{R}$ equals 010?

SOLUTION   Looking at the table in Fig. 9.7, we see that bus cycle definition code 010 identifies an I/O data read (input) bus cycle.

Three bus cycle control signals are found at pins of the 80386. They are identified in Figs. 9.3 and 9.4 as *address status* ($\overline{ADS}$), *transfer acknowledge* ($\overline{READY}$), and *next address request* ($\overline{NA}$). The $\overline{ADS}$ output is switched to logic 0 to indicate that the bus cycle definition (M/$\overline{IO}$D/$\overline{C}$W/$\overline{R}$), byte enable code ($\overline{BE_3}\overline{BE_2}\overline{BE_1}\overline{BE_0}$), and address ($A_2$ through A_{31}) signals are all stable. Therefore, it is normally applied to an input of the external bus control logic circuit and tells it that a valid bus cycle definition and address are available. In Fig. 9.7, the bus cycle definition code $M/\overline{IOD}/\overline{C}W/\overline{R} = 001$ is identified as *idle*. That is, it is the code that is output whenever no bus cycle is being performed.

$\overline{READY}$ can be used to insert wait states into the current bus cycle such that it is extended by a number of clock periods. In Fig. 9.4, we find that this signal is an input to the 80386. Normally, it is produced by the microcomputer's memory or I/O subsystem and supplied to the 80386 by way of external bus control logic circuitry. By switching $\overline{READY}$ to logic 0, slow memory or I/O devices can tell the 80386 when they are ready to permit a data transfer to be completed.

Earlier we pointed out that the 80386 supports address pipelining at its bus interface. By address pipelining, we mean that the address and bus cycle definition for the next bus cycle is output before $\overline{READY}$ becomes active to signal that the prior bus cycle can be completed. This mode of operation is optional. The external bus control logic circuitry activates pipelining by switching the next address request ($\overline{NA}$) input to logic 0. By using pipelining, delays introduced by the decode logic can be made transparent and the address to data access time increased. In this way, the same level of performance can be obtained with slower, lower-cost memory devices.

One other bus interface control output that is supplied by the 80386 is the *bus lock indication* ($\overline{LOCK}$). This signal is needed to support multiple-processor architectures. In multiprocessor systems that employ shared resources, such as global memory, this signal can be employed to assure that the 80386 has uninterrupted control of the system bus and the shared resource. That is, by switching its $\overline{LOCK}$ output to logic 0, the MPU can lock up the shared resource for exclusive use.

Interrupt Interface

Looking at Figs. 9.3 and 9.4, we find that the key interrupt interface signals are *interrupt request* (INTR), *nonmaskable interrupt request* (NMI), and *system reset* (RESET). INTR is an input to the 80386 that can be used by external devices to signal that they need to be serviced. The 80386 samples this input at the beginning of each instruction. Logic 1 on INTR represents an active interrupt request.

When an active interrupt request has been recognized by the 80386, it signals this fact to external circuitry and initiates an interrupt acknowledge bus cycle sequence. In Fig. 9.7, we see that the occurrence of an interrupt acknowledge bus cycle is signaled to external circuitry with the bus cycle definition $M/\overline{IOD}/\overline{C}W/\overline{R}$ equals 000. This bus cycle definition code can be decoded in the external bus control logic circuitry to produce an interrupt acknowledge signal. With this interrupt acknowledge signal, the 80386 tells the external device that its request for service has been granted. This completes the interrupt request/acknowledge handshake. At this point, program control is passed to the interrupt's service routine.

The INTR input is maskable. That is, its operation can be enabled or disabled with the interrupt flag (IF) within the 80386's flag register. On the other hand, the NMI input, as its name implies, is a nonmaskable interrupt input. On any 0-to-1 transition of NMI, a request for service is latched within the 80386. Independent of the setting of the IF flag, control is passed to the beginning of the nonmaskable interrupt service routine at the completion of execution of the current instruction.

Finally, the RESET input is used to provide a hardware reset to the 80386 microprocessor. Switching RESET to logic 1 initializes the internal registers of the 80386. When it is returned to logic 0, program control is passed to the beginning of a reset service routine. A diagnostic routine that tests the 80386 microprocessor can also be initiated as part of the reset sequence.

DMA Interface

Now that we have examined the signals of the 80386's interrupt interface, let us turn our attention to the *direct memory access* (DMA) interface. From Figs. 9.3 and 9.4, we find that the DMA interface is implemented with just two signals: *bus hold request* (HOLD) and *bus hold acknowledge* (HLDA). When an external device, such as a *DMA controller,* wants to take over control of the local address and data busses, it signals this fact to the 80386 by switching the HOLD input to logic 1. At completion of the current bus cycle, the 80386 enters the hold state. When in the hold state, its local bus signals are in the high-impedance state. Next, the 80386 signals external devices that it has given up control of the bus by switching its HLDA output to the 1 logic level. This completes the hold/hold acknowledge handshake sequence. The 80386 remains in this state until the hold request is removed.

Coprocessor Interface

In Fig. 9.3, we find that a coprocessor interface is provided on the 80386 microprocessor to permit it to easily interface to either the *80287* or *80387 numerics coprocessor.* The 80387 cannot perform transfers over the data bus by itself. Whenever the 80387 needs to read or write operands from memory, it must signal the 80386 to initiate the data transfers. The 80387 does this by switching the *coprocessor request* (PEREQ) input of the 80386 to logic 1.

The other two signals included in the external coprocessor interface are $\overline{\text{BUSY}}$ and $\overline{\text{ERROR}}$. *Coprocessor busy* ($\overline{\text{BUSY}}$) is an input of the 80386. Whenever the 80387 is executing a numeric instruction, it signals this fact to the 80386 by switching the $\overline{\text{BUSY}}$ input to logic 0. In this way, the 80386 knows not to request the numerics coprocessor to perform another calculation until $\overline{\text{BUSY}}$ returns to 1. Moreover, if an error occurs in a calculation performed by the numerics coprocessor, this condition is signaled to the 80386 by switching the *coprocessor error* ($\overline{\text{ERROR}}$) input to the 0 logic level.

9.4 SYSTEM CLOCK

The time base for synchronization of the internal and external operations of the 80386 microprocessor is provided by the *clock* (CLK2) input signal. At present, the 80386 is available with four different clock speeds. The standard 80386-16 MPU operates at 16 MHz and its three faster versions, the 80386-20, 80386-25, and 80386-33, operate at 20, 25, and 33 MHz, respectively. The clock signal applied to the CLK2 input of the 80386 is twice the frequency rating of the microprocessor.

Therefore, CLK2 of an 80386-16 is driven by a 32-MHz signal. This signal must be generated in external circuitry.

The waveform of the CLK2 input of the 80386 is given in Fig. 9.8. This signal is specified at CMOS-compatible voltage levels and not TTL levels. Its minimum and maximum low logic levels are $V_{ILCmin} = -0.3$ V and $V_{ILCmax} = 0.8$ V, respectively. Moreover, the minimum and maximum high logic levels are $V_{IHCmin} = V_{CC} - 0.8$ V and $V_{IHCmax} = V_{CC} + 0.3$ V, respectively. The minimum period of the 16-MHz clock signal is $t_{Cmin} = 31$ ns (measured at the 2.0 V level); its minimum high time t_{Pmin} and low time t_{Imin} (measured at the 2.0-V level) are both equal to 9 ns; and the maximum rise time t_{rmax} and fall time t_{fmax} of its edges (measured between the $V_{CC} - 0.8$V and 0.8 V levels) are both equal to 8 ns.

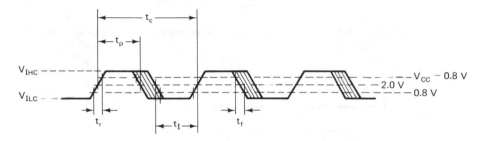

Figure 9.8 System clock (CLK2) waveform.

9.5 BUS STATES AND PIPELINED AND NONPIPELINED BUS CYCLES

Before looking at the bus cycles of the 80386, let us first examine the relationship between the timing of the 80386's CLK2 input and its bus cycle states. The *internal processor clock* (PCLK) signal is at half the frequency of the external clock input. Therefore, as shown in Fig. 9.9, one processor clock cycle corresponds to two CLK2 cycles. Notice that these CLK2 cycles are labeled as *phase 1* (ϕ_1) and *phase 2* (ϕ_2). In a 20-MHz 80386 microcomputer system, CLK2 equals 40 MHz and each clock cycle has a duration of 25 ns. In Fig. 9.9, we see that the two phases ($\phi_1 + \phi_2$) of a processor cycle are identified as one processor clock period. A processor clock period is also called a *T state*. Therefore, an internal processor clock cycle is a minimum of 50 ns long.

Nonpipelined and Pipelined Bus Cycles

A *bus cycle* is the activity performed whenever a microprocessor accesses information in program memory, data memory, or an I/O device. The 80386 can perform bus cycles with either of two types of timing: *nonpipelined* and *pipelined*. Here we will examine the difference between these two types of bus cycles.

Figure 9.10 shows a typical nonpipelined microprocessor bus cycle. Notice that the bus cycle contains two T states and that they are called T_1 and T_2. During the T_1 part of the bus cycle, the 80386 outputs the address of the storage location that is to

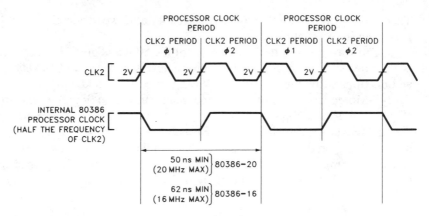

Figure 9.9 Processor clock cycles. (Reprinted by permission of Intel Corp. Copyright/Intel Corp., 1987.)

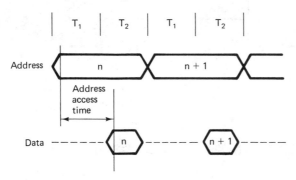

Figure 9.10 Typical read/write bus cycle.

be accessed on the address bus, a bus cycle definition code, and control signals. In the case of a write cycle, write data are also output on the data bus during T_1. The second state, T_2, is the part of the bus cycle during which external devices are to accept write data from the data bus or, in the case of a read cycle, put data on the data bus.

For instance, in Fig. 9.10 we see that the sequence of events starts with an address, denoted as n, being output on the address bus in clock state T_1. Later in the bus cycle, while the address is still available on the address bus, a read or write data transfer takes place over the data bus. Notice that the data transfer for address n is shown to occur in clock state T_2. Since each bus cycle has a minimum of two T states (four CLK2 cycles), the minimum bus cycle duration for an 80386-20 is 100 ns.

Let us now look at a microprocessor bus cycle that employs *pipelining*. By pipelining we mean that addressing for the next bus cycle is overlapped with the data transfer of the prior bus cycle. When address pipelining is in use, the address, bus cycle definition code, and control signals for the next bus cycle are output during T_2 of the prior cycle, instead of the T_1 that follows.

In Fig. 9.11, we see that address n becomes valid in the T_2 state of the prior bus cycle, and then the data transfer for address n takes place in the next T_2 state. Moreover, notice that at the same time that data transfer n occurs address n + 1 is output on the address bus. In this way, we see that the microprocessor begins addressing the

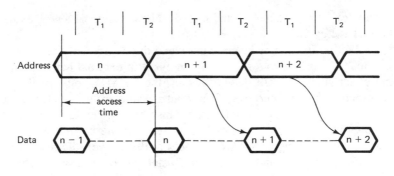

Figure 9.11 Pipelined bus cycle. (Reprinted by permission of Intel Corp. Copyright/Intel Corp., 1987.)

next storage location that it is to accessed while it is still performing the read or write of data for the previously addressed storage location. Due to the address/data pipelining, the memory or I/O subsystem actually has five CLK2 cycles (125 ns for an 80386-20 running at full speed) to perform the data transfer, even though the duration of every bus cycle is just four CLK2 cycles (100 ns).

The interval of time denoted as *address access time* in Fig. 9.10 represents the amount of time that the address must be stable prior to the read or write of data actually taking place. Notice that this duration is less than the four CLK2 cycles in a nonpipelined bus cycle. Figure 9.11 shows that in a pipelined bus cycle the *effective address access time* equals the duration of a complete bus cycle. This leads us to the benefit of the 80386's pipelined mode of bus operation over the nonpipelined mode of operation. It is that, for a fixed address access time (equal speed memory design), the 80386 pipelined bus cycle will have a shorter duration than its nonpipelined bus cycle. This results in improved bus performance.

In Fig. 9.11, we find that at completion of the bus cycle for address n another bus cycle is immediately initiated for address n + 1. Sometimes another bus cycle will not be immediately initiated. For instance, if the 80386's prefetch queue is already full and the instruction that is currently being executed does not need to access operands in memory, no bus activity will take place. In this case, the bus goes into a mode of operation known as an *idle state* and no bus activity occurs. Figure 9.12 shows a sequence of bus activity in which several idle states exist between the bus

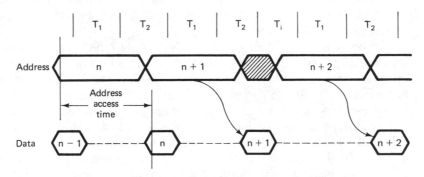

Figure 9.12 Idle states in bus activity.

cycles for addresses n + 1 and n + 2. The duration of a single idle state is equal to two CLK2 cycles.

Wait states can be inserted to extend the duration of the 80386's bus cycle. This is done in response to a request by an event in external hardware instead of an internal event such as a full queue. In fact, the $\overline{READY}$ input of the 80386 is provided specifically for this purpose. This input is sampled in the later part of the T_2 state of every bus cycle to determine if the data transfer should be completed. Figure 9.13 shows that logic 1 at this input indicates that the current bus cycle should not be completed. As long as $\overline{READY}$ is held at the 1 level, the read or write data transfer does not take place and the current T_2 state becomes a wait state (T_w) to extend the bus cycle. The bus cycle is not completed until external hardware returns $\overline{READY}$ back to logic 0. This ability to extend the duration of a bus cycle permits the use of slow memory or I/O devices in the microcomputer system.

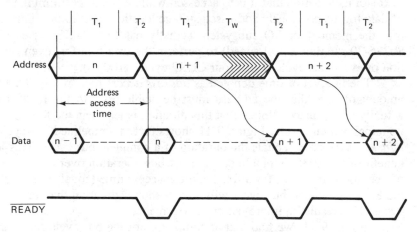

Figure 9.13 Bus cycle with wait states.

Nonpipelined Read Cycle Timing

The memory interface signals that occur when the 80386 reads data from memory are shown in Fig. 9.14. This diagram shows two separate nonpipelined read cycles. They are *cycle 1*, which is performed without wait states, and *cycle 2*, which includes one wait state. Let us now trace the events that take place in cycle 1 as data or instructions are read from memory.

The occurrence of all signals in the read bus cycle timing diagram are illustrated relative to the two timing states, T_1 and T_2, of the 80386's bus cycle. The read operation starts at the beginning of phase 1 (ϕ_1) in the T_1 state of the bus cycle. At this moment, the 80386 outputs the address of the double-word memory location to be accessed on address bus lines A_2 through A_{31}, the byte enables signals $\overline{BE}_0$ through $\overline{BE}_3$ that identify the bytes of the double word that are to be fetched, and switches address strobe ($\overline{ADS}$) to logic 0 to signal that a valid address is on the address bus. Looking at Fig. 9.14, we see that the address and cycle definition signals are maintained stable during the complete bus cycle; however, they must be latched into the external bus control logic circuitry synchronously with the pulse to

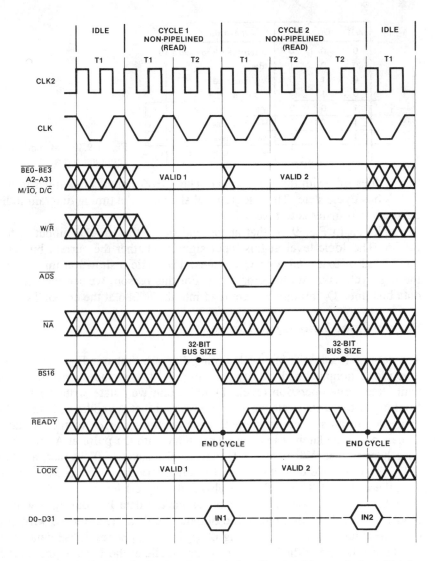

Figure 9.14 Nonpipelined read cycle timing. (Reprinted by permission of Intel Corp. Copyright/Intel Corp., 1987.)

logic 0 on $\overline{\text{ADS}}$. At the end of ϕ_2 of T_1, $\overline{\text{ADS}}$ is returned to its inactive logic 1 level.

Notice in Fig. 9.14 that the bus cycle definition signals, M/$\overline{\text{IO}}$, D/$\overline{\text{C}}$, and W/$\overline{\text{R}}$, are also made valid at the beginning of ϕ_1 of state T_1. The bus cycle definition codes that apply to a memory read cycle are highlighted in Fig. 9.15. Here we see that, if code is being read from memory, M/$\overline{\text{IO}}$D/$\overline{\text{C}}$W/$\overline{\text{R}}$ equals 100. That is, signal M/$\overline{\text{IO}}$ is set to logic 1 to indicate to the circuitry in the memory interface that a memory bus cycle is in progress, D/$\overline{\text{C}}$ is set to 0 to indicate that code memory is to be accessed, and W/$\overline{\text{R}}$ is set to 0 to indicate that data are being read from memory.

At the beginning of ϕ_1 in T_2 of the read cycle, external circuitry must signal the 80386 whether the bus is to operate in the 16- or 32-bit mode. In Fig. 9.14, we see

M/$\overline{\text{IO}}$	D/$\overline{\text{C}}$	W/$\overline{\text{R}}$	Type of Bus Cycle
0	0	0	Interrupt acknowledge
0	0	1	Idle
0	1	0	I/O data read
0	1	1	I/O data write
1	0	0	Memory code read
1	0	1	Halt/shutdown
1	1	0	Memory data read
1	1	1	Memory data write

Figure 9.15 Memory read bus cycle definition codes.

that it does this with the $\overline{\text{BS}}_{16}$ signal. The 80386 samples this input in the middle of the T_2 bus cycle state. The 1 logic level shown in the timing diagram indicates that a 32-bit data transfer is to take place.

Notice in Fig. 9.14 that at the end of T_2 the $\overline{\text{READY}}$ input is tested by the 80386. The logic level at this input signals whether the current bus cycle is to be completed or extended with wait states. The logic 0 shown at this input means that the bus cycle is to run to completion. For this reason, we see that data available on data bus lines D_0 through D_{31} are read into the 80386 at the end of T_2.

Nonpipelined Write Cycle Timing

The nonpipelined write bus cycle timing diagram shown in Fig. 9.16 is similar to that given for a nonpipelined read cycle in Fig. 9.14. It includes waveforms for both a no wait state write operation (cycle 1) and a one wait state write operation (cycle 2). Looking at the write cycle waveforms, we find that the address, byte enable, and bus cycle definition signals are output at the beginning of ϕ_1 of the T_1 state. All these signals are to be latched in external circuitry with the pulse at $\overline{\text{ADS}}$. The one difference here is that W/$\overline{\text{R}}$ is at the 1 logic level instead of 0. In fact, as shown in Fig. 9.17, the bus cycle definition code for a memory data write is M/$\overline{\text{IO}}$D/$\overline{\text{C}}$W/$\overline{\text{R}}$ equals 111; therefore, M/$\overline{\text{IO}}$ and D/$\overline{\text{C}}$ are also at the logic 1 level.

Let us now look at what happens on the data bus during a write bus cycle. Notice in Fig. 9.16 that the 80386 outputs the data the are to be written to memory onto the data bus at the beginning of ϕ_2 in the T_1 state. These data are maintained valid until the end of the bus cycle. In the middle of the T_2 state, the logic level of the BS_{16} input is tested by the 80386 and again indicates that the bus is to be used in the 32-bit mode. Finally, at the end of T_2, $\overline{\text{READY}}$ is tested and found to be at its active 0 logic level. Since the memory subsystem has made $\overline{\text{READY}}$ logic 0, the write cycle is complete and the buses and control signal lines are prepared for the next write cycle.

Wait States in a Nonpipelined Memory Bus Cycle

Earlier we showed how wait states are used to lengthen the duration of the memory bus cycle of the 80386. Wait states are inserted with the $\overline{\text{READY}}$ input signal. Upon request from an event in external hardware, for instance, slow memory, the $\overline{\text{READY}}$ input is switched to logic 1. This signals the 80386 that the current bus cycle should

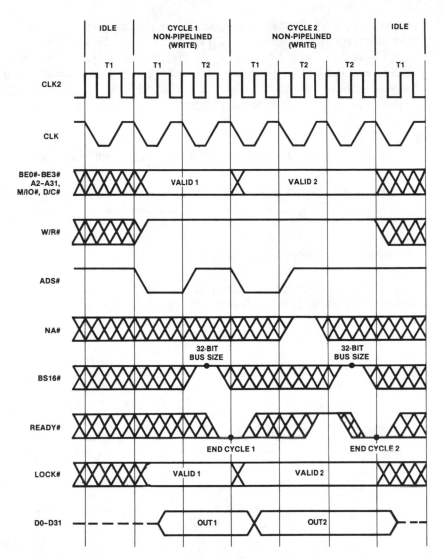

Figure 9.16 Nonpipelined write cycle timing. (Reprinted by permission of Intel Corp. Copyright/Intel Corp., 1987.)

M/$\overline{\text{IO}}$	D/$\overline{\text{C}}$	W/$\overline{\text{R}}$	Type of Bus Cycle
0	0	0	Interrupt acknowledge
0	0	1	Idle
0	1	0	I/O data read
0	1	1	I/O data write
1	0	0	Memory code read
1	0	1	Halt/shutdown
1	1	0	Memory data read
1	1	1	Memory data write

Figure 9.17 Memory write bus cycle definition code.

not be completed. Instead, it is extended by repeating the T_2 state. Therefore, the duration of one wait state ($T_w = T_2$) equals 50 ns for 20-MHz clock operation.

Cycle 2 in Fig. 9.14 shows a read cycle extended by one wait state. Notice that the address, bank enable, and bus cycle definition signals are maintained throughout the wait-state period. In this way, the read cycle is not completed until $\overline{READY}$ is switched to logic 0 in the second T_2 state.

EXAMPLE 9.6

If cycle 2 in Fig. 9.16 is for an 80386-20 running at full speed, what is the duration of the bus cycle?

SOLUTION Each T state in the bus cycle of an 80386 running at 20 MHz is 50 ns. Since the write cycle is extneded by one wait state, the write cycle takes 150 ns.

Pipelined Read/Write Cycle Timing

Timing diagrams for both nonpipelined and pipelined read and write bus cycles are shown in Fig. 9.18. Here we find that the cycle identified as *cycle 3* is an example of a pipelined write bus cycle. Let us now look more closely at this bus cycle.

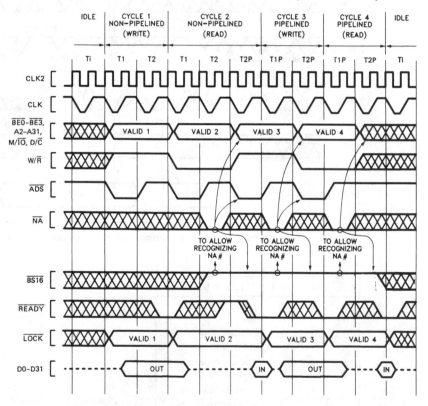

Figure 9.18 Pipelined read and write cycle timing. (Reprinted by permission of Intel Corp. Copyright/Intel Corp., 1987.)

Remember that when pipelined addressing is in use the 80386 outputs the address information for the next bus cycle during the T_2 state of the current cycle. The signal next address ($\overline{NA}$) is used to signal the 80386 that a pipelined bus cycle is to be initiated. This input is sampled by the 80386 during any bus state when $\overline{ADS}$ is not active. In Fig. 9.18, we see that ($\overline{NA}$) is first tested as 0 (active) during T_2 of cycle 2. This nonpipelined read cycle is also extended with period T_{2P} because $\overline{READY}$ is not active. Notice that the address, byte enable, and bus cycle definition signals for cycle 3 become valid (identified as VALID 3 in Fig. 9.18) during this period and a pulse is produced at $\overline{ADS}$. This information is latched externally synchronously with $\overline{ADS}$ and decoded to produce bus enable and control signals. In this way, the memory access time for a zero wait state memory cycle has been increased.

Bus cycle 3 represents a pipelined write cycle. The data to be written to memory are output on D_0 through D_{32} at ϕ_2 of T_{1P} and remain valid for the rest of the cycle. Logic 0 on $\overline{READY}$ at the end of T_{2P} indicates that the write cycle is to be completed without wait states.

Looking at Fig. 9.18, we find that $\overline{NA}$ is also active during T_{1P} of cycle 3. This means that cycle 4 will also be performed with pipelined timing. Cycle 4 is an example of a zero wait state pipelined read cycle. In this case, the address information, bus cycle definition, and address strobe are output during T_{2P} of cycle 3 (the previous cycle), and memory data are read into the MPU at the end of T_{2P} of cycle 4.

9.6 MEMORY INTERFACE

Earlier we indicated that in protected mode the 32-bit address bus of the 80386 results in a 4-GB physical memory address space. As shown in Fig. 9.19, from a software point of view, this memory is organized as individual bytes over the address range from 00000000_{16} through $FFFFFFFF_{16}$. The 80386 can also access data in this memory as words or double words.

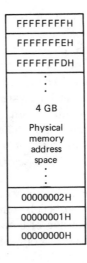

FFFFFFFFH

FFFFFFFEH

FFFFFFFDH

.
.
.

4 GB

Physical
memory
address
space

.
.
.

00000002H

00000001H

00000000H

Figure 9.19 Physical address space.

Hardware Organization of the Memory Address Space

From a hardware point of view, the physical address space is implemented as four independent byte-wide banks, and each of these banks is 1 GB in size. In Fig. 9.20, we find that the banks are identified as *bank 0, bank 1, bank 2,* and *bank 3*. Notice that they correspond to addresses that produce byte enable signals $\overline{BE}_0$, $\overline{BE}_1$, $\overline{BE}_2$, and $\overline{BE}_3$, respectively. Logic 0 at a bank enable input selects the bank for operation. Looking at Fig. 9.20, we see that address bits A_2 through A_{31} are applied to all four banks in parallel. On the other hand, each memory bank supplies just eight lines of the 80386's 32-bit data bus. For example, byte data transfers for bank 0 take place over data bus lines D_0 through D_7, while byte data transfers for bank 3 are carried over data bus lines D_{24} through D_{31}.

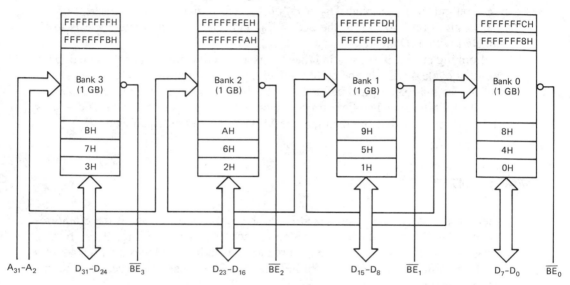

Figure 9.20 Hardware organization of the physical address space.

When the 80386 is operated in real mode, only the value on address lines A_2 through A_{19} and the $\overline{BE}$ signals are used to select the storage location that is to be accessed. For this reason, the physical address space is 1 MB in length, not 4 GB. The memory subsystem is once again partitioned into four banks, as shown in Fig. 9.20 but this time each bank is 256 KB in size.

Figure 9.20 shows that in hardware the memory address space is physically organized as a sequence of double words. The address on lines A_2 through A_{31} selects the double-word storage location. Therefore, each aligned double word starts at a physical address that is a multiple of 4. For instance, in Fig. 9.20, we see that aligned double words start at addresses 00000000_{16}, 00000004_{16}, 00000008_{16}, up through $FFFFFFFC_{16}$.

Each of the 4 bytes of a double word corresponds to one of the bank enable signals. For this reason, they are each stored in a different bank of memory. In Fig. 9.20, we have identified the range of byte addresses that corresponds to the storage locations in each bank of memory. For example, byte data accesses to addresses such as 00000000_{16}, 00000004_{16}, and 00000008_{16} all produce $\overline{BE}_0$, which enables memory bank 0, and the read or write data transfer takes place over data bus lines D_0 through D_7. Figure 9.21(a) illustrates how the byte at double-word aligned memory address X is accessed.

On the other hand, in Fig. 9.20 we see that byte addresses 00000001_{16}, 00000005_{16}, and 00000009_{16} correspond to data held in memory bank 1. Figure 9.21(b) shows how the byte of data at address X + 1 is accessed. Notice that $\overline{BE}_1$ is made active to enable bank 1 of memory.

Most memory accesses produce more than one bank enable signal. For instance, if the word of data beginning at aligned address X is read from memory, both $\overline{BE}_0$ and $\overline{BE}_1$ are generated. In this way, bank 0 and bank 1 of memory are enabled for operation. As shown in Fig. 9.21(c), the word of data is transferred to the MPU over data bus lines D_0 through D_{15}.

Let us now look at what happens when a double word of data is written to aligned double-word address X. As shown in Fig. 9.21(d), $\overline{BE}_0$, $\overline{BE}_1$, $\overline{BE}_2$, and $\overline{BE}_3$ are made 0 to enable all four banks of memory, and the MPU writes the data to memory over the complete data bus, D_0 through D_{31}.

All the data transfers we have described so far have been for what are called *double-word aligned data*. For each of these pieces of data all the bytes existed within the same double word, that is, a double word that is on an address boundary equal to a multiple of 4. The diagram in Fig. 9.22 illustrates a number of aligned words and double words of data. Byte, aligned word, and aligned double-word data transfers are all performed by the 80386 in a single bus cycle.

It is not always possible to have all words or double words of data aligned at double-word boundaries. Figure 9.23 shows some examples of misaligned words and double words of data that can be accessed by the 80386. Notice that word 3 consists of byte 3 that is in aligned double word 0 and byte 4 that is in aligned double word 4. Let us now look at how misaligned data are transferred over the bus.

The diagram in Fig. 9.24 illustrates a misaligned double-word data transfer. Here the double word of data starting at address X + 2 is to be accessed. However, this word consists of bytes X + 2 and X + 3 of the aligned double word at physical address X and bytes Y and Y + 1 of the aligned double word at physical address Y. Looking at the diagram, we see that $\overline{BE}_0$ and $\overline{BE}_1$ are active during the first bus cycle, and the word at address Y is transferred over D_0 through D_{15}. A second bus cycle automatically follows in which $\overline{BE}_3$ and $\overline{BE}_4$ are active, address X is put on the address bus, and the second word of data, X + 2 and X + 3, is carried over D_{16} through D_{31}. In this way, we see that data transfers of misaligned words or double words take two bus cycles.

EXAMPLE 9.7

Is the word at address $0000123F_{16}$ aligned or misaligned? How many bus cycles are required to read it from memory?

SOLUTION The first byte of the word is the fourth byte at aligned double word address $0000123C_{16}$ and the second byte of the word is the first byte of the aligned double word at address 00001240_{16}. Therefore, the word is misaligned and requires two bus cycles to be read from memory.

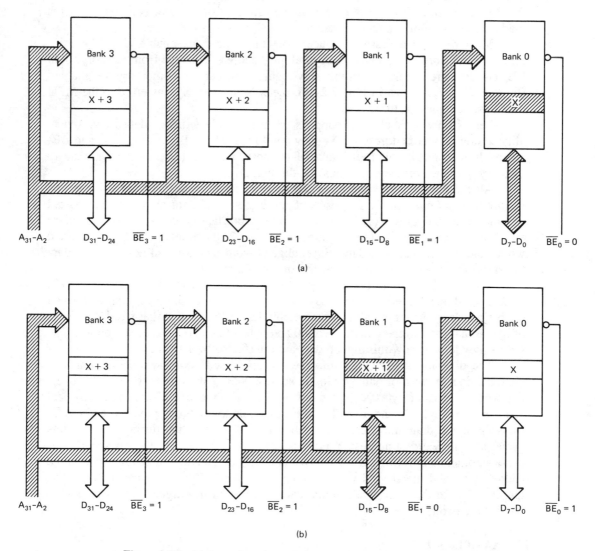

Figure 9.21 (a) Accessing a byte of data in bank 0; (b) accessing a byte of data in bank 1; (c) accessing a word of data in memory; (d) acccessing an aligned double word in memory.

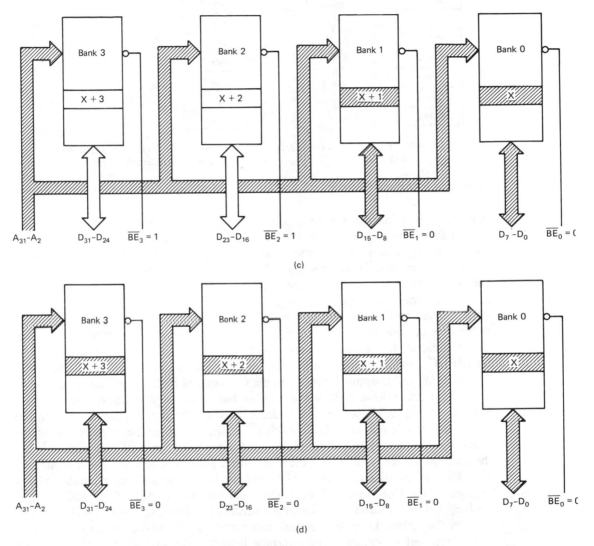

(c)

(d)

Figure 9.21 (*continued*)

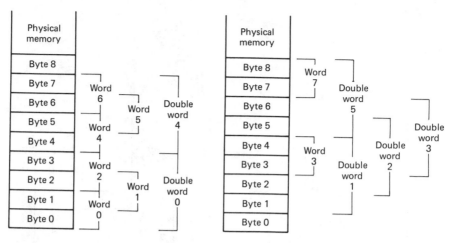

Figure 9.22 Examples of aligned data words and double words.

Figure 9.23 Examples of misaligned data words and double words.

Memory Interface Circuit

A memory interface diagram for a protected-mode, 80386-based microcomputer system is shown in Fig. 9.25. In Fig. 9.25, we find that the interface includes bus control logic, address bus latches and an address decoder, data bus transceiver/buffers, and bank write control logic. The bus cycle definition signals, $M/\overline{IO}$, $D/\overline{C}$, and $W/\overline{R}$, which are output by the 80386, are supplied directly to the bus control logic. Here they are decoded to produce the command and control signals needed to control data transfers over the bus. In Figs. 9.15 and 9.17, the status codes that relate to the memory interface are highlighted. For example, the code $M/\overline{IO}$ $D/\overline{C}$ $W/\overline{R}$ equal to 110 indicates that a data memory read bus cycle is in progress. This code changes the $\overline{MRDC}$ command output of the bus control logic switch to logic 0. Notice in Fig. 9.25 that $\overline{MRDC}$ is applied directly to the $\overline{OE}$ input of the memory subsystem.

Next let us look at how the address bus is decoded, buffered, and latched. Looking at Fig. 9.25, we see that address lines A_{29} through A_{31} are decoded to produce chip enable outputs $\overline{CE}_0$ through $\overline{CE}_7$. These chip enable signals are latched along with address bits A_2 through A_{28} and byte enable lines $\overline{BE}_0$ through $\overline{BE}_3$ into the address latches. Notice that the bus control logic produces the address latch enable (ALE) control signal from $\overline{ADS}$ and the bus cycle definition inputs. ALE is applied to the CLK input of the latches and strobes the bits of the address, byte enable, and chip enable signals into the address bus latches. These signals are buffered by the address latch devices and then output directly to the memory subsystem.

This part of the memory interface demonstrates one of the benefits of the 80386's pipelined bus mode. When working in the pipelined mode the 80386 actually outputs the address in the T_2 state of the prior bus cycle. Therefore, by putting the address decoder before the address latches, instead of after, the code at address lines A_{28} through A_{31} can be fully decoded and stable prior to the T_1 state of the next bus cycle. In this way, the access time of the memory subsystem is maximized.

During read bus cycles, the $\overline{MRDC}$ output of the bus control logic enables the

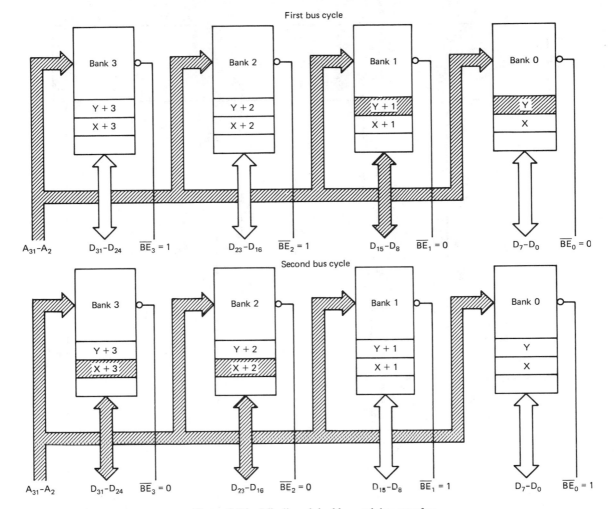

Figure 9.24 Misaligned double-word data transfers.

data at the outputs of the memory subsystem onto data bus lines D_0 through D_{31}. The 80386 will read the appropriate byte, word, or double word of data. On the other hand, during write operations to memory, the bank write control logic determines into which of the four memory banks the data are written. This depends on whether a byte, word, or double-word data transfer is taking place over the bus.

Notice in Fig. 9.25 that the latched bank enable signals $\overline{BE}_0$ through $\overline{BE}_3$ are gated with the write command signal $\overline{MWTC}$ to produce a separate bank enable signal for each of the four banks of memory. These signals are denoted as $\overline{WEB}_0$ through $\overline{WEB}_3$ in Fig. 9.25. For example, if a word of data is to be written to memory over data bus lines D_0 through D_{15}, $\overline{WEB}_0$ and $\overline{WEB}_1$ are switched to their active 0 logic level.

The bus transceivers control the direction of data transfer between the MPU and memory subsystem. In Fig. 9.25, we see that the operation of the transceivers is controlled by the data transmit/receive (DT/$\overline{R}$) and data bus enable ($\overline{DEN}$) outputs of the bus control logic. $\overline{DEN}$ is applied to the enable ($\overline{EN}$) input of the transceivers and

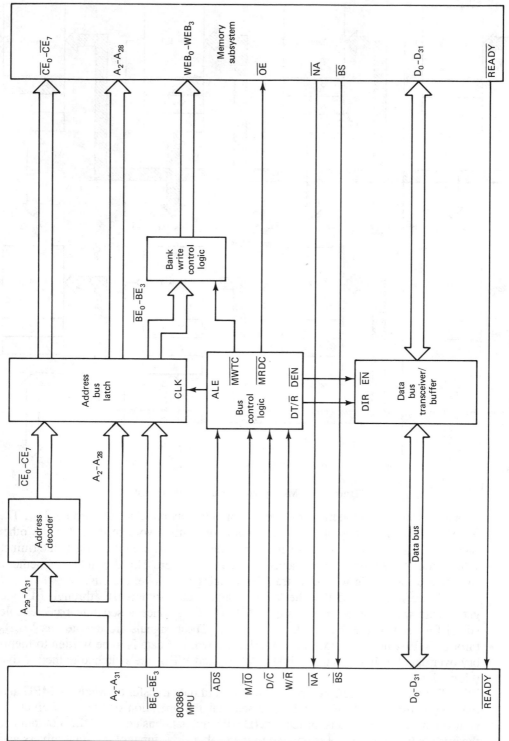

Figure 9.25 Memory interface block diagram.

enables them for operation. This happens during all read and write bus cycles. $DT/\overline{R}$ selects the direction of data transfer through the transceivers. When a read cycle is in progress, $DT/\overline{R}$ is set to 0 and data are passed from the memory subsystem to the MPU. On the other hand, when a write cycle is taking place, $DT/\overline{R}$ is switched to logic 1 and data are carried from the MPU to the memory subsystem.

9.7 INPUT/OUTPUT INTERFACE

In Section 9.6 we studied the memory interface of the 80386 microprocessor. Here we will examine another important interface of the 80386 microcomputer system, the input/output interface.

Input/Output Interface and I/O Address Space

The input/output interface of the 80386 microcomputer permits it to communicate with the outside world. The way in which the 80386 deals with input/output (I/O) circuitry is similar to the way in which it interfaces with memory circuitry. That is, input/output data transfers also take place over the data bus. This parallel bus permits easy interface to LSI peripheral devices such as parallel I/O expanders, interval timers, and serial communication controllers. Let us continue by looking at how the 80386 interfaces to its I/O subsystem.

A typical I/O interface circuit for an 80386-based microcomputer system is shown in Fig. 9.26. Notice that the interface includes the bus controller logic, an I/O address decoder, I/O address latches, I/O data bus transceiver/buffers, I/O bank write control logic, and the I/O subsystem. An example of a typical I/O device is a programmable peripheral interface (PPI) IC, such as the 8255A. This type of device is used to implement parallel input and output ports. Let us now look at the function of each of the blocks in this circuit more closely.

The I/O interface shown in Fig. 9.26 is designed to support 8-, 16-, and 32-bit I/O data transfers. Just as for the 8086 architecture, the 80386's I/O address is 16 bits in length and supports 64K independent byte-wide I/O ports. The part of the address on lines A_2 through A_{15} is used to specify the double-word I/O port that is to be accessed. When data are output to word-wide or byte-wide output ports, the logic levels of $\overline{BE}_0$ through $\overline{BE}_3$ determine which ports are enabled for operation. The more significant address bits, A_{16} through A_{31}, are held at the 0 logic level during the address period of all I/O bus cycles. The I/O address is specified as part of the instruction that performs the I/O operation. The 80386 signals external circuitry that an I/O address is on the bus by switching its $M/\overline{IO}$ output to logic 0.

Notice in the circuit diagram that part of the I/O address that is output on address lines A_2 through A_{15} of the 80386 is decoded by the I/O address decoder and then latched into the I/O address latches. Latching of the address is achieved with the pulse at the ALE output of the bus control logic. The bits of the address that are decoded produce I/O chip enable signals for the individual I/O devices. For instance, Fig. 9.26 shows that with three address bits, A_{13} through A_{15}, we produce enough chip enable outputs to select up to eight I/O devices. Notice that the outputs of the

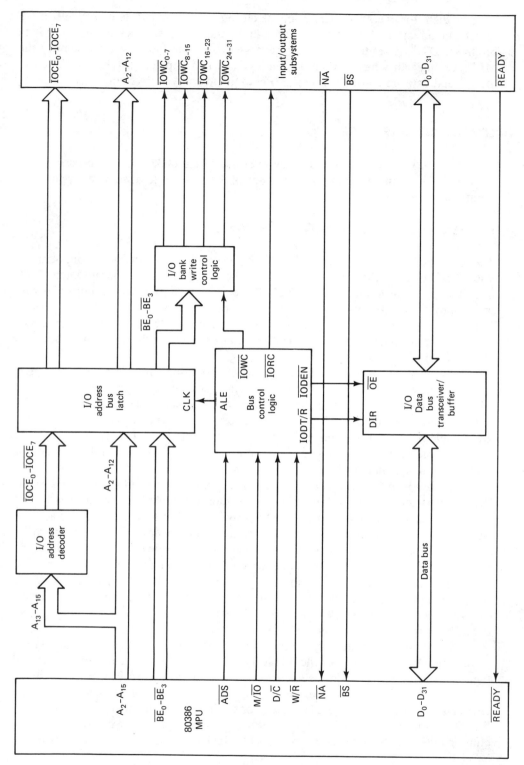

Figure 9.26 Byte, word, and double-word I/O interface block diagram.

I/O address decoder are labeled $\overline{\text{IOCE}}_0$ through $\overline{\text{IOCE}}_7$. If a microcomputer employs a very simple I/O subsystem, it may be possible to eliminate the address decoder and simply use some of the latched high-order address bits as I/O enable signals.

In Fig 9.26 all the low-order address bits are shown to be latched and sent directly to the I/O devices. Typically, these address bits are used to select the register within the peripheral device that is to be accessed. For example, with just four of these address lines, we can select any one of 16 registers.

EXAMPLE 9.8

If address bits A_7 through A_{15} are directly used as chip enable signals and address lines A_6 through A_2 are used as register select inputs for the I/O devices, how many I/O devices can be used and what is the maximum number or registers that each device can contain?

SOLUTION   The nine address lines when latched into the address latch produce the nine I/O chip enable signals, $\overline{\text{IOCE}}_0$ through $\overline{\text{IOCE}}_8$, for I/O devices 0 through 8. The lower five address bits are able to select between 2^5 equals 32 registers for each peripheral IC.

During input and output bus cycles, data are passed between the selected register in the enabled I/O device and the 80386 over data bus lines D_0 through D_{31}. Earlier we pointed out that the 80386 can input or output data in byte-wide, word-wide, or double-word format. Just as for the memory interface, the signals $\overline{\text{BE}}_0$ through $\overline{\text{BE}}_3$ are used to signal which byte or bytes of data are being transferred over the bus. Again logic 0 at $\overline{\text{BE}}_0$ identifies that a byte of data is input or output over data bus lines D_0 through D_7. On the other hand, logic 0 at $\overline{\text{BE}}_3$ means that a byte-data transfer is taking place over data bus lines D_{24} through D_{31}.

Many of the peripheral ICs that are used in the 80386 microcomputer have a byte-wide data bus. For this reason, they are normally attached to the lower part of the data bus. That is, they are connected to data bus lines D_0 through D_7. If this is done in the circuit of Fig. 9.26, all I/O addresses must be scaled by four. This is because the first byte I/O address that corresponds to a byte transfer across the lower eight data bus lines is 0000_{16}, the next byte address that represents a byte transfer over D_0 through D_7 is 0004_{16}, the third I/O address is 00008_{16}, and so on. In fact, if only 8-bit peripherals are used in the 80386 microcomputer system and they are all attached to I/O data bus lines D_0 through D_7, the bank enable signals are not needed in the I/O interface. In this case, address bit A_2 is used as the least significant bit of the I/O address and A_{15} the most significant bit. Therefore, from a hardware point of view, the I/O address space appears as 16K contiguous byte-wide storage locations over the address range from

$$A_{15}...A_3A_2 = 0000000000000_2$$

to

$$A_{15}...A_3A_2 = 1111111111111_2$$

In this case, the burden is put on software to assure that bytes of data are only input or output for addresses that are a multiples of 4 and correspond to a data transfer over data bus lines D_0 through D_7.

As in the memory interface, bus control logic is needed to produce the control signals for the I/O interface. In Fig. 9.26 we see that the inputs to the bus control logic are the bus cycle definition signals $M/\overline{\text{IO}}$, $D/\overline{\text{C}}$, and $W/\overline{\text{R}}$. They are decoded to produce the I/O read command ($\overline{\text{IORC}}$) and I/O write command ($\overline{\text{IOWC}}$) outputs. $\overline{\text{IORC}}$ is applied directly to the I/O devices and tells them when data are to be input. In this case, 32-bit data are always put on the data bus. However, the 80386 only inputs the appropriate byte. word. or double word. On the other hand, $\overline{\text{IOWR}}$ is gated with the $\overline{\text{BE}}$ signals to produce a separate write enable signal for each byte of the data bus. They are labeled $\overline{\text{IOWR}}_{0-7}$, $\overline{\text{IOWR}}_{8-15}$, $\overline{\text{IOWR}}_{16-23}$, and $\overline{\text{IOWR}}_{24-31}$. These signals are needed to support writing of 8-, 16-, or 32-bit data through the interface

The bus control logic section also produces the signals that are needed to latch the address and set up the data bus for an input or output data transfer. The data bus transceiver/buffers control the direction of data transfers between the 80386 and I/O devices. They are enabled for operation when their output enable ($\overline{\text{OE}}$) input is switched to logic 0. Notice that the signal *I/O data bus enable* ($\overline{\text{IODEN}}$) is applied to the $\overline{\text{OE}}$ inputs.

The direction in which data are passed through the transceivers is determined by the logic level of the DIR input. This input is supplied by the *I/O data transmit/ receive* (IODT/$\overline{\text{R}}$) output of the bus control logic. During all input cycles, IODT/$\overline{\text{R}}$ is logic 0 and the transceivers are set to pass data from the selected I/O device to the 80386. On the other hand, during output cycles, IODT/$\overline{\text{R}}$ is switched to logic 1 and data passes from the 80386 to the I/O device.

Another input/output interface diagram is shown in Fig. 9.27. This circuit includes a bank select multiplexer in the data bus interface. This circuit is used to multiplex the 32-bit data bus of the 80386 to an 8-bit I/O data bus for connection to 8-bit peripheral ICs. By using this circuit configuration, data can be input from or output to all 64K contiguous byte addresses in the I/O address space. In this case, hardware, instead of software, assures that byte data transfers to consecutive byte I/O addresses are performed to contiguous byte-wide I/O ports. The I/O bank select decoder circuit maps bytes of data from the 32-bit data bus to the 8-bit I/O data bus. It does this by assuring that only one bank enable ($\overline{\text{BE}}$) output of the 80386 is active. That is, it checks to assure that a byte input or byte output operation is in progress. If more that one of the $\overline{\text{BE}}$ inputs of the decoder is active, none of the $\overline{\text{OE}}$ outputs of the decoder is produced and the data transfer does not take place. Now the I/O address 0000_{16} corresponds to a I/O cycle over data bus lines D_0 through D_7 to an 8-bit peripheral attached to I/O data bus lines IOD_0 through IOD_7; 0001_{16} corresponds to an input or output of a byte of data for the peripheral over lines D_8 through D_{15}; 0002_{16} respresents a byte I/O transfer over D_{16} through D_{23}; and finally 0003_{16} accompanies a byte transfer over data bus lines D_{24} through D_{31}. That is, even though the byte of data for addresses 0000_{16} through 0003_{16} are output by the 80386 on different parts of its data bus, they are all multiplexed in external hardware to the same 8-bit I/O data bus, IOD_0 through IOD_7. In this way, the addresses of the peripheral's registers no longer need to be scaled by 4 in software.

Input and Output Bus Cycle Timing

We just found that the I/O interface signals of the 80386 microcomputer are essentially the same as those involved in the memory interface. In fact, the function, logic

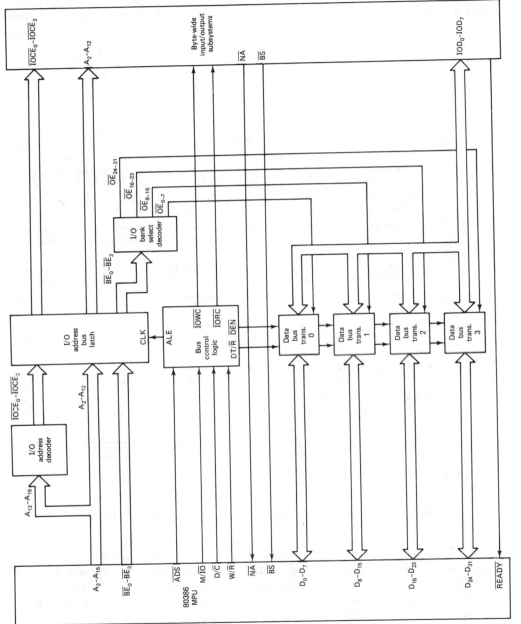

Figure 9.27 Byte-wide I/O interface block diagram.

levels, and timing of all signals other than the $M/\overline{IO}$ are identical to those already described for the memory interface in Section 9.6.

The timing diagram in Fig. 9.28 shows some *nonpipelined input* and *output bus cycles*. Looking at the waveforms for the first input/output bus cycle, which is called cycle 1, we see that it represents a zero wait state input bus cycle. Notice that the byte enable signals, $\overline{BE}_0$ through $\overline{BE}_3$, the address A_2 through A_{15}, the bus cycle definition signals $M/\overline{IO}$, $D/\overline{C}$, and $W/\overline{R}$, and address status ($\overline{ADS}$) signal are all output at the beginning of the T_1 state. This time the 80386 switches $M/\overline{IO}$ to logic 0, $D/\overline{C}$ to 1, and $W/\overline{R}$ to logic 1 to signal external circuitry that an I/O data input bus cycle is in progress.

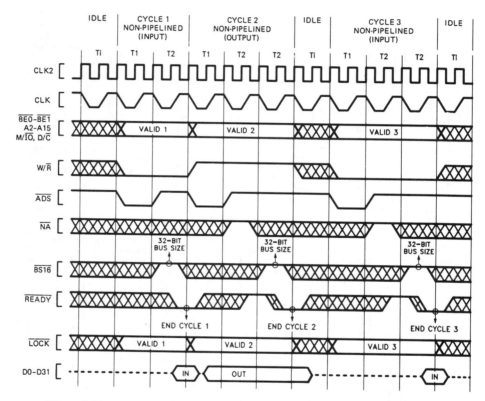

Figure 9.28 I/O read and I/O write bus cycles. (Reprinted by permission of Intel Corp. Copyright/Intel Corp., 1987.)

As shown in the block diagram of Fig. 9.28, the bus cycle definition code is input to the bus control logic and initiates an input bus control sequence. Let us continue with the sequence of events that takes place in external circuitry during the read cycle. First the bus control logic outputs a pulse to the 1 logic level on ALE. As shown in the circuit of Fig. 9.28, this pulse is used to latch the address information into the I/O address latch devices. The decoded part of the latched address ($\overline{IOCE}_0$ through $\overline{IOCE}_7$) selects the I/O device to be accessed, and the code on the lower address lines selects the register that is to be accessed. Later in the bus cycle, $\overline{IORC}$ is switched to logic 0 to signal the enabled I/O device that data are to be input to the

MPU. In response to $\overline{\text{IORC}}$, the enabled input device puts the data from the addressed register onto the data bus. A short time later, IODT/$\overline{\text{R}}$ is switched to logic 0 to set the data bus transceivers to the input direction, and then the transceivers are enabled as $\overline{\text{IODEN}}$ is switched to logic 0. At this point, the data from the I/O device are available on the 80386's data bus.

In the waveforms of Fig. 9.28, we see that at the end of the T_2 state the 80386 tests the logic level at its ready input to determine if the I/O bus cycle should be completed or extended with wait states. As shown in Fig. 9.28, $\overline{\text{READY}}$ is at its active 0 logic level when sampled. Therefore, the 80386 inputs the data off the bus. Finally, the bus control logic returns $\overline{\text{IORC}}$, $\overline{\text{IODEN}}$, and IODT/$\overline{\text{R}}$ to their inactive logic levels, and the input bus cycle is finished.

Cycle 3 in Fig. 9.28 is also an input bus cycle. However, looking at the $\overline{\text{READY}}$ waveform, we find that this time it is not logic 0 at the end of the first T_2 state. Therefore, the input cycle is extended with a second T_2 state. Since some of the peripheral devices used with the 80386 are older, slower devices, it is common to have several wait states in I/O bus cycles.

EXAMPLE 9.9

If the 80386 that is executing cycle 3 in Fig. 9.28 is running at 20 MHz, what is the duration of this input cycle?

SOLUTION   An 80386 that is running at 20 MHz has a T state equal to 50 ns. Since the input cycle takes 3 T states, its duration is 150 ns.

Looking at the output bus cycle, cycle 2 in the timing diagram of Fig. 9.28, we see that the 80386 puts the data that are to be output onto the data bus at the beginning of ϕ_2 in the T_1 state. This time the bus control logic switches $\overline{\text{IODEN}}$ to logic 0 and maintains IODT/$\overline{\text{R}}$ at the 1 level for transmit mode. From Fig. 9.26, we find that since $\overline{\text{IODEN}}$ is logic 0 and IODT/$\overline{\text{R}}$ is 1, the transceivers are enabled and set up to pass data from the 80386 to the I/O devices. Therefore, the data output on the bus are avilable on the data inputs of the enabled I/O device. Finally, the signal $\overline{\text{IOWC}}$ is switched to logic 0. It is gated with $\overline{\text{BE}}_0$ through $\overline{\text{BE}}_3$ in the I/O bank write control logic to produce the needed bank write enable signals. These signals tell the I/O device that valid output data are on the bus. Now the I/O device must read the data off the bus before the bus control logic terminates the bus cycle. If the device cannot read data at this rate, it can hold $\overline{\text{READY}}$ at the 1 logic level to extend the bus cycle.

EXAMPLE 9.10

If the output cycles performed to byte wide ports by an 80386 running at 20 MHz are to be completed in a minimum of 250 ns, how many wait states are needed?

SOLUTION   Since each T state is 50 ns in duration, the bus cycle must last at least for the

$$\text{number of T states} = 250 \text{ ns}/50 \text{ ns} = 5$$

A zero wait state output cycle lasts just two T states; therefore, all output cycles must include a minimum of three wait states.

The same bus cycle requirements exist for data transfers for I/O ports as were found for memory. That is, all word and double-word data transfers to aligned port addresses take place in just one bus cycle. However, two bus cycles are required to perform data transfers for unaligned 16- or 32-bit I/O ports.

Protected-Mode Input/Output

When the 80386 is in the protected-address mode, the input/output instructions can only be executed if the current privilege level is greater than or equal to the I/O privilege level (IOPL). That is, CPL must have a numerical value that is lower than or equal to the numerical value of IOPL. Remember that IOPL is defined by the code in bits 12 and 13 of the flags register. If the current privilege level is less than IOPL, the instruction is not executed; instead, a general protection fault occurs. The general protection fault is an example of an 80386 exception and will be examined in more detail in the next section.

In Chapter 8 we indicated that the task state segment (TSS) of a task includes a section known as the *I/O permission bit map*. This I/O permission bit map provides a second protection mechanism for the protected-mode I/O address space. Remember that the size of the TSS segment is variable. Its size is specified by the limit in the TSS descriptor. Figure 9.29 shows a typical task state segment. Here we see that the 16-bit *I/O map base* offset, which is held at word offset 66_{16} in the TSS, identifies the beginning of the I/O permission bit map. The upper end of the bit map is set by the limit field in the descriptor for the TSS. Let us now look at what the bits in the I/O permission bit map stand for.

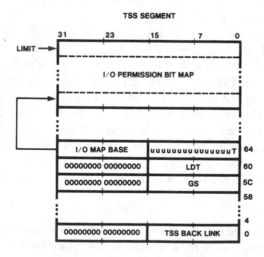

Figure 9.29 Location of the I/O permission bit map in the TSS. (Reprinted by permission of Intel Corp. Copyright/Intel Corp., 1986.)

Figure 9.30 shows a more detailed representation of the I/O permissions bit map. Notice that it contains one bit position for each of the 65,536 byte-wide I/O ports in the 80386's I/O address space. In the bit map, we find that the bit position that corresponds to I/O port 0 (I/O address 0000_{16}) is the least significant bit at the address defined with the I/O bit map base offset. The rest of the bits in this first double word in the map represent I/O ports 1 through 31. Finally, the last bit in the

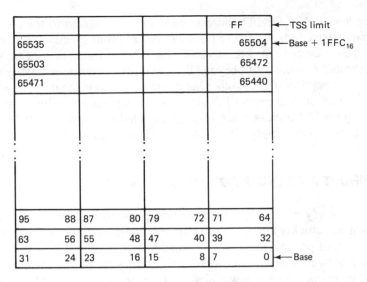

				FF	←—TSS limit
65535				65504	←—Base + 1FFC$_{16}$
65503				65472	
65471				65440	
95	88	87	80	79	72	71	64
63	56	55	48	47	40	39	32
31	24	23	16	15	8	7	0	←—Base

Figure 9.30 Contents of the I/O permission bit map.

table, which corresponds to port 65,535 and I/O address FFFF$_{16}$, is the most significant bit in the double word located at an offset of 1FFC$_{16}$ from the I/O bit map base. In Fig. 9.30, we see that the byte address that follows the map must always contain FF$_{16}$. This is the least significant byte in the last double word of the TSS. The value of the I/O map base offset must be less than DFFF$_{16}$; otherwise, the complete map may not fit within the TSS.

Using this bit map, restrictions can be put on input/output operations to each of the 80386's 65,536 I/O port addresses. In protected mode, the bit for the I/O port in the I/O permission map is checked only if the CPL when the I/O instruction is executed is less privileged than the IOPL. If logic 0 is found in a bit position, it means that an I/O operation can be performed to the port address. On the other hand, logic 1 inhibits the I/O operation. Any attempt to input or output data for an I/O address marked with a 1 in the I/O permission bit map by code with a CPL that is less privileged than the IOPL results in a general protection exception. In this way, an operating system can detect attempts to access certain I/O devices and trap to special service routines for the devices through the general protection exception. In virtual 8086 mode, all I/O accesses reference the I/O permission bit map.

The I/O permission configuration defined by a bit map only applies to the task that uses the TSS. For this reason, many different I/O configurations can exist within a protected-mode software system. Actually, a different bit map could be defined for every task.

In practical applications, most tasks would use the same I/O permission bit map configuration. In fact, in some applications not all I/O addresses need to be protected with the I/O permission bit map. It turns out that any bit map position that is located beyond the limit of the TSS is interpreted as containing a 1. Therefore, all accesses to an address that corresponds to a bit position beyond the limit of the TSS will produce a general protection exception. For instance, a protected-mode I/O address space may be set up with a small block of I/O address to which access is permitted at the low end of the I/O address space and with access to the rest of the I/O address space restricted. A smaller table can be set up to specify this configuration. By setting the values of the bit map base and TSS limit such that the bit positions for all the restricted addresses fall beyond the end of the TSS segment, they are caused to result in an exception. On the other hand, the bit positions that are located within the table are all made 0 to permit I/O accesses to their corresponding ports. Moreover, if the complete I/O address space is to be restricted for a task, the I/O permission map base address can be simply set to a value greater than the TSS limit.

9.8 INTERRUPT AND EXCEPTION PROCESSING

In our study of the 8086 microprocessor, we found that interrupts provide a mechanism for quickly changing program environments. Moreover, we identified that the transfer of program control is initiated by either the occurrence of an event internal to the microprocessor or an event in its external hardware. Finally, we determined that the interrupts employ a well-defined context switching mechanism for changing program environments.

Figure 9.31 illustrates the program context switching mechanism. Here we see that interrupt 32 occurs as instruction N of the main program is being executed. When the MPU terminates execution of the main program in response to interrupt 32, it first saves information that identifies the instruction following the one where the interrupt occurred, which is the instruction N + 1, and then picks up execution with the first instruction in the service routine. After this routine has run to completion, program control returns to the point where the MPU originally left the main program instruction N + 1, and then execution resumes.

The 80386's interrupt mechanism is essentially the same as that of the 8086. Just like the 8086-based microcomputer, the 80386 is capable of implementing any combination of up to 256 interrupts. As shown in Fig. 9.32, they are divided into five groups: *external hardware interrupts, nonmaskable interrupt, software interrupts, internal interrupts and exceptions,* and *reset*. The functions of the external hardware, software, and nonmaskable interrupts are identical to those in the 8086 microcomputer and are defined by the user. On the other hand, the internal interrupt and exception processing capability of the 80386 has been greatly enhanced. These internal interrupts and exceptions and reset perform dedicated system functions. The priority by which the 80386 services interrupts and exceptions is also indentified in Fig. 9.32.

Interrupt Vector and Interrupt Descriptor Tables

An address pointer table is used to link the interrupt type numbers to the location of their service routines in program storage memory. In a real-mode, 80386-based microcomputer system, this table is called the *interrupt vector table*. On the other hand, in a protected-mode system, the table is referred to as the *interrupt descriptor table*. Figure 9.33 shows a map of the interrupt vector table in the memory of a real-mode 80386 microcomputer. Looking at the table, we see that it contains 256 address

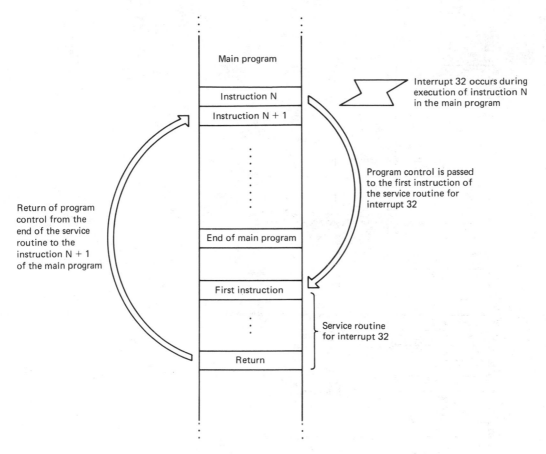

Figure 9.31 Interrupt program context switch mechanism.

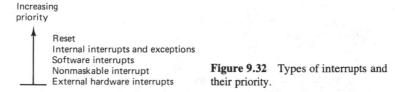

Figure 9.32 Types of interrupts and their priority.

pointers, which are identified as *Vector 0* through *Vector 255*. That is, one pointer corresponds to each interrupt type number, 0 through 255. As in the 8086 microcomputer system, these address pointers identify the starting locations of their service routines in program memory. The contents of these tables are either held as firmware in EPROMs or loaded into RAM as part of the system initialization routine.

Notice that in Fig. 9.33 the interrupt vector table is located at the low-address end of the memory address space. It starts at address 00000_{16} and ends at $003FE_{16}$. Unlike the 8086 microcomputer system, the interrupt vector table or interrupt descriptor table in an 80386 microcomputer can be located anywhere in the memory address space. Its starting location and size are identified by the contents of a register within the 80386 called the *interrupt descriptor table register* (IDTR). When

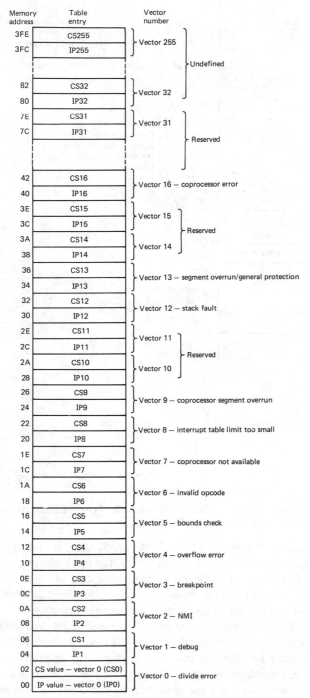

Memory address	Table entry	Vector number
3FE	CS255	Vector 255
3FC	IP255	
		Undefined
82	CS32	Vector 32
80	IP32	
7E	CS31	Vector 31
7C	IP31	
		Reserved
42	CS16	Vector 16 — coprocessor error
40	IP16	
3E	CS15	Vector 15
3C	IP15	Reserved
3A	CS14	Vector 14
38	IP14	
36	CS13	Vector 13 — segment overrun/general protection
34	IP13	
32	CS12	Vector 12 — stack fault
30	IP12	
2E	CS11	Vector 11
2C	IP11	Reserved
2A	CS10	Vector 10
28	IP10	
26	CS9	Vector 9 — coprocessor segment overrun
24	IP9	
22	CS8	Vector 8 — interrupt table limit too small
20	IP8	
1E	CS7	Vector 7 — coprocessor not available
1C	IP7	
1A	CS6	Vector 6 — invalid opcode
18	IP6	
16	CS5	Vector 5 — bounds check
14	IP5	
12	CS4	Vector 4 — overflow error
10	IP4	
0E	CS3	Vector 3 — breakpoint
0C	IP3	
0A	CS2	Vector 2 — NMI
08	IP2	
06	CS1	Vector 1 — debug
04	IP1	
02	CS value — vector 0 (CS0)	Vector 0 — divide error
00	IP value — vector 0 (IP0)	

Figure 9.33 Real-mode interrupt vector table.

the 80386 is reset at power on, it comes up in the real mode with the bits of the base address in IDTR all equal to zero and the limit set to $03FF_{16}$. This positions the interrupt vector table as shown in Fig. 9.33. Moreover, when in the real mode, the value in IDTR is normally left at this initial value to maintain compatibility with 8086/8088-based microcomputer software.

The protected-mode interrupt descriptor table can reside anywhere in the 80386's physical address space. The location and size of this table are again defined by the contents of the IDTR. Figure 9.34 shows that the IDTR contains a 32-bit *base address* and a 16-bit *limit*. The base address identifies the starting point of the table in memory. On the other hand, the limit determines the number of bytes in the table.

The interrupt descriptor table contains gate descriptors, not vectors. In Fig. 9.34, we find that the table contains a maximum of 256 gate descriptors. These descriptors are identified as *Gate 0* through *Gate 255*. Each gate descriptor can be defined as a *trap gate, interrupt gate,* or *task gate.* Interrupt and trap gates permit control to be passed to a service routine that is located within the current task. On the other hand, the task gate permits program control to be passed to a different task.

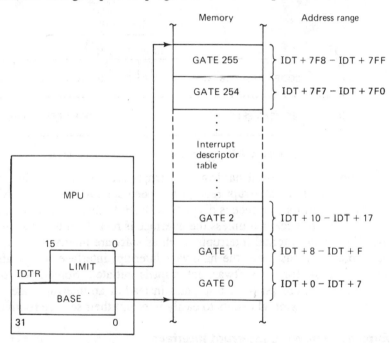

Figure 9.34 Accessing a gate in the protected-mode interrupt descriptor table.

Just like a real-mode vector, a protected-mode gate acts as a pointer that is used to redirect program execution to the starting point of a service routine. However, unlike an interrupt vector, a gate descriptor takes up 8 bytes of memory. For instance, in Fig. 9.34, we see that Gate 0 is located at addresses IDT + 0 through IDT + 7 and Gate 255 at addresses IDT + 7F8 through IDT + 7FF. If all 256 gates are not needed for an application, limit can be set to a value lower than $07FF_{16}$ to minimize the amount of memory reserved for the table.

Figure 9.35 illustrates the format of a typical interrupt or trap gate descriptor. Here we see that the two lower addressed words, 0 and 1, are the interrupt's *code offset 0 through 15* and *segment selector,* respectively. The highest-addressed word, word 3, is the interrupt's *code offset 16 through 31*. These three words identify the starting point of the service routine. The upper byte of word 2 of the descriptor is called the *access rights byte*. The settings of the bits in this byte identify whether or not this gate descriptor is valid, the privilege level of the service routine, and type of gate. For example, the *present bit* (P) needs to be set to logic 1 if the gate descriptor is to be active. The next 2 bits, identified as DPL in Fig. 9.35, are used to assign a privilege level to the service routine. If these bits are made 00, level 0, which is the most privileged level, is assigned to the gate. Finally, the setting of the *type bit* (T) determines if the descriptor works as a trap gate or an interrupt gate. T equal to 0 selects the interrupt gate mode of operation. The only difference between the operation of these two types of gates is that, when a trap gate context switch is performed, IF is not cleared to disable external hardware interrupts.

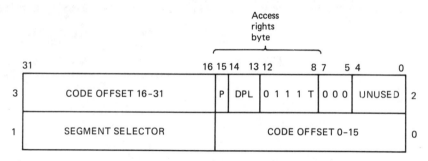

Figure 9.35 Format of a trap or interrupt gate descriptor.

Normally, external hardware interrupts are configured with interrupt gate descriptors. Once an interrrupt request has been acknowleged for service, the external hardware interrupt interface is disabled with IF. In this way, additional external interrupts cannot be accepted unless the interface is reenabled under software control. On the other hand, internal interrupts, such as software interrupts, usually use trap gate descriptors. In this case, the hardware interrupt interface in not affected when the service routine for the software interrupt is initiated. Sometimes low-priority hardware interrupts are assigned trap gates instead of an interrupt gate. This will permit higher-priority external events to easily interrupt their serivce routine.

External Hardware Interrupt Interface

Up to this point in the section, we have introduced the types of interrupts supported by the 80386, its interrupt descriptor table, and interrupt descriptor format. Let us now look at the external hardware interrupt interface of the 80386 microcomputer system.

A general interrupt interface for an 80386-based microcomputer is shown in Fig. 9.36. Here we see that it is similar to the interrupt interface of the maximum-mode 8086 microcomputer system. Notice that it includes the address and data buses, byte enable signals, bus cycle definition signals, lock output, and the ready

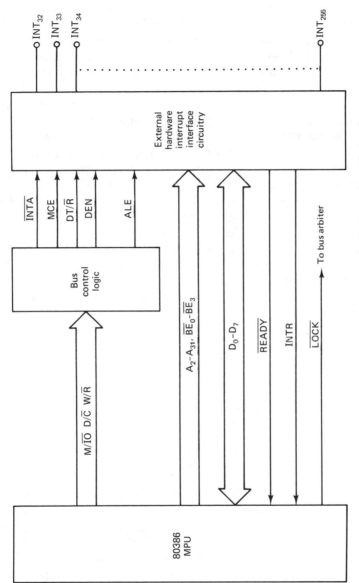

Figure 9.36 80386 microcomputer system external hardware interrupt interface.

and interrupt request inputs. Moreover, external circuitry is required to interface interrupt inputs, INT_{32} through INT_{255}, to the 80386's interrupt interface. This interface circuit must identify which of the pending active interrupts has the highest priority, perform an interrupt request/acknowledge handshake, and then set up the bus to pass a type number to the 80386.

In this circuit we see that the key interrupt interface signals are *interrupt request* (INTR) and *interrupt acknowledge* ($\overline{INTA}$). The logic level input at the INTR line signals the 80386 that an external device is requesting service. The 80386 samples this input at the beginning of each instruction execution cycle, that is, at instruction boundaries. Logic 1 at INTR represents an active interrupt request. INTR is *level triggered;* therefore, its active level must be maintained active by the external hardware until tested by the 80386. If it is not maintained, the request for service may not be recognized. For this reason, inputs INT_{32} through INT_{255} are normally latched. Moreover, the 1 at INTR must be removed before the service routine runs to completion; otherwise, the same interrupt may be acknowledged a second time.

When an interrupt request has been recognized by the 80386, it signals this fact to external circuitry by outputting the interrupt acknowledge bus cycle status code on $M/\overline{IOC}/\overline{DW}/\overline{R}$. This code, which equals 000_2, is highlighted in Fig. 9.37. Notice in Fig. 9.36 that this code is input to the bus controller logic where it is decoded to produce a pulse to logic 0 at the $\overline{INTA}$ output. Actually, two pulses are produced at $\overline{INTA}$ during the *interrupt acknowledge bus cycle sequence*. The first pulse, which is output during cycle 1, signals external circuitry that the interrupt request has been acknowledged and to prepare to send its type number to the 80386. The second pulse, which occurs during cycle 2, tells the external circuitry to put the type number on the data bus.

M/$\overline{IO}$	D/$\overline{C}$	W/$\overline{R}$	Type of Bus Cycle
0	0	0	Interrupt acknowledge
0	0	1	Idle
0	1	0	I/O data read
0	1	1	I/O data write
1	0	0	Memory code read
1	0	1	Halt/shutdown
1	1	0	Memory data read
1	1	1	Memory data write

Figure 9.37 Interrupt acknowledge bus cycle definiton code.

Notice that the lower eight lines of the data bus, D_0 through D_7, are also part of the interrupt interface. During the second cycle in the interrupt acknowledge bus cycle sequence, external circuitry puts the 8-bit type number of the highest-priority active interrupt request input onto this part of the data bus. The ready ($\overline{READY}$) input can be used to insert wait states into the bus cycle. The 80386 reads the type number off the bus to identify which external device is requesting service. Then it uses the type number to generate the address of the interrupt's vector or gate in the interrupt vector or descriptor table, respectively.

Address lines A_2 through A_{31} and byte enable line $\overline{BE}_0$ through $\overline{BE}_3$ are also shown in the interrupt interface circuit of Fig. 9.36. This is because LSI interrupt controller devices are typically used to implement most of the external circuitry.

When a read or write bus cycle is performed to the controller, for example, to initialize its internal registers after system reset, some of the address bits are decoded to produce a chip select to enable the controller device, and other address bits are used to select the internal register that is to be accessed. The interrupt controller could be I/O mapped, instead of memory mapped; in this case only address lines A_0 through A_{15} are used in the interface.

Another signal shown in the interrupt interface of Fig. 9.36 is the *bus lock indication* ($\overline{LOCK}$) output of the 80386. $\overline{LOCK}$ is used as an input to the bus arbiter circuit in multiprocessor systems. The 80386 switches this output to its active 0 logic level and maintains it at this level throughout the complete interrupt acknowledge bus cycle. In response to this signal, the arbitration logic assures that no other device can take over control of the system bus until the interrupt acknowledge bus cycle sequence is completed.

External Hardware Interrupt Sequence

In the real mode, the 80386 processes interrupts in exactly the same way as the 8086. That is, the same events that we described in Chapter 7 take place during the interrupt request, interrupt acknowledge bus cycle, and device service routine. On the other hand, in protected mode a more complex processing sequence is performed. When the 80386-based microcomputer is configured for the protected mode of operation, the interrupt request acknowledge handshake sequence appears to take place exactly the same way in the external hardware; however, a number of changes do occur in the internal processing sequence of the 80386. Let us now look at how the protected mode 80386 reacts to an interrupt request.

When processing interrupts in protected-mode, the general protection mechanism of the 80386 comes into play. The general protection rules dictate that program control can only be directly passed to a service routine that is in a segment with equal or higher privilege; that is, a segment with an equal or lower-numbered descriptor privilege level. Any attempt to transfer program control to a routine in a segment with lower privilege (higher-numbered descriptor privilege level) results in an exception unless the transition is made through a gate.

Typically, interrupt drivers are in code segments at a high privilege level, possibly level 0. Moreover, interrupts occur randomly; therefore, there is a good chance that the microprocessor will be executing application code that is at a low privilege level. In the case of interrupts, the current privilege level (CPL) is the privilege level assigned by the descriptor of the software that was executing when the interrupt occurred. This could be any of the 80386s valid privilege levels. The privilege level of the service routine is that defined in the interrupt or trap gate descriptor for the type number. That is, it is the descriptor privilege level (DPL).

When a service routine is initiated, the current privilege level may change. This depends on whether the software that was interrupted was in a code segment that was configured as *conforming* or *noncomforming*. If the interrupted code is in a conforming code segment, CPL does not change when the service routine is initiated. In this case, the contents of the stack after the context switch is as illustrated in Fig. 9.38(a). Since the privilege level does not change, the current stack (OLD SS: ESP) is used.

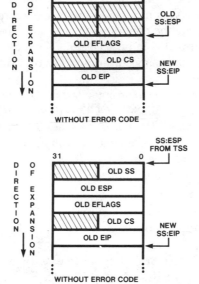

Figure 9.38 (a) Stack after context switch with no privilege-level transition (reprinted by permission of Intel Corp. Copyright/Intel Corp., 1986); (b) stack after context switch with a privilege-level transition (reprinted by permission of Intel Corp. Copyright/Intel Corp., 1986).

Notice that as part of the interrupt initiation sequence the OLD EFLAGS, OLD CS, and OLD EIP are automatically saved on the stack. Actually, the *requested privilege level* (RPL) code is also saved on the stack. This is because it is part of OLD CS. RPL identifies the protection level of the interrupted routine.

However, if the segment is nonconforming, the value of DPL is assigned to CPL as long as the service routine is active. As shown in Fig. 9.38(b), this time the stack is changed to that for the new privilege level. The MPU is loaded with a new SS and new ESP from TSS, and then the old stack pointer, OLD SS, and OLD ESP, are saved on the stack followed by the OLD EFLAGS, OLD CS, and OLD EIP. Remember that for an interrupt gate IF is cleared as part of the context switch, but for a trap gate IF remains unchanged. In both cases, the TF flag is reset after the contents of the flag register are pushed to the stack.

Figure 9.39 shows the stack as it exists after an attempt to initiate an interrupt service routine that did not involve a privilege-level transition has failed. Notice that the context switch to the exception service routine caused an *error code* to be pushed onto the stack following the values of OLD EFLAGS, OLD CS, and OLD EIP.

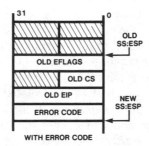

Figure 9.39 Stack contents after interrupt with an error. (Reprinted by permission of Intel Corp. Copyright/Intel Corp., 1986.)

One format of the error code is given in Fig. 9.40. Here we see that the least significant bit, which is labeled EXT, indicates whether the error was for an externally or internally initiated interrupt. For external interrupts, such as the hardware interrupts, the EXT bit is always set to logic 1. The next bit, which is labeled IDT, is set to 1 if the error is produced as the result of an interrupt. That is, it is the result of a reference to a descriptor in the IDT. If IDT is not set, the third bit indicates whether the descriptor is in the GDT (TI = 0) or the LDT (TI = 1). The next 14 bits contain the segment selector that produced the error condition. With this information available on the stack, the exception service routine can determine which interrupt attempt had failed and whether it was internally or externally initiated. A second format is used for errors that result from a protected-mode page fault. Figure 9.41 illustrates this error code and the function of its bits.

Figure 9.40 IDT error code format.

Field	Value	Description
U/S	0	The access causing the fault originated when the processor was executing in supervisor mode.
	1	The access causing the fault originated when the processor was executing in user mode.
W/R	0	The access causing the fault was a read.
	1	The access causing the fault was a write.
P	0	The fault was caused by a not-present page.
	1	The fault was caused by a page-level protection violation.

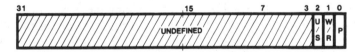

Figure 9.41 Page fault error code format and bit functions. (Reprinted by permission of Intel Corp. Copyright/Intel Corp., 1986.)

Just as in real-mode, the IRET instruction is used to return from a protected-mode interrupt service routine. For service routines using an interrupt gate or trap gate, IRET is restricted to the return from a higher privilege level to a lower privilege level, for instance, from level 1 to level 3. Once the flags, OLD CS, and OLD EIP are returned to the 80386, the RPL bits of OLD CS are tested to see if they equal CPL. If RPL = CPL, an intralevel return is in progress. In this case the return is complete and program execution resumes at the point in the program where execution had stopped.

If RPL is greater than CPL, an interlevel return is taking place, not an intralevel return. During an interlevel return, checks are performed to determine if a protection violation will occur due to the protection-level transition. Assuming that no violation occurs, the OLD SS and OLD ESP are popped from the stack into the MPU and then program execution resumes.

Internal Interrupt and Exception Functions

Earlier we indicated that some of the 256 interrupt vectors of the 80386 are dedicated to internal interrupt and exception functions. Internal interrupts and exceptions differ from external hardware interrupts in that they occur due to the result of executing an instruction, not an event that takes place in external hardware. That is, an internal interrupt or exception is initiated because an error condition was detected before, during, or after execution of an instruction. In this case, a routine must be initiated to service the internal condition before resuming execution of the same or next instruction of the program.

Internal interrupts and exceptions are not masked out with the interrupt enable flag. For this reason, occurrence of any one of these internal conditions is automatically detected by the 80386 and causes an interrupt of program execution and a vectored transfer of control to a corresponding service routine. During the control transfer sequence, no interrupt acknowledge bus cycles are produced.

Figure 9.42 identifies the internal interrupts and exceptions that are active in real mode. Here we find internal interrupts such as breakpoint and exception functions such as divide error and overflow error that were also detected by the 8086. However, the 80386 also implements several new real-mode exceptions. Examples of exceptions that are not implemented on the 8086 are invalid opcode, bounds check, and interrupt table limit too small.

Internal interrupts and exceptions are further categorized as a *fault, trap,* or *abort* based on how the failing function is reported. In the case of an exception that causes a fault, the values of CS and IP saved on the stack point to the instruction that resulted in the fault. Therefore, after servicing the exception, the faulting instruction can be reexecuted. On the other hand, for those exceptions that result in a trap, the values of CS and IP pushed to the stack point to the next instruction that is to be executed, instead of the instruction that caused the trap. Therefore, upon completion of the service routine, program execution resumes with the instruction that follows the instruction that produced the trap. Finally, exceptions that produce an abort do not preserve any information that identifies the location that caused the error. In this case the system may need to be restarted. Let us now look at the new 80386 real-mode internal interrupts and exceptions in more detail.

Debug exception. The *debug exception* relates to the debug mode of operation of the 80386. The 80386 has a set of eight on-chip debug registers. Using these registers, the programmer can specify up to four breakpoint addresses and specify conditions under which they are to be active. For instance, the activating condition

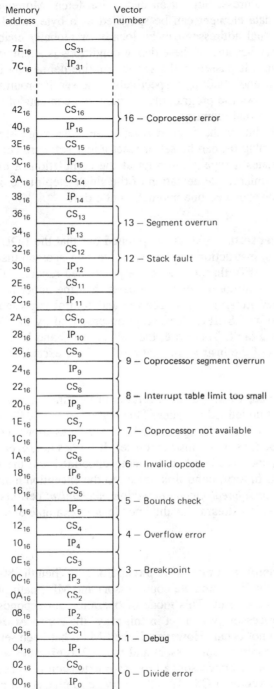

Memory address		Vector number
$7E_{16}$	CS_{31}	
$7C_{16}$	IP_{31}	
42_{16}	CS_{16}	} 16 — Coprocessor error
40_{16}	IP_{16}	
$3E_{16}$	CS_{15}	
$3C_{16}$	IP_{15}	
$3A_{16}$	CS_{14}	
38_{16}	IP_{14}	
36_{16}	CS_{13}	} 13 — Segment overrun
34_{16}	IP_{13}	
32_{16}	CS_{12}	} 12 — Stack fault
30_{16}	IP_{12}	
$2E_{16}$	CS_{11}	
$2C_{16}$	IP_{11}	
$2A_{16}$	CS_{10}	
28_{16}	IP_{10}	
26_{16}	CS_9	} 9 — Coprocessor segment overrun
24_{16}	IP_9	
22_{16}	CS_8	} 8 — Interrupt table limit too small
20_{16}	IP_8	
$1E_{16}$	CS_7	} 7 — Coprocessor not available
$1C_{16}$	IP_7	
$1A_{16}$	CS_6	} 6 — Invalid opcode
18_{16}	IP_6	
16_{16}	CS_5	} 5 — Bounds check
14_{16}	IP_5	
12_{16}	CS_4	} 4 — Overflow error
10_{16}	IP_4	
$0E_{16}$	CS_3	} 3 — Breakpoint
$0C_{16}$	IP_3	
$0A_{16}$	CS_2	
08_{16}	IP_2	
06_{16}	CS_1	} 1 — Debug
04_{16}	IP_1	
02_{16}	CS_0	} 0 — Divide error
00_{16}	IP_0	

Figure 9.42 Real-mode internal interrupt and exception vector table.

Sec. 9.8   Interrupt and Exception Processing

309

could be an instruction fetch from the address, a data write to the address, or either a data read or write for the address, but not an instruction fetch. Moreover, for data accesses the size of the data element can be specified as a byte, word, or double word. Finally, the individual addresses can be locally or globally enabled or disabled. If an access that matches any of these debug conditions is attempted, a debug exception occurs and control is passed to the service routine defined by IP_1 and CS_1 at word addresses 00004_{16} and 00006_{16}, respectively. The service routine could include a mechanism that allows the programmer to view the contents of the 80386's internal registers and its external memory.

If the trap flag (TF) bit in the flags register is set, the single-step mode of operation is enabled. This flag bit can be set or reset under software control. When TF is set, the 80386 initiates a type 1 interrupt at the completion of execution of every instruction. This permits implementation of the single-step mode of operation that allows a program to be executed one instruction at a time.

Bounds check exception. Earlier we pointed out that the BOUND (check array index against bounds) instruction can be used to test an operand that is used as the index into an array to verify that it is within a predefined range. If the index is less that the lower bound (minimum value) or greater than the upper bound (maximum value), a *bound check exception* has occurred and control is passed to the exception handler pointed to by $CS_5:IP_5$. The exception produced by the BOUND instruction is an example of a fault. Therefore, the values of CS and IP pushed to the stack represent the address of the instruction that produced the exception.

Invalid opcode exception. The exception-processing capability of the 80386 permits detection of undefined opcodes. This feature of the 80386 allows it to detect automatically whether or not the opcode to be executed as an instruction corresponds to one of the instructions in the instruction set. If it does not, execution is not attempted; instead, the opcode is identified an being undefined and the *invalid opcode exception* is initiated. In turn, control is passed to the exception handler identified by IP_6 and CS_6. This *undefined opcode detection mechanism* permits the 80386 to detect errors in its instruction stream. Invalid opcode is an example of an exception that produces a fault.

Coprocessor extension not available exception. When the 80386 comes up in the real mode, both the EM (emulate coprocessor) and MP (math present) bits of its machine status word are reset. This mode of operation corresponds to that of the 8088 or 8086 microprocessor. When set in this way, the *coprocessor extension not available exception* cannot occur. However, if the EM bit has been set to 1 under software control (do not monitor coprocessor) and the 80386 executes an ESC (escape) instruction for the math coprocessor, a processor extension not present exception is initiated through the vector at $CS_7: IP_7$. This service routine could pass control to a software emulation routine for the floating-point arithmetic operation. Moreover, if the MP and TS bits are set (meaning that a math coprocessor is available in the system and a task is in progress), when an ESC or WAIT instruction is executed an exception also takes place.

Interrupt table limit too small exception. Earlier we pointed out that the LIDT instruction can be used to relocate or change the limit of the interrupt vector table in memory. If the real-mode table has been changed, for example, its limit is set lower than address $003FF_{16}$ and an interrupt is invoked that attempts to access a vector stored at an address higher than the new limit, the *interrupt table limit too small exception* occurs. In this case, control is passed to the service routine by the vector $CS_8 : IP_8$. This exception is a fault; therefore, the address of the instruction that exceeded the limit is saved on the stack.

Coprocessor segment overrun exception. The *coprocessor segment overrun exception* signals that the 80387 numerics coprocessor has overrun the limit of a segment while attempting to read or write its operand. This event is detected by the coprocessor data channel within the 80386 and passes control to the service routine through interrupt vector 9. This exception handler can clear the exception, reset the 80387, determine the cause of the exception by examining the registers within the 80387, and then initiate a corrective action.

Stack fault exception. In the real mode, if the address of an operand access for the stack segment crosses the boundaries of the stack, a stack fault exception is produced. This causes control to be transferred to the service routine defined by CS_{12} and IP_{12}.

Segment overrun exception. This exception occurs in the real mode if an instruction attempts to access an operand that extends beyond the end of a segment. For instance, if a word access is made to the address CS:FFFF, DS:FFFF, or ES:FFFF, a fault occurs to the *segment overrun exception* service routine.

Coprocessor error exception. As part of the handshake sequence between the 80386 microprocessor and 80387 math coprocessor, the 80386 checks the status of its $\overline{ERROR}$ input. If the 80387 encounters a problem performing a numerics operation, it signals this fact to the 80386 by switching its $\overline{ERROR}$ output to logic 0. This signal is normally applied directly to the $\overline{ERROR}$ input of the 80386 and signals that an error condition has occurred. Logic 0 at this input causes a *coprocessor error exception* through vector 16.

Protected-mode internal interrupts and exceptions. In protected mode, more internal conditions can initiate an internal interrupt or exception. Figure 9.43 identifies each of these functions and its corresponding type number.

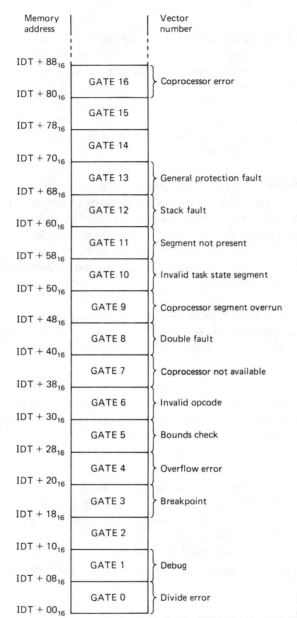

Memory address

Vector number

IDT + 88₁₆

GATE 16 — Coprocessor error

IDT + 80₁₆

GATE 15

IDT + 78₁₆

GATE 14

IDT + 70₁₆

GATE 13 — General protection fault

IDT + 68₁₆

GATE 12 — Stack fault

IDT + 60₁₆

GATE 11 — Segment not present

IDT + 58₁₆

GATE 10 — Invalid task state segment

IDT + 50₁₆

GATE 9 — Coprocessor segment overrun

IDT + 48₁₆

GATE 8 — Double fault

IDT + 40₁₆

GATE 7 — Coprocessor not available

IDT + 38₁₆

GATE 6 — Invalid opcode

IDT + 30₁₆

GATE 5 — Bounds check

IDT + 28₁₆

GATE 4 — Overflow error

IDT + 20₁₆

GATE 3 — Breakpoint

IDT + 18₁₆

GATE 2

IDT + 10₁₆

GATE 1 — Debug

IDT + 08₁₆

GATE 0 — Divide error

IDT + 00₁₆

Figure 9.43 Protected-mode internal exception gate locations.

ASSIGNMENT

Section 9.2

1. Name the technology used to fabricate the 80386 microprocessor.
2. What is the transistor count of the 80386?
3. Which signal is located at pin B7?

Section 9.3

4. How large is the real-address mode address bus and physical address space? How large is the protected-address mode address bus and physical address space? How large is the protected-mode virtual address space?
5. If the byte enable code output during a data write bus cycle is $\overline{BE_3}\,\overline{BE_2}\,\overline{BE_1}\,\overline{BE_0} = 1110_2$, is a byte, word, or double-word data transfer taking place? Over which data bus lines are the data transferred? Does data duplication occur?
6. For which byte enable codes does data duplication take place?
7. What type of bus cycle is in progress when the bus status code $M/\overline{IO}\,D/\overline{C}\,W/\overline{R}$ equals 010?
8. Which signals implement the DMA interface?
9. What processor extension is most frequently attached to the processor extension interface?

Section 9.4

10. What speed 80386 ICs are available from Intel Corporation? How are these speeds denoted in the part number?
11. At what pin is the CLK2 input applied?
12. What frequency clock signal must be applied to the CLK2 input of an 80386-25 if it is run at full speed?

Section 9.5

13. What is the duration of PCLK for an 80386 that is driven by CLK2 equals 50 MHz?
14. What two types of bus cycles can be performed by the 80386?
15. Explain what is meant by pipelining of the 80386's bus.
16. What is an idle state?
17. What is a wait state?
18. What are the two T states of the 80386's bus cycle called?
19. If an 80386-25 is executing a nonpipelined write bus cycle that has no wait states, what would be the duration of this bus cycle if the 80386 is operating at full speed?
20. If an 80386-25 that is running at full speed performs a bus cycle with two wait states, what is the duration of the bus cycle?

Section 9.6

21. How is memory organized from a hardware point of view in a protected-mode 80386 microcomputer system? Real-mode 80386 microcomputer system?

22. What are the five types of data transfers that can take place over the data bus? How many bus cycles are required for each type of data transfer?

23. If an 80386-25 is running at full speed and all memory accesses involve one wait state, how long will it take to fetch the word of data starting at address $0FF1A_{16}$? At address $0FFIF_{16}$?

24. During a bus cycle that involves a misaligned word transfer, which byte of data is transferred over the bus during the first bus cycle?

25. Overview the function of each of the blocks in the memory interface diagram of Fig. 9.25.

26. When the instruction PUSH AX is executed, what bus status code is output by the 80386, which byte enable signals are active, and what read/write control signal is produced by the bus control logic?

Section 9.7

27. Which signal indicates to external circuitry that the current bus cycle is for the I/O interface and not for the memory interface?

28. Which block produces the input (read), output (write), and bus control signals for the I/O interface?

29. Briefly describe the function of each block in the I/O interface circuit in Fig. 9.27.

30. If an 80386-25 is running at full speed inserts two wait states into all I/O bus cycles, what is the duration of a nonpipelined bus cycle in which a byte of data is being output?

31. If the 80386 in Problem 30 was outputting a word of data to a word-wide port at I/O address $1A3_{16}$, what would be the duration of the bus cycle?

32. What parameters identify the beginning of the I/O permission bit map in a TSS? At what address of the TSS is this parameter held?

33. At what double-word address in the I/O permission bit map is the bit for I/O port 64 held? Which bit of this double word corresponds to port 64?

34. To what logic level should the bit in Problem 33 be set if I/O operations are to be inhibited to the port in protected mode?

Section 9.8

35. What is the real-mode interrupt address pointer table called? Protected-mode address pointer table?

36. What is the size of a real-mode interrupt vector? Protected-mode gate?

37. The contents of which register determine the location of the interrupt address pointer table? To what value is this register initialized at reset?

38. At what addresses is the protected-mode gate for type number 20 stored in memory?

39. Assume that gate 3 consists of the four words that follow:

$$(IDT + 8) = 1000_{16}$$
$$(IDT + A) = B000_{16}$$
$$(IDT + C) = AE00_{16}$$
$$(IDT + E) = 0000_{16}$$

(a) Is the gate descriptor active?

(b) What is the privilege level?

(c) Is the gate a trap gate or an interrupt gate?

(d) What is the starting address of the service routine?

40. If values are stored in memory at locations as follows,

$$(IDT\_TABLE) = 01FF_{16}$$

$$(IDT\_TABLE + 2) = 0000_{16}$$

$$(IDT\_TABLE + 4) = 0001_{16}$$

what address is loaded into the interrupt descriptor table register when the instruction LIDT IDT_TABLE is executed? What is the maximum size of the table? How many gates are provided for in this table?

41. Explain the operation performed by the sequence of instructions that follow:

```
INIT_IDTR:    MOV     [IDT_TABLE], ILIMIT
              MOV     [IDT_TABLE + 2], IBASE_LOW
              MOV     [IDT_TABLE + 4], IBASE_HIGH
              LIDT    IDT_TABLE
              SIDT    IDT_COPY
              CMP     IDT_TABLE, IDT_COPY
              JNZ     INIT_IDTR
```

42. What is the key difference between the real-mode and protected-mode interrupt request/acknowledge handshake sequence?

43. List the real-mode internal interrupts serviced by the 80386.

44. Internal interrupts and exceptions are categorized into groups based on how the failing function is reported. List the three groups.

45. Which real-mode vector numbers are reserved for internal interrupts and exceptions?

46. Into which reporting group is the invalid opcode exception classified?

47. What is the cause of a stack fault exception?

48. Which exceptions take on a new meaning or are only active in the protected mode?

10

Software Architecture of the 68000 Microprocessor

10.1 INTRODUCTION

Up to this point in the book, we have studied Intel's 16-bit 8086 microprocessor and the 32-bit 80386 microprocessor and their microcomputer systems. We discussed their architecture, instruction set, programming, how they interface to memory and I/O devices, and their interrupt and exception-processing capabilities. Now it is time to turn our attention to Motorola's 68000 family of microprocessors. In this chapter we describe the general software architecture of the 68000 microprocessor. The three chapters that follow are devoted to its instruction set, programming, and hardware interfaces. The last two chapters in the book introduce the 68020, which is a 32-bit member of the 68000 family. The following topics are discussed in this chapter:

1. Software model
2. Memory address space and data organization
3. Dedicated and general use of memory
4. Internal registers
5. User and supervisor stacks
6. Operand addressing modes

10.2 SOFTWARE MODEL

In Chapter 2, we pointed out that the purpose of developing a *software model* is to aid the programmer in understanding the operation of the microcomputer system from a

316

software point of view. The *software model* of the 68000 microprocessor is shown in Fig. 10.1. This model specifies the resources available to programmers for implementing their program requirements. Here we see that the 68000 is represented by

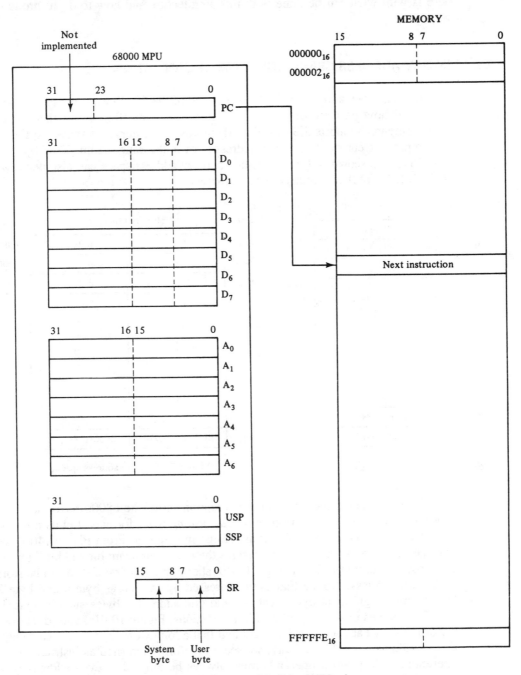

Figure 10.1 Software model of the 68000 microprocessor.

eight *data registers* (D_0 through D_7), seven *address registers* (A_0–A_6), two *stack pointers* (USP and SSP), a program counter (PC), and a status regiser (SR). Also included in the model is a 16 MB memory address space. Once again our concern here is with what can be done with this architecture and how to do it through software.

10.3 MEMORY ADDRESS SPACE AND DATA ORGANIZATION

We will begin our study of the software model of the 68000 with its memory address space and how data are organized in memory. Figure 10.2 shows that the 68000 microcomputer supports 8,388,607 (8M) words of memory. As shown in Fig. 10.2, they represent consecutive word addresses over the range from 000000_{16} through $FFFFFE_{16}$. As shown in Fig. 10.3, the memory address space can also be viewed as 16,777,214 (16M) consecutive byte addresses.

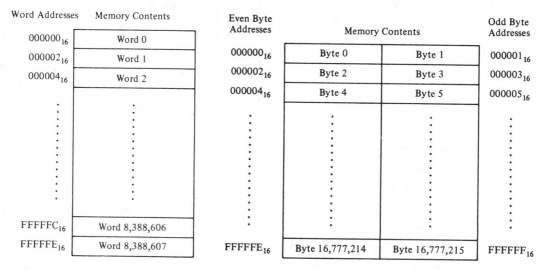

Figure 10.2   Word address space.   Figure 10.3   Byte address space.

Most of the instructions in the instruction set of the 68000 have the ability to process operands expressed in *byte, word,* or *long-word* formats. Let us now look at how data expressed in these forms are stored in memory. From Fig. 10.4(a), we see that within a byte of data, bit 0 represents the least significant bit and bit 7 represents the most significant bit. Next, Fig. 10.4(b) shows that 2 bytes of data can be stored at each word address. Notice that even-addressed bytes such as byte 0 and byte 2 are held in most significant byte locations and odd-addressed bytes such as byte 1 and byte 3 are stored in least significant byte locations. Figure 10.4(c) and (d) shows that a word is stored at each word address and that a long word is stored at two consecutive word addresses. In this way, we see that information such as instructions, word operands, or long-word operands must always be aligned at even-address boundaries.

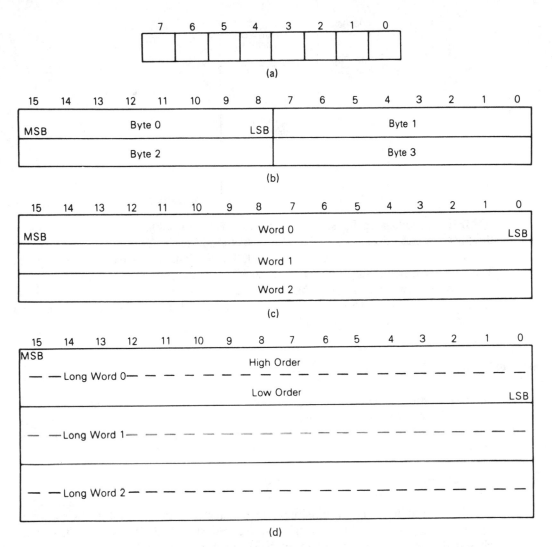

Figure 10.4 Data organization in memory. (Courtesy of Motorola, Inc.)

10.4 DEDICATED AND GENERAL USE OF MEMORY

Now that we have introduced the software model of the 68000, its address space, and data organization, let us continue by looking at which parts of the address space have dedicated uses and which parts are for general use. The 68000 supports a very large 16M-byte address space that has few limitations on its use. That is, program memory, data memory, and stack can be located almost at any address and are not limited in size.

In Fig. 10.5. we see that just the lower end of the address space has a *dedicated function*. That is, the word storage locations over the address range from 000000_{16} to

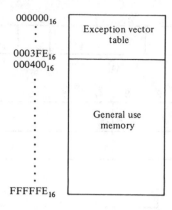

000000_{16}	Exception vector table
$0003FE_{16}$	
000400_{16}	
	General use memory
$FFFFFE_{16}$	

Figure 10.5 Memory map.

$0003FE_{16}$ are allocated for storage of an address vector table. As shown, it contains the 68000's exception vector table. Each vector address is 24 bits long and takes up two words of memory. An example of 68000 exceptions are its hardware interrupts. The exception-processing capability of the 68000 is the subject of Chapter 14.

From the *memory map* in Fig. 10.5, we see that the rest of the address space is for *general use*. Therefore, it can be used to store instructions of the program, data operands, or address information.

10.5 INTERNAL REGISTERS

Internal to the 68000 microprocessor are eighteen 32-bit registers and one 16-bit register. Figure 10.6 shows these registers. Notice that they include *eight data registers, seven address registers, two stack pointers, a program counter*, and *the status register*. The status register is the 16-bit register.

Data Registers

There are eight user-accessible data registers within the 68000. As shown in Fig. 10.6, they are called D_0 through D_7. Each register is 32 bits long and its bits are labeled 0 (least significant bit) through 31 (most significant bit). We will refer to these bits as B_0 through B_{31}, respectively.

The data registers are used to store data temporarily for use in processing. For example, they could hold the source and destination operands of an arithmetic or logic instruction. Each register can be accessed for byte operands, for word operands, or for long-word operands. Byte data are always held in the 8 least significant bits of a data register, that is, B_0 through B_7. On the other hand, words of data always reside in the lower 16 bits, B_0 through B_{15}, and long words take up all 32 bits of the register. A few instructions also permit processing of individual bits or data expressed as BCD numbers.

The size of data to be used during the execution of an instruction is generally specified in the instruction. For example, a byte move instruction could be written with register D_0 as the location of the source operand and D_7 as the location of the destination operand. Executing the instruction causes the contents of bits B_0 through

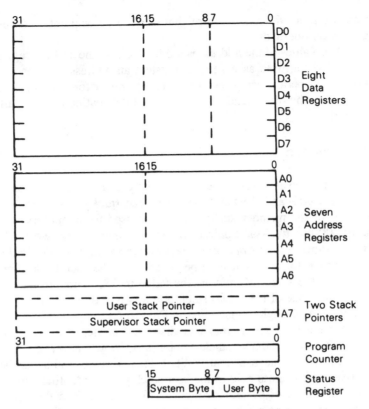

Figure 10.6 Internal registers of the 68000 microprocessor. (Courtesy of Motorola, Inc.)

B_7 of D_0 to be copied into bits B_0 through B_7 of register D_7. Alternatively, the instruction could be set up to process words of data. This time, executing the instruction would cause bits B_0 through B_{15} of D_0 to be copied into B_0 through B_{15} of D_7.

The 68000 can also use the data registers as index registers. In this case the value in the register represents an offset address that, when combined with the contents of another register, points to the location of data in the memory subsystem.

These registers are said to be truly general purpose. That is, they do not have dedicated functions. For this reason, most instructions can perform their operations on source and destination operands that reside in any of these registers.

Address Registers

The next seven registers, which are labeled A_0 through A_6 in Fig. 10.6, are the address registers. They are also 32 bits in length. These registers are not provided for storage of data for processing. Instead, they are meant to store address information such as base addresses and pointer addresses and are used to access source or destination operands that are stored in memory. Moreover, they can also act as index registers.

Just like the data registers, the address registers are general purpose. That is, an instruction can reference any of them as a base or pointer address for its source or destination operands.

The values of the addresses are loaded into the address registers under software control. When used as a source register, an address register can be accessed as a long-word operand using the complete register or for word operands using the lower 16 bits. On the other hand, when used as a destination register, all 32 bits are always affected.

Stack Pointers

Two other internal registers are used to hold address information. They are called the *user stack pointer* (USP) and the *supervisor stack pointer* (SSP). The stack is a special part of the memory subsystem that is used for temporary storage of data. Since the 68000 has two stack pointer registers, there can be two stacks in its microcomputer system, a *user stack* and a *supervisor stack*. The address in USP points to the next storage location that is to be accessed in the user stack. This location is called the top of the stack. Moreover, the value in SSP points to the top of the supervisor stack. Only one of these two stack pointers is active at a time. For this reason, they are shown as a single register, A_7 in Fig. 10.6.

Unlike the address registers discussed earlier, these two registers have dedicated functions. The user stack pointer is active whenever the 68000 is operating in a mode known as the user state. When in this mode, the supervisor stack pointer is inactive. The address held in the user stack pointer identifies the top of the user stack in the user part of system memory. This user stack is the place where return addresses, register data, and other parameters are saved during operations such as the call to a subroutine.

The 68000 can be switched to a second mode, known as the supervisor state. This causes the supervisor stack pointer to become active and the user stack pointer to become inactive. The address in the supervisor stack pointer register points to the top of a second stack. It is called the supervisor stack and resides in the supervisor part of memory. The supervisor stack is used for the same purposes as the user stack, but it is also used by *supervisory calls* such as *software exceptions, interrupts,* and *internal exceptions*.

The address values in USP and SSP can be modified through software. However, they can be modified only when the 68000 is set to operate in the supervisor mode.

Program Counter

During normal operation, the 68000 fetches one instruction after the other from memory and executes them. The address held in program counter PC points to the next instruction that is to be fetched. After the instruction is fetched, it is decoded by the 68000 and, if necessary, data operands are read from either the internal registers or memory. Then the operation specified in the instruction is performed on the operands, and the results are written to either an internal register or storage location in memory. The 68000 is now ready to execute the next instruction.

Every time an instruction is fetched from memory, the value held in PC is incremented by 2. In this way, the 68000 is ready to fetch the next word of code for execution. Each instruction can take up from one to five words of program storage memory.

In Fig. 10.6, PC is shown as a 32-bit register; however, only the lower 24 bits are actually used in currently available 68000 devices. These 24 bits can generate 16M unique memory addresses for accessing bytes of data. But instruction code is always stored at word boundaries. Therefore, the program memory address space can also be considered to represent an 8M-word address space. The range of word addresses is all even addresses from 000000_{16} through $FFFFFE_{16}$. In this way we see that program storage memory can reside anywhere in the 8M-word address space.

Status Register

Figure 10.6 also shows the 16-bit status register (SR) of the 68000 microprocessor. Here we see that this register is subdivided into two parts, called the *user byte* and the *system byte*.

The status register is shown in more detail in Fig. 10.7. Here we see that the bits implemented in the user byte are *flags* that indicate the processor state resulting from the execution of an instruction. The five conditions represented by the implemented bits are *carry* (C), *overflow* (V), *zero* (Z), *negative* (N), and *extended carry* (X). Let us now look at each of these condition flags in more detail.

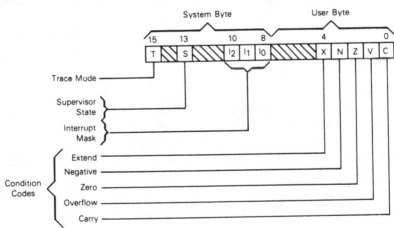

Figure 10.7 Status register. (Courtesy of Motorola, Inc.)

1. *Carry* (C): The carry flag, bit 0, is set if an add operation generates a carry-out or a subtract (or compare) operation needs a borrow. Otherwise, it is reset. During shift or rotate operations, it holds the bit that is rotated or shifted out of a register or memory location.

2. *Overflow* (V): If an arithmetic operation on signed numbers produces an incorrect result, the overflow flag (bit 1) is set; otherwise, it is reset. During an arithmetic shift operation, this flag gets set as the result of a change in the most significant bit; otherwise, it gets reset.

3. *Zero* (Z): If an operation produces a zero as its result, the zero flag (bit 2) of SR is set. A nonzero result clears Z.

4. *Negative* (N): The content of bit 3 is a copy of the most significant bit (sign bit) of the result during arithmetic, logic, shift, or rotate operations. In other words, a negative result sets the N bit and a positive result clears it.

5. *Extend* (X): During arithmetic, shift, or rotate operations, the extend flag, bit 4, receives the carry status. It is used as the carry bit in multiprecision operations.

These user bits of the status register can be tested through software to determine whether or not certain events have occurred. Typically, the occurrence of an event indicates that a change in program environment should be initiated. For instance, the overflow bit could be tested and if it is set program control is passed to an overflow service routine.

The system byte of SR contains bits that control operational options available on the 68000 microprocessor and also contains the *interrupt mask*. The implemented bits in this byte and their functions are identified in Fig. 10.7. Let us now look at these functions.

1. *Interrupt mask* ($I_2I_1I_0$): Bits 8 through 10 of SR are the interrupt mask of the 68000. This 3-bit code determines which interrupts can be serviced and which are to be ignored. Interrupting devices with priority higher than the binary value of $I_2I_1I_0$ will be accepted and those with lower or the same priority will be ignored. For example, if $I_2I_1I_0$ equals 011_2, then levels 4 through 7 are able to be active, while levels 1 through 3 are masked out.

2. *Supervisor* (S): Bit 13 of SR is used to select between the *user* and *supervisor states* of operation. A logic 1 in this bit indicates that the 68000 is operating in the supervisory state. If it is logic 0, the 68000 operates in the user state.

3. *Trace mode* (T): The T status bit is used to enable or disable *trace (single-step) mode* of operation. To activate the single-step mode, bit 15 must be set. When set in this way, the microprocessor executes an instruction, then enters the supervisor state, and vectors to a trace service routine. The service routine may pass control to a mechanism that permits initiation of execution of the next instruction or debug mode of operations for displaying the contents of the various internal registers.

The contents of the complete status register can be read at any time through software. Unimplemented bits are always read as logic 0. However, the system byte can be modified only when the 68000 is in the supervisor state.

10.6 USER AND SUPERVISOR STACKS

The 68000 employs a stack-oriented architecture. In Section 10.5, we indicated that the 68000 has two internal stack pointer registers and that these stack pointers are called the user stack pointer (USP) and supervisor stack pointer (SSP). As shown in Fig. 10.8, the addresses held in these registers point to the top storage locations in their respective stacks, that is, their tops of stacks. The storage locations identified as bottom of stack represent the locations pointed to by the initial values loaded into the

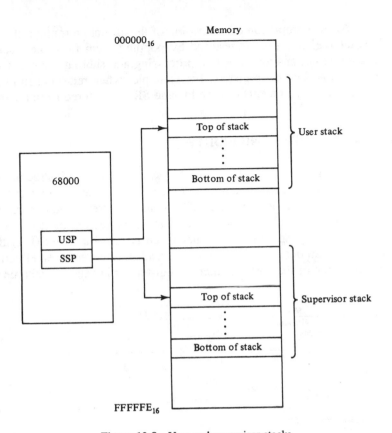

Figure 10.8 User and supervisor stacks.

stack pointers. When the stacks are empty, the stack pointers point to these locations. The *user stack* is active whenever the 68000 is in the user state, and the *supervisor stack* is active whenever it is in the supervisor state. Both stacks can be located in memory anywhere in the address space of the 68000, and they are not limited in size.

During exception processing or subroutine calls, the contents of certain internal registers of the 68000 are saved on the stack. For instance, when exception processing is initiated for a hardware interrupt, the current contents of the program counter (PC) and status register (SR) are automatically pushed to the stack. In this way, they are temporarily saved.

Additional stack operations are usually performed as part of the exception processing service routine or subroutine. These are push operations that save the contents of registers that are to be used within the service routine on the stack. For instance, instructions in a hardware interrupt service routine can cause the contents of data registers D_0, D_1, and D_2 to be pushed to the user stack. These examples all push word data to the user stack. Byte data also can be pushed to the stack; however, each byte still consumes one word of stack. The byte of data is stored in the most significant byte location of the word storage location, and the least significant byte is not affected.

At the completion of processing of the exception routine, the saved contents of internal registers can be restored by popping them from the stack. Moreover, the return instructions for exception processing and subroutines cause automatic reloading of some internal registers. For example, when returning from an exception service routine the contents of both PC and SR are restored from the top of the stack.

10.7 OPERAND ADDRESSING MODES

The operands processed by the 68000 as it executes an instruction may be specified as part of the instruction in program memory, may reside in internal registers, or may be stored in data memory. The 68000 has 14 different addressing modes. They are shown in Fig. 10.9. The objective of these addressing modes is to supply different ways for the programmer to generate an *effective address* (EA) that identifies the location of an operand. In general, operands referenced by an effective address reside either in one of the 68000's internal registers or in external data memory.

Mode	Generation
Register Direct Addressing	
Data Register Direct	EA = Dn
Address Register Direct	EA = An
Absolute Data Addressing	
Absolute Short	EA = (Next Word)
Absolute Long	EA = (Next Two Words)
Program Counter Relative Addressing	
Relative with Offset	EA = (PC) + d_{16}
Relative with Index and Offset	EA = (PC) + (Xn) + d_8
Register Indirect Addressing	
Register Indirect	EA = (An)
Postincrement Register Indirect	EA = (An), An ← An + N
Predecrement Register Indirect	An ← An − N, EA = (An)
Register Indirect with Offset	EA = (An) + d_{16}
Indexed Register Indirect with Offset	EA = (An) + (Xn) + d_8
Immediate Data Addressing	
Immediate	DATA = Next Word(s)
Quick Immediate	Inherent Data
Implied Addressing	
Implied Register	EA = SR, USP, SP, PC

NOTES:
EA = Effective Address
An = Address Register
Dn = Data Register
Xn = Address or Data Register
    used as Index Register
SR = Status Register
PC = Program Counter
( ) = Contents of

d_8 = 8-bit Offset
    (displacement)
d_{16} = 16-bit Offset
    (displacement)
N = 1 for Byte, 2 for
    Words, and 4 for Long
    Words.
← = Replaces

Figure 10.9 Operand addressing modes of the 68000 microprocessor. (Courtesy of Motorola, Inc.)

Looking at Fig. 10.9, we see that the 14 addressing modes have been subdivided into six groups based on how they generate an effective address. These groups are *register direct addressing, absolute data addressing, program counter relative addressing, register indirect addressing, immediate data addressing,* and *implied addressing.* Notice that the addressing modes in all groups other than immediate data addressing produce an effective address. Let us now look into each of these modes in detail.

Register Direct Addressing Modes

Register direct addressing modes are used when one of the data or address registers within the 68000 contains the operand that is to be processed by the instruction. In Fig. 10.9, we see that if the specified register is a data register, the addressing mode is called *data register direct addressing*. On the other hand, if an address register is used, it is known as *address register direct addressing*.

Here is an example that employs both data register direct addressing and address register direct addressing.

$$\text{MOVE.L} \quad \text{A0, D0}$$

MOVE.L is how we write the move instruction to process long-word (32-bit) data. Notice that address register A_0 is specified to contain the source operand. This is an example of address register direct addressing. On the other hand, the destination operand uses data register direct addressing and is specified as the contents of data register D_0. In this example, neither operand is located in memory.

Execution of this instruction causes the long word in address register A_0 to be copied into data register D_0. This operation can also be expressed as

$$\text{A0} \rightarrow \text{D0}$$

In Fig. 10.10(a), we see that before executing the instruction A_0 contains $76543210 and the contents of D_0 are a don't-care state. The symbol $ stands for hexadecimal number. At the conclusion of execution of the instruction, both A_0 and D_0 contain $76543210. This result is shown in Fig. 10.10(b).

Absolute Data Addressing Modes

When the effective address of an operand is included in the instruction, we are using what is called absolute data addressing mode. There are two such modes for the 68000. They are known as *absolute short addressing* and *absolute long addressing*. These addressing modes are used to access operands that reside in memory.

If an instruction uses absolute short data addressing to specify the location of an operand, a 16-bit absolute address must be included as the second word of the instruction. This word is the effective address of the storage location for the operand in memory.

As an example, let us consider the instruction

$$\text{MOVE.L} \quad \$1234, \text{D0}$$

It stands for move the long word starting at address $1234 in memory into data register D_0. Notice that the instruction is written with $1234 in the location for the source operand. This is the absolute address of the source operand and it is encoded by the assembler into the instruction as shown in Fig. 10.11(a). Notice that the address of the source operand is the next word after the instruction opcode in program memory.

The 68000 automatically does a sign extension based on the MSB of the absolute short address to give a 32-bit address (actually only 24 bits are used). For our example, the sign bit is 0; therefore, extending it gives the address 001234_{16}. Since only 16 bits can be used in absolute short data addressing, it always generates a memory address either in the range 000000_{16} through $007FFF_{16}$ or $FF8000_{16}$ through $FFFFFF_{16}$. These ranges correspond to the first 32K bytes and the last 32K bytes of the 68000's address space, respectively. Other parts of the 68000's address space cannot be accessed with this addressing mode.

The result of executing this instruction is shown in Fig. 10.11(b). Notice that the long word starting at address 001234_{16}, which equals $6789ABCD_{16}$, is copied into D_0. Here we see that the word at the lower address, 001234_{16}, is copied into the upper 16 bits of D_0, and the word at the higher address, 001236_{16}, is copied into the lower 16 bits.

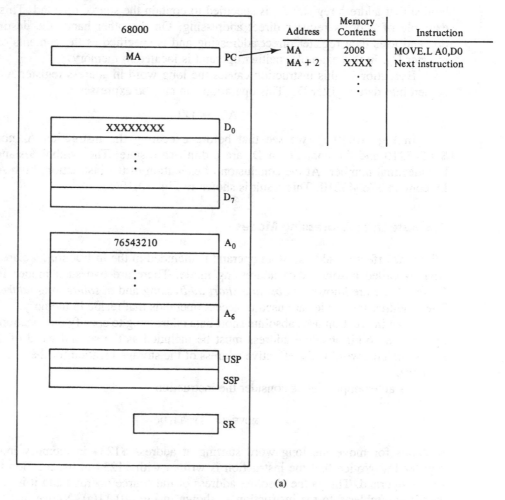

(a)

Figure 10.10 Instruction using register direct addressing: (a) before execution; (b) after execution.

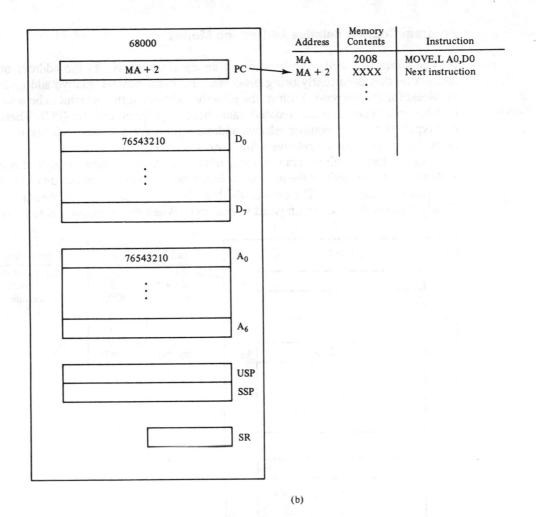

Address	Memory Contents	Instruction
MA	2008	MOVE.L A0,D0
MA + 2	XXXX	Next instruction

(b)

Figure 10.10 (*continued*)

Absolute long data addressing permits use of a full 32-bit quantity as the absolute address data. This type of operand is specified in the same way except that its absolute address is written with more than four hexadecimal digits.

For instance, the instruction

```
MOVE.L    $01234,D0
```

has the same effect as the previous instruction, but the address of the source operand is encoded by the assembler as an absolute long data address. That is, the quantity $01234 is encoded as a 32-bit number instead of a 16-bit number. This means that the instruction now takes up three words of memory instead of two.

Since all 24 bits are used, the operand specified with absolute long addressing can reside anywhere in the address space of the 68000.

Program Counter Relative Addressing Modes

It is possible to specify the location of an operand relative to the address of the instruction that is currently being processed. Program counter relative addressing is provided for this purpose. With it, the effective address of the operand to be accessed is calculated relative to the updated value held in program counter (PC). There are two types of program counter relative addressing: *program counter relative with offset* and *program counter relative with index and offset*.

Let us begin with program counter relative with offset addressing. In this case, a 16-bit quantity identifies the number of bytes the data to be accessed are offset from the updated value in PC. The offset, which is also known as the *displacement*, immediately follows the instruction word in memory. When the instruction is fetched and

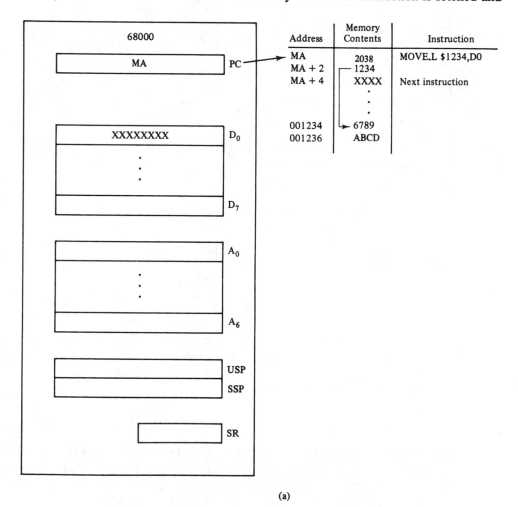

(a)

Figure 10.11 Instruction using absolute data addressing: (a) before execution; (b) after execution.

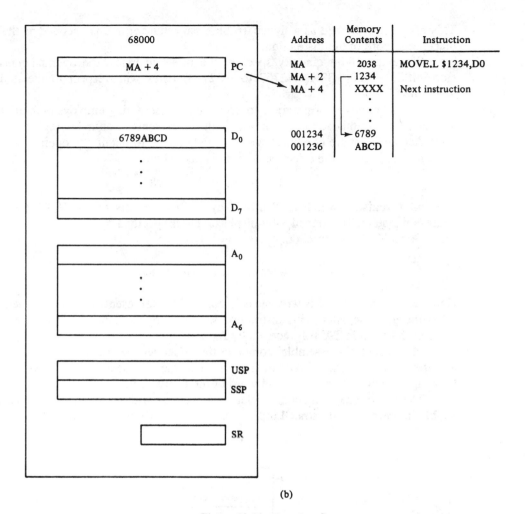

Address	Memory Contents	Instruction
MA	2038	MOVE.L $1234,D0
MA + 2	1234	
MA + 4	XXXX	Next instruction
.		
.		
.		
001234	6789	
001236	ABCD	

68000

MA + 4 — PC

6789ABCD — D_0

D_7

A_0

A_6

USP

SSP

SR

(b)

Figure 10.11 (*continued*)

executed, the 68000 sign-extends the offset to 32 bits and then adds it to the updated contents of the program counter.

$$EA = PC + d16$$

The sum that results is the effective address of the operand in memory.

An example of an instruction that employs this addressing mode is

MOVE.L   TAG,D0

This means "move the long word starting at the memory location with TAG as its label into D_0." The question arises: Where is the label TAG in memory? The answer lies with the assembler. It computes the number of bytes the displacement word in the move instruction is offset from the memory location corresponding to label TAG.

This offset is expressed as a signed 16-bit binary number and is encoded as the displacement word of the instruction.

Since the 16-bit quantity specifies the offset in bytes, the operand must reside within + or −32K(+32767 to −32768) bytes with respect to the updated value in PC.

The second type of program counter relative addressing employs both an index and an offset. In this addressing mode, both the contents of an index register and an 8-bit displacement are combined with the updated PC to obtain the operand's memory address. That is, the effective address is given by

$$EA = PC + Xn + d8$$

The index register, which is identified by X_n, can be any of the 68000's data or address registers. The signed 8-bit displacement is specified by d_8.

Consider this instruction:

MOVE.L   TABLE(A0.L),D0

Here the source operand is written such that TABLE represents the displacement and A_0 is the index register. This instruction says to copy the long word starting at the memory location in TABLE indexed by A_0 into D_0.

In this case, the assembler computes the offset between the updated value in PC and the address of label TABLE. The value of the displacement is encoded as the least significant byte in the second word of the instruction.

The use of program counter relative addressing with offset and index to access a table in memory is illustrated in Fig. 10.12. The starting point of the table in mem-

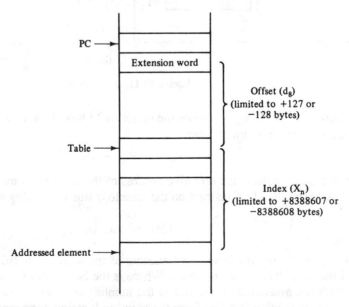

Figure 10.12 Accessing elements of a table with program counter relative with index and offset addressing.

ory is identified by the label TABLE. Since just 8 bits are provided for the offset, the table must begin within $+127$ or -128 bytes of the extension word of the instruction. The size of the table is determined by the index. The ability to specify up to a 32-bit index permits addressing of very long tables. Actually, the size of the data table is limited by the number of address lines on the 68000, which is 24.

Address Register Indirect Addressing Modes

Address register indirect addressing is similar to the register direct addressing we discussed earlier in that an internal register is specified when writing the instruction. However, in this case, only address registers A_0 through A_6 can be used. Moreover, the register does not represent the location of the operand; instead, it contains the effective address of the operand in memory. Notice that register indirect addressing enables the 68000 to access information that resides in external memory.

There are five different kinds of register indirect addressing supported by the 68000. As shown in Fig. 10.9, they are called *register indirect addressing, postincrement register indirect addressing, predecrement register indirect addressing, register indirect with offset addressing,* and *indexed register indirect with offset addressing.* We will now look at each of these types in more detail.

Register indirect is the simplest form of address register indirect addressing. When it is specified, one of the address registers contains the address of the source or destination operand. For instance, in the instruction

MOVE.L   (A0),D0

the source operand employs register indirect addressing. Notice that this type of addressing is specified by enclosing the name of the address register, which in our example is A_0, with parentheses. The destination operand is specified as D_0 using register direct addressing.

Figure 10.13 illustrates the result of using this addressing mode. In Fig. 10.13(a), we see that the contents of A_0 are $1234. Moreover, we see that the long word stored at address $1234 through $1237 is $ABCDEF89. As shown in Fig. 10.13(b), execution of the instruction causes this value to be copied into destination register D_0.

Postincrement register indirect addressing works essentially the same as the register indirect addressing we just demonstrated. However, there is one difference. This is that after the operation specified by the instruction is completed the contents of the address register are automatically incremented by 1, 2, or 4, depending on whether byte, word, or long-word data are processed. In this way, the address points to the next sequential element of data.

Our earlier example can be rewritten to use postincrement register indirect addressing. This gives

MOVE.L   (A0)+,D0

Here we see that including a $+$ symbol after the operand specifies the postincrement operation.

If we assume that the state of the 68000 just prior to execution of this instruction is as shown in Fig. 10.14(a), the results are similar to those shown in Fig. 10.13(b) for register indirect addressing. Again $ABCDEF89 is copied into D_0. But this time the contents of A_0 are also incremented by 4 to give $1238, as shown in Fig. 10.14(b). Therefore, it points to the start of the next long word in data memory.

Predecrement register indirect addressing is the same as postincrement register indirect addressing except that the contents of the selected address register are decremented instead of incremented. Moreover, the decrement operation takes place prior to performing the operation specified in the instruction.

For instance, in the instruction

MOVE.L   −(A0),D0

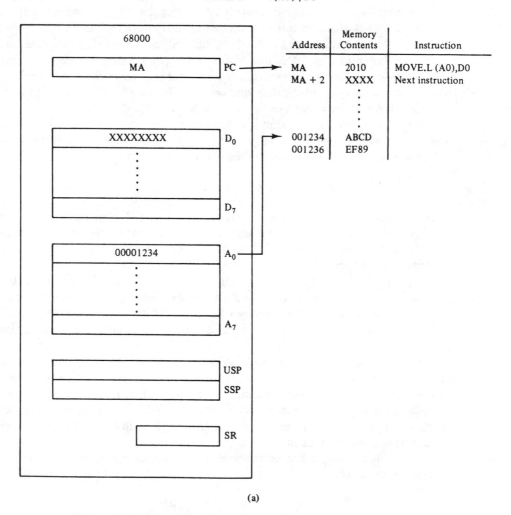

(a)

Figure 10.13 Instruction using address register indirect addressing: (a) before execution; (b) after execution.

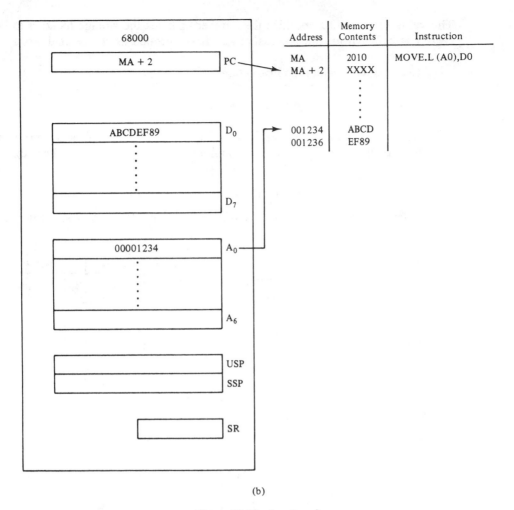

Address	Memory Contents	Instruction
MA	2010	MOVE.L (A0),D0
MA + 2	XXXX	
.		
.		
.		
001234	ABCD	
001236	EF89	

(b)

Figure 10.13 (*continued*)

the $-$ symbol identifies predecrement indirect addressing. If this instruction is executed with the 68000 in the state shown in Fig. 10.15(a), the address in A_0 is first decremented by 4 and equals $1230. Therefore, the contents of memory locations $1230 through $1233 are copied into D_0. This result is illustrated by Fig. 10.15(b).

Postincrement and predecrement indirect addressing allows a programmer to implement memory scanning operations without the need to update the address pointer with additional instructions. This type of addressing is useful for performing data processing operations such as block transfer and string searches.

In the address register indirect with offset addressing mode, a sign-extended 16-bit offset value and an address register are specified in the instruction. The effective address of the operand is generated by adding the offset to the contents of the selected address register; that is,

$$EA = An + d16$$

The value of offset d_{16} specifies the number of bytes the storage location to be accessed is offset from the address in A_n. It is encoded as the second word of the instruction.

Let us now consider the instruction

$$\text{MOVE.W} \quad 16\text{(A0), D0}$$

Here we find that an offset of 16 (16 bytes) is specified for the source operand. Execution of this instruction for the conditions in Fig. 10.16(a) produces the effective address

$$EA = 1234_{16} + 16_{10} = 1244_{16}$$

As shown in Fig. 10.16(b), the word contents of address $1244, which equals

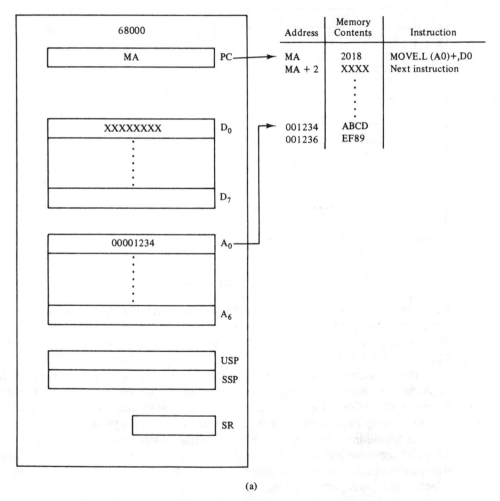

(a)

Figure 10.14 Instruction using postincrement register indirect addressing: (a) before execution; (b) after execution.

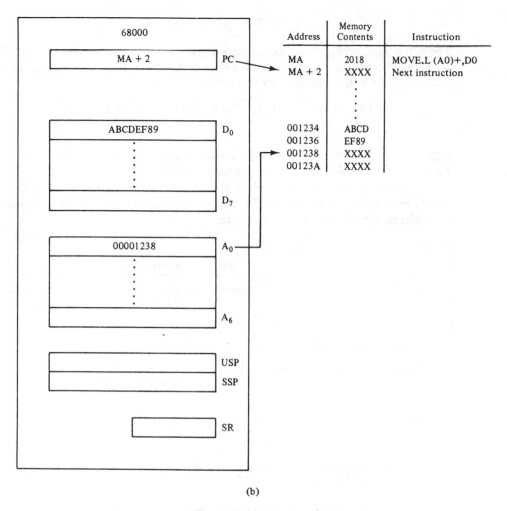

Address	Memory Contents	Instruction
MA	2018	MOVE.L (A0)+,D0
MA + 2	XXXX	Next instruction
.		
.		
.		
001234	ABCD	
001236	EF89	
001238	XXXX	
00123A	XXXX	

(b)

Figure 10.14 (*continued*)

$ABCD, are copied into the least significant 16 bits of D_0.

Since the offset is a signed 16-bit integer number, the operand to be accessed must be within +32767 or −32768 bytes of the storage location pointed to by the contents of the address register.

The last register indirect addressing mode, indexed register indirect with offset addressing, allows specification of an address register, an offset, and an index register for formation of the effective address. The offset value is limited to a signed 8-bit quantity. On the other hand, the index register can be the contents of any of the 68000's data or address registers. The effective address is computed by adding the contents of the address register, the contents of the index register, and the offset. That is,

$$EA = An + Xn + d8$$

Here is an instruction that uses this addressing mode for its source operand.

The offset equals 16_{10}, A_0 is the address register, and A_1 is the index register. Figure 10.17(a) shows that A_0 contains \$1234 and A_1 contains \$2344. In this case, the address of the source operand is obtained as

$$EA = A0 + A1 + 16_{10} = 1234_{16} + 2344_{16} + 10_{16}$$
$$= 3588_{16}$$

Figure 10.17(b) shows that the word contents at this memory location are $ABCD_{16}$. This value is copied into the least significant word of D_0.

Since the offset value is an 8-bit signed integer, the address offset is limited to $+127$ or -128 bytes relative to the location specified by the sum of the contents of the address register and the index register.

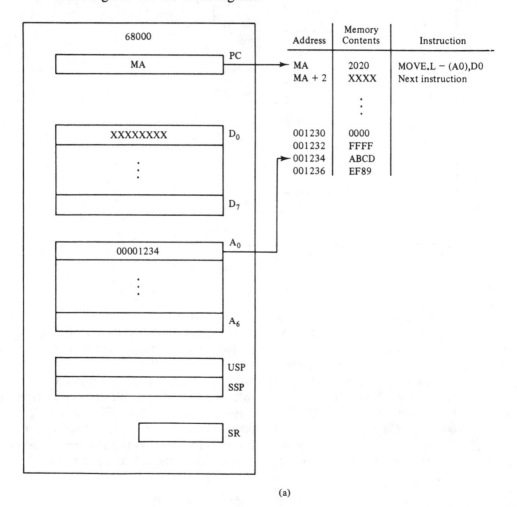

(a)

Figure 10.15 Instruction using predecrement register indirect addressing: (a) before execution; (b) after execution.

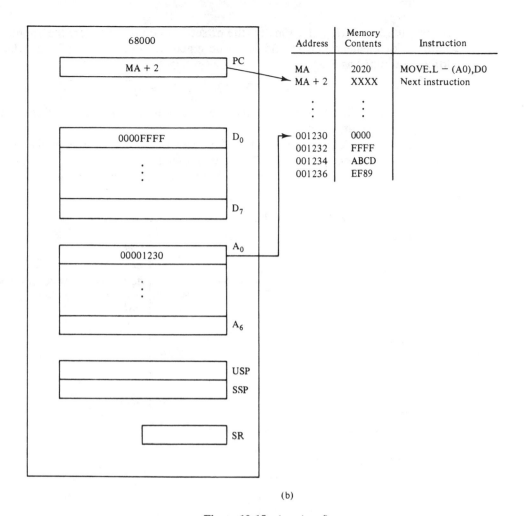

Address	Memory Contents	Instruction
MA	2020	MOVE.L − (A0),D0
MA + 2	XXXX	Next instruction
.	.	
.	.	
.	.	
001230	0000	
001232	FFFF	
001234	ABCD	
001236	EF89	

(b)

Figure 10.15 (*continued*)

Address register indirect with index and offset addressing is very useful when accessing elements of an array in memory. For example, the two-dimensional array of Fig. 10.18(a), which has a size of $m + 1$ rows by $l + 1$ columns, can be stored in memory as shown in Fig. 10.18(b). Notice that the first $l + 1$ addresses, with starting address at $00F000_{16}$, contain the elements of row 0 of the array, that is, the elements located at columns 0 through l of row 0. In both figures, these are identified as E(0,0) through E(0,l). The elements of row 0 are followed in memory by those for rows 1 through m.

Let us look at how to access the element located at column j of row i (E(i,j)). To access this element, the first address register A_0 can be loaded with the beginning address, $00F000, of the array in memory. In this way, it points to the first element in the first row of the array. A_1 can be used as the index register and loaded with an index number such that it points to row i in the array. Assuming that each element uses a word for storage, the value required in index register A_1 in order to access row i is computed as 2i $(l + 1)$. Finally, the offset can be used to select the appropriate column. For element j, it should be made equal to 2j. In this way, the effective address computed as

$$EA = A0 + 2i\,(l + 1) + 2j$$

points to element E(i,j). Notice that the 8-bit offset limits the number of columns in the array to a maximum of 128.

For instance, let us determine the effective address needed to copy the word in element E(5,6) of the array in Fig. 10.18 with $m = 8$ into D_0. Assume that the array of words is stored starting at address \$00F000. First we must load registers A_0 and A_1 as follows:

$$A0 = 00F000_{16}$$

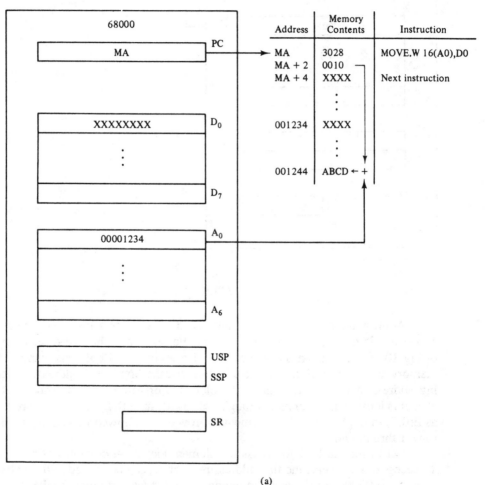

(a)

Figure 10.16 Instruction using register indirect with offset addressing: (a) before execution; (b) after execution.

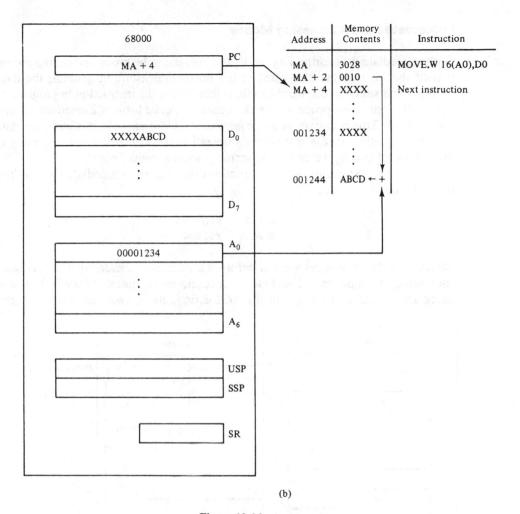

68000		Address	Memory Contents	Instruction
MA + 4	PC	MA	3028	MOVE.W 16(A0),D0
		MA + 2	0010	
		MA + 4	XXXX	Next instruction
XXXXABCD	D_0	001234	XXXX	
	D_7	001244	ABCD ← +	
00001234	A_0			
	A_6			
	USP			
	SSP			
	SR			

(b)

Figure 10.16 (*continued*)

$$A1 = 2i(l + 1) = 2(5)(8 + 1) = 90_{10} = 5A_{16}$$

Then the offset is obtained by multiplying the column dimension of the array element by 2. This gives

$$d8 = 2j = 2(6) = 12_{10} = C_{16}$$

Therefore, the effective address of the element is

$$EA = A0 + A1 + d8 = 00F000_{16} + 5A_{16} + C_{16}$$
$$= 00F066_{16}$$

This element can be copied into D_0 by executing the instruction

```
MOVE.W   12(A0,A1.L),D0
```

Immediate Data Addressing Modes

With immediate data addressing mode, the operand to be processed during the execution of the instruction is supplied in the instruction itself. In general, the data are encoded and stored in the word locations that follow the instruction in program memory. If the instruction processes bytes of data, a special form of immediate addressing can be used. This is known as *quick immediate addressing*. In this case, the data are encoded directly into the instruction's operation word. For this reason, using quick immediate addressing takes up less memory and executes faster.

Here are two examples of instructions that employ immediate data addressing for their source operands.

```
MOVEQ     #$C5,D0
MOVE.W    #$1234,D0
```

Notice that the # symbol written before the operand indicates that immediate data addressing is employed. The first instruction, move quick (MOVEQ), illustrates quick immediate addressing. In this instruction, the immediate source operand is

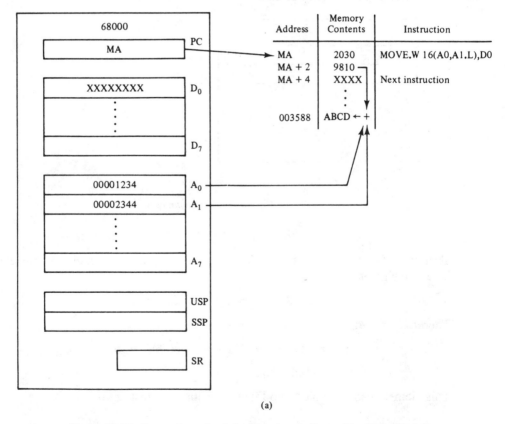

(a)

Figure 10.17 Instruction using indexed register indirect with offset addressing: (a) before execution; (b) after execution.

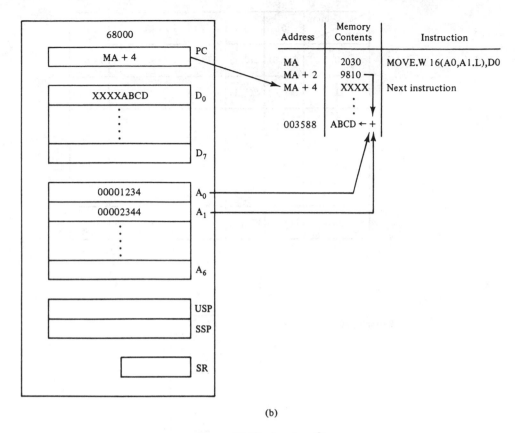

Address	Memory Contents	Instruction
MA	2030	MOVE.W 16(A0,A1.L),D0
MA + 2	9810	
MA + 4	XXXX	Next instruction
003588	ABCD ← +	

68000

PC: MA + 4

D₀: XXXXABCD

D₇

A₀: 00001234

A₁: 00002344

A₆

USP

SSP

SR

(b)

Figure 10.17 (*continued*)

$C5_{16}$. As shown in Fig. 10.19(a), it gets encoded as $70C5, where the least significant byte of the instruction word is the immediate operand. Executing this instruction loads D_0 with the sign-extended long-word value of $C5; that is.

$$\$FFFFFFC5 \longrightarrow D0$$

Looking at the second instruction, we see that its immediate source operand is the word 1234_{16}. Figure 10.19(b) illustrates how its immediate operand gets encoded into the second word of the instruction. When the instruction is executed, sign extension is not performed; instead, the value $1234 is loaded into the least significant 16 bits of D_0. That is,

$$\$1234 \longrightarrow \text{least significant 16 bits of } D_0$$

The most significant 16 bits of D_0 are not affected.

Implied Addressing Mode

Some of the 68000's instructions do not make direct reference to operands. Instead, inherent to their execution is an automatic reference to one or more of its internal registers. Typically, these registers are the stack pointers, the program counter, or

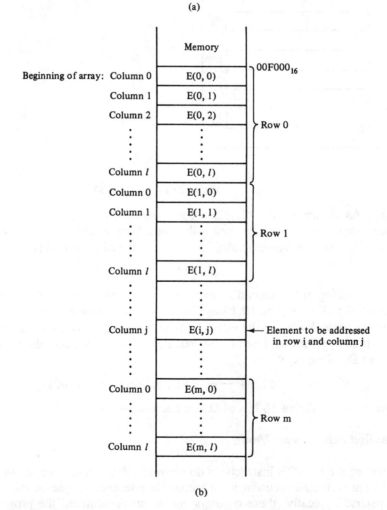

Figure 10.18 (a) An $(m + 1) \times (l + 1)$ two-dimensional array; (b) storage of the array in memory.

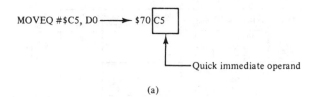

(a)

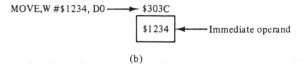

Immediate operand

(b)

Figure 10.19 (a) Coding of a move instruction using a quick immediate operand; (b) coding of a move instruction using a general immediate operand.

the status register. An example is the instruction

BSR   SUBRTN

It stands for branch to the subroutine at label SUBRTN. Both the contents of the program counter and active stack pointer are always referenced during the execution of this instruction.

Functional Addressing Categories

The addressing modes that we have discussed in this section can be divided into four categories based on the manner in which they are used. These functional categories are *data addressing, memory addressing, control addressing,* and *alterable addressing.* The relationship between the addressing modes and these four categories is summarized by the table in Fig. 10.20.

If an addressing mode can be used to reference data operands, it is categorized as data addressing. Looking at Fig. 10.20, we see that all addressing modes other than address register direct are classified as data addressing. Address register direct is not included because it only allows access to address information.

Similarly, if an addressing mode provides the ability to reference operands in memory, it is classified as memory addressing. Notice in Fig. 10.20 that just the data register direct and address register direct addressing modes are not classified in this way. This is because their use is restricted to accessing information that resides in the internal registers of the 68000.

An addressing mode is considered control addressing if it can be used to reference an operand in memory without specification of the size of the operand. Notice in Fig. 10.20 that all direct addressing modes, indirect addressing modes with either predecrement or postincrement, and the immediate addressing modes are not included in this category.

Moreover, if an addressing mode permits reference to operands that are being written to, it is called an *alterable addressing mode.* That is, alterable addressing modes can be used in conjunction with destination operands. Looking at Fig. 10.20, we see that immediate data addressing is an example of an addressing mode that cannot be used to specify a destination operand. It only can be used to reference source operands.

Sec. 10.7   Operand Addressing Modes   **345**

Addressing Mode	Mode	Register	Addressing Categories				Assembler Syntax
			Data	Mem	Cont	Alter	
Data Reg Dir	000	reg no.	X	–	–	X	Dn
Addr Reg Dir	001	reg no.	–	–	–	X	An
Addr Reg Ind	010	reg no.	X	X	X	X	(An)
Addr Reg Ind w/Postinc	011	reg no.	X	X	–	X	(An)+
Addr Reg Ind w/Predec	100	reg no.	X	X	–	X	–(An)
Addr Reg Ind w/Disp	101	reg no.	X	X	X	X	d(An)
Addr Reg Ind w/Index	110	reg no.	X	X	X	X	d(An, Ri)
Absolute Short	111	000	X	X	X	X	XXX
Absolute Long	111	001	X	X	X	X	XXXXXX
Prog Ctr w/Disp	111	010	X	X	X	–	d(PC)
Prog Ctr w/Index	111	011	X	X	X	–	d(PC, Ri)
Immediate	111	100	X	X	–	–	#XXX

Figure 10.20 Effective addressing mode categories. (Courtesy of Motorola, Inc.)

ASSIGNMENT

Section 10.2

1. How many registers are available to the programmer in the 68000 software model?
2. How large is the 68000's memory address space?

Section 10.3

3. What is the size of the 68000's memory address space when expressed in words?
4. What is the highest word address in the 68000's address space? The lowest word address?
5. What three data formats are supported by the 68000 and how many bits are in each format?
6. Can a word or long word of data start at an odd address boundary?
7. Show how the long word $5555AAAA_{16}$ is stored in memory starting at address 001000_{16}.

Section 10.4

8. How many bytes of the memory address space are dedicated?
9. What function does the dedicated memory perform?

Section 10.5

10. How are the data registers identified?
11. Which bits of a data register are used to hold byte data? Word data? Long-word data?
12. If a data register is used as an index register, does it contain a source operand, destination operand, or offset address?
13. How many address register does the 68000 have?
14. What kind of information is held in the address registers?
15. When reading from an address register, what data formats are permitted? When writing into an address register?
16. What does SSP stand for?

17. When USP is active, what mode is the 68000 operating in?
18. What mode must the 68000 be in to permit modification of the values in USP and SSP?
19. How is the program counter identified?
20. How large is the value in the program counter?
21. Are code accesses bytes or words?
22. What are the two parts of SR called?
23. Make a list of the flags and their mnemonics.
24. What does flag bit N = 1 mean?
25. If $I_2I_1I_0 = 100_2$, which interrupt levels are masked out?
26. If the 68000 is in the user state, what is the setting of the S bit?
27. What does the T bit stand for?

Section 10.6

28. What is a stack used for?
29. What are the two stacks in a 68000 microcomputer called?
30. What is the maximum size of a stack?
31. What term is used to describe the act of putting data onto the stack? Removing data from the stack?
32. How much stack space does a double word take up? Word? Byte?

Section 10.7

33. Make a list of the addressing modes available on the 68000.
34. Identify the addressing modes for both the source and destination operands in the instructions that follow.
    (a) MOVE.W   D3,D2
    (b) MOVE.B   D3,A2
    (c) MOVE.L   D3,$ABCD
    (d) MOVE.L   XYZ,D2
    (e) MOVE.W   XYZ(D0.L),D2
    (f) MOVE.B   D3,(A2)
    (g) MOVE.L   A1,(A2)+
    (h) MOVE.L   -(A2),D3
    (i) MOVE.W   10(A2),D3
    (j) MOVE.B   10(A2,A3.L),$A123
    (k) MOVE.W   #$ABCD,$1122
35. Compute the memory address for the source operand and/or destination operand in each of the instruction in Problem 34.
36. Specify the conditions that make the following instructions equivalent.

    MOVE.L   D0,$ABCD
    MOVE.L   D0,$10(A1)
    MOVE.L   D0,$100(A2,D1.L)
    MOVE.L   D0,(A3)

11

68000 Microprocessor Programming 1

11.1 INTRODUCTION

Chapter 10 was devoted to the general software architectural aspects of the 68000 microprocessor. In this chapter we introduce a large part of its instruction set. These instructions provide the ability to write simple straight-line programs. Chapter 12 covers the rest of the instruction set and more sophisticated programming concepts. The following topics are presented in this chapter:

1. Instruction set
2. Data transfer instructions
3. Integer arithmetic instructions
4. Decimal arithmetic instructions
5. Logic instructions
6. Shift and rotate instructions

11.2 INSTRUCTION SET

Motorola, Inc., has applied *orthogonality* in the design of the instruction set of the 68000. That is, instead of having a large number of instructions that include many special-purpose instructions, they have included a smaller number of general-purpose instructions. But the 68000 is equipped with more powerful addressing modes, and most of the instructions can use all the addressing modes. This makes its general instructions very versatile. Moreover, it results in fewer instruction mnemonics for the programmer to remember and less restrictions on how operands can be accessed during instruction execution.

The 68000 microprocessor provides a very powerful minicomputerlike instruction set. It has 56 basic instruction types. A summary of the instructions is shown in Fig. 11.1. These basic instruction types coupled with their variations, shown in Fig. 11.2, the 14 addressing modes, and five data types produce a large number of executable instructions at the machine code level.

Mnemonic	Description
ABCD	Add Decimal with Extend
ADD	Add
AND	Logical And
ASL	Arithmetic Shift Left
ASR	Arithmetic Shift Right
Bcc	Branch Conditionally
BCHG	Bit Test and Change
BCLR	Bit Test and Clear
BRA	Branch Always
BSET	Bit Test and Set
BSR	Branch to Subroutine
BTST	Bit Test
CHK	Check Register Against Bounds
CLR	Clear Operand
CMP	Compare
DBcc	Test Condition, Decrement and Branch
DIVS	Signed Divide
DIVU	Unsigned Divide
EOR	Exclusive Or
EXG	Exchange Registers
EXT	Sign Extend
JMP	Jump
JSR	Jump to Subroutine
LEA	Load Effective Address
LINK	Link Stack
LSL	Logical Shift Left
LSR	Logical Shift Right
MOVE	Move
MOVEM	Move Multiple Registers
MOVEP	Move Peripheral Data
MULS	Signed Multiply
MULU	Unsigned Multiply
NBCD	Negate Decimal with Extend
NEG	Negate
NOP	No Operation
NO	Ones Complement
OR	Logical Or
PEA	Push Effective Address
RESET	Reset External Devices
ROL	Rotate Left without Extend
ROR	Rotate Right without Extend
ROXL	Rotate Left with Extend
ROXR	Rotate Right with Extend
RTE	Return from Exception
RTR	Return and Restore
RTS	Return from Subroutine
SBCD	Subtract Decimal with Extend
Scc	Set Conditional
STOP	Stop
SUB	Subtract
SWAP	Swap Data Register Halves
TAS	Test and Set Operand
TRAP	Trap
TRAPV	Trap on Overflow
TST	Test
UNLK	Unlink

Figure 11.1 Instruction set summary. (Courtesy of Motorola, Inc.)

Instruction Type	Variation	Description
ADD	ADD ADDA ADDQ ADDI ADDX	Add Add Address Add Quick Add Immediate Add with Extend
AND	AND ANDI ANDI to CCR ANDI to SR	Logical AND AND Immediate AND Immediate to Condition Code AND Immediate to Status Register
CMP	CMP CMPA CMPM CMPI	Compare Compare Address Compare Memory Compare Immediate
EOR	EOR EORI EORI to CCR EORI to SR	Exclusive OR Exclusive OR Immediate Exclusive Immediate to Condition Codes Exclusive OR Immediate to Status Register
MOVE	MOVE MOVEA MOVEQ MOVE to CCR MOVE to SR MOVE from SR MOVE to USP	Move Move Address Move Quick Move to Condition Codes Move to Status Register Move from Status Register Move to User Stack Pointer
NEG	NEG NEGX	Negate Negate with Extend
OR	OR ORI ORI to CCR ORI to SR	Logical OR OR Immediate OR Immediate to Condition Codes OR Immediate to Status Register
SUB	SUB SUBA SUBI SUBQ SUBX	Subtract Subtract Address Subtract Immediate Subtract Quick Subtract with Extend

Figure 11.2 Variations of instruction types. (Courtesy of Motorola, Inc.)

For ease of learning, we will divide the instructions of the 68000's instruction set into functionally related groups. In this chapter the groups covered are the *data movement instructions,* the *integer arithmetic instructions,* the *decimal arithmetic instructions,* the *logic instructions,* and the *shift and rotate instructions.* The rest of the instruction set will be presented in Chapter 12.

11.3 DATA TRANSFER INSTRUCTIONS

The instruction set of the 68000 provides instructions to transfer data between its internal registers, between an internal register and a storage location in memory, or between two locations in memory. The basic instructions in the data transfer group are shown in Fig. 11.3. Notice that it includes the following instructions: *move* (MOVE), *move multiple* (MOVEM), *load effective address* (LEA), *exchange* (EXG), *swap* (SWAP), and *clear* (CLR).

Move Instruction: MOVE

The first of the basic data transfer instructions in Fig. 11.3 is the MOVE instruction.

Mnemonic	Meaning	Type	Operand Size	Operations
MOVE	Move	MOVE EAs,EAd	8, 16, 32	(EAs) → EAd
		MOVE EA,CCR	8	(EA) → CCR
		MOVE EA,SR	16	(EA) → SR
		MOVE SR,EA	16	SR → EA
		MOVE USP,An	32	USP → An
		MOVE An,USP	32	An → USP
		MOVEA EA,An	16, 32	(EA) → An
		MOVEQ #XXX,Dn	8	#XXX → Dn
MOVEM	Move multiple	MOVEM Reg_list,EA	16, 32	Reg_list → EA
		MOVEM EA,Reg_list	16, 32	(EA) → Reg_list
LEA	Load effective address	LEA EA,An	32	EA → An
EXG	Exchange	EXG Rx,Ry	32	Rx ↔ Ry
SWAP	Swap	SWAP Dn	16	Dn 31:16 ↔ Dn 15:0
CLR	Clear	CLR EA	8, 16, 32	0 → EA

Figure 11.3 Data transfer instructions.

This instruction has the ability to perform all three of the earlier mentioned data transfer operations. That is, data transfers from register to register, between register and memory, or memory to memory. Looking at Fig. 11.3, we see that there are eight different forms of this instruction. Notice that they differ in both the size of operands they process and the types of operands that they can access.

The first form of the MOVE instruction is

MOVE EAs, EAd

It permits movement of a source operand location identified by effective address EAs into a destination location identified by effective address EAd. The source and destination operands can be located in data registers, address registers, or storage locations in memory. Moreover, this instruction can be used to process byte, word, or long-word operands.

Whenever this instruction is processing word or long-word data, the source operand can be specified using any addressing mode. However, for operation on byte data, address register direct addressing mode cannot be used. This is because the address registers can be accessed only as word or long-word operands.

For the destination operand, only the alterable addressing modes are allowed. The addressing modes in this group were identified in Fig. 10.20. In other words, program counter relative and the immediate data addressing modes cannot be used to specify the location of the destination operand. Moreover, when processing byte operands, address register direct addressing cannot be used.

Another thing that may be important to note is how the condition code bits in the user byte of the 68000's status register are affected by execution of the MOVE instruction. The condition codes affected are the negative (N) bit, the zero (Z) bit, the overflow (V) bit, and the carry (C) bit. N and Z are set or cleared based on the result of the instruction; that is, the value copied into the destination location. If the result is negative, N is set; otherwise, it is cleared. Similarly, if the result is zero, Z is set, and if it is nonzero, it is cleared. The V and C bits are always cleared.

Here is an example of the move instruction that performs a word-copy operation.

$$\text{MOVE.W} \quad \text{D0,D1}$$

The source operand in D_0 is specified using data register direct addressing mode. Let us assume that the contents of register D_0 are 12345678_{16}. The destination operand in D_1 is also specified using data register direct addressing mode. Execution of the instruction causes the least significant word in D_0, which equals 5678_{16}, to be copied into the lower16 bits of D_1. Since the result in D_1 is positive and nonzero, the condition codes are affected as follows: N = 0, Z = 0, V = 0, C = 0, and X is not affected.

The next two forms shown in Fig. 11.3 for the MOVE instruction are provided for initialization of the status register. The instruction

$$\text{MOVE} \quad \text{EA,CCR}$$

allows only the condition code part of the status register to be specified as the destination operand. This operand is identified by CCR. On the other hand, any of the data addressing modes can be used for the source operand. This instruction can be used to load the user byte of SR from memory or an internal register. Even though the source operand size is specified as a word, just its eight least significant bits are used to modify the condition code bits in SR.

The second instruction

$$\text{MOVE} \quad \text{EA,SR}$$

is used to load all 16 bits of the status register. Therefore, its execution loads both the system byte and user byte. Since this instruction updates the most significant byte in SR, it can be executed only when the 68000 is in the supervisor state (privileged instruction).

EXAMPLE 11.1

What will be the result of executing the following sequence of instructions?

$$\text{MOVE.W} \quad \text{\#12,D0}$$
$$\text{MOVE} \quad \text{D0,SR}$$

Assume that the 68000 is in the supervisor state.

SOLUTION   Execution of the first instruction loads the lower word of D_0 with immediate source operand 12_{10}.

$$12_{10} = 000C_{16} = 0000000000001100_2$$

After execution of this instruction, the condition code bits of SR are as follows:

$$X = \text{unchanged}$$
$$N = 0$$
$$Z = 0$$
$$V = 0$$
$$C = 0$$

Check Fig. 10.7 for the meaning of each of these bits. The result of executing the second instruction depends on the state of the 68000. We have assumed that it is operating in the supervisor state; therefore, SR is loaded with the lower word of D_0, which is 0000000000001100_2.

$$D0 = \text{XXXXXXXXXXXXXXXX}0000000000001100_2$$

$$SR = 0000000000001100_2$$

This gives the condition codes that follow:

$$X = 0$$
$$N = 1$$
$$Z = 1$$
$$V = 0$$
$$C = 0$$

The next form of the MOVE instruction shown in Fig. 11.3 is

MOVE SR, EA

Notice that its source operand is always the contents of SR and the destination operand is represented by the effective address EA. Therefore, this instruction permits the programmer to save the contents of the status register in an address register, data register, or a storage location in data memory. In specifying the destination operand, only those addressing modes identified in Fig. 10.20 as alterable can be used.

For example, executing the instruction

MOVE SR, D7

causes the contents of SR to be copied into data register D_7. No condition codes are affected due to the execution of this instruction. Since this instruction reads but does not modify the contents of SR, it can be executed when the 68000 is in either the user state or the supervisor state.

The move user stack pointer instructions are shown in Fig. 11.3 to be

MOVE USP, An

and

MOVE An, USP

Notice that the data transfer that takes place is always between the user stack pointer (USP) register and one of the address registers. For this reason, these instructions are used to read and to modify the user stack pointer, respectively. Since USP is a 32-bit register, both the source and destination operands are always long word in size. Both of the instructions are privileged and must only be executed when the 68000 is in the supervisor state.

An efficient way of loading an address register from another address register, data register, or storage location in memory is with the *move address instruction.* In Fig. 11.3, this form of the MOVE instruction is given as

MOVEA EA, An

This instruction allows the operand to be either 16 bits or 32 bits in length. If the source operand is specified as a word, the address word is sign-extended to give a long word before it is moved into the address register.

The source operand can be specified using any of the 68000's addressing modes. For instance, the instruction

MOVEA.L (A0) , A6

employs address register indirect addressing. Execution of this instruction causes the long-word contents of the memory location pointed to by the address in A_0 to be loaded into address register A_6. Condition codes are not affected by execution of this instruction.

The last form of the MOVE instruction we find in Fig. 11.3 is

MOVEQ #XXX, Dn

This instruction, *move quick,* is used to load a data register efficiently with a byte-wide immediate operand. An example is the instruction

MOVEQ #4, D1

The immediate operand, which is decimal number 4, is encoded directly into the instruction operation word. When this instruction is executed, the immediate data are loaded into data register D_1. However, before the value is loaded, it is sign extended to 32 bits. Therefore, the value loaded into D_1 is 00000004_{16}.

Move Multiple Registers Instruction: MOVEM

The move multiple registers (MOVEM) instruction provides an efficient mechanism for saving the contents of the internal registers into memory or to restore their contents from memory. One use of this instruction is to initialize a group of registers from a table in memory. This operation can be done with a series of MOVE instructions or with just one MOVEM instruction.

Another operation for which it can be useful is when working with subroutines.

For instance, if a subroutine is to be initiated, typically the contents of the registers that are used during its execution must be saved in memory. Moreover, after its execution is complete, their contents must be restored. In this way, when program control is returned to the main program, the registers reflect the same information that they contained prior to entry into the subroutine. Either the save or restore operation can be performed with a single MOVEM instruction.

The two forms of MOVEM are shown in Fig. 11.3. The first form,

```
MOVEM  Reg-list,EA
```

is employed to save the contents of the registers specified in *register list* (Reg-list) in memory. They are saved at consecutive addresses in memory starting at the address specified by the destination operand. Any of the control addressing modes and address register indirect with predecrement can be used in conjunction with the destination operand.

The register list can include any combination of data and address registers. A list of the registers to be saved is coded into a second word of the instruction. This word is called the *register list mask*. As shown in Fig. 11.4(a), each bit of this mask corresponds to one of the 68000's internal registers. Setting a bit to 1 indicates that the corresponding register is included in the list and 0 indicates that it is not included. Notice that data registers D_0 through D_7 correspond to bits 0 through 7 of the mask, respectively, and address registers A_0 through A_7 correspond to bits 8 through 15, respectively. When address register indirect with predecrement addressing is used, the meaning of the bits of the mask word are changed as shown in Fig. 11.4(b). The register corresponding to the first set bit is saved first, followed by the register corresponding to the next set bit, and so on. The last saved register corresponds to the last set bit.

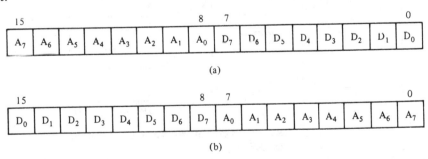

(a)

(b)

Figure 11.4 (a) Register list mask word format for control mode and postincrement addressing; (b) format for address register indirect with predecrement addressing.

This instruction can be written to perform word or long-word data transfers. In a word operation, only the least significant word parts of the specified registers are saved in memory. In this case, it requires one word of memory storage for each register. However, if long-word transfers are specified, each register needs two words of memory.

The second form of the MOVEM instruction shown in Fig. 11.3 permits the internal registers of the 68000 to be initialized or restored from memory. It is written as

$$\text{MOVEM EA, Reg-list}$$

Execution of this instruction causes the word or long-word contents of the registers in Reg-list to be loaded one after the other from memory. When specifying the source operand, the starting address of the table of values to be loaded can only use the control or postincrement addressing modes.

EXAMPLE 11.2

Write an instruction that will do the reverse of the instruction

$$\text{MOVEM.W D0/D1/A5, \$AF00}$$

SOLUTION This instruction will save the lower words of registers D_0, D_1, and A_5 in memory at word addresses $AF00_{16}$, $AF02_{16}$, and $AF04_{16}$, respectively. To restore the registers, the instruction is written as

$$\text{MOVEM.W \$AF00, D0/D1/A5}$$

Figure 11.5 illustrates what happens due to the execution of these two instructions.

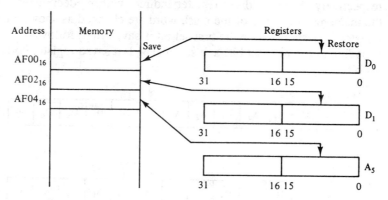

Figure 11.5 Save and restore of processor register contents as implemented with the MOVEM instructions.

Load Effective Address Instruction: LEA

A way of directly loading an address register with an address is with the load effective address (LEA) instruction. The form of this instruction is given in Fig. 11.3 as

$$\text{LEA EA, An}$$

Execution of this instruction does not load the destination operand with the contents of the specified source operand. Instead, it computes an effective address based on the addressing mode used for the source operand and loads this value into the address register specified as the destination. Only the control addressing modes listed in Fig. 10.20 can be used to describe the source operand.

EXAMPLE 11.3

Describe what happens when the instruction

$$\text{LEA} \quad 6\,(\text{A1},\text{D0})\,,\text{A2}$$

is executed. Assume that $A_1 = 00004000_{16}$ and $D_0 = 000012AB_{16}$.

SOLUTION This instruction uses address register indirect with index addressing for the source operand. Its destination is simply address register A_2. Execution of the instruction causes A_2 to be loaded with the effective address

$$A2 = A1 + D0 + 6_{10}$$

Using the values given for the contents of A_1 and D_0, we find that the effective address loaded into A_2 equals

$$A2 = 00004000_{16} + 000012AB_{16} + 6_{16}$$

$$= 000052B1_{16}$$

Exchange Instruction: EXG

Earlier we showed how the MOVE instruction could be used to move the contents of one of the internal registers of the 68000 to another internal register. Another type of requirement for some applications is to exchange efficiently the contents of two registers. It is for this reason that the exchange (EXG) instruction is included in the instruction set of the 68000.

This instruction is shown in Fig. 11.3 and has the form

$$\text{EXG} \quad \text{Rx},\text{Ry}$$

Here Rx and Ry stand for arbitrarily selected data or address registers. An example is the instruction

$$\text{EXG} \quad \text{D0},\text{A3}$$

It will load data register D_0 with the contents of address register A_3 and A_3 with the earlier contents of D_0. For example, if D_0 contains $FFFFFFFF_{16}$ and A_3 contains 00000000_{16}, the result after executing the instruction is that D_0 now contains 00000000_{16} and A_3 contains $FFFFFFFF_{16}$. The data transfers that take place are always 32 bits long and no condition code bits are affected.

Swap Instruction: SWAP

The swap (SWAP) instruction is similar to the exchange instruction in that it has the ability to exchange two values. However, it is used to exchange the upper and lower words in a data register. The general form of SWAP is given in Fig. 11.3 as

SWAP   Dn

An example is

SWAP   D0

When this instruction is executed, the contents of the lower 16 bits of D_0 are swapped with its upper 16 bits. If the original contents of D_0 are $FFFF0000_{16}$, execution of the instruction results in the value $0000FFFF_{16}$ in D_0. The 32-bit value that results in D_0 after the swap operation is used to set or reset the condition code flags.

Clear Instruction: CLR

The CLR instruction can be used to initialize the contents of an internal register or storage location in data memory to zero. Figure 11.3 shows that the instruction is written in general as

CLR   EA

and that it can perform its operation on byte, word, or long-word operands. All alterable addressing modes except address register direct can be used to access the operand.

For instance, to clear the least significant 8 bits of D_0, the following instruction is executed:

CLR. B   D0

Whenever this instruction is executed, the Z bit of SR is set and the N, V, and C bits are cleared. Moreover, the X bit is not affected.

11.4 INTEGER ARITHMETIC INSTRUCTIONS

The instruction set of the 68000 provides instructions to perform binary arithmetic operations, such as add, subtract, multiply, and divide. These instructions can process both signed and unsigned numbers. Moreover, the data being processed can be organized as bytes, words, or long words. The instructions in this group are shown in Fig. 11.6.

The condition code bits in the SR register are set or reset as per the result of arithmetic instruction. For ADD, SUB, and NEG instructions the five condition code bits are affected as follows:

N is set if the result is negative, cleared otherwise

Z is set if the result is zero, cleared otherwise

Mnemonic	Meaning	Type	Operand Size	Operation
ADD	Add	ADD EA, Dn	8, 16, 32	(EA) + Dn → Dn
		ADD Dn, EA	8, 16, 32	Dn + (EA) → EA
		ADDI #XXX, EA	8, 16, 32	#XXX + (EA) → EA
		ADDQ #XXX, EA	8, 16, 32	#XXX + (EA) → EA
		ADDX Dy, Dx	8, 16, 32	Dy + Dx + X → Dx
		ADDX ⁻(Ay), ⁻(Ax)	8, 16, 32	⁻(Ay) + ⁻(Ax) + X → (Ax)
		ADDA EA, An	16, 32	(EA) + An → An
SUB	Subtract|	SUB EA, Dn	8, 16, 32	Dn − (EA) → Dn
		SUB Dn, EA	8, 16, 32	(EA) − Dn → EA
		SUBI #XXX, EA	8, 16, 32	(EA) − #XXX → EA
		SUBQ #XXX, EA	8, 16, 32	(EA) − #XXX → EA
		SUBX Dy, Dx	8, 16, 32	Dx − Dy − X → Dx
		SUBX ⁻(Ay), ⁻(Ax)	8, 16, 32	⁻(Ax) − ⁻(Ay) − X → (Ax)
		SUBA EA, An	16, 32	An − (EA) → An
NEG	Negate	NEG EA	8, 16, 32	0 − (EA) → EA
		NEGX EA	8, 16, 32	0 − (EA) −X → EA
MUL	Multiply	MULS EA	16	(EA) · Dn → Dn
		MULU EA	16	(EA) · Dn → Dn
DIV	Divide	DIVS EA, Dn	32 ÷ 16	Dn ÷ (EA) → Dn
		DIVU EA, Dn	32 ÷ 16	Dn ÷ (EA) → Dn
EXT	Extend sign	EXT.W Dn	8 → 16	Dn byte → Dn word
		EXT.L Dn	16 → 32	Dn word → Dn long word

Figure 11.6 Integer arithmetic instructions.

V is set if an overflow occurs, cleared otherwise

X and C are set if carry is generated or borrow is taken, cleared otherwise

For MUL, DIV, and EXT instructions, V and C are always cleared, X is not affected, and N and Z are set or cleared as in other arithmetic instructions: ADD, SUB, and NEG.

Addition Instructions: ADD, ADDI, ADDQ, ADDX, and ADDA

For implementing the binary addition operation, the 68000 provides five types of add instructions. All five forms together with their permitted operand sizes are shown in Fig. 11-6. The different types of instructions are provided for dealing with different kinds of addition requirements. For instance, when addresses are manipulated, we want to operate on data in the address registers and do not want to affect the condition codes in SR. Thus for this situation a special address addition (ADDA) instruction is provided.

The first four forms of the add instruction in Fig. 11.6 are generally used to process data and the last form is for modifying addresses. Two forms of the basic *add* (ADD) instruction are shown. The first form

ADD   EA, Dn

adds the contents of the location specified by the effective address EA to the contents of data register D_n; that is,

$$(EA) + Dn \rightarrow Dn$$

The source operand can be located in an internal register or a storage location in memory. Moreover, its effective address can be specified with any of the addressing modes of the 68000. The only exception is that the size of the operand cannot be specified as a byte when address register direct addressing mode is used.

For instance, the instruction

```
ADD.L  D0,D1
```

causes the contents of D_0 to be added to the contents of D_1. If the original contents of D_0 are \$00013344 and that of D_1 are \$00000FFF, the sum that is produced equals \$00014343 and it is saved in D_1.

The second form is similar except that it represents the addition of the contents of a source data register to the contents of a destination operand that is identified by the effective address EA.

```
ADD  Dn,EA
```

$$Dn + (EA) \rightarrow EA$$

In this case only the alterable memory addressing modes are applicable to the destination operand.

EXAMPLE 11.4

Write an instruction sequence that can be used to add two long words whose locations in memory are specified by the contents of address registers A_1 and A_2, respectively. The sum is to replace the contents of the storage location pointed to by the address in A_2.

SOLUTION We will use D_0 as an intermediate storage location for implementing the memory-to-memory add. The instruction sequence is

```
CLR.L    D0
ADD.L    (A1),D0
ADD.L    D0,(A2)
```

The instruction *add immediate* (ADDI) operates similarly to the ADD instruction we just introduced. The important difference is that now the value of the source operand is always located in program memory as an immediate operand. That is, it is encoded as the second word of the instruction for byte and word operands or as a second and third word for long-word operands. The general instruction format as shown in Fig. 11.6 is

```
ADDI  #XXX,EA
```

Here #XXX stands for the immediate source operand and EA is the effective address of the destination operand. For example, the instruction

ADDI.L #$0FFFF,D0

causes the value $FFFF_{16}$ to be added to the long-word contents of D_0.

The *add quick* (ADDQ) instruction of Fig. 11.6 is a special variation of the add-immediate instruction. It limits the size of the source operand to the range 1 through 8.

An example is the instruction

ADDQ #3,D1

It stands for add the number 3 to the contents of D_1. These immediate data are encoded directly into the instruction word. For this reason, ADDQ encodes in fewer bytes and executes faster than ADDI. Therefore, it is preferred when memory requirement and execution times are to be minimized. The addition that is performed cannot involve a number larger than 8 as the source operand.

The next type of addition instruction in Fig. 11.6 is the *add extend* (ADDX) instruction. It differs from the earlier instructions in that the addition it performs involves the two operands along with the extend (X) bit of SR. One form of the instruction is

ADDX Dy,Dx

and the arithmetic operation it performs is

$$Dy + Dx + X \rightarrow Dx$$

That is, the contents of data register Dy are added to the contents of data register Dx and extend bit X. The sum that results is placed in Dx. Notice that both operands must always be in data registers.

The other form of the ADDX instruction, as shown in Fig. 11.6, specifies its operands with predecrement address register indirect addressing. It permits access to data stored in memory.

The last form of the addition instruction in Fig. 11.6 is the *add address* (ADDA) instruction. Its form is

ADDA EA,An

and its execution results in

$$(EA) + An \rightarrow An$$

The source operand can employ any of the addressing modes of the 68000. For this reason, the source operand can reside in an internal register or storage location in memory. On the other hand, the destination is always an address register. Since the destination operand is always an address register, only word or long-word operations are permitted.

EXAMPLE 11.5

If the values in D_3 and A_3 are 76543210_{16} and $0000ABCD_{16}$, respectively, what is the result produced by executing the instruction

$$\text{ADDA.W} \quad \text{D3,A3}$$

SOLUTION Execution of this instruction causes the word value in D_3 to be added to the contents of A_3. This gives

$$A_3 = 00003210_{16} + 0000ABCD_{16}$$
$$= 0000DDDD_{16}$$

Subtraction Instructions: SUB, SUBI, SUBQ, SUBX, and SUBA

Having covered the addition instructions of the 68000, let us look at the instructions provided to perform binary subtraction. As shown in Fig. 11.6, the subtraction instruction also has five basic forms. Notice that these forms are identical to those already described for the addition operation. For this reason, we will present the subtraction instructions in less detail.

The general *subtraction* (SUB) instruction of the 68000 can be written in general using either the form

$$\text{SUB} \quad \text{EA,Dn}$$

or

$$\text{SUB} \quad \text{Dn,EA}$$

The first form permits the cotents of an internal register or storage location in memory to be subtracted from the contents of a data register. The difference that is obtained is stored in the selected destination data register. This operation can be expressed as

$$\text{Dn} - (\text{EA}) \rightarrow \text{Dn}$$

For instance, the instruction

$$\text{SUB} \quad \text{D0,D1}$$

performs a register-to-register subtraction. The difference $D_1 - D_0$ is saved in D_1.

The second SUB instruction in Fig. 11.6 performs the opposite subtraction operation. Its source operand is a data register within the 68000, and the location of the destination is specified by an effective address. Therefore, it can be a data register, address register, or storage location in data memory.

The next two subtraction instructions in Fig. 11.6, *substract immediate* (SUBI) and *subtract quick* (SUBQ), permit an immediate operand in program memory to be subtracted from the destination operand identified by EA. The destination operand can be a data register or a storage location in data memory. These instructions operate the same as their addition counterparts except that they calculate the difference between their source and destination operands instead of their sum.

For instance,

$$\text{SUBI.W} \quad \#\$1234, \text{D0}$$

causes the value 1234_{16} to be subtracted from the contents of D_0. Assuming that D_0 initially contains 0000FFFF_{16}, the difference produced in D_0 is

$$\text{FFFF}_{16} - 1234_{16} = \text{EDCB}_{16}$$

Extend subtract (SUBX), just like ADDX, includes the extend (X) bit of SR in the subtraction. Moreover, the same source and destination operand variations are permitted as for the ADDX instruction. For example, the first form in Fig. 11.6 is

$$\text{SUBX} \quad \text{Dy, Dx}$$

and it performs the subtraction

$$\text{Dx} - \text{Dy} - \text{X} \rightarrow \text{Dx}$$

For example, if D_1 and D_2 contain the values 76543210_{16} and 0000ABCD_{16}, respectively, and the extend bit is 1_2, the result produced by executing the instruction

$$\text{SUBX.W} \quad \text{D1, D2}$$

is

$$D_2 = 0000\text{ABCD}_{16} - 00003210_{16} - 1_{16}$$
$$= 79\text{BC}_{16}$$

Finally, *subtract address* (SUBA) of Fig. 11.6 is used to modify addresses in A_0 through A_6 subtraction. For example, it can be used to subtract the contents of data register D_7 from the address in A_5 with the instruction

$$\text{SUBA} \quad \text{D7, A5}$$

Negate Instructions: NEG and NEGX

Another type of arithmetic instruction is the negate instruction. Two forms of this instruction are shown in Fig. 11.6. The negate instructions are similar to the subtract instructions in that the specified operand is subtracted from another operand. However, in this case, the other operand is always assumed to be zero. Subtracting any number from zero gives its negative.

The basic *negate* (NEG) instruction is used to form the negative of the specified operand. It is given in general by

NEG   EA

and an example is the instruction

NEG. W   D0

If the original contents of D_0 are $00FF_{16}$, execution of the instruction produces the result $FF01_{16}$.

Negate with extend (NEGX) differs from NEG in that it subtracts both the contents of the specified operand and the extend (X) flag from 0. That is, it performs the operation

$$0 - (EA) - X \rightarrow EA$$

Both instructions can be written to process bytes, words, or long words of data. Moreover, the addressing modes permitted for the operand are the alterable addressing modes that were shown in Fig. 10.20.

Multiplication Instructions: MULS and MULU

The 68000 provides instructions that perform the multiplication arithmetic operation on unsigned or signed numbers. Separate instructions are provided to process these two types of numbers. As shown in Fig. 11.6, they are signed multiply,

MULS EA, Dn

and unsigned multiply,

MULU EA, Dn

Both MULS and MULU have two 16-bit operands that are labeled EA and Dn. The source operand EA can be specified with any of the data addressing modes, and the destination operand always uses data register direct addressing. Both the source and destination operands are treated as signed numbers when executing MULS and as unsigned numbers when executing MULU. The result, which is a 32-bit number, is placed in the destination data register.

Here is an example of the instruction needed to multiply the unsigned word number in data register D_1 by the unsigned word number in D_0.

MULU   D0, D1

At completion of execution of the instruction, the long-word product that results is in D_1.

As in most arithmetic instructions, the condition code bits of SR are updated based on the product that results. Two of the condition code bits, zero (Z) and negative (N), are affected based on the results. On the other hand, carry (C) and overflow (V) are always cleared.

Division Instructions: DIVS and DIVU

Similar to the multiplication instructions of the 68000, there is a *signed divide* (DIVS) instruction and an *unsigned divide* (DIVU) instruction. They are expressed in general as

$$\text{DIVS EA, Dn}$$

and

$$\text{DIVU EA, Dn}$$

The destination operand, which is the dividend, must be the contents of one of the data registers. The source operand, which is the divisor, can be accessed using any of the data addressing modes of the 68000.

Execution of either of these instructions causes the 32-bit dividend identified by the destination operand to be divided by the 16-bit divisor specified by the effective address. The 16-bit quotient that results is produced in the lower word of the destination data register, and the remainder is placed in the upper word of the same register. The sign of the remainder produced by a signed division is always the same as that of the dividend.

The condition codes that are affected by the division instruction are zero (Z) and negative (N). They are set or reset based on the quotient value and its sign. Furthermore, the carry flag is always cleared. If the result turns out to be over 16 bits, the overflow condition code bit is set and the destination operand is not changed. Thus one should check the V flag for an overflow after executing a division instruction. An attempt to divide by zero is also automatically detected by the 68000.

Sign Extend Instruction: EXT

The 68000 provides the *sign extend* (EXT) instruction for *sign extension* of byte or word operands. As shown in Fig. 11.6, the general form of this instruction is given by

$$\text{EXT Dn}$$

Notice that its operand must be located in a data register. When EXT is executed, the sign bit of the operand is copied into the most significant bits of the register.

For instance, when the word value in D_1 must be extended to a long word, the instruction

$$\text{EXT.L D1}$$

can be executed. It causes the value in bit 15 (the sign bit) to be copied into bits 16 through 31 of D_1.

Sign extension is required before data of unequal lengths can be involved in signed arithmetic operations. For instance, if one of the operands for an addition instruction that is written to process word data is expressed as a signed byte, it must first be extended to a signed word.

┌─ **EXAMPLE 11.6**

Assume that data registers D_0, D_1, and D_2 contain a signed byte, a signed word, and a signed long word in 2's-complement form, respectively. Write a sequence of instructions that will produce the signed result of the operation that follows:

$$D_0 + D_1 - D_2 \rightarrow D_0$$

SOLUTION   Before any addition or subtraction can be performed, we must extend each value of data to a signed long word. To convert the byte in D_0 to its equivalent long word, we must first convert it to a word and then a long word. This is done with the following instructions:

```
EXT. W   DO
EXT. L   DO
```

Similarly, to convert the word in D_1 to a long word, we execute the instruction

```
EXT. L   D1
```

Since the contents of D_2 are already a signed long word, no sign extension is necessary.

To do the required arithmetic operations, we just use the appropriate arithmetic instructions. For instance, to add the contents of D_0 and D_1, we use ADD, and to subtract the contents of D_2 from this sum, we use SUB. This leads us to the following sequence of instructions.

```
ADD. L   D1, DO
SUB. L   D2, DO
```

The complete program is listed in Fig. 11.7.

```
EXT.W    DO
EXT.L    DO
EXT.L    D1
ADD.L    D1, DO
SUB.L    D2, DO
```

Figure 11.7   Addition and subtraction of signed numbers.

11.5 DECIMAL ARITHMETIC INSTRUCTIONS

The arithmetic instructions we considered in the preceding section process data that are expressed as binary numbers. However, data are frequently provided that are coded as BCD numbers instead of as binary numbers. Traditionally, BCD-to-binary and binary-to-BCD conversion routines are used to process BCD data. However, the 68000 microprocessor has the ability to perform the add, subtract, and negate arithmetic operations directly on packed BCD numbers. Three BCD arithmetic instructions, ABCD, SBCD, and NBCD, are provided for this purpose. They provide an efficient and easy-to-use method for implementing BCD arithmetic. As a result of these instructions, the condition code bits, Z, C, and X, are affected, whereas N and V are undefined.

Add Decimal with Extend Instruction: ABCD

Let us begin with the *add binary-coded decimal* (ABCD) instruction. In Fig. 11.8, we see its permitted operand variations, operand size, and the operation it performs. Notice that only two addressing modes can be used to specify its operands.

Mnemonic	Meaning	Type	Operand Size	Operation
ABCD	Add BCD numbers	ABCD Dy, Dx ABCD $^-$(Ay), $^-$(Ax)	8 8	Dy + Dx + X → Dx $^-$(Ay) + $^-$(Ax) + X → (Ax)
SBCD	Subtract BCD numbers	SBCD Dy, Dx SBCD $^-$(Ay), $^-$(Ax)	8 8	Dx − Dy − X → Dx $^-$(Ax) − $^-$(Ay) − X → (Ax)
NBCD	Negate BCD numbers	NBCD EA	8	0 − (EA) − X → EA

Figure 11.8 Binary-coded decimal arithmetic instructions.

The first form,

$$ABCD \quad Dy, Dx$$

uses data register direct addressing for both source and destination operands. Therefore, both operands must reside in internal data registers of the 68000.

The other form,

$$ABCD \quad -(Ay), \quad -(Ax)$$

employs predecrement address register indirect addressing to specify both operands. Use of this addressing mode permits access of data stored in memory.

Execution of either of the ABCD instructions adds the contents of the source and destination operands together with the extend (X) bit of SR. The sum that results is saved in the destination operand location.

These instructions perform decimal addition operations; therefore, we must start with decimal operands instead of binary operands. These decimal operands are expressed in packed BCD. The sum that is produced is also a decimal number coded in packed BCD. However, the operand size is always byte wide; therefore, two BCD digits can be processed at a time.

An example is the instruction

$$ABCD \quad D0, D1$$

If D_0 initially contains the value $12_{10} = 00010010_{BCD}$, D_1 contains $37_{10} = 00110111_{BCD}$, and X is clear, execution of the instruction produces the sum

$$D0 + D1 + X = 12_{10} + 37_{10} + 0_{10}$$

$$= 49_{10}$$

At completion of the instruction, D_0 still contains 12_{10} but the contents of D_1 are changed to 49_{10}. X remains cleared because no carry results.

Condition code bits Z, X, and C are affected based on the result produced by the addition. Bits C and X are always set to the same logic level. The other two condition code bits, V and N, are undefined after execution of the instruction and do not provide any usable information.

Subtract Decimal with Extend Instruction: SBCD

The *subtract binary-coded decimal* (SBCD) instruction works similar to the ABCD instruction just discussed. In this case, the subtraction arithmetic operation is performed and not the addition operation.

As shown in Fig. 11.8, the two forms of the instruction are

$$SBCD \quad Dy,Dx$$

and

$$SBCD \quad -(Ay),-(Ax)$$

Notice that the permitted addressing modes are identical to those employed by the ABCD instruction.

An example is the instruction

$$SBCD \quad -(A0),-(A1)$$

When this instruction is executed, the byte-wide (two BCD digits) contents of the source operand and X bit of SR are subtracted from the destination operand. The difference that is produced is saved at the destination location.

In our example, we are using address register indirect with predecrement addressing. Therefore, the contents of address registers A_0 and A_1 are first decremented by 1. For instance, if their original contents were $0000110F_{16}$ and $0000120F_{16}$, respectively, decrementing by 1 gives $A_0 = 0000110E_{16}$ and $A_1 = 0000120E_{16}$. These are the addresses that are used to access the operands in memory. Then the BCD data at memory location $00110E_{16}$ and X are subtracted from the BCD value at $00120E_{16}$. We will assume that the value stored at $00120E_{16}$ is 37_{10}, the value at $00110E_{16}$ is 12_{10}, and X is 1. Then the difference calculated by the instruction is

$$(00120E_{16}) - (00110E_{16}) - (X) = 37_{10} - 12_{10} - 1_{10}$$

$$= 24_{10}$$

This value is saved at destination address $00120E_{16}$, and the condition code bits Z, X, and C are cleared.

Negate Decimal Instruction: NBCD

The last of the decimal arithmetic instructions in Fig. 11.8 is *negate binary-coded decimal* (NBCD). It is expressed in general as

$$\text{NBCD} \quad \text{EA}$$

NBCD is effectively an SBCD instruction in which the subtrahend always equals zero. For this reason, it implements the operation

$$0 - (\text{EA}) \rightarrow \text{EA}$$

The operand identified as EA can be specified using the alterable addressing modes. One exception is address register direct addressing, which cannot be used.

Here is an example with the operand accessed through address register indirect addressing mode with postincrement:

$$\text{NBCD} \quad (\text{A5})+$$

The condition code bits affected by the NBCD instruction are the same as those affected by the SBCD instruction.

EXAMPLE 11.7

Write a program segment that will add two four-digit packed BCD numbers that are held in registers D_0 and D_1 and place their sum in D_0. The organization of the original BCD data in the data registers is shown in Fig. 11.9(a).

SOLUTION   Remember that only the contents of the eight least significant bits of a data register can be processed with the BCD instructions. Moreover, up to this point in the chapter we have not shown any direct way of exchanging the most significant byte of a word in a data register with its least significant byte. One solution to this problem is to move the contents of D_0 and D_1 to memory. This reorganizes the BCD digits at separate byte addresses, as shown in Fig. 11.9(b). To move D_0 and D_1 to memory, say D_0 to address MEM0 and D_1 to address MEM1 the following instructions can be used:

```
MOVE.W  D0,MEM0
MOVE.W  D1,MEM1
```

Now we can use the predecrement address register indirect form of the BCD addition instruction to perform the decimal arithmetic operations. Therefore, address registers must be loaded with pointers to the data in memory. Let us use A_0 and A_1 for this purpose. Since the predecrement mode of addressing must be used, A_0 should be loaded with MEM0 +2 and A_1 with MEM1 +2. This is done with the instructions

```
LEA  MEM0+2,A0
LEA  MEM1+2,A1
```

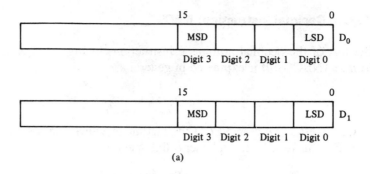

Digit 3 Digit 2 Digit 1 Digit 0

Digit 3 Digit 2 Digit 1 Digit 0

(a)

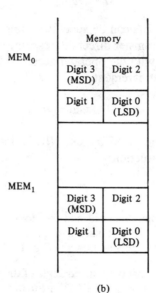

(b)

```
MOVE.W    D0, MEM0
MOVE.W    D1, MEM1
LEA       MEM0 + 2, A0
LEA       MEM1 + 2, A1
MOVE      #0, CCR
ABCD      -(A1), -(A0)
ABCD      -(A1), -(A0)
MOVE.W    MEM0, D0
```

(c)

Figure 11.9 (a) Four-digit BCD numbers in data registers D_0 and D_1; (b) storage of the BCD numbers in memory; (c) program for adding two four-digit BCD numbers.

Moreover, to use the BCD instruction, we must start with X = 0. To do this, we execute the instruction

$$\text{MOVE} \quad \#0, \text{CCR}$$

Now that the address pointers and the extend bit of SR are initialized, we are ready to perform the addition operation. Executing the instructions

$$\text{ABCD} \quad -(\text{A1}), \; -(\text{A0})$$

and

$$\text{ABCD} \quad -(\text{A1}), \; -(\text{A0})$$

gives the sum in MEM0. To put the sum into D_0, the instruction is

$$\text{MOVE.W} \quad \text{MEM0,D0}$$

The complete program is repeated in Fig. 11.9(c).

11.6 LOGIC INSTRUCTIONS

To implement logic functions, such as AND, OR, exclusive-OR, and NOT, the instruction set of the 68000 provides a group of logic instructions. The instructions in this group are shown in Fig. 11.10 together with their different forms, operand sizes, and operations. The execution of a logic instruction sets the condition code bits N and Z as per result, clears V and C, and does not affect the X bit.

Mnemonic	Meaning	Type	Operand Size	Operation
AND	Logical AND	AND EA,Dn	8, 16, 32	$(\text{EA}) \cdot \text{Dn} \to \text{Dn}$
		AND Dn,EA	8, 16, 32	$\text{Dn} \cdot (\text{EA}) \to \text{EA}$
		ANDI #XXX,EA	8, 16, 32	$\#\text{XXX} \cdot (\text{EA}) \to \text{EA}$
		ANDI #XXX,CCR	8	$\#\text{XXX} \cdot \text{CCR} \to \text{CCR}$
		ANDI #XXX,SR	16	$\#\text{XXX} \cdot \text{SR} \to \text{SR}$
OR	Logical OR	OR EA,Dn	8, 16, 32	$(\text{EA}) + \text{Dn} \to \text{Dn}$
		OR Dn,EA	8, 16, 32	$\text{Dn} + (\text{EA}) \to \text{EA}$
		ORI #XXX,EA	8, 16, 32	$\#\text{XXX} + (\text{EA}) \to \text{EA}$
		ORI #XXX,CCR	8	$\#\text{XXX} + \text{CCR} \to \text{CCR}$
		ORI #XXX,SR	16	$\#\text{XXX} + \text{SR} \to \text{SR}$
EOR	Logical exclusive-OR	EOR Dn,EA	8, 16, 32	$\text{Dn} \oplus (\text{EA}) \to \text{EA}$
		EORI #XXX,EA	8, 16, 32	$\#\text{XXX} \oplus (\text{EA}) \to \text{EA}$
		EORI #XXX,CCR	8	$\#\text{XXX} \oplus \text{CCR} \to \text{CCR}$
		EORI #XXX,SR	16	$\#\text{XXX} \oplus \text{SR} \to \text{SR}$
NOT	Logical NOT	NOT EA	8, 16, 32	$\overline{(\text{EA})} \to \text{EA}$

Figure 11.10 Logic instructions.

AND Instructions—AND and ANDI

As shown in Fig. 11.10, there are four forms of the AND instruction. The general form, which uses the mnemonic AND, permits the contents of a data register and an operand specified by the effective address EA to be ANDed together. Let us look at the first form of the instruction:

$$\text{AND} \quad \text{EA, Dn}$$

The source operand can use the data addressing modes to generate EA. Therefore, the source operand can use any addressing mode except address register direct addressing. On the other hand, the destination operand can be specified only with data register direct addressing and will always be one of the eight data registers inside the 68000.

An example of the instruction, which uses register direct addressing for both the source and destination operands, is

AND.B D0,D1

Execution of this instruction causes a bit by bit AND operation to be performed on the byte contents of D_0 and D_1. The result is saved in destination register D_1.

For instance, if D_1 contains $0000ABCD_{16}$ and D_0 contains $00000F0F_{16}$, the AND operation between the least significant bytes gives

$$CD_{16} \cdot 0F_{16} = 11001101_2 \cdot 00001111_2$$
$$= 00001101_2$$
$$= 0D_{16}$$

Therefore, the new contents of D_1 are $0000AB0D_{16}$. Notice that the four most significant bits of the least significant byte of D_1 have been masked off. The affected condition code bits in SR are Z, N, C, and V. The C and V bits are always cleared, but Z and N are set or reset based on the result produced in the destination register.

The second form,

AND Dn,EA

permits the contents of a source operand held in a data register to be ANDed with a destination operand identified by EA. This time the location of the destination operand can be specified using any of the alterable memory addressing modes. These addressing modes are identified in Fig. 10.20.

The next three types of the AND group are *AND immediate* (ANDI) instructions. These instructions AND an immediate source operand identified as #XXX with the contents of a specified destination operand. The immediate operand is stored as part of the instruction in program memory.

The first form,

ANDI #XXX,EA

permits ANDing of an immediate source operand with the contents of a destination operand whose location is specified by effective address EA. This destination operand can be in a data register, address register, or storage location in data memory.

An example is the instruction

ANDI.B #7,D1

Execution of this instruction causes the binary form of decimal number 7 to be ANDed with the contents of D_1. Let us assume that D_1 originally contained $FFFFFFFF_{16}$; then, executing the instruction gives

$$D_1 = FFFFFFFF_{16} \bullet 7_{16}$$

$$= FFFFFFF7_{16}$$

The next two forms,

```
ANDI   #XXX, SR
```

and

```
ANDI   #XXX, CCR
```

are used to AND the contents of the complete status register and the condition code byte part of SR with immediate data, respectively. The first of these two operations is privileged and can only be executed when the 68000 is in the supervisor state.

OR Instructions: OR and ORI

The OR instruction has the same five forms that we just introduced for the AND instruction. Figure 11.10 shows that they include two forms of the *general OR* instruction and three forms of the *OR immediate* (ORI) instruction.

The general OR instruction permits the OR logic operation to be performed between the contents of a data register specified using one operand and the contents of another data register, an address register, or a location in memory specified by the data addressing mode of the other operand. For example, the instruction

```
OR.B   (A0), D0
```

ORs the contents of the byte location whose effective address is the contents of A_0 with the byte contents of D_0. The result is saved in D_0. That is, it performs the logic operation

$$(EA) + D0 \rightarrow D0$$

Assuming that the contents of the storage location pointed to by the address in A_0 are $AAAAAAAA_{16}$ and the data held in D_0 are 55555555_{16}, the result obtained by executing the instruction is

$$D0 = AAAAAAAA_{16} + 55555555_{16}$$

$$= FFFFFFFF_{16}$$

The OR immediate forms of the instruction allow an immediate operand to be ORed with the contents of a storage location in data memory, a data register, or the status register. An example is the instruction

```
ORI   #FF00, SR
```

Execution of this instruction causes all the bits in the upper byte of SR to be set to 1 without changing the bits in the lower byte. Since the status register's upper byte is changed, the operation can only be performed when in the supervisor state.

Exclusive-OR Instructions: EOR and EORI

Looking at Fig. 11.10, we see that the same basic instruction forms are also provided for the *exclusive-OR* (EOR) instruction. The difference here is that they perform the exclusive-OR logic function on the contents of the source and destination operands.

Let us now look at some examples. A first example of the instruction is

$$\text{EOR.L} \quad \text{D0,A0}$$

When it is executed, the operation performed is

$$\text{D0} \oplus \text{A0} \rightarrow \text{A0}$$

Another example is

$$\text{EOR} \quad \text{\#\$0F,CCR}$$

Execution of this instruction performs the operation

$$\text{\$0F} \oplus \text{CCR} \rightarrow \text{CCR}$$

NOT Instruction: NOT

The *NOT* instruction differs from the AND, OR, and EOR instructions we just described in that only one operand is specified. Its general form, as shown in Fig. 11.10, is

$$\text{NOT} \quad \text{EA}$$

When this instruction is executed, the contents of the specified operand are replaced by its 1's complement. To address the operand, only the alterable addressing modes can be used. However, one exception exists: it is that address register direct addressing is not permitted.

> **EXAMPLE 11.8**
>
> Write a sequence of logic instructions that will clear the bits in register D_1 that correspond to the bits that are set in D_0.
>
> **SOLUTION** To clear a bit that is set, it should be ANDed with logic 0. Moreover, to obtain a logic 0 from logic 1, it should be inverted. Thus, if the contents of D_0 are inverted and then ANDed with D_1, the required result will be generated in D_1. The instructions that do this are
>
> $$\text{NOT.L} \quad \text{D0}$$
> $$\text{AND.L} \quad \text{D0,D1}$$

11.7 SHIFT AND ROTATE INSTRUCTIONS

The shift and rotate instructions of the 68000 are used to change bit positions of the data bits in an operand. These types of operations are useful to multiply or divide a given number by a power of 2, check the status of individual bits in an operand, or simply shift the position of data bits in a register or memory location.

Shift Instructions: LSL, LSR, ASL, and ASR

There are two kinds of shift operations: the *logical shift* and the *arithmetic shift*. Moreover, each of these two shifts can be performed in the *left direction* or *right direction*. As shown in Fig. 11.11, these variations lead to four basic shift instructions.

Mnemonic	Meaning	Type	Operand Size	Operation
LSL	Logical shift left	LSL #XXX,Dy LSL Dx,Dy LSL EA	8, 16, 32 8, 16, 32 16	X/C ← ← 0
LSR	Logical shift right	LSR #XXX,Dy LSR Dx,Dy LSR EA	8, 16, 32 8, 16, 32 16	0 → → X/C
ASL	Arithmetic shift left	ASL #XXX,Dy ASL Dx,Dy ASL EA	8, 16, 32 8, 16, 32 16	X/C ← ← 0
ASR	Arithmetic shift right	ASR #XXX,Dy ASR Dx,Dy ASR EA	8, 16, 32 8, 16, 32 16	→ → X/C MSB

Figure 11.11 Shift instructions.

The two logical shift instructions are *logical shift left* (LSL) and *logical shift right* (LSR). The operation of these instructions is illustrated with diagrams in Fig. 11.11. Looking at the illustration for LSL, we see that its execution causes the bits of the operand to be shifted to the left by a specific number of bit positions. At the same time, the vacated bit positions on the least significant bit end of the operand are filled with zeros and bits are shifted out from the most significant bit end. The last bit shifted out on the left is copied into both the extend (X) and carry (C) bits of SR.

Notice in Fig. 11.11 that there are three forms of the LSL instruction. The first two forms differ in the way the shift count is specified. In the first form,

$$\text{LSL} \quad \text{\#XXX, Dy}$$

the count is specified by the immediate operand #XXX. The value of this operand can be from 0 through 7. A value of zero stands for "shift left eight bit positions." In this way, we see that this form of the instruction limits the shift left to the range of from 1 to 8 bits. For instance,

$$\text{LSL.W} \quad \text{\#5, D4}$$

initiates a shift left by five bit positions for the word contents of data register D_4.

The second form

$$LSL \quad Dx, Dy$$

specifies the count as residing in data register Dx. Only the six least significant bits of this register are used for the shift count. Therefore, the shift count is extended to a range of from 1 to 63 bit positions.

An example is the instruction

$$LSL.L \quad D0, D1$$

Assuming that D_0 contains 4_{16} and D_1 contains $0000FFFF_{16}$, execution of the instruction results in

$$D_1 = 000FFFF0_{16}$$

and

$$C = 0$$

Both forms of the LSL instruction that we have considered up to this point only have the ability to shift the bits of an operand that is held in one of the internal data registers of the 68000. The third form,

$$LSL \quad EA$$

permits a shift left operation to be performed on the contents of a storage location in memory. Actually, any of the data-alterable addressing modes that relate to external memory can be used to specify EA. One restriction is that the size specified for the operand must always be a word. Moreover, since no shift count is specified, execution of the instruction causes a shift left of just one bit position.

Looking at Fig. 11.11, we see that the logical shift right (LSR) instruction can be written using the same basic forms as the LSL instruction. Moreover, the operations that they perform are the exact opposite of that just described for their corresponding LSL instruction. Now data are shifted to the right instead of to the left; zeros are loaded into vacated bits from the MSB end instead of the LSB end; and the last bit shifted out from the LSB is copied into both X and C.

There are also two basic arithmetic shift instructions: *arithmetic shift left* (ASL) and *arithmetic shift right* (ASR). Their forms and operations are also shown in Fig. 11.11. Here we see that the operation performed by ASL is essentially the same as that performed by the LSL instruction. However, there is a difference in the way in which the overflow flag is handled by the two instructions. It is always 0 for the LSL instruction, but for ASL it is set to 1 if the MSB changes logic level.

On the other hand, ASR is not the same as LSR. Notice that it does not only shift the bits of its operand but also preserve its sign. The illustration of operation of ASR in Fig. 11.11 shows that vacated more significant bit positions are filled with the original value for the MSB, that is, the sign bit.

Rotate Instructions: ROL, ROR, ROXL, and ROXR

The rotate instructions of the 68000 are similar to its shift instructions in that they can be used to shift the bits of data in an operand to the left or right. However, the shift operation they perform differs in that the bits of data that are shifted out at one end are shifted back in at the other end. Hence, the bits of data appear to have been rotated.

Based on the path in which bits are rotated, two kinds of rotate operations are defined. As shown in Fig. 11.12, the basic rotate operation performed by the *rotate left* (ROL) instruction or *rotate right* (ROR) instruction use a path in which bits are shifted out from one end of the operand into the carry (C) bit of SR, and at the same time they are reloaded at the other end. Notice that the path for the other two instructions, ROXL and ROXR, differs in that both C and X are loaded with the bits as they are shifted out. Moreover, bits that are reloaded at the other end pass through X.

Mnemonic	Meaning	Type	Operand Size	Operation
ROL	Rotate left	ROL #XXX,Dy ROL Dx,Dy ROL EA	8, 16, 32 8, 16, 32 16	C ← ←
ROR	Rotate right	ROR #XXX,Dy ROR Dx,Dy ROR EA	8, 16, 32 8, 16, 32 16	→ C
ROXL	Rotate left through extend	ROXL #XXX,Dy ROXL Dx,Dy ROXL EA	8, 16, 32 8, 16, 32 16	C ← ← X
ROXR	Rotate right through extend	ROXR #XXX,Dy ROXR Dx,Dy ROXR EA	8, 16, 32 8, 16, 32 16	X → C

Figure 11.12   Rotate instructions.

Let us begin with the ROL instruction. Looking at the diagram of its operation in Fig. 11.12, we see that it causes the bits of the specified operand to be rotated to the left. Bits shifted out from the most significant bit position are both loaded into C and the least significant bit position. The number of bit positions through which the data are to be rotated are specified as part of the instruction.

Notice that the allowed operand variations for ROL are identical to those shown in Fig. 11.11 for the shift instructions. The first form,

ROL #XXX,Dy

permits an immediate operand in the range 0 to 7 to specify the count. This limits the amount of rotation to 1 to 8 bit positions. A value of 0 for XXX is actually a special case. It causes an 8-bit rotate to the left. The next form,

ROL Dx,Dy

uses the contents of the six least significant bits of data register Dx to specify the count. This extends the rotate range to from 1 to 63 bit positions. When either of these instructions is used, the operand that is to be processed by the rotate operation must reside in one of the data registers.

An example is the instruction

$$\text{ROL.L} \quad \text{D0,D1}$$

If D_0 contains 00000004_{16}, execution of the instruction causes the long-word contents of D_1 to be rotated four bit positions to the left. For instance, if the original contents of D_1 were $0000FFFF_{16}$, after the rotate operation is complete, the new contents of D_1 are $000FFFF0_{16}$ and C equals 0.

The last form of the rotate left instruction,

$$\text{ROL} \quad \text{EA}$$

permits the operand to reside in a storage location in memory. This instruction may only be used to perform a 1-bit rotate left on a word operand.

In Fig. 11.12, we see that the rotate right (ROR) instruction is capable of performing the same operations as ROL. However, in this case, the data are rotated in the opposite direction.

As we indicated earlier, the *rotate left with extend* (ROXL) and *rotate right with extend* (ROXR) instructions essentially perform the same rotate operations as ROL and ROR, respectivley. However, this time the last bit rotated out is loaded into both X and C, not just C, and bits that are reloaded at the other end pass through X. Therefore, execution of the instruction

$$\text{ROXL.L} \quad \text{D0,D1}$$

when $D_0 = 4_{16}$, $D_1 = 000FFFF0_{16}$, C = 1, and X = 1, results in $D_1 = 00FFFF08_{16}$ with C = 0 and X = 0.

EXAMPLE 11.9

Implement the operation described in Example 11.7 using the rotate and decimal arithmetic instructions to add two four-digit packed BCD numbers that are held in D_0 and D_1, respectively. Place the result in D_0.

SOLUTION We first start with X = 0 and add the two least significant digits. The instructions required to do this are

$$\begin{array}{ll} \text{MOVE} & \text{\#0,CCR} \\ \text{ABCD} & \text{D1,D0} \end{array}$$

Let us save this result in D_2 by executing the instruction

$$\text{MOVE.B} \quad \text{D0,D2}$$

To add the most significant digits, we can rotate the words in D_1 and D_0 8 bits to the right. The instructions for this are

```
ROR.W      #0,D0
ROR.W      #0,D1
```

This does not change the X bit, which must be used in the addition. Now the least significant bytes in D_0 and D_1 can be added as BCD numbers by the instruction

```
ABCD       D1,D0
```

The result of D_0 can now be rotated to the left and the least significant result saved in D_2 can be placed back in D_0. The instructions to do this are

```
ROL.W      #0,D0
MOVE.B     D2,D0
```

This completes the BCD addition. The entire program is shown in Fig. 11.13.

```
MOVE       #0,CCR
ABCD       D1,D0
MOVE.B     D0,D2
ROR.W      #0,D0
ROR.W      #0,D1
ABCD       D1,D0
ROL.W      #0,D0
MOVE.B     D2,D0
```

Figure 11.13 BCD addition program.

ASSIGNMENT

Section 11.3

1. Describe the operation that is performed by each of the following instructions
   (a) MOVE.L   #$A0001000,D0
   (b) MOVE.B   #$06,A0
   (c) MOVE.W   D0,A1
   (d) MOVE.L   D0,$A000
   (e) MOVE.B   D0,(A1)+
   (f) MOVE.W   D0,9(A1)
   (g) MOVE.L   D0,9(A1,A0.B)

2. Assume that the data registers and address registers are all initialized to 00000000_{16} and that all data storage memory has been cleared. Determine the location and value of the destination operand as instructions (a) through (g) from Problem 1 are executed as a sequence.

3. Write an instruction sequence that will load the condition code part of the status register with the value 10100_2.

4. Describe the function that is performed by the instruction sequence

```
MOVE.L     $12345678,A0
MOVE       A0,USP
```

5. Given that $D_0 = 12345678, $D_1 = $ABCDEF01$, and $A_0 = 87654321, specify the memory contents of address A000 to address A002 after executing the instruction.

```
MOVEM.B    D0/D1/A0,$A000
```

6. Write an instruction that places the long-word contents of memory locations $B000, $B004, and $B008 into registers D_5, D_6, and D_7, respectively.

7. What is the value in A_1 after the instruction

$$\text{LEA} \quad \text{A(A0,D0.B),A1}$$

Assume that the initial contents of A_0 equals 00100000_{16} and D_0 equals $AABBCCDD_{16}$.

8. Write a single instruction that will exchange the contents of registers A_0 and A_1.

9. If register D_1 contains the value $AAAA5555_{16}$, what are the the contents of this registers after executing the instruction

$$\text{SWAP} \quad \text{D1}$$

10. What happens when the instruction CLR.W A0 is executed?

11. What are the contents of D_0 and D_1 after executing the following sequence of instructions?

```
MOVE.L    #$13579BDF,D0
MOVE.L    #$02468ACE,D1
SWAP      D0
EXG       D0,D1
```

Section 11.4

12. Describe the operation performed by each of the instructions that follows:

(a) ADD.B   D1,D0   (e) ADDX.B   D0.D1
(b) SUB.W   D1,-(A1)   (f) SUBX.W   -(A1),-(A0)
(c) ADDI.W   #$1234,$10000 (g) ADDA.L   (A1),A0
(d) SUBQ   #7,3(A1)

13. Assume that the state of the 68000's registers and memory is as follows:

$$D0 = 11223344_{16}$$
$$D1 = 01234567_{16}$$
$$A0 = 00010010_{16}$$
$$A1 = 00010020_{16}$$
$$(\$00010000) = FFFF0000_{16}$$
$$(\$0001000E) = FFFFFFFF_{16}$$
$$(\$00010010) = AABBCCDD_{16}$$
$$(\$0001001E) = FF00FF00_{16}$$
$$(\$00010020) = 0000FFFF_{16}$$
$$(\$00010023) = 00000002_{16}$$
$$X = 1$$

just prior to execution of each of the instructions in Problem 12. What are the results produced in the destination operand by executing instructions (a) through (g).

14. Write a negate with extend instruction that will form the negative of the byte contents of memory location $F100.

15. What happens when the instruction NEG.B (A0) is executed? Assume that the value in A_0 and the memory location pointed to by this address are those specified in Problem 13.

16. Assuming that D_0 contains 00000123_{16} and D_1 contains 00000010_{16}, what will be the new contents of D_0 after executing the instruction DIVU D1,D0?

17. Write an instruction that will sign extend the byte contents of register D_0 to a word.

18. Assuming that D_1 initially contains $0000A03F_{16}$, what is the result in D_1 after executing the instruction EXT.L D1?

19. Two word-wide unsigned integers are stored at the memory address $A000 and $B000, respectively. Write an instruction sequence that computes and stores their sum, difference, product, and quotient. Store these results at consecutive memory locations starting at address $C000 in memory. To obtain the difference, subtract the integer at $B000 from the integer at $A000. For the division, divide the integer at $A000 by the integer at $B000. Use register indirect relative addressing mode through register A_1 to store the various results.

Section 11.5

20. Explain what operation is performed by the instruction

$$ABCD \quad -(A0), -(A1)$$

21. If D_0 contains 56_{10}, D_1 contains 92_{10}, and X is 1, what is the result produced in D_1 after executing the instruction

$$SBCD \quad D0, D1$$

22. Write an instruction that will negate the byte of BCD data that is held at address $100F0.

23. Two long-word BCD integers are stored at the symbolic addresses NUM1 and NUM2, respectively. Write an instruction sequence to generate their difference and store it at NUM3. The difference is to be formed by subtracting the value at NUM1 from that at NUM2. Use the predecrement indirect mode of addressing.

Section 11.6

24. Describe the operation performed by each of the following instructions.
   (a) AND.W   (A0), D0
   (b) ANDI.B   #$F0, (A0)
   (c) OR.B   D0, (A1)
   (d) ORI   #01, CCR
   (e) EOR.B   D0, 20 (A0)
   (f) EORI   #$0300, SR
   (g) NOT.B $10020

25. Assume that the state of the 68000's registers and memory is as follows:

$$D0 = F0F0A5A5_{16}$$

$$A0 = 00100000_{16}$$

$$A1 = 00100010_{16}$$

$$(\$00100000) = 5555AAAA_{16}$$

$$(\$00100010) = 0000F05A_{16}$$

$$(\$00100020) = 0000A50F_{16}$$

$$SR = 0400_{16}$$

just prior to the execution of each of the instruction in Problem 24. What are the results produced in the destination operands after executing instructions (a) through (g)?

26. The result in Problem 25(d), sets a condition code bit. What condition is indicated by the set bit?

27. In the result obtained in Problem 25(f), what is the interrupt mask before and after execution of the instruction?

28. Assuming that the 68000 is in the user state, write an instruction that will switch the 68000 to the supervisor state.

29. Write an instruction that will initialize the interrupt mask to 000_2.

30. Write an instruction sequence that generates a byte-size integer in the memory location identified by label RESULT. The value of the byte integer is to be calculated using logic operations as follows:

$$(RESULT) = D0 \cdot NUM1 + NUM2 \cdot D0 + D1$$

Assume that all parameters are byte size.

Section 11.7

31. Explain what operation is performed by each of the instructions:
    (a) LSL. L   #$F, D0   (d) LSR $100000
    (b) LSL. B   D1, D0   (e) ASL. L   #$F, D0
    (c) LSR. L   #$F, D0   (f) ASR   (A0)

32. Assume that the state of the 68000's registers and memory is

$$D0 = 12345678_{16}$$

$$D1 = 00000005_{16}$$

$$A0 = 00100010_{16}$$

$$(\$00100000) = 0F0F0F0F_{16}$$

$$(\$00100010) = FF00FF00_{16}$$

$$X = 0$$

$$C = 0$$

just prior to the execution of each of the instructions in Problem 30. What are the results produced by executing the instructions (a) through (f)?

33. Implement the following operation using shift and arithmetic instructions.

$$7 \cdot D1 - 5 \cdot D2 - 1/8 \cdot D2 \rightarrow D0$$

Assume that the parameters are all long word in size.

34. Explain what operation is performed by each of the instructions that follow:
    (a) ROL. L   #$F, D0   (d) ROR $100000
    (b) ROL. B   D1, D0   (e) ROXL. L   #$F, D0
    (c) ROR. L   #$F, D0   (f) ROXR   (A0)

35. Assume that the state of the 68000's registers and memory are as follows:

$$D0 = 12345678_{16}$$
$$D1 = 00000005_{16}$$
$$A0 = 00100010_{16}$$
$$(\$00100000) = 0F0F0F0F_{16}$$
$$(\$00100010) = FF00FF00_{16}$$
$$X = 0$$
$$C = 0$$

just prior to the execution of each of the instrucitons in Problem 34. What are the results produced by executing instructions (a) through (f)?

36. Write a program that stores the long-word contents of D_0 into memory starting at address location \$B001.

12

68000 Microprocessor Programming 2

12.1 INTRODUCTION

In Chapters 10 and 11, we introduced the addressing modes and many of the instructions in the instruction set of the 68000 microprocessor. Using these instructions, we also covered some preliminary programming techniques. Here we will cover the rest of the instructions and introduce more complex programming methods. Specifically, the following topics are presented in this chapter:

1. Compare and test instructions
2. Jump and branch instructions
3. Test condition, decrement, and branch instruction
4. Subroutines and subroutine-handling instructions
5. Bit manipulation instructions

12.2 COMPARE AND TEST INSTRUCTIONS

The instruction set of the 68000 includes instructions to compare two operands or an operand with zero. The comparison is done by subtracting the source operand from the destination operand. The result of the subtraction does not modify either of the operands; instead, it is used to set or reset condition code bits (flags) in the status register. The flags affected are negative (N), zero (Z), overflow (V), and carry (C). These flags can then be examined by other instructions to make the decision as to whether to execute one part of the program or another.

The instructions that have the ability to compare operands are shown in Fig. 12.1. Basically, two types of instructions are available: the *compare* (CMP) instruction and *test* (TST) instruction. Notice that the CMP instruction always compares two operands. On the other hand, the TST instruction compares the specified operand with zero.

Mnemonic	Meaning	Type	Operand Size	Status Bits Affected
CMP	Compare	CMP EA,Dn	8, 16, 32	N, Z, V, C
		CMPA EA,An	16, 32	N, Z, V, C
		CMPI #XXX,EA	8, 16, 32	N, Z, V, C
		CMPM $(Ay)^+,(Ay)^+$	8, 16, 32	N, Z, V, C
TST	Test	TST EA	8, 16, 32	N, Z, V, C

Figure 12.1 Compare and test instructions.

Let us begin by looking in detail at the compare instruction of the 68000. Looking at Fig. 12.1, we see that there are four forms of this instruction. These forms are *compare* (CMP), *compare address* (CMPA), *compare immediate* (CMPI), and *compare memory* (CMPM). They differ in the manner their operands are obtained for comparison.

The CMP instruction is used to compare a source operand with the contents of a data register. To specify the location of the source operand, any of the 68000's addressing modes can be used. On the other hand, the destination operand must always be one of the internal data registers. As indicated in Fig. 12.1, the specified operand size may be a byte, a word, or a long word. However, when an address register contains the source operand, byte-size comparisons cannot be made.

The result of the comparison is reflected by changes in four of the 68000's status flags. Notice in Fig. 12.1 that it affects the sign, zero, overflow, and carry flags. The logic state of these flags can be referenced by instructions in order to make a decision whether or not to alter the sequence in which the program executes.

The process of comparison performed by the CMP instruction is basically a subtraction operation. The source operand is subtracted from the destination operand. However, the result of this subtraction is not saved in the destination. Instead, based on the result the appropriate flags are set or reset.

An example of the instruction is

CMP.W   D1,D0

When this instruction is executed, the word contents of D_1 are subtracted from that of D_0 and the flags are affected according to the result produced by the subtraction. For instance, if the value in D_1 is the same as that in D_0, the Z bit in SR is set and N, V, and C are all reset. Even though a subtraction is performed to determine this status, the values in D_1 and D_0 are not changed.

For instance, if the word contents of D_1 and D_0 are 1000_{16} and 4000_{16}, respectively, execution of the instruction CMP.W   D1,D0 subtracts 1000_{16} from 4000_{16} and sets or resets the status flags based on the difference that results. Since this result is positive and nonzero, both N and Z are reset. Moreover, no carry is generated by the subtraction; therefore, C is also reset. Finally, in the process of performing the subtraction, an overflow condition does not occur and V is also reset. In this way, we find that at completion of execution of the instruction the status flags are: $N = 0$, $Z = 0$, $V = 0$, and $C = 0$.

Compare address (CMPA) is the same as CMP except that the destination operand must reside in an address register instead of a data register. For this reason only word and long-word operands can be specified. A word source operand is sign extended to a long word before making the comparison. Here is an instruction that does a long-word comparison of the value of a long word in memory to the contents of A_0.

CMPA.L   (A1),A0

Notice that the address in A_1 is used to point to the long word in memory.

The next instruction, compare immediate (CMPI), is used to compare a byte, word, or long-word immediate operand to a destination operand that resides in a data register, address register, or storage location in memory. The location of the destination operand can be specified using any of the data-alterable addressing modes of the 68000. An example is the instruction

CMPI.B   #$FF,D0

The last type of compare instruction in Fig. 12.1 is compare memory (CMPM). Here both operands are located in memory and must be specified using the automatic postincrement indirect address register addressing modes. Since this instruction updates the address pointers each time it is executed, we are always ready to compare the next two pieces of data in memory. For this reason, it is very useful for performing string comparisons.

EXAMPLE 12.1

Determine how the condition codes will change as the following instructions are executed.

CLR.L   D0
MOVE.B   #$5A,D0
CMP.B   D0,D0
CMPI.B   #$60,D0

SOLUTION What happens to the condition codes as these instructions are executed is summarized in Fig. 12.2. Here we see that the first instruction clears data register D_0. This is written as a long-word instruction; therefore, all 32 bits of D_0 are cleared. That is, it is loaded with 00000000_{16}. Due to the execution of the first instruction, the Z condition code bit is set while N, V, and C are cleared.

The next instruction loads the lower byte of D_0 with the number $5A_{16}$. Since this number is positive and greater than zero, the N and Z bits of SR are cleared. Moreover, it always clears the V and C bits.

The third instruction compares the contents of D_0 with itself. Thus the Z bit is set and N, V, and C are cleared.

The last instruction compares 60_{16} with the contents of D_0. Therefore, it subtracts 60_{16} from $5A_{16}$. This subtraction yields a negative result; therefore, the N bit is set. Furthermore, to subtract a larger number from a smaller one, a borrow is required. Thus the C bit is also set. The result of subtracting the two numbers can be correctly represented as a byte. That is, no overflow has occurred. Therefore, V is reset. Moreover, the result is not zero, therefore, Z is also reset.

Instruction	Function	Condition Codes				
		X	N	Z	V	C
CLR.L D0	Clear D_0	X	0	1	0	0
MOVE.B #$5A,D0	Load $5A_{16}$ into D_0	X	0	0	0	0
CMP.B D0,D0	Compare D_0 with D_0	X	0	1	0	0
CMPI.B #$60,D0	Compare 60_{16} with D_0	X	1	0	0	1

Figure 12.2 Example program employing compare instructions.

Test Instruction: TST

The last instruction in Fig. 12.1 is the test (TST) instruction. This instruction performs an operation that is similar to the compare instruction except that its source operand is always assumed to be zero. Zero is subtracted from the specified destination operand and, based on the result, the condition code bits in SR are set or reset. Any of the data-alterable addressing modes can be used to specify the destination operand and it can be a byte, word, or long word.

The same four condition code bits are affected by the TST instruction. But in this case only N and Z are set or reset based on the result of the comparison. The other two bits, V and C, are always cleared.

An example is the instruction

$$\text{TST.B} \quad \text{D0}$$

Let us assume that D_0 contains 10_{16}. Executing the instruction causes 0_{16} to be subtracted from $1D_{16}$, and then the flags are set or reset based on the difference that results. For this value of data, the difference that is produced is positive and nonzero; therefore, N and Z are both cleared to 0.

Set According to Condition Instruction: Scc

Earlier we pointed out that the condition code bits set or reset by the compare and test instructions are examined through software to decide whether or not branching should take place in the program. One way of using these bits is to test them directly with the branch instructions. Another approach is to test them for a specific condition and then save a flag value representing whether the tested condition is true or false. This flag value can then be used for program branching decisions. An instruction that performs this operation is *set according to condition* (Scc).

The form of the Scc instruction is shown in Fig. 12.3(a). The cc part of the mnemonic stands for a general condition code relationship and must be replaced with a specific relationship when writing the instruction. Figure 12.3(b) is a list of the mnemonics and condition code relationships that can be used to replace cc. For in-

Mnemonic	Meaning	Format	Operand Size	Operation
Scc	Set according to condition code	Scc EA	8	$11111111 \rightarrow$ EA if cc is true $00000000 \rightarrow$ EA if cc is false

(a)

Mnemonic	Meaning	Condition Code Relationship
SCC	Set if carry clear	$C = 0$
SCS	Set if carry set	$C = 1$
SEQ	Set if equal	$Z = 1$
SNE	Set if not equal	$Z = 0$
SMI	Set if minus	$N = 1$
SPL	Set if plus	$N = 0$
SVC	Set if overflow clear (signed)	$V = 0$
SVS	Set if overflow set (signed)	$V = 1$
SHI	Set if higher (unsigned)	$\overline{C} \cdot \overline{Z} = 1$
SLS	Set if lower or same (unsigned)	$C + Z = 1$
SGT	Set if greater than (signed)	$NV\overline{Z} + \overline{N}\overline{V}\overline{Z} = 1$
SGE	Set if greater or equal (signed)	$NV + \overline{N}\overline{V} = 1$
SLT	Set if less than	$N\overline{V} + \overline{N}V = 1$
SLE	Set if less or equal (signed)	$Z + N\overline{V} + \overline{N}V = 1$

(b)

Figure 12.3 (a) Set according to condition code instruction; (b) condition tests of the Scc instruction.

stance, replacing cc by LE gives the instruction mnemonic SLE. This stands for *set if less than or equal to* and tests status to determine if the logical value of

$$Z + N \cdot \overline{V} + \overline{N} \cdot V$$

is equal to 0 or 1.

Looking at Fig. 12.3(a), we see that a byte-wide destination operand is also specified in the instruction. Its location can be identified using any of the data-alterable addressing modes. For example, an instruction could be written as

$$\text{SGT} \quad \text{D0}$$

When this instruction is executed, it causes the condition code bits to be checked to determine if the relationship

$$N \cdot V \cdot \overline{Z} + \overline{N} \cdot \overline{V} \cdot \overline{Z} = 1$$

is satisfied. If this relationship is true, the bits of the byte part of destination register D_0 are all set. On the other hand, if the relationship is false, they are all reset. For example, if $N = V = 0$, and $Z = 1$, the condition code relationship evaluates as

$$N \cdot V \cdot \overline{Z} + \overline{N} \cdot \overline{V} \cdot \overline{Z} = 0 \cdot 0 \cdot 0 + 1 \cdot 1 \cdot 0$$
$$= 0$$

Therefore, the relationship is false and the byte part of D_0 becomes 00_{16}.

12.3 JUMP AND BRANCH INSTRUCTIONS

For all the programs we have studied up to this point, the sequence in which the instructions were written was also the sequence in which they were executed. In other words, after execution of an instruction the program counter always points to the next sequential instruction.

For most applications, we must be able to alter the sequence in which instructions of the program execute. The changes in sequence may have to be unconditionally done or may be subject to satisfying a conditional relationship. To support these types of operations, the 68000 is equipped with jump and branch instructions.

Unconditional Jump and Branch Instructions: JMP and BRA

Unconditional changes in the execution sequence of a program are supported by both the jump and branch instructions. The first instruction in Fig. 12.4 is the *jump* (JMP) instruction. The effect of executing this instruction is to load the program counter with the contents of the effective address specified by the operand in the instruction. Therefore, program execution resumes at the location specified by the effective address.

Mnemonic	Meaning	Format	Operand Size	Operation
JMP	Jump	JMP EA	$--$	$EA \rightarrow PC$
BRA	Branch always	BRA Label	8, 16	$PC + d \rightarrow PC$

Figure 12.4 Jump and branch always instructions.

An example of the instruction is

$$JMP \quad A0$$

In this case, program execution is directed to the instruction at the address specified by the contents of address register A_0. Only the control addressing modes can be used to specify the operand.

A second way of initiating unconditional changes in the program execution sequence is by means of the *branch always* (BRA) instruction. The format of this instruction is also shown in Fig. 12.4. Notice that BRA differs from JMP in the manner by which the address of the next instruction to be executed is encoded. In JMP, this address is specified directly by an EA operand. This permits it to reside in a data register or a storage location in memory. On the other hand, in BRA the difference between the address of the new instruction and that of the BRA instruction (displacement) is encoded following the opcode. Thus, for the BRA instruction the microprocessor computes the next address by adding the displacement to the current value in PC.

The branch instruction allows the displacement to be encoded either as an 8-bit (*short-form*) integer or 16-bit (*long-form*) integer. With an 8-bit displacement, the instruction is encoded as one word, but the branch to location must reside within $+129$ or -126 bytes of the current value in PC. On the other hand, the 16-bit displacement is encoded as a second instruction word, thereby making it a two-word instruction. This long displacement extends the range of the branch operation to $+32769$ to -32766 bytes relative to the current PC.

The programmer does not normally specify the displacement in the branch instruction. Instead, a label is written in the program to identify the branch to location. For example, the instruction

BRA   START

causes a transfer of program control to the instruction in the program with the label START. It is the duty of the assembler program to compute the actual displacement and encode it into the instruction. In this example, the displacement will be encoded as a 16-bit word. If displacement must be encoded as a byte, the instruction should be written as

BRA.S   START

JMP and BRA are called *unconditional branch* instructions. This is because the change in instruction sequence that they initiate takes place independent of any processor status.

Conditional Branch Instruction:Bcc

The 68000 provides a *conditional branch* instruction called *branch conditionally* (Bcc). As shown in Fig. 12.5(a), its general form is

Bcc   LABEL

Here cc is used to specify one of many conditional relationships. Figure 12.5(b) is a list of all the valid relationships and their mnemonics. For instance, selecting EQ we get the *branch on equal* (BEQ) instruction.

The conditional branch instruction passes control to the specified label only if the conditional relationship is true. In the example BEQ, the Z bit of SR is tested. If it is set, the branch takes place to the location specified by LABEL. If it is not set, the next sequential instruction is executed. The amount of displacement allowed with the conditional branch instruction is the same as for the branch always instruction.

Let us now consider an example. The instruction

BVS   START

means branch to the instruction identified by START if the overflow (V) bit is set. If V is not set, the instruction that follows the BVS instruction is executed. The displacement between the address of BVS plus two and the instruction with label START is computed by the assembler and encoded into the instruction as a 16-bit integer. For encoding the displacement as a byte, the instruction should be written as

Mnemonic	Meaning	Format	Operand Size	Operation
Bcc	Branch conditionally	Bcc Label	8, 16	$(PC) + d \rightarrow PC$ if cc is true; otherwise, next sequential instruction executes

(a)

Mnemonic	Meaning	Conditional Code Relationship
BCC	Branch if carry clear	$C = 0$
BCS	Branch if carry set	$C = 1$
BEQ	Branch if equal	$Z = 1$
BNE	Branch if not equal	$Z = 0$
BMI	Branch if minus	$N = 1$
BPL	Branch if plus	$N = 0$
BVC	Branch if overflow clear (signed)	$V = 0$
BVS	Branch if overflow set (signed)	$V = 1$
BHI	Branch if high (unsigned)	$\overline{C} \cdot \overline{Z} = 1$
BLS	Branch if less or same (unsigned)	$C + Z = 1$
BGT	Branch if greater than (signed)	$NV\overline{Z} + \overline{N}\,\overline{V}\,\overline{Z} = 1$
BGE	Branch if greater or equal (signed)	$NV + \overline{N}\,\overline{V} = 1$
BLT	Branch if less than (signed)	$N\overline{V} + \overline{N}V = 1$
BLE	Branch if less or equal (signed)	$Z + N\overline{V} + \overline{N}V = 1$

(b)

Figure 12.5 (a) Branch conditionally instruction; (b) conditional tests of the Bcc instruction.

BVS. S   START

EXAMPLE 12.2

It is required to move a set of N 16-bit data points that are stored in a block of memory that starts at location BLK1 to a new block that starts at location BLK2. Write a program to implement this operation.

SOLUTION The flowchart in Fig. 12.6(a) shows a plan for implementing the block move function. Initially, we set up two pointers, one for the beginning of BLK1 and the other for the beginning of BLK2. Address registers A_1 and A_2, respectively, can be used as these pointers. The count for the number of points to be moved is placed in D_0. This can be accomplished by the instruction sequence

```
LEA       BLK1, A1
LEA       BLK2, A2
MOVE. L   N, D0
```

To move a word from BLK1 to BLK2, we can use a move word instruction with address register indirect addressing with postincrement mode for both its source and destination operands. Moreover, each time a data point is moved, the count in D_0 must be decreased by 1. The move instruction must be repeated if the count has not reached zero. The instructions that follow will perform these operations.

```
NXTPT     MOVE.W    (A1)+, (A2)+
          SUBQ.L    #1,D0
          BNE       NXTPT
```

The entire program is shown in Fig. 12.6(b).

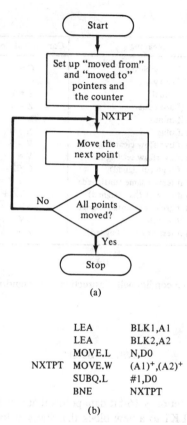

(a)

```
          LEA       BLK1,A1
          LEA       BLK2,A2
          MOVE.L    N,D0
NXTPT     MOVE.W    (A1)+,(A2)+
          SUBQ.L    #1,D0
          BNE       NXTPT
```

(b)

Figure 12.6 (a) Block transfer flow-chart; (b) program.

12.4 TEST CONDITION, DECREMENT, AND BRANCH INSTRUCTION

The program we considered in the preceding section was an example of a *software loop*. In the earlier example we found that when a software loop is executed, a group of instructions are executed repeatedly. The repetition may be unconditional or conditional. To design a loop, we can use the previously introduced compare, jump, and branch instructions. This was the approach employed in Example 12.2. However, the 68000 provides another instruction that is especially useful for handling loops. This instruction is called *test condition, decrement, and branch* (DBcc) and has the general form

DBcc   Dn, Label

Here cc represents the same conditions that were available for the Bcc instruction. They are listed in the table of Fig. 12.5(b). In fact, two more conditions, always true (T) and always false (F), are also available for the DBcc instruction. Dn is the data register that contains the count of how many times the loop is to be repeated, and Label identifies the location to which control is to be returned by the branch operation.

When the DBcc instruction is executed, first the condition identified by cc is tested. If it is true, no branch takes place; instead, the loop is terminated and the next sequential instruction is executed. On the other hand, if the condition is not true, the contents of the specified data register are decremented by 1. Then another test is performed. This one is on the count in Dn. If it is equal to -1, the branch does not take place because the loop operation has run to completion. In this case, execution continues with the next sequential instruction. However, if the count is not -1, program control branches to the location corresponding to Label.

An example of the instruction is as follows:

$$\text{DBLE} \quad \text{D0, NXTPT}$$

During the execution of this instruction, first the condition code bits of SR are tested to determine if the relationship

$$Z + N \cdot \overline{V} + \overline{N} \cdot V = 1$$

is satisfied. If true, the instruction following the DBLE instruction is executed. If false, D_0 is decremented. Next, D_0 is tested to determine if it has become -1. If it has, the next sequential instruction is executed. But if D_0 is any number other than -1, execution continues at the label NXTPT.

For example, if $Z = 0$, $N = 1$, $V = 1$, and the contents of D_0 are 03_{16}, the condition code relationship evaluates as

$$Z + N \cdot \overline{V} + \overline{N} \cdot V = 0 + 1 \cdot 0 + 0 \cdot 1$$
$$= 0$$

Since the result is 0, the relationship is false. Thus, the value in D_0 is decremented by 1, which gives 02_{16}, and tested for -1. Since D_0 does not contain -1, control is passed to the instruction corresponding to label NXTPT.

EXAMPLE 12.3

Given N data points that are signed 16-bit numbers stored in consecutive memory locations starting at address DATA, write a program that finds their average value. The average value that results is to be stored at location AVERAGE in memory . Assume that N is in the range $0 < N < 32K$.

SOLUTION A flowchart that solves this problem is shown in Fig. 12.7(a). It implements an algorithm that finds the average of N data points by adding their values and then dividing the sum by N.

Initially we set the sum, which will reside in D_7, to 0, the address pointer in A_1 to DATA so that it points to the first data point, and the counter in D_0 equal to $N - 1$. Notice that the value of the count is 1 less than the number of data to be processed.

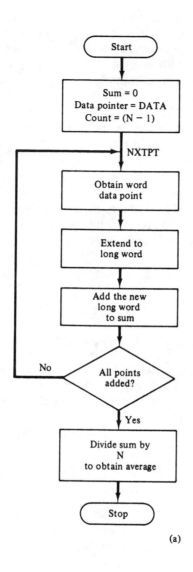

D_0 = counter
D_7 = sum
A_1 = pointer to data points
D_1 = temporary register for
    holding data point

(a)

```
        CLR.L      D7
        LEA        DATA,A1
        MOVE.L     #(N−1),D0
NXTPT   MOVE.W     (A1)⁺,D1
        EXT.L      D1
        ADD.L      D1,D7
        DBF        D0,NXTPT
        DIVS       #N,D7
        MOVE.W     D7,AVERAGE
```

(b)

Figure 12.7 (a) Flowchart of a program for finding the average of N signed numbers; (b) program.

The reason for this is that we intend to use the DBcc instruction that branches out of the loop when the count in a data register becomes equal to -1 and not 0. This initialization is performed by executing the following instructions

```
CLR.L      D7
LEA        DATA, A1
MOVE.L     #(N - 1), D0
```

To add a new data point to sum, we first move it into D_1. Since the data point is of word length, it must be sign extended to a long word before it can be added to the previous sum. Then the sign-extended data point in D_1 is added to the sum in D_7. Next the count in D_0 is decremented by 1 and checked to determine if it has become equal to -1. A value of -1 means that all points have been added. If it is not -1, there are still data points to be added and we must repeat the set of instructions that add a new data point. On the other hand, if the count shows that all points have been added, we are ready to divide the sum in D_7 by N to obtain the average. This value can then be moved from D_7 to the storage location AVERAGE in memory. All this can be done by the following sequence of instructions.

```
NXTPT   MOVE.W    (A1)+, D1
        EXT.L     D1
        ADD.L     D1, D7
        DBF       D0, NXTPT
        DIVS      #N, D7
        MOVE.W    D7, AVERAGE
```

The complete program is listed in Fig. 12.7(b).

12.5 SUBROUTINES AND SUBROUTINE-HANDLING INSTRUCTIONS

A *subroutine* is a segment of program separate from the main part of the program. It can be called upon to execute by the main program whenever its function is needed. The instructions provided to transfer control from the main program to a subroutine and return control back to the main program are called *subroutine-handling instructions*. Let us now examine the instructions provided for this purpose.

Subroutine Control Instructions: JSR, BSR, RTS, and RTR

The four subroutine-handling instructions of the 68000 microprocessor are shown in Fig. 12.8. These instructions include *jump to subroutine* (JSR), *branch to subroutine* (BSR), *return from subroutine* (RTS), and *return and restore condition codes* (RTR). These instructions provide for efficient subroutine handling and nesting.

The instructions jump to subroutine (JSR) and branch to subroutine (BSR) serve essentially the same purpose. This is to pass control to the starting point of a subroutine. As shown in Fig. 12.8 they both save the current contents of PC by pushing it to the active stack. This preserves a return address for use at completion of the subroutine. Then they pass control to the starting point of the subroutine.

These two instructions differ in how they specify the starting address of the subroutine. For the JSR instruction, this address is specified as an effective address and only the control addressing modes are allowed. Therefore, the starting address can reside in a data register, address register, or in either program or data storage memory. For instance, using address register indirect addressing through register A_1, we get

$$\text{JSR} \quad \text{(A1)}$$

Mnemonic	Meaning	Format	Operand Size	Operation
JSR	Jump to subroutine	JSR EA	32	PC → ⁻(SP) EA → PC
BSR	Branch to subroutine	BSR Label	8, 16	PC → ⁻(SP) PC + d → PC
RTS	Return from subroutine	RTS	——	(SP)⁺ → PC
RTR	Return and restore	RTR	——	(SP)⁺ → CCR (SP)⁺ → PC

Figure 12.8 Subroutine control instructions.

On the other hand, in the BSR instruction, the *displacement* between the current instruction and the first instruction of the subroutine is determined and encoded into the instruction. That is, it is stored in program storage memory. An example is

$$\text{BSR} \quad \text{STARTSUB}$$

Thus JSR provides the ability to jump to a subroutine that resides anywhere in the 16M-byte address space of the 68000. But BSR only permits branching to a subroutine that is located within the maximum allowable displacement value. The displacement can be either 8 bits for the short form of the BSR instruction or 16 bits for the long form.

The other two instructions return from subroutine (RTS) and return and restore (RTR) provide the means for returning from a subroutine back to the calling program. In Fig. 12.8 we see that executing RTS simply restores the program counter by popping the value that was saved on the active stack when the subroutine was called. The second instruction RTR restores both the condition code part of SR and PC from the stack. One of these instructions is always the last instruction of a subroutine.

EXAMPLE 12.4

In a Fibonacci series, the first number is 0, the second is 1, and each subsequent number is obtained by adding the previous two numbers. For example, the first 10 numbers of the series are

0, 1, 1, 2, 3, 5, 8, 13, 21, 34

Write a program to generate the first 20 elements of a Fibonacci series. The numbers of the series are to be stored at consecutive locations in memory starting at address FIBSER. Use a subroutine to implement the part of the procedure by which the next number of the series is obtained from the previous two numbers.

SOLUTION A flowchart for this program together with the assignments of various registers is shown in Fig. 12.9(a). The first part of the program initializes the registers and stores the first two numbers. The instructions used for this purpose are

MOVE.L	#$11,D0	SET THE COUNTER TO 17
LEA	FIBSER,A1	SET THE POINTER TO FIBSER
CLR.W	D1	D1 = 0
MOVEQ.W	#1,D2	D2 = 1
MOVE.W	D1,(A1)+	STORE THE FIRST NUMBER
MOVE.W	D2,(A1)+	STORE THE SECOND NUMBER

The next-to-last instruction causes 0 to be loaded into address FIBSER and increments the pointer in A_1 by 2 such that it points to the storage location of the next number in the series. Then a similar instruction is executed to load FIBSER+2 with 1 and A_1 is again incremented.

We are now ready to call the subroutine that does the addition to form the next number in the series. Since the subroutine will be called repeatedly, the BRS instruction is identified by a label to which the program can loop back. This instruction is

NXTNM   BRS.S   SBRTF

The subroutine starts at the instruction with label SBRTF. The purpose of the subroutine is to add the contents of D_1 and D_2 so that the next number in the series is generated, temporarily save this number in D_3, and then return back to the main program. This can be done by the instruction sequence

SBRTF	ADD.W	D2,D1
	MOVE.W	D1,D3
	RTS	

At this point in the main program, we get ready for generating the next number. This is done by saving the contents of D_2 in D_1 and that of D_3 in D_2. Next we save the new number that was generated in D_3 by moving it to memory. To do this, the instructions are

MOVE.W	D2,D1
MOVE.W	D3,D2
MOVE.W	D3,(A1)+

Now the count in D_0 is decremented and tested for -1. If it is not equal to -1, we loop back to the label NXTNM. However, if it is -1, we are done. The instruction for this is

	DBF	D0,NXTNM
DONE	BRA	DONE

The entire program is repeated in Fig. 12.9(b).

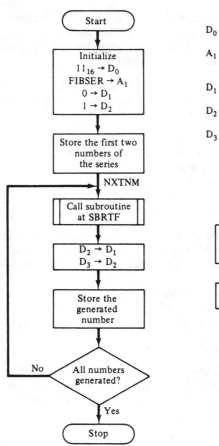

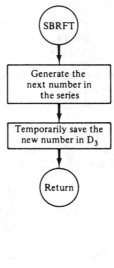

D_0 = counter for the numbers to be generated

A_1 = pointer to the address at which the number is to be stored

D_1 = first number used in the generation

D_2 = second number used in the generation

D_3 = generated number

(a)

```
              MOVE.L      #$11,D0
              LEA         FIBSER,A1
              CLR.W       D1
              MOVEQ.W     #1,D2
              MOVE.W      D1,(A1)+
              MOVE.W      D2,(A1)+
NXTNM         BSR.S       SBRTF
              MOVE.W      D2,D1
              MOVE.W      D3,D2
              MOVE.W      D3,(A1)+
              DBF         D0,NXTNM
DONE          BRA         DONE
SBRTF         ADD.W       D2,D1
              MOVE.W      D1,D3
              RTS
```

(b)

Figure 12.9 (a) Flowchart for the Fibonacci series program; (b) program.

Link and Unlink Instructions: LINK and UNLK

Before the main program calls a subroutine, quite often it is necessary for the calling program to pass the values of some *variables* (*parameters*) to the subroutine. It is a common practice to push these variables onto the stack before calling the routine. Then during the execution of the subroutine, they are accessed by reading them from the stack and used in computations. Two instructions are provided to allocate and deallocate a data area called a *frame* in the stack part of memory. This data area is used for local storage of parameters or other data. The two instructions, as shown in Fig. 12.10 are *link and allocate* (LINK) and *unlink* (UNLK). They make the process of passing and retrieving parameters much easier.

Mnemonic	Meaning	Format	Operation
LINK	Link and allocate	LINK An, d	$An \rightarrow {}^-(SP)$ $SP \rightarrow An$ $SP - d \rightarrow SP$
UNLK	Unlink	UNLK An	$An \rightarrow SP$ $(SP)^+ \rightarrow An$

Figure 12.10 Link and unlink instructions.

The LINK instruction is used at the beginning of a subroutine to create a data frame. Looking at the format of the instruction in Fig. 12.10, we see that it has two operands. The one denoted A_n is always an address register. The address held in A_n is known as the *frame pointer,* and it points to the lowest addressed storage location in the data frame. The other operand is an immediate operand that specifies the value of a displacement. This displacement specifies the size of the data space. Since it can be as long as 16 bits, a *frame data space* can be as large as 32K words.

As example of this instruction is

```
LINK    A1,-#$A
```

Execution of this instruction causes the current contents of A_1 to be pushed onto the active stack; then the updated contents of the active SP register are loaded into A_1; finally, A_{16} is subtracted from the new value in SP.

Figure 12.11 shows what happens by executing this instruction. First we see that pushing the contents of A_1 to the stack saves the frame pointer for the prior data frame. This is identified as "Prior frame pointer" and is stored at A_{1new}. Loading A_1 with the contents of SP establishes a frame pointer to the new data frame. Subtracting the displacement from (SP) modifies the stack pointer so that the active stack is located in memory just below the data frame. Since the displacement is A_{16}, the data frame is 10 bytes in length.

The frame pointer A_1 provides a fixed reference into the data frame and old stack. Parameters that were loaded into the stack prior to calling the subroutine can be accessed using address register indirect with displacement addressing for the operand. For example, the instruction

```
MOVE.W    4(A1),D0
```

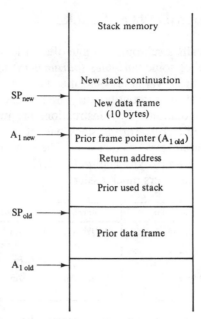

Stack memory

New stack continuation

SP_{new} → New data frame
(10 bytes)

$A_{1\,new}$ → Prior frame pointer ($A_{1\,old}$)

Return address

Prior used stack

SP_{old} →

Prior data frame

$A_{1\,old}$ →

Figure 12.11 Creation of a data frame with the link instruction.

causes the word parameter stored four bytes from frame pointer A_1 to be copied into D_0. This parameter is in the old stack.

After performing the operation defined by the subroutine and just before returning to the calling program, the prior data frame must be restored. The UNLK instruction is used for this purpose. Notice in Fig. 12.10 that it causes address register A_n, which is used for the frame pointer, to be loaded into the active stack pointer register. Then the address held at the top of the stack is popped into A_n.

For our example, the unlink instruction would be

        UNLK   A1

Earlier we pointed out that execution of the LINK instruction saved the old frame pointer on the stack and then created a new data frame. Executing UNLK A1 causes SP to be loaded from A_1. Looking at Fig. 12.11 we find that the stack pointer now points to the location of the prior frame pointer. Then A_1 is loaded from the stack. Therefore, the prior frame pointer is put back in A_1 and the prior stack and data frame environment is restored.

To understand this concept better, let us consider the example illustrated in Fig. 12.12. As we begin to execute the first instruction of the program segment shown in Fig. 12.12(a), we will assume that the active SP points to the top of the data frame identified in Fig. 12.12(b) as local storage area for the calling routine. Execution of the first two instructions

        MOVE.W   D0, - (SP)
        MOVE.W   D1, - (SP)

passes the contents of D_0 and D_1 as parameters onto the stack. Looking at Fig.

```
              MOVE.W        D0, ⁻(SP)              parameter 1 passed to stack
              MOVE.W        D1, ⁻(SP)              parameter 2 passed to stack
    AA        JSR           SBRT                   call subroutine SBRT
              •             •
              •             •
              •             •
              •             •
              •             •

    SBRT      LINK          A0, ⁻#$8               FP and local storage established for called routine
              •             •
              •             •
              MOVE.W        10(A0), D5             parameter 1 accessed
              •             •
              •             •
              UNLK        ᐧ A0                     FP for the calling routine established
              RTS                                  return to main program
```

(a)

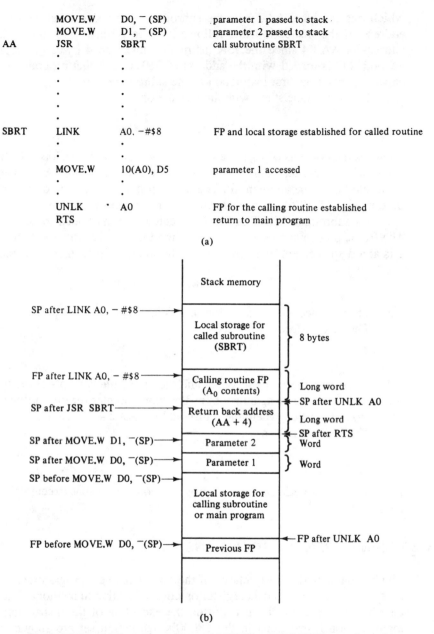

(b)

Figure 12.12 (a) Example program with LINK and UNLINK instructions; (b) stack for the example program.

12.12(b), we see that at the completion of these two instructions SP points to the location where parameter 2 is stored.

The next instruction,

JSR   SBRT

which has the label AA, calls the subroutine starting at label SBRT. It causes the address of the instruction that follows it to be pushed onto the stack. This return address is AA+4 since the JSR instruction takes up 4 bytes of program memory. Second, PC is loaded with the address of SBRT such that program control picks up execution from the first instruction of the subroutine.

The subroutine starts with the instruction

LINK   A0,−#$8

It causes the contents of A_0 to be saved on the stack and then loads A_0 from the active stack pointer register. This sets up a new frame pointer FP (A_0 register). Then 8 is subtracted from the value in SP. Therefore, it points to the top of the data area identified in Fig. 12.12(b) as *local storage* for the called subroutine.

As subroutine SBRT is being executed, we may need to access parameter 1. The frame pointer serves as a reference into the called routines data frame. Parameter 1 is at a displacement of 10 bytes from the frame pointer; therefore, the instruction

MOVE.W   10(A0),D5

can be used to access it. Execution of this instruction copies parameter 1 into D_5.

The next instruction we see is

UNLK   A0

It loads SP with the contents of A_0 and then pops the contents at the top of the stack into A_0. Now A_0 once again contains the frame pointer for the calling routine and SP points to the location where the return address AA+4 is stored.

The last instruction

RTS

loads the return address into the program counter so that execution resumes in the calling routine.

12.6 BIT MANIPULATION INSTRUCTIONS

The bit manipulation instructions of the 68000 enable a programmer to test the logic level of a bit in either a data register or storage location in memory. The tested bit can also be set, reset, or changed during the execution of the instruction. The four bit manipulation instructions in the 68000's instruction set are shown in Fig. 12.13. They are *test a bit* (BTST), *test a bit and set* (BSET), *test a bit and clear* (BCLR), and *test a bit and change* (BCHG).

Test a Bit Instruction: BTST

The test a bit (BTST) instruction has the ability to test any one bit in a 32-bit data register or any one bit of a byte storage location in memory. The logic state of the tested bit is inverted and copied into the Z bit of SR. That is, when the bit is tested as 1, Z is set to 0 or when the bit is tested as 0, Z is set to 1. The two valid forms of the BTST instruction are shown in Fig. 12.13. In both forms, the destination operand, which contains the bit to be tested, is specified by an effective address.

Mnemonic	Meaning	Format	Operand Size	Operation
BTST	Test a bit	BTST #XXX,EA BTST Dn,EA	8, 32 8, 32	$\overline{\text{EA bit}} \to \text{Z}$
BSET	Test a bit and set	BSET #XXX,EA BSET Dn,EA	8, 32 8, 32	$\overline{\text{EA bit}} \to \text{Z}$ $1 \to \text{EA bit}$
BCLR	Test a bit and clear	BCLR #XXX,EA BCLR Dn,EA	8, 32 8, 32	$\overline{\text{EA bit}} \to \text{Z}$ $0 \to \text{EA bit}$
BCHG	Test a bit and change	BCHG #XXX,EA BCHG Dn,EA	8, 32 8, 32	$\overline{\text{EA bit}} \to \text{Z}$ $\overline{\text{EA bit}} \to \text{EA bit}$

Figure 12.13 Bit-manipulation instructions.

These two forms differ in the way the number of the bit to be tested is specified. In the first form, the number of the bit is supplied as an immediate source operand that gets coded as part of the instruction in program memory. An example is the instruction

BTST   #5,D7

Execution of this instruction tests bit 5 in data register D_7. The complement of the value found in this bit position is copied into Z. For example, if D_7 contains 25_{16}, that is

$$D_7 = 00000000000000000000000001001012$$

bit 5 is logic 1. Thus, the complement of 1, which is 0, is copied into the Z flag.

The second form uses the contents of one of the data registers to specify the bit position. For instance, if D_0 contains number 5, then executing the instruction

BTST   D0,D7

produces the same result as the instruction that employed an immediate operand.

Other Test Bit Instructions: BSET, BCLR, and BCHG

The other instructions in Fig. 12.13, BSET, BCLR, and BCHG, operate similarly to BTST. However, they not only copy the complement of the tested bit into Z, but also set, clear, or invert the bit in the destination operand, respectively.

An example is the instruction

BSET   #7,(A1)

When this instruction is executed, bit 7 of the memory location pointed to by (A1) is tested. The complement of its logic level is copied into Z and then bit 7 is set to 1. For instance, if the byte memory location pointed to by the address in A_1 contains $7F_{16}$, which is 01111111_2 in binary form, bit 7 is logic 0. Therefore, execution of the instruction causes Z to be set to 1 and the contents of the memory location to be changed to FF_{16}.

When a memory bit is addressed, BTST allows use of the data addressing modes to specify the effective address of the destination operand. The instructions BSET, BCLR, and BCHG allow the use of data-alterable addressing modes for EA.

Test and Set Operand Instruction: TAS

Another instruction that is similar to the test bit instruction is *test and set operand* (TAS). As shown in Fig. 12.14 TAS differs from BTST in that it tests a byte operand in a data register or storage location in memory. The test is performed by comparing the operand with zero and setting or resetting condition code bits N and Z based on the result. N is set to the logic level of the most significant bit of the operand and Z is set if the operand is zero. Second, independent of the result of the test, the most significant bit of the accessed byte is set to 1. An example is the instruction

TAS   D0

Mnemonic	Meaning	Format	Operand Size	Operation
TAS	Test and set an operand	TAS EA	8	If destination is zero, $1 \rightarrow Z$; otherwise, $0 \rightarrow Z$ If destination is negative, $1 \rightarrow N$; otherwise, $0 \rightarrow N$ $0 \rightarrow V$ $0 \rightarrow C$ $1 \rightarrow$ most significant bit of byte addressed by EA

Figure 12.14   TAS instruction.

The TAS instruction is specifically designed to support *multiprocessing* and *multitasking system environments*. For instance, in a multiprocessing system, a bit called a semaphore in a byte in memory is set for resolving which processor can access a memory section reserved for a specific resource. If a processor needs to access this resource, it will first test and set the memory byte. If the resource is already in use, the test will indicate that condition and the processor can wait until it is available. Once it is done using the resource, it resets the *semaphore* bit, thus allowing access by other processors. This is illustrated in Fig. 12.15.

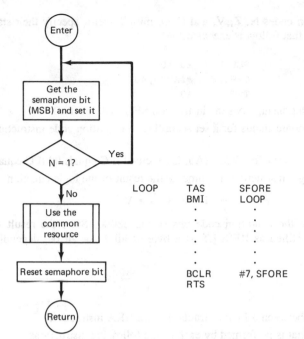

```
                LOOP    TAS     SFORE
                        BMI     LOOP
                        .       .
                        .       .
                        .       .
                        .       .
                        .       .
                        BCLR    #7, SFORE
                        RTS
```

Figure 12.15 Use of TAS for multi-processing.

ASSIGNMENT

Section 12.2

1. Which status bits are used to reflect the result of a compare instruction?
2. Describe the operation that is performed by each of the instructions that follows:
   (a) CMP.B $10000, D0   **(c)** CMPI.W   #$1234, (A0)
   (b) CMPA.W D1, A0   **(d)** CMPM.B   (A1)+, (A2)+
3. What are the states of the 68000's condition code bits after executing the instructions in Problem 2. Assume that the following initial state exists before executing each instruction.

$$D0 = FFFFFFFF_{16}$$
$$D1 = 00001000_{16}$$
$$A0 = 00010010_{16}$$
$$A1 = 00010020_{16}$$
$$A2 = 00010030_{16}$$
$$N = Z = V = C = 0$$

4. Which bits of SR are used to reflect the result of a test instruction?
5. What operation is performed by the instruction

   TST.L   (A0)

6. Write a test instruction that will perform a test operation on the word contents of memory location 100010_{16}.

7. Assuming that condition codes N, Z, V, and C are initially zero, specify their status as each of the instructions that follow is executed.

```
SUB.L    A0,A0
CMPI.W   #$A000,A0
TST      A0
```

8. What condition code relationship does the instruction SEQ D0 test for?

9. Which instruction mnemonic stands for a set according to condition code instruction that tests for N equals 0?

10. What happens when the instruction SCC (A0) is executed if C equals 0? If C equals 1?

11. Use move, shift, and logic instructions to compute the result of the logic equation

$$F = Z + N \bullet \overline{V} + \overline{N} \bullet V$$

where N, V, and Z are the condition code bits of the 68000. Store the result F at a location in memory identified as RESULT as a byte of all 1s or all 0s, depending on whether F is 1 or 0.

Section 12.3

12. Describe the difference between a JMP instruction and a BRA instruction.

13. Describe the operation that is performed by each of the following instructions:
(a) JMP $10000
(b) JMP   5(A0)
(c) JMP   (A0,A1.B)

14. Assume the following initial state exists before executing each instruction in Problem 13.

$$A0 = 00010010_{16}$$
$$A1 = 00000020_{16}$$

To what address is program control passed by executing each jump instruction?

15. What is the maximum-size jump that can be coded with a short-form displacement? With a long-form displacement?

16. Describe the operation that is performed by the instruction

```
BRA      SERVICE_ROUTINE
```

where the value of SERVICE_ROUTINE equals 40_{16}.

17. Identify whether the jump or branch performed by the JMP, BRA, and Bcc instructions is unconditional or conditional.

18. What condition code relationship does the instruction BMI SERVICE_ROUTINE test for?

19. Write an instruction that will branch to the service routine OUT_OF_RANGE if an unsigned integer is too high?

20. Consider the delay loop program that follows:

```
         MOVE.B   #$10,D7
DLY      SUBQ.B   #1,D7
         BGT      DLY
NXT      —        —
```

(a) How many times is the instruction BGT DLY executed?

(b) Change the program so that BGT DLY is executed just 17 times.

(c) Change the program so that BGT DLY is executed 2^{32} times.

Section 12.4

21. What instruction does the mnemonic DBCS stand for?

22. What condition code relationship does the instruction DBLS D0,OUT_OF_RANGE test for?

23. Describe the operation performed by the instruction in Problem 22 if D_0 contains the value 00000000_{16}.

24. Given a number N in the range $0 < N \leq 5$, write a program that computes its factorial and saves the result in the memory location corresponding to FACT.

25. Write a program that compares the elements of two array, A(I) and B(I). Each array contains one hundred 16-bit integer numbers. The comparison is to be done by comparing the corresponding elements of the two arrays until either two elements are found to be unequal or all elements of the arrays have been compared and found to be equal. Assume that the arrays start at addresses $A000 and $B000, respectively. If the two arrays are found to be unequal, save the address of the first unequal element of A(I) at memory location FOUND. On the other hand, if all elements are equal, write a byte of 0s into FOUND.

26. Given an array A(I) with one hundred 16-bit signed numbers, write a program to generate two new arrays, P(J) and N(K). P(J) is to contain all the positive numbers from A(I), and N(K) is to contain all of its negative numbers. A(I) starts at address $A000 in memory and the two new arrays, P(J) and N(K), are to start at addresses $B000 and $C000, respectively.

27. Given an array A(I) of one hundred 16-bit signed integers, write a program to generate a new array, B(I), according to the following directions:

$$B(I) = A(I), \qquad \text{for I} = 1, 2, 99, \text{ and } 100$$

and

$$B(I) = \text{ median of } A(I - 2), A(I - 1), A(I), A(I + 1), \text{ and } A(I + 2),$$
$$\text{for all other I's}$$

Section 12.5

28. Describe the difference between the JSR and BSR instructions.

29. What gets automatically pushed to the stack when a BSR instruction is executed?

30. How large is the short-form displacement for a BSR instruction? The long-form displacement?

31. Describe the difference between the RTS and RTR instructions.

32. Write a subroutine the converts a given 32-bit binary number to its equivalent BCD number. The binary number is to be passed to the subroutine as a parameter in D_7, and the subroutine also returns the result in D_7.

33. Given an array A(I) of 100 signed 16-bit integer numbers, generate another array B(I) given by

$$B(I) = A(I), \qquad \text{for I} = 1 \text{ and } 100$$

and

$$B(I) = 1/4(A(I - 1) + 2A(I) + A(I + 1)), \qquad \text{for all other I's}$$

Use a subroutine to generate the terms of B(I). Parameters $A(I - 1)$, $A(I)$, and $A(I + 1)$ are to be passed to the subroutine on the stack, and the subroutine returns the result B(I) on the stack.

34. What is the data area created by the LINK instruction called?

35. What points to the lowest addressed storage location in the data area created with the LINK instruction?

36. What specifies the size of the data area set up with the LINK instruction?

37. Describe the operations performed when the instruction

```
LINK    A3, #$7
```

gets executed.

Section 12.6

38. Write an instruction that will perform a test and set operation on bit 5 in the byte-wide memory location at address 10000_{16}.

39. If the memory location pointed to by address 10000_{16} in the instruction written for Problem 38 contains the value 90_{16}, what happens when the instruction is executed?

40. Rewrite the instruction for Problem 38 such that the bit position to be tested is specified by data register D_3 instead of as an immediate operand.

41. What operation is performed when the instruction

```
BCLR    #4, 5 (A3)
```

is executed?

42. What happens to the contents of D_0 and the Z flag when the instruction

```
BCHG    #3, D0
```

is executed. Assume that D_0 contains the value $000F_{16}$.

43. Write the segment of main program and show its subroutine structure to perform the following operations. The program is to check repeatedly the three least significant bits of D_0 and, depending on their settings, executes one of three subroutines: SUBA, SUBB, or SUBC. The subroutines are selected according to the priority that follows:

3 LSB of D_0	Execute
XX1	SUBA
X10	SUBB
100	SUBC

If a subroutine is executed, before returning to the main program, the corresponding bit or bits in register D_0 are to be cleared. After returning from the subroutine, the main program continues.

13

The 68000 Microprocessor: Memory and Input/Output Interfaces

13.1 INTRODUCTION

The preceding three chapters were devoted to the software architecture of the 68000, its instruction set, and assembly language programming. In this chapter we study the *memory and input/output interfaces* of this microprocessor together with the instructions that are provided to perform I/O operations. In particular, the following topics are the subject of this chapter:

1. 68000 microprocessor
2. Interfaces of the 68000 microprocessor
3. Clock input and waveform
4. Asynchronous memory and I/O interface
5. Hardware organization of the address space
6. Program and data storage memory and the function codes
7. Memory and I/O read and write cycles
8. 64K-byte software-refreshed dynamic RAM subsystem
9. I/O instruction: MOVEP
10. 6821 peripheral interface adapter
11. Asynchronous bus interface I/O circuitry
12. Dual 16-Bit ports for the 68000 microcomputer using 6821s
13. Synchronous memory and I/O interface

13.2 THE 68000 MICROPROCESSOR

The 68000 is a very powerful 16-bit microprocessor whose development was announced by Motorola, Inc., in 1979. Since then Motorola has concentrated on bringing the device up to production, providing tools to support hardware and software development, and developing a new family of LSI support peripherals. With apparent success in these areas, they have continued the growth of the product family by introducing other microprocessors, such as the 68008, 68010, 68020, and 68030.

The 68000 is manufactured using HMOS (high-density N-channel MOS) technology. The present-day advances in circuit design, process technology, and chip fabrication techniques have enabled Motorola to implement very high performance operation and complex functions for the 68000. The circuitry within the 68000 is equivalent to approximately 68000 MOS transistors.

The 68000 microprocessor is packaged into a 64-pin package. This package is shown together with its pin assignments in Fig. 13.1. Notice that use of this large package eliminates the need for multifunction pins. For instance, the address bus and data bus are not multiplexed. The fact that each lead serves just one electrical function simplifies design of the external hardware interfaces in a 68000 microcomputer system.

The 68000 employs a very powerful 32-bit general-purpose internal architecture. It has 15 internal general-purpose registers that are all 32 bits in length. Eight of these registers are *data registers* and the other seven are *address registers*.

The architecture of the 68000 was planned to permit all types of data and address operations to be performed from its data registers and address registers, respectively. That is, none of its data registers has dedicated functions such as for use as an accumulator or for input/output. Therefore, instructions can be written such that their operands reside in any of the data registers or storage locations in memory. Moreover, data processed by the 68000 can be expressed in five different types. They are *bit, BCD (4-bit), byte, word,* and *long word (32-bit)*.

The address registers are also designed for general use and do not have dedicated functions. For instance, if the MOVE instruction was to have its source operand located in memory instead of in one of the internal registers, any one of the address registers can be specified to contain this address.

The architecture of the 68000 includes a number of powerful hardware and software functions. From a hardware point of view, we see that the 68000 has a large 23-bit external address bus. This gives it a very large 16M-byte logical address space. A software function that has been included in the architecture is the ability to create a *user/supervisor environment* for the 68000 microcomputer system. This feature helps the programmer to protect the operating system software and provides support for *multiprocessing* and *multitasking* applications.

13.3 INTERFACES OF THE 68000 MICROPROCESSOR

Now that we have briefly introduced the 68000 microprocessor, let us look at its electrical interfaces. From the block diagram in Fig. 13.2, we see that the signal lines

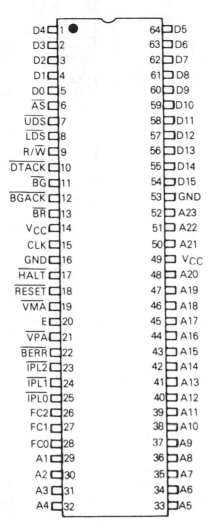

Figure 13.1 Pin layout of the 68000 microprocessor. (Courtesy of Motorola, Inc.)

can be grouped into seven interfaces: the *address/data bus, asynchronous bus control, processor status lines, system control bus, interrupt control bus, bus arbitration control bus,* and *synchronous control bus.* It is through these buses and lines that the 68000 is connected to external circuitry such as memory and input/output peripherals.

Address and Data Bus

Earlier we pointed out that the 68000 microprocessor has independent address and data buses. This simplifies the design of the memory and I/O interfaces because the address and data signals need not be demultiplexed with external circuitry. Moreover, the address bus, data bus, and memory address space are used to interface to input/output devices in addition to interface to the memory subsystem. That is, all I/O devices in the 68000 microcomputer system are memory mapped.

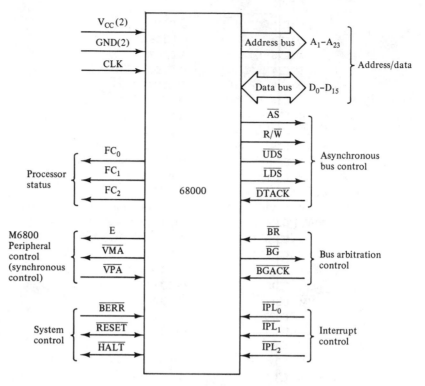

Figure 13.2 Block diagram of the 68000 microprocessor. (Courtesy of Motorola, Inc.)

Earlier we indicated that the 68000 has a 23-bit *unidirectional address bus*. The function of the signals at these lines, A_{23} through A_1, is to supply addresses to the memory and input/output subsystems. A_{23} represents the most significant bit of the address and A_1 the least significant bit. Bit A_0, which is maintained internal to the 68000, indicates whether the upper or lower byte of a word is to be used when processing byte data.

The 16 *bidirectional data lines* are labeled D_{15} through D_0. They either carry read/write data between microprocessor and memory or input/output data between the microprocessor and I/O peripherals.

Asynchronous Control Bus

The control of the 68000's bus is *asynchronous*. By this we mean that once a bus cycle is initiated, it is not completed until a signal is returned from external circuitry. The signals that are provided to control address and data transfers are *address strobe* ($\overline{AS}$), *red/write* (R/$\overline{W}$), *upper data strobe* ($\overline{UDS}$), *lower data strobe* ($\overline{LDS}$), and *data transfer acknowledge* ($\overline{DTACK}$).

The 68000 must signal external circuitry when an address is available and whether a read or write operation is to take place over the bus. It does this with the signals $\overline{AS}$ and R/$\overline{W}$, respectively. At the moment a valid address is present on the address bus, the 68000 produces the address strobe ($\overline{AS}$) control signal. The pulse to logic 0 that is output as $\overline{AS}$ is used to signal memory or I/O devices that an address is available.

Read/write (R/$\overline{W}$) signals which type of data transfer is to take place over the data bus. During a read or input bus cycle, when the microprocessor reads data from bus lines D_0 through D_{15}, the R/$\overline{W}$ output is switched to logic 1. Similarly, when data are written or output to memory or I/O devices, the 68000 indicates this condition by a logic 0 on this line.

Since the bus cycle is asynchronous, external circuitry must signal the 68000 when the bus cycle can be completed. Data transfer acknowledge ($\overline{DTACK}$) is an input to the microprocessor that indicates the status of the current bus cycle. During a read or input cycle, logic 0 at $\overline{DTACK}$ signals the microprocessor that valid data are on the data bus. In response, it reads and latches the data internally and completes the bus cycle. On the other hand, during a write or output operation, $\overline{DTACK}$ informs the microprocessor that the data have been written to memory or a peripheral device. Thus we see that in both cases $\overline{DTACK}$ is used to terminate the bus cycle.

Two other control outputs provided on the 68000 are upper data strobe ($\overline{UDS}$) and lower data strobe ($\overline{LDS}$). These two signals act as an extension of the address bus and signal whether a byte or word of data is being transferred over the data bus. In the case of a byte transfer, they also indicate if the data will be carried over the upper eight or lower eight data lines. Logic 0 at $\overline{UDS}$ signals that a byte of data is to be transferred across upper data lines D_{15} through D_8, and logic 0 at $\overline{LDS}$ signals that a byte of data is to be transferred over lower data lines D_7 through D_0.

Figure 13.3 shows the logic levels of $\overline{UDS}$, $\overline{LDS}$, and R/$\overline{W}$ for each type of data transfer operation. For instance, if $\overline{UDS} = 0$, $\overline{LDS} = 0$, and R/$\overline{W} = 1$, a read operation is taking place over the complete data bus.

$\overline{UDS}$	$\overline{LDS}$	R/$\overline{W}$	Operation
0	0	0	Word → memory/IO
0	1	0	High byte → memory/IO
1	0	0	Low byte → memory/IO
1	1	0	Invalid data
0	0	1	Word → microprocessor
0	1	1	High byte → microprocessor
1	0	1	Low byte → microprocessor
1	1	1	Invalid data

Figure 13.3 Memory access relationships for $\overline{UDS}$, $\overline{LDS}$, and R/$\overline{W}$ (Courtesy of Motorola, Inc.)

EXAMPLE 13.1

Specify the address and control signals that occur to read the lower byte from the word stored at address $001B36_{16}$.

SOLUTION The address lines A_{23} through A_1 directly specify an even (upper) byte address. The odd (lower) byte address is obtained by $\overline{LDS}$ being active. Thus we get

$$A_{23}A_{22} \ldots A_1A_0 = 001B37_{16}$$

$$= 0000000000011011001101111_2$$

and

$$\overline{LDS} = 0$$

$$\overline{UDS} = 1$$

Since a byte of data is to be read,

$$R/\overline{W} = 1$$

and the data are supplied to the 68000 on the lower data lines D_0 through D_7.

Processor Status Bus and the Function Codes

During every bus cycle executed by the 68000, it outputs a 3-bit processor status code. These status codes are also known as *function codes* and are output on lines FC_0 through FC_2. They tell external circuitry which type of bus cycle is in progress, that is, whether data or program is being accessed and if the microprocessor is in the *user* or *supervisor state*.

The table in Fig. 13.4(a) shows the implemented fuction codes and also the ones that are reserved for future expansion. For instance, the code 110_2 on

FC2	FC1	FC0	Cycle Type
Low	Low	Low	(Undefined, Reserved)
Low	Low	High	User Data
Low	High	Low	User Program
Low	High	High	(Undefined, Reserved)
High	Low	Low	(Undefined, Reserved)
High	Low	High	Supervisor Data
High	High	Low	Supervisor Program
High	High	High	Interrupt Acknowledge

(a)

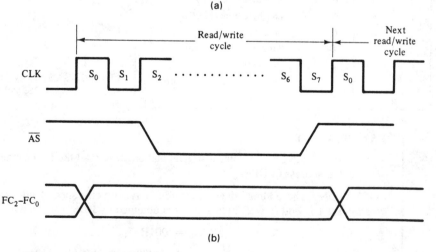

(b)

Figure 13.4 (a) Function code table (courtesy of Motorola, Inc.); (b) relationship between $FC_2FC_1FC_0$, CLK, and $\overline{AS}$.

$FC_2FC_1FC_0$ indicates that an instruction or immediate operand aquisition bus cycle is in progress from *supervisor program memory*. Notice that 111_2 has a special function. It is the *interrupt acknowledge code*.

These codes are output by the 68000 at the beginning of each read or write cycle and remain valid until the beginning of the next read or write cycle. The timing relationship between the function code lines, the clock, and $\overline{AS}$ is shown in Fig. 13.4(b). Notice that the function code outputs are valid during the address strobe $\overline{AS}$ pulse. Therefore, they can be combined with $\overline{AS}$ to generate device or memory select signals. As an example, the function code 001_2 can be used to gate AS to the user data section of memory.

System Control Bus

The group of control signals that are labeled as the system control bus in Fig. 13.2 are used either to control the function of the 68000 microprocessor or to indicate its operating state. There are three system control signals: *bus error* ($\overline{BERR}$), *halt* ($\overline{HALT}$), and *reset* ($\overline{RESET}$).

The control line bus error ($\overline{BERR}$) is an input that is used to inform the 68000 of a problem with the bus cycle currently in progress. For instance, it could be used to signal that the bus cycle has not been completed even after a set period of time has elapsed.

On the other hand, $\overline{HALT}$ can be used to implement a hardware mechanism for stopping the processing of the 68000. An external signal applied to the $\overline{HALT}$ input stops the microprocessor at completion of the current bus cycle. In this state all its buses and control signals are inactive. $\overline{HALT}$ is actually a bidirectional line; that is, it has both an input and output function. When the processor stops instruction execution due to a halt condition, it informs external devices by producing an output signal at the same $\overline{HALT}$ pin.

The $\overline{RESET}$ input can be used to initiate initialization of the 68000 based on the occurrence of a signal generated in external hardware. Typically, this is done at the time of power-up. When an external reset signal is applied, the processor initiates a system initialization sequence.

The $\overline{RESET}$ line is also bidirectional, but unlike $\overline{HALT}$, its output function is initiated through software. This $\overline{RESET}$ output is used to initialize external devices such as LSI peripherals. To reset external devices connected to the $\overline{RESET}$ line, the 68000 must execute the RESET instruction. Execution of this instruction does not affect the internal state of the processor; instead, it just causes a pulse to be output at $\overline{RESET}$.

Interrupt Control Bus

In a 68000 microcomputer system, external devices request interrupt service by applying a 3-bit *interrupt request code* to the $\overline{IPL_2}$ through $\overline{IPL_0}$ inputs. This code is supplied to the microprocessor from the interrupting device to indicate its priority level. The value of $\overline{IPL_2}\overline{IPL_1}\overline{IPL_0}$ is compared to the interrupt mask value in the 68000's status register. If the encoded priority is higher than the mask, the interrupting device is serviced; otherwise, it is ignored.

Bus Arbitration Control Bus

The bus arbitration control signals provide a handshake mechanism by which control of the 68000's system bus can be transferred between devices. The device that has control of the system bus is known as the *bus master*. It controls the system address, data, and control buses. Other devices are attached to the bus but are not active. Examples of devices that can be used as masters are host processors or external devices such as *DMA controllers* or *attached processors*.

As shown in Fig. 13.2, the 68000 microprocessor has three control lines for this purpose. They are *bus request* ($\overline{BR}$), *bus grant* ($\overline{BG}$), and *bus grant acknowledge* ($\overline{BGACK}$). A device requests control of the bus by asserting the bus request ($\overline{BR}$) input. After synchronization, the 68000 responds by switching the bus grant ($\overline{BG}$) control output to its active low level. This means that it will give up control of the bus at completion of the current bus cycle.

At this point, the requesting device waits for the 68000 to complete its bus cycle. The fact that the bus cycle is complete is indicated by address strobe ($\overline{AS}$) and data transfer acknowledge ($\overline{DTACK}$) returning to their inactive levels. After this happens, the requesting device asserts bus grant acknowledge ($\overline{BGACK}$) and also removes bus grant request ($\overline{BR}$). The 68000 responds by removing the bus grant ($\overline{BG}$) signal. This completes the bus arbitration handshake. The requesting device has now taken over control of the bus and assumes the role of bus master. When the device has completed its function, it releases control of the bus by negating $\overline{BGACK}$ for rearbitration or return of bus mastership to the 68000.

Synchronous Control Bus

The 68000 microprocessor also has control signals that can make data transfers over its system bus occur in a synchronous fashion. Three control signals are provided for this purpose. In Fig. 13.2, we see that they are *enable* (E), *valid peripheral address* ($\overline{VPA}$), and *valid memory address* ($\overline{VMA}$). These signals provide for simple interface between, say, a 10-MHz 68000 microprocessor and 1-MHz synchronous LSI peripheral devices such as those available for use in 6800 microcomputer systems.

Let us now look at the function of each of these signals. The enable (E) output of the 68000 is used by 6800 peripherals to synchronize its data read/write operations. It is a free-running clock with a frequency equal to one-tenth of that of the 68000 clock frequency. This signal allows 1-MHz LSI peripheral ICs to be used with the 10-MHz 68000. It is applied to the $\overline{E}$ or PHI_2 input of a 6800 family peripheral.

The valid peripheral address ($\overline{VPA}$) line is an input to the 68000 that is used to tell it to perform a synchronous transfer over its asynchronous system bus. When the address output on the address bus is decoded and found to correspond to an external 6800 peripheral, $\overline{VPA}$ must be switched to logic 0. This tells the microprocessor to synchronize the next data transfer with the enable (E) signal.

The valid memory address ($\overline{VMA}$) output is supplied by the 68000 in response to an active $\overline{VPA}$ input. It indicates to external circuitry that a valid address is on the address bus and that the next data transfer over the data bus will by synchronized with enable (E).

13.4 CLOCK INPUT AND WAVEFORM

Looking at Fig. 13.2, we find that the 68000 has a single *clock input* that is labeled CLK. The clock generator circuitry is not provided on the chip. Instead, the CLK signal must be generated in external circuitry and fed to the 68000. Internally, this signal is used to produce additional clock signals that synchronize the operation of the 68000's circuitry.

The 68000 is available with clock frequencies over the range from as low as 4 MHz to as high as 12.5 MHz. Figure 13.5 shows the CLK waveform. For 10-MHz operation, the cycle time (t_{CYC}) is 100 ns. The corresponding maximum pulse width low (t_{CL}) and pulse width high (t_{CH}) are both equal to 45 ns. The maximum rise and fall times of its edges, t_{Cr} and t_{Cf}, are both 10 ns. CLK is at TTL-compatible voltage levels.

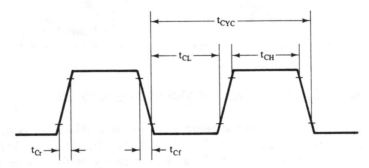

Figure 13.5 Clock waveform.

13.5 ASYNCHRONOUS MEMORY AND I/O INTERFACE

The *asynchronous memory and input/output interface* of the 68000 is shown in Fig. 13.6. It consists of the address bus, data bus, function code bus, and control bus. Earlier we indicated that the address and data buses of the 68000 are *demultiplexed*. That is, they do not share pins on the package of the IC. The advantage of this is that the interface circuitry between microprocessor and memory is simplified.

Moreover, we pointed out that I/O devices in the 68000 microcomputer are always *memory mapped*. By this we mean that memory and I/O do not have separate address spaces. Instead, the designer allocates a part of the memory address space to the I/O devices. Therefore, both memory and I/O are accessed in the same way through the asynchronous bus interface.

We have indicated several times that the bus between the 68000 and memory or I/O is *asynchronous*. By asynchronous we mean that once a bus cycle is initiated to read (input) or write (output) instructions or data, it is not completed until a response is provided by the memory or I/O subsystem. This response is an acknowledge signal that tells the 68000 that it should complete its current bus cycle. For this reason, the timing of the bus cycle in a 68000 microcomputer system can be easily matched to slow memories or I/O devices. This results in efficient use of the system bus.

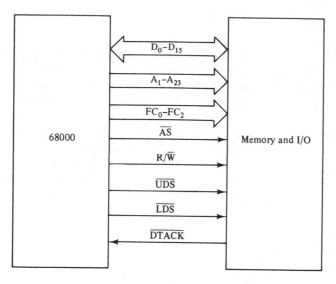

Figure 13.6 Asynchronous memory and I/O interface.

13.6 HARDWARE ORGANIZATION OF THE ADDRESS SPACE

Notice in Fig. 13.6 that the address bus of the 68000 consists of 23 independent address lines, which are labeled A_1 through A_{23}. The address information output on these lines selects the storage location in memory or the I/O device that is to be accessed. With this large 23-bit address, the 68000 is capable of generating 8M unique addresses.

Coupling the upper data strobe ($\overline{UDS}$) and lower data strobe ($\overline{LDS}$) control signals with this address bus gives the 68000 the ability to access bytes of data. Figure 13.7 illustrates how these two signals can be used to enable *byte-wide upper* and *lower data banks* in memory. Address lines A_1 through A_{23} are applied in parallel to both memory banks. When viewed in this way, the size of the *physical address space* is said to be 16M bytes.

The address strobe ($\overline{AS}$) control signal is output by the 68000 along with the address on A_1 through A_{23}. It is used to signal memory and I/O devices that valid address information is available on the bus.

In Fig. 13.6, we find a second bus between the 68000 and the memory or I/O device. It is the data bus and consists of the 16 bidirectional data lines D_0 through D_{15}. Data are input to the microprocessor over these lines during read (input) operations and are output by the processor over these lines during write (output) operations.

The control signals that coordinate the data transfers that take place between the 68000 and memory or I/O devices are also shown in Fig. 13.6. They are the read/write ($R/\overline{W}$) output and the data transfer acknowledge ($\overline{DTACK}$) input. The 68000 sets $R/\overline{W}$ to the appropriate logic level to tell external circuitry whether data are being input or output by the microprocessor during the current bus cycle.

On the other hand, $\overline{DTACK}$ acknowledges that the transfer between microprocessor and memory or I/O subsystem has taken place. When the 68000 executes a

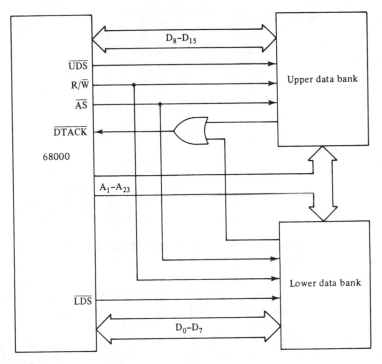

Figure 13.7 Memory organized as upper and lower data banks.

read operation, it always waits until the $\overline{\text{DTACK}}$ input goes active before completing the bus cycle. $\overline{\text{DTACK}}$ is asserted by the memory or I/O device when the data it has put on the bus are valid. In response to $\overline{\text{DTACK}}$ equal to 0, the 68000 latches in the data from the bus and completes the read cycle. During a write operation, $\overline{\text{DTACK}}$ indicates to the 68000 that data have been written; therefore, it terminates the bus cycle.

Looking at the memory subsystem hardware configuration in Fig. 13.7, we see that for an addressed word storage location the upper 8 bits of the word are in the upper data bank. This is the even byte and it is transferred between memory and microprocessor over data bus lines D_8 through D_{15}. The lower 8 bits of the word, the odd byte, are in the lower data bank. They are transferred between microprocessor and memory over D_0 through D_7.

For a word transfer to take place over the bus, both $\overline{\text{UDS}}$ and $\overline{\text{LDS}}$ must be active at the same time. Therefore, they are both switched to the 0 logic level. Moreover, the direction in which data are transferred is identified by the logic level of $R/\overline{W}$. For instance, if the word of data is to be written into memory, $R/\overline{W}$ is set to logic 0. $\overline{\text{UDS}}$ and $\overline{\text{LDS}}$ can also be set to access just the upper byte or lower byte of data. In this case, either $\overline{\text{UDS}}$ or $\overline{\text{LDS}}$ remains at its inactive 1 logic level.

Figure 13.8 summarizes the types of data transfers that can take place over the data bus and the corresponding control signal logic levels. For example, when an even byte is read from the high memory bank $\overline{\text{UDS}} = 0$, $\overline{\text{LDS}} = 1$, $R/\overline{W} = 1$ and data are transferred from memory to the 68000 over data lines D_8 through D_{15}.

UDS	LDS	R/W	D8-D15	D0-D7
High	High	—	No valid data	No valid data
Low	Low	High	Valid data bits 8-15	Valid data bits 0-7
High	Low	High	No valid data	Valid data bits 0-7
Low	High	High	Valid data bits 8-15	No valid data
Low	Low	Low	Valid data bits 8-15	Valid data bits 0-7
High	Low	Low	Valid data bits 0-7	Valid data bits 0-7
Low	High	Low	Valid data bits 8-15	Valid data bits 8-15

Figure 13.8 Relationship between bus control signals and data bus transfers. (Courtesy of Motorola, Inc.)

13.7 PROGRAM AND DATA STORAGE MEMORY AND THE FUNCTION CODES

In the preceding section, we showed how the memory address space of the 68000 is partitioned into upper and lower data banks. Another way of partitioning the memory subsystem in a 68000 microcomputer system is in terms of *program and data storage memory*. In general, the program segment of memory contains the opcodes of the instructions in the program, direct addresses of operands, and data of immediate source operands. It can be implemented with ROM or RAM.

On the other hand, the data segment is generally implemented with RAM. This is because it contains data operands that are to be processed by the instructions. Therefore, it must be able to be read from or written into.

During all bus cycles to memory, the 68000 outputs bus status codes to indicate whether it is accessing program or data memory. The bus status code is known as the *function code* and is output on function code bus lines FC_0 through FC_2. The table in Fig. 13.9 lists all function codes output by the 68000 and the corresponding types of bus cycles. Notice that program and data memory accesses are further categorized based on whether they occur when the 68000 is in the user state or supervisor state. For instance, an instruction acquisition bus cycle performed when the 68000 is in the

Function code output			Reference class
FC_2	FC_1	FC_0	
0	0	0	(Unassigned)
0	0	1	User data
0	1	0	User program
0	1	1	(Unassigned)
1	0	0	(Unassigned)
1	0	1	Supervisor data
1	1	0	Supervisor program
1	1	1	Interrupt acknowledge

Figure 13.9 Memory function codes. (Courtesy of Motorola, Inc.)

user state is accompanied by the function code $FC_2FC_1FC_0 = 010$, but the same type of access when in the supervisor state is accompanied by $FC_2FC_1FC_0 = 110$.

One use of the function codes is to partition the memory subsystem hardware. This can be done by decoding the function codes in external logic to produce enable signals for the *user program segment, user data segment, supervisor program seg-met,* and *supervisor data segment.*

One approach is illustrated in Fig. 13.10. Here the memory subsystem has been partitioned into a user memory segment and a supervisor memory segment. Looking at Fig. 13.9, we see that the logic level of function code line FC_2 indicates whether the 68000 is in the user or supervisor state. Notice that in this circuit FC_2 is gated with address strobe $\overline{AS}$ to produce select input $\overline{S}_1$ for the supervisor memory bank. In this way, the 68000 can access either the user or supervisor memory banks when it is in the supervisor state, but when it is in the user state the supervisor memory bank is locked out.

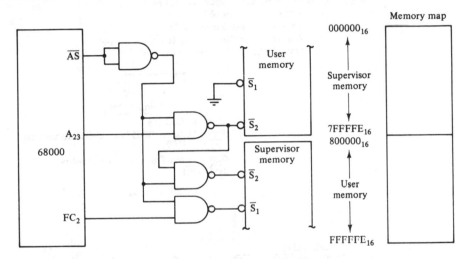

Figure 13.10 Partitioning memory into user and supervisor segments. (Courtesy of Motorola, Inc.)

Another approach would be to partition the memory subsystem such that it has an independent 16M byte program memory segment and a 16M byte data memory segment. This expands the address space of the 68000 to 32M bytes in a segmented fashion.

13.8 MEMORY AND I/O READ CYCLE TIMING

To read a word or byte from an input device or memory, the signal lines that are used are address lines A_1 through A_{23}, data lines D_0 through D_{15}, and asynchronous control lines: address strobe $(\overline{AS})$, upper and lower data strobes $(\overline{UDS}$ and $\overline{LDS})$, read/write $(R/\overline{W})$, and data transfer acknowledge $(\overline{DTACK})$. Figure 13.11(a) is a flowchart that shows the sequence of events that take place in order to read a byte of data from the memory subsystem in Fig. 13.7. A timing diagram for an upper bank *read bus cycle* is shown in Fig. 13.11(b).

From the timing diagram, we see that a read cycle can be completed in as few as four clock cycles. Each clock cycle consists of a high and low state for a total of eight states. They are labeled S_0 through S_7 in the timing diagram. With the 100-ns clock cycle of the 10-MHz 68000, this gives a minimum read bus cycle time of 400 ns.

In Fig. 13.11(a), we see that the read bus cycle begins with $R/\overline{W}$ being switched to logic 1. As shown in Fig. 13.11(b), this happens at the leading edge of state S_0. During S_0, a function code $FC_2FC_1FC_0$ is output and address lines A_1 through A_{23} are put in the high-Z state. Next the address is output during the S_1 state

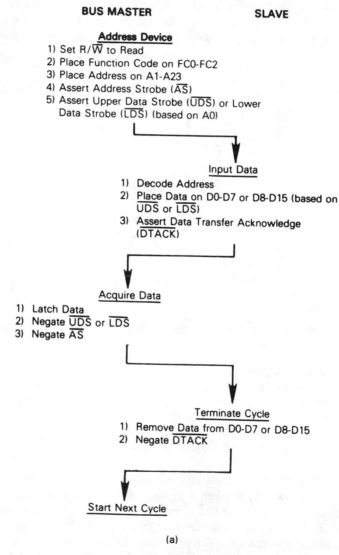

(a)

Figure 13.11 (a) Byte read cycle flowchart (courtesy of Motorola, Inc.); (b) upper byte read timing diagram.

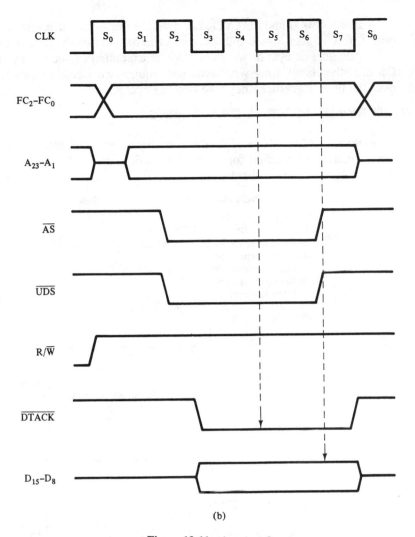

(b)

Figure 13.11   (*continued*)

followed by address strobe $\overline{\text{AS}}$ and the appropriate data strobes during S_2. In our example, we are to read only the upper byte; therefore, $\overline{\text{UDS}}$ is switched to its active 0 logic level. The address phase of the bus cycle is now complete.

Next the memory or I/O subsystem must decode the address and put the sclected data on bus lines D_8 through D_{15}. This must happen during S_3. Then in S_4 it must assert $\overline{\text{DTACK}}$ by switching it to logic 0. This signals the 68000 that valid data are on the bus and that the bus cycle should be continued through to completion.

$\overline{\text{DTACK}}$ is tested by the 68000 during S_5. If it is active (logic 0), data are read off the bus at the end of S_6. During S_7, the 68000 returns $\overline{\text{AS}}$ and $\overline{\text{UDS}}$ to their inactive logic levels and the address bus and data lines to the high-Z state. Moreover, the memory or I/O subsystem must return $\overline{\text{DTACK}}$ to the 1 level before another bus cycle can be initiated.

If the 68000 finds $\overline{\text{DTACK}}$ not asserted during S_5, it inserts wait clock cycles until $\overline{\text{DTACK}}$ goes low to indicate that valid data are on the data bus.

Accesses of byte or word data require execution of one bus cycle by the 68000. On the other hand, long-word accesses require two words of data to be transferred over the bus. Therefore, they take two bus cycles.

13.9 MEMORY AND I/O WRITE CYCLE TIMING

To write a word or a byte of data to memory or an I/O device, the same basic interface signals we identified for the read operation are used. The flowchart and timing diagram for a bus cycle that writes a word of data are shown in Fig. 13.12(a) and (b),

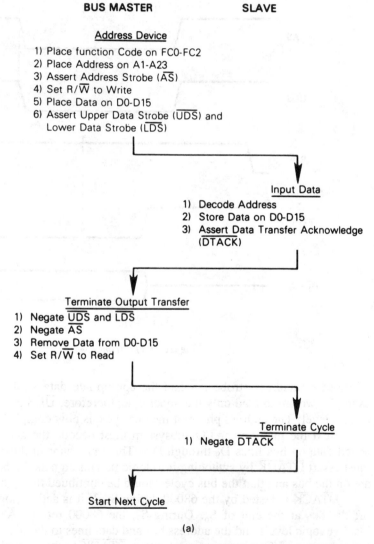

BUS MASTER   SLAVE

Address Device
1) Place function Code on FC0-FC2
2) Place Address on A1-A23
3) Assert Address Strobe ($\overline{\text{AS}}$)
4) Set R/$\overline{\text{W}}$ to Write
5) Place Data on D0-D15
6) Assert Upper Data Strobe ($\overline{\text{UDS}}$) and Lower Data Strobe ($\overline{\text{LDS}}$)

Input Data
1) Decode Address
2) Store Data on D0-D15
3) Assert Data Transfer Acknowledge ($\overline{\text{DTACK}}$)

Terminate Output Transfer
1) Negate $\overline{\text{UDS}}$ and $\overline{\text{LDS}}$
2) Negate $\overline{\text{AS}}$
3) Remove Data from D0-D15
4) Set R/$\overline{\text{W}}$ to Read

Terminate Cycle
1) Negate $\overline{\text{DTACK}}$

Start Next Cycle

(a)

Figure 13.12 (a) Word write cycle flowchart (courtesy of Motorola, Inc.); (b) timing diagram.

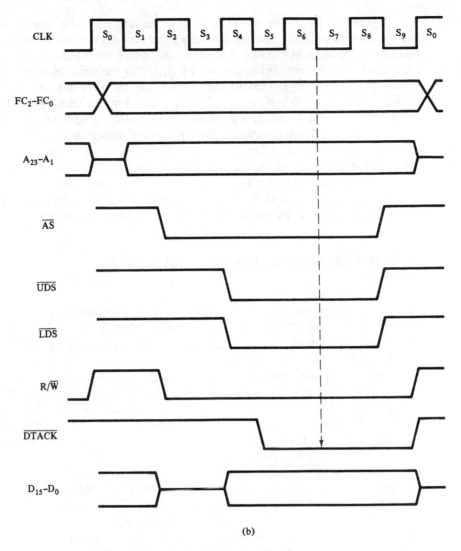

(b)

Figure 13.12 (*continued*)

respectively. Here we see that a minimum of five clock cycles, which equals 10 states S_0 through S_9, are required to perform a *write bus cycle*. At 10 MHz this takes 500 ns.

Looking at Fig. 13.12(a), we see that the bus cycle begins with a function code being output on the FC bus during S_0. The address lines that are floating during S_0 are asserted with a valid address during S_1 and $\overline{AS}$ and R/$\overline{W}$ go active during S_2. This time, R/$\overline{W}$ is set to 0 to indicate that a write operation is to take place and data are output on the complete bus D_0 through D_{15} during S_3.

Selection of byte or word data is made by the 68000 asserting the data strobe signals. For a word access, both $\overline{UDS}$ and $\overline{LDS}$ are switched to their active 0 logic level. This is done during the S_4 state.

Up to this point, the 68000 has output the address of the storage location and put the data on the bus. External circuitry must now decode the address to select the memory location or I/O device. Then the data, which were put on the bus during S_3, are written into the enabled device during S_4. After the write of data has been completed, the memory or I/O device must inform the 68000 of this condition by pulling $\overline{DTACK}$ to its active 0 logic level. $\overline{DTACK}$ is tested by the 68000 at the beginning of S_7 and, if it is not asserted, wait clock cycles are inserted between the S_6 and S_7 states. This extends the duration of the write cycle. However, if $\overline{DTACK}$ is found to be at its active 0 level, $\overline{UDS}$, $\overline{LDS}$, and $\overline{AS}$ are returned to their inactive 1 logic levels at the beginning of the S_9 state. Furthermore, at the end of S_9, the address and data lines are returned to the high-Z state and R/$\overline{W}$ is switched to 1.

Before the S_0 state of the next bus cycle, $\overline{DTACK}$ must be returned to logic 1. However, this is done by the memory or I/O subsystem, not the 68000.

13.10 64K-BYTE SOFTWARE-REFRESHED DYNAMIC RAM SUBSYSTEM

The circuit diagram in Fig. 13.13 shows one way of implementing a dynamic RAM subsystem for a 68000 microcomputer system. This circuit is designed to provide 64K bytes of memory that are mapped into the address range 008000_{16} through $017FFF_{16}$ of the 68000's address space.

Due to the large memory support capability of the 68000, it is essential to buffer all the memory interface signals. This is done by the leftmost group of circuits in Fig. 13.13. For example, two 74245 devices are used to buffer bidirectional data bus lines D_0 through D_{15}, and two 74LS244 devices are used to buffer address lines A_1 through A_{16}. These buffers increase the drive capability of the address and data buses over that supplied directly by the lines of the 68000.

Let us next look at the storage array of the memory subsystem. It is located at the right of the circuit diagram and employs thirty-two 16K by 1 dynamic RAMs. The type of memory device used is the MCM4116. The circuit is set up to implement a structure similar to that shown in Fig. 13.7. The upper 16 devices form a 32K-byte upper data bank. This bank is used to store even-addressed bytes of data, and they are transferred between microprocessor and memory over data bus lines D_8 through D_{15}. The lower 16 devices form a 32K-byte lower data bank. It stores odd bytes of data, which are carried between the 68000 and memory over data lines D_0 through D_7.

Since dynamic RAMs are in use instead of static RAMs, the address output by the 68000 on A_1 through A_{14} must be multiplexed into separate row and column address before it can be applied to the memory devices. In Fig. 13.13, we see that these address lines are input to two 74LS157 multiplexers, which produce 7-bit row and column addresses at their outputs, A_1 through A_7. The timing of the address output on these lines is determined by the PTND output of a 74LS74 flip-flop in IC U_9.

Both bank and byte/word selection is performed through the generation of $\overline{RAS}$ signals. Notice that the control logic implemented with ICs U_2, U_4, U_5, and U_9 produces four RAS signals. They are denoted as $\overline{RAS}_{1U}$, $\overline{RAS}_{2U}$, $\overline{RAS}_{1L}$, and $\overline{RAS}_{2L}$. Also, two CAS signals, $\overline{CAS}_U$ and $\overline{CAS}_L$, are produced by this section of circuitry. The inputs from which the row select and column select signals are derived are address bits A_{14} through A_{16}, upper and lower data select $\overline{UDS}$ and $\overline{LDS}$, and the system clock SYSTEM 0.

For example, to perform a word access from the group 1 RAMs, both $\overline{LDS}$ and $\overline{UDS}$ are logic 0. This makes both the $\overline{RAS}_L$ and $\overline{RAS}_U$ signals active. At the same time, the address code $A_{16}A_{15}A_{14}$ is decoded by ICs U_2 and U_5 to enable both $\overline{RAS}_{1U}$ and $\overline{RAS}_{1L}$ to the memory array. These signals are synchronized to the output of the row address from the multiplexer. A short time later, the $\overline{CAS}_U$ and $\overline{CAS}_L$ signals are produced. They are synchronized to the output of the column address from the multiplexer.

Notice that the data acknowledge ($\overline{DTACK}$) signal is also produced by this section of control logic. It is buffered and then sent to the 68000.

This memory subsystem employs *software refresh* and not *hardware refresh*. The 6840 device is provided for this purpose. It contains a timer that is set up to initiate an interrupt to the 68000 every 1.9 ms. This interrupt has a priority level of 7, and execution of its service routine performs the software refresh function. The advantage of software refresh is that the interface hardware is simplified. However, it also has a disadvantage—the software and time overhead required to perform the refresh operation.

13.11 AN I/O INSTRUCTION: MOVEP

The 68000 microprocessor has one instruction that is specifically designed for communicating with LSI peripherals that interface over an 8-bit data bus. It is the *move peripheral data* (MOVEP) instruction. An example of an LSI peripheral that can be used in the 68000 microcomputer system is the *6821 peripheral interface adapter* (PIA). Internal to this device is a group of byte-wide control registers. When the device is built into the microcomputer system, these registers will all reside at either odd addresses or even addresses. This poses a problem if we attempt to make multibyte transfers by specifying word or long-word data operands. For instance, a MOVE instruction for word data would cause the two bytes to be transferred to consecutive byte addresses, one of which is even and the other is odd. This problem is overcome by using the MOVEP instruction.

The general formats of the instruction are

    MOVEP   Dn, d(An)

and

    MOVEP   d(An), Dn

The first form of the instruction is for output of data. It copies the contents of a source operand that is in data register D_n to the location at the effective address specified by the destination operand. Notice that the destination operand must always

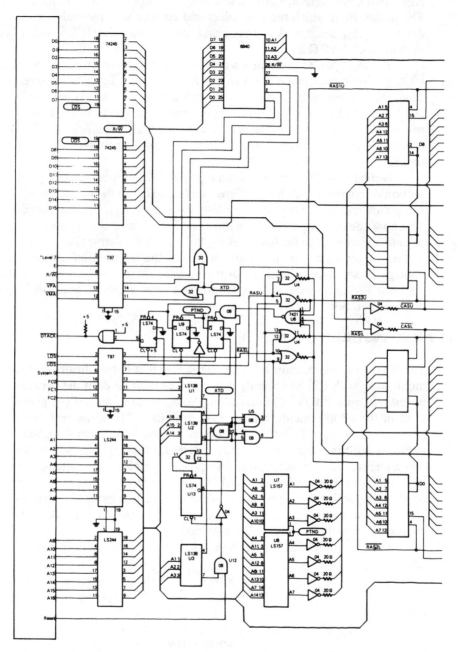

Figure 13.13 Software-refreshed dynamic RAM subsystem. (Courtesy of Motorola, Inc.)

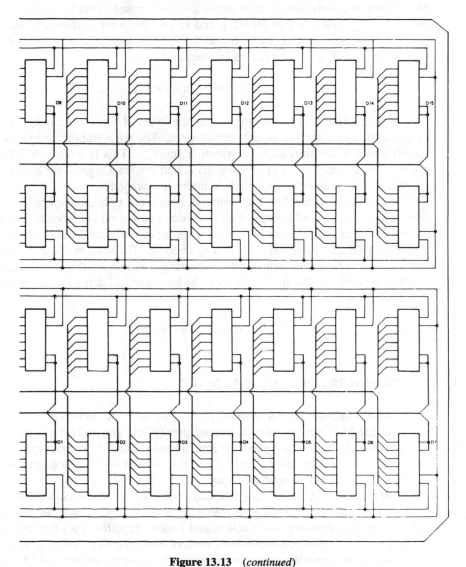

Figure 13.13 (*continued*)

be specified using address register indirect with displacement addressing.

As an example, let us write an instruction that will transfer a word of data that is in D_0 to two consecutive output ports. Assume that the contents of A_0 are 16000_{16} and it is a pointer to the first of a group of eight byte-wide registers in an LSI peripheral. These registers are at consecutive even addresses. That is, register 0 is at address 16000_{16}, register 1 at 16002_{16}, and so on. We want to transfer data to the last two of these registers, registers 6 and 7. The displacement of register 6 from the address in A_0 is C_{16}; therefore, the instruction is

$$\text{MOVEP.W} \quad \text{D0,12(A0)}$$

Execution of this instruction causes the bytes of the word contents of D_0 to be output to two consecutive even-byte addresses. The most significant byte is output to the effective destination address, which is $1600C_{16}$. This is register 6. Then the address is incremented by 2 to give $1600E_{16}$, and the least significant byte is output to register 7. The pointer address in A_0 remains unchanged.

A MOVEP instruction that employs long-word operands operator in a similar way except that it would output 4 bytes to consecutive odd or even addresses. As an example, let us assume that four byte-wide input ports are located at odd-byte addresses 16001_{16}, 16003_{16}, 16005_{16}, and 16007_{16}. The data at these 32 inputs lines can be read into a data register by executing a single MOVEP instruction. If A_1 contains a pointer to the first input port, the long word of data can be input to D_1 with the instruction

$$\text{MOVEP.L} \quad \text{0(A1),D1}$$

13.12 6821 PERIPHERAL INTERFACE ADAPTER

In the 68000 microcomputer system, parallel input/output ports can be implemented by using the 6821 peripheral interface adapter (PIA). The 6821 is one of the simpler LSI peripherals that is designed for implementing parallel input/output. It has two byte-wide I/O ports called A and B. Each line at both of these ports can be independently configured as an input or output.

Figure 13.14 is a block diagram that shows the internal architecture of the 6821 device. Here we find six programmable registers. They include an *output register* (OR), *data direction register* (DDR), and *control register* (CR) for each of the I/O ports. Let us overview the function of each of these registers before going on.

All input/output data transfers between the microprocessor and PIA take place through the output data registers. These registers are 8 bits wide and their bits correspond to the I/O port lines. For example, to set the logic level of an output line at port A to logic 1, we simply write logic 1 into the corresponding bit in port A's output register.

Each I/O line of the 6821 also has a bit corresponding to it in the A or B data direction register. The logic level of this bit decides whether the corresponding line

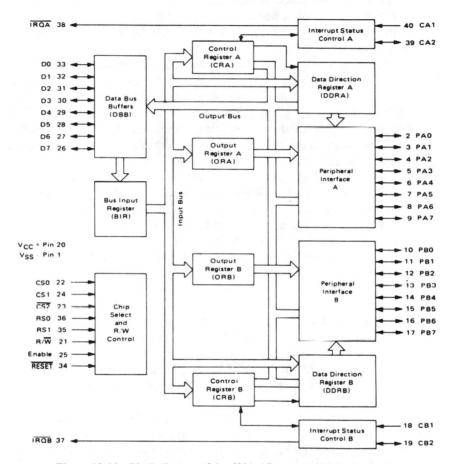

Figure 13.14 Block diagram of the 6821. (Courtesy of Motorola, Inc.)

works as an input or an output. Logic 0 in a bit position selects input mode of operation for the corresponding I/O line and logic 1 selects output operation. For instance, port A can be configured as a byte-wide output port by initializing its data direction register with the value FF_{16}.

The control register (CR) serves three main functions. First, it is used to configure the operation of *control inputs* CA_1, CA_2, CB_1, and CB_2. A second function is that it can be read by the 68000 to identify control status. However, its third function is what we are interested in right now. This is how it is used to select between the DDR and OR registers when they are loaded or read by the 68000. In Fig. 13.15, we see that the logic level of bit b_2 in CR selects DDR when it is zero and OR when it is 1.

Looking at Fig. 13.14, we find that the microprocessor interface of the 6821 is shown on the left. The key signals here are the eight *data bus lines* D_0 through D_7. It is over these lines that the 68000 can initialize the registers of the 6821, write commands to the control registers, read status from the control registers, and read from or write into the peripheral data registers. The direction in which data are to be transferred is signaled to the 6821 by the logic level of $R/\overline{W}$. For example, logic 0 on $R/\overline{W}$ indicates that data are to be written into one of its registers.

Even though the 6821 has six addressable registers, only two *register select lines* have been provided. They are labeled RS_0 and RS_1. The table in Fig. 13.16 shows how they are used together with bit b_2 of the control registers to select the internal registers. Notice that if both RS_1 and RS_0 are logic 0 the data direction register and output register for port A are selected. As we pointed out earlier, the setting of b_2 in the A control register selects between the two registers. For instance, if this bit is logic 0, the data transfer takes place between the microprocessor and the DDR for port A. In this way we see that bit 2 in control register A must be set to select the appropriate register before initiating the data transfer.

As part of the microprocessor interface, there are also three *chip select inputs*. They are labeled CS_0, CS_1, and $\overline{CS_2}$ and must be 1, 1, and 0, respectively, to enable the microprocessor interface.

At the right side of the 6821 block diagram in Fig. 13.14, we find the A and B byte-wide I/O ports. The individual I/O lines at these ports are labeled PA_0 through PA_7 and PB_0 through PB_7, respectively.

Two more lines are associated with each I/O port. They are control lines. For instance, looking at the A port, we find control lines CA_1 and CA_2. Notice that CA_1 is a dedicated output, but CA_2 is bidirectional and can be configured to operate as either an input or an output. The mode of operation of these control lines is determined by the settings of the bits in port A's control register.

These control lines permit the user of the 6821 to implement a variety of different *I/O handshake mechanisms*. For example, port A could be configured for a *strobed mode* of operation. If this is the case, a pulse is output at CA_2 whenever new data are available at PA_0 through PA_7. Moreover, the 6821 can be configured such that the pulse at CA_2 is automatically produced by the 6821 or is generated under software control from the 68000. In the *automatic mode*, the pulse that is output is of a fixed duration. But if the pulse is initiated by the 68000, it can be set to any duration.

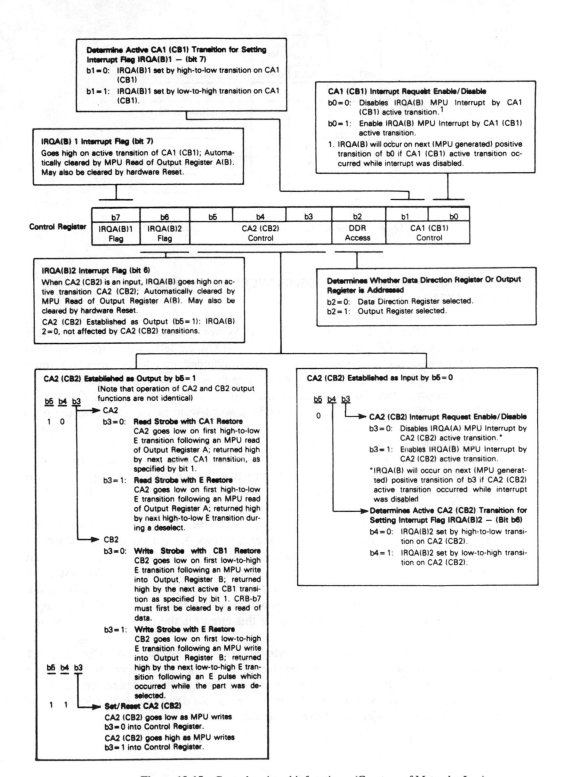

Figure 13.15 Control register bit functions. (Courtesy of Motorola, Inc.)

		Control register bit		
RS1	RS0	CRA-2	CRB-2	Location selected
0	0	1	X	Peripheral register A
0	0	0	X	Data direction register A
0	1	X	X	Control register A
1	0	X	1	Peripheral register B
1	0	X	0	Data direction register B
1	1	X	X	Control register B

X — Don't care

Figure 13.16 User-accessible register selection. (Courtesy of Motorola, Inc.)

13.13 DUAL 16-BIT PORTS FOR THE 68000 MICROCOMPUTER USING 6821s

The circuit in Fig. 13.17 shows how 6821 PIAs can be used to implement a parallel I/O interface for a 68000 microcomputer system. At the left of the circuit diagram, we find the asynchronous interface bus signals. Included are address lines A_1 through A_{16}, data lines D_0 through D_{15}, and control signals $\overline{AS}$, R/$\overline{W}$, and $\overline{DTACK}$.

To construct two 16-bit ports, we use two 6821 ICs, U_{14} and U_{15}. The A ports on the two 6821 ICs are cascaded to make a word-wide output port. On the other hand, the B ports on the two devices are cascaded to make a word-wide input port.

This circuit has been designed such that the registers of the PIAs reside in the address range 18000_{16} through 18007_{16}. The chart in Fig. 13.18(a), (page 438) shows the address for each register. Notice that the data direction registers corresponding to the bytes of the 16-bit output port are at addresses 18000_{16} and 18001_{16}. Those of the 16-bit input port are at 18004_{16} and 18005_{16}.

The address decoding for selecting between the two chips and their internal registers is shown in Fig. 13.18(b). Notice that bits A_1 and A_2 of the address are applied to register select inputs RS_0 and RS_1, respectively. Moreover, A_3 and A_4 are applied to the CS_1 and CS_0 chip select inputs of both 6821 devices. The rest of the address lines, A_5 to A_{16}, and $\overline{AS}$ are decoded by gates U_{9A}, U_{9B}, U_{10E}, U_{11A}, and U_{11B}. Their output is synchronized with a 2-MHz externally generated clock signal by flip-flops U_{13A} and U_{13B}. The output of this circuit is the third chip select signal, $\overline{CS}_2$, for the PIAs.

The data bus lines are simply buffered and then applied to both PIAs in parallel. Notice that the upper PIA device is coupled to the 68000 over the lower eight data bus lines and the lower PIA by the upper eight data lines. Therefore, as shown in Fig. 13.18(a), the registers of the upper device reside at odd byte addresses and those of the lower device are at even byte addresses.

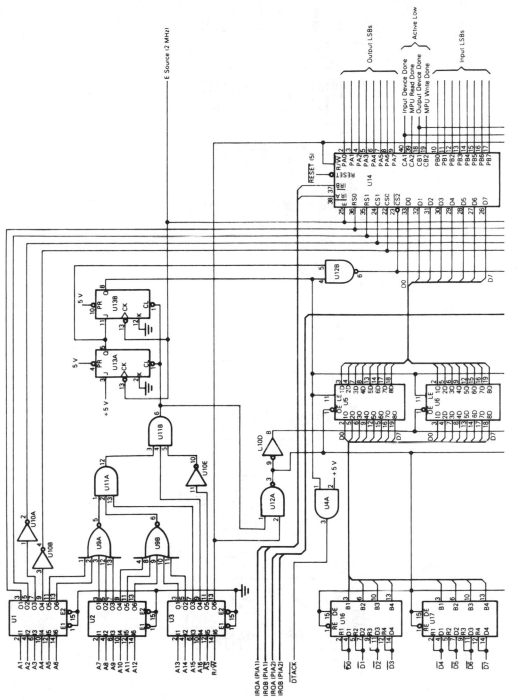

Figure 13.17 Dual 16-bit I/O ports using the 6821. (Courtesy of Motorola, Inc.)

435

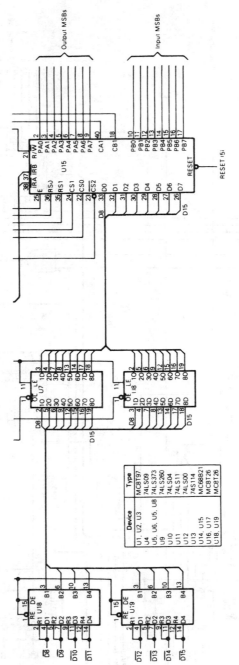

Figure 13.17 (continued)

To use the B ports on the two 6821 devices as inputs, their B port DDRs must be initialized with all zeros. These two registers are located at addresses 18004_{16} and 18005_{16}, respectively. However, to select these DDRs, bit 2 in the corresponding control registers must be loaded with logic 0. These control registers are located at addresses 18006_{16} and 18007_{16}. Thus, to configure the B ports as inputs, we can execute the following instruction sequence:

```
MOVE.W  #$0,$18006   SELECT DATA DIRECTION REGISTERS B
MOVE.W  #$0,$18004   PORT B IS INPUT PORT
```

Execution of these instructions loads the word-wide memory locations at addresses 18006_{16} and 18004_{16} with 0000_{16}.

To configure the A ports on the two chips, we first select the DDRs for port A by clearing bit 2 in their control registers. These CRs are located at addresses 18002_{16} and 18003_{16}. The DDRs are located at 18000_{16} and 18001_{16}. To configure the A ports as outputs, we must load their DDRs with all 1s. This gives the following instruction sequence:

```
MOVE.W  #$0,$18002      SELECT DATA DIRECTION REGISTERS A
MOVE.W  #$FFFF,$18000   PORT A IS OUTPUT PORT
```

Now to use the ports for inputting or outputting of data, we must select the peripheral data (output) registers. To select the two output registers for port A, we must load their control registers so that bit 2 is logic 1. A similar configuration is needed for port B. To do this, the following instructions can be executed:

```
MOVE.W  #$0404,$18002   SELECT DATA REGISTERS A
MOVE.W  #$0404,$18006   SELECT DATA REGISTERS B
```

Now the two ports are ready to perform I/O operations.

As an example of how data are input and output, let us show how to read a 16-bit word from the input port, increment it by 1, and output the new value to the output port. This can be accomplished by the following instructions:

```
MOVE.W  $18004,D1
ADDQ.W  #1,D1
MOVE.W  D1,$18000
```

The first instruction moves the contents of the input port to D_1. Then we increment the value in D_1 by 1. Finally, the third instruction outputs the value in D_1 to the output port.

13.14 SYNCHRONOUS MEMORY AND I/O INTERFACE

Up to this point in the chapter, we have been considering the asynchronous bus interface of the 68000 microprocessor. However, the 68000 also provides a *synchronous*

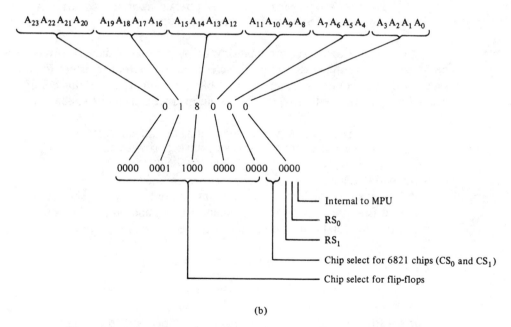

18000	Peripheral Data/DDRA	(U15)
18001	Peripheral Data/DDRA	(U14)
18002	CRA	(U15)
18003	CRA	(U14)
18004	Peripheral Data/DDRB	(U15)
18005	Peripheral Data/DDRB	(U14)
18006	CRB	(U15)
18007	CRB	(U14)

(a)

$A_{23} A_{22} A_{21} A_{20}$ $A_{19} A_{18} A_{17} A_{16}$ $A_{15} A_{14} A_{13} A_{12}$ $A_{11} A_{10} A_9 A_8$ $A_7 A_6 A_5 A_4$ $A_3 A_2 A_1 A_0$

0 1 8 0 0 0

0000 0001 1000 0000 0000 0000

Internal to MPU

RS_0

RS_1

Chip select for 6821 chips (CS_0 and CS_1)

Chip select for flip-flops

(b)

Figure 13.18 (a) 6821 register address map (courtesy of Motorola, Inc.); (b) address decoding for port selection.

bus interface. This capability is provided primarily for interface with 8-bit LSI peripherals such as those in the 6800 family. The synchronous interface is shown in Fig. 13.19. This interface looks quite similar to the asynchronous interface of Fig. 13.6. It includes the complete address bus A_1 through A_{23}, the 16-bit data bus D_0 through D_{15}, and control signals $\overline{UDS}$, $\overline{LDS}$, $\overline{AS}$, and R/$\overline{W}$. Notice that $\overline{DTACK}$ is not part of this interface. Instead, it is replaced by three synchronous bus control signals. They are valid peripheral address ($\overline{VPA}$), valid memory address ($\overline{VMA}$), and enable (E).

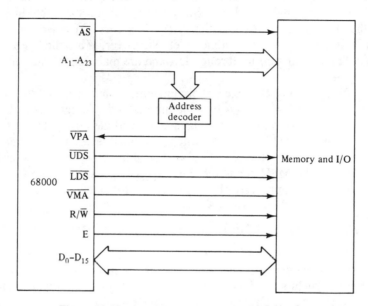

Figure 13.19 Synchronous memory and I/O interface.

Let us look briefly at the function of each of these control signals. $\overline{VPA}$ is an input to the 68000. It must be switched to the 0 logic level to tell the 68000 to perform a synchronous bus cycle. As shown in Fig. 13.9, external decoder circuitry is supplied in the interface to detect that the address on the bus is in the address space of the synchronous peripherals. On the other hand, $\overline{VMA}$ is an output produced by the 68000 only during synchronous bus cycles. It signals that a valid address is on the bus.

E is an enable clock that is produced within the 68000. It is at a rate equal to 1/10 that of the system clock. For instance, in a 10-MHz 68000 microcomputer system, E is at 1 MHz. The duty cycle of this signal is such that the pulse is at the 1 logic level for four clock states and at the 0 logic level for six clock states. This signal is applied to the E clock input of 6800 LSI peripherals.

Synchronous Bus Cycle

A flowchart of the 68000's *synchronous bus cycle* is shown in Fig. 13.20(a). Moreover, a general timing diagram for the key interface signals involved in a synchronous read/write operation is shown in Fig. 13.20(b). Notice that the waveforms of the FC, R/$\overline{\text{W}}$, $\overline{\text{UDS}}$, and $\overline{\text{LDS}}$ signals are not shown. They have the same function and timing as in the asynchronous bus cycle.

The synchronous bus cycle starts out just like an asynchronous bus cycle with a function code being output on the FC bus during state S_0. It is followed by the address on A_1 through A_{23} during S_1. When the address is stable in S_2, $\overline{\text{AS}}$ is switched to the 0 logic level. At this time R/$\overline{\text{W}}$ is set to 0 if a write cycle is in progress; otherwise, it stays at the 1 logic level. Moreover, if a write operation is in progress, the data are output on D_0 through D_{15} and are maintained valid during the rest of the bus cycle.

By the end of S_4, external circuitry must have decoded the address on the bus. At this time, it asserts $\overline{\text{VPA}}$ by switching it to the 0 logic level. In response to this, the 68000 begins to assert wait states to extend the bus cycle. At the end of the next clock state, the $\overline{\text{VMA}}$ output is switched to the 0 level. This signals external circuitry that an address is on the bus. The peripheral transfers the data after E is active. For a read cycle, the MPU reads the data when E goes low. The data transfer cycle is terminated by the processor by negating control signals $\overline{\text{VMA}}$, $\overline{\text{AS}}$, $\overline{\text{UDS}}$, and $\overline{\text{LDS}}$.

Interfacing the 6821 PIA to the Synchronous Interface Bus

The circuit diagram of Fig. 13.17 illustrates how 6821 PIAs are interfaced to the 68000's asynchronous bus. This circuit can be easily modified so that the LSI peripherals work off a synchronous bus cycle instead of an asynchronous bus cycle. Figure 13.21 shows a simple circuit that makes this modification. First, the ICs U_{11A}, U_{12B}, U_{13A}, and U_{13B} are removed from the circuit of Fig. 13.17. This is because $\overline{\text{DTACK}}$ is not required to support the synchronous bus. Moreover, the E output of the 68000 now gets directly connected to the E input of both 6821 devices in parallel.

Looking at Fig. 13.21, we see that the chip select (CS) output at pin 6 of U_{11B} gets connected to one input of the 74LS00 NAND gate. The other input of this gate is supplied by the $\overline{\text{VMA}}$ output of the 68000 after it is inverted. The output of the NAND gate goes to the $\overline{\text{CS}}_2$ input of both 6821 devices in parallel. In this way, we see that the 6821s get chip-selected only when one of their addresses is on the bus and the 68000 has signaled that a valid address is on the bus during a synchronous bus cycle.

The upper NAND gate in this circuit also has CS as one of its inputs and $\overline{\text{AS}}$ as the other. Therefore, it detects when an address corresponding to one of the LSI peripherals is on the bus. When this condition occurs, it switches $\overline{\text{VPA}}$ to logic 0, thereby signaling to the processor that a synchronous bus cycle should be performed.

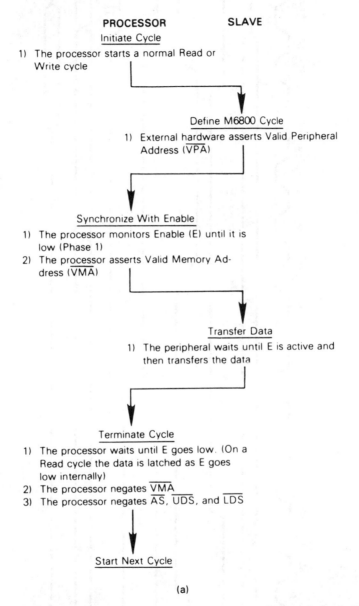

PROCESSOR   **SLAVE**

Initiate Cycle

1) The processor starts a normal Read or Write cycle

Define M6800 Cycle

1) External hardware asserts Valid Peripheral Address ($\overline{VPA}$)

Synchronize With Enable

1) The processor monitors Enable (E) until it is low (Phase 1)
2) The processor asserts Valid Memory Address ($\overline{VMA}$)

Transfer Data

1) The peripheral waits until E is active and then transfers the data

Terminate Cycle

1) The processor waits until E goes low. (On a Read cycle the data is latched as E goes low internally)
2) The processor negates $\overline{VMA}$
3) The processor negates $\overline{AS}$, $\overline{UDS}$, and $\overline{LDS}$

Start Next Cycle

(a)

Figure 13.20 (a) Synchronous bus cycle flowchart (courtesy of Motorola, Inc.); (b) timing diagram (courtesy of Motorola, Inc.).

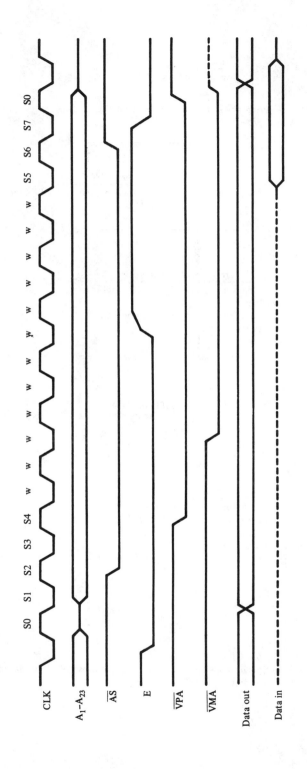

Figure 13.20 (continued)

442

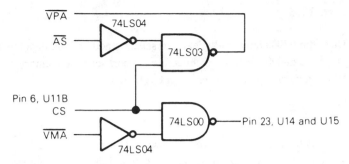

Figure 13.21 Conversion circuit for implementing synchronous bus cycles. (Courtesy of Motorola, Inc.)

ASSIGNMENT

Section 13.2

1. Name the technology used to fabricate the 68000 microprocessor.
2. In what size package is the 68000 housed?
3. How many general-purpose registers does the 68000 have? What are they called? Specify the size of each register.
4. What basic data types is the 68000 able to process directly?

Section 13.3

5. How many address lines are on the 68000 IC? How many unique memory or I/O addresses can be generated using these lines?
6. How many data lines does the 68000 have?
7. What is meant by asynchronous bus?
8. What function is served by $\overline{\text{DTACK}}$ during read/write operations?
9. How is byte addressing accomplished by the 68000?
10. Specify the address and asynchronous bus control signals that occur to write a word of data to memory address $A000.
11. What function code is output by the 68000 when it fetches an instruction while in the supervisor state?
12. Describe briefly the function of system control lines, $\overline{\text{BERR}}$, $\overline{\text{RESET}}$, and $\overline{\text{HALT}}$.
13. How does the 68000 prioritize interrupts?
14. Why are the bus arbitration control signals provided on the 68000?
15. Why is synchronous bus operation also provided for the 68000?

Section 13.4

16. At what number pin is the clock input applied to the 68000?
17. What is the duration of the clock cycle of a 68000 that is operating at 8 MHz?

Section 13.5

18. Does the 68000 have multiplexed or separate address and data bus lines?

19. Does the 68000 hardware architecture support separate memory and I/O address spaces?

20. What is meant by an asynchronous bus interface?

Section 13.6

21. What is the maximum size of the lower data bank in Fig. 13.7?

22. Which output of the 68000 supplies the bank select for the upper data bank in Fig. 13.7?

23. If the control signals in Fig. 13.7 are $\overline{UDS} = 1$, $\overline{LDS} = 0$, and $R/\overline{W} = 0$, are data being read from or written to memory? Is a byte or word data transfer taking place? Which data bus lines will be carrying valid data?

Section 13.7

24. What function code would be anticipated on the FC lines when the result of an ADD instruction is written to the destination location in memory? Assume that the 68000 is operating in the user state.

25. Why would a user/supervisor system environment be employed?

26. Draw a circuit similar to the one in Fig. 13.10 in which a 16M byte memory address space is implemented as four 4M byte blocks: the user program memory, user data memory, supervisor program memory, and supervisor data memory. The supervisor is to have access to all memory areas.

Section 13.8

27. What is the minimum amount of time needed to read a long-word operand from memory? Assume that the 68000 in the microcomputer is running at 8 MHz.

28. Give an overview of the sequence of events that occurs when a word of instruction code is read from address $A000.

Section 13.9

29. What is the minimum amount of time needed to write a long-word operand to memory? Assume that the 68000 in the microcomputer is running at 8 MHz.

30. Give an overview of the sequence of events that occurs when a byte of data is written to address $A001.

Section 13.10

31. List the type of IC that is used to perform each of the functions that follows in the circuit of Fig. 13.13.

   (a) Data bus buffer/transceiver

   (b) Address bus buffer

   (c) Data storage memory

(d) Row and column address generation

(e) Refresh interval timer

32. Give an overview of the circuit in Fig. 13.13 for an upper byte access from the group 2 RAMs.

Section 13.11

33. Describe the operation performed by the instruction

$$\text{MOVEP.L} \quad \text{D7,0(A3)}$$

Assume that A_3 contains $01A000_{16}$.

34. Describe the operation performed by the instruction

$$\text{MOVEP.W} \quad \text{6(A4),D6}$$

Assume that A_4 contains $0A1000_{16}$.

35. Write an instruction sequence that will output the long-word contents of D_0 to 4-byte-wide output ports starting at address $16000. The output ports are located at consecutive even addresses.

36. Write an instruction that will input a word of data from 2-byte-wide input ports and store it in D_1. Assume that the input ports are located at consecutive odd addresses that are displaced by 10 bytes in the positive direction from an input address pointer held in register A_1.

Section 13.12

37. Make a list of the programmable registers of the 6821.

38. Which user-accessible register is being accessed if the code at the register select lines is $RS_1RS_0 = 11$?

39. What should be loaded into the data direction register for port B if all port lines are to be configured as inputs?

40. What must be loaded into bit b_2 of CRB if output register B is to be accessed?

41. To what values must b_1b_0 and $b_5b_4b_3$ in CRB be set to enable the occurrence of the $\overline{IRQ}_B$ interrupt output for a 1-to-0 transition at CB_1 or CB_2?

42. What does bit b_7 in CRB stand for?

43. What mode of operation does making $b_5b_4b_3 = 100$ in CRB specify?

Section 13.13

44. For the circuit in Fig. 13.17 and the address map in Fig. 13.18(a), write instructions that do the following:

(a) Configure the B port of both U_{14} and U_{15} as output ports.

(b) Configure the A port of both U_{14} and U_{15} as input ports.

(c) Configure the B output ports such that they produce a fixed duration strobe pulse at their CB_2 output and select its data output register.

(d) Configure the A input ports such that they initiate an interrupt request through their CA_1 inputs; the interrupt is to be initiated by a high-to-low transition at CA_1; and the output register is to be selected.

45. Write a program that moves 5 bytes of data from a table in memory starting at address $A000 to the B port of U_{14} in the circuit of Fig. 13.17. Assume that the B port is configured as defined in Problem 44(c).

Section 13.14

46. What is the primary use of the synchronous memory I/O interface?
47. What is meant by synchronous bus operation for the 68000?
48. How does the synchronous bus cycle of Fig. 13.20(a) differ from the asynchronous bus cycle in Fig. 13.11(a)?

14

Exception Processing of the 68000 Microprocessor

14.1 INTRODUCTION

In the last chapter, we covered the memory and input/output interfaces for the 68000-based microcomputer. Here we will consider the exception-processing capability of the 68000 and a special input interface, the *external hardware interrupt interface*. The topics covered are as follows:

1. Types of exceptions
2. Exception vector table
3. Exception priorities
4. External hardware interrupts
5. General interrupt processing sequence
6. General interrupt interface of the 68000
7. Autovector interrupt mechanism
8. Autovector interface support circuit
9. Exception instructions
10. Internal exception functions

14.2 TYPES OF EXCEPTIONS

For the 68000 microcomputer system, Motorola, Inc., has defined the concept of *exception processing*. Exception processing is similar to what is more generally known as interrupt processing. Just like the interrupt capabilities of other microprocessors, the exception mechanism allows the 68000 to respond quickly to special internal or external events. Based on the occurrence of this type of event, the main program is terminated and a context switch is initiated to a new program environment. This new program environment, the exception service routine, is a segment of program designed to service the requesting condition. At completion of exception processing, program control can be returned to the point at which the exception occurred in the main program.

The 68000 has a broad variety of methods by which exception processing can be initiated. They include the *external exception functions, hardware reset, bus error,* and *user-defined interrupts.* Furthermore, the 68000 has a number of instructions that can initiate exception processing. Some examples of these instructions are TRAP, TRAPV, and CHK. The 68000 also has extensive internal exception capability. It includes exceptions for internal error conditions (*address error, illegal/ unimplemented opcodes,* and *privilege violation*) and internal functions (*trace* and *spurious interrupt*).

14.3 EXCEPTION VECTOR TABLE

Each of the exception functions that is performed by the 68000 has a number called the *vector number* assigned to it. For external interrupts, the interrupting device supplies the vector number to the 68000. On the other hand, for other types of interrupts, the vector number is generated within the microprocessor. The 68000 converts the vector number to the address of a corresponding long-word storage location in memory. Held at this memory location is a 24-bit address known as the *vector address* of the exception. It defines the starting point of the service routine in program storage memory. Figure 14.1 shows the format in which the address vector is stored in memory. As shown, it takes up two word locations. The lower addressed word is the high word of the new program counter and the higher addressed word is the low word of PC. Only the 8 LSBs of the high word are used.

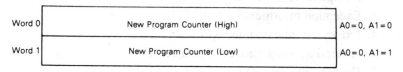

Figure 14.1 Exception vector organization. (Courtesy of Motorola, Inc.)

The vector addresses are stored in a part of the 68000's memory system known as the *exception vector table.* As shown in Fig. 14.2, the vector table contains up to 256 vectors, which are labeled with vector numbers 0 through 255. Notice that the table must reside in the address range 000000_{16} through $0003FF_{16}$, which is the first 1024 bytes of the 68000's 16M-byte address space. All vectors other than vector 0 must reside in supervisor data memory. Vector 0, which is assigned to the hardware reset function, must be stored in supervisor program memory.

The hexadecimal address at which each vector is located in memory is also provided in the table of Fig. 14.2. The address of the most significant word of any

Vector Number(s)	Address Dec	Address Hex	Address Space	Assignment
0	0	000	SP	Reset: Initial SSP
–	4	004	SP	Reset: Initial PC
2	8	008	SD	Bus Error
3	12	00C	SD	Address Error
4	16	010	SD	Illegal Instruction
5	20	014	SD	Zero Divide
6	24	018	SD	CHK Instruction
7	28	01C	SD	TRAPV Instruction
8	32	020	SD	Privilege Violation
9	36	024	SD	Trace
10	40	028	SD	Line 1010 Emulator
11	44	02C	SD	Line 1111 Emulator
12*	48	030	SD	(Unassigned, reserved)
13*	52	034	SD	(Unassigned, reserved)
14*	56	038	SD	(Unassigned, reserved)
15	60	03C	SD	Uninitialized Interrupt Vector
16-23*	64	04C	SD	(Unassigned, reserved)
	95	05F		–
24	96	060	SD	Spurious Interrupt
25	100	064	SD	Level 1 Interrupt Autovector
26	104	068	SD	Level 2 Interrupt Autovector
27	108	06C	SD	Level 3 Interrupt Autovector
28	112	070	SD	Level 4 Interrupt Autovector
29	116	074	SD	Level 5 Interrupt Autovector
30	120	078	SD	Level 6 Interrupt Autovector
31	124	07C	SD	Level 7 Interrupt Autovector
32-47	128	080	SD	TRAP Instruction Vectors
	191	0BF		–
48-63*	192	0C0	SD	(Unassigned, reserved)
	255	0FF		–
64-255	256	100	SD	User Interrupt Vectors
	1023	3FF		–

Figure 14.2 Vector table. (Courtesy of Motorola, Inc.)

vector can be determined by multiplying its vector number by 4. For instance, vector 8 is stored starting at address $4_{10} \times 8_{10} = 32_{10} = 000020_{16}$.

The low-numbered vectors serve special functions of the 68000 microcomputer system. Examples are the *bus error exception vector* at address 000008_{16}, *address error exception vector* at $00000C_{16}$, *CHK instruction vector* at 000018_{16}, and *spurious interrupt vector* at 000060_{16}. Within this group we also find a small number of reserved vector locations. For instance, vectors 12 through 14 are unassigned and reserved for future use.

The next group, vectors 25 through 31 at addresses 000064_{16} through

$00007C_{16}$, is dedicated to what are known as the *autovector interrupts*. They are followed by the *trap instruction vectors* in the address range 000080_{16} through $0000BF_{16}$ and some more reserved vector locations. The last 192 vectors, which are said to be user definable, are used for the external hardware interrupts. Since the addresses that are held in this table are defined by the programmer, the corresponding exception service routines can reside anywhere in the 68000's 16M-byte address space.

EXAMPLE 14.1

At what address is the vector for TRAP #5 stored in the memory? If the service routine for this exception is to start at address 010200_{16}, what will be the stored vector?

SOLUTION   The TRAP #5 instruction corresponds to vector number 37. Therefore, its address is calculated as

$$4_{10} \times 37_{10} = 148_{10} = 000094_{16}$$

The vector address 010200_{16} is broken into two words for storage in memory. These words are

$$\text{Most significant word} = 0001_{16}$$

$$\text{Least significant word} = 0200_{16}$$

They get stored as

$$0001_{16} \text{ at address } 000094_{16}$$

$$0200_{16} \text{ at address } 000096_{16}$$

14.4 EXCEPTION PRIORITIES

The exception processing of the 68000 is handled on a *priority* basis. The *priority level* of an exception or interrupt function determines whether or not its operation can be interrupted by another exception. In general, the 68000 will acknowledge a request for service by an exception only if there is no other exception already in progress or if the requesting function is at a higher-priority level then the currently active exception.

Figure 14.3 shows that the exception functions are divided into three basic priority groups and then assigned additional priority levels within these groups. Here *group 0* represents the highest-priority group. It includes the exception functions of external events such as reset and bus error, as well as the the internal address error detection condition. Within group 0, reset has the highest priority. It is followed by bus error and address error in that order.

Exception functions from group 0 always override an active exception from *group 1* or *group 2*. Moreover, a group 0 function does not wait for completion of execution of the current instruction; instead, it is initiated at the completion of the bus cycle that is in progress.

Group	Exception	Processing
0	Reset Bus Error Address Error	Exception processing begins within two clock cycles.
1	Trace Interrupt Illegal Privilege	Exception processing begins before the next instruction
2	TRAP, TRAPV, CHK, Zero Divide	Exception processing is started by normal instruction execution

Figure 14.3 Exception priority groups. (Courtesy of Motorola, Inc.)

The next-to-highest priority group, group 1, includes the external hardware interrupts and internal functions: trace, illegal/unimplemented opcode, and privilege violation. In this group, trace has the highest priority and it is followed in order of descending priority by external interrupts, illegal/unimplemented instruction, and privilege violation.

In all four cases in group 1, exception processing is initiated with the completion of the current instruction. If a group 1 exception is in progress, its service routine can be interrupted only by a group 0 exception or another exception from group 1 with higher priority. For instance, if an interrupt service routine is in progress when an illegal instruction is detected, the interrrupt service routine will run to completion before service is initiated for the illegal opcode.

Group 2 is the lowest-priority group and its exceptions will be interrupted by any group 0 or group 1 exception request. This group includes the software exception functions TRAP, TRAPV, CHK, and divide by zero. These exceptions differ from those in the other groups in that they are initiated through execution of an instruction. Therefore, there are no individual priority levels within group 2.

Let us assume that a TRAP exception is in progress when an external device requests service using an interrupt input. In this case the hardware interrupt is of higher priority. Therefore, the trap routine is suspended and execution resumes with the first instruction of the interrupt service routine.

14.5 EXTERNAL HARDWARE INTERRUPTS

The first type of 68000 exception that we will consider in detail is the *external hardware interrupts*. The external hardware interrupt interface can be considered to be a special-purpose input interface. It allows the 68000 to respond quickly and efficiently to events that occur in its external hardware. Through it, external devices can signal the 68000 whenever they need to be serviced. For this reason, the processor does not have to dedicate any of its processing time for checking to determine which of the external devices needs service. For example, the occurrence of a power failure can be detected by an external power failure detection circuit and signaled to the microprocessor as an interrupt.

The General Interrupt Interface

Figure 14.4 shows the *general interrupt interface* of the 68000. Here we have shown the signals that are involved in the interface and see that some circuitry is required to interface external devices to the interrupt request inputs of the 68000. Notice that as many as 192 unique devices could apply interrupt requests to the 68000. However, few applications require this many.

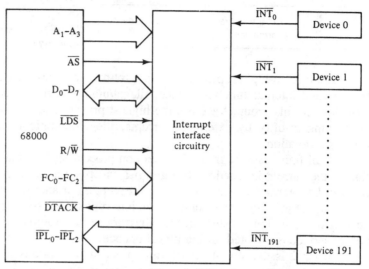

Figure 14.4 General interrupt interface.

Let us now look just briefly at the function of each of the signals involved in the interrupt interface. First we find that three address lines, A_1 through A_3, are in use. They carry an interrupt priority number that is output during the interrupt acknowledge bus cycle. The logic level of $\overline{AS}$ signals external circuitry when this code is available at $A_3A_2A_1$. Accompanying this priority-level number is the *interrupt acknowledge* (IACK) *function code* at outputs FC_2 through FC_0.

During the interrupt acknowledge bus cycle, external circuitry must return an 8-bit vector number to the 68000. Data bus lines D_0 through D_7 are used to input this vector number. The external device signals that the vector number is available on the bus with the data transfer acknowledge ($\overline{DTACK}$) signal. $R/\overline{W}$ and $\overline{LDS}$ control the direction and timing of data transfer over the bus.

External devices must issue a request for service to the 68000. The external *interrupt request inputs* of the 68000 are labeled $\overline{IPL_2}$, $\overline{IPL_1}$, and $\overline{IPL_0}$. The code 000_2 at these inputs represents no interrupt request. On the other hand, a nonzero input represents an active interrupt request.

External Hardware Interrupt Priorities

The external hardware interrupts of the 68000 have another priority scheme within their group 1 priority assignment. The number of priority levels that can be assigned is determined by the number of interrupt inputs. As shown in Fig. 14.5, for three

Priority Level	Interrupt Code		
	$\overline{IPL_2}$	$\overline{IPL_1}$	$\overline{IPL_0}$
None	0	0	0
1	0	0	1
2	0	1	0
3	0	1	1
4	1	0	0
5	1	0	1
6	1	1	0
7	1	1	1

Figure 14.5 External interrupt priorities.

interrupt inputs we get seven independent priority levels. They are identified as 1 through 7 and correspond to interrupt codes $\overline{IPL_2}\,\overline{IPL_1}\,\overline{IPL_0}$ equal to 001_2 through 111_2, respectively. Here 7 represents the highest priority level and 1 the lowest priority level.

The external interrupt circuitry can be designed to allow a large number of devices to respond at each of these interrupt levels. It is for this reason that we have identified 192 external devices in Fig. 14.4. Any number of these 192 devices can be assigned to any one of the interrupt levels. Moreover, additional external priority logic circuitry can be added to prioritize the interrupts into 192 unique priority levels.

Interrupt Mask

Bits 8 through 10 in the system byte of the status register are used as a mask for the external hardware interrupts. Figure 14.6 shows that these bits are labeled I_0 through I_2, respectively. Only active interrupts with a priority level higher than the current value of the mask are enabled for operation. Those of equal or lower priority level are masked out.

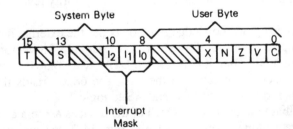

Interrupt Mask

Figure 14.6 Interrupt mask bits in the status register. (Courtesy of Motorola, Inc.)

When the 68000 is reset at power-up, the mask is automatically set to 111_2. This disables interrupts from occurring. For the interrupt interface to be enabled, the mask must be modified to a lower priority level through software. For instance, it could be set to 000_2. This would enable all interrupts for operation.

Whenever a higher-priority interrupt occurs, the mask is automatically changed so that equal- or lower-priority interrupts are masked out. For instance, with initiation of a level 5 interrupt it is changed to 101_2. This masks out from level 5 down through level 1.

The level 7 interrupt request code is not actually masked out with the interrupt mask. Even if the mask is set to 111_2, it remains enabled. For this reason, it can be used to implement a nonmaskable interrupt for the 68000 microcomputer system.

14.6 GENERAL INTERRUPT PROCESSING SEQUENCE

Whenever the code at interrupt inputs $\overline{IPL}_2\overline{IPL}_1\overline{IPL}_0$ is nonzero, an external device is requesting service. It is said that an interrupt is *pending*. At the completion of the current instruction, the 68000 compares this code to the contents of the interrupt mask, $I_2I_1I_0$ in bits 10 through 8 of the status register. If the priority level of the active request is higher than that already in the mask, the request for service is accepted. Otherwise, execution continues with the next instruction in the currently active program or routine.

Upon accepting the exception service request, the 68000 initiates a sequence by which it passes control to the service routine located at the address specified by the interrupt's vector. First, the contents of the status register are temporarily saved. Next, the S-bit, bit 13, of the status register is set to 1 and the T-bit, bit 15, is cleared to 0. They enable the supervisor mode of operation and disable the trace function, respectively. Then interrupt mask $I_2I_1I_0$ is set to the priority level of the interrupt request just accepted.

Now the 68000 initiates an *interrupt acknowledge (IACK) bus cycle*. The sequence of events that occurs during this bus cycle is summarized in Fig. 14.7(a) and shown by waveforms in Fig. 14.7(b). Here we see that it first signals external devices that service has been granted. It does this by outputting the interrupt code of the device to which service was granted on address bus lines A_1 through A_3 and then makes control signals R/$\overline{W}$ = 1, $\overline{AS}$ = 0, and $\overline{LDS}$ = 0. When R/$\overline{W}$ = 1 and $\overline{LDS}$ = 0, a byte of data will be transferred over data bus lines D_0 through D_7. At the same time, it outputs the interrupt acknowledge function code. This code is $FC_2FC_1FC_0$ equal to 111. In this way, it tells the external circuitry which priority level interrupt is being processed.

In response to the interrupt acknowledge function code, the external device that corresponds to the interrupt code on A_1 through A_3 must put an 8-bit vector number on data bus lines D_0 through D_7. Then it must switch $\overline{DTACK}$ to logic 0 to signal the 68000 that the vector number is available on the bus. The 68000 reads the vector number off the bus and then returns both $\overline{LDS}$ and $\overline{AS}$ to logic 1.

It is this 8-bit code that tells the 68000 which of the devices associated with the active interrupt level is requesting service. Notice in Fig. 14.2 that not all the 256 vectors in the table are to be used with the user-defined external hardware interrupts. Only the 192 vectors from vector 64 through 255 should be used for this purpose. Finally, the interrupt knowledge bus cycle is completed when the external device returns $\overline{DTACK}$ to the 1 logic level.

Next, the 68000 pushes the current contents of its program counter onto the top of the supervisor stack. Since PC is 24 bits long, it requires two words of stack and takes two write bus cycles. Then the contents of the old status register, which were saved earlier, are also pushed to the supervisor stack. It takes just one word of memory and is accomplished with one write cycle.

Now the address of the interrupt's vector, which the 68000 calculates from the interrupt vector number, is put on the address bus. The value at this address in the vector table is read over the data bus and loaded into PC. It takes two read bus cycles to fetch the complete vector. During the first bus cycle, the most significant word is carried over the bus and during the second bus cycle, the least significant word. The 68000 now has the new address at which it begins executing the routine that services the interrupt.

A return from exception (RTE) instruction must be included at the end of the service routine. Its execution initiates return of software control to the original program environment.

Figure 14.8 shows how the 68000 internally generates a *vector address* from an

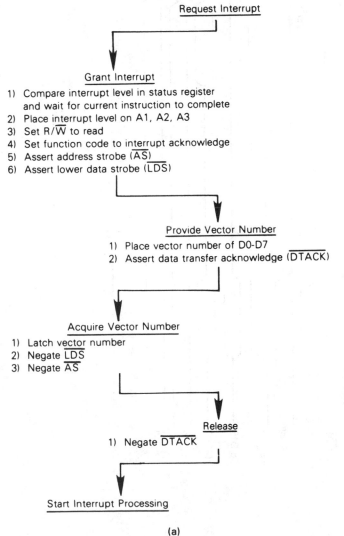

Request Interrupt

Grant Interrupt
1) Compare interrupt level in status register and wait for current instruction to complete
2) Place interrupt level on A1, A2, A3
3) Set R/$\overline{\text{W}}$ to read
4) Set function code to interrupt acknowledge
5) Assert address strobe ($\overline{\text{AS}}$)
6) Assert lower data strobe ($\overline{\text{LDS}}$)

Provide Vector Number
1) Place vector number of D0-D7
2) Assert data transfer acknowledge ($\overline{\text{DTACK}}$)

Acquire Vector Number
1) Latch vector number
2) Negate $\overline{\text{LDS}}$
3) Negate $\overline{\text{AS}}$

Release
1) Negate $\overline{\text{DTACK}}$

Start Interrupt Processing

(a)

Figure 14.7 (a) IACK bus cycle flowchart (courtesy of Motorola, Inc.); (b) IACK bus cycle waveforms (courtesy of Motorola, Inc.).

Sec. 14.6   General Interrupt Processing Sequence

455

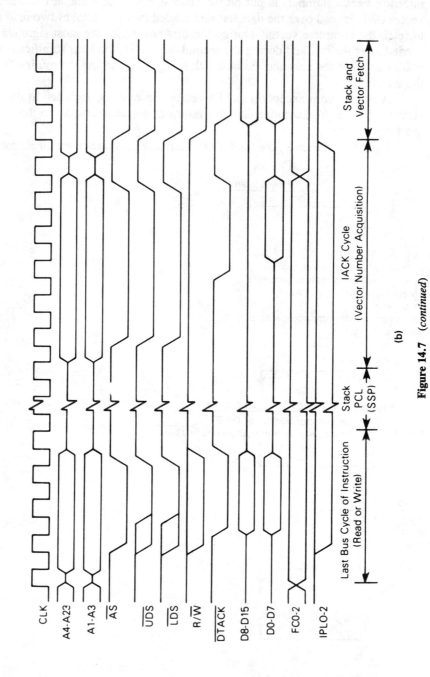

CLK
A4-A23
A1-A3
$\overline{AS}$
$\overline{UDS}$
$\overline{LDS}$
$R/\overline{W}$
$\overline{DTACK}$
D8-D15
D0-D7
FC0-2
IPL0-2

Last Bus Cycle of Instruction (Read or Write)

Stack PCL (SSP)

IACK Cycle (Vector Number Acquisition)

Stack and Vector Fetch

(b)

Figure 14.7 *(continued)*

456

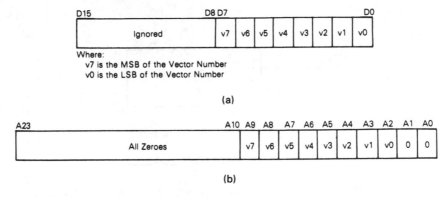

Figure 14.8 (a) Vector for address generation (courtesy of Motorola, Inc.); (b) generated address (courtesy of Motorola, Inc.).

8-bit *vector number*. As shown in Fig. 14.8(a), the vector number was read off of the lower eight data bus lines, D_0 through D_7. First, the 68000 multiplies the vector number by 4. This is done by performing a shift left by two bit positions. Then it fills the upper 14 bits with 0s to form a 24-bit address. This gives the address shown in Fig. 14.8(b), which points to the vector in the table.

14.7 GENERAL INTERRUPT INTERFACE OF THE 68000

The block diagram of Fig. 14.9 illustrates the type of circuitry needed to support a general interrupt interface for the 68000 microcomputer system. This circuit has 192 interrupt request inputs, which are labeled IRQ_0 through IRQ_{191}. These inputs are synchronized by latching them into an *interrupt latch circuit*.

The 192 outputs of the interrupt latch circuit are applied to inputs of the *interrupt absolute priority encoder circuit*. Here they are prioritized and encoded to produce an 8-bit output code that identifies the highest-priority active interrupt request. These codes are in the range IRQ_0 equal to $00000000_2 = 0_{10}$ to IRQ_{191} equal to $10111111_{16} = 191_{10}$.

Remember that in the vector table of Fig. 14.2 the vectors assigned to the user-defined external interrupts are in the range from 64 through 255, not 0 to 191. For this reason, the priority codes that are produced by the *encoder circuit* must be displaced by 64 before they are applied to the data bus of the 68000 during the IACK bus cycle. The circuit labeled *add 64* is provided for this purpose. It simply adds 64 to the 8-bit code at its input.

The output of the add 64 circuit, which is the correct vector number, is latched into the *three-state output vector number latch circuit*. Notice that the outputs of this latch are enabled by $\overline{IACK}$. In this way, the vector number is put on data bus lines D_0 through D_7 only during the interrupt acknowledge bus cycle. At all other times, the outputs of the latch are in the high-Z state.

Up to this point, we have just described the part of the interrupt interface circuit that is used to generate the vector number. But, at the same time, another circuit

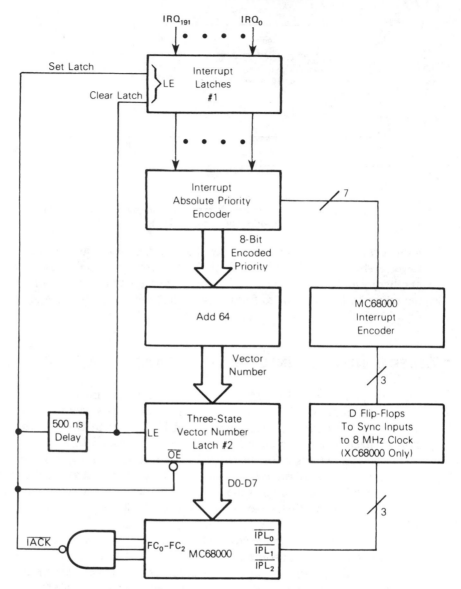

Figure 14.9 Typical general interrupt interface circuit. (Courtesy of Motorola, Inc.)

path, which includes the *interrupt encoder* and *synchronization flip-flops,* must produce an interrupt request to the 68000.

Notice that the *interrupt absolute priority encoder circuit* outputs a 7-bit code in addition to the 8-bit priority code. The 7-bit code is input to the interrupt encoder circuit. In this code, just one bit is set to 0 and it identifies the priority level of the interrupt request. In response, the encoder produces a 3-bit request code for this priority level at its output. This code is latched onto the $\overline{IPL}_2$ through $\overline{IPL}_0$ inputs of the 68000, where it represents an interrupt request.

14.8 AUTOVECTOR INTERRUPT MECHANISM

In 68000 microcomputer systems that do not require more than seven interrupt inputs, a modified interrupt interface configuration can be used. This interface decreases the amount of external support circuits and at the same time shortens the response time from interrupt request to initiation of the service routine. This simplified interrupt mechanism uses what is known as the *autovector mode* of operation.

The *autovector interrupt interface* is shown in Fig. 14.10. It simplifies the interface requirements between external devices and the 68000. In this case, external hardware need just recognize the IACK function code at $FC_2FC_1FC_0$ and respond by switching $\overline{VPA}$ to logic 0. This signals the 68000 to follow its *autovector interrupt sequence*.

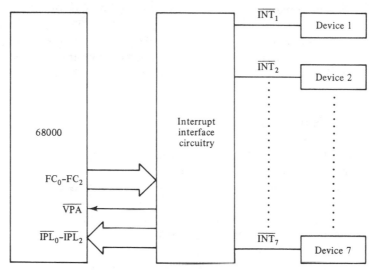

Figure 14.10 Autovector interrupt interface.

When using autovector exception processing, the source of the interrupt vector is determined in a different way. Instead of external circuitry supplying an 8-bit vector number on D_7 through D_0, the 68000 generates the vector address internally from the interrupt request code $\overline{IPL_2}\,\overline{IPL_1}\,\overline{IPL_0}$, and the address of the service routine is fetched from the autovector section of the vector table in Fig. 14.2. In this way, we see that the interrupt acknowledge sequence is shortened. This is the reason that the response time between interrupt request and entry of the service routine is decreased.

As an example, assume that autovector interrupt request code 101_2 is applied to $\overline{IPL_2}$ through $\overline{IPL_0}$. Looking at the table in Fig. 14.2, we see that vector 29 is fetched from addresses 000074_{16} and 000076_{16} and loaded into the PC of the 68000.

14.9 AUTOVECTOR INTERFACE SUPPORT CIRCUIT

Now that we have introduced the autovector interrupt mechanism of the 68000, let us look at a simple circuit that can be used to implement the external hardware interface.

The circuit of Fig. 14.11 can be used to implement the autovector interface in a 68000 microcomputer system. Here we find the seven interrupt request inputs identified as levels 1 through 7. The logic levels at these inputs are latched into the 74LS273 octal latch synchronously with the CLK signal from the 68000. This latch is provided to synchronize the application of interrupt inputs to the priority encoder.

Interrupt requests must be prioritized and encoded into a 3-bit interrupt request code for input to the 68000. This is done by the 74LS348 8-line to 3-line priority encoder. Notice that the inputs of this device are active low, with input 7 corresponding to the highest-priority input and 0 to the lowest-priority input. The binary code corresponding to the highest-priority active input is output at $A_2A_1A_0$. This interrupt code is latched in a 74LS175 latch and its outputs applied to the $\overline{IPL}_2$ through $\overline{IPL}_0$ inputs of the 68000.

In addition to this interrupt request code interface circuit, another circuit is required to support the autovector interrupt interface. This circuit is required to detect the IACK code when it is output by the 68000 and in response assert the $\overline{VPA}$ signal. Typically, this is done by the function decoder circuit of the 68000 microcomputer system. Alternatively, a single three-input NAND gate can be used.

14.10 EXCEPTION INSTRUCTIONS

The instruction set of the 68000 includes a number of instructions that use the exception-processing mechanism. They differ from the hardware-initiated exceptions that we have covered up to this point in that they are initiated as the result of the 68000 executing an instruction. Some of these instructions make a conditional test to determine whether or not to initiate exception processing.

There are five such instructions. They are *trap* (TRAP), *trap on overflow* (TRAPV), *check register against bounds* (CHK), *signed divide* (DIVS), and *unsigned divide* (DIVU). The operation of these instructions is summarized in Fig. 14.12. Let us now look at the exception processing for each of these instructions in more detail.

Trap Instruction: TRAP

The TRAP instruction can be considered to be the software interrupt instruction of the 68000. It permits the programmer to perform a vectored call of an exception service routine. We can call this routine the trap service routine, and it is typically used to perform vectored subroutine calls such as *supervisory calls*.

The trap instruction is simply written as

TRAP #n

Here n represents the *trap vector number* that is to be used to locate the starting point of the exception-processing routine in program memory. Looking at the vector table in Fig. 14.2, we see that the 24-bit starting addresses for the trap instructions are located at addresses in the range 000080_{16} through $0000BF_{16}$. This gives a total of 32

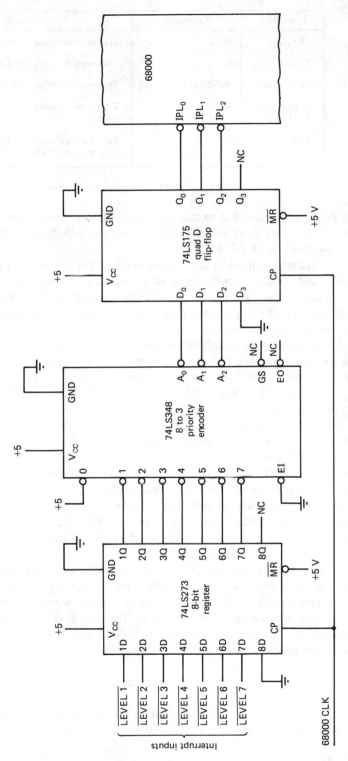

Figure 14.11 Typical autovector interrupt interface circuit. (Courtesy of Motorola, Inc.)

Instruction	Condition	Operation
TRAP #n	None	Trap sequence using trap vector n
TRAPV	V = 1	Trap sequence using TRAPV vector
CHK EA,Dn	Dn < 0 or Dn > (EA)	Trap sequence using CHK vector
DIVS EA,Dn DIVU EA,Dn	(EA) = 0	Trap sequence using zero divide vector
RTE		Return from exception routine to the program in which exception occurred

Figure 14.12 Exception instructions.

words of memory allocated to storage of trap vectors. Since each vector requires two words of memory, there is room for 16 vectors, which correspond to instructions TRAP #0 through TRAP #15.

For instance, the most significant word of the vector for TRAP #0 is held at 000080_{16} and its least significant word at 000082_{16}. Execution of the TRAP #0 instruction causes the 24-bit value stored at these locations to be loaded into the PC of the 68000. Therefore, program execution resumes with the first instruction of the TRAP #0 service routine.

Let us look more closely at the series of events that takes place to pass control to the exception service routine of a trap instruction. After the 68000 executes the trap instruction, it first saves the current contents of its status register in a temporary holding register. Then the S-bit of SR is set. This enables the supervisor system environment. Next, bit T of SR is cleared to disable the trace mode of operation.

Now the 68000 preserves the current program environment such that it can be reentered at completion of exception processing. It does this by pushing the current contents of PC onto the supervisor stack. This value of PC points to the instruction following the TRAP instruction that just initiated exception processing. Then the status word is pushed onto the supervisor stack.

We are now ready to enter the exception service routine. The address of the trap vector is automatically calculated by the 68000 from the trap number. The trap vector is read from this location and loaded into PC. Execution picks up with the first instruction of the service routine.

Notice that just the old PC and SR are automatically saved on the supervisor stack by the exception-processing mechanism. Frequently, the exception service routine will require use of the 68000's data or address registers. For this reason, their contents may also be saved on the stack. The 68000 does not have PUSH or POP instructions for this purpose. Instead, its MOVE instruction is used to perform these types of operations. For example, the instruction

MOVE.L D0, - (SP)

will effectively push the 32-bit contents of D_0 on to the top of the supervisor stack. Typically, this is done with the first few instructions of the service routine.

Just as for interrupts, the return mechanism of the TRAP instruction is the return from exception (RTE) instruction. Execution of this instruction at the end of the service routine causes the saved values of PC and SR to be popped from the supervisor stack. Prior to executing the RTE instruction, the contents of any additional registers saved on the stack must also be popped back into the 68000. Again, this can be done with the MOVE instruction. For example,

$$\text{MOVE.L} \quad (\text{SP})+, \text{D0}$$

causes the 32-bit value at the top of the stack of effectively be popped into register D_0.

TRAPV, CHK, and DIVU/DIVS Instructions

The rest of the exception instructions initiate a trap to an exception service routine only upon detection of an abnormal processing condition. For instance, the trap on overflow (TRAPV) instruction checks overflow bit V, bit 1 of the status register, to determine whether or not an overflow has resulted from execution of the previous instruction. If V is found to be set, an overflow has occurred and exception processing is initiated with an overflow service routine. In this case control is passed to the overflow service routine pointed to by the TRAPV vector at addresses $00001C_{16}$ and $00001E_{16}$ of the vector table. On the other hand, if V is not set, execution continues with the next sequential instruction in the program.

The check register against boundaries (CHK) instruction, as its name implies, can determine if the contents of a register lie within a set of minimum/maximum values. The minimum value (boundary) is always 0000_{16}. On the other hand, the maximum value (boundary), $MMMM_{16}$, is specified as a source operand and can reside in an internal register or a location in external memory.

An example is the instruction

$$\text{CHK} \quad \#\$5A, \text{D0}$$

Here register D_0 contains the parameter under test and $5A is the maximum boundary. If during execution of the instruction the contents of D_0 are found to be within the range 0000_{16} to the value $5A_{16}$, the parameter is within bounds and exception processing is not initiated. On the other hand, if it is negative or greater than $5A_{16}$, it is out of bounds and exception processing is initiated. The change in program environment is to the address defined by vector 6 at addresses 000018_{16} and $00001A_{16}$ in the vector table.

The last two exception instructions, DIVU and DIVS, cause a trap to a service routine if the division they perform involves a divisor equal to zero. This divide-by-zero exception is initiated through the vector at address 000014_{16} and 000016_{16}.

14.11 INTERNAL EXCEPTION FUNCTIONS

The 68000 also has a number of internally initiated exception functions. In fact, it has four such functions: address error, privilege violation, trace, and illegal/unimplemented opcode detection. We will look next at each of these internal exception functions in detail.

Address Error Exception

In Chapter 13 we discussed how data are organized in the memory of a 68000 microcomputer system. At that time, we pointed out that instructions, words of data, and long words of data all must always reside at even-address boundaries. However, software can be written that incorrectly attempts to access one of these types of information from an odd-address boundary. It is to detect and correct for this error condition that the address error feature is provided on the 68000.

Address error detection does not have to be done with external circuitry as we saw earlier for bus error detection. Instead, this capability is built within the 68000 as an internal exception function. Whenever an attempt is made to read or write word-wide data from an odd-address boundary, the 68000 automatically recognizes the memory access as an address error condition. Upon detection, the exception-processing sequence is initiated and control is passed to the address error exception service routine. This routine can attempt to correct the error condition, or if correction is not possible, its occurrence can be signaled in some way. For instance, the address and type of access could be displayed on a panel of LEDs.

The control transfer sequence that takes place for address error exceptions causes the contents of SR and PC, the first word of the current instruction, the address that was in error, and an access-type error word. The format of the access-type error word saved on the stack during an address error exception is shown in Fig. 14.13. Vector 2 is used to locate the service routine. As shown in Fig. 14.2, this vector resides at address $00000C_{16}$ and $00000E_{16}$ of the vector table.

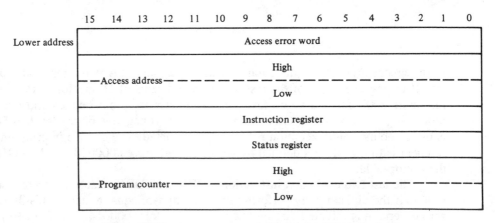

Figure 14.13 Access error word. (Courtesy of Motorola, Inc.)

Exception Processing of the 68000 Microprocessor   Chap. 14

Privilege Violation Exception

In earlier chapters, we found that the 68000 has the ability to easily implement a *user/supervisor microcomputer system environment* and that the state of operation can be selected under software control. The importance of this capability lies in that it permits certain system resources to be accessible only by the supervisor. In this way, it provides a level of security in the system design.

Another internal exception feature of the 68000 that we have not yet considered gives it the ability to identify when a user attempts to use a supervisor resource. These illegal accesses are referred to as *privilege state violations*.

Remember that the S-bit in the system byte of the status register determines whether the 68000 is in the user state or the supervisor state. For instance, when S is set to logic 0, the user state of operation is selected. The user state is the lower security level. Switching S to logic 1 under software control puts the microprocessor at the higher security level or supervisor state.

When in the supervisor state, the 68000 can execute all the instructions of its instruction set. However, when in the user mode, certain instructions are considered privileged and cannot be executed. For example, instructions that AND, OR, or exclusive-OR an immediate word operand with the contents of the status register are not permitted. Any attempt to execute one of these privileged instructions, while in the user state, results in a privileged state violation exception. The privilege violation exception service routine can signal the occurrence of the violation and provide a mechanism for recovery. Figure 14.2 shows that the privilege mode violation uses vector 8 at addresses 000020_{16} and 000022_{16} of the vector table.

Trace Exception

The 68000 has a trace option that allows for implementation of the single-step mode of operation. Just like the privileged state, this option can be enabled or disabled under software control by toggling a bit in the status register. Trace is controlled by the T-bit in the system byte of SR. Trace is turned on by setting T to logic 1 and turned off by clearing it to 0.

When *trace mode* is enabled, the 68000 initiates a trace exception through vector 9 at completion of execution of each instruction. This exception routine can pass control to a monitor that allows examination of the MPU's internal registers or external memory. This type of information is necessary for debugging software. The monitor can also be used to initiate execution of the next instruction. In this way, the instructions of the program can be stepped through one after the other and their operations verified.

Illegal/Unimplemented Instructions

The last internal exception function of the 68000 is its *illegal/unimplemented instruction detection* capability. This feature of the 68000 permits it to detect automatically whether or not the opcode fetched as an instruction corresponds to one of the instructions in the instruction set. If it does not, execution is not attempted; instead, the opcode is identified as being illegal and exception processing is initiated. This *illegal opcode detection mechanism* permits the 68000 to detect errors in its instruction stream.

Occurrence of an illegal opcode initiates a change of program context through the illegal instruction vector, vector 4 in the table of Fig. 14.2. The exception service routine that gets initiated can signal the occurrence of the error condition.

The *unimplemented instruction* concept is an extension of the illegal instruction detection mechanism by which the instruction set of the 68000 can be expanded. It lets us use two ranges of unused opcodes to define new instructions. They correspond to all opcodes of the from $FXXX_{16}$ and $AXXX_{16}$. Here the X's stand for don't-care digits and can be any hexadecimal numbers.

Whenever an opcode of the form $FXXX_{16}$ is detected by the 68000, control is passed to an exception-processing routine through vector 11 at addresses $00002C_{16}$ and $00002E_{16}$ of the exception vector table. The service routine pointed to by this vector should be a *macroinstruction emulation routine* for the new instruction. For example, floating-point arithmetic or double-precision arithmetic emulation routines can be implemented. The emulation routine is written and debugged in assembly language and then stored in main memory as machine code. To use the new instruction in a program, we just insert this opcode, $FXXX_{16}$, as an instruction statement.

As shown in Fig. 14.2, the other unimplemented instruction opcode, $AXXX_{16}$, vectors out of address 000028_{16} and $00002A_{16}$.

ASSIGNMENT

Section 14.2

1. Name three external exception functions.
2. Give three instructions that initiate exception processing.
3. List three internal functions that lead to exception processing.

Section 14.3

4. What is the range of exception vector numbers?
5. What is held in the exception vector table?
6. How large is the exception vector table? What is its address range?
7. Find the vector number of the TRAP 3 exception.
8. What addresses in the exception vector table are reserved for the zero divide exception?
9. What addresses in the exception vector table are reserved for user-defined exception 50?
10. Show how the address 010123_{16} would be stored in the address error location of the exception vector table.
11. If the TRAPV vector has the values 0034_{16} and 0012_{16} at address $00001C and $00001E, respectively, what is the address of the service routine?

Section 14.4

12. Does the bus error exception or the privilege violation exception have the higher group priority?

13. What group priority do the TRAP exceptions have?
14. Which interrupt has the higher priority level: level 1 autovector interrupt or level 7 autovector interrupt?
15. Which exception is at the highest priority level in group 1?
16. If external hardware interrupt 50 is in progress when an address error exception occurs, will the INT 50 service routine be interrupted?

Section 14.5

17. How many exception numbers are reserved for external hardware interrupts?
18. Which vector numbers are assigned to external hardware interrupts?
19. What is output on $A_3A_2A_1$ during the interrupt acknowledge bus cycle?
20. What function code is output on $FC_2FC_1FC_0$ during the interrupt acknowledge bus cycle?
21. How large is the interrupt vector number that is put on the 68000's data bus during the interrupt acknowledge bus cycle?
22. When no interrupts are active, what is the code at $\overline{IPL_2}\,\overline{IPL_1}\,\overline{IPL_0}$?
23. How many priority levels exist for external hardware interrupts?
24. Does external hardware priority level 2 or 6 represent the higher of the two priority levels?
25. Where is the interrupt mask located?
26. To what value is the interrupt mask set after reset?
27. If the interrupt mask is set to 010_2, which priority levels are masked out? Which levels are active?
28. What external hardware interrupt priority level should be assigned to the nonmaskable interrupt input?
29. If the interrupt mask value is 5 when the 68000 receives an external hardware interrupt request with code 100_2, will the request be acknowledged or ignored?
30. Write a sequence of instructions to load the interrupt mask with the value 011_2 without changing any of the other bits in the status register. Assume that the 68000 is in the supervisor state.

Section 14.6

31. Overview the sequence of events that takes place during the interrupt processing sequence for $\overline{IPL_2}\,\overline{IPL_1}\,\overline{IPL_0} = 011$. Assume that no other interrupts are currently active.
32. The contents of which registers are automatically saved on the stack during interrupt processing? To which stack do they get pushed? How much stack space do they consume?
33. Into which register is the vector address for the exception loaded?

Section 14.7

34. What two functions are performed by the interrupt absolute priority encoder circuit?
35. Why is an add 64 circuit needed in the circuit of Fig. 14.9?
36. Overview the response of the circuit in Fig. 14.9 to an active IRQ_{60} input. Assume that this is the only active interrupt input and that it is assigned priority level 4.

Section 14.8

37. What is the maximum number of interrupts that can be directly supported off of the autovector interrupt interface?

38. What signal is part of the autovector interrupt interface in Fig. 14.10, but is not part of the general interrupt interface in Fig. 14.9? Which signal is part of the general interrupt interface of Fig. 14.9, but is not part of the autovector interrupt interface of Fig. 14.10?

39. How is the vector number for the active autovector interrupt produced?

Section 14.9

40. If the level 2 input of the circuit in Fig. 14.11 is active, which vector number identifies the location of the address for the service routine? What is the address of the vector?

41. Overview the operation of the autovector interrupt interface circuit in Fig. 14.11 when a level 2 request for service is received.

42. Show how an octal decoder (three line to eight-line decoder) can be used in the circuit of Fig. 14.11 to decode the function codes and apply $\overline{VPA}$ to the 68000.

Section 14.10

43. Which vector number corresponds to the instruction TRAP #3? What is the address of the vector?

44. How many trap instructions can be written?

45. What instruction does TRAPV stand for? What vector number is assigned to this exception?

46. Assume that D_0 contains the value 00001000_{16} and D_1 contains 00001234_{16}; what is the result of executing the instruction

    CHK D0,D1

47. Write an instruction sequence that will check the index of an array. The index is stored in memory location INDEX, and the upper bound of the array is stored at UBD.

48. Under what conditions will the DIVS instruction cause an exception?

49. What instruction must be included at the end of an interrupt service routine?

50. Show the general structure of a TRAP service routine. Assume that the service routine uses registers D_0, D_1, and A_2.

Section 14.11

51. What internal exceptions are implemented in the 68000?

52. Explain what is meant by an address error exception.

53. Which state has the lower privilege level; user state or supervisor state?

54. Which state must the 68000 be in to permit all instructions of the instruction set to be executed?

55. What mode of operation is implemented with the T-bit in SR and the trace exception.

56. What happens when the unused opcode $F100_{16}$ is encountered during instruction execution?

57. Which vector number is used to specify the service routine when an illegal opcode is detected?

15

Software Architecture of the 68020 Microprocessor

15.1 INTRODUCTION

Having described the 68000 microprocessor in the previous chapters, we now start a study of the 68020 microprocessor. The 68020 is the fourth member of the 68000 family and brings both higher performance and a number of advanced features to the architecture. For instance, the software architecture is enhanced with new addressing modes and instructions. This chapter is devoted to the software architecture of the 68020. Here we will concentrate on the differences between the original 68000 and the 68020. The hardware architecture of the 68020 is also enhanced to make it more versatile. Hardware architecture is the subject of the next chapter. The material in this chapter assumes that the reader is already familiar with the 68000 microprocessor. Specifically, the following topics are covered.

1. Software model
2. Addressing modes
3. Instruction set
4. Enhancements to instructions in the base instruction set
5. Bit field instructions
6. BCD pack and unpack instructions
7. Modular programming support instructions
8. Multiprocessing/multitasking support instructions
9. Coprocessor interface support instructions

15.2 SOFTWARE MODEL

In Chapter 2 we discussed the software model of the 68000 microprocessor. In this section we begin our study of the 68020's software architecture with its software model. The user-mode software model is illustrated in Fig. 15.1. This is the register model that is active when the 68020 is configured for user mode of operation.

Let us first compare the 68020's *user-mode software model* to that shown for the 68000 in Fig. 2.1. Like the 68000, the 68020 has eight 32-bit data registers, eight 32-bit address registers, and a 16-bit status register. These registers serve the exact same functions for both the 68000 and 68020 microprocessors. There are two differences found in these models. First, the program counter (PC) in the 68000 is just 24 bits in length, while that in the 68020 is 32 bits. Second, the address range of the memory address space is shown to be from 00000000_{16} to $FFFFFFFC_{16}$ for the 68020. In this way; we see that the memory address space has been extended from 16 MB to 4 GB (gigabytes).

When the 68000 is switched to the supervisor mode, the only change in the software model of Fig. 2.1 is that the user stack pointer (USP) becomes inactive and the supervisor stack pointer (SSP) becomes active. This is not true of the 68020. Switching the 68020 into supervisor mode enables a software model that includes a number of new registers. These registers are provided to support advanced features such as cache memory and operating system.

The *supervisor mode register model* of the 68020 is given in Fig. 15.2. Here we find seven new registers: the *interrupt stack pointer* (ISP), *master stack pointer* (MSP), *vector base register* (VBR), two *alternate function code registers* (SFC and DFC), *cache control register* (CACR), and the *cache address register* (CAAR). Let us now look at the function of some of these registers in detail.

Notice that the SSP register of the 68000 microprocessor is replaced by two stack pointer registers, ISP and MSP, in the 68020. This shows that supervisor mode of operation can support separate stacks for interrupt handling and supervisor-level subroutine handling. Remember that a third stack also exists in the system software. This is the user stack that is used for subroutine and interrupt handling in the user mode. When operating in supervisor mode, the programmer can select between the interrupt stack and master stack with a bit in the status register.

In our study of the 68000 microprocessor, we found that the exception vector table always started at address 000000_{16}. This is not true of the vector table in a 68020-based microcomputer system. The beginning of the table is defined by the value of the 32-bit address in the vector base register (VBR). At reset, the contents of this register are initialized to 00000000_{16}. This locates the table as in the 68000 system. But the programmer can relocate the table anywhere in the 68020's 4-GB address space by simply loading an address into VBR. Moreover, it is possible to have more than one exception vector table. A new table is activated by just changing the contents of VBR.

The source function code register (SFC) and destination function code register (DFC) can be used in some instructions to specify a specific address space for the source or destination operand, respectively. Remember that during all operand accesses a function code, $FC_2FC_1FC_0$, is output by the 68000. This function code iden-

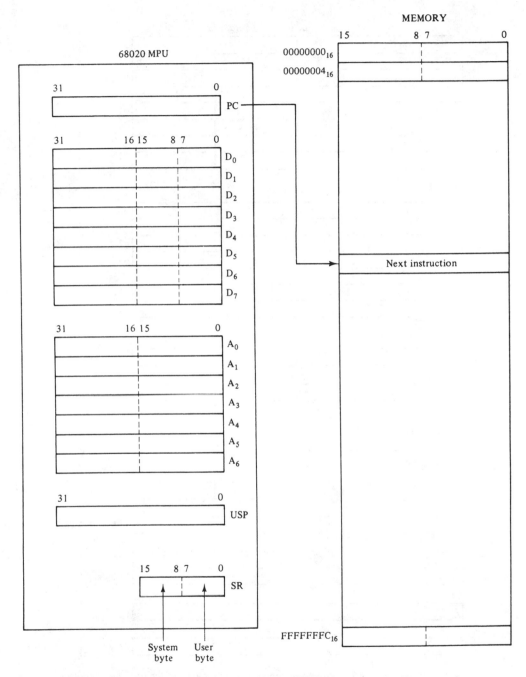

Figure 15.1 User-mode software model of the 68020 microprocessor. (Courtesy of Motorola, Inc.)

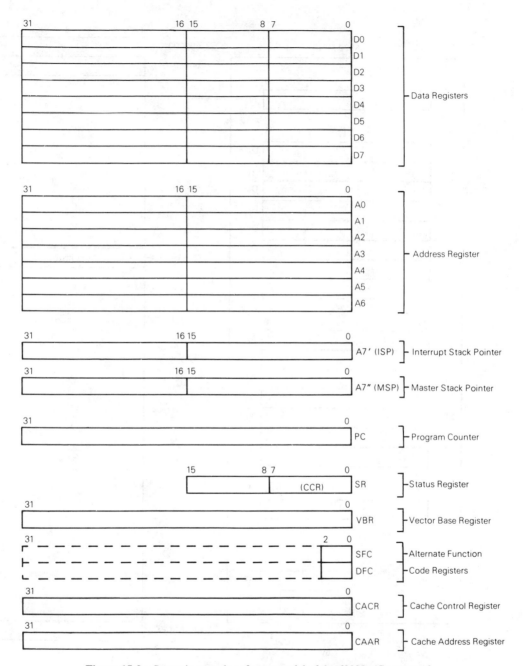

Figure 15.2 Supervisor-mode software model of the 68020. (Courtesy of Motorola, Inc.)

tifies whether the operand is in the user data address space or supervisor data address space. If an instruction that references an alternate function code register is executed, the 3-bit code in the register is output on the FC lines during the operand access instead of the normal code. That is, the function code held in the referenced alternate function code register overrides the normal function code. For example, to write an operand to a storage location in the user data address space while in supervisor mode, DFC would first be loaded with 001_2 and then the instruction executed must reference DFC for its destination operand. In this way, we see that the alternate function code registers implement a mechanism that permits an instruction to access data in a different address space.

The status register (SR) of the 68020 microprocessor is shown in Fig. 15.3. Comparing it to that of the 68000 in Fig. 2.7, we find that their user bytes are identical. On the other hand, two additional bits are defined in the system byte. Bit 12, M, is the master/interrupt stack select bit. This is the bit that allows the programmer to select between the two types of supervisor-mode system stacks, the master stack and the interrupt stack. For instance, M equal to 1 enables the master stack for operation.

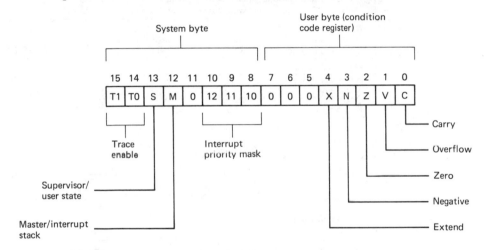

Figure 15.3 Status register of the 68020. (Courtesy of Motorola, Inc.)

The trace bit (T) of the 68000 is split into two trace bits T_0 and T_1 in the 68020's SR. These 2 bits are not used together; instead, they control separate modes of trace operation. T_1 performs the same operation as T does for the 68000. That is, it is used to enable/disable single-step mode of operation. On the other hand, T_0 enables/disables a mode of trace operation known as trace on change of control flow. This mode of trace operation causes a break in program execution whenever the MPU executes a branch, return from subroutine, or a trap instruction. Thus, T_0 can be set to trace when such events occur. This is a trace mechanism commonly implemented with breakpoints and is very useful while debugging programs.

The 68020 employs an on-chip instruction cache. The cache control register (CACR) and cache address register (CAAR) provide support for cache operations. The cache and the function of these registers are discussed in the next chapter.

15.3 ADDRESSING MODES

Just like the 68000 microprocessor, the 68020 provides a number of addressing modes to access operands. These addressing modes permit access to operands in internal registers, program memory, or data memory. The table in Fig. 15.4 identifies the addressing modes implemented by the 68020.

The addressing modes supported by the 68020 are a superset of those provided by the 68000. Figure 2.10 lists the addressing modes of the 68000. In Fig. 15.4, we

Addressing Modes	Syntax
Register Direct Data Register Direct Address Register Direct	Dn An
Register Indirect Address Register Indirect Address Register Indirect with Postincrement Address Register Indirect with Predecrement Address Register Indirect with Displacement	(An) (An)+ -(An) (d_{16},An)
Register Indirect with Index Address Register Indirect with Index (8-Bit Displacement) Address Register Indirect with Index (Base Displacement)	(d_8,An,Xn) (bd,An,Xn)
Memory Indirect Memory Indirect Postindexed Memory Indirect Preindexed	([bd,An],Xn,od) ([bd,An,Xn],od)
Program Counter Indirect with Displacement	(d_{16},PC)
Program Counter Indirect with Index PC Indirect with Index (8-Bit Displacement) PC Indirect with Index (Base Displacement)	(d_8,PC,Xn) (bd,PC,Xn)
Program Counter Memory Indirect PC Memory Indirect Postindexed PC Memory Indirect Preindexed	([bd,PC],Xn,od) ([bd,PC,Xn],od)
Absolute Absolute Short Absolute Long	(xxx).W (xxx).L
Immediate	#(data)

NOTES:

Dn = Data Register, D7–D0

An = Address Register, A7–A0

d_8, d_{16} = A twos-complement, or sign-extended displacement; added as part of the effective address calculation; size is 8 (d_8) or 16 (d_{16}) bits; when omitted, assemblers use a value of zero.

Xn = Address or data register used as an index register; form is Xn.SIZE*SCALE, where SIZE is .W or .L (indicates index register size) and SCALE is 1, 2, 4, or 8 (index register is multiplied by SCALE); use of SIZE and/or SCALE is optional.

bd = A twos-complement base displacement; when present, size can be 16 or 32 bits.

od = Outer displacement, added as part of effective address calculation after any memory indirection; use is optional with a size of 16 or 32 bits.

PC = Program Counter

(data) = Immediate value of 8, 16, or 32 bits

( ) = Effective Address

[ ] = Use as indirect access to long word address.

Figure 15.4 Addressing modes of the 68020. (Courtesy of Motorola, Inc.)

have highlighted those addressing modes that are new with the 68020. Here we find six new modes: *address register indirect with index (base displacement)*, *memory indirect postindexed*, *memory indirect preindexed*, *PC indirect with index (base displacement)*, *PC memory indirect postindexed*, and *PC memory indirect preindexed*. Moreover, addressing modes that use an index, support what is called scaling. Let us now examine scaling and each of these new addressing modes.

Index Scaling

Many of the addressing modes that are common to the 68000 and 68020 use what is called indexing. That is, they specify a value called an index, which is in either a data register or an address register, for use in the address calculation. We just pointed out that the 68020 supports what is called *scaling* of indices. Scaling permits the value of the index to be automatically multiplied by 1, 2, 4, or 8 as part of the effective address calculation.

An example of an addressing mode that uses indexing is address register indirect with index addressing. In Fig. 15.4, we see that the address syntax is (d8,An,Xn). Here An stands for an address register, Xn is the index register, and d8 is an 8-bit displacement. In the 68000, this effective address is calculated in general as

$$EA = An + Xn.SIZE + d8$$

On the other hand, in the 68020 it is calculated by the expression

$$EA = An + Xn.SIZE * SCALE + d8$$

Notice that SCALE, which can be equal to 1, 2, 4, or 8, has been included to multiply the value of the index.

We have shown what SCALE does in the effective address calculation, but not how it is specified in an instruction. If no value of scale is specified, it is assumed to be equal to 1. On the other hand, a value of 2 stands for word and is specified as W. For instance, in the instruction

        MOVE.W   16(A0,A1.L*W),D0

the source operand uses address register indirect with index addressing. Notice that the index is in the long-word address register A_1 and its value is scaled by 2. Therefore, the effective address of the operand in memory is given by

$$EA = A0 + A1 * 2 + 16$$

A SCALE value of 4, which is specified in the instruction as L, means long word. Finally, SCALE equal to 8 specified by Q identifies a quad word.

Address Register and Program Counter Indirect with Index (Base Displacement) Addressing Modes

The second form of register indirect with index addressing shown in Fig. 15.4 is address register indirect with index (base displacement) addressing. This is one of the addressing modes that is new with the 68020. The only difference between this form of the addressing mode and the one supported on the 68000 is the size of the displacement. Notice that the syntax of the effective address is now

$$(bd, An, Xn)$$

where bd stands for base displacement. Therefore, the effective address is computed as

$$EA = An + Xn.SIZE * SCALE + bd$$

The base displacement (bd) can be 16 or 32 bits in size. Its value must be specified in 2's-complement form. An example is the instruction

$$MOVE.L \quad \$FFF0(A0,D0.L*Q),D1$$

Looking at Fig. 15.4, we find that the program counter indirect with index addressing mode is also enhanced with a version that supports a base displacement. In this case, the effective address is obtained with the expression

$$EA = PC + Xn.SIZE * SCALE + bd$$

Memory Indirect Addressing Modes

The memory indirect addressing modes identified in Fig. 15.4 are not supported on the 68000. The addressing modes of the 68000 could only use the contents of an internal register (IP, Dn, or An) to access operands in memory. With the memory indirect addressing modes, the 68020 can also use the contents of a storage location in memory as the address to access an operand held elsewhere in memory. Notice that two forms of memory indirect addressing are available on the 68020 microprocessor. One is called *memory indirect postindexed* and the other *memory indirect preindexed*.

The syntax of an operand specified with memory indirect postindexed addressing is given in Fig. 15.4 as

$$([bd, An], Xn, od)$$

and the expression used to obtain the effective address of the operand is

$$EA = [bd+An] + Xn.SIZE * SCALE + od$$

Here bd stands for a 16- or 32-bit base displacement and od for a 16- or 32-bit outer displacement. Furthermore, the brackets around bd + An mean that the contents of the memory location whose address is equal to bd + An are to be used in the computation of the effective address, not the value of bd plus the value in An. By *postindexed* we mean that the value in the index register is added after (post) the value of the indirect address is obtained from memory.

Let us consider an example where the destination operand is specified with memory indirect postindexed addressing mode. Consider the following:

$$\text{MOVE.W} \quad \text{D0, ([\$1111, A1], A2.L*W, \$20)}$$

From the instruction, we find that bd = $1111 and od = $20. Assuming that A1 = $00001234 and A2 = $12340000, the memory address bd + A1 is

$$\text{MA} = \$00001111 + \$00001234 = \$00002345$$

We will further assume that the long-word contents of memory location $2345 are $000ABCD. Then the effective address of the word size destination operand is given by

$$\text{EA} = \$0000ABCD + \$12340000 * 2 + \$20$$

$$= \$2468ABED$$

Therefore, the lower 16 bits of D0 are moved to the word storage location starting at $2468ABED in memory.

The other memory indirect addressing mode, memory indirect with preindex, is similar to memory indirect with postindex addressing in that the value of the indirect address is fetched from memory. The difference here is that the index is added along with the base displacement and address register to obtain the address of the storage location of the indirect address in memory. That is, the value in the index register is used before (pre) the effective address is calculated. This is what is meant by *preindex*. In this case, the effective address is found as

$$\text{EA} = [\text{bd} + \text{An} + \text{Xn.SIZE} * \text{SCALE}] + \text{od}$$

For example, the source operand in the instruction

$$\text{MOVE.W} \quad \text{([\$1111, A1, A2.L*W], 10), D0}$$

uses memory indirect preindexed addressing. Assuming that A_1 and A_2 again contain $00001234 and $12340000, respectively, the address of the memory location for the indirect address is

$$\text{MA} = \$00001111 + \$00001234 + \$12340000 * 2$$

$$= \$24682345$$

Let the contents at this address be equal to $12345678. Then the address of the source operand is given as

$$\text{EA} = \$12345678 + \$20 = \$12345698$$

Program Counter Memory Indirect Addressing Modes

The last two of the new addressing modes identified in Fig. 15.4 are the program counter memory indirect addressing modes. There are two types: *program counter memory indirect postindexed* and *program counter memory indirect preindexed*. These modes are similar to the memory indirect addressing modes just discussed; however, they use the value of the program counter (PC) in the indirect address calculation instead of the contents of an address register.

For example, the instruction

$$\text{MOVE.W} \quad ([bd, PC], Xn.SIZE*SCALE, od), D0$$

uses program counter memory indirect postindexed addressing for the source operand. In this case, the effective address of the source operand is calculated as

$$EA = [bd + PC] + Xn.SIZE * SCALE + od$$

15.4 INSTRUCTION SET

The table in Fig. 15.5(a) shows all the instructions in the 68020's instruction set. Figure 15.5(b) shows that this instruction set is a superset of that of the 68000. By this we mean that it includes all the instructions that can be performed by the 68000, the *base instruction set* of the 68000, plus a number of enhancements. The instructions that represent enhancement are highlighted in Fig. 15.5(a). These enhancements fall into two categories. First, the capability of some of the instructions in the 68000's instruction set have been extended in the 68020. For example, the function of some instructions have been extended to support larger-size displacements and more addressing modes and to process larger-size operands or even new forms of operands. Second, a number of new instruction types have been added to the base instruction set of the 68000. For instance, instructions have been added to support bit field operations, system-level operations, and coprocessor operations.

Since the 68020's instruction set includes all the instructions of the 68000's base instruction set, *upward object code compatibility* is achieved. By upward object code compatibility we mean that object code produced by writing programs for earlier processors such as the 68000 or 68008 can be directly run on the 68020. Therefore, they can be easily ported from these processors to the 68020. However, better performance and more code efficiency may be obtained by rewriting them and using some of the enhanced instruction available in the 68020.

15.5 ENHANCEMENTS TO INSTRUCTIONS IN THE BASE INSTRUCTION SET

In this section, we will examine just those instructions from the base instruction set of the 68000 that are provided with enhanced functionality in the 68020's instruction set. In the sections that follow, we will introduce instructions that are new with the 68020's software architecture.

The tables in Figs. 15.6 and 15.7 list instructions from the base instruction set of the 68000 that have been enhanced in the 68020 microprocessor. Figure 15.6 is a list of integer arithmetic instructions whose functions have been expanded. Notice that it includes the multiply, divide, and sign extend instructions.

For the 68000, the signed multiply (MULS) and unsigned (MULU) instructions only supported the multiplication of 16-bit operands. In Fig. 15.6, we find that for the 68020 the function of these instructions is expanded to support 32-bit operands.

Mnemonic	Description
ABCD	Add Decimal with Extend
ADD	Add
ADDA	Add Address
ADDI	Add Immediate
ADDQ	Add Quick
ADDX	Add with Extend
AND	Logical AND
ANDI	Logical AND Immediate
ASL, ASR	Arithmetic Shift Left and Right
Bcc	Branch Conditionally
BCHG	Test Bit and Change
BCLR	Test Bit and Clear
BFCHG	Test Bit Field and Change
BFCLR	Test Bit Field and Clear
BFEXTS	Signed Bit Field Extract
BFEXTU	Unsigned Bit Field Extract
BFFFO	Bit Field Find First One
BFINS	Bit Field Insert
BFSET	Test Bit Field and Set
BFTST	Test Bit Field
BKPT	Breakpoint
BRA	Branch
BSET	Test Bit and Set
BSR	Branch to Subroutine
BTST	Test Bit
CALLM	Call Module
CAS	Compare and Swap Operands
CAS2	Compare and Swap Dual Operands
CHK	Check Register Against Bound
CHK2	Check Register Against Upper and Lower Bounds
CLR	Clear
CMP	Compare
CMPA	Compare Address
CMPI	Compare Immediate
CMPM	Compare Memory to Memory
CMP2	Compare Register Against Upper and Lower Bounds
DBcc	Test Condition, Decrement and Branch
DIVS, DIVSL	Signed Divide
DIVU, DIVUL	Unsigned Divide
EOR	Logical Exclusive OR
EORI	Logical Exclusive OR Immediate
EXG	Exchange Registers
EXT, EXTB	Sign Extend
ILLEGAL	Take Illegal Instruction Trap
JMP	Jump
JSR	Jump to Subroutine
LEA	Load Effective Address
LINK	Link and Allocate
LSL, LSR	Logical Shift Left and Right
MOVE	Move
MOVEA	Move Address
MOVE CCR	Move Condition Code Register
MOVE SR	Move Status Register
MOVE USP	Move User Stack Pointer
MOVEC	Move Control Register
MOVEM	Move Multiple Registers
MOVEP	Move Peripheral

Mnemonic	Description
MOVEQ	Move Quick
MOVES	Move Alternate Address Space
MULS	Signed Multiply
MULU	Unsigned Multiply
NBCD	Negate Decimal with Extend
NEG	Negate
NEGX	Negate with Extend
NOP	No Operation
NOT	Logical Complement
OR	Logical Inclusive OR
ORI	Logical Inclusive OR Immediate
ORI CCR	Logical Inclusive OR Immediate to Condition Codes
ORI SR	Logical Inclusive OR Immediate to Status Register
PACK	Pack BCD
PEA	Push Effective Address
RESET	Reset External Devices
ROL, ROR	Rotate Left and Right
ROXL, ROXR	Rotate with Extend Left and Right
RTD	Return and Deallocate
RTE	Return from Exception
RTM	Return from Module
RTR	Return and Restore Codes
RTS	Return from Subroutine
SBCD	Subtract Decimal with Extend
Scc	Set Conditionally
STOP	Stop
SUB	Subtract
SUBA	Subtract Address
SUBI	Subtract Immediate
SUBQ	Subtract Quick
SUBX	Subtract with Extend
SWAP	Swap Register Words
TAS	Test Operand and Set
TRAP	Trap
TRAPcc	Trap Conditionally
TRAPV	Trap on Overflow
TST	Test Operand
UNLK	Unlink
UNPK	Unpack BCD

COPROCESSOR INSTRUCTIONS

Mnemonic	Description
cpBcc	Branch Conditionally
cpDBcc	Test Coprocessor Condition, Decrement and Branch
cpGEN	Coprocessor General Instruction

Mnemonic	Description
cpRESTORE	Restore Internal State of Coprocessor
cpSAVE	Save Internal State of Coprocessor
cpScc	Set Conditionally
cpTRAPcc	Trap Conditionally

(a)

Figure 15.5 (a) New instructions of the 68020 (courtesy of Motorola, Inc.); (b) 68020 extensions to the base instruction set of the 68000.

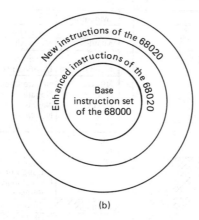

(b) **Figure 15.5** (*continued*)

For instance, the instruction

$$\text{MULS.L} \quad (\text{A1}), \text{D0}:\text{D1}$$

performs a signed multiplication of the 32-bit number held in the memory storage location specified by the address in A_1 with the 32-bit contents of D_1. The 64-bit result is placed in D_0 (most significant 32-bits) and D_1 (least significant 32-bits).

> **EXAMPLE 15.1**
>
> Write an instruction that will multiply the unsigned long-word contents of data register D_4 by the long-word value in D_0. The product produced is 32 bits in length.
>
> **SOLUTION** In Fig. 15.6, this multiplication operation is described by the operand size
>
> $$32 \times 32 = 32$$
>
> Therefore, it is performed with the instruction
>
> $$\text{MULU.L} \quad \text{D4}, \text{D0}$$

Similar to the multiplication instructions, the function of the division instructions has also been extended in the 68020. In the 68000, the DIVS and DIVU instruction could only perform a division of a 32-bit operand by a 16-bit operand. Notice in Fig. 15.6 that in the 68020 they also support division of either a 32-bit or a 64-bit operand by a 32-bit operand. An example is the instruction

$$\text{DIVU.L} \quad (\text{A1}), \text{D0}:\text{D1}$$

It implements the division of a 64-bit number held in D_0 and D_1 by a 32-bit divisor stored in memory at the address in A_1. The 32-bit quotient that results is placed in D_1 and the remainder is placed in D_0.

The last instruction in Fig. 15.6 is the extend sign instruction. In the 68000, this instruction has the ability to extend an 8-bit operand to 16 bits or a 16-bit operand to 32 bits. An EXTB form of the instruction has been added in the 68020 to allow a byte operand to be directly extended to a long word.

Mnemonic	Meaning	Type	Operand size	Operations	Enhancements
MULS	Signed multiply	MULS.W EA, Dn	16 × 16 → 32	(EA) · Dn → Dn	
		MULS.L EA, Dℓ	32 × 32 → 32	(EA) · Dℓ → Dℓ	32-bit operand (Dℓ)
		MULS.L EA, Dh : Dℓ	32 × 32 → 64	(EA) · Dℓ → Dh : Dℓ	32-bit operand (Dℓ) and 64-bit result (Dh and Dℓ)
MULU	Unsigned multiply	MULU.W EA, Dn	16 × 16 → 32	(EA) · Dn → Dn	
		MULU.L EA, Dℓ	32 × 32 → 32	(EA) · Dℓ → Dℓ	32-bit operand (Dℓ)
		MULU.L EA, Dh : Dℓ	32 × 32 → 64	(EA) · Dℓ → Dh : Dℓ	32-bit operand (Dℓ) and 64-bit result (Dh and Dℓ)
DIVS	Signed divide	DIVS.W EA, Dn	32/16 → 16 : 16	Dn/(EA) → Dn	
		DIVS.L EA, Dr : Dq	64/32 → 32 : 32	Dr : Dq/(EA) → Dr : Dq	64-bit dividend, 32-bit divisor, 32-bit quotient, and 32-bit remainder
		DIVS.L EA, Dq	32/32 → 32	Dn/(EA) → Dq	32-bit dividend, 32-bit divisor, 16-bit quotient, and 16-bit remainder
		DIVSL.L EA, Dr : Dq	32/32 → 32 : 32	Dr : Dq/(EA) → Dr : Dq	32-bit dividend, 32-bit divisor, 32-bit quotient, and 32-bit remainder
DIVU	Unsigned divide	DIVU.W EA, Dn	32/16 → 16 : 16	Dn/(EA) → Dn	
		DIVU.L EA, Dr : Dq	64/32 → 32 : 32	Dr : Dq/(EA) → Dr : Dq	64-bit dividend, 32-bit divisor, 32-bit quotient, and 32-bit remainder
		DIVU.L EA, Dq	32/32 → 32	Dq/(EA) → Dq	32-bit dividend, 32-bit divisor, 16-bit quotient, and 16-bit remainder
		DIVUL.L EA, Dr : Dq	32/32 → 32 : 32	Dr : Dq/(EA) → Dr : Dq	32-bit dividend, 32-bit divisor, 32-bit quotient, and 32-bit remainder
EXTB	Extend size	EXTB.L Dn	8 → 32	Dn byte → Dn long word	Direct byte to long word sign

Dn = 32 bit operand
Dℓ = lower 32 bits of a 64 bit operand
Dh = upper 32 bits of a 64 bit operand
Dq = quotient operand
Dr = remainder operand

Figure 15.6 Enhanced integer arithmetic instructions.

Mnemonic	Meaning	Type		Operand size	Operations	Enhancements
TST	Test	TST	EA	8, 16, 32	Set condition codes as per (EA) − 0	Allows program counter relative addressing mode for the source operand
CMPI	Compare immediate	CMPI	#XXX, EA	8, 16, 32	Set condition codes as per (EA) − XXX	Allows program counter relative addressing mode for the source operand
CMP2	Compare register against bounds	CMP2	EA, Rn	8, 16, 32	Rn is compared to upper and lower bounds at EA 1 → Z if Rn = upper or lower bound C = 1 if Rn < lower bound or > upper bound	Allows the contents of a register to be checked to determine if these are within a specific range
BRA	Branch always	BRA	Label	8, 16, 32	PC + d → PC	Allows a 32-bit displacement
Bcc	Branch conditionally	Bcc	Label	8, 16, 32	PC + d → PC if cc is true; otherwise next sequential instruction executes	Allows a 32-bit displacement
BSR	Branch to subroutine	BSR	Label	8, 16, 32	PC → (SP) SP − 4 → SP PC + d → PC	Allows a 32-bit displacement
LINK	Link and allocate	LINK	An, #d	16, 32	An → (SP) SP − 4 → SP SP → An SP + d → SP	Allows a 32-bit displacement
MOVEC	Move CCR	MOVEC	Rc, Rn	32	Rc → Rn	Supports new control registers
		MOVEC	Rn, Rc	32	Rn → Rc	Supports new control registers
MOVES	Move address space	MOVES	EA, Rn	8, 16, 32	(EA) → Rn	Moves to address space defined by DFC
		MOVES	Rn, EA	8, 16, 32	Rn → (EA)	Moves from address space defined by SFC

Figure 15.7 Other instructions with enhanced functionality.

EXAMPLE 15.2

If the byte contents of D_1 are 88_{16}, what is the long-word contents of D_1 after the instruction

$$\text{EXTB.L} \quad \text{D1}$$

is executed?

SOLUTION Executing this instruction sign extends the byte contents of D_1, which equals 10001000_2, to a long word. Since the sign bit of the byte value is 1, the long word that results is

$$D_1 = \text{FFFFFF88}_{16}$$

The table in Fig. 15.7 identifies the rest of the instructions of the base instruction set that have been enhanced in the 68020. In this table, we have identified the enhancements made to each instruction. Looking at the table, we see that only a small change has been made to the function of the test (TST) and compare immediate (CMPI) instructions. This is that the addressing modes supported for their source operand now includes program counter relative addressing.

In addition, a new form of the compare instruction has been included, *compare register against bounds* (CMP2). This instruction is used to determine if the value in register Rn, which can be a data register or address register, is within a specified range. The upper and lower boundaries of the range are held in memory starting at the effective address EA. The lower boundary is the lower addressed word at the long-word storage location and the upper boundary is the higher addressed word. Both the operand to be checked must be placed in the register and the boundaries into memory at the effective address before executing the instruction. In Fig. 15.7, we see that if the contents of Rn equals the value of either boundary when the instruction is executed, the zero flag (Z) is set. Moreover, if it contains a value that is less than the lower boundary or more than the upper boundary, the value is out of bounds, the carry flag (C) is set. On the other hand, if the contents of Rn are within the bounds, then both Z and C are cleared.

The next four instructions in Fig. 15.7, BRA, Bcc, BSR, and LINK, represent a second type of expanded functionality. Here the allowed operands have been expanded to support 32-bit displacements. For example, in the 68000, the branch always (BRA) instruction allowed just 8- or 16-bit displacements. This limits the range of a branch operation to $+$ or $-$ 32K bytes from the current value of PC. With the expansion of the displacement to 32 bits, the range is extended to the full 4-GB address space of the 68020.

Finally, two new forms of the move instruction are provided to directly access the control registers and additional function code registers of the 68020. The instruction *move control register (MOVEC) is used to load or save the contents of a control register* (R_c). Figure 15.8 lists the control registers that can be accessed with this instruction. For instance, executing the instruction

$$\text{MOVEC} \quad \text{MSP,D0}$$

Mnemonic	Control register
SFC	Source function code
DFC	Destination function code
CACR	Cache control register
USP	User stack pointer
VBR	Vector base register
CAAR	Cache address register
MSP	Master stack pointer
ISP	Interrupt stack pointer

Figure 15.8 Control registers accessed with the MOVEC instruction.

saves the current contents of the master stack pointer register in data register D_0. On the other hand, the instruction

MOVEC   D1,MSP

loads the master stack pointer register from data register D_1.

EXAMPLE 15.3

Write an instruction that will load the source function code register from data register D_3.

SOLUTION   The SFC register is loaded from D_3 with the instruction

MOVEC   D3,SFC

The second new form of the move instruction, *move address space* (MOVES), is used to write a data operand to a storage location in the address space defined by the function code in the destination function code (DFC) register or read an operand from an address in the address space selected by the source function code (SFC) register. An example is the instruction

MOVES.L   D1, (A1)

When executed, this instruction copies the value held in data register D_1 into the long-word memory location pointed to by the address in address register A_1 in the address space selected by the function code in DFC.

EXAMPLE 15.4

Describe what happens when the instruction MOVES.B   (A1),D0 is executed.

SOLUTION   Execution of this instruction causes the byte of data held at the address in A_1 in the address space selected by the function code in SFC to be copied into data register D_0.

The registers affected by the MOVEC and MOVES instructions are active in the supervisor mode, and their values can only be modified when the 68020 is in the privilege mode. For this reason, they are called privileged instructions.

15.6 BIT FIELD INSTRUCTIONS

Earlier we pointed out that the instruction set of the 68020 is enhanced with instructions that have the ability to operate on fields of bits. Its bit field instructions are given in Fig. 15.9. Before examining the operation of these instructions, let us first look at the bit field data type.

Meaning	Mnemonic	Type		Operand size	Operations
BFTST	Bit field test	BFTST	EA{oddset : width}	1–32 bits	MSB of FIELD → N If all bits in FIELD are 0, 1 → Z; otherwise, 0 → Z
BFCHG	Bit field test and change	BFCHG	EA{offset : width}	1–32 bits	BFTST instruction FIELD → FIELD
BFCLR	Bit field clear	BFCLR	EA{offset : width}	1–32 bits	BFTST instruction 0s → FIELD
BFEXTS	Bit field extract sign	BFEXTS	EA{offset : width}, Dn	1–32 bits	BFTST instruction Sign extend FIELD → Dn
BFEXTU	Bit field extract unsigned	BFEXTU	EA{offset : width}, Dn	1–32 bits	BFTST instruction Zero extend FIELD → Dn
BFFFO	Bit field find first one	BFFFO	EA{offset : width}, Dn	1–32 bits	BFTST instruction Offset of first bit from MSB and that is set in FIELD → Dn
BFINS	Bit field insert	BFINS	Dn, EA{offset : width}	1–32 bits	BFTST instruction Dn → FIELD
BFSET	Bit field test and set	BFSET	EA{offset : width}	1–32 bits	BFTST instruction 1s → FIELD

Figure 15.9 Bit field instructions.

By *bit field* we mean a group of bits in a long-word operand. The location of the MSB of the field is identified by a parameter known as the *offset*. As shown in Fig. 15.10, the offset equals the difference between the MSB end of the register or memory location, bit 31, and the value of the bit position of the MSB in the field. The number of bits in the field are specified by another parameter known as the *width*. For instance, if the offset and width of a field in a data register are specified as 4 and 8, respectively, the field consists of bit positions 20 through 27 of the register. In this field, bit 20 represents the LSB and bit 27 the MSB.

Bit Field (0≤Offset<32, 0<Width≤32)

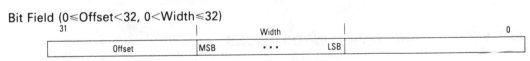

Note: If width + offset<32, bit field wraps around within the register.

Figure 15.10 Bit field data format. (Courtesy of Motorola, Inc.)

Figure 15.9 lists each bit field instruction along with its type, operand size, and a brief description of the operation performed by the instruction. Here we see that the operations that can be done on the bits of a field include complementing each bit in the field (BFCHG), replacing the bits of the field with 0s (BFCLR), copying the bits of the field to a data register (BFEXTS and BFEXTU), scanning the bits of a field to find the first bit that is 1 (BFFFO), replacing the bit field (BFINS), setting all bits of the field to 1 (BFSET), and testing a bit field for the sign and zero (BFTST). During the execution of all bit field instructions, the negative (N) bit is set if the MSB of the field is 1 and cleared if it is 0. That is, the original sign bit of the field is saved in the N flag. Also, the zero (Z) flag is cleared to 0 if all bits of the field are zero. Otherwise, it is set to 1. In this way, we see that the Z flag identifies whether or not the original contents of the field are zero.

EXAMPLE 15.5

Describe the operation performed by each instruction in the program that follows:

```
              MOVE.L    #$00001234,A1
              MOVE.L    #$0000ABCD,A2
              BFTST     (A1){4:8}
              BEQ       BYPASS
              BFCHG     (A2){5:8}
              BRA       DONE
   BYPASS     BFSET     (A2){5:8}
   DONE
```

What function does the instruction sequence perform?

SOLUTION The first two instructions load address registers A_1 and A_2 with the values 00001234_{16} and $0000ABCD_{16}$, respectively. Then the BFTST instruction tests bits 20 through 27 of the long word pointed to in memory by the address in A_1. The test makes N equal to the value in bit 27 and sets Z to 1 if all 8 bits are logic 0. If any of the bits in the range 20 through 27 are not zero, Z is cleared to 0. The BEQ instruction tests the zero flag, and if it is 1, control is passed to the instruction with the label BYPASS. This instruction, BFSET, sets the 8 bits 26 through 19 in the long-word memory location pointed to by the address in A_2 to 1s. On the other hand, if Z is 0, the BFCHG instruction is executed. This instruction causes the values in bits 26 through 19 of the long-word storage location identified by the value in A_2 to be complemented. Then the BRA instruction is executed and control is passed to the instruction with the label DONE.

In summary, the instruction sequence tests bits 20 through 27 of the long-word memory storage location pointed to by the address in A_1 to determine if they are all zero. If they are all zero, bits 19 through 26 of the long-word storage location pointed to by A_2 are set. Otherwise, they are complemented.

15.7 BCD PACK AND UNPACK INSTRUCTIONS

Both the 68000 and 68020 have the ability to directly add, subtract, or negate BCD numbers. However, we found that, when the 68000 processes data with the BCD arithmetic instructions BCD numbers need to be expressed in what is called packed BCD format. Packed BCD means that two BCD digits are stored in a single byte. With the 68000, multiple instructions would need to be executed to take BCD digits in separate bytes and put them into a single byte as packed BCD digits. Special instructions have been added in the instruction set of the 68020 to both pack and unpack BCD digits.

Figure 15.11 describes the operation of the *pack* (PACK) and *unpack* (UNPK) instructions of the 68020. Notice that the pack instruction takes two BCD digits that are in separate bytes of a word-wide source register or storage location in memory and concatenates them as packed BCD digits in a byte-wide destination register or memory location, respectively. For example, if the contents of register D_0 are as shown in Fig. 15.12(a), executing the instruction

PACK   D0,D1

results in packed BCD digits in D_1. Notice in Fig. 15.12(b) that BCD digit 4321, which is in bits 8 through 11 of D_0, and BCD digit $4'3'2'1'$, which is in bits 0 through 3 of D_0, are copied into bits 0 through 7 of D_1. The upper 8 bits of the destination are unchanged. Notice that the instruction types show that only the data register direct and address register indirect with predecrement addressing modes are supported by the instruction.

Mnemonic	Meaning	Type	Operand size	Operations
PACK	Pack BCD	PACK Dx, Dy, #adj PACK −(Ax), −(Ay), #adj	$16 \rightarrow 8$ $16 \rightarrow 8$	Unpacked BCD + adj → packed BCD Unpacked BCD + adj → packed BCD Ax − 2 → Ax Ay − 2 → Ay
UNPK	Unpack BCD	UNPK Dx, Dy, #adj UNPK −(Ax), −(Ay), #adj	$8 \rightarrow 16$ $8 \rightarrow 16$	Packed BCD → unpacked BCD + adj Packed BCD → unpacked BCD + adj Ax − 1 → Ax Ay − 1 → Ay

Figure 15.11   BCD pack and unpack instructions.

(a)

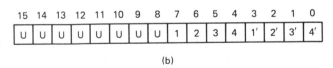

(b)

Figure 15.12   (a) Unpacked BCD numbers before packing with the PACK instruction (courtesy of Motorola, Inc.); (b) BCD numbers after execution of the PACK instruction. (Courtesy of Motorola, Inc.)

In Fig. 15.11, we see that an adjustment may also be included in the instruction. The value of the adjustment is added to the BCD digits of the source before they are copied into the destination. For instance, the instruction

PACK   D0,D1,#5

adds 5_{16} as an extended word to D0 and then packs it.

The unpack instruction performs the exact opposite of the operation just described for the pack instruction. That is, it takes two packed BCD digits in a byte-wide source data register or storage location in memory and splits them into separate bytes in a word-wide destination register or memory location, respectively. Figure

15.13(a) shows packed BCD digits $4'3'2'1'$ and 4321 in register D_1. Executing the instruction

UNPK   D1,D0

splits the digits into separate bytes as shown in Fig. 15.13(b). Similarly the UNPK instruction allows adjustment to the unpacked result.

15	14	13	12	11	10	9	8	7	6	5	4	3	2	1	0
U	U	U	U	U	U	U	U	1	2	3	4	$1'$	$2'$	$3'$	$4'$

(a)

15	14	13	12	11	10	9	8	7	6	5	4	3	2	1	0
U	U	U	U	1	2	3	4	U	U	U	U	$1'$	$2'$	$3'$	$4'$

(b)

Figure 15.13 (a) Packed BCD numbers before unpacking with the UNPK instruction (courtesy of Motorola, Inc.); (b) BCD numbers after execution of the UNPK instruction (courtesy of Motorola, Inc.).

EXAMPLE 15.6

A table of 100 pairs of unpacked BCD numbers is stored in word memory locations starting at address SOURCE. Write a program that will convert the elements of this table into a table of byte-wide packed BCD numbers starting at memory address DESTINATION.

SOLUTION We will begin by setting up a counter in register D_0 to represent the number of unpacked BCD elements, a pointer to the first element in the source table in register A_1, and a pointer to the first element in the destination table in register A_2. These operations are done with the instructions

```
MOVE.L   #100,D0
LEA      SOURCE,A1
LEA      DESTINATION,A2
```

The next segment of program must read a word of data that contains unpacked BCD digits from the source table, pack these BCD digits into a byte, and then copy the packed byte of data into the destination table. This is done with the instruction sequence

```
NEXT   MOVE.W   (A1)+,D1
       PACK     D1,D1
       MOVE.B   D1,(A2)+
```

Notice that the first word in the source table is read into data register D_1 and then the source pointer in A_1 is incremented. In this way, it automatically points to the next word of data. Then the individual BCD digits in word register D_1 are converted to packed digits in byte register D_1. Finally, the packed BCD data are stored in the first byte storage location of the destination table. The destination pointer is also incremented so that it automatically points to the next byte location of the destination table.

This operation must be repeated until all 100 of the unpacked BCD numbers have been read and converted to their equivalent packed BCD numbers. For this reason, the first instruction of the conversion routine has the label NEXT. After each element is converted, the count in D_0 is decremented by 1 with the instruction

SUBQ.L   #1,D0

Then a branch on not-equal instruction

BNE   NEXT

is executed to test the zero flag. If Z is not zero, control is returned to NEXT and the next element is converted. This loop repeats until all 100 elements of the source table are packed. After the 100th element has been converted, execution of the SUBQ instruction makes Z equal to 1. In this case, the branch is not taken; instead, the program is done. The complete routine is shown in Fig. 15.14.

```
        MOVE.L    #100, D0
        LEA       SOURCE, A1
        LEA       DESTINATION, A2
NEXT    MOVE.W    (A1)+, D1
        PACK      D1, D1
        MOVE.B    D1, (A2)+
        SUBQ.L    #1, D0
        BNE       NEXT
DONE
```

Figure 15.14   Program for converting unpacked BCD data to packed BCD data.

15.8 MODULAR PROGRAMMING SUPPORT INSTRUCTIONS

The instruction set of the 68020 microprocessor is enhanced with instructions that are designed to support *modular programming*. When using modular programming, the function that is to be performed by a program is broken down into a number of smaller subfunctions. These subfunctions may be used just once or many times during the execution of the program. Each subfunction is implemented and tested as a separate module of code. Also, a main function module is developed and tested. This main module is used to call the subfunction modules in the sequence needed to perform the overall function for which the program was written. Finally, the subfunction modules are combined with the main function module to produce the complete program. Figure 15.15 shows this type of program structure.

The two instructions added to the instruction set of the 68020 to support program modules are *call module* (CALLM) and *return from module* (RTM). The formats of these instructions are shown in Fig. 15.16. Together these instructions provide the mechanism for calling a new module from another module and initiating a return back to the original module. The program structure that employs these instructions is shown in Fig.15.17. Notice that a CALLM instruction is inserted into the current module to transfer control to the new module, and a RTM instruction is used at the end of the new module to return back to the calling module. As part of the module switching operation, the linkage information needed to return to the original module is saved on the stack. This information is saved in what is called the *module stack frame* of the new module.

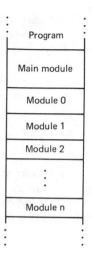

Figure 15.15 Structure of a modular program.

Mnemonic	Meaning	Type	Operations
CALLM	Call module	CALLM #d, EA	Save current module state on stack, load new module state from EA.
RTM	Return from module	RTM Rn	Reload saved module state from stack.

Figure 15.16 Modular programming support instructions.

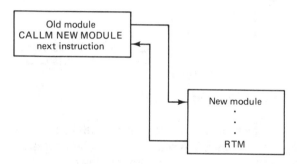

Figure 15.17 Using the CALLM and RTM instructions.

Let us now look more closely at the module switching operation. When a CALLM instruction is executed, it references what is called a *module descriptor*. As shown in Fig. 15.18, this descriptor contains the information needed to pass control to the module, that is, the state of the new module. Notice that the descriptor can be as large as 32 bytes in length and contains seven fields: *opt, type, access level, module entry word pointer, module data area pointer, module stack pointer,* and *additional user-defined information.* The location of the module descriptor is specified in CALLM instruction using the effective address (EA) operand.

In Fig. 15.16, we find that a byte count of the arguments (parameters) that are to be passed to the module are also specified as an operand. The 3-bit *options* (OPT) field in the descriptor is used to tell how these arguments are to be passed from the calling module to the called module. Only two argument-passing mechanisms are supported by the 68020. A code of 000_2 in the OPT field means that the parameters are located on the stack just before the module stack frame. On the other hand, if OPT is coded as 100_2, it tells the called module that the parameters are in the stack of the calling module and that a pointer to this stack is included in the module stack frame.

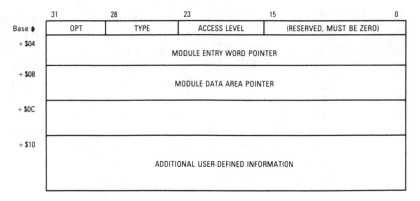

Figure 15.18 Module descriptor format. (Courtesy of Motorola, Inc.)

The next field, TYPE, is 5 bits in length and defines the type of the module. Again only two options are available, 00000_2 and 00001_2. The value 00000_2 identifies a module that does not involve a change in access level. This means that it creates the stack frame at the top of the current stack. The other option, 00001_2, means that the module may involve a change in access level. For this case, the byte-wide access-level field defines the access level for a new stack, the old stack pointer is saved in the module stack frame, and the new stack pointer is loaded with the value in the module stack pointer field.

Let us assume that execution of a CALLM instruction initiates a call to a type 00000_2 module. Earlier we pointed out that in this case the 68020 simply creates a stack frame at the top of the current stack. Figure 15.19 shows the typical contents of a stack frame. Notice that the first two long words contain the opt, type, and access-level fields from the calling modules descriptor, the current values of the CCR

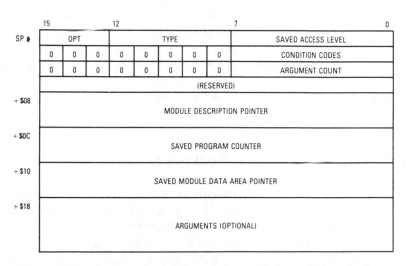

Figure 15.19 Contents of a module stack frame. (Courtesy of Motorola, Inc.)

bits of the 68020's status register, and the number of arguments specified in the CALLM instruction. This information is followed in the stack frame by the address of the module descriptor used in the module call, the old value of PC, which now points to the instruction following the CALLM instruction, and the address of the data area for the calling module. The rest of the stack frame locations, which are reserved for storage of a copy of the arguments being passed to the module, are only used in type 00001_2 module calls where OPT is set to 000_2.

After the module stack frame is automatically created, the module entry word pointer from the descriptor, which is the starting address of the called module, is accessed. The first word at this address does not contain instruction code; instead, it holds what is called the *module entry word*. The instructions of the module follow this module entry word in program memory. Figure 15.20 shows the format of this word. The contents of this word identify the register that is to be used as the module data area pointer. Here we see that it has just four implemented bits. The setting of the D/A bit determines whether a data register or address register is used, and the 3-bit register code selects the specific register.

15	14	13	12	11	10	9	8	7	6	5	4	3	3	1	0
D/A	REGISTER			0	0	0	0	0	0	0	0	0	0	0	0
OPERATION WORD OF FIRST INSTRUCTION															

Figure 15.20 Module entry word format. (Courtesy of Motorola, Inc.)

As part of the module call sequence, the current value in this register is saved in the module stack frame as the module data area pointer. Then the new value of the module data area pointer is loaded into the specified register from the module descriptor. This completes the module call process and execution picks up with the first instruction of the new module.

At the end of the module, a RTM instruction is used to return control to the old module. For a type 000_2 module, execution of this instruction first reloads the saved values of CCR, PC, the data or address register used as the data module area pointer from the module stack frame. Then the stack frame area is deallocated from the stack, and the argument count is added to the stack pointer to clear arguments passed to the module on the stack. This restores the stack for use by the prior module. Finally, program control is resumed in the old module at the instruction following the CALLM instruction.

15.9 MULTIPROCESSING/MULTITASKING INSTRUCTIONS

The 68000 has just one instruction that is meant to support multiprocessing/multitasking operations, the test and set an operand (TAS) instruction. In the 68020, two other instructions are available to support multiple processors. They are *compare and swap with operand* (CAS) and *compare and swap with operand double* (CAS2). Let us next look at the operation performed by each of these instructions.

The operation of these instructions is described in Fig. 15.21. Here we find that the CAS instruction has three operands. The first two are source operands. They are

Mnemonic	Meaning	Type	Operand size	Operations
CAS	Compare and swap	CAS Dc, Du, EA	8, 16, 32	(EA) − Dc → CCR if Z = 1, then Du → (EA) else (EA) → Dc
CAS2	Double compare and swap	CAS2 Dc1 : Dc2 : Du1 : Du2, (Rn1) : (Rn2)	16, 32	Two operand CAS compare operations

Figure 15.21 Multiprocessor/multitasking support instructions.

in data registers and are called the compare operand (Dc) and update operand (Du). The third operand, which is identified as EA, is the destination operand and represents a byte, word, or long word of data in memory. When executed, the CAS instruction compares the value of the destination operand pointed to by EA with the value of the compare operand in Dc, and if they are the same the Z flag is set, and the destination operand is replaced with the value of the update operand in Du. On the other hand, if they are not the same (Z equals 0), the compare operand in Dc is replaced with the value of the destination operand at EA. In both cases, a compare and swap has taken place. This compare and swap uses an indivisible read–modify–write bus cycle. For this reason, no other processor or task can access the destination operand before the CAS operation is done.

As a demonstration of the use of the CAS instruction, let us consider a global variable called GLOBAL_CTR that can be incremented by any of the tasks in a multitasking system or by any of the processors in a multiprocessor system. This count is to be updated each time the global process it corresponds to is performed. The problem is to assure that, during the period when one processor or task is executing the instructions needed to increment the count, another processor or task does not change it.

The sequence of instruction in Fig. 15.22 can be used to ensure that the updating of the count takes place properly. It begins by reading the value of the global counter from memory into compare register D_0. This value is copied into update register D_1 and incremented by 1. Next the CAS instruction compares the original value of the global counter, which is held in D_0, to the current value of the global counter in memory. If the two values are the same, no other processor or task has modified GLOBAL_CTR since its value was read into D_0. Moreover, because the CAS instruction performs an indivisible read–modify–write operation, GLOBAL_CTR cannot change once this instruction is initiated. Therefore, the updated count in D_1 is correct and is written to the global counter.

```
            MOVE.W    GLOBAL_CTR, D0
TRY_AGAIN   MOVE.W    D0, D1
            ADDQ.W    #1, D1
            CAS.W     D0, D1, GLOBAL_CTR
            BNE       TRY_AGAIN
```

Figure 15.22 Routine for updating a global counter in a multitasking or multiprocessor system.

However, if the two values are found not to be equal by the CAS instruction, this means that another processor or task has modified the count since its value was read into D_0. In this case, the counter is not updated; instead, the modified value of

GLOBAL_CTR is copied into D_0 and the branch to TRY_AGAIN is taken to repeat the comparison. This loop sequence repeats until execution of the CAS instruction finds the contents of D_0 equal to GLOBAL_CTR. Notice that not until a match is found in the updated count is D_1 used to replace the value of GLOBAL_CTR.

Looking at Fig. 15.21, we see that the CAS2 instruction performs the same operation as CAS except it has the ability to check two separate compare and swap operations. However, CAS2 only supports word or long-word operands.

15.10 COPROCESSOR INTERFACE SUPPORT INSTRUCTIONS

The 68020 microprocessor can be supported by coprocessors to implement functions that are not directly provided by the 68020. An example of a type of function that can be performed by a coprocessor is floating-point arithmetic. In fact, a special device, the 68881 floating-point coprocessor, is available to perform these functions for the 68020-based microcomputer system. Another example is the 68851 paged memory management unit coprocessor. Special instructions are provided in the 68020's instruction set to initiate coprocessor operations. However, none of the coprocessor devices is covered in this book. For this reason, we wil just briefly introduce these instructions.

The seven instructions that can be executed by the 68020 microprocessor in support of coprocessor operations are listed in Fig. 15.23. These coprocessor instructions can be included in any program just as 68020 instructions.

Mnemonic	Meaning	Operations
cpGEN	Coprocessor general function	Send a coprocessor's general instruction.
cpBcc	Branch on coprocessor condition	Branch if the condition expressed by the coprocessor status is true. Otherwise just proceed.
cpDBcc	Test coprocessor condition decrement and branch	Decrement and branch if Dn is not = −1. Otherwise just proceed.
cpScc	Set on coprocessor condition	Set if the condition expressed by the coprocessor status is true, otherwise reset.
cpTRAPcc	Trap on coprocessor condition	Trap if the condition expressed by the coprocessor status is true, otherwise just proceed.
cpSAVE	Coprocessor save function (privileged operation)	Save internal state of the coprocessor.
cpRESTORE	Coprocessor restore function (privileged operation)	Restore the internal state of the coprocessor.

Figure 15.23 Coprocessor instructions.

The coprocessor support instructions fall into one of four categories: *general, conditional, context save,* and *context restore.* The cpGEN instruction is the only instruction in the general category. It is used to pass a command word to the coprocessor to specify the general data processing or data movement operation that is to be performed. An example of this type instruction is

This is a floating-point coprocessor instruction that moves a long word from the memory location addressed by A_0 to floating-point register FP0 in the 68881 coprocessor.

The next four instructions are in the conditional group, and the operations they perform are similar to the corresponding 68020 instruction. The difference is that they use condition code bits in the coprocessor, not those in the 68020's status register. For example, the instruction cpScc sets the destination to 1s or 0s depending on whether the specified condition code relationship is true or false, respectively.

The last two instructions are for saving and restoring the coprocessor's status. These two instructions are privileged instructions and can be executed only in the supervisor mode.

ASSIGNMENT

Section 15.2

1. Give two ways in which the 68020's user-mode software model differs from that of the 68000.
2. Make a list of the registers in the 68020's supervisor-mode software model that do not exist in the 68000's supervisor-mode software model.
3. How many stacks exist in the supervisor-mode 68020 microcomputer system?
4. What is the function of the VBR register? To what value is it initiated?
5. Over which lines are the contents of SFC and DFC output?
6. What does logic 1 in status bit M mean?
7. What does status bit T_0 stand for?

Section 15.3

8. Make a list of the new addressing modes supported by the 68020 microprocessor.
9. What values of scale factors are supported in 68020 index scaling?
10. What is the value of the scale factor in the instruction MOVE.W   16 (A0, A1.W*Q), D0?
11. Determine the value of the effective address for the instruction in Problem 10 for $A_0 = 00100000_{16}$ and $A_1 = 00002000_{16}$.
12. What sizes of base displacement are supported by the address register indirect with index addressing mode? In what form must the base displacement be expressed?
13. What addressing mode is used for the destination operand in the instruction MOVE.W D0,$FFF0 (PC,A1.W*B)? What is the value of the base displacement?
14. In the instruction MOVE.W   ([$ABCD,A1],A2.W*B,$0020),D1, what addressing mode is used by the source operand? What is the value of the outer displacement?
15. For the instruction in Problem 14, what is the value of the indirect address if $A_1 = 00100000_{16}$ and $A_2 = 00002000_{16}$?

16. How do the program counter memory indirect addressing modes differ from the memory indirect addressing modes?

17. What addressing mode is used for the destination operand in the instruction MOVE.L D1,([$1111,PC,A2.W*B],$0020)?

18. What is the value of the indirect address in Problem 17 if $PC = 00101000_{16}$ and $A_2 = 00000200_{16}$?

Section 15.4

19. Into what two categories do the enhancements of the 68020's instruction set fall?

20. What is meant by upward object code compatibility in the 68000 software architecture?

Section 15.5

21. After execution of the instruction MULS   D0,D3:D4, where are the most significant 32 bits of the product found? The least significant 32 bits of the product?

22. Write an instruction sequence that will perform an unsigned multiply of the long-word contents of memory location 00200000_{16} by the long-word contents of register D_0. The 64-bit product is to reside in D_0 and D_1.

23. What size numbers does the instruction DIVSL   D4,D0:D1 divide? What size quotient does it produce? What size remainder?

24. If the original contents of D_0 are 00000055_{16}, what is the result in D_0 after the instruction EXTB.L   D0 is executed?

25. What new addressing modes are supported by the TST and CMPI instructions of the 68020?

26. Describe the operation performed by the instruction sequence

```
MOVE.L   HIGH_LOW,A0
CMPI     (A0),D0
```

27. What size displacements are supported by the BRA, Bcc, and BSR instructions of the 68000? Of the 68020?

28. What operation is performed by the instruction sequence

```
MOVE.L   TABLE,D0
MOVEC    D0,VBR
```

29. Write an instruction that will save the value in the destination function code register in data register D_3.

30. What value must be in the SFC register if the instruction

```
MOVES.L   (A0),D0
```

when executed, reads the contents of a storage location in the user code space into D_0?

Section 15.6

31. If data register D_0 contains the value 12345678_{16}, what is the binary contents of the bit field with offset equal to 8 and width equal to 6?

32. Write an instruction that will clear the field of bits from bit 7 through 14 of data register D_0.

33. If the memory location pointed to by the address in A_0 contains $5A5A5A5A_{16}$, what result is produced when the instruction

$$\text{BFEXTS} \quad (A0)\{4:8\},D0$$

is executed?

34. If the instruction in Problem 33 is BFEXTU (A0){4:8},D0, what result is produced?

35. If D_1 contains $A5A5A5A5_{16}$. When the instruction

$$\text{BFFFO} \quad D1\{4:8\},D0$$

is executed, what result is produced in D_0?

36. Write an instruction that will insert the contents of the eight least significant bits of D_0 into bits 16 through 23 of data register D_1.

Section 15.7

37. Write an instruction that will pack the BCD contents of the word-wide memory location pointed to by the address in A_0 in the memory location pointed to by the address in A_1. What happens to the addresses in A_0 and A_1 during the execution of the instruction?

38. If the contents of D_0 are 00560029_{16}, what is the result of executing the instruction PACK D0,D1?

39. Write an instruction that will unpack the packed BCD contents of the word-wide memory location pointed to by the address in A_1 in the memory location pointed to by the address in A_0. What happens to the addresses in A_0 and A_1 during the execution of the instruction?

40. Assume that before the instruction written in Problem 39 is executed the addresses in A_0 and A_1 are 00300300_{16} and 00300200_{16}, respectively. Moreover, assume that the data held at address $003001FE_{16}$ are 00001234_{16}. At what address is the result produced and what is its value?

Section 15.8

41. What is meant by modular programming?

42. What instruction is inserted into a module to call a new module?

43. What instruction is used to pass control back to the calling module at completion of a called module?

44. What information is supplied in a module descriptor?

45. What does OPT equals 100 stand for?

46. What does TYPE equals 00001 mean?
47. What are the contents of a module stack frame for a TYPE 00000 module?
48. What function is performed by the module entry word?

Section 15.9

49. What instructions of the 68020's instruction set are intended for supporting multiprocessing and multitasking operations?
50. Overview the operation performed by the CAS instruction.
51. Write an instruction sequence that, when executed, tests the value of a byte-wide semaphore that identifies whether a process is available or busy. The value of the semaphore is FF_{16} if the process is busy and 00_{16} when available. Use the CAS instruction to assure that the semaphore cannot be changed during the execution of the test routine. If the process is available, the semaphore is to be marked busy and the process initiated. However, if it is busy, the semaphore should be retested until the process becomes available.

Section 15.10

52. What is the mnemonic of the coprocessor interface support instruction in the general group?
53. What function is performed by the cpSAVE instruction?
54. Which coprocessor interface support instruction performs the reverse operation of cpSAVE?

16

Hardware Architecture of the 68020 Microprocessor

16.1 INTRODUCTION

In the last chapter, we examined the software architecture of the 68020 microprocessor. In this chapter we will continue our study of the 68020 with its hardware architecture. As in Chapter 9, it is assumed that the reader is already familiar with the architecture of the 68000. The focus in this chapter is on differences between the 68000 and the 68020 hardware architectures and the 68020's advanced features. The topics covered are as follows:

1. 68020 microprocessor
2. Signal interfaces
3. System clock
4. Bus cycles
5. Instruction cache memory
6. Exception processing

16.2 THE 68020 MICROPROCESSOR

The 68020 is Motorola Corporation's fourth member of the 68000 family of microprocessors. The 68020, which was announced in 1984, was the first fully 32-bit MPU in the 68000 family. In earlier chapters we found that the original 68000 device has a 32-bit internal architecture, but does not have either a 32-bit external data bus or 32-bit address bus. On the other hand, the 68020 is equipped with 32-bit internal registers, and both the external address bus and data bus are 32 bits in length.

The 68020 microprocessor has been designed to provide more powerful and flexible operations than the earlier 68000 microprocessors. To increase performance, the internal hardware architecture has been enhanced with an internal code cache memory and pipelining. This on-chip caching of code and parallel processing speed up instruction execution. These internal architectural features are key to the high level of performance obtained with the 68020.

The external hardware architecture has also been improved with a number of new features. We already mentioned that the address and data buses are expanded to 32 bits in length. The memory and I/O interface has been further enhanced with what is called *dynamic bus sizing*. This permits the 68020 to be easily interfaced to 8-, 16-, or 32-bit memory or I/O devices.

To simplify interfacing and provide more flexibility, additional control signals are provided in the 68020's interfaces. For instance, the *interrupt pending* ($\overline{\text{IPEND}}$) output has been added to the external hardware interrupt interface. This signal tells external devices that interrupt service is pending. Finally, a coprocessor interface has been added that allows easy connection to external devices such as a 68881 floating-point coprocessor.

Figure 16.1 shows a 68020 IC. Unlike the 68000 MPU, which was only available in NMOS, the 68020 is also manufactured using the CMOS technology. The circuits within the device are equivalent to approximately 103,000 transistors. Looking at Fig. 16.1, we see that the device is housed in a pin grid array (PGA) package.

Figure 16.1 68020 IC. (Courtesy of Motorola, Inc.)

The illustration in Fig. 16.2(a) identifies the location of each pin on the PGA package. Notice that the pins are arranged in rows and columns and that the rows are identified by letters A through N, while the columns are labeled with numbers 1 through 13. There are a total of 120 pins on this package. The location of a pin is identified by a row/column coordinate. For example, the pin in the lower-left corner is called A1.

Just like for the original 68000 IC, all the signals of the 68020 are available at separate pins of the 68020's package. That is, no signal is multiplexed with another signal at the same pin. Figure 16.2(b) lists each pin number and its corresponding signal on the package. For example, pin A1, supplies the $\overline{\text{BGACK}}$ signal.

EXAMPLE 16.1

What signal is supplied by the pin at the upper-left corner of the PGA package in Fig. 16.2(a)?

SOLUTION In Fig. 16.2(a), we find that the coordinates of the pin at the upper-left corner are N1. Figure 16.2(b) shows that this pin provides line D_{31} of the data bus.

16.3 SIGNAL INTERFACES

Up to this point in the chapter, we have introduced the 68020 microprocessor and its internal architecture. Let us continue by looking at the signals at its interfaces. Figure 16.3 is a block diagram that shows the interface signals provided on the 68020 microprocessor. In this diagram, the signals are grouped according to their function. In Fig. 16.4, we have listed the mnemonic and function of each signal along with its type and active level. For example, we find that $\overline{\text{AS}}$ stands for the address strobe signal function. This output line of the 68020 is used to signal external circuitry that the address on the address bus is valid. Its active 0 level should be used to latch the value of this address into external circuitry. Many of these signals are identical to those available on the 68000.

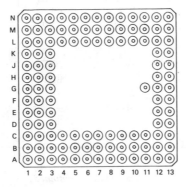

Figure 16.2 (a) Pin layout (courtesy of Motorola, Inc.); (b) signal locations (courtesy of Motorola, Inc.).

Pin Number	Signal	Pin Number	Signal	Pin Number	Signal
A1	$\overline{BGACK}$	D1	V_{CC}	K1	GND
A2	A_1	D2	V_{CC}	K2	$\overline{HALT}$
A3	A_{31}	D3	N.C.	K3	N.C.
A4	A_{28}	D4–D11	–	K4–K11	–
A5	A_{26}	D12	A_4	K12	D_1
A6	A_{23}	D13	A_3	K13	D_0
A7	A_{22}			L1	$\overline{AS}$
A8	A_{19}			L2	$R/\overline{W}$
A9	V_{CC}	E1	FC_0	L3	D_{30}
A10	GND	E2	$\overline{RMC}$	L4	D_{27}
A11	A_{14}	E3	V_{CC}	L5	D_{23}
A12	A_{11}	E4–E11	–	L6	D_{19}
A13	A_8	E12	A_2	L7	GND
		E13	$\overline{OCS}$	L8	D_{15}
				L9	D_{11}
				L10	D_7
B1	N.C.	F1	SIZ_0	L11	N.C.
B2	$\overline{BG}$	F2	FC_2	L12	D_3
B3	$\overline{BR}$	F3	FC_1	L13	D_2
B4	A_{30}	F4–F11	–		
B5	A_{27}	F12	N.C.	M1	$\overline{DS}$
B6	A_{24}	F13	$\overline{IPEND}$	M2	D_{29}
B7	A_{20}			M3	D_{26}
B8	A_{18}			M4	D_{24}
B9	GND	G1	$\overline{ECS}$	M5	D_{21}
B10	A_{15}	G2	SIZ_1	M6	D_{18}
B11	A_{13}	G3	$\overline{DBEN}$	M7	D_{16}
B12	A_{10}	G4–G10	–	M8	V_{CC}
B13	A_6	G11	V_{CC}	M9	D_{13}
		G12	GND	M10	D_{10}
		G13	V_{CC}	M11	D_6
				M12	D_5
C1	$\overline{RESET}$			M13	D_4
C2	CLK	H1	$\overline{CDIS}$		
C3	N.C.	H2	$\overline{AVEC}$	N1	D_{31}
C4	A_0	H3	$\overline{DSACK_0}$	N2	D_{28}
C5	A_{29}	H4–H11	–	N3	D_{25}
C6	A_{25}	H12	IPL_2	N4	D_{22}
C7	A_{21}	H13	GND	N5	D_{20}
C8	A_{17}			N6	D_{17}
C9	A_{16}			N7	GND
C10	A_{12}	J1	$\overline{DSACK_1}$	N8	V_{CC}
C11	A_9	J2	$\overline{BERR}$	N9	D_{14}
C12	A_7	J3	GND	N10	D_{12}
C13	A_5	J4–J11	–	N11	D_9
		J12	$\overline{IPL_0}$	N12	D_8
		J13	$\overline{IPL_1}$	N13	N.C.

(b)

Figure 16.2 (*continued*)

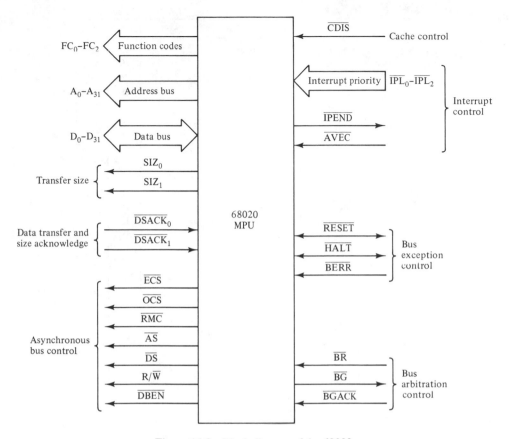

Figure 16.3 Block diagram of the 68020.

Address Bus and Data Bus

Let us begin our examination of the interface signal groups with the address and data buses. Just like the 68000, the 68020 MPU has demultiplexed address and data lines. The address lines are outputs and supply address information to the memory and I/O devices. The 24-bit address bus of the 68000 is expanded to 32 bits on the 68020. These lines are labeled A_0 through A_{31} in Fig. 16.3. With this 32-bit address, the address space contains 2^{32} unique addresses. This means that the physical address space is 4 gigabytes (GB) in size.

The external data bus is also expanded on the 68020. Notice in Fig. 16.3 that there are 32 bidirectional lines, D_0 through D_{31}, in the data bus. These lines are used to carry data between the MPU and its memory and I/O devices. Therefore, it is the path over which read and write data transfers take place.

The data bus supports transfers of three data types: byte (8-bit), word (16-bit), and long word (32-bit). Figure 16.5 shows what are called aligned long words. Here we see that aligned long words are all located on address boundaries equal to a multiple of 4. That is, long word 0 is at address 0_{16}, long word 1 is at address 4_{16}, long word 2 is at address 8_{16}, and so on.

Mnemonic	Function	Type	Level
A_0-A_{31}	Address bus	O	1
D_0-D_{31}	Data bus	I/O	1
FC_0-FC_2	Function codes	O	1
SIZ_0	Size	O	1
SIZ_1		O	1
$\overline{RMC}$	Read-modify-write cycle	O	0
$\overline{ECS}$	External cycle start	O	0
$\overline{OCS}$	Operand cycle start	O	0
$\overline{AS}$	Address strobe	O	0
$\overline{DS}$	Data strobe	O	0
$R/\overline{W}$	Read/write	O	1/0
$\overline{DBEN}$	Data buffer enable	O	0
$\overline{DSACK_0}$	Data transfer and size acknowledge	I	0
$\overline{DSACK_1}$		I	0
$\overline{CDIS}$	Cache disable	I	0
$\overline{IPL_0}-\overline{IPL_2}$	Interrupt priority level	I	0
$\overline{AVEC}$	Autovector	I	0
$\overline{IPEND}$	Interrupt pending	O	0
$\overline{BR}$	Bus request	I	0
$\overline{BG}$	Bus grant	O	0
$\overline{BGACK}$	Bus grant acknowledge	I	0
$\overline{RESET}$	Reset	I/O	0
$\overline{HALT}$	Halt	I/O	0
$\overline{BERR}$	Bus error	I	0
CLK	Clock	I	-

Figure 16.4 Signals of the 68020.

Figure 16.5 Aligned data stored in memory.

The diagram in Fig. 16.5 also shows how bytes are organized within a long-word storage location. Notice that long word 0 contains 4 bytes of data, bytes 0, 1, 2, and 3. The lowest addressed byte, byte 0, is stored at byte address 0_{16} and is located at the most significant byte location of the long word. The next byte, byte 1, is held at byte address 1_{16}.

Address bits A_0 and A_1 form what are called the *byte offset*. Figure 16.6 shows

A_1	A_0	Offset
0	0	+0 bytes
0	1	+1 bytes
1	0	+2 bytes
1	1	+3 bytes

Figure 16.6 Address selection of bytes.

how these bits select the bytes within a long word. For example, the most significant byte, byte 3, of the long word at aligned long-word address C_{16} in Fig. 16.5 has an offset of $+3$. Therefore, it is at byte address F_{16}.

EXAMPLE 16.2

What is the address of byte 2 of long word 2 in Fig. 16.5?

SOLUTION   Long word 2 starts at address 8_{16}. Byte 2 is offset by $+2$ from this address; therefore, its address is A_{16}.

In long words 4 through 7 of Fig. 16.5, aligned words of data are shown. Here word 8 starts at address 10_{16} and word 9 begins at address 12_{16}. Also, bytes 2 and 3 of long word 0 can be treated as a word of data. Together they represent word 1 at address 2_{16}.

EXAMPLE 16.3

At what word address is the most significant word of the long word at address $2C_{16}$?

SOLUTION   The most significant word of a long word is located at the higher word address. Therefore, the most significant word of long word 7, which is the aligned long word that starts at address $2C_{16}$, is at address $2E_{16}$.

The 68020 also supports long-word or word data stored at misaligned address boundaries. A word operand is misaligned if it starts at an odd address. Notice in Fig. 16.7 that misaligned words 0 and 1 are located at word addresses 1_{16} and 3_{16}, respectively. Notice that the least significant byte of word 0, byte 0, is at byte address 1_{16} and the most significant byte, byte 1, at address 2_{16}. A long word is misaligned if its starting address is not a multiple of 4. Several misaligned long words are shown in Fig. 16.8.

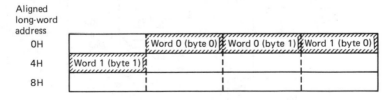

Figure 16.7   Misaligned words of data.

EXAMPLE 16.4

What is the address of misaligned long word 2 (LW2) in Fig. 16.8

Aligned long-word address				
0H		LW0 (byte 0)	LW0 (byte 1)	LW0 (byte 2)
4H	LW0 (byte 3)		LW1 (byte 0)	LW1 (byte 1)
8H	LW1 (byte 2)	LW1 (byte 3)		LW2 (byte 0)
CH	LW2 (byte 1)	LW2 (byte 2)	LW2 (byte 3)	

Figure 16.8 Misaligned long words of data.

SOLUTION LW2 starts with byte 3 of aligned long-word address 8_{16}. Since this byte is offset by $+3$, the address of LW2 is B_{16}.

The data bus of the 68020 supports dynamic bus sizing. This means that the width of the data bus can be dynamically set to 8, 16, or 32 bits. In Fig. 16.9 we find that, when the data bus is set to the byte-wide mode of operation, all data transfers take place as bytes over data bus lines D_{31} through D_{24}. Data line D_{31} carries the MSB of the byte and D_{24} the LSB. If the bus is set to word-wide mode, data are transferred as words and passed between the MPU and memory or I/O devices over data lines D_{31} through D_{16}. Again, D_{31} represents the MSB, but this time bit D_{16} carries the LSB. Finally, in 32-bit mode long words are shown to be carried over the complete 32-bit data bus.

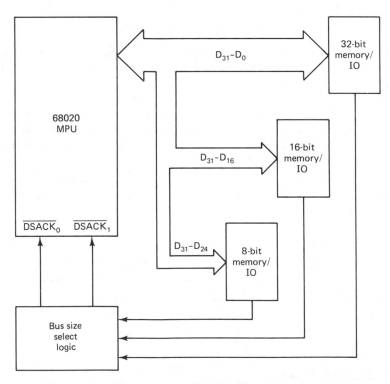

Figure 16.9 Byte, word, and long-word data bus configurations.

Bus width is determined by the code at the *data transfer and size acknowledge* inputs. These inputs are labeled $\overline{DSACK_0}$ and $\overline{DSACK_1}$ in the block diagrams of Figs. 16.3 and 16.9. Figure 16.10 describes the relationship between these inputs and bus size. For example, $\overline{DSACK_1}\ \overline{DSACK_0} = 00$ indicates that the bus is operated in 32-bit mode. Figure 16.11(a) shows how bytes, words, and long words of data are transferred over a 32-bit bus.

On the other hand, if $\overline{DSACK_1}\ \overline{DSACK_0} = 01$, it means that the current bus cycle is to be performed over a word-wide data bus. Earlier we pointed out that in

$\overline{DSACK_1}$	$\overline{DSACK_0}$	Cycle status/bus width
0	0	Complete cycle — 32-bit bus width
0	1	Complete cycle — 16-bit bus width
1	0	Complete cycle — 8-bit bus width
1	1	Insert wait states into current bus cycle

Figure 16.10 Data transfer and size acknowledge signals.

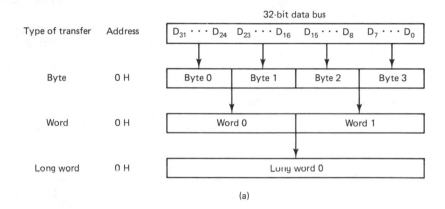

(a)

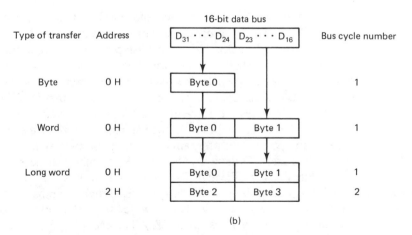

(b)

Figure 16.11 (a) Byte, word, and long-word data transfers over a 32-bit data bus; (b) byte, word, and long-word data transfers over a 16-bit data bus.

this case the active bus corresponds to data lines D_{31} through D_{16}. However, as shown in Fig. 16.11(b), transfers can still involve a byte, word, or long word of data. In the case of a byte transfer, the data are carried over data bus lines D_{31} through D_{24} and the transfer takes place in one bus cycle. A long-word transfer also takes place over the upper 16 data bus lines, but this transfer takes place as two consecutive word transfers. Looking at Fig. 16.11(b), we see that the lower 16 bits of the long word, byte 0 and byte 1, are passed over the bus during the first bus cycle and that the upper 16 bits, byte 2 and byte 3, are transferred during the second cycle. The $\overline{\text{DSACK}}$ signals must be supplied to the 68020 by the memory subsystem or I/O device.

EXAMPLE 16.5

If the $\overline{\text{DSACK}}$ input code is 00, over which data bus lines would the byte of data at address 13_{16} be carried? How about if $\overline{\text{DSACK}}_1$ $\overline{\text{DSACK}}_0$ equals 10?

SOLUTION When $\overline{\text{DSACK}}_1$ $\overline{\text{DSACK}}_0$ = 00, the data bus is configured for 32-bit mode of operation. Therefore, the byte at address 13_{16} is transferred over data bus lines D_7 through D_0.
   If $\overline{\text{DSACK}}_1$ $\overline{\text{DSACK}}_0$ = 10, the bus is set up for byte-wide mode. In this case the byte at address 13_{16} is transferred over data bus lines D_{31} through D_{24} instead of D_7 through D_0.

EXAMPLE 16.6

If $\overline{\text{DSACK}}_1$ $\overline{\text{DSACK}}_0$ = 10 and the long word at address 14_{16} is to be transferred over the bus, how many bus cycles take place and what is the address of the byte that is transferred first?

SOLUTION Since $\overline{\text{DSACK}}_1$ $\overline{\text{DSACK}}_0$ = 10, the data bus is in 8-bit mode and the data transfer is performed as four consecutive byte data transfers. The first byte transferred is the byte at address 14_{16}.

Just as for the 68000's system bus, the 68020's bus is asynchronous. This means that the 68020 will not complete the current bus cycle until it is signaled to do so by external circuitry. The $\overline{\text{DSACK}}$ inputs also perform this function. That is, they are used to acknowledge whether the current bus cycle should be run to completion or be extended with wait states. In the 68000 microcomputer system, this function was performed by $\overline{\text{DTACK}}$. Looking at Fig. 16.10, we see that $\overline{\text{DSACK}}_1\overline{\text{DSACK}}_0$ = 11 indicates that wait states are to be inserted into the current bus cycle. The bus cycle is not completed until the $\overline{\text{DSACK}}$ code signals the size of the system data bus. In a typical system application, program and data memory may be accessed over the full 32-bit data bus and I/O devices, such as LSI peripherals, accessed as 8-bit devices over data bus lines D_{31} through D_{24}. Moreover, wait states may be inserted into these bus cycles by controlling when the $\overline{\text{DSACK}}$ signals become active.

During a bus cycle such as a read or write, the 68020 always outputs a 2-bit code on the data *transfer size* lines (SIZ_1SIZ_0). The encoding for these bits is given in the table of Fig. 16.12. This code represents the number of bytes that remain to be transferred. For example, if a long-word transfer of aligned data is to be performed

SIZ_1	SIZ_0	Bytes remaining
0	0	4 bytes
0	1	1 byte
1	0	2 bytes
1	1	3 bytes

Figure 16.12 Data transfer size code.

across a 32-bit bus, the code 00 is output at SIZ_1SIZ_0. This indicates that 4 bytes of data remain to be transferred and they are all transferred in one bus cycle. On the other hand, if the long word is transferred over an 8-bit bus, four bus cycles are required. In this case, the first byte transfer is accompanied by the code 00. Again, this means that 4 bytes remain to be transferred. The byte transfer during the second bus cycle is accompanied by 11, meaning that 3 bytes remain to be transferred. The third byte transfer bus cycle is accompanied by 10 (2 bytes remaining) and the fourth transfer by 01 (last byte).

EXAMPLE 16.7

If the code $\overline{DSACK_1}\overline{DSACK_0} = 01$ during a write bus cycle in which a long word of data is transferred to address $1C_{16}$, how many bus cycles are required to perform the transfer and what SIZ code is output by the 68020 during each cycle?

SOLUTION The long word at $1C_{16}$ is at a long-word aligned address. Since $\overline{DSACK_1}\overline{DSACK_0} = 01$, the data bus is configured for 16-bit mode and the data transfer is performed as two consecutive word transfers. During the first word transfer, $SIZ_1SIZ_0 = 00$, meaning that a long word (4 bytes) remains to be transferred. During the second cycle, just 2 bytes remain to be transferred and 10 is output on the SIZ lines.

Asynchronous Bus Control

Up to this point we have examined the address bus, data bus, size signals, and data transfer and size acknowledge signals. Earlier we pointed out that the bus of the 68020 operates asynchronously. A number of signals are provided to control the transfer of data across the 68020's data bus. These signals are identified as the *asynchronous bus control* signals in Fig. 16.3.

Comparing the asynchronous bus control signals in Fig. 16.3 to those of the 68000, we see that some are the same and others are new. For example, the signals *address strobe* ($\overline{AS}$) and *read/write* ($R/\overline{W}$) perform the same functions for both MPUs. Two signals that are new with the 68020 interface are *operand cycle start* ($\overline{OCS}$) and *external cycle start* ($\overline{ECS}$). $\overline{ECS}$ provides the earliest indication that the 68020 is starting a bus cycle. This output is switched to logic 0 at the beginning of all bus cycles. It even becomes active during instruction fetch cycles for which the instruction is obtained from the internal instruction cache. $\overline{OCS}$ is also an output, but it is only at the active 0 logic level for instruction fetch cycles or operand transfer cycles. In fact, during operand transfers, it is only active during the first bus cycle.

The signals *data strobe* ($\overline{DS}$) and *data buffer enable* ($\overline{DBEN}$) are used to time the data transfer during a bus cycle. $\overline{DS}$ is another asynchronous bus control signal that is new with the 68020. During read cycles, $\overline{DS}$ is switched to logic 0 to signal external devices when to put the read data onto the bus. On the other hand, for write cycles, $\overline{DS}$ signals external devices that valid data are available on the data bus. $\overline{DBEN}$ is used to enable the external data bus buffer/transceivers during both read and write bus cycles.

The 68020 has the ability to perform read–modify–write bus cycles, as well as the traditional read and write cycles. This type of cycle must be completed before the bus is made available to another processor. Whenever a read–modify–write cycle is in progress, the 68020 outputs the signal *read modify write cycle* ($\overline{RMC}$). The logic 0 at $\overline{RMC}$ can be used by external circuitry to lock other devices off the bus until the current bus cycle is complete. $\overline{RMC}$ is not provided in the 68000's asynchronous bus interface.

Function Code Lines

In our study of the 68000, we found that function codes are output on the function code lines during each bus cycle. The function code lines FC_0 through FC_2 of the 68020 are essentially the same as those of the 68000. They provide status about the microprocessor's operational mode. The table in Fig. 16.13 summarizes the various codes output by the microprocessor. Function codes 000_2 through 110_2 are identical to those implemented on the 68000. They tell external circuitry whether the microprocessor is operating in the user or supervisor mode and if it is accessing instructions or data. For instance, the code 001 indicates that the microprocessor is accessing data in the user data space.

FC_2	FC_1	FC_0	Cycle type
0	0	0	(Undefined reserved)*
0	0	1	User data space
0	1	0	User program space
0	1	1	(Undefined reserved)*
1	0	0	(Undefined reserved)*
1	0	1	Supervisor data space
1	1	0	Supervisor program space
1	1	1	CPU space

*Address space 3 is reserved for user definition, while 0 and 4 are reserved for future use by Motorola.

Figure 16.13 Function codes. (Courtesy of Motorola, Inc.)

For the 68000, function code 111 served a single function. It meant that an interrupt acknowledge bus cycle was in progress. This code occurs for several special functions performed by the 68020. In Fig.16.13, we see that this code specifies what is called *CPU space*. The 68020 operates in the CPU space for four special cycles: the *interrupt acknowledge cycle, coprocessor communication cycle, module access level control cycle,* and *breakpoint acknowledge cycle.* When $FC_2FC_1FC_0 = 111$, another code is output on address lines A_{16} through A_{19} to identify the four types of CPU space activities. Figure 16.14 lists these four codes. Notice that $A_{19}A_{18}A_{17}A_{16}$ equals 0010 indicates that the 68020 is communicating with a coprocessor.

A_{19}	A_{18}	A_{17}	A_{16}	CPU space cycles
0	0	0	0	Breakpoint acknowledge
0	0	0	1	Module access level control
0	0	1	0	Coprocessor communication
1	1	1	1	Interrupt acknowledge

Figure 16.14 CPU space cycle codes.

EXAMPLE 16.8

What type of bus cycle is taking place if $FC_2FC_1FC_0$ equals 110?

SOLUTION From Fig. 16.13, we find that $FC_2FC_1FC_0 = 110$ means that code in the supervisor program address space is being accessed.

Bus Exception Control

The bus exception control lines give external circuitry the ability to control the operation of the 68020. In Fig. 16.3, the three signals identified for bus exception control are system *reset* ($\overline{RESET}$), *halt* ($\overline{HALT}$) and *bus error* ($\overline{BERR}$), and they serve the same functions as for the 68000 microprocessor. $\overline{RESET}$ is again a bidirectional line that is used in the initialization of the MPU. That is, input of logic 0 at $\overline{RESET}$ initiates reset exception processing. On the other hand, as an output, the reset operation is caused by executing the reset instruction. In this case, the active 0 logic level output at $\overline{RESET}$ is applied to external hardware and causes its initialization.

$\overline{HALT}$ is also a bidirectional signal line. Just as for the 68000, making this input active halts operation at the completion of the current bus cycle and puts the MPU in the inactive halt state. As an output, $\overline{HALT}$ becomes active to acknowledge that the halt state has been entered. An example is a halt that results due to a double bus fault.

The $\overline{BERR}$ signal serves the same function as it did in the 68000 microcomputer system. External circuitry uses this input to inform the MPU that there is a problem with the current bus cycle and that it cannot be completed. For instance, it could be used to signal that the addressed I/O device is not responding.

Interrupt Control

The interrupt interfaces of the 68000 and 68020 are similar. Comparing the interface of the 68000 to that of the 68020 in Fig. 16.3, we find that the 68020's interface has two new signal lines. They are *interrupt pending* ($\overline{IPEND}$) and *autovector* ($\overline{AVEC}$). To initiate an interrupt, the external device applies a 3-bit code to the *interrupt priority level* ($\overline{IPL_0}$ through $\overline{IPL_2}$) inputs of the MPU. If this code represents a higher priority level than the current value in the interrupt mask part of the status register, the request for service is accepted and will be acknowledged. $\overline{IPEND}$ is an output that can be used to tell external circuitry that the interrupt has been accepted and is pending service. When it is switched to the 0 level, an interrupt acknowledge cycle will be initiated at completion of the current instruction.

Sec. 16.3   Signal Interfaces
511

The $\overline{\text{AVEC}}$ input serves the same function in the 68020's interrupt interface as the $\overline{\text{VPA}}$ signal did in the 68000's interrupt interface. That is, it is the request input for autovector mode of interrupt interface operation. When an external device asserts $\overline{\text{AVEC}}$ during the interrupt acknowledge bus cycle, the 68020 automatically generates the interrupt vector numbers from the code at the $\overline{\text{IPL}}$ inputs.

Bus Arbitration Control

The bus arbitration control signals implement a mechanism for designing multimaster microcomputer systems with the 68020 MPU. The signals *bus request* ($\overline{\text{BR}}$), *bus grant* ($\overline{\text{BG}}$), and *bus grant acknowledge* ($\overline{\text{BGACK}}$) provide the same function as they did for the 68000 microprocessor. $\overline{\text{BR}}$ is an input that signals that an external device wants to take over control of the system bus; $\overline{\text{BG}}$ is an output by which the 68020 signals the device that it will give up control of the system bus at completion of the current bus cycle; and $\overline{\text{BGACK}}$ is an input over which the external device tells the 68020 that it has taken control of the bus. In this way, we see that together these three signals implement the handshake sequence needed to pass control of the system bus to a bus master.

Cache Control

Earlier we indicated that the 68020 has an internal instruction cache memory. At times, it is desirable to disable the use of this cache. For example, when either emulating the 68020 chip or running tests to determine the effect of the cache on performance, the cache needs to be turned off. The *cache disable* $\overline{\text{CDIS}}$) input allows the operation of the cache to be dynamically enabled or disabled. Asserting the signal enables the cache for operation and negating the signal disables the cache. The contents of the cache are not flushed when it is disabled.

16.4 SYSTEM CLOCK

In our study of the 68000, we found that it does not have an on-chip clock generator circuit. This is also true of the 68020. The system clock signal must be produced in external circuitry and applied to the CLK input. The 68020 is available in various speeds ranging from 12.5 to 33.33 MHz. Let us now look at the timing and electrical characteristics of the CLK signal.

The clock signal waveform is shown in Fig. 16.15(a). Figure 16.15(b) lists the timing specifications for the clock signal for five versions of the microprocessor: the 68020RC12 (12.5 MHz), 68020RC16 (16.67 MHz), 68020RC20 (20 MHz), 68020RC25 (25 MHz), and 68020RC33 (33.33 MHz). Notice that the specifications include the range of clock frequency, range of cycle time, range of clock pulse width, and the maximum rise or fall time of its edges. For instance, the 68020RC12 can be operated over a frequency range from 8 to 12.5 MHz; the minimum and maximum cycle times are 80 and 125 ns, respectively; and the rise and fall times of the clock edges must be 5 ns or less. If the clock specifications are not met, the microprocessor is not guaranteed to operate correctly.

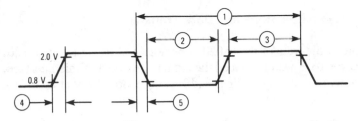

Num.	Characteristic	12.5 MHz		16.67 MHz		20 MHz		25 MHz*		33.33 MHz		Unit
		Min	Max	Min	Max	Min	Max	Min	Max	Min	Max	
	Frequency of Operation	8	12.5	8	16.67	12.5	20	12.5	25	12.5	33.33	MHz
1	Cycle Time	80	125	60	125	50	80	40	80	30	80	ns
2, 3	Clock Pulse Width (Measured from 1.5 V to 1.5 V for 25 and 33.33 MHz)	32	87	24	95	20	54	19	61	14	66	ns
4, 5	Rise and Fall Times	—	5	—	5	—	5	—	4	—	3	ns

*These specifications represent an improvement over previously published specifications for the 25 MHz MC68020 and are valid only for product bearing date codes of 8827 and later.

Figure 16.15 (a) Clock waveform (courtesy of Motorola, Inc.); (b) clock timing specification (courtesy of Motorola, Inc.).

The clock signal applied to the CLK input must be at TTL-compatible voltage levels. That is, the minimum high-voltage level (V_{IHmin}) equals 2.0 V and the maximum high-voltage level (V_{IHmax}) is V_{CC}. For the low logic level, the minimum and maximum values are V_{ILmin} equals −0.5 V and V_{ILmax} equals 0.8V, respectively.

> **EXAMPLE 16.9**
>
> What is the cycle time of the clock if a 68020RC12 is operated at 10 MHz?
>
> **SOLUTION** The cycle time is calculated as
>
> $$t_{CYC} = 1/f$$
> $$= 1/10 \text{ MHz}$$
> $$= 100 \text{ ns}$$

16.5 BUS CYCLES

A bus cycle is the process by which an MPU transfers information such as instruction code, data, or interrupt vector numbers to or from memory devices, I/O devices, or the interrupt interface circuit. The function code table in Fig. 16.13 shows us that the 68020 performs three different classes of bus cycles. They are *program space bus cycles* for accessing code in user or supervisor program memory, *data space bus cycles* for accessing operands in user or supervisor data memory, and special *CPU space bus cycles,* such as the interrupt acknowledge cycle, coprocessor communication cycle, and breakpoint acknowledge cycle. Here we will examine the bus interface and bus cycles for the memory and I/O interface. The interrupt acknowledge bus cycle will be covered separately later in this chapter.

Bus Cycle Functions and Data Transfers

A block diagram of the 68020's memory and I/O interface is shown in Fig. 16.16. In Section 16.3 we introduced the signals involved in this interface. Let us continue by reviewing these signal lines and looking more closly at their functions relative to the bus cycle operation.

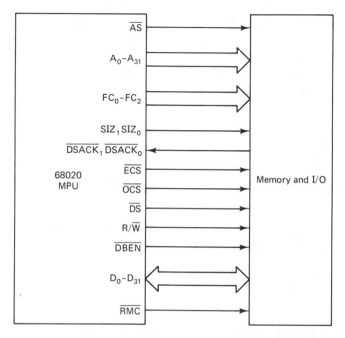

Figure 16.16 Memory interface of the 68020.

The bus cycle operation involves the address bus to identify the location that is to be accessed, the data bus to provide a path to carry data, and control signals to initiate, sequence, and complete the data transfer. Both the 68000 and 68020 use an asynchronous bus protocol to implement data transfer operations. Remember that by asynchronous we mean that the microprocessor starts a data transfer operation and then waits for a code from the memory or I/O subsystem to confirm that the cycle should be completed. Earlier we pointed out that this code is applied at its $\overline{DSACK_1}$ $\overline{DSACK_0}$ inputs. The table in Fig. 16.14 shows that as long as this code equals 11 the current bus cycle is not completed; instead, it is extended with wait states. When either or both of the inputs switch to logic 0, the cycle is run to completion.

In Section 16.3, we found that the 68020 microprocessor is capable of reading from and writing to memory and I/O ports over a byte-wide, word-wide, or long-word data bus. Moreover, the size of the bus can be dynamically changed. For instance, a 68020 microcomputer system configuration could be implemented with a 32-bit data bus to program storage and data storage memory and an 8-bit I/O bus. We also found out earlier that during each bus cycle the 68020 determines the size of the data bus for the devices that are being accessed from the value of the code at the $\overline{DSACK}$ inputs. These signals are returned by the device that the address output on the address bus has selected to receive or transmit data. In this way, we find that the

$\overline{\text{DSACK}}$ inputs not only tell the MPU when the cycle should be completed, but also whether the data path to the device is configured as 8, 16, or 32 bits wide.

The 68020 also supports all types of data transfers over each size of data bus. For instance, it can initiate a word data transfer to a byte-size port that is attached to data bus lines D_{31} through D_{24}. Figure 16.17 represents this type of data transfer for an aligned word address. Since the data bus has just eight lines, this data transfer takes place in two consecutive bus cycles.

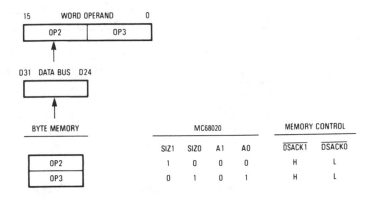

Figure 16.17 Word data transfer to a word aligned address over an 8-bit data bus. (Courtesy of Motorola, Inc.)

Earlier we indicated that the code output on $SIZ_1 SIZ_0$ tells the device being accessed how many byte transfers still need to be performed. That is, it allows the device to know how many bytes have been transferred and how many more remain to be transferred. In our example, the size signals are equal to 10 during the first byte transfer bus cycle. As shown in Fig. 16.17, this means that a word (2 bytes) remains to be transferred. During this bus cycle, the first byte of data, operand 2 (OP_2), is transferred over data bus lines D_{31} through D_{24}. During the second byte transfer bus cycle, $SIZ_1 SIZ_0$ is set to 01 and indicates that just 1 byte remains to be transferred. The second byte of the word, OP_3, is automatically output on the same data bus lines, D_{31} through D_{24}, during bus cycle 2.

We just saw that depending on the type of data transfer taking place and the size of the bus, the 68020 must automatically channel the bytes of the operand between the source or destination register and the appropriate data bus lines. The 68020 contains an internal multiplexer circuit that maps the data from the 68020's 32-bit internal bus to the external data bus lines. Figure 16.18 shows how the bytes of a 32-bit internal long word are mapped to a 32-, 16-, and 8-bit data bus. For example, if the data bus is set up for word-wide mode and the word of data held in an internal register as bytes OP_2 and OP_3 are to be written to an even address, Fig. 16.18 shows that the multiplexer outputs the complete word on data lines D_{31} through D_{16}. On the other hand, if we want to read a long word of data from even address XXXXXXX0 into an internal register over a 16-bit data bus, Fig. 16.18 shows that this transfer will use two bus cycles. During the first bus cycle, it reads a word of data and loads it into the destination register as bytes OP_0 and OP_1. Notice in Fig. 16.19 that during this

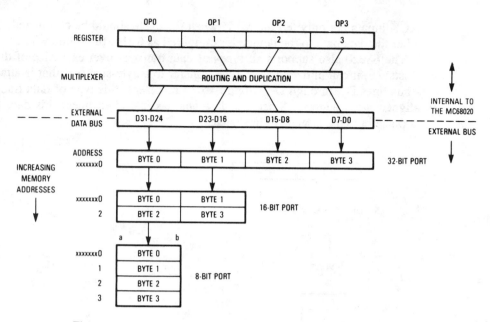

Figure 16.18 Internal data bus multiplexer. (Courtesy of Motorola, Inc.)

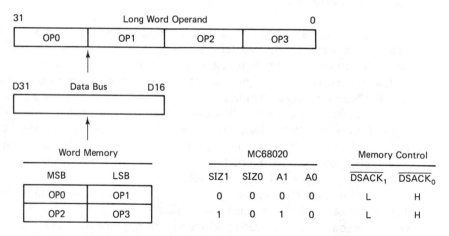

Figure 16.19 Long-word data transfer from a long-word aligned address over an 8-bit data bus. (Courtesy of Motorola, Inc.)

cycle address bits A_1A_0 equal 00 and point to the upper word of the long word. During the second bus cycle, A_1A_0 equals 10 and points to the lower word. The word is read from memory and stored as OP_2 and OP_3 in the same register. This demonstrates how the multiplexer reassembles a long word that was stored as two words in 16-bit wide memory.

Read Cycle

When the 68020 executes an instruction that transfers data from an external I/O port or a storage location in memory to one of its internal registers, it performs a read cycle. An example is the instruction

$$\text{MOVE.L} \quad \text{(A1), D0}$$

Here the MPU reads a long word from the device addressed by the contents of address register A_1 into data register D_0. Let us assume that the device being accessed is attached to the complete 32-bit data bus, D_{31} through D_0, and that the operand resides in the user data space. In this case, the read operation can be accomplished in just one bus cycle.

A flowchart that shows the sequence of events that takes place during an aligned long-word read bus cycle is given in Fig. 16.20. Waveforms that show the timing relationship of the various bus signals during this data transfer are given in Fig. 16.21. Notice that the 68020, which is identified as the processor in Fig. 16.20, starts the bus cycle by asserting both $\overline{\text{ECS}}$ and $\overline{\text{OCS}}$. Figure 16.21 shows that they are pulsed to logic 0 for one-half of clock cycle S_0. $\overline{\text{ECS}}$ tells the external circuitry that a bus cycle has started, and $\overline{\text{OCS}}$ means that either code or a data operand access is taking place. At the same time, the MPU outputs the address (A_{31} through A_0) of the external device. The address is accompanied by the function code $FC_2FC_1FC_0 = 001$ to specify a user data space cycle, transfer size ($SIZ_1SIZ_0 = 00$) to specify a long-word (4-byte) transfer, and logic 1 on R/$\overline{\text{W}}$ to indicate that a read transfer is to

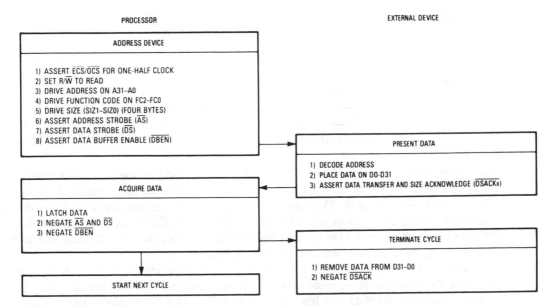

Figure 16.20 Long-word read cycle flowchart. (Courtesy of Motorola, Inc.)

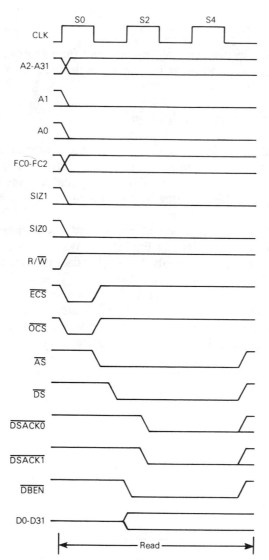

Figure 16.21 Timing diagram for an aligned long-word read bus cycle over a 32-bit data bus. (Courtesy of Motorola, Inc.)

take place. Later, in S_0, address strobe ($\overline{AS}$) is switched to logic 0. This output should be used to latch the address in external circuitry. During the second half of S_0, $\overline{DS}$ is switched to logic 0. This tells the external device to put the data from the addressed storage location onto the data bus. Finally, $\overline{DBEN}$ is set to 0 and enables the data bus buffer/transceiver devices for operation. This completes the *address device* phase of the bus cycle sequence shown in Fig. 16.20.

Now the *present data* part of the bus cycle sequence begins. In Fig. 16.20, we find that the external device decodes the address and then places the data at this storage location onto data bus lines D_{31} through D_0. This takes place during clock cycle S_2 in the waveforms of Fig. 16.21. A short time later the external device outputs the $\overline{DSACK}$ code 00. This code tells the 68020 that the bus cycle should be completed and that the bus width is 32 bits. This completes the present data phase.

Looking at Fig. 16.21, we see that the bus cycle continues with the *acquire data* phase. First the 68020 latches the data off the bus and loads it into the D_0 register. Then, in clock cycle S_4, $\overline{AS}$, $\overline{DS}$, and $\overline{DBEN}$ are negated. As shown in the waveforms of Fig. 16.21, all three signals return to their inactive logic level. In response to the removal of these signals, the external device terminates the cycle by removing the data from D_{31} through D_0 and negating the $\overline{DSACK}$ signals. In Fig. 16.21, we see that $\overline{DSACK_1}$ and $\overline{DSACK_0}$ are negated by switching them back to the 1 logic level.

Write Cycle

Figure 16.22 shows a flowchart that outlines the sequence of events that takes place during a write bus cycle. Notice that the address device part of the write cycle is essentially the same as that found in the read cycle. One difference is that the processor outputs data to the addressed device on the data lines. A second difference is that the R/$\overline{W}$ output is set to 0 to signal that a write operation is taking place.

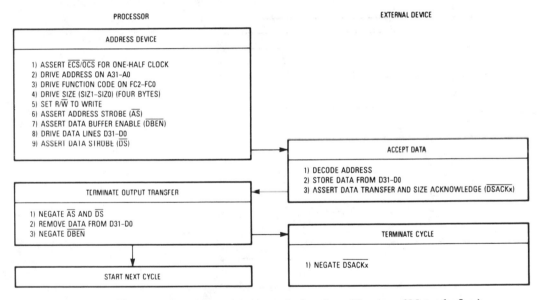

Figure 16.22 Long-word write cycle flowchart. (Courtesy of Motorola, Inc.)

In the write cycle flowchart, an *accept data* phase replaces the present data phase found in the read cycle flowchart. This is because during a write cycle the external device accepts data off the bus and stores them into the addressed location. That is, the external device presents the data to the MPU. This operation completes the data transfer, and then the bus cycle is terminated by both the processor and external device.

The 68020 writes data to a memory location or an I/O port as the result of executing a data transfer instruction such as

MOVE.L D0, (A3)

When this instruction is executed, it transfers the long word in data register D_0 to the location specified by the address in A_3.

Let us assume that this location is a 16-bit I/O port at an even-address boundary that is a multiple of 4. This means that the external device is at a long-word aligned address. Therefore, the write operation will take place as two word transfers in consecutive bus cycles. Figure 16.23 shows the timing relationships of the various signals and operand transfers involved in these bus cycles. During each bus cycle, the data are carried over the upper part of the data bus, that is, data lines D_{31} through D_{16}. For the first cycle, the processor informs external circuitry that it is transferring

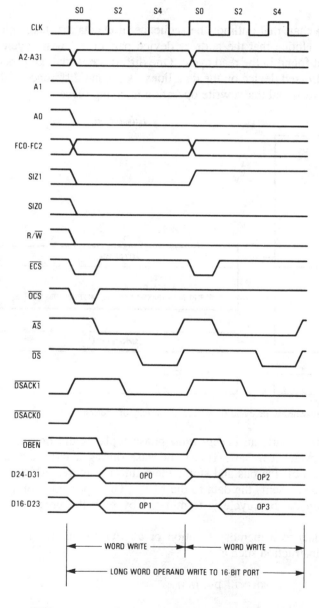

Figure 16.23 Timing diagram for a bus cycle that performs a long-word write to an aligned 16-bit I/O port. (Courtesy of Motorola, Inc.)

a long word by outputting the code 00 on the SIZ lines. Notice that the I/O interface responds with $\overline{DSACK_1}\overline{DSACK_0}$ equals 01 to tell the microprocessor that the bus is 16 bits wide. In Fig. 16.23, we see that the upper word of the long-word operand, OP_0OP_1, is transferred during this bus cycle. At the completion of the bus cycle, the I/O device returns the acknowledge signals to 11, telling the microprocessor that the word of data has been received. Then, the microprocessor increments the address by 2 ($A_1A_0 = 10$) and initiates another bus cycle to output the lower word of the register, OP_2OP_3. During this cycle, the SIZ code equals 10. This means that a word of data remains to be transferred. The transfer takes place and the bus cycle is terminated. Figure 16.24 summarizes the data transfers and control signals for this bus cycle.

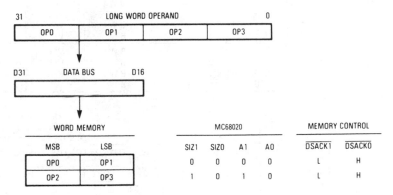

Figure 16.24 Data transfers and bus control signals for an aligned long-word write data transfer over a 16-bit data bus. (Courtesy of Motorola, Inc.)

Bus Cycles for Misaligned Data

Both the bus cycles we described so far transferred aligned data. That is, the data transfer was assumed to take place from or to a long-word address boundary. The 68020 microprocessor also supports data transfer operations on misaligned data. Earlier we found that long-word storage locations that start at an address that is not a multiple of 4 and word storage locations at an odd address are misaligned. Even though the 68020 has the ability to transfer misaligned data, this type of operand access takes more bus cycles. For example, a misaligned long word read over a 32-bit bus will take a minimum of two bus cycles, while an aligned long-word read is done in one bus cycle. The tables in Figs. 16.25(a) and (b) show what data the 68020's bus multiplexer outputs on the data bus during aligned and misaligned write cycles. The table in Fig. 16.26 shows similar information for read cycles.

Figure 16.27(a) illustrates a misaligned long-word write bus cycle. This cycle assumes that the misaligned word starts at an address that is a multiple of 3. Therefore, the address of the storage location to be written into has the form XXXXXXX3. Notice in Fig. 16.27(a) that during the first bus cycle $SIZ_1SIZ_0 = 00$ and $A_1A_0 = 11$. In Fig. 16.25(a), we find that for this output combination during a long-word data transfer (L) only data bus lines D_7 through D_0 carry active data. Moreover, Fig. 16.25(b) shows that the multiplexer outputs $OP_0OP_0OP_1OP_0$ on the data bus.

Transfer Size	SIZ1	SIZ0	A1	A0	Data Bus Active Sections Byte (B) – Word (W) – Long Word (L) Ports			
					D31:D24	D23:D16	D15:D8	D7:D0
Byte	0	1	0	0	B W L	—	—	—
	0	1	0	1	B	W L	—	—
	0	1	1	0	B W	—	L	—
	0	1	1	1	B	W	—	L
Word	1	0	0	0	B W L	W L	—	—
	1	0	0	1	B	W L	L	—
	1	0	1	0	B W	W	L	L
	1	0	1	1	B	W	—	L
3 Byte	1	1	0	0	B W L	W L	L	—
	1	1	0	1	B	W L	L	L
	1	1	1	0	B W	W	L	L
	1	1	1	1	B	W	—	L
Long Word	0	0	0	0	B W L	W L	L	L
	0	0	0	1	B	W L	L	L
	0	0	1	0	B W	W	L	L
	0	0	1	1	B	W	—	L

(a)

Transfer Size	Size		Address		External Data Bus Connection			
	SIZ1	SIZ0	A1	A0	D31:D24	D23:D16	D15:D8	D7:D0
Byte	0	1	x	x	OP3	OP3	OP3	OP3
Word	1	0	x	0	OP2	OP3	OP2	OP3
	1	0	x	1	OP2	OP2	OP3	OP2
3 Byte	1	1	0	0	OP1	OP2	OP3	OP1*
	1	1	0	1	OP1	OP1	OP2	OP3
	1	1	1	0	OP1	OP2	OP1	OP2
	1	1	1	1	OP1	OP1	OP2*	OP1
Long Word	0	0	0	0	OP0	OP1	OP2	OP3
	0	0	0	1	OP0	OP0	OP1	OP2
	0	0	1	0	OP0	OP1	OP0	OP1
	0	0	1	1	OP0	OP0	OP1*	OP0

*Due to the current implementation, this byte is output but never used.
x = don't care
NOTE: The OP tables on the external data bus refer to a particular byte of the operand that is written on that section of the data bus.

(b)

Figure 16.25 (a) Active data bus sections for the various data types, size codes, and address boundaries (courtesy of Motorola, Inc.); (b) data transfer combinations for aligned and misaligned write operations (courtesy of Motorola, Inc.).

Transfer Size	Size		Address		Long Word Port External Data Bytes Required				Word Port External Data Bytes Required		Byte Port External Data Bytes Required
	SIZ1	SIZ0	A1	A0	D31:D24	D23:D16	D15:D8	D7:D0	D31:D24	D23:D16	D31:D24
Byte	0	1	0	0	OP3				OP3		OP3
	0	1	0	1		OP3				OP3	OP3
	0	1	1	0			OP3		OP3		OP3
	0	1	1	1				OP3		OP3	OP3
Word	1	0	0	0	OP2	OP3			OP2	OP3	OP2
	1	0	0	1		OP2	OP3			OP2	OP2
	1	0	1	0			OP2	OP3	OP2	OP3	OP2
	1	0	1	1				OP2		OP2	OP2
3 Byte	1	1	0	0	OP1	OP2	OP3		OP1	OP2	OP1
	1	1	0	1		OP1	OP2	OP3		OP1	OP1
	1	1	1	0			OP1	OP2	OP1	OP2	OP1
	1	1	1	1				OP1		OP1	OP1
Long Word	0	0	0	0	OP0	OP1	OP2	OP3	OP0	OP1	OP0
	0	0	0	1		OP0	OP1	OP2		OP0	OP0
	0	0	1	0			OP0	OP1	OP0	OP1	OP0
	0	0	1	1				OP0		OP0	OP0

Figure 16.26 Data transfer combinations for aligned and misaligned read operations. (Courtesy of Motorola, Inc.)

Figure 16.27(b) shows what data are written into memory during each bus cycle. Here we find that byte OP_0, which is the most significant byte in the long-word register, is multiplexed to the least significant byte position of the long word storage location at address XXXXXXX0 in memory.

In Fig. 16.27(a), we see that for the second bus cycle $SIZ_1 SIZ_0 = 11$ and $A_1 A_0 = 00$. Looking at Fig. 16.25(a), we find that this means that a 3-byte transfer is taking place over D_{31} through D_8. Figure 16.25(b) shows that the contents of the data bus will be $OP_1 OP_2 OP_3 OP_0$. This combination is consistent with that shown in Fig. 16.27(a).

Figure 16.27(b) shows that during the second bus cycle the contents of the three lower bytes of the long-word register, OP_1, OP_2, and OP_3, are transferred over the bus and loaded into the three most significant byte locations of the next consecutive long-word storage location. This is the long-word storage location at address XXXXXXX4. This completes the misaligned data transfer.

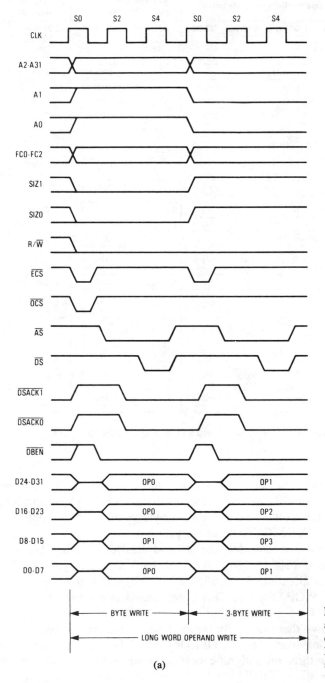

Figure 16.27 (a) Timing diagram for a write transfer of misaligned long-word data over a 32-bit data bus (courtesy of Motorola, Inc.); (b) data write cycle summary (courtesy of Motorola, Inc.).

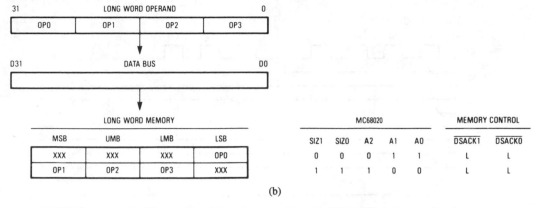

LONG WORD MEMORY				MC68020					MEMORY CONTROL	
MSB	UMB	LMB	LSB	SIZ1	SIZ0	A2	A1	A0	DSACK1	DSACK0
XXX	XXX	XXX	OP0	0	0	0	1	1	L	L
OP1	OP2	OP3	XXX	1	1	1	0	0	L	L

(b)

Figure 16.27 (*continued*)

Read-Modify-Write Bus Cycle

We pointed out earlier that the 68020 has the ability to perform a read-modify-write bus cycle in addition to the separate read and write cycles. During a read-modify-write bus cycle, the contents of a memory location or I/O port are first read into a register within the 68020; their value is modified based on the operation specified by the instruction; and then the result is written back into its original storage location. The waveforms in Fig. 16.28 illustrate a typical read-modify-write bus cycle. Here we see that the $\overline{RMC}$ output is held at its active 0 logic level throughout the complete bus cycle. This signal is used in a multiple-processor system to tell other processors that they cannot have access to the bus until the read-modify-write operation is complete.

16.6 INSTRUCTION CACHE MEMORY

An important improvement of the 68020 microprocessor over the 68000 is the on-chip instruction *cache memory*. In the past, external cache memories were widely used in high-performance minicomputer and microcomputer systems. In a computer system with a cache, a second smaller but very fast memory section is added for use together with the large, slow main memory section. Figure 16.29(a) illustrates this type of system architecture. The small, high-speed memory section is known as the *cache*. The purpose of the cache is to obtain close to 0 wait-state memory system operation even though accesses of the main memory, which is built with low-cost, slow-speed memory devices, require one or more wait states. External caches typically range is size from 32 to 256K bytes and are used to cache both data and code. As shown in Fig. 16.29(b), the 68020's cache differs in that it is on-chip, very small in size (256 bytes), and, as its name implies, only caches instructions. But it still provides many important benefits to 68020-based microcomputer systems. For example, it results in both higher performance for the microcomputer and increases bus availability for external devices.

Let us begin our examination of the 68020's instruction cache by looking briefly at what an instruction cache is used for in a microcomputer system. The first

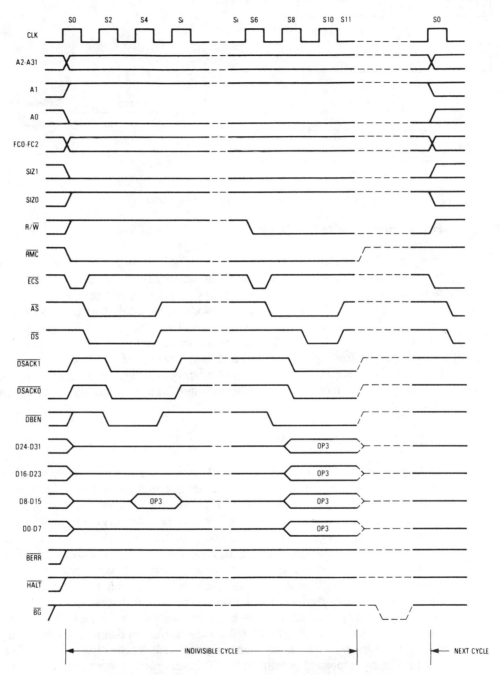

Figure 16.28 Read–modify–write bus cycle timing diagram. (Courtesy of Motorola, Inc.)

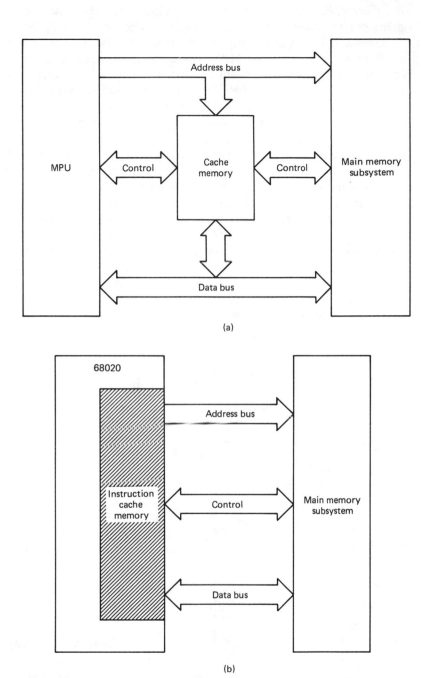

Figure 16.29 (a) External cache system architecture; (b) internal code cache of the 68020.

time the 68020 executes a segment of program it fetches one instruction after the other from external program storage memory. The most recently fetched instructions are automatically saved on-chip in the cache memory. That is, a copy of these instructions is held within the MPU. For example, a segment of a program that implements a loop operation could be fetched and placed in the cache. In this way, we see that the 68020 always holds 128 words of instruction code on-chip.

Now that we know what the code cache holds, let us continue by looking at how the cached instructions are used during program execution. Many software operations involve repeated execution of the same sequence of instructions. A loop is a good example of this type of operation. In Fig. 16.30, we find that the first execution of the loop references code in the slow external program memory. During this access, the routine is copied into the on-chip cache. When the instructions of the loop are repeated, the MPU reaccesses the routine by using the instructions held in the cache, instead of refetching them from external memory. Accesses to code in the internal cache are performed with no wait states, while those of code in external program memory normally require wait states. The more the code held in the cache is used the closer 0 wait-state operation is achieved and the more the overall execution time of the program is decreased. The execution time is further reduced because the 68020 permits operand accesses to external memory to be performed simultaneously with code accesses from the internal cache. This shows us how a cache increases overall system performance.

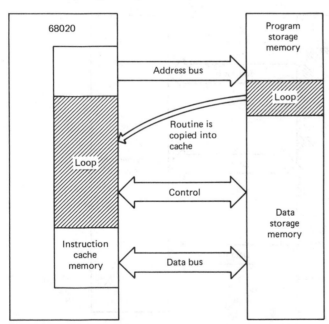

Figure 16.30 Caching of a loop routine.

We mentioned earlier that another advantage of a cache is that it reduces bus activity. In our example of a loop routine, we saw that repeated accesses of the instructions that perform the loop operation were made from the internal cache, not from external program memory. Therefore, fewer code fetch cycles are performed across the bus. This freed-up bus bandwidth is available to other bus masters, such as DMA controllers or other processors in a multiple processor system.

A block diagram of the 68020's instruction cache array is shown in Fig. 16.31. Here we see that the cache contains 64 entries. Each entry is made up of three pieces of information: a *tag* (TAG), a *valid bit* (V), and a *long-word storage location*. The long-word storage locations hold the cached code. Notice that they are organized as two separate instruction words. The tag is 24 bits in length and its value corresponds to the upper 24 bits of the address of the cached code entry in external memory. Finally, the valid bit tells whether or not the long word of code is valid. The code entry is valid if this bit is 1 and invalid if it is 0. When the 68020 MPU is reset, the cache is automatically cleared by resetting all the valid bits. Notice that the instruction contents of the cache array are not cleared at reset; instead, they are simply marked as invalid.

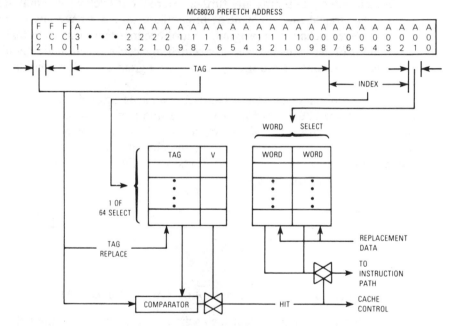

Figure 16.31 Block diagram of the 68020's instruction cache. (Courtesy of Motorola, Inc.)

Everytime an instruction address is generated by the 68020, its value is first checked by the cache circuitry to determine if the long word of code that is to be fetched is already held on-chip. In Fig. 16.31 we see that bits A_2 through A_7 of the address are used as an index into the cache array. This 6-bit code selects one of the 64 long-word entries in the array. Next, the tag of the selected entry is compared with bits A_8 through A_{31} of the address. If they are the same, a second check is made. That is, the valid bit is tested, and if it is 1, a *cache hit* has occurred. A cache hit means that the long word of instruction code does exist in the cache. In this case, the instruction word selected by bit A_1 is read from the cache, and no external instruction fetch bus cycle is initiated.

If either the tag does not match the code on A_8 through A_{31} or V equals 0, there is a *cache miss*. That is, the long word of code is not already in the cache. For this case, the MPU must fetch the code from the storage location at this address in external program storage memory. When the 68020 fetches the long word, it automatically gets written into the cache, V is set, and A_{31} through A_8 are used to update the tag. In this way, the long word is cached and the next access to this address may result in a cache hit.

Remember that the instruction cache only hold 128 words of code. Therefore, it contains just the most recently used instructions. The amount of performance improvement achieved with the cache depends on the code that is being executed. In our example of the loop, the caching of instructions can have a great effect. This is because the complete loop routine may fit into the cache, and once cached it can be reexecuted without initiating any further external bus cycles. But, in other cases, for instance, a straight-line segment of program, it may not have any effect at all. In fact, whenever a change in program control occurs or an instruction that can change the contents of the status register is executed, the cache is automatically flushed. That is, all its current entries are invalidated. As program execution continues, the cache is refilled.

To control the operation of the cache, a *cache control register* (CACR) is provided within the 68020. In Fig. 16.32, we find that just 4 of its 32 bits are implemented. They provide the ability to perform functions, such as enable/disable the cache, freeze the cache, clear an entry, and clear the entire cache, through software. When the 68020 is reset, the E and F bits of CACR are cleared. Let us now look at the function of each of these bits.

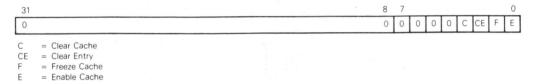

C = Clear Cache
CE = Clear Entry
F = Freeze Cache
E = Enable Cache

Figure 16.32   Cache control register (CACR). (Courtesy of Motorola, Inc.)

Earlier we pointed out that the cache is cleared whenever the 68020 recieves a hardware reset. The cache can also be cleared under software control. This is the function performed by the *clear cache* bit (C) in CACR. Writing 1 into C clears all the valid bits in the cache. In this way, the contents of the cache are flushed by invalidating them.

The cache can also be dynamically enabled or disabled under software control. The *enable cache* (E) bit is used for this purpose. Making E equal to 1 enables the cache for operation. Disabling the cache does not flush the entries within the cache; instead, its contents remain valid and will continue to be used if the cache is reenabled. An example of a use for disabling the cache is in benchmarking the effect of the cache on application code. The execution time for the code can be measured first with the cache enabled and then again with it disabled. The difference between the two measurements identifies the increased performance achieved by the caching of instructions.

The *freeze cache* (F) bit is used to freeze the contents of the cache. When F is set to 1, the current contents of the cache are frozen. The entries in the cache remain valid and are still used if a cache hit occurs. The difference is that if a miss occurs the code is fetched from external memory, but not loaded into the cache. In this way, we see that the contents of the cache are accessed, but not updated. This feature of the cache may be used after loading a critical piece of code into the cache to assure that it always executes in minimum time.

The last of the implemented bits in CACR, which is called *clear entry in cache* (CE), is used to selectively clear individual entries in cache memory. This bit works in conjunction with the *cache address register* (CAAR). Figure 16.33 shows that CAAR contains a 6-bit index. The value of this index points to one of the 64 entries in the cache memory. When CE is switched to 1, the cache entry identified by the index in CAAR is cleared. That is, the valid bit for this long-word entry is cleared to make it invalid.

31	8	7	2	1	0
CACHE FUNCTION ADDRESS		INDEX			

Figure 16.33 Cache address register (CAAR). (Courtesy of Motorola, Inc.)

A special instruction is provided in the instruction set of the 68020 to modify the contents of the CACR register. This is the *move control register* (MOVEC), which is a privileged instruction. For instance, to initiate a freeze cache function, we execute the following instructions

```
MOVEC   CACR, D0    READ CACR
ORI     #2, D0      SET F=1
MOVEC   D0, CACR    RELOAD CACR
```

The first instruction copies the current contents of the cache control register into data register D_0. Then the ORI instruction sets bit 1 in D_0, which corresponds to F, without affecting any other bits. Finally, the second MOVEC instruction updates the cache control register with the new contents of D_0, thereby setting the freeze bit.

16.7 EXCEPTION PROCESSING OF THE 68020

In Chapter 14, we described the exception-processing capability of the 68000 microprocessor. We found that exception processing provides a mechanism for quickly changing program environments. External hardware interrupts permit the transfer of program control to be initiated by an event in external circuitry. On the other hand, exceptions represent program control transfers that are initiated due to an internal event such as a privilege violation. Here we will focus on how the exception processing capability of the 68020 differs from that of the 68000.

Exception Vector Table

The exception program transfer mechanism of the 68020 is identical to that of the 68000. That is, program control is passed to the exception service routine through a vector address held in a vector table. The exceptions supported by the 68020 are shown in the vector table of Fig. 16.34. Comparing this table to that shown for the 68000 in Fig. 14.2, we see that all the vectors assigned for the 68000 perform the

Vector Number(s)	Vector Offset Hex	Vector Offset Space	Assignment
0	000	SP	Reset Initial Interrupt Stack Pointer
1	004	SP	Reset Initial Program Counter
2	008	SD	Bus Error
3	00C	SD	Address Error
4	010	SD	Illegal Instruction
5	014	SD	Zero Divide
6	018	SD	CHK, CHK2 Instruction
7	01C	SD	cpTRAPcc, TRAPcc, TRAPV Instructions
8	020	SD	Privilege Violation
9	024	SD	Trace
10	028	SD	Line 1010 Emulator
11	02C	SD	Line 1111 Emulator
12	030	SD	(Unassigned, Reserved)
13	034	SD	Coprocessor Protocol Violation
14	038	SD	Format Error
15	03C	SD	Uninitialized Interrupt
16 Through 23	040 05C	SD SD	Unassigned, Reserved
24	060	SD	Spurious Interrupt
25	064	SD	Level 1 Interrupt Autovector
26	068	SD	Level 2 Interrupt Autovector
27	06C	SD	Level 3 Interrupt Autovector
28	070	SD	Level 4 Interrupt Autovector
29	074	SD	Level 5 Interrupt Autovector
30	078	SD	Level 6 Interrupt Autovector
31	07C	SD	Level 7 Interrupt Autovector
32 Through 47	080 0BC	SD SD	TRAP #0-15 Instruction Vectors
48	0C0	SD	FPCP Branch or Set on Unordered Condition
49	0C4	SD	FPCP Inexact Result
50	0C8	SD	FPCP Divide by Zero
51	0CC	SD	FPCP Underflow
52	0D0	SD	FPCP Operand Error
53	0D4	SD	FPCP Overflow
54	0D8	SD	FPCP Signaling NAN
55	0DC	SD	Unassigned, Reserved
56	0E0	SD	PMMU Configuration
57	0E4	SD	PMMU Illegal Operation
58	0E8	SD	PMMU Access Level Violation
59 Through 63	0EC 0FC	SD SD	Unassigned, Reserved
64 Through 255	100 3FC	SD SD	User-Defined Vectors (192)

SP = Supervisor Program Space   SD = Supervisor Data Space

Figure 16.34 Exception vector table of the 68020. (Courtesy of Motorola, Inc.)

same functions for the 68020. However, the functions of a few of these exceptions have been expanded. For example, vector 7, which only occurred for the TRAPV instruction in the 68000, now is produced for two other instructions, *coprocessor trap on condition* (cpTRAPcc) *and trap on condition* (TRAPcc).

Some of the vector numbers identified as reserved in the table of Fig. 14.2 have been implemented in the 68020. For example, in Fig. 16.34 we find that vectors 13 and 14 represent *coprocessor protocol violation* and *format error,* respectively. Also, Fig. 16.34 shows that all vectors in the range 48 through 54 provide exception functions for the 68881 floating-point coprocessor, and those in the range from 56 through 58 implement exception functions for the 68851 paged memory management unit.

Exception Priorities

Similarly to the 68000, the 68020 processes exceptions on a priority basis. Figure 16.35 summarizes the group priorities of the various types of exceptions. Earlier we found that the importance of priority is that higher priority exceptions are always serviced first. In this table, the group 0 exception is at the highest priority level and those in group 4 are at the lowest. In this way, we see that the reset exception is at the highest group priority level.

Looking at Fig. 16.35, we find that within some groups their are subgroup priority levels. As an example, let us look at group 1. Here *address error* is at the higher sublevel, level 1.0, and *bus error* at the lower level, 1.1. This means that within group 1 the address error exception takes precedence over the bus error exception. This means that if both were active at the same time, the address error service routine would be executed to completion and then the bus error routine initiated.

Group Priority	Exception and Relative Priority	Processing
0	0.0 — Reset	Aborts all processing (instruction or exception) and does not save old context.
1	1.0 — Address Error 1.1 — Bus Error	Suspends processing (instruction or exception) and saves internal context.
2	2.0 — BKPT #n, CALLM, CHK, CHK2, cp Midinstruction, Cp Protocol Violation, cpTRAPcc, Divide by Zero, RTE, RTM, TRAP #n, TRAPV	Exception processing is part of instruction execution.
3	3.0 — Illegal Instruction, Line A, Unimplemented Line F, Privilege Violation, cp Preinstruction	Exception processing begins before instruction is executed.
4	4.0 — cp Postinstruction 4.1 — Trace 4.2 — Interrupt	Exception processing begins when current instruction or previous exception processing is completed.

Figure 16.35 Exception priority groups. (Courtesy of Motorola, Inc.)

EXAMPLE 16.10

What type of exceptions are at the lowest priority level?

SOLUTION In Fig. 16.35, we find that the lowest priority level in group 4 correspond to external hardware interrupts. They are at priority level 4.2.

External Hardware Interrupt Interface

The 68020's external hardware interrupt interface, which is shown in Fig. 16.36, is similar to that shown for the 68000 in Fig. 14.4. Again, the interface supports interrupt inputs from up to 192 devices. In the table of Fig. 16.34, we find that the service routines for these devices correspond to vector numbers 64 through 255. Some of the signal lines provided by the 68020 are different from those in the 68000's interface. For example, one difference is the addition of an $\overline{\text{IPEND}}$ output. Another difference is that $\overline{\text{DTACK}}$ is replaced by the signals $\overline{\text{DSACK}}_1$ and $\overline{\text{DSACK}}_0$.

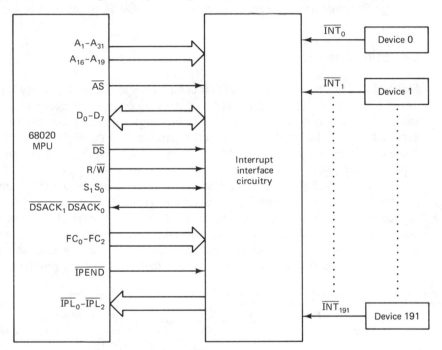

Figure 16.36   General interrupt interface of the 68020.

The flowchart in Fig. 16.37 outlines the events that take place in the interrupt request/acknowledge handshake sequence between an interrupting device and the 68020. Waveforms for the interrupt acknowledge bus cycle are given in Fig. 16.38. The handshake sequence begins with the external device issuing a request for service. This is done by applying a code to the IPL inputs. If at least one of these inputs is logic 1, an interrupt request is pending. Just as for the 68000, the 192 interrupt inputs are assigned to one of the priority levels. These levels correspond to $\overline{\text{IPL}}_2\overline{\text{IPL}}_1\overline{\text{IPL}}_0 = 001$ through $\overline{\text{IPL}}_2\overline{\text{IPL}}_1\overline{\text{IPL}}_0 = 111$. Code 111 represents the highest-priority external hardware interrupt request.

Bits 8 through 10 of the status register are the interrupt mask. When the code at $\overline{\text{IPL}}_2\overline{\text{IPL}}_1\overline{\text{IPL}}_0$ represents a priority level that is higher than the value currently held in the interrupt mask, the 68020 switches its $\overline{\text{IPEND}}$ output to the 0 logic level. This signal, which is not provided in the 68000's interrupt interface, tells external circuitry that an interrupt is pending for service.

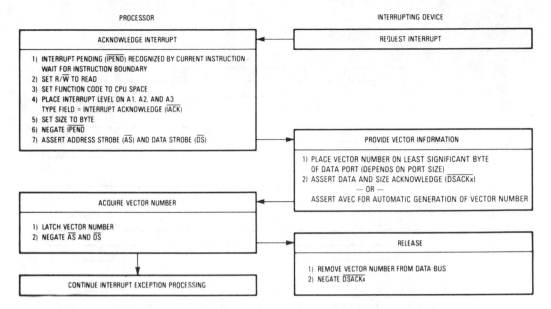

PROCESSOR   INTERRUPTING DEVICE

ACKNOWLEDGE INTERRUPT

1) INTERRUPT PENDING ($\overline{\text{IPEND}}$) RECOGNIZED BY CURRENT INSTRUCTION · WAIT FOR INSTRUCTION BOUNDARY
2) SET R/$\overline{\text{W}}$ TO READ
3) SET FUNCTION CODE TO CPU SPACE
4) PLACE INTERRUPT LEVEL ON A1, A2, AND A3. TYPE FIELD = INTERRUPT ACKNOWLEDGE ($\overline{\text{IACK}}$)
5) SET SIZE TO BYTE
6) NEGATE $\overline{\text{IPEND}}$
7) ASSERT ADDRESS STROBE ($\overline{\text{AS}}$) AND DATA STROBE ($\overline{\text{DS}}$)

REQUEST INTERRUPT

PROVIDE VECTOR INFORMATION

1) PLACE VECTOR NUMBER ON LEAST SIGNIFICANT BYTE OF DATA PORT (DEPENDS ON PORT SIZE)
2) ASSERT DATA AND SIZE ACKNOWLEDGE ($\overline{\text{DSACKx}}$)
— OR —
ASSERT AVEC FOR AUTOMATIC GENERATION OF VECTOR NUMBER

ACQUIRE VECTOR NUMBER

1) LATCH VECTOR NUMBER
2) NEGATE $\overline{\text{AS}}$ AND $\overline{\text{DS}}$

RELEASE

1) REMOVE VECTOR NUMBER FROM DATA BUS
2) NEGATE $\overline{\text{DSACKx}}$

CONTINUE INTERRUPT EXCEPTION PROCESSING

Figure 16.37 Hardware interrupt request/acknowledge handshake sequence flowchart. (Courtesy of Motorola, Inc.)

In Figs. 16.37 and 16.38, we see that in response to an interrupt request the processor initiates a read cycle to the CPU space. Notice that R/$\overline{\text{W}}$ is set to 1 for read cycle; $A_{19}A_{18}A_{17}A_{16}$ equals 1111 for interrupt acknowledge cycle, SIZ_1SIZ_0 equals 01 for byte transfer; and both the $\overline{\text{AS}}$ and $\overline{\text{DS}}$ outputs are at their active levels. In response to these signals, the interrupt interface must put the vector number of the active interrupt onto the data bus and then activate the $\overline{\text{DSACK}}$ inputs of the 68020. The code on $\overline{\text{DSACK}_1}\overline{\text{DSACK}_0}$ tells the 68020 what size data bus is in use. Looking at Fig. 16.38, we see that for a 32-bit bus the type number is transferred over D_0 through D_7. The 68020 latches the type number off the bus and then completes the interrupt acknowledge bus cycle.

At this point, the 68020 knows the type number, but it has not yet fetched the vector address. The flowchart in Fig. 16.39 shows what happens next. Notice that at the next instruction boundary the contents of the status register (SR) are saved in a temporary register (TEMP) and then later pushed onto the stack along with the current value in the program counter (PC). Finally, the vector address for the interrupt is read out of the vector table in memory and loaded into PC. Then, the instructions of the service routine are prefetched.

The 68020 also supports the autovector mode of initiating external hardware interrupts. An autovector interrupt interface diagram for the 68020 is shown in Fig. 16.40. The only differences between this interface and that shown for the 68000 in Fig. 14.10 are that the autovector input is called $\overline{\text{AVEC}}$, instead of $\overline{\text{VPA}}$, and the addition of $\overline{\text{IPEND}}$. Other than these changes, the autovector mode of operation on the 68020 is identical to that provided by the 68000. The autovector bus interface sequence is shown in Fig. 16.41. Notice that the autovector mode of operation is initiated by asserting $\overline{\text{AVEC}}$, instead of supplying the interrupt level to the MPU.

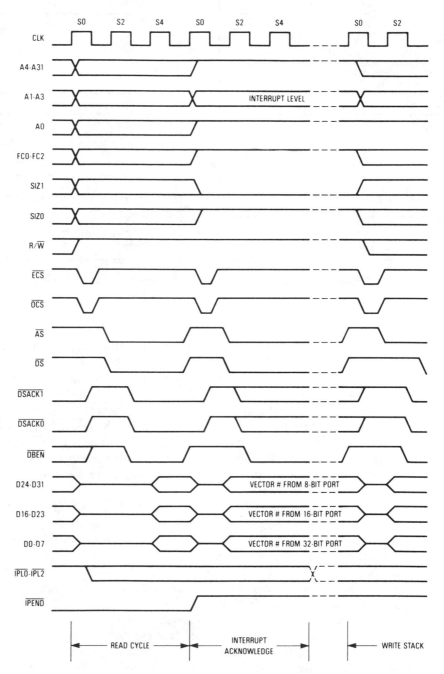

Figure 16.38 Interrupt acknowledge bus cycle waveforms. (Courtesy of Motorola, Inc.)

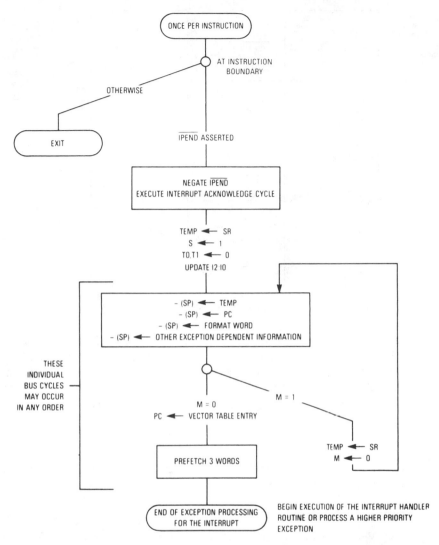

Figure 16.39 Interrupt processing flowchart. (Courtesy of Motorola, Inc.)

Exception Instructions

In Section 14.10, we examined exception processing for the TRAP, TRAPV, CHK, DIVS, and DIVU instructions. For the 68020, these instructions involve the same exception functions that they did for the 68000. However, the 68020 has three new instructions that result in exception processing. They are trap on condition (TRAPcc), trap on coprocessor condition (cpTRAPcc), and check register against bounds (CHK2). The formats of these instructions are shown in Fig. 16.42. Let us now look at the operations they perform.

The TRAPcc instruction permits the programmer to test for a variety of different status conditions and, if they exist, pass program control to an exception service

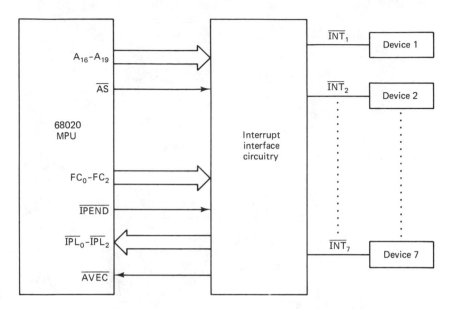

Figure 16.40 Autovector interrupt interface.

routine. Remember that the TRAPV instruction that is provided in both the 68000 and 68020 tests for just one status condition. This is whether or not the overflow bit, V, is set. Figure 16.43 shows all the condition code (cc) combinations that can be tested for with the TRAPcc instruction. For example, the condition code cc equals CS means trap on carry set. The instruction is written as

TRAPCS

When this instruction is executed, status bit C is tested and, if it is equal to 1, exception processing is initiated.

EXAMPLE 16.11

What condition code relationship is tested for by the instruction TRAPGE?

SOLUTION Looking at Fig. 16.43, we find that the trap on greater than or equal to instruction initiates exception processing based on the condition code relationship

$$N.V + \bar{N}.\bar{V}$$

All the variations of the TRAPcc instruction pass control to the service routine through vector 7. However, the TRAPcc instruction can also include an immediate data operand. This operand will reside in program memory following the instruction word for the instruction. The exception routine pointed to by the address in vector location 7 can access this data. For example, the data could be a pointer to the service routine that will service the specific condition code relationship. An example of a trap on not equal instruction with a long-word operand equal to 12345678_{16} is

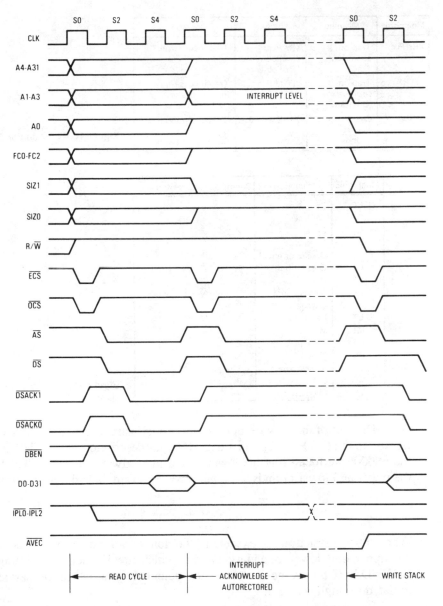

Figure 16.41 Autovector bus cycle waveforms. (Courtesy of Motorola, Inc.)

TRAPNE.L #$12345678

The trap on coprocessor condition instruction is similar to the TRAPcc instruction we just described. The only difference is that it performs the test specified by cc on the state of the condition code bits in a coprocessor, not those in the 68020's status register. For instance, it can initiate exception processing based on the setting of condition code bits in the 68881 floating-point coprocessor.

Mnemonic	Meaning	Format	Operations
TRAPcc	Trap on condition	TRAPcc TRAPcc.W #d TRAPcc.L #d	Trap if cc is true.
cpTRAPcc	Trap on coprocessor condition	cpTRAPcc cpTRAPcc #d	Trap if cc is true in coprocessor.
CHK2	Check register against bounds	CHK2 EA, Rn	CHK exception if Rn < lower bound or Rn > upper bound.

Figure 16.42   Additional exception instructions.

Mnemonic	Function	Condition code relationship
CC	Carry clear	$\overline{C}$
CS	Carry set	C
EQ	Equal	Z
F	Never true	0
GE	Greater or equal	$N \cdot V + \overline{N} \cdot \overline{V}$
GT	Greater than	$N \cdot V \cdot \overline{Z} + \overline{N} \cdot \overline{V} \cdot \overline{Z}$
HI	High	$\overline{C} \cdot \overline{Z}$
LE	Less or equal	$Z + N \cdot \overline{V} + \overline{N} \cdot V$
LS	Low or same	$C + Z$
LT	Less than	$N \cdot \overline{V} \cdot \overline{N} \cdot V$
MI	Minus	N
NE	Not equal	$\overline{Z}$
PL	Plus	$\overline{N}$
T	Always true	1
VC	Overflow clear	$\overline{V}$
VS	Overflow set	V

Figure 16.43   Condition code relationships.

The last of the new exception processing instructions, CHK2, is simply an extension to the 68000's CHK instruction. In our description of the CHK instruction for the 68000, we found that the lower bound must always be zero. CHK2 allows both the upper and lower bounds to be nonzero. An example is the instruction

$$\text{CHK2.L   BOUNDS, D1}$$

When this instruction is executed, the long-word value in D_1 is compared to the upper and lower boundary values, which are in memory starting at address BOUNDS. If this value is outside the boundaries, an exception service routine is initiated through vector 6.

Internal Exceptions

In our study of the 68000, we found that it automatically detects and initiates exception processing for address errors, privilege violations, trace operations, and illegal or unimplemented opcodes. This internal exception capability has also been expanded in the 68020. Earlier we pointed out that a number of vector numbers are assigned to the floating-point coprocessor and paged memory management unit of the 68020 microcomputer system. In additiion to this, two new internal exceptions are defined for the 68020 *coprocessor protocol violation* and *format error*. A coprocessor protocol violation occurs as the result of an error in the handshake sequence between the 68020 and a coprocessor such as the 68881 floating-point coprocessor. It passes control to a service routine through vector 13 at address 34_{16}. The format error exception can result from an error in the format of data for control transfer operations such as module calls, restores to a coprocessor, and returns from exceptions and modules. If an error is detected in the format of the data for one of these operations, exception processing is initated through vector 14.

ASSIGNMENTS

Section 16.2

1. Name two enhancements of the 68020's internal hardware architecture over that of the 68000.
2. List three improvements of the external hardware architecture of the 68020 that are not available on the 68000.
3. What process technology is used to manufacture the 68020?
4. What signal is supplied at pin A2 of the package?
5. At which pin of the 68020's package is the signal R/$\overline{\text{W}}$ found?

Section 16.3

6. How large is the 68020's physical address space?
7. What type of data transfers are supported over the data bus?
8. In Fig. 16.5, which byte in long word 2 is in the least significant byte position? What is its address?
9. Which is the most significant word of long word 6 in the Fig. 16.5? What is its word address?
10. Is the word starting at address $0000101F_{16}$ aligned or misaligned? The word at address 00001020_{16}?
11. If a long word begins at address $0000202A_{16}$, is it aligned or misaligned? The word at address $0000202B_{16}$?
12. What does dynamic bus sizing permit?
13. What two functions are provided by the $\overline{\text{DSACK}}$ signals?
14. If $\overline{\text{DSACK}_1}\overline{\text{DSACK}_0}$ equals 00, over which data bus lines would the word of data at word address 22_{16} be carried? How about if the $\overline{\text{DSACK}}$ code is 01?
15. How many bus cycles are required to transfer the word of data in Problem 14 if $\overline{\text{DSACK}_1}\overline{\text{DSACK}_0}$ equals 00? How about if $\overline{\text{DSACK}_1}\overline{\text{DSACK}_0}$ equals 01? If $\overline{\text{DSACK}_1}\overline{\text{DSACK}_0} = 10$?
16. Make a drawing like that in Fig. 16.11 to show the data transfers and bus cycles for an 8-bit data bus.
17. What does a slow I/O device need to do to extend a bus cycle to it with wait states?
18. List the mnemonic and name of each of the 68020's asynchronous bus control signals that are not available on the 68000.

19. If the function code outputs are $FC_2FC_1FC_0 = 111$ and the CPU space code output on $A_{19}A_{18}A_{17}A_{16}$ is 1111, what type of bus cycle is in progress?

20. Which interrupt control signal is new with the 68020?

21. What does $\overline{CDIS}$ stand for?

Section 16.4

22. At what pin is the clock signal input to the 68020?

23. What is the maximum operating frequency of the 68020RC33? Its minimum operating frequency?

24. What is the maximum cycle time of the 68020RC16?

25. What is the minimum clock pulse width of the 68020RC25?

26. What number in the waveform of Fig. 16.15(a) identifies fall time?

27. If the minimum cycle time of a 68020RC25 is 45 ns, at what frequency is the device operating?

Section 16.5

28. Are SIZ_0 and SIZ_1 inputs or outputs? What function do they provide?

29. Make a drawing like that in Fig. 16.17 to show how an aligned long word of data is read over a byte-wide data bus.

30. For the waveforms in Fig. 16.44 answer the following:
   (a) What are the values of $\overline{DSACK_1}\,\overline{DSACK_0}$, SIZ_1SIZ_0, and A_1A_0 for bus cycle 1?
   (b) What are the values of $\overline{DSACK_1}\,\overline{DSACK_0}$, SIZ_1SIZ_0, and A_1A_0 for bus cycle 2?
   (c) What are the values of $\overline{DSACK_1}\,\overline{DSACK_0}$, SIZ_1SIZ_0, and A_1A_0 for bus cycle 3?

31. If a long-word write data transfer is performed to a misaligned address that has the form XXXXXXX1, how many bus cycles are needed to perform the transfer, what are A_1A_0 equal to during each cycle, what is the SIZ code during each cycle, and what bytes of data are transferred during each bus cycle?

32. During what type of bus cycle is the signal $\overline{RMC}$ active?

Section 16.6

33. How large is the 68020's instruction cache?

34. Does the 68020's on-chip cache store code, data, or both?

35. What are the three pieces of information held in each cache storage location?

36. What is meant by the expression cache hit?

37. What happens if a cache miss occurs?

38. Can the contents of the cache be cleared through software? Through hardware?

39. How is the instruction cache disabled under software control? Under hardware control?

40. What happens when the F bit of CACR is set to 1?

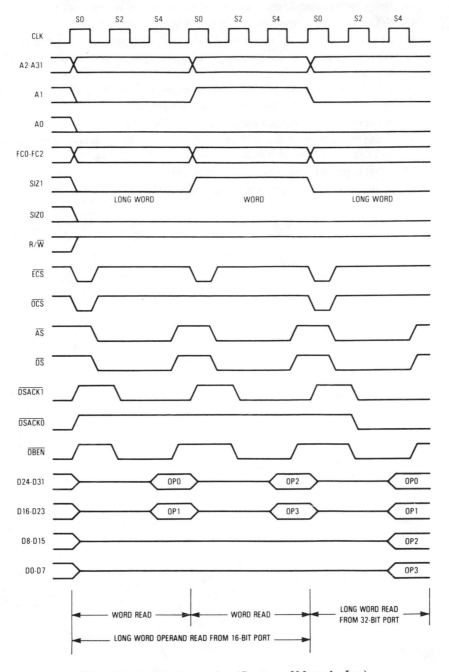

Figure 16.44 Read bus cycles. (Courtesy of Motorola, Inc.)

41. For what additional functions does an exception for vector 6 occur in the 68020?

42. Which exception, breakpoint or trace, is at the higher priority?

43. At what address is the vector for the floating-point overflow exception held?

44. What external hardware interrupt code can be used to implement a nonmaskable interrupt request?

45. If $\overline{DSACK_1}\,\overline{DSACK_0}$ = 10 during an interrupt acknowledge bus cycle, over which data bus lines will the type number transfer take place?

46. What does the instruction mnemonic TRAPVC stand for?

47. Write an instruction that will produce a trap for the condition code relationship C + Z and that has a byte-wide immediate operand equal to 03_{16}.

48. What is the difference between the CHK and CHK2 instructions?

49. Name two internal exceptions detected by the 68020 and not by the 68000.

Bibliography

BRADLEY, DAVID J., *Assembly Language Programming for the IBM Personal Computer.* Englewood Cliffs, NJ: Prentice-Hall, Inc. 1984.

BRYCE, HEATHER, "Microprogramming Makes the MC68000 a Processor for the Future," *Electronic Design* 22, Oct. 25, 1979.

CIARCIA, STEVEN, "The Intel 8086," *Byte,* Nov. 1979.

COFFRON, JAMES W., *Programming the 8086/8088.* Berkeley, CA: Sybex Inc., 1983.

DAVIS, REX, *Prioritized Individually Vectored Interrupts for Multiple Peripheral Systems with the 68000.* Austin, TX: Motorola, Inc., 1981.

GRADEN, DUANE, *Software Refreshed Memory Card for the MC68000 (AN-816).* Austin, TX: Motorola, Inc., 1981.

INTEL CORPORATION, *Components Data Catalog.* Santa Clara, CA: Intel Corporation, 1980.

——, *80386 Microprocessor Hardware Reference Manual.* Santa Clara, CA: Intel Corporation, 1987.

——, *80386 Programmer's Reference Manual.* Santa Clara, CA: Intel Corporation, 1987.

——, *80386 System Software Writer's Guide.* Santa Clara, CA: Intel Corporation, 1987.

——, *iAPX86, 88 User's Manual.* Santa Clara, CA: Intel Corporation, July 1981.

——, *Introduction to the 80386.* Santa Clara, CA: Intel Corporation, Sept. 1985.

——, *MCS-86™ User's Manual.* Santa Clara, CA: Intel Corporation, Feb. 1979.

——, *Peripheral Design Handbook.* Santa Clara, CA: Intel Corporation, Apr. 1978.

KANE, GERRY, DOUG HAWKINS, and LANCE LEVENTHAL, *68000 Assembly Language Programming.* Berkeley, CA: Osborne/McGraw-Hill, 1981.

McKENZIE, JAMES, *Dual 16-Bit Ports for the MC68000 Using Two MC6821s (AN-810).* Austin, TX: Motorola, Inc., 1981.

MORSE, STEPHEN P., *The 8086 Primer*. Rochelle Park, NJ: Hayden Book Company, Inc., 1978.

MOTOROLA, INC., *MC68000 16-bit Microprocessor User's Manual,* 3rd ed. Englewood Cliffs, NJ: Prentice-Hall, Inc., 1982.

————, *MC68020 32-bit Microprocessor User's Manual,* 3rd ed. Englewood Cliffs, NJ: Prentice-Hall, Inc., 1989.

————, *MC68000 Educational Computer Board User's Manual*. Austin, TX: Motorola, Inc., 1981.

————, *Motorola Microprocessors Data Manual*. Austin, TX: Motorola, Inc., 1981.

————, *32-Bit Computer Design Using 68020/68881/68851*. East Kilbride, Scotland: Motorola, Inc., 1987.

NORTON, PETER, *Inside the IBM PC*. Bowie, MD: Robert J. Brady Co., 1983.

RECTOR, RUSSELL, and GEORGE ALEXY, *The 8086 Book*. Berkeley, CA: Osborne/McGraw-Hill, 1980.

SCANLON, LEO J., *IBM PC Assembly Language*. Bowie, MD: Robert J. Brady Co., 1983.

SCANLON, LEO J., *The 68000: Principles and Programming*. Indianapolis, IN: Howard W. Sams & Company, Inc., Publishers, 1981.

SCHNEIDER, AL, *Fundamentals of IBM PC Assembly Language*. Blue Ridge Summit, PA: Tab Books, Inc., 1984.

SINGH, AVTAR, and WALTER A. TRIEBEL, *The 8088 Microprocessor: Programming, Interfacing, Software, Hardware, and Applications*. Englewood Cliffs, NJ: Prentice-Hall, Inc., 1989.

————, and ————, *The 8086 and 80286 Microprocessors: Architecture, Software, and Interface Techniques*. Englewood Cliffs, NJ: Prentice-Hall, Inc., 1990.

————, and ————, *IBM PC/8088 Assembly Language Programming*. Englewood Cliffs, NJ: Prentice-Hall, Inc., 1985.

STARNES, THOMAS W., "Compact Instructions Give the MC68000 Power While Simplifying its Operation," *Electronic Design* 20, Sept. 27, 1979.

————, "Handling Exceptions Gracefully Enhances Software Reliability," *Electronics,* Sept. 11, 1980.

————, "Powerful Instructions and Flexible Registers of the MC68000 Make Programming Easy," *Electronic Design* 9, Apr. 26, 1980.

STRITTNER, SKIP, and TOM GUNTER, "A Microprocessor Architecture for a Changing World: The Motorola 68000," *Computer*, Feb. 1979.

TRIEBEL, WALTER A., *Integrated Digital Electronics*. Englewood Cliffs, NJ: Prentice-Hall, Inc., 1979.

————, and ALFRED E. CHU, *Handbook of Semiconductor and Bubble Memories*. Englewood Cliffs, NJ: Prentice-Hall, Inc., 1982.

TRIEBEL, WALTER A., and AVTAR SINGH, *The 68000 Microprocessor: Architecture, Software, and Interfacing Techniques*. Englewood Cliffs, NJ: Prentice-Hall, Inc., 1986.

WILLEN, DAVID C., and JEFFREY I. KRANTZ, *8088 Assembler Language Programming: the IBM PC*. Indianapolis, IN: Howard W. Sams & Co., Inc., 1983.

Answers to Selected Assignments

Section 1.6

25. TMS1000 or PPS-4
29. 8088, 68000

CHAPTER 2

Section 2.2

3. 13

Section 2.3

5. $FFFFF_{16}$ and 00000_{16}
7. $00FF_{16}$

Section 2.4

9. Up to 256K bytes
11. Up to 128K bytes

Section 2.5

13. Pointers to interrupt and exception service routines

Section 2.6

17. IP is incremented such that it points to the next sequential instruction.

Section 2.7

19. With a postscript X. AX, BX, CX, and DX.
21. Count for string and multibit shift and rotate instructions.

Section 2.8

23. Base pointer (BP) and stack pointer (SP)
25. DS

Section 2.9

29. Instructions can be used to test the state of these flags and, based on their setting, modify the sequence in which instructions of the program are executed.

Answers to Selected Assignments

31. Instructions are provided that can load the complete register or modify specific flag bits.

Section 2.10

43. Offset and base
35. $A000_{16}$

Section 2.11

39. 128 words

Section 2.12

41. Separate
43. Page 0

Section 2.14

45. Instruction	Source	Destination
(a)	Register	Register
(b)	Register	Immediate
(c)	Register indirect	Register
(d)	Register indirect	Register
(e)	Based	Register
(f)	Indexed	Register
(g)	Based indexed	Register

CHAPTER 3

Section 3.3

1. (a) Value of immediate operand 0110 is moved into AX.
   (b) Contents of AX are copied into DI.
   (c) Contents of AL are copied into BL.
   (d) Contents of AX are copied into memory address DS:0100.
   (e) Contents of AX are copied into the memory location pointed to by BX + DI.
   (f) Contents of AX are copied into the memory location pointed to by DI + 4.
   (g) Contents of AX are copied into the memory location pointed to by BX + DI + 4.

3. MOV   AX, 1010
       MOV   ES, AX

7. $10750_{16} + 100_{16} + 10_{16} = 10860_{16}$

Section 3.4

13. ADC DX,111F
17. DAA
19. $(AX) = FFA0_{16}$

Section 3.5

23. (a) $(DS:300) = 0A_{16}$ (e) $(AX) = AA55_{16}$
    (b) $(DS:100) = 0H_{16}$, $(DS:101) = A0_{16}$ (f) $(DS:300) = 55_{16}$
    (c) $(DS:210) = FFFF_{16}$ (g) $(DS:300) = 55_{16}$, $DS:301 = AA$
    (d) $(DS:220) = F5_{16}$

25. AND WORD PTR [100H] , 80

Section 3.6

31. MOV CL, 08
    SHL WORD PTR [DI] , CL

Section 3.7

35. (a) $(DX) = 2222_{16}$, $CF = 0$ (d) $(DS:210) = AA_{16}$, $CF = 1$
    (b) $(DS:400) = 5A_{16}$, $CF = 1$ (e) $(DS:210, 211) = D52A_{16}$, $CF = 1$
    (c) $(DS:200) = 01_{16}$, $CF = 0$ (f) $(DS:220, 221) = AAAD_{16}$, $CF = 0$

CHAPTER 4

Section 4.2

1. Executing the first instruction causes the contents of the status register to be copied into AH. The second instruction causes the value of the flags to be saved in memory at the location pointed to by BX + DI.
3. STC; CLC.

Section 4.3

7. (a) The byte of data in AL is compared to the byte of data in memory at address DS:100 by subtraction and the status flags are set or reset to reflect the results.
   (b) The word contents of the data storage memory location pointed to by SI is compared to the contents of AX by subtraction and the status flags are set or reset to reflect the results.
   (c) The immediate data 1234 is compared to the word contents of the memory location pointed to by the value in DI by subtraction and the status flags are set or reset to reflect the results.

Section 4.4

11. IP; CS and IP

13. Intersegment

17. SF = 0

21. **(a)** $1000_{16} = 2^{12} = 4096$ times.

(b)
```
            MOV     CX, 11
    DLY:    DEC     CX
            JNZ     DLY
    NXT:    —
```

(c)
```
            MOV     AX, 0FFFF
    DLY1:   MOV     CX, 0
    DLY2:   DEC     CX
            JNZ     DLY2
            DEC     AX
            JNZ     DLY1
    NXT:    —
```

25. ; For the given binary number B, the BCD number's digits are
    ; (D0) = R (B/10)
    ; (D1) = R (Q (B/10) /10)
    ; (D2) = R (Q (Q (B/10) /10) /10)
    ; (D3) = R (Q (Q (Q (B/10) /10) /10) /10)

```
                    MOV     SI, 0         ; Result = 0
                    MOV     CH, 4         ; Counter
                    MOV     BX, 10        ; Divisor
                    MOV     AX, DX        ; Get the binary number
                    MOV     DX, 0         ; For division make (DX) = 0
    NEXTDIGIT:      DIV     BX            ; Compute the next BCD digit
                    CMP     DX, 9         ; Invalid if > 9
                    JG      INVALID
                    MOV     CL, 12        ; Position as most signicant digit
                    SHL     DX, CL
                    OR      SI, DX
                    DEC     CH            ; Repeat for all four digits
                    JZ      DONE
                    MOV     CL, 4         ; Prepare for next digit
                    SHR     SI, CL
                    JMP     NEXTDIGIT
    INVALID:        MOV     DX, 0FFFF     ; Invalid code
                    JMP     DONE1
    DONE:           MOV     DX, SI
    DONE1:          —
```

Section 4.5

27. The call instruction saves the value in the instruction pointer (and maybe both segment registers) in addition to performing the jump operation.

29. IP; IP and CS

31. (a) 1075:1000   **(b)** 1075:1000   **(c)** 1000:0100

35. ; For the decimal number = $D_3 D_2 D_1 D_0$,
; the binary number = $10(10(10(0+D_3)+D_2)+D_1)+D_0$

```
                    MOV    BX, 0           ; Result = 0
                    MOV    SI, 10          ; Multiplier = 10
                    MOV    CH, 4           ; Number of digits = 4
                    MOV    CL, 4           ; Rotate counter = 4
                    MOV    DI, DX
NXTDIGIT:           MOV    AX, DI          ; Get the decimal number
                    ROL    AX, CL          ; Rotate to extract the digit
                    MOV    DI, AX          ; Save the rotated decimal number
                    AND    AX, 0F          ; Extract the digit
                    ADD    AX, BX          ; Add to the last result
                    DEC    CH
                    JZ     DONE            ; Skip if this is the last digit
                    MUL    SI              ; Multiply by 10
                    MOV    BX, AX          ; and save
                    JMP    NXTDIGIT        ; Repeat for the next digit
DONE:               —                      ; Result = (AX)
```

Section 4.6

39. ZF

41. Jump size = -126 to $+129$

43.
```
            MOV    AL, 1
            MOV    CX, N
            JCXZ   DONE          ; N = 0 case
            LOOPZ  DONE          ; N = 1 case
            INC    CX            ; Restore N
AGAIN:      MUL    CL
            LOOP   AGAIN
DONE:       MOV    FACT, AL
```

Section 4.7

45. DF

47. (a) CLD   **(b)** CLD   **(c)** STD
       MOVSB   LODS   CMPLS

CHAPTER 5

Section 5.2

1. HMOS
5. 1 MB

Section 5.3

7. The logic level of input $MN/\overline{MX}$
9. $\overline{WR}$; $\overline{LOCK}$

Section 5.4

11. 20-bit, 16-bit
15. $\overline{BHE}$
17. $\overline{WR}$
19. HOLD, $\overline{HLDA}$

Section 5.5

23. $\overline{MRDC}$, $\overline{MWTC}$, $\overline{AMWC}$, $\overline{IORC}$, $\overline{IOWC}$, $\overline{AIOWC}$, $\overline{INTA}$, and $\overline{MCE/PDEN}$
25. 101_2
27. 10_2

Section 5.6

30. 24 MHz
32. $V_{Hmin} = 3.9$ V and $V_{Hmax} = Vcc + 1$ V, $V_{Lmin} = -0.5$ V and $V_{Lmax} = 0.6$ V

Section 5.7

34. 400 ns
36. An extension of the current bus cycle by a period equal to one or more T states because the READY input is tested and found to be logic 0.

Section 5.8

38. 8086; 8288

Section 5.9

40. High bank; $\overline{BHE}$

Section 5.10

44. 01

Section 5.11

46. $\overline{S_2}\overline{S_1}\overline{S_0} = 100$, $\overline{MRDC}$
48. $S_3S_4 = 10$; $\overline{S_2}\overline{S_1}\overline{S_0} = 110$; $\overline{MWTC}$ and $\overline{AMWC}$

Section 5.12

Section 5.13

52. Local bus consists of AD_0 through AD_{15}, A_{16} through A_{19}, $\overline{BHE}$, ALE, $M/\overline{IO}$, $DT/\overline{R}$, $\overline{DEN}$, $\overline{WR}$, and $\overline{RD}$. System bus consists of A_0 through A_{19}, D_0 through D_{15}, $\overline{BHE}$, $M/\overline{IO}$, $\overline{WR}$, and $\overline{RD}$.

Section 5.14

56. 00000_{16} through $07FFE_{16}$
58. 6

CHAPTER 6

Section 6.2

1. Address lines A_0 through A_{15} and $\overline{BHE}$ carry the address of the I/O port to be accessed, while address lines A_{16} through A_{19} are held at the 0 logic level. Data bus lines D_0 through D_{15} carry the data that are transferred between the MPU and I/O port.
3. 8288.

Section 6.3

5. 16 bits
7. No

Section 6.4

9.
```
MOV    AX, 1A
IN     DX, AX
```

Section 6.5

13. 1200 ns

Section 6.7

17.
```
MOV    AX, 0
MOV    DS, AX
MOV    AL, 92
MOV    BX, 0100
MOV    [BX] , AL
```

Section 6.8

19.
```
IN     AL, 08    ; Read port A
MOV    BL, AL    ; Save in BL
IN     AL, 0A    ; Read port B
ADD    AL, BL    ; Add the two numbers
OUT    0C, AL    ; Output to port C
```

CHAPTER 7

Section 7.2

1. Hardware interrupts, software interrupts, internal interrupts, software interrupts, and reset

5. Higher priority.

Section 7.3

7. 4 bytes

9. Overflow

11. $IP_{40} \rightarrow B0$ and $CS_{40} \rightarrow B2$

Section 7.4

13. Arithmetic; overflow flag

Section 7.5

15.
```
CLI    ; Disable interrupts at entry point of
       ; Noninterruptible subroutine

   .
   .
   .   ; Body of subroutine
   .
   .
STI    ; Reenable interrupts at end of
       ; subroutine
RET    ; Return to main part of program
```

Section 7.6

19. D_0 through D_7

Section 7.7

23. $1.8 \ \mu s$

Section 7.8

25. $D0 = 0$ ICW4 not needed
$D_1 = 1$ Single device
$D3 = 0$ Edge triggered
and assuming that all other bits are logic 0 gives $ICW1 = 00000010_2 = 02_{16}$

29. MOV AL, [0A001]

31. ; Assume that a copy of OCW3 is kept in memory location OCW3.

```
MOV    AL, OCW3    ; Extract the RR bit
NOT    AL          ; Toggle it
AND    AL, 2
OR     AL, OCW3    ; New OCW3
MOV    OCW3, AL
```

Section 7.9

33. 22

Section 7.10

35. Divide error, single step, breakpoint, overflow error

CHAPTER 8

Section 8.2

3. 32 bits; 16 bits

Section 8.3

5. The immediate value 1234 is pushed to the stack.

9. The data held at the word-wide input port at I/O address 1000 are read in and stored at memory address 1075:100 = 10850 and the value in DI is incremented to 102.

11. Assures that the value in DI will only be in the range 0 through 255

13. Double precision shift left

15. MOVZX EAX, DATA_WORD

Section 8.4

21. Defines the location and size of the global descriptor table

23. System segment descriptor

25. $0FFF_{16}$

27. Local descriptor table

29. CR_0

33. Switch the PG bit in CR_0 to 1

35. 4 KB

37. Selector; selects a task state segment descriptor

39. BASE and LIMIT of the TSS descriptor

43. 00130020_{16}

45. Level 2

47. Selector and offset

49. 64 TB, 16,384 segments

Section 8.5

61. LIMIT $= 00110_{16}$, BASE $= 00200000_{16}$

63. 00200226_{16}

65. $R/\overline{W} = 0$ and $U/\overline{S} = 0$ or $R/\overline{W} = 1$ and $U/\overline{S} = 0$

67. Dirty bit

Section 8.7

71. The running of multiple processes in a time-shared manner

75. Level 0, level 3

77. LDT and GDT

79. Level 0

83. A task can access code in segments at the CPL or at higher privilege levels, but cannot modify the code at a higher privilege level.

85. The call gate is used to transfer control within a task from code at the CPL to a routine at a higher privilege level.

87. Identifies a task state segment

Section 8.8

93. Active, level 3

95. Yes

CHAPTER 9

Section 9.2

1. CHMOSIII

3. INTR

Section 9.3

5. Byte, D_0 through D_7, no
7. I/O data read

Section 9.4

11. F12

Section 9.5

13. 40 ns
17. An extension of the current bus cycle by a period equal to one or more T states because the $\overline{READY}$ input was tested and found to be logic 1
19. 80 ns

Section 9.6

21. Four independent banks each organized as 1 GB × 8 bits; four banks each organized as 256 KB × 8 bits.
23. 120 ns; 240 ns

Section 9.7

27. $M/\overline{IO}$
31. 320 ns
33. BASE + 8; LSB (bit 0)

Section 9.8

35. Interrupt vector table; interrupt descriptor table
37. Interrupt descriptor table register; 0000000003FF
39. (a) Active;   (b) privilege level 2;   (c) interrupt gate;   (d) B000:1000
43. Divide error, debug, breakpoint, overflow error, bounds check, invalid opcode, coprocessor not available, interrupt table limit to small, coprocessor segment overrun, stack fault, segment overrun, and coprocessor error
45. 0 through 31

CHAPTER 10

Section 10.2

1. 19

Section 10.3

3. 8,388,607 words
5. Byte = 8 bits, word = 16 bits, and double word = 32 bits

Section 10.4

9. Holds the exception vector table

Section 10.5

11. B_0 through B_7, B_0 through B_{15}, and B_0 through B_{31}
13. 7
15. Word and long word; long word only
17. User mode
19. PC
21. Words
25. Levels 1 through 4
27. Trace mode control bit

Section 10.6

29. User stack, supervisor stack
31. Push; pop

Section 10.7

33. Register direct addressing, absolute data addressing, program counter relative addressing, register indirect addressing, immediate data addressing, implied addressing

CHAPTER 11

Section 11.3

3. MOVE.W   #$14,D0
   MOVE   D0,CCR
5. ($A000) = 78_{16}
   ($A001) = 01_{16}
   ($A002) = 21_{16}
9. $5555AAAA_{16}$
11.   D0 = $02468ACE_{16}$
        D1 = $9BDF1357_{16}$

Section 11.4

13. **(a)** D0 = $112233AB_{16}$ **(e)** D1 = $112233AC_{16}$
   (b) ($0001001E) = $FF00B999_{16}$ **(f)** ($0001000E) = $FFFF00FE_{16}$
   (c) ($00010000) = $FFFF1234_{16}$ **(g)** A0 = $0002000F_{16}$
   (d) ($00010023) = 00000009_{16}

17. EXT.B   D0

Section 11.5

21. D1 = 35_{10}

Section 11.6

25. **(a)** D0 = $F0F0A0_{16}$ **(b)** ($00100000) = $5555AAA0_{16}$ **(c)** ($00100010) = $0000F0FF_{16}$
27. $I_2I_1I_0 = 4$ before execution; $I_2I_1I_0 = 7$ after execution
29. ANDI   #F8FF,SR

Section 11.7

35. **(a)** D0 = 56781234_{16},   C = 0   **(d)** D0 = $0F0F8787_{16}$,   C = 1
   (b) D0 = $1234560F_{16}$,   C = 1   **(e)** D0 = $5678091A_{16}$,   C = 0, X = 0
   (c) D0 = 56781234_{16},   C = 0   **(f)** D0 = $FF007F80_{16}$,   C = 0, X = 0

CHAPTER 12

Section 12.2

1. N, Z, V, and C
5. The long-word contents of the memory location pointed to by the address in A_0 are compared to 0. Then the N and Z bits in SR are set or reset to reflect the result of the comparision.
9. SPL

Section 12.3

13. **(a)** The absolute address value 10000_{16} is loaded into PC.
   (b) The address held in the memory location pointed to by the value in A_0 combined with the offset of 5 is loaded into PC.
   (c) The address held in the memory location pointed to by the value in A_0 combined with the index in A_1 is loaded into PC.
15. +129 bytes or −126 bytes; +32,769 bytes or −32,766 bytes
19. BHI   OUT_OF_RANGE

Section 12.4

21. Test condition, decrement, and branch if carry set

Section 12.5

29. PC
31. RTS pops the saved value of PC from the stack. However, RTR first pops the saved value of CCR from the stack and then the value of PC.
35. Frame pointer

Section 12.6

39. $Z = 1$, bit $5 = 1$, $(A1) = B0_{16}$

41. The Z flag is set equal to the complement of the value in bit 4 of the long-word memory location offset by 5 from the address in register A_3 and then bit 4 is cleared.

CHAPTER 13

Section 13.2

1. High-density N-channel MOS (HMOS)
3. 15 general-purpose registers, 8 data registers D_0 through D_7, and 7 address registers A_0 through A_6, and all are 32 bits in length.

Section 13.3

5. 23 address lines A_1 through A_{23}; 2^{23} unique addresses
9. The address lines A_1 through A_{23} present a word address and the upper and lower bytes of that word are accessed using the $\overline{UDS}$ and $\overline{LDS}$ signals.
11. $FC_2FC_1FC_0 = 110$
15. To provide interface signals so that low-speed 6800 synchronous peripheral devices can be used with the high-speed 68000 MPU

Section 13.4

17. 125 ns

Section 13.5

19. No; memory and I/O exist in the same address space. That is, I/O is memory mapped.

Section 13.6

21. 8 MB

23. Write; byte; D_0 through D_{15}

Section 13.7

25. Provide a protection model that permits some system resources to only be accessible at the supervisor level of protection and others to be accessed from both the user and supervisor levels of protection

Section 13.8

27. 1000 ns $= 1 \mu s$

Section 13.9

29. 1250 ns $= 1.25 \mu s$.

Section 13.10

31. (a) Data bus buffer/transceiver $= 74245$
   (b) Address bus buffer $= 74LS244$
   (c) Data storage memory $= MCM4116$
   (d) Row and column address generation $= 74LS157$
   (e) Refresh interval timer $= 6840$

Section 13.11

35. MOVE.L   #$16000,A0
   MOVEP.L   D0,0(A0)

Section 13.12

39. 00_{16}

41. $b_1b_0 = 01$; $b_5b_4b_3 = 001$

43. CB_2 is an output configured for read strobe with CA_1 restore mode of operation.

Section 13.14

47. A special fixed duration bus cycle operation that is initiated by the $\overline{VPA}$ signal from external circuitry

CHAPTER 14

Section 14.2

1. Hardware reset, bus error, and user-defined interrupts
3. Address error, illegal/unimplemented opcode, privilege violation

Section 14.3

5. Vector addresses
7. 35
11. 340012_{16}
13. Group 2 priority

Section 14.5

17. 192
21. 8 bits
23. 7
25. Status register
29. Ignored

Section 14.6

33. PC

Section 14.7

35. The IRQ inputs for the external interrupts are labeled 0 through 191; however, in the 68000 architecture external interrupts correspond to vector 64 through 255. It is the function of the add 64 circuit to scale the 8-bit codes at the output of the interrupt absolute priority encoder into the range 64 through 255.

Section 14.8

37. 7
39. Automatically generated within the 68000

Section 14.9

41. When 68000 CLK is pulsed, output 2Q of the 74LS273 becomes active. This makes the input 2 of the 74LS348 active and causes the code $A_2A_1A_0 = 010_2$ to be output. This code is latched into the 74LS175 flip-flop and applied to the IPL inputs of the 68000.

Section 14.10

43. 35; $8C_{16}$ and $8E_{16}$
47. CHK UBD, INDEX
49. RTE = return from exception

Section 14.11

51. Address error exception, privilege violation, trace, and illegal/unimplemented opcode detection
53. User state
55. Single-step mode of operation
57. 4

CHAPTER 15

Section 15.2

3. Two, the master stack and interrupt stack
5. $FC_2FC_1FC_0$
7. Enable the master stack

Section 15.3

9. 1, 2, 4, and 8
11. EA = 00100000_{16} + 2000_{16} × 8 + 16_{16} = 00110016_{16}
15. $0010ABCD_{16}$
17. Program counter memory indirect preindexed

Section 15.4

19. Enhancements to the instructions of the 68000; new instructions of the 68020

Section 15.5

21. D_3, D_4
23. 32 bits/32 bits; 32-bit; 32-bit
27. 8 bit and 16 bit; 8 bit, 16 bit, and 32 bit
29. MOVEC DFC, D3

Section 15.6

31. 001101_2
33. $FFFFFFA5_{16}$

35. $0000001A_{16}$

Section 15.7

37. PACK   `-(A0),-(A1)`; both addresses are decremented before the pack operation takes place.

39. UNPACK `-(A1),-(A0)`; both addresses are decremented before the unpack operation takes place.

Section 15.8

43. RTM

45. It tells the called module that the parameters are in the stack of the calling module and that a pointer to this stack is included in the module stack frame.

Section 15.9

49. TAS, CAS, and CAS2

51.

```
                MOVE.B   #$FF,D1]
TEST_AGAIN      CLR.B    D0
                CAS.B    D0, D1, SEMAPHORE
                BNE      TEST_AGAIN
                BRA      NEW_PROCESS
```

Section 15.10

53. Save the internal state of the coprocessor

CHAPTER 16

Section 16.2

1. Instruction cache memory and pipelining

3. CMOS

5. L2

Section 16.3

7. Byte, word, and long word

9. Word D; $1A_{16}$

11. Misaligned; misaligned

15. 1, 1, 2

19. Interrupt acknowledge

21. Cache disable

Section 16.4

23. 33.33 MHz; 12.5 MHz
25. 19 ns
27. 22.2 MHz

Section 16.5

31. Two bus cycles; cycle 1: $SIZ_1SIZ_0 = 00$, $A_1A_0 = 01$, D_{23} through $D_0 = $ OP0 OP1 OP2; cycle 2: $SIZ_1SIZ_0 = 01$, $A_1A_0 = 00$, D_{31} through $D_{24} = $ OP3

Section 16.6

33. 256 bytes
35. Tag, valid bit, long word of code
37. The long word of code is read from external memory and copied into the cache.

Section 16.7

41. TRAPcc and cpTRAPcc instructions
43. $D4_{16}$
45. D_{31} through D_{24}
47. TRAPLS.B #3

Index

Index

REC'D